THE ESSENTIAL THEATRE

The Essential Theatre

NINTH EDITION

Oscar G. Brockett
University of Texas at Austin

Robert J. Ball
University of the Incarnate Word

WADSWORTH
CENGAGE Learning

Australia • Brazil • Japan • Korea • Mexico • Singapore • Spain • United Kingdom • United States

WADSWORTH
CENGAGE Learning

The Essential Theatre: Ninth Edition
Oscar G. Brockett, Robert J. Ball

Publisher: Michael Rosenberg

Managing Development Editor: Karen Judd

Senior Development Editor: Greer Lleuad

Assistant Editor: Christine Halsey

Editorial Assistant: Megan Garvey

Technology Project Manager: Lucinda Bingham

Marketing Manager: Erin Mitchell

Marketing Assistant: Kassie Tossiello

Marketing Communications Manager:
Stacey Purviance

Content Project Manager:
Karen Stocz/Catherine Morris

Creative Director: Rob Hugel

Art Director: Maria Epes

Print Buyer: Doreen Suruki

Cover Image Research: Sheri Blaney

Production Service: Katie O'Keeffe-Swank,
Lachina Publishing Services

Text Designer: Gopa

Copy Editor: Barbara Armentrout

Illustrator: Heidi Grosch, Carla Martin

Cover Designer: Marsha Cohen

Compositor: Lachina Publishing Services

Cover Image: © Michael Daniel, 2006

For product information and technology assistance, contact us at
Cengage Learning Customer & Sales Support, 1-800-354-9706

For permission to use material from this text or product,
submit all requests online at **cengage.com/permissions**
Further permissions questions can be emailed to
permissionrequest@cengage.com

Library of Congress Control Number: 2006938701

ISBN-13: 978-0-495-09037-3

ISBN-10: 0-495-09037-9

Wadsworth Cengage Learning
25 Thomson Place
Boston, MA 02210-1202
USA

Cengage Learning is a leading provider of customized learning solutions with office locations around the globe, including Singapore, the United Kingdom, Australia, Mexico, Brazil, and Japan. Locate your local office at:
international.cengage.com/region

Cengage Learning products are represented in Canada by Nelson Education, Ltd.

For your course and learning solutions, visit **academic.cengage.com**

Purchase any of our products at your local college store or at our preferred online store **www.ichapters.com**

Printed in the United States of America
2 3 4 5 6 7 13 12 11 10 09 08

Brief Contents

Preface xiii

PART ONE: FOUNDATIONS 2

CHAPTER 1 *The Nature of Theatre* 4
CHAPTER 2 *Performance, Audience, and Critic* 22
CHAPTER 3 *The Play* 36

PART TWO: VARIETIES OF THEATRICAL EXPERIENCE 54

CHAPTER 4 *Festival Theatre: Greek, Roman, and Medieval Theatre Experiences* 56
CHAPTER 5 *Creating a Professional Theatre: Elizabethan England,
              Italian Commedia dell'Arte, and Seventeenth-Century France* 94
CHAPTER 6 *From Romanticism to Realism* 132
CHAPTER 7 *The Modernist Temperament: 1885–1940* 160
CHAPTER 8 *Reevaluation, Decentralization, and Subsidization* 186
CHAPTER 9 *Contemporary Theatre and Its Diversity* 218
CHAPTER 10 *Asian and African Theatre* 252

PART THREE: THEATRICAL PRODUCTION 276

CHAPTER 11 *Theatrical Space and Production Design* 278
CHAPTER 12 *Playwriting and Dramaturgy* 294
CHAPTER 13 *Directing and Producing* 310
CHAPTER 14 *Acting* 336
CHAPTER 15 *Scene Design* 354
CHAPTER 16 *Costume Design and Makeup* 376
CHAPTER 17 *Lighting and Sound Design* 396

Glossary 419

Bibliography 427

Credits 437

Index 439

Contents

Preface   xiii

Part One: Foundations   2

CHAPTER 1: *The Nature of Theatre*   4

The Basic Elements of Theatre   6
Theatre as a Form of Art   9
Special Qualities of Theatre   16
Art and Value   18
Additional Opportunities with InfoTrac College Edition   21

CHAPTER 2: *Performance, Audience, and Critic*   22

Watching a Performance   24
Who Is the Audience?   26
The Audience and Critical Perspective   29
The Basic Problems of Criticism   32
Qualities Needed by the Critic   34
Additional Opportunities with InfoTrac College Edition   35

CHAPTER 3: *The Play*   36

On Reading a Play   37
Dramatic Action   38
Methods of Organizing Dramatic Action   39
Plot   41
     The Beginning   41
     The Middle   42
     The End   43

Character and Characterization   44
     Thought   45
     Diction   45
     Music   47
     Spectacle   47
Form in Drama   47
     Tragedy   49
     Comedy   50
     Other Forms   51
Style in Drama   51
Differing Styles of Production Applied to the Same Play   53
Additional Opportunities with InfoTrac College Edition   52

Part Two: Varieties of Theatrical Experience   54

CHAPTER 4: *Festival Theatre: Greek, Roman, and Medieval Theatre Experiences*   56

The Theatre of Ancient Greece   57
The Theatre of Dionysus   60
The Performers   62
Oedipus Rex and Its Performance   66
Greek Comedy   70
The Roman Theatre Experience   72
The Roman Theatrical Context   74
The Menaechmi   76
Other Roman Drama and Theatre   78

The Revival of Drama
in the Middle Ages   79

Trade Guilds and the Corpus
Christi Festival   80

Conventions of Medieval Theatre   83

The Wakefield Cycle   86

Noah and His Sons   88

Other Medieval Theatre and Drama   90

Comparing Greek, Roman,
and Medieval Theatre   92

*Additional Opportunities
with InfoTrac College Edition*   92

CHAPTER 5: *Creating a Professional
Theatre: Elizabethan England, Italian
Commedia dell'Arte, and Seventeenth-
Century France*   94

Creating a Professional Theatre   95

Shakespeare and the Globe Theatre   97

Hamlet   103

The Theatre Experience
in Renaissance Italy   107

Commedia dell'Arte   111

The Servant of Two Masters   117

The French Background   119

Molière and Seventeenth-Century
French Theatre Practice   121

Tartuffe   124

The Elizabethan, Italian,
and French Traditions   128

*Additional Opportunities
with InfoTrac College Edition*   130

CHAPTER 6: *From Romanticism
to Realism*   132

The Emergence of Romanticism   134

Monte Cristo   138

The Advent of Realism   144

Realism and Naturalism   145

A Doll's House   146

Zola and Naturalism   149

The Emergence of the Director   150

The Independent Theatre Movement   153

*Additional Opportunities
with InfoTrac College Edition*   159

CHAPTER 7: *The Modernist
Temperament: 1885–1940*   160

Symbolism   161

"Art for Art's Sake"   163

The Importance of Being Earnest   163

The Modernist Influence
on Theatrical Visionaries   165

New Artistic Movements   168

"The Hairy Ape"   172

The Postwar Era   174

The Federal Theatre
and the Group Theatre   176

Epic Theatre   177

The Good Person of Setzuan   180

Artaud and the Theatre of Cruelty   181

*Additional Opportunities
with InfoTrac College Edition*   185

CHAPTER 8: *Reevaluation,
Decentralization, and Subsidization*   186

Postwar American Theatre   187

Cat on a Hot Tin Roof   188

The Musical in Postwar America   190

Postwar Europe   193

Absurdist Drama   195

Happy Days   195

Decentralization and Subsidization   196

The Postwar British Theatre   197

Off-Broadway and Off-Off-
Broadway   202

Regional Theatres   205

Subsidization of the Arts
in the United States   207

Broadway and Musicals
after Subsidization   209

American Playwrights
after 1960   212

Buried Child   214

*Additional Opportunities
with InfoTrac College Edition*   217

CHAPTER 9: *Contemporary Theatre
and Its Diversity*   218

Alternative Theatre Groups   219

Poor and Environmental Theatres   221

Multimedia, Happenings,
and Performance Art   224

Postmodernism   227

Trends in Directing   229

Cultural Diversity   230

African American Theatre   231

Ma Rainey's Black Bottom   233

Latino Theatre   236

Roosters   237

Asian American Theatre   240

Native American Theatre   243

Theatre by and for Women   245

How I Learned to Drive   247

Gay and Lesbian Theatre   248

Epilogue   249

*Additional Opportunities
with InfoTrac College Edition*   251

CHAPTER 10: *Asian and African
Theatre*   252

Theatre in Japan   253

Noh Theatre   254

The Shrine in the Fields (Nonomiya)   257

Other Japanese Theatre Forms   258

Japanese Interest in Western
Drama and Theatre   261

Theatre in China   261

Other Asian Countries   264

Wayang Kulit   264

Theatre in Africa   265

Performance in Nigeria   267

The Strong Breed   269

South Africa   271

North Africa   273

Other African Countries   274

Epilogue   274

*Additional Opportunities
with InfoTrac College Edition*   275

Part Three: Theatrical Production   276

CHAPTER 11: *Theatrical Space
and Production Design*   278

The Influence of Theatrical Space   279

The Proscenium-Arch Stage   281

The Thrust Stage   281

The Arena Stage   282

Flexible Space   283

Auxiliary Spaces   285

Using the Theatrical Space   285

Collaborative Production Design   287

*Additional Opportunities
with InfoTrac College Edition*   293

CHAPTER 12: *Playwriting
and Dramaturgy*   294

The Playwright   295

The Dramaturg   302

Dramaturgy and Literary
Management   302

Production Dramaturgy   307

*Additional Opportunities
with InfoTrac College Edition*   309

CHAPTER 13: *Directing and Producing*   310

The Producer   311

The Director   314

Analyzing and Studying the Play   315

Approaches to Directing   316

The Director and the Designers 321

Auditions and Castings 323

Working with the Actors 324

The Director's Means 324

Stage Images 325

Movement, Gesture, and Business 327

Voice and Speech 330

Rehearsing the Play 331

The Director's Assistants 334

Thinking about the Director's Work 335

*Additional Opportunities
with InfoTrac College Edition* 335

CHAPTER 14: *Acting* 336

The Actor's Training and Means 338

The Actor's Instrument 338

Observation and Imagination 340

Concentration 342

Stage Vocabulary 342

Scene Study 344

From Training to Performing 344

Creating a Role 345

*Psychological and Emotional
Preparation* 348

Movement, Gesture, and Business 349

Vocal Characterization 349

Memorization and Line Readings 350

Refining the Role 351

Dress Rehearsals and Performance 351

Thinking about the Actor's Work 352

*Additional Opportunities
with InfoTrac College Edition* 353

CHAPTER 15: *Scene Design* 354

The Functions of Scene Design 355

The Scene Designer's Skills 357

Working Plans and Procedures 359

Basic Scenic Elements 361

Soft-Scenery Units 363

Framed Units 364

Three-Dimensional Units 365

Innovative Materials and Methods 365

Assembling and Painting Scenery 366

Shifting Scenery Onstage 368

Set Decoration and Properties 369

Technical Rehearsals, Dress
Rehearsals, and Performances 371

The Scene Designer's
Assistants and Coworkers 371

Thinking about the Scene
Designer's Work 373

*Additional Opportunities
with InfoTrac College Edition* 374

CHAPTER 16: *Costume Design
and Makeup* 376

The Functions of Costume Design 377

The Costume Designer's Skills 380

Working Plans and Procedures 382

Realizing the Designs 384

The Costume Designer
and the Actor 387

Makeup 388

Types of Makeup 389

The Costume Parade, Dress
Rehearsals, and Performances 391

The Costume Designer's Assistants 391

Thinking about Costume
and Makeup 392

*Additional Opportunities
with InfoTrac College Edition* 394

CHAPTER 17: *Lighting
and Sound Design* 396

The Controllable Qualities
of Light 397

The Functions of Stage Lighting 399

The Lighting Designer's Skills 402

The Lighting Designer's
Working Procedures 403

Organizing the Distribution
of Light   405

Setting the Lights, Rehearsals,
and Performances   410

The Lighting Designer's Assistants   411

The Increasing Role
of Sound Design   412

The Functions of Sound Design   412

The Sound Designer's
Working Methods and Resources   413

Mixed-Media Productions   415

Thinking about Stage Lighting
and Sound   417

Afterword   418

*Additional Opportunities
with InfoTrac College Edition*   418

Glossary   419

Bibliography   427

Credits   437

Index   439

Preface

BEHIND THIS EDITION lies more than forty years of publication. Although *The Essential Theatre* was first published in 1976, it began as an abridged version of another book, *The Theatre: An Introduction,* which first appeared in 1964. *The Essential Theatre* has since taken on an identity of its own and is now in its ninth edition.

Like the earlier versions, this edition is divided into three parts. Part One addresses basic issues and features related to the nature of theatre, to the role of audiences, to the varied criteria for judging theatrical performances, and to dramatic structure and style. Part Two looks at various theatrical experiences from theatre's past and present. These experiences suggest that, as a vital form of creative expression, theatre changes to reflect the dynamics of the cultures within which it exists. Part Three provides an overview of theatre production today: the principles, practices, and procedures used in the creation of theatre.

As with the previous editions, *The Essential Theatre* is intended to assist in two different kinds of courses: an introductory course in which an overview serves as a foundation for those intending to major in theatre (future theatre-makers) and a theatre appreciation course in which an overview provides insights and understanding for audience members (future theatregoers). Although these two courses may address the same topics, they usually do so with somewhat different emphases. Because instructors will often use the material in ways suited to their individual needs, we have sought to provide a logically organized, comprehensive overview of the theatre. But instructors need not follow the sequence we have chosen nor use all of the material in the book. Some instructors may wish to use only some of the chapters in Part Two, for instance, while others may wish to assign Part Three prior to or concurrently with Part Two. Regardless, our aim has been to provide helpful discussions of topics pertinent to introductory and theatre appreciation courses rather than to prescribe how the courses should be organized.

This edition also contains an extensive bibliography appended to the book as a guide to additional sources about the topics discussed in each chapter, and each chapter ends with an InfoTrac® College Edition activity to facilitate research and further discussion of issues related to the text. A Premium Book Companion website helps students further explore and test their comprehension of concepts via web links, an interactive glossary, and chapter-by-chapter self-quizzing. For instructors, an Instructor's Resource

Manual and a Multimedia Manager/Instructor's Resources CD-ROM (with ExamView®) are available as guides to using the materials in the text.

We have assumed that those who use this book will both read plays and attend theatrical performances. Ideally, students should be able to read a script and then see a performance of that script. This is not always possible, but reading a play and seeing a performance, even if both are not of that script, illustrate the difference between text on the printed page and the enacted script on stage—the difference between drama and theatre. Because students typically will not have read a wide variety of plays, fifteen examples cited in *The Essential Theatre*, ninth edition, are also included in a companion anthology titled *Plays for the Theatre*, ninth edition, edited by Oscar G. Brockett and Robert J. Ball and published by Cengage Learning. These scripts serve as foundations for discussions of various types of theatrical experience and include Sophocles' *Oedipus the King,* the anonymously composed *Noah and His Sons,* Shakespeare's *Hamlet,* Goldoni's *The Servant of Two Masters,* Molière's *Tartuffe,* Ibsen's *A Doll's House,* Wilde's *The Importance of Being Earnest,* O'Neill's *"The Hairy Ape,"* Williams' *Cat on a Hot Tin Roof,* Shepard's *Buried Child,* Wilson's *Ma Rainey's Black Bottom,* Sanchez-Scott's *Roosters,* Vogel's *How I Learned to Drive,* the Noh drama *The Shrine in the Fields,* and Soyinka's *The Strong Breed.*

New to This Edition

- In Part One, changes have been made to address several issues more effectively. For example, more material has been formatted as bulleted lists to help visual learners and highlight essential information, and Chapter 3 features a new discussion of climactic and episodic plot structures and the unique advantages to each. In Part Two, all of the chapters have been brought up to date, and

Chapter 10, "Asian and African Theatre," has been expanded to provide even greater variety and to make our overview more comprehensive. In addition, Part Two discusses more plays in depth. In Part Three, updates have been made so that the discussions of theatre production reflect standard practices, and some technical details have been trimmed to maintain focus on significant processes, practices, and procedures.

- In-depth discussions of two new plays have been added to Chapters 7 and 8: *The Importance of Being Earnest* by Oscar Wilde and *Buried Child* by Sam Shepard. The full text of these plays is provided in the *Plays for the Theatre.*

- New "Building a Broad Context" timelines appear near the ends of Chapters 4 through 9 to help students establish a broader context for the historical and cultural developments and activities discussed within those chapters.

- The feature boxes throughout the book have been considerably revamped. Several new boxes replace previous ones; others have been revised or expanded; and several new boxes have been added. These boxes are used to give special emphasis to topics of broad social and cultural interest and to address pertinent theories, practices, and people in concrete detail. These boxes are categorized and color-coded to identify related concerns.

- In addition to changes in content, this edition features many new photos and drawings that illustrate significant concepts, practices, and features.

Acknowledgments

It is impossible to list all the people to whom we are indebted. The bibliography indicates most of the sources we have used, and the captions indicate the people and organizations who have permitted us to include their illustrations. In addition to these, we wish to thank Melissa Gaspar for her valuable assistance, as well as the following colleagues for their insightful and useful comments: Richard Borthwick, *Central New Mexico Community College;* Wallace Bridges, *Eastern Michigan University;* Patricia C. Caple, *North Carolina State University;* Bud Coleman, *University of Colorado, Boulder;* Thomas Ellis, *California State University, Fresno;* Josh Foldy, *Southeastern Louisiana University;* Kent G. Gallagher, *Northern Illinois University;* and Darrell Lawrence Willis, Sr., *Brookdale Community College.*

Finally, we thank the staff at Cengage Learning: Holly J. Allen, Barbara Armentrout, Meghan Bass, Lucinda Bingham, Megan Garvey, Christine Halsey, Karen Judd, Greer Lleuad, Carla Martin, Michael Massmann, Erin Mitchell, Catherine Morris, Katie O'Keeffe-Swank, Stacey Purviance, Michael Rosenberg, Amy Schneider, and Karen Stocz.

Oscar G. Brockett
Robert J. Ball

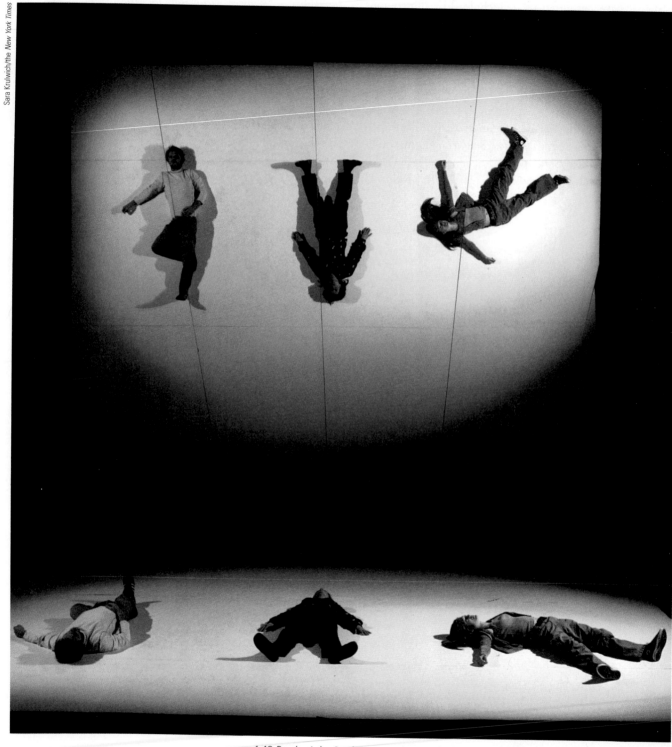

4:48 Psychosis by Sarah Kane as presented at St. Ann's Warehouse (Brooklyn, NY) as produced on tour by the Royal Court Theatre. Directed by James MacDonald; scene and costume designs by Jeremy Herbert; lighting by Nigel Edwards; sound by Paul Arditti.

PART 1

Foundations

THEATRE IS A COMPLEX art at least twenty-five hundred years old. Over such a long span, it has undergone many changes and followed diverse paths. When we attend the theatre today, we and a few hundred other people come together, usually in the evening, to see a performance that will last approximately two hours on an indoor stage illuminated by artificial light. But theatregoing has not always been this way. Our experience of theatregoing would have seemed strange indeed to Greeks living in the fifth century B.C. as they assembled at dawn in an outdoor theatre seating some seventeen thousand people to watch a series of plays that lasted all day under the bright sunlight. Our experience would have seemed equally strange to a fifteenth-century A.D. English audience that gathered at various places along a route to watch a series of short biblical plays performed on wagons that moved from one performance site to the next. These examples by no means exhaust the possibilities, because theatrical experience has been as varied as the cultures in which it has appeared. The practices we are familiar with today encompass only a limited range of the theatre's possibilities.

Such diversity invites questions about what theatre's varied manifestations have in common and the significance of their differences. It also invites questions about the appeal of theatre: Why do people create theatre? What attracts audiences to it? What makes one production seem better to us than another?

Let us begin our look at the theatre by examining some basic issues: the nature and function of theatre; the relationship of theatre to other forms of art; criteria for judging theatrical performances; how plays, the usual starting point of theatrical production, are structured; and other related topics. These initial explorations will help build the foundation for a fuller understanding and appreciation of theatre and the processes of theatrical production.

The "mousetrap," the play-within-a-play that Hamlet instructs the players to perform so that he might "catch the conscience of the king," from Shakespeare's *Hamlet* as produced by the Long Wharf Theatre. Directed by Mladen Kiselov, lighting design by Jennifer Tipton, scene design by Douglas Stein, costume design by Paul Tazewell and Michael McAleer, sound design and original music composed by John Gromada.

> "Theatre" consists in this: in making live representations of reported or invented happenings-between human beings, and doing so with a view to entertainment.
> —Bertolt Brecht, *A Short Organum for the Theatre*

The Nature of Theatre

IT IS UNCERTAIN just how and when theatre originated. As far back as we can trace human history, various kinds of rituals considered vital to the well-being of the tribe were already using the elements needed for theatre: a performance space, performers, masks or makeup, costumes, music, dance, and an audience. The function of these early rites was only incidentally theatrical; they were addressed to supernatural forces thought to control the return of spring, success in hunting and war, the fertility of human beings and the land, and the place of humans in the cosmic scheme. Other activities that contributed to theatre, such as storytelling and mimicry, also were already evident.

Although exactly how it emerged from these beginnings is unclear, theatre achieved its own distinct identity at least twenty-five hundred years ago. During its existence, it has at times been highly developed and highly prized. In ancient Greece, it was performed for the entire community at religious festivals financed by the state and wealthy citizens. At other times, theatre has existed on the fringes of respectability, as it did from the fifth to the tenth century A.D., when small bands of itinerant performers traveled around playing wherever they could for whatever they could collect from those who came to watch. In other times, theatre has been forbidden altogether, as it was in England between 1642 and 1660 when the Puritans then in power considered it not only morally unacceptable but also an activity that tempted people away from more honest work. During its long life, theatre has as often been denounced as praised, and its value—even its right to exist—has frequently been questioned.

Such ambivalent response has been encouraged in part by theatrical terminology (*play, show, acting*) that suggests that theatre is the product of grown-ups who have prolonged their childhood by dressing up and playing games to divert themselves and others. Furthermore, because dramas are fictional, they have at times been denounced as a form of lying, as they were in colonial New England. Because they tend to emphasize human crises (often involving deception, violence, and socially reprehensible behavior), they have been accused of exerting dangerous influence on the young (as many claim much television drama does today). Nevertheless, in almost all periods at least some people have considered theatre not only an acceptable form of entertainment but also a truthful reflection of human behavior.

The theatre, then, has had its detractors and its advocates. Nevertheless, those who value it often find themselves on the defensive with those who question whether it has a valid place in a college curriculum or whether a world dominated by film and television would miss theatre if it disappeared altogether.

■ The Basic Elements of Theatre

ONE REASON for the varying responses can be found in the theatre's range and diversity, both of which are evident in its three basic elements:

■ What is performed (a play, scenario, or plan)
■ The performance (including all of the processes involved in the creation and presentation of a production)
■ The audience (the perceivers)

Each of these elements is essential and they affect not only each other, but also the totality of what is expressed and how it may be perceived.

What is performed can be extremely varied—from a comic routine performed by a single entertainer to a Shakespearean tragedy performed by a large company of actors. Some people consider such events as street carnivals and parades types of theatre. Because of this great range, theatre is not easy to define. The critic Eric Bentley has argued that all of the many definitions of theatre can be reduced to: *A performs B for C.* That is, the most basic definition of theatre is: someone performing something for someone else.

Though theatre is varied, typically it is thought of as the staged performance of a written text. But it is important to remember that theatre does not require a written text, dialogue, or conflict. Juggling and tumbling, for example, have often been presented as theatrical entertainments. But even if we restrict our definition of theatre to performances that involve some degree of storytelling, we are still faced with great diversity because improvised scenes, pantomimes, vaudeville sketches, musical plays, and spoken dramas are all theatrical entertainments. Further-

more, they may be brief or lengthy; they may deal with the everyday or the unusual, the comic or the serious.

With so much diversity, it is not surprising that some people think of theatre primarily as entertainment, whereas others find the essence of theatre to be its capacity to provoke thought or action about significant issues. John Millington Synge, one of the leading Irish dramatists of the twentieth century, argued that drama is at its best not when it is dealing with social problems that will soon be forgotten but rather when it feeds the imagination: "We should not go to the theatre as we go to a [pharmacy] . . . , but as we go to dinner, where the food we need is taken with pleasure and excitement. . . ." Conversely, Peter Brook, one of the world's great directors, sees theatre as serving an important social and political role: "the basic function of theatre is to be anti-government, anti-establishment and anti-social. What we all recognize as feeble theatre is the theatre that enters into the public lie of pretending that everything's okay." If we are to understand the theatre, we must acknowledge its great range and recognize that its potential (like that of most human creations) can be developed in many ways, some of which we may like and some of which we may even consider dangerous.

Theatre's second ingredient, the performance, is equally complex. It translates the potential of a play, scenario, or plan into actuality. What the audience usually sees when it goes to the theatre is the fleshing out of a written text or plan through the application of theatrical processes. The performance takes place in a space that can vary from a building intended specifically for theatrical performances to a street, park, or nightclub. Spaces may vary from those that seat fewer than a hundred people to those (as in ancient Greece) that seat fifteen to twenty thousand. The arrangement of this space may also vary: It may permit the audience to surround the performers, require the audience to sit in rows facing a platform on which the performance occurs, or utilize other audience–performer configurations, each of which alters the

Joan Marcus

The Lion King, adapted for the stage from Disney's animated feature film (music and lyrics by Elton John and Tim Rice). Direction and design of costumes, masks, and puppets by Julie Taymor (aided by a number of others).

total theatrical experience. (This subject is explored more fully in Chapter 11.)

Most performances require the creative efforts and cooperation of many people: playwright, director, actors, designers, and technicians. A musical involves even more: composer, instrumentalists, singers, choreographer, and dancers. Any component of production (a play, acting, scenery, costumes, lighting, music, dance) can be manipulated to create varied effects. All of the components may be so skillfully integrated that the spectator is aware only of a single unified impression; or one or more of the components—such as acting or spectacle—may completely overshadow the others. Today, for example, many people argue that spectacular effects overwhelm the other elements in such popular musicals as *Phantom of the Opera, Les Miserables,* or *The Lion King.*

The components may be handled in a way easily understood by almost everyone or in ways so strange that all but a few are puzzled. A performance may seem to one part of the audience original and entertaining and to another obvious and boring; conversely, what to one group may seem strange and incomprehensible may be judged insightful and brilliant by another. Although the possibilities and results of performance may be infinite, the beginning point of the theatrical experience has been reduced to its essentials by Peter Brook in his book *The Empty Space:* "I can take any empty space and call it a bare stage. A man walks across this empty space whilst someone else is watching him, and this is all that is needed for an act of theatre to be engaged."

The third ingredient of the theatre is the audience, because until material is performed and seen by a public, we usually do not call it theatre.

Brook has said: "The only thing that all forms of theatre have in common is the need for an audience. This is more than a truism: In the theatre the audience completes the steps of creation." For all the arts, a public is imperative, but for some this public may be thought of as individuals—the reader of a novel or poem, the viewer of a painting or a piece of sculpture—each of whom may experience the work in isolation. But a theatre audience (as well as the audience for music and dance) is assembled as a group at a given time and place to experience a performance.

The audience affects the theatre in many ways, perhaps most clearly through the immediate feedback it provides the performers. Continuous interaction occurs not only between stage and auditorium, but also among spectators involved in a communal experience. For example, if one segment of the audience begins to laugh at what the director intended to be serious, the rest of the audience may come to respond in the same way; in turn, such unexpected response will probably disrupt the actors' concentration and alter their performance. Conversely, the shared enthusiastic laughter of an audience during scenes intended to be comic may lift the actors to greater effectiveness. This live three-way interaction is a distinctive characteristic of theatre and a major cause of variations in performances from night to night.

Audiences also affect the theatre through their expectations and motives for attending. Some members of the audience come to the theatre wanting only to be entertained, to be diverted from personal cares and the problems of their world. This group is likely to consider it the job of the playwright and director to make everything clear; it may see no need to make an effort to understand unfamiliar ideas or conventions. Such spectators may resent or avoid any production that questions conventional moral, political, or cultural values. Other members of

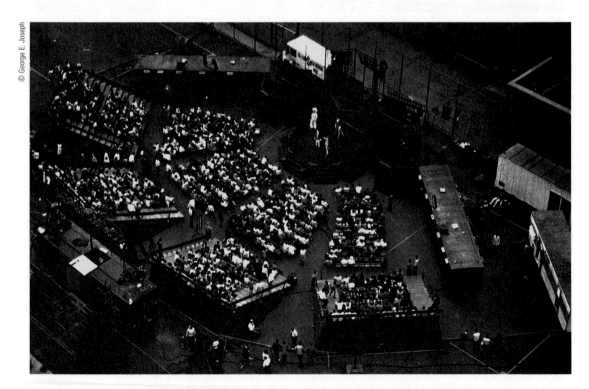

© George E. Joseph

A mobile unit, used by the New York Shakespeare Festival to take free performances to neighborhoods where audiences may have little experience with theatre, is shown here in Harlem. Unfortunately, the festival no longer offers this program.

the audience may prefer productions that challenge accepted values, raise provocative issues, advocate action about political or social issues, or use innovative theatrical means. Ultimately, various segments of the public make their preferences felt through attendance or nonattendance. They support what appeals to them and fail to support what they do not like or do not understand. Now that the cost of tickets to some Broadway productions is more than one hundred dollars, audiences understandably hesitate to attend the theatre unless they feel confident that a performance will suit their tastes. In turn, Broadway producers, who need to recover the large sums required to mount a play on Broadway, often avoid controversial subject matter or unfamiliar staging conventions that might reduce attendance. Off-Broadway and regional theatres, with lower costs and ticket prices, can afford to take greater chances and may seek a more restricted audience than that wooed by Broadway. Audience taste thus significantly influences what is performed, how it is performed, and where it is performed.

These three elements—play, performance, and audience—although they may be treated separately in discussion, interact and modify each other in practice. Playwrights may have specific intentions when they write, but they can seldom control how directors and others involved in production will interpret their plays. Therefore, different productions of the same play can vary drastically. Nor can directors dictate what audiences will get from their productions, and individual members of a single audience may have widely different reactions to the same performance. Because what is performed, how it is performed, and audience taste and perception are so diverse, not all theatre will appeal to all segments of the public. Responses to theatre are inescapably varied.

Theatre as a Form of Art

THEATRE SHOULD ENTERTAIN. No one seriously questions that. But not everyone finds the same things entertaining. When a performance begins to violate our sense of propriety by presenting things we believe should not be put on the stage, we may be too offended to be entertained. But theatre is a form of art, and art

Richard Anderson; courtesy of Center Stage

Henrik Ibsen's *Ghosts* was originally denied production (either by government censorship or by audience opposition) but is now considered one of the modern theatre's most important dramas. It was considered scandalous largely because it portrayed syphilis as a major factor in the destruction of a family. Shown here are Oswald (Greg Naughton) and his mother, Mrs. Alving (Pamela Payton-Wright) in the Center Stage (Baltimore) production, directed by Irene Lewis; scene design by John Conklin; costume design by Catherine Zuber; lighting by James F. Ingalls.

is not always comfortable or comforting. It often insists on its right to look at the world in unpopular ways and to challenge our ways of looking at ourselves and the standards of the culture that has shaped the way we view the world.

What is art? Probably no term has been discussed so frequently or defined so ambiguously. Until the eighteenth century, art always meant the systematic application of known principles to achieve some predetermined result. The word is still used in this sense when we speak of the art of medicine, politics, or persuasion. During the eighteenth century, critics began to divide the arts into two groups, "useful" and "fine." Into the latter category were placed literature (including drama), painting, sculpture, architecture, music, and dance. (Today, this list has been extended to include other forms, such as cinema and photography.) The reasoning was that whereas the useful arts may be taught and mastered, the fine arts, as products of genius, cannot be reduced to rules or principles that, even if learned, would enable just anyone to create significant works of art. As a result, since about 1800 art has often been depicted as too complex to be fully understandable. Many critics have implied that only those with superior sensitivity can fully appreciate art and that the average person often mistakes an inferior product (usually some type of popular entertainment) for authentic artistic expression. Therefore, those who view the theatre as an art form are often contemptuous of those who think of it as "show business." Similarly, in the visual arts, a distinction is usually made between works considered worthy of the museum or gallery and works created for advertisements or as illustrations; and in music, a clear line is usually drawn between compositions considered appropriate to a symphony orchestra and those played by a rock band.

Many people are uneasy at the very mention of "art." Uncertain of what art is or how they should respond to it, they feel inadequate or resentful. This is probably one of the principal reasons why many people do not visit museums or attend concerts or theatrical performances and why they may discount altogether the importance of these types of art. Their reluctance might be overcome if they could be convinced that there are no right or wrong responses to art: One responds as one does. Through multiple experiences we begin to perceive distinctions and patterns that permit us to develop our own standards. But we can never begin this process if we are unwilling to open ourselves to the unfamiliar.

We are faced less with distinctions between art and non-art than with two attitudes about what is worthwhile. All art is "made" (that is, artworks are not produced by nature the way human beings, animals, and plants are). Art comes into being through the application of certain processes, which are basically the same for all works in the same category. For example, in painting, all works, whether a sunset depicted on black velvet or a nonfigural composition on canvas, utilize the same basic elements: line, mass, color, light, and shadow, all of which are used to create spatial relationships. Unfortunately in modern times, the word *art* has come to be used as a value judgment. Consequently, though both works were created using the same process, artistic status would probably be denied the velvet painting but accorded the nonfigural composition.

Perhaps this will become clearer if we relate the issue to two broad categories used by cultural historians: popular culture and elitist culture. As the terms imply, popular culture is usually thought to reflect the tastes of a broad, general public, whereas elitist culture reflects the tastes of a smaller group whose members apply what they consider to be more demanding standards, often ones with which the general public is unfamiliar. Proponents of each category may speak contemptuously of the other using such terms as "lowbrow" for those who favor popular culture and "highbrow" for those who take the elitist view. Although the boundaries are fluid, popular culture today would probably encompass such forms of expression as pop music, television sitcoms, advertising art, and musical comedy; elitist forms would encompass those kinds of music

SOCIETY, ART,
AND CULTURE

Prior Censorship
and Self-Censorship

Although art may entertain us or illuminate various aspects of human experience, it may also offend some people when it includes subject matter they find morally offensive. Those offended often propose to control art through a form of prior censorship (forbidding the printing, performance, or display of works without prior approval). In the United States, even though the Constitution protects freedom of expression, attempts to exert prior censorship—usually through threat or intimidation—are common. The most common threat is the boycott. Groups may threaten not to buy the products of companies who sponsor works of which they disapprove. They may also mount campaigns against government subsidization or corporate support of specific arts organizations or artists or of art in general. More direct intimidation may also be used.

In 1998, the Manhattan Theatre Club announced that it was abandoning its planned production of a new play by Terrence McNally, *Corpus Christi,* in response to a bomb threat made against the theatre. (Those condemning the play hadn't read it but were basing their objections on a report that the play included a Christlike figure who is homosexual.) Athol Fugard, an internationally famous South African playwright who also had a play scheduled for presentation by the Manhattan Theatre Club, withdrew his work in protest against the theatre's decision, and TWA, one of the theatre's corporate sponsors, withdrew its financial support. Many theatre organizations in New York (and elsewhere) denounced the decision to cancel. The Manhattan Theatre Club later reinstated the production, but the implications of the cancellation remained: Threats of violence can be used to prevent the production of *any* play that one doesn't like.

Many theatre companies have been intimidated into adopting a kind of self-censorship under which they avoid presenting anything that might be interpreted as a challenge to some group's notions about religion, race, patriotism, or sexuality. Self-censorship is ultimately stultifying, because if art never goes beyond what is already familiar, it risks being dull and predictable. Art may and does encompass the familiar, but it is crippled if it is not allowed to strike out in new directions as well. No one should be forced to accept art they consider offensive, but should they be able to prevent others who do not consider it offensive from experiencing this same art? Where should the line between acceptability and unacceptability be drawn? And who should draw it?

As produced by the Huntington Theatre, Naomi Iizuka's play *36 Views* raises questions about the authenticity of a work of art as well as about the truth of our identities and interpersonal relationships. Directed by Evan Yionoulis; scene design by Adam Stockhausen; costume design by Teresa Snider-Stein; lighting by Chris Parry and sound by David Budries.

usually heard in concert halls, the visual art shown in galleries and museums, and many of the theatrical productions seen in not-for-profit or regional theatres. Nevertheless, no clear-cut distinctions exist between low and high art; they may and often do overlap or intermingle, and what was at one time looked upon as mere popular diversion (such as the plays of Shakespeare or the films of Charlie Chaplin) may later come to be considered significant art. Today the distinctions between high and low art have eroded as elements of each have increasingly been intermingled.

The type of theatre associated with popular culture seeks primarily to provide entertainment for a general audience by telling a story in a way that engages and builds interest. It employs easily recognizable character types, situations, and dramatic conventions, manipulating them with sufficient inventiveness to be entertaining but

usually without raising disturbing questions that challenge the audience's values and assumptions. Perhaps the most obvious examples of this kind of entertainment are the prime-time, network television series that, though they often show characters violating societal values, do so within a framework that ultimately reaffirms those values. These series are certifiably popular because the networks retain only those programs that attract audiences in sufficiently large numbers to please the advertisers who sponsor them. Anything so controversial as to alienate viewers is avoided. Such performances entertain, reaffirm values, divert audiences from their cares, and offer a change from the routine of existence. The majority of people feel most at ease with this type of art.

Popular entertainment is sometimes grouped with games, sports, and other recreational pastimes. Dramatic performances share many char-

Easily recognizable characters, a suspense-driven plot, and highly imaginative spectacle helped make *The Phantom of the Opera* appeal to a broad audience. Featured here are the Phantom (Michael Crawford) and Christine Daaé (Sarah Brightman). Music, book, and lyrics by Andrew Lloyd Webber, Richard Stilgoe and Charles Hart; directed by Harold Prince; musical staging and choreography by Gillian Lynne; production design by Maria Björnson; lighting by Andrew Bridge.

acteristics with sports and games, because all of these forms pit one side against another, build suspense, and reach an outcome. Games and theatre also share a dependence on conventions—that is, agreed-upon and understood rules, practices, and procedures. In football, the size and layout of the playing field, the number of downs and players, the uniforms, the system of scoring, and the length of the game are conventions that are understood by both players and spectators.

The theatre, too, depends on conventions, although more flexible ones: the stage as a place where fictional events occur; the use of scenery to suggest locales; the use in some periods of masks, or of males to play female roles; the singing (rather than speaking) of lines in opera. If we introduce new (or alter old) conventions, we are likely to confuse spectators, at least at first, although the changes may be accepted once understood. When Samuel Beckett's *Waiting for Godot* was first performed in the 1950s, many spectators were unable to relate to a play in which there was no discernible storyline beyond two tramps waiting for someone who never arrived. The response of many to this innovative play was summed up in one of the play's speeches: "Nobody comes, nobody goes. It's terrible." But the conventions of this play, now considered one of the most important of the twentieth century, have become so familiar as to be commonplace.

Despite the similarities between games and theatre, we usually do not confuse them, not only because of differences in conventions but also because in most scripted drama the outcome is predetermined before the performance begins. For example, Hamlet always avenges the death of his father and dies himself because Shakespeare's text dictates these actions. In addition, the attitudes of audiences to the characters and their struggles are determined by information revealed during the performance, whereas in games, loyalties that existed before the action begins usually determine which side spectators will root for.

Although much of the theatre's appeal lies in its ability to entertain, if it does not offer additional challenges, it may be (and often is) dismissed as an easily forgotten, momentary diversion—especially by those who consider the functions of art to include raising disturbing questions, challenging accepted values and assumptions, and searching for new types of theatrical expression, even though these often are the very elements that alienate the general public. Elitists have so fully coopted the term *art* that the general public seldom applies it to the works it admires. Nevertheless, art (in the broad sense of something that is made and the process by which it is made) encompasses the whole range of theatre.

If no definition of art is universally accepted, some of its distinguishing characteristics can be explored by comparing it with other approaches to experience. First and most broadly, art is one way human beings seek to understand their world. In this respect, it can be compared with history, philosophy, or science, each of which strives to discover and record patterns in human experience. All of these approaches recognize that human experience is composed of innumerable happenings that have occurred to an infinite number of people through countless generations and that each person's life is made up of a series of momentary occurrences, many seemingly determined wholly by chance. One question these disciplines seek to answer is: What unifying patterns can be perceived behind the apparent randomness? The questions raised and the methods used to discover possible truths differ in each field, but they are always directed toward finding those relationships that reveal some pattern. As one approach, art shapes perceptions about human experience into forms (or patterned relationships) that help to order our views about humanity and the world in which we live.

Many students of contemporary American culture have argued that our notions about love and marriage, for example, are determined much more by what we see on television (in both dramatic programs and advertising) than by our real-life experiences with our own family and acquaintances. One may argue that the notions absorbed from television are inaccurate or harmful, but they suggest nevertheless the power of art to shape or reflect perceptions.

The methods used in various approaches to human experience differ significantly. Historians, philosophers, and scientists isolate a limited problem, do their research or experiments, and then set down their conclusions in logical, expository prose; they direct their appeal primarily to the intellect. Artists, on the other hand, work primarily from their own perceptions and seek to involve the audience's emotions, imagination, and intellect directly. A play consequently shows events as though occurring at that moment before our eyes; we absorb them in the way we absorb life itself—through their direct operation on our senses. Art differs from life by stripping away irrelevant details and by organizing and telescoping events so that they compose a connected pattern. Thus a play illuminates and comments (though sometimes indirectly) on human experience even as it creates it. Nevertheless, a play often is not perceived to be a way of knowing and understanding because we are aware that it is fiction.

How, then, can imagined experience be a way of knowing and understanding? Shakespeare offers one answer in *As You Like It* (Act II, Scene 7): "All the world's a stage, /And all the men and women merely players." This speech states not only that we may think of the world as a stage upon which each person plays a role but also, conversely, that the stage is a symbol of the world where it is possible to see reflected fundamental patterns of human behavior. Such representations, however, need not be realistic; they may represent experience in alternative ways. (For some examples, see the illustrations on pages 2 and 25.) The stage can also serve as a

In some of Shakespeare's comedies, female characters disguise themselves as men to gain a greater scope of action than that permitted to most women in Shakespeare's society. The resulting complications and misidentifications provide considerable comedy. Here, Rosalind (Sara Kathryn Bakker) dresses as a man to enter the forest of Arden, joined by Touchstone (Michael David Edwards) and Celia (Saren Nofs-Synder) in the Utah Shakespearean Festival's production of *As You Like It*.

magnifying glass through which we examine some aspect of human experience. What we see onstage, even though not factually real, are embodiments of types of human beings, situations, motivations, and actions. Thus, though fictional, plays may provide insights about human behavior that are as "truthful" as those obtained from a statistical study of actual human beings. What they show us also reflects basic assumptions of the society from which the plays have come. For example, the range of activities and values permitted female characters in the drama of any period reflects (by supporting or challenging) that period's cultural assumptions about women.

As spectators, our responses to a play differ from those to an actual event. Just as we do not mistake a statue for a real person, we do not mistake stage action for reality. We usually view a play with what Samuel Taylor Coleridge called a "willing suspension of disbelief"—although we know the events of a play are not real, we agree for the moment not to disbelieve them. We are nevertheless not moved to immediate action by what we see on the stage as we might be by real-life events. We watch one man seemingly kill another, but we make no attempt to rescue the victim or to call the police. We are aware that we are watching actors impersonate characters, but we acquiesce in granting them temporary reality. This state, in which we are sufficiently detached to view an artistic event semiobjectively, is sometimes called esthetic distance. At the same time, the distance must not be so great as to induce indifference. Although a degree of detachment is necessary, involvement is of equal importance. This feeling of involvement is sometimes called empathy. Art lifts us above the everyday fray and gives us something like a "god's-eye" view of experience.

Art, then, is one method of discovering and presenting patterns that provide insights and perceptions or of raising questions about ourselves and our world. Thus art may be viewed as one form of knowledge or way of knowing. In addition, it is an imaginative reshaping of experience that operates directly on our senses in a way that involves us both esthetically and empathically, allowing us to be simultaneously at a distance from and involved in the experience so that we participate in it emotionally even as we gain insights from it. Art lays claim to being serious (in the sense of having something important to communicate), but because its methods are indirect (it presents experience but does not attempt to explain all of its ramifications), it is often ambiguous and almost always open to alternative interpretations.

■ Special Qualities of Theatre

W ITHIN THE FINE ARTS, theatre holds a special place. It has a set of qualities that help to distinguish it from other arts:

- Lifelikeness
- Ephemerality
- Objectivity
- Complexity of means
- Immediacy

Although some of these qualities may also be present in other arts, theatre combines and manifests them in a special way.

Theatre is the art that comes closest to life as it is lived day by day. Shakespeare has Hamlet say (Act III, Scene 2), "the purpose of playing . . . is to hold . . . the mirror up to nature; to show virtue her own feature, scorn her own image, and the very age and body of the time his form and pressure." Not only is human experience its subject, but theatre also uses live human beings (actors) as its primary means of communicating with an audience. Often the speech of the performers approximates that heard in real life, and the actors may wear costumes that might be seen on the street; they may perform in settings that recall actual places. Not all theatre attempts to be realistic, and at times it may approximate other arts (such as dance, music, or visual arts), but it remains the art (along with film and television) most capable of re-creating everyday human experience.

Such lifelikeness is one of the reasons why theatre is often insufficiently valued: A play, a setting, and the acting may so resemble what is familiar to spectators that they fail to recognize how difficult it is to produce this lifelikeness skillfully. To a certain degree all people are actors; they vary the roles they play (almost moment by moment) according to the people they encounter and their relationship to them (parent, priest, friend, lover, enemy, and so on). In doing so, they utilize the same tools as the actor does: voice, speech, movement, gesture, and psychological motivation. Consequently, many people do not fully recognize or appreciate the problems actors face.

The theatre further resembles life in being ephemeral. As in life, each episode is experienced and then immediately becomes part of the past. When the performance ends, its essence can never be fully recaptured, because—unlike a film, novel, painting, or statue, each of which remains relatively unchanged—when a theatrical production ends, it lives only in the memories of those who were present, and in artifacts from the production, such as programs, pictures, and reviews.

Theatre resembles life also in being the most objective of the arts, because characteristically it presents both outer and inner experience through speech and action. As in life, we come to know characters both externally and internally through listening and watching. What we learn about their minds, personalities, and motivations comes from what they say and do and from what others tell us about them. But these are also conditions that make it necessary that each spectator interpret what is seen and heard—and, as in real

IDEAS AND
INFLUENCES

Thornton Wilder
on the Nature of Theatre

Thornton Wilder, author of *Our Town*, one of the best known and most popular of all American plays, argued that four things distinguish theatre from the other arts:

1. The theatre is an art which reposes upon the work of many collaborators;
2. It is addressed to the group-mind;
3. It is based upon a pretense and its very nature calls out a multiplication of pretenses;
4. Its action takes place in a perpetual present time.

—"Some Thoughts on Playwriting,"
in *The Intent of the Artist*, ed. Augusto Centeno

Might the same be said of television drama and film? What distinguishes dramatic presentations in theatre from those in other media?

life, interpretations may differ markedly. Thus, though theatre is objective in its presentation, it demands subjective response.

The theatre can be said to resemble life because of the complexity of its means, because like a scene from life itself it is made up of intermingled sound, movement, place, dress, lighting, and so on. Theatre draws on all of the other arts: literature in its play; painting, architecture, and sculpture (and sometimes dance) in its spectacle; and speech and music in its audible aspects.

Furthermore, theatre is psychologically the most immediate of the arts. Several contemporary critics have argued that the essence of the theatre (what distinguishes it from other dramatic media such as television and film) lies in

the simultaneous presence of live actors and spectators in the same room. On the surface, theatre may seem to have several drawbacks compared with other dramatic media. For example, more people often see a filmed or televised show on a single evening than attend the live theatre during an entire year. In fact, the theatre may be likened to a handcrafted product in an age of mass production, because it must be re-created at each performance and for a relatively small group of spectators. Conversely, thousands of copies of a film may be printed and shown throughout the world simultaneously and year after year, and a televised program may be videotaped and repeated at will. These media may make performers world famous almost overnight, whereas the actor who works only in the theatre may build up an international reputation only over a considerable period of time, if ever.

Nevertheless, the theatre has important attributes that television and film do not duplicate. The most significant of these are the three-dimensionality of the theatrical experience and the interactive relationship between performers and spectators. In film and television, the camera is used to select what the audience can see and to ensure that it will see nothing more; the camera can frame the picture to restrict our view to a facial expression, the twitch of a hand, or a small object. In the theatre, the director uses various means to focus the audience's attention on a specific character or object, but—because the full acting area remains visible and close-ups are impossible—the audience may choose to watch something else. Perhaps most important, during a live performance, there is continuous interaction between performer and spectator; the pacing of a scene, for example, affects how the audience responds, and in turn the audience response may stimulate the actors to alter the pace. Because of such interaction, each performance differs in many details. The audience thus plays a far more active role in the theatre than it does in film or television. Ultimately, there is an important difference in the psychological responses aroused in the spectator by electronic media and theatre, because the former present pictures of events, whereas the latter performs the actual events in the same space as that occupied by the audience. This difference results in one unique characteristic of the theatre: the simultaneous presence of live actors and audience. Film is also more literal than theatre; it usually seeks to show every detail of setting and action, whereas theatre requires the audience to imagine what it cannot show. Some critics have charged that film dulls the imagination, whereas theatre stimulates it.

These special qualities—lifelikeness, ephemerality, objectivity, complexity, and immediacy—define both the weaknesses and strengths of the theatre.

Art and Value

ART IS VALUABLE for its capacity to improve the quality of life—by bringing us pleasure, by sharpening our perceptions, by increasing our sensitivity to others and our surroundings, by suggesting that moral and societal concerns should take precedence over materialistic goals. Of all the arts, theatre has perhaps the greatest potential as a humanizing force, because much of it asks us to enter imaginatively into the lives of others so we may understand their aspirations and motivations. Through role-playing (either in daily life or in the theatre), we come to understand who and what we are and see ourselves in relation to others. Perhaps most important, in a world given increasingly to violence and tensions among ethnic and other diverse groups, the value of being able to understand and feel for others as human beings cannot be overestimated, because violence depends on dehumanizing others so that we no longer think of their hopes, aims, and sufferings but rather treat them as objects to be manipulated or on whom to vent our frustrations. To experience (emotionally, imaginatively, and intellectually) what it means to be human in the broadest sense ought to be one of the primary goals of both education and life; few approaches have greater potential than theatre for reaching this goal, because humanity is its subject and human beings its primary medium.

Theatre is also valued as a form of cultural expression. Every culture has some type of theatrical expression, the nature of which and the degree to which it is accepted tell us much about the society in which it exists. Greek tragedies and comedies, and the circumstances under which they were presented, reveal much about a culture that considered theatre its highest form of expression. Ancient Rome, whose theatrical activities were far more extensive and varied than those of Greece, favored entertainments such as mimes, chariot races, gladiatorial contests, and animal baiting, strong indicators that Rome valued popular-culture forms more highly than did Greece. We can gain insight into any culture by examin-

Joan Marcus

Perhaps due to their use of movement, music, spatial compositions, and intense energy, musical entertainments are particularly appealing to many people. Seen here is Broadway's *Thoroughly Modern Millie*, featuring Sutton Foster in her Tony Award–winning role. Directed by Michael Mayer; scene design by David Gallo; costume design by Martin Pakledinaz; and lighting by Donald Holder.

ing the range, prestige, and relative popularity of its entertainment forms. We can also measure the theatre's value to a culture by studying the relative emphasis it places on the theatre's capacity to provide diversion, recreation, or artistic expression.

Most people probably give little thought to the arts as an integral part of their lives. But try to conceive of life without any music, dance, drama (whether in theatre, television, or film), or visual art of any kind. Without these, the quality of our lives would be greatly diminished. Still, many people think of the arts as expendable "frills" that can be eliminated when financial stress occurs. Many also devalue the arts because they do not yield concrete benefits of the type derived from medicine or engineering. For these reasons, most artists have a difficult time making a living, although a few (including performers) win enormous fame and wealth. Parents typically try to discourage their children,

especially as they approach adulthood, from viewing the arts as appropriate career choices. Because of such attitudes, many Americans by the time they become adults have suppressed whatever artistic inclinations they may have had. They are thereby cut off from, or are only partly utilizing, one of the primary ways of knowing the world and understanding themselves.

One purpose of this book is to affirm the value of theatre. The chapters that follow seek to acknowledge and encourage understanding and appreciation of the theatre by providing an overview of its various aspects: how plays are structured; varieties of theatre experience, both past and present; how the theatre functions today; and how each theatre artist makes use of available materials and techniques. Taken together, these discussions should provide a foundation for intelligent and sensitive reactions to the theatre and its role in its culture.

Multiple Intelligences Theory and the Arts

Attitudes regarding the devaluation of the arts may (in part) be a by-product of a lack of understanding among educators and the general public regarding the nature of intelligence. Human intelligence long has been treated as a very narrow group of abilities measurable by IQ tests. The two clusters of abilities that education has sought to cultivate most are the linguistic/verbal and the logical/mathematical, and achievements or abilities in these two areas are the only ones addressed by the most commonly used standardized tests. In fact, the effectiveness of the educational system is often judged by how well students perform on standardized tests. However, psychologists have posited that there are many types of intelligence. Howard Gardner, a professor at Harvard University, argues that in addition to linguistic (verbal) and logical (mathematical) there are six types of intelligence:

- musical—sensitivity to melody, rhythm, pitch, and tone
- spatial—the ability to envision and manipulate spatial relationships
- bodily-kinesthetic—the ability to use the body and handle objects
- interpersonal—the ability to understand others and human relationships
- intrapersonal—the ability to use one's own emotions as a key to understanding oneself and others
- naturalistic—sensitivity to the natural world and ability to interface with it

If Gardner is correct, much education has failed to cultivate major aspects of human intelligence and potential. Of these, most are related to one or more of the arts, especially music, dance, visual arts, and theatre. If education and society are to stimulate and develop the full range of human intelligence, the potential of the arts in this process and the value of the arts in society need to be more fully acknowledged and encouraged.

Additional Opportunities with InfoTrac College Edition

Access your InfoTrac College Edition account. You'll see that you are able to research topics via a simple subject or keyword search, or via an advanced search—choose the search method you'd like from the lefthand menu. For the exercise shown below, you might want to use the Subject Guide to explore the subject of *acting*. (If you'd like a demonstration of how to operate InfoTrac College Edition and its many features, click on the link "InfoTrac Demo" in the lefthand menu that appears after you register and log on.)

1. Because *acting* is a broad subject and results in so many hits (search results), InfoTrac College Edition divides them into subdivisions by subject and indicates what types of articles you will find in the subdivisions (i.e., newspaper or periodical articles). You can explore a specific subdivision or try again by limiting your current search.

2. Search on *acting opportunities* through the Keyword Search.
   - How many hits appear? What sort of information do the results seem to provide? How current are the articles listed? How many years back do some of the articles date?

3. Limit your current search to those entries published after January 1, 2005, that mention *acting opportunities* in the article's title, citation, or abstract.

4. Click on the article "Acting Opportunities in London: From the West End to the Fringe" by Mark Shenton in *Back Stage,* which details some of the practical challenges facing American actors hoping to work in London.
   - Which American actor does the author use as an example of an actor finding success on the London stage?
   - What makes the "fringe" theatres in London more accessible to American actors? And what are the associated risks?

Plays are performed outdoors in many major cities during the summer months. Pictured here is the Commonwealth Shakespeare Company production of *Twelfth Night,* presented free of charge on the Boston Common. Directed by Steven Maler; scene design by Alexander Dodge; lighting by John R. Malonoxski.

> The audience is the most revered member of the theatre. Without an audience there is
> no theatre. Every technique learned by the actor, every curtain and flat on the stage,
> every careful analysis by the director, every coordinated scene, is for the enjoyment
> of the audience. . . . They make the performance meaningful.
> —Viola Spolin, *Improvisation for the Theatre*

2: Performance, Audience, and Critic

ALL TYPES OF THEATRICAL performance require an audience, because it is in the mind and imagination of the spectator that the final step in the creative process occurs. No matter what the playwright or performers had in mind, audience members observing the theatrical event as it unfolds arrive at their own interpretations of what was intended. There is no guarantee that a spectator's interpretation will accord with the playwright's or director's or that one spectator's interpretation will be the same as those of other spectators. Nevertheless, shaping the theatrical medium to arouse the desired audience response is the primary challenge that playwright, director, and performers seek to meet.

Although not all theatrical performances are based on plays, this book is concerned primarily with those that translate a play from the medium of words on a page into the concrete language of the stage—acting, costumes, scenery, lighting, sound, and so on. When such a translation is effective, it allows spectators to experience directly and immediately the developing action, the relationships among the characters, the rhythms, the spectacle, and the overall implications of the production as a whole. Thus spectators absorb the play as they would events from real life—through watching and listening—rather than, as in reading, seeking inwardly both to see and to hear everything.

During the theatrical performance, spectators are carried along at the pace the performers set. The spectator who fails to hear a line or to see a piece of business cannot go back and recover it; there are no instant replays or fast-forwards. Readers of plays may proceed at their own pace, turn back, look ahead, or reread the entire play. The reader may decide that there are several possible interpretations of a line or scene and can leave all possibilities open, whereas the spectator in the theatre is offered only the one chosen by the director. What the spectator sees is one interpretation, but never the only possible interpretation, of a play. Productions of the same play by other directors may offer drastically different interpretations, resulting in drastically different visual and aural styles. Nevertheless, an effective performance can be far more satisfying than a reading because it makes what had been words on a page immediate and present in the living flesh and voices of the actors and the physical environment created by the designers.

Watching a Performance

ATTENDING THE PERFORMANCE of a play differs in several ways from going to a film. A live performance has more of a sense of special occasion. Except in large cities, live performances are not always readily available. One must usually buy tickets in advance and go to the theatre at a specified time; usually there is only one performance a day, although some theatres offer afternoon matinees twice each week. Because tickets for a live performance usually specify the seat in which one is to sit, much more attention is given to such matters as ushering spectators to their seats than at movie theatres. At live performances, spectators are usually provided with programs listing the author, director, designers, cast of actors, and the production staff—much like the on-screen credits shown at the end of movies. Programs may also contain statements or articles about the play or information about the persons involved in the production. Because today the stage is seldom hidden by a curtain, the spectator can usually examine the stage and scenery and gain some idea of the production approach before the performance begins. Music is frequently used to get the audience into the appropriate mood. Most live performances have one or more intermissions, during which audience members may leave their seats, mingle, and discuss what they have seen or what is to come.

In the theatre, interior and exterior settings may be suggested with the addition or subtraction of a few properties or multi-purpose scenic units as they are here in *The Umbrellas of Cherbourg* (music by Michel Legrand, adapted by Sheldon Harnick and Charles Burr from the film by Jacques Demy). Produced at Two River Theater Company under the direction of Jonathan Fox; scene design by Neil Prince; costume design by Moira Shaughnessy; lighting by Aaron Black.

T. Charles Erickson

Theatres use various devices to prepare audiences for experiencing performances in an informed and perceptive manner. Some of the most common are advance press releases, articles in newsletters sent to subscribers, lobby displays, and programs (sometimes very elaborate) containing articles and documents that place the production that the audience is about to see within an interpretive context.

There are no rules about how to experience a theatrical performance. Willingness to give one's full attention to what is happening onstage moment by moment is the prime requisite. As a performance unfolds, many questions that a reader can answer only in the imagination are given immediate form, at least in this production of the play: What is the appearance of the stage setting? How are the characters dressed? How do the characters move and relate to each other? Unlike a film, in which the settings are usually realistic (often actual places), a live performance may use little scenery. The spectator may need to imagine much that is merely suggested by a few set pieces, projected images, lighting, or dialogue; and the same basic setting may be used to represent quite different locales. Costumes may be based on the dress of some historical period, or actors may wear ordinary street attire even though the characters are mythical, biblical, or historical personages. The audience may be asked to accept visual styles that alter ordinary modes of perception. These and other conventions may make great demands on the spectators' imagination.

In addition to using imagination, spectators need to concentrate. Unless they let their eyes and ears be carried along by the production, spectators may miss what is significant. Theatre requires more collaboration between director and spectator than does film, because in the theatre, although directors seek to focus audience attention on what is significant at any given moment, they cannot force attention as film directors can through such devices as close-ups and other camera shots that deny the audience the possibility of seeing anything other than

what the director wishes. In the theatre, the entire stage space is visible, and consequently the spectator may choose what to look at regardless of what the director wishes. The size and configuration of the auditorium and the stage may also affect audience response. A large auditorium may make seeing and hearing difficult, whereas a small auditorium may make it possible to see and hear every detail. How the seating area is related to the acting area can also affect audience response. (The typical arrangements—arena, thrust, proscenium, and flexible stages—are explained at length in Chapter 11.)

Richard Feldman

The Theatre for a New Audience produces bold treatments of new and classical plays. In their production of Shakespeare's *The Tempest,* directed and designed by Julie Taymor, Caliban (played by AveryBrooks and pictured here) begins the performance imprisoned in a mask, because of which he is considered to be a monster. Eventually the mask is broken, freeing the man within.

Theatre for a New Audience

Founded in 1979 by Jeffrey Horowitz, Theatre for a New Audience is a nonprofit organization that produces modern and classical plays in New York (Off-Broadway) as well as for national and international tours. Some of its collaborators include Mark Rylance (Artistic Director of London's Globe Theatre), the Royal Shakespeare Company, and Tony Award–winning director Julie Taymor (who has directed several productions for the group, including *The Tempest* and *Titus Andronicus*).

Perhaps no group has been more active in audience development, especially among a diverse population of young students, than the Theatre for a New Audience. Over the course of its more than twenty-five-year history, over 125,000 elementary, middle, and high school students have attended one of its performances or participated in one of its initiatives to make theatre and drama more accessible. Its World Theatre Project introduces young students to Shakespeare and other world-renowned playwrights by bringing artist-teachers into the classroom to help students and their teachers read, interpret, and perform one of these plays. Its New Voices Project brings professional actors into the classroom to help students write and rehearse their original plays, and to perform some of the students' completed plays in staged readings before an invited audience. Both programs attempt to build appreciation by getting students creatively involved in writing or performing plays.

Theatre for a New Audience has long been an itinerant theatre, renting different spaces for its performances and rehearsals, but recently announced plans for a permanent theatre building in the Williamsburg waterfront district of Brooklyn, New York. The new building will contain a 299-seat theatre that would permit different performance space configurations (proscenium, thrust, arena), a fifty-seat rehearsal and performance space, and a permanent home for the theatre's administrative offices and educational programs.

Who Is the Audience?

THOUGH WE MAY speak of audiences as though they were all much the same, in actuality audiences vary widely in terms of tastes, education, economic status, race, age, and other factors. Those who produce theatre usually feel it necessary, in the choice of plays and production styles, to consider to whom they wish to appeal. Broadway, in part because of its elevated ticket prices, tends to cater to the well-to-do middle class, a large percentage of whom are tourists who, with limited time in town, must choose one or two shows from among the many avail-

IDEAS AND INFLUENCES

Conditioned Audience Response

Although we tend to think of an audience's responses as immediate and spontaneous, they are conditioned by conventions almost as complex as those used by the performers. Today's theatre audiences typically are seated and are expected to behave in a respectful manner that does not divert attention from the staged event—they refrain from talking, moving about, and other distracting behavior. At a rock concert, on the other hand, such audience behavior would be considered deadly. Without the audience's high-decibel verbal and high-energy physical responses, the performance would be judged disappointing. In both situations, the audience is playing its expected role.

Conventions of audience behavior can change markedly over time. The quiet, sedate behavior of today's theatre audiences contrasts sharply with that of earlier times. In the eighteenth and early nineteenth centuries, audiences at plays were quick to let their responses be known. They often hissed and booed, threw things at the actors, and occasionally rioted—storming the stage or creating noise so intense and prolonged that no one could hear the actors. In the English theatre during the late eighteenth century, a soldier with a bayonet-equipped rifle faced the audience on either side of the proscenium arch as a deterrent to violent behavior.

Audience behavior may change gradually. In the early twentieth century, standing ovations were extremely rare, reserved for performances of the highest quality. Now it is rare to attend a theatrical event that is not greeted with a standing ovation. If a few people near the front of the theatre stand, others seem to accept that they are expected to join in and do so even if they have found the production unexciting. Peter Marks, writing in the *New York Times*, observes: "In the absence of standards shared by a wide range of informed theatregoers, it may be unsurprising that audiences stand to applaud anything, regardless of how mediocre."

able to them. The productions are usually tailored, polished, and marketed to appeal to the greatest number possible from this group. Both the population of New York and the number of visitors to it encourage Broadway producers to aim for the longest possible run, and the success of plays is often judged by the number of performances they achieve. For example, *The Phantom of the Opera,* which has been performing on Broadway since 1988, recently overtook *Cats* as the Broadway musical with the greatest number of performances.

But many theatres exist in communities where long runs are not possible and may not be

Disruptive audience behavior was common in eighteenth-century England, as illustrated here by the beginning of a riot at London's Covent Garden Theatre in 1763.

considered desirable. Most not-for-profit theatres in the United States stage plays for limited runs (usually no more than six weeks and often less). Over the course of a season, these theatres usually offer a series of plays of varying types drawn from both the past and present. They, too, have tended to attract primarily white, well-educated, middle-class (and, it is often said, middle-aged) spectators. In recent years, concern has grown about how to enlarge the theatre audience and especially how to attract the young and others who do not have a history of theatregoing.

Attracting new audiences is not easy and when successful sometimes alienates existing patrons. Plays that appeal to a new constituency may polarize audiences over artistic, racial, class, or gender issues. An increase in productions of interest to specific racial or minority groups has been encouraged by foundations and corporations by providing funding earmarked for this purpose. Such funding in many instances has become controversial. Minority theatres argue that these grants should have come to them (to strengthen their work) rather than being used to encourage mainstream theatres to broaden their repertories (and in doing so attract audiences away from minority theatres). This controversy, in turn, raises questions as to whether minority theatres should cater only to minority audiences and

whether any theatre can adequately serve the needs of all members of a community or geographical area. Ongoing questions for many theatres are: How many audiences are there? Of these, which ones do we wish to attract? How may the differing interests of multiple audiences be met?

Some theatres consider it important to challenge audiences to move beyond what they have become accustomed to and to enlarge their experience and appreciation of unfamiliar forms of theatre. Some theatres devote their entire program to these goals, but more typically theatres include one unusual piece among an otherwise traditional repertory. For most, the goal is not merely to follow but to lead audiences. Some theatres pursue this goal more aggressively than others.

Because the majority of the theatregoing public in America is middle-aged or older, and because relatively few spectators have come from lower economic classes and from racial minorities, how can theatres attract young audiences, and how can they increase attendance from groups for whom theatregoing has not been customary? A number of different approaches to this issue have been taken. One approach involves outreach programs designed to bring school children to the theatre or take productions to schools or to community centers. The hope is that, once new audiences become familiar with theatre, they will con-

T. Charles Erickson

Suzan-Lori Parks writes intellectually challenging and emotionally charged plays that often draw a younger and more diverse audience. Pictured here is her Pulitzer Prize–winning play *Topdog/Underdog,* which treats (among other things) the sibling rivalry of two brothers, Lincoln (David Rainey) and Booth (K. Todd Freeman) as produced at the Hartford Stage. Directed by Amy Morton.

tinue to attend. Some theatres have developed expansive websites for today's online culture to provide information, particularly of a visual nature, about the plays they are producing. Many of these websites also make tickets available for purchase online and may offer special discounts. There have been some indications of success. The number of under-twenty ticket holders more than doubled for Broadway productions during the 1990s, but today they still make up less than nineteen percent of the audience.

A theatre's attempts to identify its potential audience (or audiences) and its concerns as well as to devise means of reaching them are important because the theatre cannot exist without audiences. Sensitivity to varying audience tastes and interests is essential to achieving a diversified theatre.

The Audience and Critical Perspective

DO WE NEED a critical perspective to enjoy theatre? Most of us go to the theatre hoping to be fully caught up in the performance. When this happens, we are too involved to pass judgment on what we are seeing, although our involvement itself may be an acknowledgment of the production's power. Only after the performance has ended can we fully process our response to it. At an ineffective performance, however, we are likely to pass judgment even as we watch, largely because we are not able to become absorbed in it. Even if we have liked a production, we may have trouble formulating our responses to it when it is over. Most of us restrict ourselves to such generalized responses as

"I really enjoyed it" or "I thought the actors did a good job with a weak play." If we are to be more articulate, we must not only examine our overall response but also look more analytically at the elements that went into the production (the play, the directing, acting, scenery, costumes, lighting) and develop criteria for judging the individual elements as well as the overall achievement. This can be viewed as a three-step process: One has an experience, one analyzes the experience, and then one communicates one's response to another. If we can reason through our subjective response to art, we may discover more about our own thoughts and feelings as well as express ourselves in a more coherent way. Although a critical perspective is not required to enjoy theatrical performance, it increases our understanding of the experience and helps us to communicate our response to others. This book, taken as a whole, seeks to assist in this process.

Although every member of the audience is in some sense a "critic," this title is usually reserved for those who formulate their judgments for dissemination. Such critics should have had considerable theatregoing experience (an inexperienced theatre critic is comparable to a sports columnist who has never seen a baseball game); they need to understand what goes into a production (the potentials and limitations of the various theatre arts) so they can assess the contributions of each element of a production. Critics need to be aware of the audience for whom they are writing so they can express themselves in terms meaningful to it.

Usually, the critic has a particular type of audience in mind. The production reviews published in daily newspapers are addressed to a general public that may have no extensive knowledge of theatre, whereas the critical articles written for literary quarterlies or scholarly journals are addressed to a more restricted, often an academic, audience. A single piece of criticism seldom serves the needs of all audiences.

Critics who write reviews for newspapers often think of themselves as consumer guides, alerting readers to which productions are worth their time and money and which are not. In recent years, many television stations have begun reviewing plays (usually in short spots of two

Les Miserables, adapted by Alain Boublil and Claude-Michel Schönberg from the Victor Hugo novel; lyrics by Herbert Kretzmer (additional lyrics by James Fenton); directed by Trevor Nunn and John Caird; scene design by John Napier; costumes by Adreane Neofitou, and lighting by David Hersey.

Bob Marshak

SOCIETY, ART,
AND CULTURE

Influence
of Criticism

Although many persons insist that published critiques of plays have no influence on their own reactions, this certainly is not true for everyone. It used to be said that a negative review in the *New York Times* spelled failure for a Broadway production. This is not necessarily true anymore, if it ever was, but newspaper reviews do serve as a kind of shopping guide, and theatregoers are understandably reluctant to pay high prices to attend a production that has been panned by reviewers. In several instances, however, positive "word of mouth" passed along by those who have seen the production has overcome negative reviews and has led to long runs. Initially, many theatre critics gave *Les Miserables,* a musical based on Victor Hugo's novel, unfavorable reviews. Some reported that the musical cheapened Hugo's novel by treating it too sentimentally. Others said that a Victor Hugo novel wasn't appropriate source material for a musical. Despite less than rave reviews, which normally might close a production then and there, audiences flocked to see it and in a few days the production was sold out for months in advance. *Les Miserables* played for long runs in London and New York as well as on tour and in cities throughout the world for several years.

Reviewers may influence in other ways how audiences respond in the theatre. Michael Gambon, one of England's most admired actors, tells of his experience of performing in David Hare's *Skylight* in New York after a long and much praised run in London, where audiences laughed appreciatively during performances. The same response greeted the production in New York during preview performances, but once the play was reviewed by critics, the laughter largely ceased. According to Gambon, audiences "were told it's a serious play," and they seemed thereafter to feel it in bad taste to laugh.

to five minutes). Both newspaper and television reviews have had substantial impact on ticket sales.

To many, criticism means adverse response, but the true meaning of the word is "the act of making judgments." The best criticism requires attention to both excellence and shortcomings. Not all critics provide balanced discussions. Benedict Nightingale, theatre critic for the *London Times,* states: "So often criticism seems to be a courtroom in which theatre practitioners are arraigned. If that is so, then perhaps the critic should think of himself as court recorder and defense attorney at least as much as a prosecutor and judge."

Some critics may provide less-than-balanced discussion either because they lack the space or because they believe a play or a production is so good or so inadequate that nothing of importance need be said on the other side. Some reviews concentrate primarily on the acting or the playwriting, and other aspects of production may be ignored altogether.

Some commentaries on productions are almost wholly descriptive. A critic may explain how a play is structured or may provide information about certain aspects of the production (the visual appearance of the costumes, the use of lighting, the innovative conventions, how the production differs from previous ones of the same play, and so on) without passing any judgment on these features. Such descriptive pieces can help an audience appreciate a production or a play that it might otherwise find baffling because of unfamiliar conventions or a controversial directorial interpretation.

Some reviewers have a tendency to be flippant or condescending. Legendary examples of flippancy are Dorothy Parker's comment that Katharine Hepburn ran the gamut of emotion from A to B (in a Broadway production of *The Lake* in 1933) and John Mason Brown's statement "Tallulah Bankhead barged down the Nile last night and sank" (in his review of her performance in Shakespeare's *Antony and Cleopatra*). Examples of condescension include John Simon's remarks on Jerzy Grotowski's production of *The Constant Prince*—"I was so dumbfounded by the infantilism and coarseness of the proceedings that sheer amazement kept me from even trying [to take notes]." Such quips may be amusing, but they can be infuriating and discouraging to theatre workers whose efforts are callously dismissed out of hand. Such reviews contribute significantly to the antipathy that often exists between theatre artists and critics.

■ The Basic Problems of Criticism

THE CRITIC IS CONCERNED with three basic problems: understanding, effectiveness, and ultimate worth. What were the playwright, director,

and other theatre artists trying to do? How well did they do it? How valuable was the experience?

Critics follow any of several paths to answering the first question. If the play is available, they may study it carefully prior to attending its production. They may find out more about the author's life and other works and about what other critics have said about the dramatist's plays. They may refresh their memory of previous work by the director and production team or of previous productions of the same play. Some reviewers avoid any preparation for viewing a production on the grounds that they wish to attend it much as any other spectator might, so they may react without any preconceptions about the play or how it should be performed.

By choice or necessity, many reviewers write about the production of plays they have not read and know only from a single performance. In such circumstances, reviewers are often guilty of damning a play rather than its inadequate production, or a performance rather than its inadequate play, because of the difficulty in judging the sources of strengths and weaknesses based on a single viewing or without any prior knowledge of the play.

In dealing with effectiveness—How successful were the playwright, director, and other theatre artists in accomplishing what they set out to do?—the critic may focus on the play's intention or the director's interpretation. Rarely do playwrights state their intentions directly. Intention is indicated by the way conflicts, characters, and ideas are handled and by the look and sound of the production. Evidence of the director's interpretation usually comes from what one sees and hears during the performance, although sometimes the director explains his or her approach in notes printed in the program, in interviews before the opening, or in publicity releases. Many directors try to embody the play's intention as faithfully as possible. But some directors use the written text (somewhat like acting, scenery, and lighting) as raw material to be shaped according to the director's vision. Contemporary directors often interpret plays in ways that are at variance with the playwright's appar-

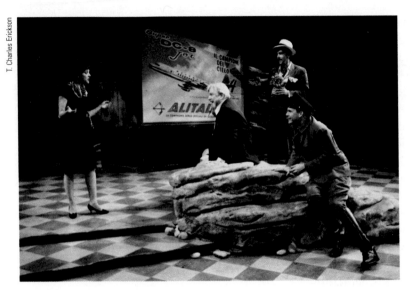

As produced by the Long Wharf Theatre, Shakespeare's *Twelfth Night* is set somewhere in the mid-twentieth-century Mediterranean to give this classic play a fresh look and underscore certain themes. Directed by David Warren; scene design by James Youmans; costume design by Toni-Leslie James; lighting by Peter Maradudin.

ent intentions on the grounds that by doing so one gains a new perspective on the issues dealt with in the play or that a close examination of the play reveals unconscious motives or biases that need to be brought out or that certain changes make a play from the past more relevant to today's world. For example, Peter Sellars moved the action of Mozart's *Don Giovanni,* an opera dealing with an amoral, compulsive womanizer in seventeenth-century Spain, to present-day New York and used drug addiction and street violence to clarify the characters' behavior. In evaluating such productions, the critic may assess how the director's interpretation is related to, or differs from, the play's apparent intention. Although the critic may believe that the director is misguided, this belief is irrelevant in the critic's assessment of whether the director has achieved what he or she set out to do.

Even though a play or production is understandable and effective, a critic may still consider it unsatisfactory when seeking to answer the third basic question: How valuable was the experience? Any response to this question assumes some standard against which value can be measured. Unfortunately, there are no universally accepted standards of worth, and no standard can be proven incontestably better than another.

Often we are puzzled by other people's pronouncements because we do not know what criteria have been used in making them. Why do friends detest a play or movie we have greatly admired? If we discuss with them our conflicting responses, we often find that each of us is looking at the same work from a different perspective. One of us may praise a production's comic inventiveness, whereas another may find the work's treatment of women (or some other element) so appalling that nothing can compensate for this shortcoming.

Many contexts are used in evaluating the relative worth of plays or productions. Some critics consider the only meaningful context to be other plays or productions of the same type. Each critic may value a production for a different reason: its emotional power, its relevance to contemporary issues, its insights into human behavior, its innovations, its embodiment of the written text, its ability to entertain. At times, critics seem to damn productions for failing to satisfy criteria that the playwright or director never intended to meet. Furthermore, critics do not necessarily adhere to a single context in making their judgments and often shift their ground within a single review. Examining carefully any review to uncover the stated or implied criteria that underlie the various value judgments expressed can be instructive. In turn, this may lead us to a greater awareness of the preconceptions and prejudices that underlie our own judgments.

We should define what, for us, makes a production satisfying or unsatisfying. Many believe that the most satisfying production is one that so fully absorbs their attention that they completely forget themselves. Others have argued that to enter so fully into a production makes it impossible to watch critically or to be aware of the ideology or prejudices implied by the action.

In assessing our own critical stance, here are some questions that may be helpful:

■ Am I open to unfamiliar subjects, ideas, or conventions?
■ In the theatre, am I uncomfortable with moral stances that differ from my own?
■ Are there subjects I think should not be treated on the stage? If so, which?
■ What standards do I use in judging a play or performance? Why?

Such questions suggest the need for each of us to understand our own convictions and biases, because these influence (usually quite unconsciously) our critical judgments.

Critical responses, whether those of the casual spectator or the professional critic, ultimately involve the three major questions already posed:

■ What was attempted?
■ How fully was it accomplished?
■ How valuable was the experience?

In addition, an informed and perceptive reviewer usually deals with elaborations on the following major questions:

■ What play was performed? Who is the playwright? What information about the playwright or the play is important for understanding the production?
■ Where and when did the performance take place? Will there be additional performances?

■ Who was involved in the production—producer, director, actors, designers? (Not everyone need be named, and comments about those who are may be scattered throughout the reviews.)
■ What were the apparent goals of the play or production?
■ How effectively and fully were the goals realized (in the directing, acting, design elements)?
■ Should others see it? Why?

A critic may not deal with all of these questions or in this order, and answers to each question may vary in length and complexity.

■ Qualities Needed by the Critic

BECAUSE THE THEATRE is a composite art and because each of us is subject to many influences, it is difficult to become a good theatre critic. A reliable critic usually has had years of theatregoing on which to draw, as well as a firm foundation of studying and reading about the theatre, its processes, and its cultural context.

A critic should strive:

■ to be sensitive to feelings, images, and ideas.
■ to become as well acquainted as possible with the theatre of all periods and of all types.
■ to be willing to explore plays and production processes.
■ to be tolerant of innovation.
■ to be aware of his or her own prejudices and values.
■ to be articulate and clear in expressing judgments and their bases.
■ to be courteous.

Perhaps most important, the critic should avoid becoming dogmatic or unwilling to consider alternative views. The theatre is constantly changing, and critics must be willing to reassess their standards in light of innovations even as they seek to evaluate the changes.

Additional Opportunities with InfoTrac College Edition

To learn more about the possible variance in critical response, use InfoTrac College Edition to find and read two very different responses to the same production: "Which Witch Is Wicked?" by Don Shewey in *The Advocate* and "Wicked" by Frank Scheck in *Hollywood Reporter*.

1. How do these two reviewers address the three basic critical questions: What was attempted? How fully was it accomplished? How valuable was the experience?

2. Are there any points on which these two reviewers agree? What are they?

3. Which review do you think is the more convincing and why?

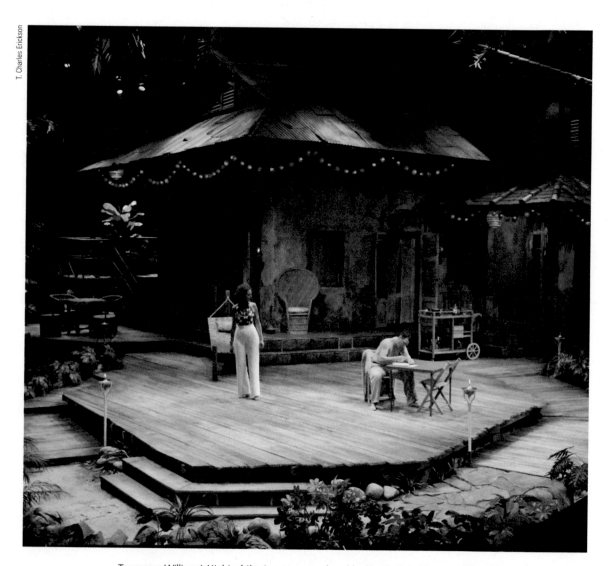

Tennessee Williams' *Night of the Iguana* as produced by the Guthrie Theatre (Minneapolis, Minn). Directed by John Miller-Stephany; scene design by James Youmans; costume design by Mathew J. LeFebvre; lighting by Marcus Dilliard; sound by Scott Edwards.

It is almost as if you were frantically constructing another world while the world that you live in dissolves beneath your feet, and that your survival depends on completing this construction at least one second before the old habitation collapses.
–Tennessee Williams, from the Foreword of *Camino Real*

3: The Play

THE PLAY IS BOTH the typical starting point for a theatrical production and the most common residue of production, because it usually remains intact after its performance ends. It is useful to distinguish the play—the written text—from a theatrical production of it because the same play may serve as a basis for many different productions. A play has greater permanence than its theatrical representations and may come to be considered a literary work. Drama is consequently often taught apart from theatre; many people who read plays have never seen a live theatre performance, and most students get their first glimpse of theatre through reading plays in literature classes. But a play may seem unsatisfactory or puzzling, because it is essentially a blueprint demanding from both reader and performer the imaginative creation of much that is only implied on the printed page. Learning to read, understand, and fill out the play (either in the mind or on the stage) is essential if its power is to be fully realized.

On Reading a Play

THERE ARE NO RULES about how one should read a play. Nevertheless, some observations may be helpful to those who are new to play reading. First, they must accept that the ability to read imaginatively and perceptively is a basic skill that everyone needs, because without this skill much of human experience is lost, and intellectually we suffer from historical and cultural amnesia.

Because all writers do not express themselves in the same form, all written works cannot be read in the same way. Each form has its own characteristics, and each makes distinctive demands on the reader. If we read a play in the same way we read a historical treatise, an essay, a biography, a novel, or a poem, we will miss out on its dramatic power and nuances of meaning. To read a play adequately, we must adjust our minds to the dramatic form. A play is distinctive in part because it is made up primarily of dialogue constructed with great care to convey its intentions and to create the sense of spontaneous speech by characters involved in a developing action. A play is both a highly controlled structure and a simulated reflection of human experience.

Drama requires readers to contribute more than most other forms of fiction do. Not only must readers see and understand what is explicitly said and done, but also they must be aware of all that is implied. The dramatist may use stage directions to clarify setting, situation, or tone but usually conveys intentions through dialogue. In reading a play, we should assume that what is written is what the writer wished to say. But because the dramatist must convey intentions through a likeness of conversation, we must be sensitive—as in life—to what is left unspoken. The reader must be alert to the nuances of interactions among characters. Although it is not a simple undertaking to inwardly and imaginatively see and hear what a written text suggests, we can become adept with practice. Perhaps the best place to begin is with a look at how plays are constructed and how their structure is related to dramatic effectiveness and meaning. (How playwrights function in today's theatre is discussed in Chapter 12.)

Dramatic Action

Broadly speaking, a play is—as the ancient Greek philosopher Aristotle wrote in his *Poetics*—a representation of human beings "in action." By *action* he did not mean mere physical movement. Rather, he was concerned not only with *what* characters do but also with *why* they do it. In turn, the actions of the individual characters relate to some question, problem, or theme that forms the central focus, or dramatic action, of the play as a whole.

Francis Fergusson, a twentieth-century American critic, has argued that a dramatic action builds through three steps: purpose, passion, and perception. By *purpose* he means awareness of some desire or goal; by *passion* he means the strength of desire or suffering that makes characters act to fulfill their goals, along with the emotional turmoil they undergo while doing so; and by *perception* he means the understanding that eventually comes from the struggle. In Ibsen's *A Doll's House* (a discussion of which can be found in Chapter 6), we see Nora attempt desperately to conceal that she has borrowed money without her husband's knowledge, the increasing anguish into which this attempt leads her, and her eventual discovery that her marriage has been a lie based on a misunderstanding of her husband's character.

The range of human motivation and behavior is so great that no single play can depict more than a small part of the totality. Because each playwright's view of the human condition differs, each drama is in some respects unique. Still, all plays share certain qualities that allow us to draw some conclusions about the characteristics of effective dramatic action:

- It is complete and self-contained.
- It is deliberately shaped.
- It has variety.
- It engages and maintains interest.
- It is internally consistent.

Aristotle stated that a dramatic action should have a beginning, middle, and end. On the surface, this statement seems obvious, but it summarizes a fundamental principle: A dramatic action should be *complete and self-contained* (that is, everything essential for understanding it should be in or implied in the play). If this principle is not observed, the action will probably seem incomplete or unsatisfying. Effective dramatic action is *deliberately shaped* or organized to reveal its purpose and goal and to evoke from the audience specific responses (pity, fear, laughter, ridicule, and so on). Effective dramatic action, in addition to having purpose, must also have *variety* (in story, characterization, idea, mood, spectacle) to avoid monotony. Effective dramatic action *engages and maintains interest.* The situation must be sufficiently compelling to arouse curiosity, the characters interesting enough to awaken sympathy or antipathy, the issues vital enough to provoke concern, or the spectacle and sound novel enough to attract attention. Effective dramatic action is *internally consistent.* Even if the events might be impossible in real life, they should be consistent with the "rules of the game" established in the opening section of the play. For example, when during the opening speech of Eugene Ionesco's *The Bald Soprano* the clock strikes seventeen times and a character announces that it is nine o'clock, we are warned that in this play we should be prepared for

Aristotle's

Poetics

Probably no one has exerted greater influence on ideas about the nature of drama, dramatic structure, and dramatic form than the Greek philosopher Aristotle (384–322 B.C.). The son of a physician, he was sent to Athens at the age of eighteen to study at the Academy, the school headed by Plato, another of the great Greek philosophers. Aristotle remained for twenty years, becoming a teacher there. Beginning in 343, he was for seven years tutor to the future Alexander the Great. When Alexander succeeded to the throne in 336, Aristotle returned to Athens, where he founded his own school, the Lyceum. When Alexander died in 323, a reaction against those who had been associated with the ruler made it prudent for Aristotle to flee Athens. Aristotle died the next year at the age of sixty-two or sixty-three.

Aristotle was a biologist by training, but he studied and wrote in a number of other fields. His study of drama led to the *Poetics* (c. 335–323), the oldest surviving treatise on drama. After it was rediscovered in the fifteenth century A.D., the *Poetics* came to be considered authoritative on drama, especially tragedy. Although its influence began to decline in the nineteenth century, it continues to be one of the works most frequently referred to in discussions of the nature and structure of drama. It seems likely that only a part of the *Poetics* has survived, because although it divides drama into two basic types—tragedy and comedy—and promises to treat both, it discusses only tragedy at length. While describing tragedy, it outlines several principles of dramatic writing. It recommends the cause-to-effect arrangement of incidents, progressing through complications and resolution, as the most effective means of unifying action. It also considers internal consistency to be the basis of believability. The *Poetics* is too complex to summarize briefly, especially because the meaning of almost every line has been heatedly debated. Because it has been so influential, it is a work with which serious students of drama should be familiar.

things to deviate from normal modes of perception—and they do. It is consistency within the framework of the particular play, not whether the events would have happened this way in real life, which leads us to accept events in drama as believable.

■ Methods of Organizing Dramatic Action

A PLAY IS COMPOSED of incidents organized to accomplish a purpose. This organization directs attention to relationships that create a meaningful pattern. In analyzing a play, it is helpful to pinpoint the source of unity; otherwise, the play may seem a collection of unrelated happenings rather than a whole. The most common sources of unity are cause-to-effect arrangement of events, character, and thought. (The following discussion uses a number of plays contained in *Plays for the Theatre* as examples.)

The majority of plays from the past are organized through cause-to-effect arrangement of events. This is the organizational principle used in *A Doll's House.* Using this method, in the opening scenes a playwright sets up the necessary conditions—the situation, the desires and motivations of the characters—out of which later events develop. The goals of one character come into conflict with those of another, or two conflicting desires within the same character lead to a crisis. Attempts to surmount the obstacles make up the substance of the play, each scene growing logically out of those that precede it. Any organizational pattern other than cause-to-effect is likely to seem loose, often giving the effect of randomness.

Less often, a dramatist uses a character as the source of unity. Such a play is held together primarily because all of the events focus on one person. Few plays are unified predominantly through character, however, because, to create a sense of purpose, more is required than that all the incidents involve one person. They must also either tell a connected story or embody a theme. Paula Vogel's *How I Learned to Drive* is unified in part through the character of Li'l Bit but ultimately through its central metaphor that relates learning how to handle an automobile to learning how to navigate one's way through life—from adolescence to maturity. Similarly, *A Doll's House* gains much of its sense of purpose from Nora Helmer, but the play is organized mainly through the structure of its incidents. Plays with primary emphasis on character are usually biographical, as, for instance, a play about Abraham Lincoln or Richard Nixon.

Many contemporary dramatists organize plays around thought, with scenes linked through a theme or set of ideas. Vogel's *How I Learned to Drive* shows its central character in various

Nora (René Augesen) and her husband Torvald (Stephen Caffrey) in *A Doll's House* at the American Conservatory Theatre (San Francisco), as directed by Carey Perloff.

moments in the protagonist's life, moving easily back and forth from one period to another as they become relevant to her feelings or anxieties. It is organized somewhat like a musical composition, in which a theme or motif is introduced and then elaborated upon in a series of variations; ultimately, these variations fuse to create a vision of human existence and illuminate a central thought.

Although a play usually has one major source of unity, it also uses secondary sources, because every play involves a sequence of incidents, uses characters, and implies a theme or set of ideas. Other sources of unity are a dominant mood, visual style, and distinctive use of language.

The organization of dramatic action may also be approached through the parts of drama, which, according to Aristotle, are plot, character, thought, diction, music, and spectacle.

▇ Plot

P LOT IS OFTEN considered merely the summary of a play's incidents, but it also refers to the organization of all the elements into a meaningful pattern. Thus plot is the overall structure of a play. The plot of a play may be structured in many different ways, but two of the most common plot structures are *episodic* and *climactic.* Climactic plots normally follow the action in a cause-to-effect manner to its conclusion, and, because they frequently begin late in the overall storyline, they are often successful in creating a sense of compression or dramatic tension. Episodic plots jump from one scene to the next, often separated by time or place, without necessarily building a cause-to-effect relationship between them. Because episodic plots usually treat some central character or concern over time or through a number of variations, they are often successful in creating a broad perspective.

▇ THE BEGINNING

T HE BEGINNING of a play establishes some or all of these: the place, the occasion, the characters, the mood, the theme, and the internal logic (the rules of the game) that will be followed. Viewing a play is like coming upon previously unknown places and people. Initially, the novelty may excite interest, but as information about the place and people unfolds, interest either wanes or increases. The playwright is faced with a double problem: to give essential information and at the same time to make the audience want to stay and see more.

The beginning of a play involves *exposition,* or the setting forth of information—about earlier events, the identity and relationship of the characters, and the present situation. Although exposition is a necessary part of the opening scenes, it is not confined to those scenes, because information is gradually revealed throughout most plays.

The amount of exposition required about past events is partly determined by the *point of attack:* the moment at which the story is taken up. Shakespeare typically uses an early point of attack (that is, he begins the play near the beginning of the story and tells it chronologically). Thus he needs relatively little exposition. Greek tragic dramatists, on the other hand, use late points, which require that many previous events be summarized for the audience's benefit. Thus Greek tragedies actually show only the final parts of their stories. In *Oedipus Rex,* all of the action seems to take place in one day, but to uncover the truth on which the action turns, we must be told about events that begin before Oedipus' birth. Some modern plays have a late point of attack but show, in flashbacks, events that range through many years.

Playwrights motivate the giving of exposition in many ways. Ibsen, as in *A Doll's House,* frequently introduces a character that has returned after a long absence; questions about happenings while the character was away motivate the giving of background information needed by the audience to understand the situation. On the other hand, some plays offer exposition without attempting to make it seem natural. Many of Euripides' Greek tragedies open with a monologue-prologue that summarizes events up to

Oedipus the King, as produced in a new adaptation by the Hartford Stage. Directed by Jonathan Wilson; scene design by Scott Bradley; costume design by Susan Hilferty; lighting by Kevin Snow; sound by Stephen Baker, with original music by René McLean.

T. Charles Erickson

this time. In a musical play, exposition may be given in song and dance.

In most plays, attention is focused early on a question, potential conflict, or theme. The beginning of such plays includes what may be called an *inciting incident,* an occurrence that sets the main action in motion. In Sophocles' *Oedipus Rex,* a plague is destroying the city of Thebes; the oracle at Delphi declares that the murderer of the former king, Laius, must be found and punished before the plague can end. This is the event (introduced in the prologue) that sets the action in motion.

The inciting incident usually leads directly to a *major dramatic question* around which the play is organized, although this question may change as the play progresses. For example, the question first raised in *Oedipus Rex* is: Will the murderer of Laius be found and the city saved? Later, this question changes as interest shifts to Oedipus' involvement in the crime. *A Doll's House* asks: Can Nora conceal her criminal act from Torvald, and, if not, what will he do?

Not all plays include inciting incidents or clearly identifiable major dramatic questions. All have focal points, nevertheless, frequently a theme or controlling idea around which the action is centered. *How I Learned to Drive* exemplifies this alternative pattern as Li'l Bit seeks to cope with having been sexually abused.

■ THE MIDDLE

THE MIDDLE of a play normally consists of rising action composed of a series of *complications*. A complication is any new element that changes the direction of the action—the discovery of new information, for example, or the arrival of a character. The substance of most complications is discovery (any new information of sufficient importance to alter the direction of action). Discoveries may involve objects (a wife discovers in her husband's pocket a weapon of the kind used in a murder), people (a young man discovers that his rival in love is his father), facts (a young man about to leave home discovers that his mother has cancer), values (a woman discovers that self-esteem is more important than marriage), or self (a man discovers that he has been acting from purely selfish motives when he thought he was acting out of love for his children). Each complication normally has a beginning, middle, and end—its own development, climax, and resolution—just as the play as a whole does.

Other means than discoveries can be used to precipitate complications. Natural or mechanical disasters (earthquakes, storms, airplane crashes, automobile accidents) are sometimes used, but these are likely to seem contrived if they resolve the problem (for example, if the villain is killed in an automobile accident and as a result the struggle automatically ends).

The series of complications culminates in the *climax,* the highest point of interest or suspense. It is often accompanied by the *crisis,* that discovery or event that determines the outcome of the action. For example, the title character in *Oedipus Rex* sets out to discover the murderer of Laius; the interest steadily grows as events increasingly focus attention on Oedipus, and the turning point comes when Oedipus realizes that he himself is the guilty person and becomes the pursued rather than the pursuer. Not all plays have a clear-cut series of complications leading to climax and crisis. Nevertheless, usually interest is maintained by the frequent introduction of new elements and an ongoing pattern of tension

and relaxation. One way of analyzing such plays (and all others as well) is to divide them into beats, or units, the beginnings and endings of which are indicated by shifts in motivation or the introduction of some new element. One can then examine the function of each of these units both at that point in the action and in the overall development of the play.

■ THE END

THE FINAL PORTION of a play, the *resolution* or *denouement* (unraveling or untying), extends from the crisis to the final curtain. It may resolve the conflict, make sense of the various strands of action, answer the questions raised earlier, or solidify the theme. It typically returns the situation to a state of balance and satisfies audience expectations.

Plays may also have *subplots,* in which events or actions of secondary interest are developed, often providing contrast to or commentary on the main plot. In *A Doll's House,* the relationship of Krogstad and Mrs. Linde contrasts sharply with that of Nora and Torvald. Often a subplot becomes a major factor in resolving the main plot, as in *Hamlet,* when Laertes, a morally upright character, is provoked by the death of his father, Polonius, and the madness of his sister, Ophelia, to agree to help Claudius in his plan to kill Hamlet.

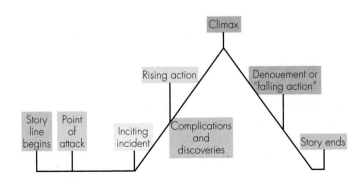

Climactic Plot Structure Note that the overall story line may be much longer than the plot's treatment of it. Exposition is used to relate events within the story line that occurred prior to the play's point of attack. The inciting incident establishes the dramatic question, and rising action ensues as complications arise in its pursuit until the play's climax. The falling action or denouement follows the climax.

Character and Characterization

CHARACTER IS THE PRIMARY material from which plots are created, because incidents are developed through the speech and behavior of dramatic personages. *Characterization* is anything that delineates a person or differentiates that person from others. It operates on four levels:

- Physical or biological (defining gender, age, size, coloration, and general appearance)
- Societal (defining economic status, profession or trade, religion, family relationships, and all other factors that place a character in a particular social environment)
- Psychological (defining a character's habitual responses, desires, motivation, likes, and dislikes—the inner workings of the character's mind)
- Moral (defining a character's value system through choice and action—it reveals what characters are willing to do to get what they want)

A playwright may emphasize one or more of these levels and may develop many or few traits, depending on *how the character functions in the play.* For example, the audience needs to know very little about a maid who appears only to announce dinner, whereas the principal characters need to be drawn in considerable depth. Even the major characters in a play may be depicted more through certain levels of characterization than others due to the nature of the play or the playwright's intentions. For example, Sophocles gives only very basic information regarding the physical level of characterization for his characters in *Oedipus Rex.* Because drama most often arises from conflicting desires, the psychological and moral levels of characterization are often the most essential. The moral level is developed most fully in serious plays because it shows what characters actually do when faced with making a difficult choice (as opposed to

what they have said they or others should do in such situations). Moral decisions differentiate characters more fully than any other type, because deliberating about such decisions causes characters to examine their values and motives, in the process of which their true natures are revealed both to themselves and to the audience. (Analyzing Torvald in *A Doll's House* and Oedipus in *Oedipus Rex* in terms of the four levels will reveal much about these characters and the plays in which they appear.)

A character is revealed in several ways:

- Through descriptions in stage directions, prefaces, or other explanatory material not part of the dialogue
- Through what the character says
- Through what others in the play say about the character
- Most importantly, through what the character does

Dramatic characters are usually both *typified* and *individualized.* On the one hand, spectators would be unable to relate to a character that was totally unlike any person they had ever known. Therefore, characters can usually be placed in one of several large categories of people. On the other hand, audiences may be dissatisfied unless the playwright goes beyond this to give characters individualizing traits that set them apart from other characters of the same type. The most satisfactory dramatic characters are usually easily recognizable types with some unusual or complex qualities.

A playwright may be concerned with making characters *sympathetic* or *unsympathetic.* Normally, sympathetic characters are given major virtues and lesser foibles, whereas the reverse is true of unsympathetic characters. A character that is either completely good or bad is likely to seem unconvincing as a reflection of human behavior. Acceptability varies, however, with the type of play. Melodrama, for example, oversimplifies human psychology and clearly divides characters into good or evil. Tragedy, on the other hand, normally depicts more complex forces at work both within and without characters and requires greater depth and range of characterization.

THOUGHT

THE THIRD BASIC element of a play is *thought*. Thought includes the themes, arguments, and overall meaning of the action. It is present in all plays, even the most lighthearted farce, because a playwright cannot avoid expressing some attitudes, because events and characterization always imply some view of human behavior. As we have already seen, thought may also be used to unify a play's dramatic action.

Meaning in drama is usually implied rather than stated directly. It is suggested by the relationships among characters; the ideas associated with unsympathetic and sympathetic characters; the conflicts and their resolution; and such devices as spectacle, music, and song. Playwrights often use their characters to advocate a certain line of action, point of view, or specific social reform.

Dramatists in different periods have used various devices to project ideas. Greek playwrights made extensive use of the *chorus,* a group representing some segment of society, just as those of later periods employed such devices as *soliloquies, asides,* and other forms of statement made directly to the audience. Other tools for projecting meaning are *allegory* and *symbol.* In allegory, characters are personifications of abstract qualities (mercy, greed, and so on), as in the medieval play *Everyman.* A symbol is an object, event, or image that, although meaningful itself, also suggests a concept or set of relationships. In *Buried Child,* the disinterred buried child carried by Tilden up the stairs to Halie at the end of the play serves as a powerful symbol and visually sums up the play's thought.

Just because plays imply or state meaning, we should not conclude that there is a single correct interpretation for each play. Most plays permit multiple interpretations, as different pro-

T. Charles Erickson

Peter Macon as Oedipus and Isabell Monk O'Connor as Jocasta in *Oedipus,* a new version of Sophocles' play by Ellen McLaughlin at the Guthrie Theatre. Directed by Lisa Peterson; scene design by Riccardo Hernandez; costume design by David Zinn; lighting by Christopher Akerlind; music by Zeitgeist (Heather Barringer and Pat O'Keefe).

ductions of, and critical essays about, the same play clearly indicate. Nevertheless, each interpretation should be supported by evidence found in the play.

DICTION

PLOT, CHARACTER, and thought are the basic subjects of drama. To convey these to an audience, playwrights have at their disposal two means: sound and spectacle. *Sound* includes language, music, and other aural effects; *spectacle* includes the visual elements of a production (the physical appearance and movement of performers, the costumes, scenery, properties, and lighting).

Language is the playwright's primary means of expression. When a play is performed, other expressive means (music, sound effects, and spectacle) may be added; but to convey intentions to others, the dramatist depends almost entirely on dialogue and stage directions. Thus language (diction) is the playwright's primary tool.

Diction serves many purposes. It is used to impart information, to characterize, to direct attention to important plot elements, to reveal the themes and ideas of a play, to establish tone or mood and internal logic, and to establish tempo and rhythm.

The diction of every play, no matter how realistic, is more abstract and formal than that of normal conversation. A dramatist always selects, arranges, and heightens language. In a realistic play, although the dialogue is modeled after and may retain the rhythms and basic vocabulary of everyday usage, the characters are usually more articulate and state their ideas and feelings more precisely than their real-life counterparts would.

The dialogue of nonrealistic plays (such as Greek and Shakespearean tragedies) deviates markedly from everyday speech. It employs a larger vocabulary, abandons the rhythms of conversation, and makes extensive use of imagery

Joan Marcus

Striking music and spectacle are major features of *Wicked*. The Tony Award–winning Broadway musical written by Winnie Holzman and Stephen Schwartz is based on the novel by Gregory Maguire. Directed by Joe Mantello; choreography by Wayne Cilento; scene design by Eugene Lee; costume design by Susan Hilferty; lighting by Kenneth Posner; sound by Tony Meloa.

and meter. Other types of nonrealistic plays may emphasize the clichés and repetitiveness of conversation as a means of commenting on the mechanical quality and meaninglessness of exchanges that pass for communication.

The basic criterion for judging diction is its appropriateness to characters, situation, internal logic, and type of play.

MUSIC

MUSIC, AS WE ordinarily understand the term, does not occur in every play. But if the term is extended to include all patterned sound, it is an important ingredient in every production, except those wholly silent.

Language has been described as the playwright's principal means of expression. But a play is not fully realized until the performers transform words into sound. The elements of pitch, stress, volume, tempo, duration, and quality convey meaning. For example, though the words of a sentence may remain constant, its meaning can be varied by manipulating emphasis or tone ("You say *he* told her?" as contrasted with "You say he told *her*?" or the differences that result if the tone in the same speech is shifted from joy to sarcasm). Because written language is imprecise in emphasis or tone, actors and directors may interpret a passage in ways the playwright did not intend.

The spoken aspect of language varies in its formal qualities. In some plays, among them *A Doll's House,* it simulates the loose rhythms of everyday speech; in others, such as Shakespeare's *Hamlet,* it is shaped into formalized metrical patterns.

In addition to the sound of the actors' voices, a play may also use music in the form of incidental songs and background music, or—as in musical comedy and opera—it may utilize song and instrumental accompaniment as integral structural means. Music (especially in combination with lyrics) may serve many functions. It may establish mood, it may characterize, it may suggest ideas, it may compress characterization or exposition (by presenting information, feelings, or motivations in a song), it may lend variety, and it may be pleasurable in itself.

SPECTACLE

SPECTACLE ENCOMPASSES all the visual elements of a production: the movement and spatial relations of characters, the lighting, settings, costumes, and properties. Because others normally supply these elements, the playwright does not have full control over them; and because playwrights seldom describe the spectacle precisely, the other theatre artists must discover the play's intentions through careful study of the text. Similarly, the reader of a play must try to envision the spectacle in order to grasp a play's full power. The visual image of Gallo fighting/dancing with Zapata (a performer costumed to represent a rooster) is essential to *Roosters.*

Some playwrights give the reader more help than others. Many older plays (including Greek and Shakespearean tragedies) contain almost no stage directions, and most clues to spectacle must be sought in the dialogue. When place or action is important, such plays usually have a character describe them. Beginning in the nineteenth century, when visual elements were given added prominence, stage directions became usual. Since that time, the printed texts of plays have typically included many aids designed to help the reader visualize the action. In evaluating spectacle, the characteristics we should be most concerned with are appropriateness and distinctiveness. (The chapters that make up Part Three treat the process of transferring the play to the stage more fully.)

Form in Drama

PLAYS ARE FREQUENTLY classified according to form: tragedy, comedy, tragicomedy, melodrama, farce, and so on. Considerable emphasis is sometimes placed on understanding the essential qualities of each dramatic form and the

Analyzing Plays

Dramatic structure can best be understood by analyzing specific plays. Here is a list of questions useful in that process.

1. What are the given circumstances? (Location? Period? Time of day? Socioeconomic environment? Attitudes and relationships of the characters at the beginning of the play? Previous action?) How is this information conveyed?

2. Where in the overall story is the play's point of attack? What sets the dramatic action in motion? How is the action resolved?

3. What is the major conflict, dramatic question, or unifying theme? Are there subplots? If so, how is each related to the main plot? How is the dramatic action unified?

4. Are the play's characters typified or individuated? What is each character willing to do to achieve his/her desires?

5. What is the dominant tone of the play? Serious? Comic? Ironic? Is the tone consistent throughout, or does it change often? How is its tone established?

6. What are the major ideas/themes/implications of the dramatic action? Are there a number of possible interpretations of the play? If so, which seems most valid based on the play's action, characterizations, and other elements?

7. To what extent do the vocabulary, rhythm, and tempo of speeches follow or deviate from everyday colloquial usage? What information is given or implied about sound, music, settings, costumes, makeup, and lighting? Is this information significant to the dramatic action? If so, how?

8. For what kind of theatrical space was the play written? What characteristics of the play are explained by the theatrical or dramatic conventions in use at the time the play was written?

Not all of these questions need be answered for every play. Additional questions may be needed for some plays or for specialized interests (to meet the needs of actors, designers, and others) or for atypical plays.

proper classification of each play. Arthur Miller's *Death of a Salesman,* for example, provoked a lengthy controversy over whether it was a true tragedy. Since the 1960s concern over dramatic form has lessened, in part because much recent drama defies formal classification. Nevertheless, one cannot read plays without encountering formal labels. Consequently, some understanding of dramatic form is helpful.

Basically, *form* means the shape given to something for a particular purpose. A sentence is a form created by words arranged in a particular order to convey a thought. Similarly, a play is a form created by arranging incidents in a particular order to create a dramatic action. Most plays have in common certain formal elements that permit us to recognize them as plays rather than as novels, epic poems, or essays. Still, those works we recognize as plays are not all alike. Critics have divided them into a number of dramatic forms on the basis of certain characteristics, the most important of which are type of action, overall tone, and basic emotional appeals. Throughout much of history, tragedy and comedy have been considered the two basic forms.

TRAGEDY

THE OLDEST KNOWN form of drama, tragedy, presents a genuinely serious action and maintains a serious tone throughout, although there may be moments of comic relief. It raises significant issues about the nature of human existence, morality, or human relationships. The protagonist, or leading character, of tragedy is usually someone who arouses our sympathy and admiration but who encounters disaster through the pursuit of some goal, worthy in itself, that conflicts with another goal or principle. The emotional effect of tragedy is the arousal of a strong empathy for those who strive for integrity and dignity.

Courtesy of the Goodman Theatre

Lee Breuer and Bob Telson's *Gospel at Colonus* is a retelling of Sophocles' *Oedipus at Colonus* through American gospel music and preaching. Pictured here in a production at the Goodman Theatre (Chicago) is Martin Jacob (a member of the gospel group Soul Stirrers) separating the Balladeer at left (Sam Butler Jr.) and Polyneices at right (Terrence A. Carson).

SOCIETY, ART,
AND CULTURE

The Possibility of Writing
Tragedy Today

I s it still possible to write tragedy? This question has been debated frequently during the past century. Few dramatists since the mid-nineteenth century have called their serious plays tragedies, and today, though we still study tragedy and talk about tragic form, when we do so we usually look back to the Greeks or to Shakespeare for our examples. Joseph Wood Krutch, a university professor and critic, argued in his essay "The Tragic Fallacy" that it is impossible to write tragedy in modern times because we consider human beings too petty to be capable of tragic action:

> [T]he idea of nobility is inseparable from the idea of tragedy, which cannot exist without it. . . . [A] tragedy . . . must . . . have a hero, and from the universe as we see it both the Glory of God and the Glory of Man have departed. Our cosmos may be farcical or it may be pathetic but it has not the dignity of tragedy. . . . The death of tragedy is, like the death of love, one of those emotional fatalities as the result of which the human as distinguished from the natural world grows more and more a desert.

Not everyone agrees with Krutch's conclusions. Arthur Miller was driven to offer a different point of view when *Death of a Salesman*, following its original production, became the subject of a lengthy debate over whether it could be considered a "true tragedy." Miller responded in an essay entitled "Tragedy and the Common Man":

> For one reason or another, we are often held to be below tragedy—or tragedy above us. . . . I believe that the common man is as apt a subject for tragedy in its highest sense as kings were. . . . [T]he tragic feeling is evoked in us when we are in the presence of a character who is ready to lay down his life, if need be, to secure one thing—his sense of personal dignity.

Tragedy is a form associated especially with ancient Greece and Elizabethan England. (In later chapters, two of the world's greatest tragedies, Sophocles' *Oedipus Rex* and Shakespeare's *Hamlet* will be discussed in detail.) Few modern plays have been called tragedies, perhaps because, as some critics have argued, we no longer consider human beings capable of the kind of heroic action associated with the great tragic heroes.

■ COMEDY

A DRAMATIC FORM that had its origins in ancient Greece, comedy is based on some deviation from normality in action, character, or thought. It must not pose a serious threat, and an "in-fun" tone is usually maintained. Comedy demands that an audience view the situation objectively. Henri Bergson argues that comedy requires "an anesthesia of the heart," because it is difficult to laugh at anything about which we feel deeply. We may find it funny to see a person slip on a banana peel, but if we discover that the person is a close relative who is just recovering from a serious operation, our concern will destroy the laughter. Similarly, we may dislike some things so intensely that we cannot see their ridiculous qualities. Nevertheless, any subject, however trivial or important, can become the subject of comedy if we place it in the right framework and distance ourselves sufficiently from its serious implications. Comedy arouses emotions ranging between joy and scorn, with laughter as their common response.

■ OTHER FORMS

NOT ALL PLAYS are wholly serious or comic. The two are often intermingled to create mixed effects, as in tragicomedy, a serious play that ends happily. Perhaps the best known of the mixed types is *melodrama,* the favorite form of the nineteenth century and still the dominant form among television dramas dealing with crime and danger. A melodrama develops a temporarily serious action that is initiated and kept in motion by the malicious designs of a villain; a happy resolution is made possible by destroying the villain's power. Melodrama depicts a world in which good and evil are sharply differentiated; there is seldom any question where the audience's sympathies should lie. The appeals are strong and basic, creating a desire to see the "good guys" triumph and the "bad guys" punished. This desire is usually met in a double ending, one outcome for the good, another for the bad. Melodrama is related to tragedy through its serious action and to comedy through its happy ending. It is a popular form, perhaps because it assures audiences that good triumphs over evil.

Concern for giving formal labels to plays has greatly diminished, probably because people no longer consider it possible to categorize situations and people precisely. Boundaries have come to seem so fluid that a single event might be viewed almost simultaneously as serious, comic, threatening, or grotesque. Thus tone might shift rapidly; elements that in the past were associated with tragedy or comedy might be intermingled or be transformed into their opposites. As a result, the old formal categories have lost much of their significance. Since World War II, plays have been labeled "tragic farce," "anti-play," "tragedy for the music hall," and a variety of other terms that suggest how elements from earlier categories and from popular culture have been intermingled.

Despite all of the changes, we need to recognize that each play has a form; otherwise, we would not be able to read or comprehend it. It is perhaps best to remember that the form of each play is in some respects unique—no two plays are exactly alike—but that there are sufficient similarities among certain plays to group them into a common category. Whether or not we have precise notions about tragedy, comedy, or other forms, we are aware of distinctions between the serious and the funny, and most of us freely use *tragic, comic,* and *melodramatic* to describe events in the world around us. Basic awareness of dramatic form will be helpful in many of the subsequent discussions in this book.

■ Style in Drama

EVEN PLAYS OF THE SAME FORM vary considerably. One reason for this variety is style. Like *form,* the word *style* is difficult to define because it has been used to designate many things. Basically, however, style results from a distinctive mode of expression or method of presentation. For example, style may stem from traits attributable to a period, a nation, a movement, or an author. In most periods, the drama of all Western nations has certain common qualities caused by prevailing cultural concepts (religious, philosophical, psychological, economic) and by then-current theatrical conventions. Thus we may speak of an eighteenth-century style. Within a period, national differences permit us to distinguish a French from an English style. Furthermore, the dramas written by neoclassicists have qualities that distinguish them from those written by romantics, expressionists, or absurdists. Finally, the plays of individual authors have distinctive qualities that set them off from the work of all other writers. Thus we may speak of Shakespeare's or Sophocles' style.

Style in theatre results from three basic influences. First, it is grounded in assumptions about what is truthful and valuable. Dramatists of all movements or periods have sought to convey truthful pictures of humanity, but they have differed widely in their answers to the following questions: What is ultimate truth? Where is it to be found? How can we perceive reality? Some have argued that surface appearances only disguise truth, which is to be found in some inner or spiritual realm. Others have maintained that truth can be discovered only by objective study of things that can be felt, tasted, seen, heard, or smelled. To advocates of the latter view, observable details hold the key to truth; to advocates of the former view, the same details only hide the truth. Although all writers attempt to depict the truth as they see it, the individual playwright's conception of truth is determined by basic temperament and talent and by the culture in which he or she lives.

Second, style results from the manner in which a playwright manipulates the means of expression. All dramatists have at their disposal the same means—sound and spectacle. Nevertheless, the work of each playwright is distinctive, because each perceives the human condition from a different point of view, and these perceptions are reflected in situations, characters, and ideas; in manipulation of language; and in suggestions for the use of spectacle. In the process of writing, playwrights set their distinctive stamp (or style) on their plays.

Third, style results from the manner in which the play is presented in the theatre. The directing, acting, scenery, costumes, and lighting used to translate the play from a written text to the stage may each be manipulated in many ways; the distinctive manner in which these elements are handled in a production characterizes its style. Because so many people are involved in producing a play, it is not unusual to find conflicting or inconsistent styles in a single production. Typically, unity is a primary artistic goal. Each theatre artist usually seeks to create qualities analogous to those found in the written text, and the director then coordinates all of the parts into a unified whole. In recent times, postmodernism has intermingled different styles, although this intermingling may itself be considered a style. Ultimately, style results from the way in which means are adapted to ends.

Part One has introduced and discussed several basic issues related to the nature of theatre, to the role of audiences, to varied criteria for judging theatrical performances, and to dramatic structure, form, and style. Such discussions remain somewhat abstract, however, until they are made concrete through specific examples. Consequently, the chapters that follow explore how these issues have been manifested in the theatrical practices of diverse times and places, both past and present.

Additional Opportunities with InfoTrac College Edition

How long does a play need to be in order to be effective? The length of a play may depend upon its subject and plot, but short plays have become increasingly popular. Read about short play festivals and events by using InfoTrac College Edition to find the article "The One-Act Takes Center Stage" by Leonard Jacobs in *Back Stage.*

1. What accounts for the popularity of shorter plays? In what types of venues are they performed?

2. Are there special challenges regarding the organization of dramatic action in a short play? If so, what are they?

Differing Styles of Production Applied to the Same Play

Courtesy of the Atlanta Shakespeare Company

Hamlet as directed by Drew Reeves for the Atlanta Shakespeare Company at the New American Shakespeare Tavern. Performed on a simulated Elizabethan stage and using Elizabethan styled costumes and properties.

T. Charles Erickson

Hamlet as directed by Brian MacEleny for the Trinity Repertory Theatre Company (Boston) and performed on a modern modified thrust stage. The costumes, scenery, and properties place the action in a 1930s manor house. The production foregrounds the social class distinctions in Shakespeare's play by portraying Laertes (pictured holding a tray) and Ophelia as servants in this *Upstairs/Downstairs, Gosford Park* styled *Hamlet.*

T. Charles Erickson

Hamlet as produced by the McCarter Theatre (Princeton, N.J.) under the direction of Daniel Fish. The scene design by John Conklin (complete with mirrored sidewall and folding metal table) and contemporary dress costumes by Kaye Voyce characterize the performance space as a rehearsal hall rather than Gertrude's bedroom. Seen here is Hamlet after killing the eavesdropping Polonius, who, in this production of the play, has been eavesdropping along with the audience on their side of the theatre's proscenium curtain.

PART 2

Varieties of Theatrical Experience

SINCE THE VERY EARLIEST times, some form of theatrical activity has existed, although surviving records permit us to trace it back with any certainty for only about twenty-five hundred years. When we look at today's theatre, we see only a small part of what the theatre is capable of. If we are to appreciate the full range of possibilities, however, we need to be aware of its multiple manifestations and the transformations it has undergone. This awareness of the diverse forms theatre has taken can alert us to possibilities for reshaping theatre in the present and future. Creative artists do not repeat past forms so much as reshape them by exploring alternative possibilities.

In the theatre, awareness of the past is important for other reasons as well. Many plays from the past are still performed regularly. Each of these plays was written with a particular kind of theatre structure, set of theatrical conventions, and audience in mind. Each also reflects the cultural assumptions and values of its time. Although plays may transcend the conditions of time and place (otherwise they would not communicate with us today), we can perhaps understand them most fully in the context within which they originated. Plays are among the best indicators we have of the culture out of which they came. They are simultaneously specific to a particular context and universal in their ability to speak to us in the much broader context of human experience in general.

In a book of this length, it is impossible to treat every form the theatre has taken in the past and present. Therefore, only representative types of theatrical experience will be discussed. Those chosen do not provide a comprehensive survey of the theatre's development, but they do touch on most major periods. Taken all together, these discussions should contribute to a fuller understanding of today's theatre.

Over its more than twenty-five–hundred–year history, theatre has taken diverse forms that alert us to the creative possibilities for reshaping theatre in the present and future. A scene from the English Romantic poet Percy Shelley's 1819 play, *The Cenci,* given an imaginative staging at the Jean Cocteau Repertory Theatre in New York.

©Gerry Goodstein

Electra by Sophocles, adapted by Frank McGuinness, as presented by the McCarter Theatre Center (Princeton, N.J.) with Zoë Wanamaker (at the bottom of the stairs) in the title role. Directed by David Leveaux; scene and costume design Johan Engels; lighting by Paul Pyant.

The second phase [in the development of theatre brings it] to as elaborate a scale
of great festival performance as one can reach, but still acted under the . . . open sky. . . .
[The offerings] are performed only on special, ritual occasions in the year. There is still
a dominating . . . religious element. There is no, or very little, professionalism.
—Richard Southern, *The Seven Ages of the Theatre*

4: Festival Theatre:

GREEK, ROMAN, AND MEDIEVAL THEATRE EXPERIENCES

DURING THE FIRST two thousand years of its existence, Western theatre was markedly different from the professional and commercial theatre that we know today and that has flourished only during the past four hundred years. Until the sixteenth century A.D., theatre in the Western world was performed primarily as part of festivals. Financed by the community and performed for the community, it was available only for brief periods each year when theatrical performances were presented as offerings to a god and for the enjoyment of the general populace. This type of theatre flourished in ancient Greece and Rome and medieval Europe, although in each the differences were as important as the similarities.

The Theatre of Ancient Greece

THEATRE IN THE WESTERN world can be traced back to ancient Greece, and especially to Athens, usually considered the cradle of Western civilization. The Athenians, inventors of democracy, were the first to have sufficient faith in humanity to let citizens be responsible for making the laws that governed their lives. Nevertheless, the Greeks did not consider everyone equal: Their economy depended on slave labor, and women were permitted no public role.

The belief in the ability of human beings to make significant decisions contrasted sharply with the beliefs of earlier societies that people are pawns of supernatural forces or all-powerful tyrants. This new attitude may have been a major factor in the development of Greek drama, which usually emphasized the attempts of human characters to control their own destinies. The Greeks nevertheless considered happiness to depend on harmony between human and supernatural forces and believed that this harmony could easily be broken. Greek tragedy often shows the results of human attempts to escape fate or the will of the gods. From the beginning, Greek drama was presented exclusively at festivals honoring Dionysus, one of the many gods worshiped by the Greeks, who conceived of their gods essentially as immortal human beings. Each god had power over a limited sphere of activity. Like human beings, these gods had many failings: They were jealous of each other, bickered among themselves, were vindictive when slighted, took sides in both human and divine quarrels, indulged frequently in adulterous affairs, and in general made human existence unpredictable. The Greeks did not observe a holy day comparable to the Sabbath but had a series of religious festivals throughout the year, one or more dedicated to each of the gods.

Dionysus, the god in whose honor plays were presented, was the god of wine (one of the principal products of Greece) and fertility. His blessing was sought in order to ensure fertility of both human beings and the land. Supposedly the son of Zeus (the greatest of Greek gods) and Semele (a mortal), Dionysus was killed (allegedly at the behest of Zeus' jealous wife, Hera), dismembered, resurrected, and deified. The myths associated with him were closely related to the life cycle and seasonal changes: birth, growth, decay, death, and rebirth; summer, fall, winter, and especially spring, the season of rebirth and the return of fertility. As the god of wine and revelry, he was also associated with a number of irrational forces.

By the fifth century B.C. Athens held four festivals in honor of Dionysus each year, at three of which theatrical performances were offered. Plays were not presented at the festivals of other gods. The major Dionysian festival in Athens was the City Dionysia. Extending over several days near the end of March, it was one of the most important occasions of the year and a major showcase for Athenian wealth and power. The festival was both a religious and civic celebration under the supervision of the principal state official. Theatrical performances were viewed in a radically different light than they are today.

They were offerings of the city to a god. At the same time, they were expressions of civic pride—indications of the cultural superiority of Athens over the other Greek states, which only later developed their own theatres. (Eventually there were theatres throughout the eastern Mediterranean in areas now parts of Turkey, Lebanon, Syria, Israel, southern Italy, and elsewhere.)

Our first record of a theatrical event in Athens is the establishment in 534 B.C. of a contest for the best tragedy, a form that also originated in Athens. The first winner was Thespis, the earliest playwright and actor whose name has come down to us. From his name we derive the term *thespian,* still used in reference to actors. During the fifth century, three tragic dramatists competed at each City Dionysia, each writer presenting a group of four plays: three tragedies and one satyr play.

A *satyr play* was short, comic or satiric in tone, poked fun at some Greek myth using a chorus of satyrs, and was presented following the tragedies. Thus, nine tragedies were produced at each City Dionysia, a total of nine hundred during the fifth century. Of these, only thirty-two have survived, all written by three dramatists—Aeschylus (523–456 B.C.), Sophocles (496–406 B.C.), and Euripides (480–406 B.C.)—who are ranked among the world's greatest playwrights.

From Baumeister, *Denkmäler des Klassischens Altertums*, 1888

Actors of a satyr play as depicted on a Greek vase of the late fifth century B.C. The embroidered robes resemble those thought to have been worn by some tragic actors. Notice at bottom center the flute player who provided the musical accompaniment for dramatic performances.

Performance in Ancient Egypt

Theatrical performances may have taken place in Egypt long before the Greeks held their first City Dionysia festival in Athens. At Abydos, the most sacred spot in Egypt, some kind of event relating to the myth of the Egyptian god Osiris occurred annually from around 2500 to 550 B.C. But it is unclear if this was a ceremonial rite, a theatrical performance, or a combination of the two.

According to the myth, Osiris, son of Geb (the earth) and Nut (the sky), succeeded his father as ruler and married his sister, Isis. His brother, Set, was jealous of Osiris' power. Set killed and dismembered Osiris, burying parts of his body throughout Egypt. However, Isis found these parts and with help Osiris was resurrected. Osiris went to dwell in the afterworld, where he became the judge of souls. His body was buried at Abydos, and Horus, Osiris' son, defeated Set and won back his father's kingdom. This is the most revered of all the Egyptian myths. Osiris is associated with the life-giving power of the Nile (water), fertility, and everlasting life.

No text for any play or plays (dating back to ancient Egypt) connected with the myth exists. Most of what scholars know about the event they have deduced from an account by one of its participants, Ikhernofret, who described his participation on a stone in approximately 1868 B.C. However, scholars disagree on how to interpret Ikhernofret's account.

Some scholars argue that each major event of Osiris' life was reenacted in an enormous spectacle staged at different locations over a period of weeks or months. Ikhernofret's account tells of ships sailing, battles, processions, and burial ceremonies. These scholars suggest the principal roles were taken by priests and that the spectators participated by representing crowds whenever crowds were called for by the events. If these scholars are correct, this was perhaps the most spectacular form of festival theatre ever performed.

Other scholars argue that the evidence does not indicate that the life or death of Osiris was reenacted. They see the event as a rite commemorating all of the dead pharaohs, each of whom was symbolized in Osiris, and that this ritual consequently took on the character of a royal funeral. Scholars who argue that the events were commemorated rather than reenacted reason that equating the Egyptian ritual with the Christian passion plays of the medieval period suggests a projection of one culture upon another without taking into account their many differences or the scarcity of existing evidence.

Because so many things may be deemed "performance," the debate over whether the event at Abydos was ritual or theatre is likely to continue.

Of the surviving tragedies, *Oedipus Rex* by Sophocles is often considered the finest. Performed about 430 B.C.—approximately a hundred years after the establishment of the contest for tragedy—it continues to be produced frequently. Before we look more closely at this play and its performance, let us examine some features of Greek theatre buildings and other conventions that affected staging.

The Theatre of Dionysus

PLAYS WERE PERFORMED in the Theatre of Dionysus, on the slope of the hill just beneath the Athenian Acropolis (a fortified area including the Parthenon, the city treasury, and other buildings considered essential to the city's survival). The theatre was located within a compound that included a temple and a large outdoor altar dedicated to the worship of Dionysus. Originally, the slope (without any seating) served as the *theatron* ("seeing place," the origin of our word *theatre*). A flat terrace below the slope served as the *orchestra* ("dancing place"), in the middle of which was an altar (*thymele*) dedicated to Dionysus.

This arrangement was gradually converted into a permanent structure. The auditorium eventually became a semicircle of stadium-like stone seats extending up the hill to the retaining walls of the Acropolis (the structure was not fully completed until the late fourth century B.C.). It held at least fourteen thousand and perhaps as many as seventeen thousand spectators. This seating curved about halfway around a circular orchestra, measuring about sixty-five feet in diameter, which was used as performance space, especially for the chorus. On the side of the orchestra opposite the audience was the *skene* ("hut" or "tent," the origin of our word *scene*). The term suggests that the original structure was used as a place to which the actors could retire or where they could change costumes. Once its possibilities as a background for the action were recognized, the *skene* was elaborated into a structure seventy-five to a hundred feet long and probably two stories high. It is thought that this scene house had three doors—a large central doorway flanked on either side by smaller doors—all opening onto the acting area. The roof of this structure could be used as an acting area to represent high places or for the appearance of gods. The *skene* was not architecturally joined to the auditorium; the spaces (called *parodoi*) at either side between the *skene* and the auditorium were used for entrances and exits by performers (especially the chorus) and

From Dorpfeld-Reisch, *Das Griechische Theatre*, 1896

Plan of the precinct devoted to the worship of Dionysus in Athens: at bottom, the temple and altar; at top, the theatre. Notice the rectangular structure (the *skene*) immediately below the circular area (the *orchestra*), and the passageways (the *parodoi*), used for the entrance of the chorus and others, between the ends of the *skene* and the auditorium.

Courtesy of the Embassy of Greece

The theatre at Epidaurus, the best preserved of all ancient Greek theatres, is still used for festival performances. The *skene* or scene house, at left, is a temporary structure erected on the ruins of the original. A tragic chorus of fifteen is performing in the orchestra. Notice the large size of the theatre and the audience–performer relationship.

perhaps by spectators before and after performances. Because the original *skene* has long since disappeared, no one knows exactly how it looked. (Some possibilities are shown in the illustrations in the adjacent illustration.)

The *skene* (or scene house) served as a formalized architectural background for all plays, even those set in woods, on seashores, or outside caves. This convention meant that dialogue, not representational scenery, probably established locale. The action in Greek plays usually took place outdoors, but occasionally the outcome of events that occurred indoors was shown. Most of the latter scenes involved the corpses (effigies) of characters slain offstage that were then shown onstage. To show the corpses, the large central doorway was probably opened and a wheeled platform (the *eccyclema*) pushed out. Another common occurrence in Greek plays was the appearance of a god. Sometimes the roof was used, but in many plays the god had to descend to ground level or to be lifted from the orchestra to roof level. For this purpose, a cranelike device (the *machina*) was used. (The overuse of gods to resolve difficult dramatic situations led to any contrived ending being labeled a *deus ex machina*—

From Ernst Fiechter, *Antike Griechische Theaterbauten*, 1936; courtesy of Dr. Charlotte Fiechter

No one knows precisely the appearance of the scene house used for the Theatre of Dionysus in the fifth century B.C. These drawings show four possibilities.

god from the machine—ending.) Probably nothing better illustrates the nonrepresentational conventions of the Greek theatre than the *machina,* because its fulcrum arm, ropes, and pulleys were visible to the audience. It was not intended to fool anyone; rather, it was used to suggest the idea of flying, a power possessed by the gods and denied to human beings (except for a few who had been granted special powers by the gods).

From our standpoint, one of the most remarkable things about the Theatre of Dionysus is its size. Today, a theatre with an audience capacity of even three thousand is considered almost unusable for drama because of the difficulty of seeing and hearing. We expect realistic visual effects and acting, and we feel cheated if we cannot see every detail as we do on the movie or television screen. Obviously, the Greeks had expectations that differed from ours, as is clear from the conventions they developed and accepted. The structures today that most resemble Greek theatres are sports arenas. (Keeping in mind the scale of such structures will help us understand many other conventions of the Greek theatre.)

■ The Performers

ONE MAY DIVIDE performers in the Greek theatre into four categories: actors, chorus, supernumeraries, and musicians. All were male.

By the time *Oedipus Rex* was produced, around 430 B.C., the rules of the contests restricted the number of speaking actors to three for each author. This rule did not restrict the number of roles to three; rather, all speaking parts had to be assumed by three actors, which meant that the same actor might have to play several roles and that the same three actors appeared in all three of the tragedies presented by a competing dramatist. *Supernumeraries* (extras) could be used, but they were not permitted to speak lines. This convention was probably developed to ensure fairness in the competition.

A principal actor was assigned by lot to playwrights, who usually staged their own plays. The playwright and the leading actor then probably chose the other two actors. A prize was offered for the best tragic actor at each festival, but only the leading actors were eligible to win.

The tragic chorus was composed of fifteen men. A playwright wishing to present his plays at the City Dionysia had to apply to the principal government official for a chorus. We do not know how this official decided which playwrights would be granted choruses, but it is clear that being granted a chorus was the mark that a playwright had been accepted as a competitor. This official also paired the dramatist with a *choregus,* a wealthy citizen who bore the expense of training and costuming that dramatist's choruses and of the musicians who accompanied the choruses during their training and during performances. The well-to-do citizens of Athens were required to take turns serving as *choregoi,* and most seem to have done so willingly. Thus, the state and a few wealthy citizens financed the productions. The playwright and his *choregus* shared the prize awarded for the best group of plays. We are not sure what the prizes consisted of; they may have included money, but the honor of winning seems to have mattered most, just as winning an Oscar or an Olympic medal does today.

Choruses were assigned approximately eleven months prior to the next festival. How much time was spent in training is unknown, but apparently the routine was not unlike that today in training athletes. Exercises and diets were controlled, and the chorus worked under the strict and strenuous supervision of a trainer. A great deal of emphasis was placed on singing and dancing, because the fifteen members both sang and danced the choral passages. Thus much of their training resembled that of opera singers and dancers. Usually they performed in unison, but at times they were divided into semi-choruses of seven members. The chorus leader sometimes had solo lines, but the rest of the chorus usually responded as a group or as two thereafter until the end of the play. The choral odes, performed between episodes, divided the action into segments something like the acts of a modern play. The chorus served several functions in Greek drama:

- It formed a collective character who expressed opinions, gave advice, and occasionally threatened to interfere in the action.
- It often seemed to express the author's point of view and establish a standard against which the actions of the characters could be judged.
- It frequently served as the ideal spectator, reacting to events and characters as the author would like the audience to react.
- It helped to establish mood and heighten dramatic effects.
- It added color, movement, and spectacle as it sang and danced the choral interludes.

The principal musical accompaniment in Greek tragedy was provided by a flute player, who preceded the chorus as it made its entrance and then (like the chorus) remained onstage throughout. The source of the musical accompaniment was thus visible to the audience and not kept offstage, as in most modern productions. The flute player wore sandals, one with a clapper on its sole for beating time. Both percussionist and flutist, he also seems to have composed the music he played.

Although much music was used in Greek theatrical performances, almost none of it has survived; the texts of Greek plays do little to make us aware that we should be hearing certain passages sung or recited to musical accompaniment. (Attempts to unite music and text as they had been in Greek tragedy gave rise to opera in Italy during the late sixteenth and early seventeenth centuries.) Greek music had a great variety of musical modes, each with a particular tonal quality that was thought appropriate to certain kinds of subjects or emotions. It probably more nearly approximated the sounds of traditional music from the Near East than that of

From *Monumenti Inediti*, 2, 1879

The Greek statuette of a tragic actor depicts the performer in a mask, headdress, and long robe. This figure is from a period later than the fifth century B.C. and is more exaggerated in appearance than would have been typical in Sophocles' time. The projections below the statuette are pegs used to anchor it in a base.

subgroups that performed and responded to each other alternately.

The chorus was one of the distinctive conventions of the Greek theatre. It usually made its entrance following the prologue and was present

Greek Tragic
Dramatists

Aeschylus, Sophocles, and Euripides are the only tragic authors whose plays have survived. Aeschylus (523–456 B.C.), a member of the Athenian nobility who distinguished himself in the wars against Persia, wrote approximately eighty plays, of which seven survived: *The Persians, Seven against Thebes, The Suppliants, Prometheus Bound,* and the *Oresteia* (a trilogy of plays: *Agamemnon, The Libation Bearers,* and *The Furies*). Some scholars believe that all of Aeschylus' surviving plays were parts of trilogies (three plays based on a single story or theme) treating philosophical issues. The *Oresteia,* for example, shows the evolution of the concept of justice as personal revenge is replaced by the impersonal judgment of the state. Aeschylus' plays, the oldest that have survived, are somewhat crude in comparison with Sophocles', but they show heroic figures wrestling with significant philosophical issues.

Sophocles (496–406 B.C.) was from a wealthy family, well educated, handsome, and popular. For a time, he served as one of ten generals, the highest elective office of the Athenian state. Sophocles wrote more than 120 plays and won 24 contests, more than any other Greek dramatist. Of his plays, only seven have survived: *Ajax, Antigone, Oedipus Rex, Electra, Trachiniae, Philoctetes,* and *Oedipus at Colonus.* Sophocles wrote his final play, *Oedipus at Colonus,* when he was almost ninety years old; it was produced the year after his death. His reputation as one of the world's great dramatists has remained constant since his lifetime, probably because of his masterful dramatic structure, moving stories, complex characters, beautiful poetry, and universal themes.

Euripides (480–406 B.C.), the last of the great Greek tragic dramatists, wrote about ninety plays, of which eighteen have survived. His best-known plays are *Alcestis, Medea, Hippolytus, The Trojan Women, Electra, The Bacchae,* and *Iphigenia in Aulis.* He is also author of *Cyclops,* the only surviving satyr play. Because he questioned many Athenian beliefs and customs, he was rarely honored during his lifetime but later became the most popular of tragic writers. Often denounced for writing about subjects considered unfit for the stage (such as Medea killing her children and Phaedra falling in love with her stepson), he was also disliked for suggesting that the gods of Greek myth are morally corrupt. Writing at the end of the fifth century, Euripides raised doubts about many of the values that Aeschylus had championed at the beginning of that century.

Euripides' plays challenged the prevailing social and religious standards of his time. Pictured here is *The Bacchae* as presented by the Guthrie Theatre (Minneapolis). Agave (second from right) has just discovered that while possessed she killed her son. Direction and scene design by Liviu Culei; costumes by Patricia Zipprodt; masks by Mary Walker; lighting by Marcus Dilliard.

western Europe or America. In Greek theatre, music may have had much in common with film music, enhancing the mood and emotion of the action it accompanied.

All of the performers, except the musician, wore masks of lightweight wood, cork, or linen. The use of masks, another of the Greek theatre's distinctive conventions, served several purposes: It facilitated the rapid change of roles when three actors had to play all of the parts; it made it easier for male performers to embody female roles; it helped the actor in assuming roles that differed widely in age or character type; and it assisted communication in the large theatres by capturing and emphasizing the essential qualities of each character. Because each mask covered the entire head and included the appropriate hair and headdress, the actor's appearance could be changed instantaneously with a change of mask.

A variety of clothing was used for stage purposes. Some characters wore a long-sleeved, heavily embroidered tunic, but because there are references in the plays to characters in rags, in mourning, and in Greek or in foreign dress, it seems unlikely that all characters were dressed alike. The selection of costume was probably determined by its appropriateness to the role. The sleeved, embroidered tunic, which was not a garment the Greeks wore in daily life, may have been reserved for supernatural or non-Greek characters, whereas native dress was used for Greeks. The usual dress in Greece was an ankle-length or knee-length garment called a *chiton*. On his feet the tragic actor wore soft, flexible, high-topped boots in common use at that time.

These conventions suggest that performance in the Greek theatre was highly formalized:

- A group of performers formed a chorus.
- One actor often played several roles in a single play.
- Men played both male and female roles.
- Performers wore masks and character appropriate dress.
- Performers sang, chanted, and danced much of the text.
- The scale of the theatre prevented small details from being seen.

Thus it was a performance mode quite different from that of the present day. That this mode was pleasing to the Greeks emphasizes a

Sophocles' *Oedipus the King* at the Stratford Shakespearean Festival (Canada). Oedipus (at center), played by Douglas Campbell, surrounded by the Chorus; Jocasta (Ellen Stuart) and Creon (Robert Goodier) in background. Directed by Tyrone Guthrie; designed by Tanya Moiseiwitch.

Donald McKague; courtesy of the Stratford Shakespearean Festival Foundation of Canada

simple truth: What any group accepts as effective theatrical performance depends to a great extent upon the group's familiarity with, and acceptance of, a particular set of conventions and upon the skill with which those conventions are handled.

Oedipus Rex and Its Performance

THE CITY DIONYSIA included five days of performances. In addition to the tragedies, there were comedies and dithyrambs (hymns to Dionysus sung and danced by groups of fifty men or boys). At the end of the festival, prizes were awarded. The performance of *Oedipus Rex* was thus embedded within a much larger festival framework.

The performances were open to everyone, but the audience was composed primarily of men and boys, although some accounts suggest that women, children, and even slaves attended. Officials were responsible for keeping order, and violence in the theatre was punishable by death.

Performances probably lasted all day, because several plays were presented. The audience at times expressed itself noisily and occasionally hissed actors off the stage. The atmosphere probably resembled a mixture of religious festival and athletic event.

Performances seem to have begun at dawn. There was no artificial lighting in the theatre, no proscenium arch or curtain. The auditorium rose sharply up the hill, so that most of the spectators looked down on the acting areas and could see over the stage house across a plain to the sea. The total visual context was immense.

The beginning of *Oedipus Rex* was signaled by the entrance through one of the *parodoi* of a group of people of all ages carrying branches, the symbol of the suppliant. Oedipus, masked and in full-length *chiton*, appeared through the central doorway of the stage house (which in this play represented a palace) to hear their petition that something be done to end the plague that had been ravishing Thebes for some time. Then Creon, returning from Delphi—where he had been sent to consult the oracle about how to end the plague—arrived through the other *parodos*.

After the suppliants left, the chorus of fifteen elderly Thebans, all as identical in appearance as possible and preceded by the flute player, marched into the orchestra and performed the first choral song. As this description of the opening suggests, spectacle was important throughout the performance.

Let us look more closely at the play. The skill with which *Oedipus Rex* is constructed can be appreciated if we compare the complex story (which actually begins with a prophecy prior to the birth of Oedipus) to Sophocles' ordering of the events. In the play, there is a simultaneous movement backward and forward in time during which the revelation of the past moves Oedipus ever nearer to his doom in the present.

The division of the play into a prologue and five episodes or scenes separated by choral passages is typical of Greek tragedy. The prologue is devoted principally to exposition: A plague is destroying the city of Thebes; Creon returns from Delphi with a command from the oracle to find and punish the murderer of Laius, the former king; Oedipus promises to obey the command. All of the necessary information is given in this very brief scene, and the first important question—Who is the murderer of Laius?—is raised. The prologue is followed by the *parodos,* or entry of the chorus, and the first choral song, which offers prayers to the gods for deliverance from the plague.

The first episode begins with Oedipus' proclamation demanding that anyone with knowledge of the crime come forward and placing a curse on the murderer. This proclamation has great dramatic power because Oedipus is unknowingly pronouncing a curse on himself. Then Tiresias, the blind seer, enters. His refusal to answer questions about the past provokes Oedipus' anger, the first display of a response that is developed forcefully throughout the first four episodes. Oedipus' quick temper, we later discover, has caused him to kill Laius. When Tiresias suggests that the truth is too painful to reveal, Oedipus suspects some trickery. The scene ends in a stalemate of accusations.

It is interesting to note that while the first four episodes move forward in the present, they go successively further back in time. This first episode reveals only that part of the past immediately preceding Oedipus' arrival at Thebes. The choral passage that follows the first episode reflects upon the previous scene, stating the confusion that Sophocles probably wished the audience to feel.

The second episode builds logically upon the first. Creon returns to defend himself against Oedipus' accusation that he is involved in a conspiracy with Tiresias. Queen Jocasta is drawn to the scene by the quarrel, and she and the chorus persuade Oedipus to let his anger cool. This quarrel illustrates Oedipus' complete faith in his own righteousness. Ironically, Jocasta's attempt to placate Oedipus leads to his first suspicion about himself. She tells him that oracles are not to be believed and points out that Laius' death did not occur in the manner prophesied. But her description of how Laius was killed recalls to Oedipus the circumstances under which he killed a man. He insists that Jocasta send for the sole survivor of Laius' party. This scene continues the backward exploration of the past, because in it Oedipus tells of his life in Corinth, his visit to the oracle of Delphi, and his killing of a man who is later discovered to have been Laius. The choral song that follows concludes that if oracles are proven untrue, then the gods themselves are to be doubted.

Though Jocasta has called oracles into question, she seems to believe in the gods, for at the beginning of the third episode she makes offerings to them. She is interrupted by the entrance of the Messenger from Corinth, who brings news of the death of Oedipus' supposed father, Polybos. But this news, rather than arousing grief, as one would expect, is greeted with rejoicing, for it seems to disprove the oracle's prediction that Oedipus would kill his father. Oedipus still fears returning to Corinth because the oracle also has prophesied that he will marry his own mother. Thinking that he will set Oedipus' mind at ease, the Messenger reveals that he himself brought Oedipus as an infant to Polybos. The circumstances under which the Messenger acquired the child reveal the truth to Jocasta. This discovery leads to a complete reversal for Jocasta; the oracles she cast doubt upon in the preceding scene have suddenly been vindicated. She strives to stop Oedipus from making further inquiries, but he interprets her entreaties as fear that he may be of humble birth. Jocasta goes into the palace; it is the last we see of her.

The scene not only reveals the truth to Jocasta, but also it diverts attention from the murder of Laius to the birth of Oedipus. The scene goes backward in time to the infancy of Oedipus. The choral song that follows speculates on Oedipus' parentage and suggests such possibilities as the god Apollo and the nymphs. The truth is deliberately kept at a distance to make the following scene more powerful.

The fourth scene begins with the entry of the Shepherd (the sole survivor of Laius' party at the time of the killing and the person from whom the Corinthian Messenger had acquired the infant). The Shepherd does not wish to speak, but Oedipus' servants torture him into doing so. In this very rapid scene, everything that has gone before is brought to a climax. We are taken back to the beginning of the story (Oedipus' birth). We learn that he is the son of Laius and Jocasta, that Oedipus killed Laius, and that Oedipus is married to his mother. The climax is reached in Oedipus' cry of despair and disgust as he rushes into the palace.

The final episode is divided into two parts. A Messenger enters and describes what has happened offstage. The "messenger scene" is a standard part of Greek drama. Because Greek sensibilities dictated that acts of extreme violence take place offstage, a messenger often appears to tell us of these acts. The results of the violence (the bodies of the dead, or in this case Oedipus' self-inflicted blindness) might be shown. Following the Messenger's part of scene, Oedipus returns to the stage and seeks to prepare himself for the future.

Oedipus Rex is structurally unusual, for the resolution scene is the longest in the play. Sophocles was not solely concerned with discovering the murderer of Laius, for in this lengthy final scene interest shifts to the question: What will Oedipus do now that he knows the truth? Up to this scene, the play has concentrated upon Oedipus as the ruler of Thebes, but in the resolution, Oedipus as a man and a father becomes the center of interest. At this point, he has ceased to be the ruler of Thebes and has become the lowest of its citizens.

Oedipus' act of blinding himself grows believably out of his character, for his very uprightness and deep sense of moral outrage cause him to

Courtesy of Guthrie Theatre

Oedipus (standing center), flanked by Guards, forces the Shepherd (kneeling) to tell him the truth. Oedipus doesn't realize that the truth he seeks will eventually implicate him as the killer of King Laius.

punish himself by thrusting pins into his eyes. Although he is innocent of intentional sin, he considers the deeds themselves (killing a blood relative and incest) to be so horrible that ignorance cannot wipe away the moral stigma. Part of the play's power resides in the revulsion with which people in all ages have viewed patricide and incest. That an essentially good man might commit these acts only makes them more terrible.

In drawing his characters, Sophocles pays little attention to the physical level. The principal characters—Oedipus, Creon, and Jocasta—are mature people, but Sophocles says almost nothing about their age or appearance. One factor that is likely to distract modern readers—the relative ages of Jocasta and Oedipus—is not even mentioned by Sophocles. When Oedipus answered the Sphinx's

riddle, his reward, being made king, carried the stipulation that he marry the queen, Jocasta. Sophocles never questions the suitability of the marriage on the grounds of disparity in age.

On the sociological level of characterization, Sophocles again indicates little. Oedipus, Creon, and Jocasta hold joint authority in Thebes, although the power has been delegated to Oedipus. Vocational designations—priest, seer, shepherd, servants—are used for some of the characters.

Unlike a modern play, then, in which characterization is usually built from numerous realistic details, here the characterization is drawn with a few bold strokes. For example, Oedipus' quick temper, his arrogance, his love for his children, and his willingness to take responsibility for his actions once they have been made clear to him

T. Charles Erickson

Oedipus leaves Thebes in exile at the end of *Oedipus Rex*. Pictured here is Ellen McLaughlin's new version of Sophocles' play at the Guthrie Theatre. Directed by Lisa Peterson; scene design by Riccardo Hernandez; costume design by David Zinn; lighting by Christopher Akerlind.

are all qualities that help us to understand Oedipus, although a limited number of traits are used. Jocasta is similarly restricted. She strives to help and comfort Oedipus, to mediate between him and Creon, and to stop Oedipus when she suspects that his quest may bring about his ruin. She commits suicide when the truth becomes clear. We know nothing of her as a mother, and the existence of the children is not mentioned until after her death. In Sophocles' play characterization is pared down to essential attributes and the most important traits are psychological and moral.

All of the speaking roles had to be played by three actors. Discovering which actor played which roles is revealing. The first actor played Oedipus throughout, because he is present in every scene. The second actor probably played Creon and the Messenger from Corinth; the third actor probably played the Priest, Tiresias, Jocasta, the Shepherd, and the second Messenger. The greatest range is required of the third actor, whereas the greatest individual power is required of the first.

In addition to the three speaking actors, a great many supernumeraries are required, many of whom no doubt appeared in more than one scene. For example, the band of suppliants in the prologue includes children, two of whom could later appear as Antigone and Ismene. Some who portrayed suppliants probably also later appeared as servants and attendants. To the actors must be added the chorus of fifteen members. The total number in the cast of *Oedipus Rex* was probably no fewer than thirty-five.

In reading the play, it is sometimes difficult to perceive that there were so many participants and that the visual and aural appeals were so numerous and continuous. However, the power of the play and of the production was so great that *Oedipus Rex* became one of the most admired plays in ancient Greece. It is still among the most frequently performed Greek plays.

Why has *Oedipus Rex* continued to attract audiences? We have already looked at its skillful construction and its concern with the moral

taboos of incest and patricide. In addition, it develops themes of universal relevance. The fall of Oedipus from the place of highest honor to that of an outcast demonstrates the uncertainty of human destiny. This is related to another theme: the limited ability of human beings to control their fate. Oedipus has done everything he can to avoid the oracle's prediction that he will kill his father and marry his mother but, in doing so, he unknowingly fulfills the oracle. The contrast between human beings seeking to control their destiny and external forces shaping destiny is clearly depicted.

It is significant that no attempt is made in the play to explain why destruction comes to Oedipus. It is implied that human beings must submit to fate and that in struggling to avoid it, they only become more entangled. No one in the play asks who or what has determined Oedipus' fate. The truth of the oracle is established, but the purpose is unclear. It is possible to interpret this play as suggesting that the gods, rather than having decreed the characters' fates, have merely foreseen and foretold what will happen. Such an interpretation shifts the emphasis, but it does not contradict the picture of humanity as a victim of forces beyond its control.

Greek Comedy

I N ADDITION TO TRAGEDY and satyr plays, Athens developed a distinctive comic drama. Comedy became an official part of the Dionysian festivals about fifty years later than tragedy. Although comedy was performed at the City Dionysia with the tragedies, it eventually found its most sympathetic home at another Dionysian festival, the Lenaia, which was held during the winter, when few outsiders were present and at which the playwrights were allowed to ridicule Athenian events more pointedly.

Five comic dramatists competed each year at the Lenaia, but each presented only one play. The conventions of comedy differed significantly from those of tragedy. Greek comedy was usually concerned with current issues in politics or art, with questions of war and peace, or with persons or practices disliked by the author. Occasionally playwrights used mythological material as a framework for satire, but usually they invented their own stories. Comedy used a chorus of twenty-four members, not always identical in appearance or all of the same sex. Sometimes the choruses were depicted as everyday citizens but often as nonhuman (birds, wasps, frogs, clouds). Many of the male characters wore a very tight, too-short *chiton* over flesh-colored tights, creating a ludicrous effect of partial nakedness. This effect was emphasized by an enormous phallus attached to the costumes of most male characters. This not only was a source of humor but also was a constant reminder of the purpose of the Dionysian festival: the celebration of fertility. Masks contributed to the ridiculous appearance of the characters.

Numerous authors wrote *Old Comedy,* as the plays written prior to 400 B.C. are called, but only eleven comedies have survived and all of these are by Aristophanes (448–380 B.C.). His plays mingle slapstick, fantasy, lyrical poetry, personal abuse, literary and musical parody, and serious commentary on contemporary affairs. The plot of an Old Comedy revolves around a "happy idea" (a farfetched premise) and the results of putting it into practice. For example, in *Lysistrata,* probably the best known of all Greek comedies, the women of Greece successfully use a sex strike to end a war. Old Comedy has several typical features:

- A *prologue* (introducing the happy idea)
- A *parodos* or entry of the chorus
- An *agon* (a debate over the merits of the happy idea, ending in its adoption)
- A *parabasis* (a choral passage addressed to the audience, most frequently filled with advice on civic or other contemporary problems)
- A series of episodes showing the happy idea in practice
- A *komos* (an exit to feasting and revelry)

From Robert, *Die Masken der Neueren Attischen Komoedie,* 1911

A figure from Old Comedy.

The unity of Old Comedy is found in its ruling idea rather than in a series of causally related events. Sometimes days or weeks are assumed to have passed during one or two speeches, and place may change often. Stage illusion is broken frequently as characters make comments about or to the audience.

After the fifth century, Greek drama declined in quality, although not in quantity. During the fourth century B.C., especially after Alexander the Great conquered most of the Middle East and Egypt, Greek theatres were built throughout the eastern Mediterranean areas, and plays began to be performed at festivals other than those in honor of Dionysus. Comedy underwent the most drastic change, no longer treating major political, artistic, or social issues, turning instead to the intrigues of everyday domestic life. Although Old Comedy (the type written by Aristophanes) is now considered superior to the New Comedy that replaced it, Old Comedy exerted little influence after its own time. New

Comedy, especially after it was taken over, adapted, and expanded by the Romans, set the pattern followed by most popular comic drama down to the present.

The Roman Theatre Experience

AROUND TWO HUNDRED years after the first performance of *Oedipus Rex,* Rome became a major power, eventually gaining control of Greece, the entire eastern Mediterranean, and most of western Europe and northern Africa. For seven hundred years, the Romans reigned over an extensive empire.

As in Greece, theatrical performances were part of religious festivals, although in Rome they might be for any of several gods. The Roman term for these festivals was *ludi* ("games"). At the *ludi,* in addition to religious ceremonies and sacrifices, many other activities were offered for the pleasure of the god being honored—as well as for the diversion of the Roman people whose tastes were considered to coincide with those of the gods. Such attitudes led increasingly to theatrical offerings that appealed to the greatest common denominator. The activities (other than the ceremonies and sacrifices) varied from festival to festival and from year to year, but all involved tests of skill, frequently with prizes for the most skillful or popular competitors. The theatrical company that won the greatest favor with the audience received extra payments, as did the winners of chariot races, horse races, animal baiting, acrobatic feats, and other activities. The Romans apparently placed their theatrical performances in the same category as sports and other forms of diversion.

The Romans were great assimilators, accepting, borrowing, or changing those things that seemed useful or desirable. When they encountered Greek drama in the mid-third century B.C., they imported a Greek writer, Livius Andronicus, to adapt Greek drama to Roman tastes. The first of his plays was produced in 240 B.C., and soon native Romans began to write plays. But the taste for this Greek-style drama seems to have peaked quickly, because the major period of this type of Roman drama was over by about 150 B.C. Roman taste favored novelty and variety. When Greek-style plays were introduced in 240 B.C., they were novelties to be elaborated and exploited. When their appeal faded, they were displaced by other kinds of entertainment, although they did not disappear altogether.

A conjectural reconstruction of one of the oldest Roman theatres (in Ostia, near Rome), built between 30 and 12 B.C.

D'Espouy, *Fragments d'Architecture Antique,* 1, 1901

Roman

Dramatists

Plays by only three Roman dramatists have survived: Plautus and Terence (both of whom wrote comedies) and Seneca (who wrote tragedies). Titus Maccius Plautus was born in 254 B.C. and apparently had worked at several trades, including that of baker and perhaps actor, before turning to playwriting in 205 when he was almost fifty years old. Thereafter, he was a prolific author up to the time of his death in 184 B.C. After his death, as many as 130 plays were attributed to him, but only 21, all of which have survived, are considered certainly his. *The Braggart Warrior, Pot of Gold, Pseudolus, The Captives,* and *The Menaechmi* are among his best-known works. Owing to his witty dialogue, distinctive characters, and farcical plots, Plautus was extremely popular in his own day and for long after his death.

Publius Terentius Afer (195 or 185–159 B.C.) is said to have been born in Carthage, brought to Rome as a slave, educated, and freed. He wrote six plays, all of which have survived: *Andria, Mother-in-Law, Self-Tormentor, Eunuch, Phormio,* and *The Brothers.* The chief interest in his plays lies in character and the double plots that provided him opportunities for showing contrasts in human behavior. In the Renaissance, Plautus and Terence were major influences on comic writing, in part because their plays were among the few that had survived from the classical era.

Lucius Annaeus Seneca (c. 5 B.C.–A.D. 65) was born in Spain but came to Rome at an early age. A philosopher, he was tutor to the future emperor Nero, who, coming to distrust and fear him, forced Seneca to commit suicide. Nine of his tragedies have survived, among them *Medea, Oedipus,* and *Phaedra.* Though Seneca wrote about many of the same subjects treated by Greek dramatists, his plays differ markedly from theirs, most notably in the amount of violence they include. Seneca's *Oedipus,* for example, dramatizes the same story as Sophocles' *Oedipus Rex,* but Seneca graphically depicts the horrors of the plague; a bull is sacrificed onstage so that the prophet Tiresias can read the entrails. In the final scene, Jocasta rips open her womb onstage with Oedipus' sword. In part because of such onstage actions, scholars believe that Seneca wrote plays to be read rather than performed. Seneca's were the tragedies from the classical world with which most Renaissance writers were most familiar, because most of them could read Latin but not Greek. The many bloodthirsty scenes in the English plays of Shakespeare's time owe much to Seneca.

Although the taste for full-length scripted drama sharply declined after the mid-second century B.C., the demand for other types of theatrical entertainment steadily increased. These entertainments included short comic plays, dancing, singing, juggling, tightrope-walking, acrobatics, trained animals, gladiatorial contests, animal baiting, water ballets, mock sea fights, and a host of other events. From a single day given over to theatrical entertainments in 240 B.C., the number had grown to 101 by A.D. 354.

Because plays, as written texts, survive and artifacts relating to other kinds of theatrical entertainment often do not, accounts of theatrical activities usually emphasize performances based on full-length written plays. Accounts of Roman theatre typically concentrate on theatrical production between 205 and 159 B.C., when Plautus (c. 254–184 B.C.) and Terence (195–159 B.C.) wrote the twenty-six surviving Roman comedies. Nine tragedies by Seneca (5 B.C.–A.D. 65) have survived, but they apparently were not intended for public performance. Let us look at the theatrical experience in the age of Plautus and Terence.

■ The Roman Theatrical Context

THE ROMAN THEATRE resembled that of Greece in many ways, but it also differed in significant ways. The Romans were ambivalent about anything derived from Greece, which they considered to be decadent. This ambivalence about drama is probably reflected in Roman comedy, all surviving examples of which are adapted from Greek plays. In these adaptations, the setting and characters remain Greek, even though, as many critics have pointed out, the manners and customs depicted in the plays are far more Roman than Greek. In the period when the Roman comedies were written, Rome placed great emphasis on "gravity" (*gravitas*, seriousness of purpose) in its citizens. Historians have suggested that the Greek setting was

retained in the comedies so as not to offend the Roman authorities that controlled the festivals and their contents.

As in Greece, the state assumed the expenses of theatrical production. The government made an appropriation for each festival as a whole; the officials in charge, usually wealthy citizens who often used the occasion to curry favor with the Roman populace, frequently contributed additional funds. Rather than choosing the plays, as seems to have been the rule in Greece, these officials contracted with the heads of theatrical companies for productions. The officials probably viewed the productions before they were presented, more for the sake of guarding against unacceptable material than for judging artistic merit.

In addition to underwriting production expenses, the Roman state also supplied the theatre in which the plays were presented. In the time of Plautus and Terence, all theatres were temporary structures (no permanent theatre was built in Rome until 55 B.C.). We cannot be certain about the appearance of these temporary structures, but it is usually assumed that they were less elaborate versions of the one depicted in the illustration on page 72. Tiered seating for several thousand people apparently surrounded a semicircular orchestra (half of the Greek full-circle orchestra). A long stage (probably more than one hundred feet long and twenty or more feet deep) rose five feet above the orchestra; it was enclosed at either end and across the back by a facade (the *scaenae frons*). This facade apparently had three doors in the back wall and one at either end. In comedy, the stage was treated as a street, with the doors in the back wall serving as entrances to houses fronting on the street, and the doors at the ends serving as continuations of the street. The facade also had windows and a second story that could be used as needed by the action. Roman comedies take place outdoors, most frequently in a street in front of one or more houses. The orchestra area seems never to have been used in the comedies, which did not include a chorus.

The scale of the Roman theatre was comparable to that of the Greek. It, too, was an outdoor structure, but the stage house and the auditorium were joined and of the same height, and consequently the audience could not see over the stage house. The individual performer was also much more prominent because of the raised stage and the absence of a chorus.

Admission to this theatre was free, seats were not reserved, and audiences were often unruly. In the prologue to his *The Carthaginian,* Plautus lists several types of distracting behavior that apparently were common among Roman audiences: "Let no worn out prostitutes sit in the front part of the auditorium, nor the guards make any noise with their weapons, nor the ushers move about in front of spectators or show anyone to seats while the actors are onstage. . . . Don't let slaves take up seats meant for free men. . . , let nursemaids keep little children at home. . . . Let matrons . . . refrain from gossiping." Guards were present to enforce order, but because a series of plays was presented each day, comings and goings were frequent. The plays had to compete with other attractions, and consequently the actors had to provide entertainment that would satisfy a mass audience. Terence states in the prologue to one of his plays that it is the third attempt to present the play; the earlier two attempts had been abandoned because one time the audience left to see rope dancers and another time to see gladiators. The total context of attractions was akin to the multiple channels on our television sets, which permit us to move from one attraction to another, seeking the most entertaining.

By the time of Plautus and Terence, there seems to have been a number of theatre companies. We do not know what they did when they were not performing at the festivals, but probably they traveled about or gave private performances for wealthy Romans. In any case, more than one company was hired to give performances at the festivals. Once hired, they were responsible for all details of production: finding plays, providing the actors, costumes, musicians, and so on. Although each company was assured a certain payment, special incentives were offered to those companies receiving the most favorable audience response.

The actors wore Greek costumes similar to those of Greek daily life, although there may have been some exaggeration for comic purposes. Because most of the characters were types, certain colors came to be associated with particular groups, such as red with slaves and yellow with courtesans. This conventional use of color extended to wigs as well, making distinctions among the types of characters instantly visible to audiences. All of the performers were male and wore masks.

Roman comedy does not deal with political or social issues but rather with everyday domestic affairs. Almost invariably, the plots turn on misunderstandings of one sort or another: mistaken identity (frequently involving long-lost children), misunderstood motives, or deliberate deception. They show the well-to-do middle class (the older man concerned with his wealth or children; the young man who rebels against authority) and those around them (slaves, slave dealers, hangers-on, courtesans, cowardly soldiers). Of all the characters, the most famous is perhaps the "clever slave" who, to help his master, devises all sorts of schemes, most of which go awry and lead to further complications. Very few respectable women appear in Roman plays, and although love affairs may be the source of a play's intrigues, the women involved seldom appear onstage.

While reading a Roman play, we should try to remember the musical element. In Plautus' plays, about two-thirds of the lines were accompanied by the flute. The flute player remained on stage throughout the play, although the actors ignored his presence. There were a number of songs by the characters (rather than by the chorus, as had been the practice in Greek drama). In performance, a Roman comedy closely resembled a modern musical.

Plautus' *The Menaechmi*. Directed
by Harold Shiffler; designed by
Richard Baschky.

Courtesy of the University of Iowa Theatre

■ *The Menaechmi*

O F ALL ROMAN comedies, Plautus' *The Menaechmi* has perhaps been the most popular.
It served as the basis for Shakespeare's *Comedy of
Errors* as well as for a number of others, including the American musical *The Boys from Syracuse*
by Richard Rodgers.

As in most of Plautus' plays, *The Menaechmi*
begins with a prologue that carefully lays out the
background of the action and goes over important points more than once. By the time the play
begins, the audience has been given a summary
of the prior action: Twin brothers were separated when very young, and one, who has been
looking for the other, arrives in Epidamnus
without knowing that this is where his twin now
is. Because the prologue has given the audience
this information, the introductory scenes are
used to establish the present conditions out
of which the comedy will grow: the dispute
between Menaechmus I and his wife; the visit
of Menaechmus I to the courtesan Erotium, his

gift to her of a dress stolen from his wife, their
plans for an elaborate meal and party later in
the day, and the departure of Menaechmus I to
the Forum; the entrance of Menaechmus II and
his slave, Messenio. When Menaechmus II is
addressed by name by Erotium and her servants,
he and Messenio assume that they are being set
up for some con game by people who have
learned Menaechmus' name at the dock where
their ship has just put in. The remainder of the
play presents a series of scenes in which the two
Menaechmi are in turn mistaken for each other,
and each is mystified and maddened by being
accused of doing things that the other has done.
The two are kept apart until the final scene,
when their meeting solves the mystery and
resolves the complications.

Although Plautus' comic sense is everywhere
evident, it may be seen at work especially in the
reunion, which might have concluded the play
on a sentimental note. Instead, the final lines
give the story a twist in keeping with the cynical
tone of earlier scenes: Menaechmus I, intending

A mosaic from Pompeii shows Roman actors preparing for a performance. Note the masks and musical instruments.

to go away with his twin, offers all of his goods for sale—including his wife, if anyone is foolish enough to buy her.

Plautus has little interest in social satire. Instead, he concentrates on the ridiculous situation growing out of mistaken identity. Consequently, when his characters indulge in adultery, stealing, or deception, they merely contribute to the overall tone of good-humored cynicism—with a considerable touch of misogyny.

As in most Roman comedy, the characters in *The Menaechmi* are types rather than individuals. Some roles are summed up in their names: Peniculus ("Brush") suggests the parasite's (or flattering sponger's) ability to sweep the table clean; the cook is called Cylindrus ("Roller"); and the courtesan is named Erotium ("Sexy"). Each character has a restricted number of motivations: The twins wish to satisfy their physical appetites; the wife wants to reform her husband; the father-in-law desires to keep peace in the family; and the quack doctor, who is sent for when the wife decides that Menaechmus I has gone mad, is seeking a patient on whom he can practice a lengthy and costly treatment.

A company of six actors could easily perform the ten speaking roles in *The Menaechmi*. Doubling of roles was common in the Roman theatre, and in changing roles all of the actors had the advantage of masks and conventionalized costumes and colors of garments and wigs. The play does not require actors who are skilled in the subtle portrayal of a wide range of emotions; rather, they need that highly developed comic technique that produces precision in the timing of business and dialogue. The scenes of quarreling, drunkenness, and simulated madness indicate that physical nimbleness is essential. Most of the actors also must be skilled singers, because the main characters have "entering songs" when they first appear and sometimes additional songs later in the action. The musical accompaniment was played on a flute with two pipes, each about twenty inches long. Sometimes it was bound to the player's head to free his hands for playing the instrument. Its sound resembled that of a modern oboe. (Some sense of the overall stage conventions can be derived from the illustration on page 76, although it does not give an adequate sense of the size of the stage.)

PRACTICES
AND STYLES

Roman Paratheatrical Entertainments

Roman religious festivals included entertainments—many of them quite violent and bloodthirsty—extending far beyond theatrical performances. The oldest and most popular of these was chariot racing, for which structures (circuses) were built that allowed twelve chariots to race abreast of each other. One of these, the Circus Maximus, held sixty thousand people. The circuses also were used for other forms of entertainment: horseracing (sometimes with trick riding), cavalry battles, footraces, acrobatics, prizefighting, wrestling, exhibitions of wild and trained animals, and fights between animals or between animals and men.

Another popular form of entertainment was gladiatorial contests. Originally gladiatorial combat was confined to funeral games and did not become part of state religious festivals until 105 B.C. The number of combatants steadily increased. In A.D. 109, five thousand pair were featured at one festival. It was primarily as places for gladiatorial contests and animal fights that amphitheatres were built, the most famous of which is the Colosseum (seating fifty thousand), which opened in A.D. 80 when nine thousand animals were killed during the hundred-day inaugural program. It was also here that Christians were placed in the arena with lions, for which they quickly became prey, as a form of entertainment and religious persecution.

Among the most spectacular of all of the entertainments were the *naumachiae* or sea battles. Sometimes these were staged on lakes, but amphitheatres also were sometimes flooded for such events. The largest of the *naumachiae* was given in A.D. 52 on the Fucine Lake east of Rome; many of the nineteen thousand participants it involved perished in the battles.

Although our own entertainments are not always as bloody, they match the Roman in their variety, especially as made available by television.

▓ Other Roman Drama and Theatre

BY THE BEGINNING of the Christian era, Rome seemed to have forgotten its earlier emphasis on gravity. As power came to rest almost wholly with emperors and armies, the people were offered increasing numbers of public entertainments, many of them bloodthirsty. During this time, theatres and amphitheatres were built throughout the empire, which included most of western Europe, northern Africa, and the Middle East.

In addition to comedy, the Romans also wrote tragedy. The only surviving examples of Roman tragedy, nine plays by Seneca, are from this period, but were probably not intended for production. Like Greek tragedies, Seneca's are based on myths but emphasize exaggerated emotions and onstage

From Laumann, *La Machinerie au Théâtre*, 1897

A conjectural drawing of a Roman *naumachia* (a staged sea battle) in the late first century A.D. (drawn during the Renaissance).

violence, features that centuries later would influence the tragic writers of Shakespeare's age.

The Roman preference for variety entertainment and short plays drove regular comedy and tragedy from the stage. The favorite form in late Rome was the mime, a short, topical, usually comic, often improvised playlet. (It was not silent, as today's mime is.) Women played the female roles in the mime, mime apparently being the first form in which female performers were permitted to appear. None of the mime actors seem to have worn masks. Mime used more realistic conventions than tragedy or comedy did. The dramatic action of mimes in late Rome often centered on sexual encounters, and the dialogue was often obscene. As Christianity grew, its sacraments and beliefs were frequently ridiculed in the mimes.

In addition to the mimes, late Roman festivals increasingly emphasized blood sports, which, along with mimes and variety entertainment, remained integral parts of religious festivals until around A.D. 400. Perhaps not surprisingly, the emerging Christian church became a strong opponent of the theatre—not only because of what was performed but also because it was associated with the worship of pagan gods.

The Roman Empire rapidly disintegrated after being overrun by invaders in A.D. 476. One consequence was the loss of the official and financial support that had sustained the theatre for more than a thousand years. During the following five hundred years, theatrical activity in western Europe was reduced to small bands of players or individuals who traveled about performing wherever they could. These performers were often denounced by the Christian church (by then the dominant and most stable institution) and denied its sacraments. It is ironic, therefore, that the revival of the theatre owed most to the church's discovery (during the last half of the tenth century) that the dramatization of biblical episodes was an effective means of teaching.

■ The Revival of Drama in the Middle Ages

HISTORIANS USUALLY divide the Middle Ages (or medieval period) into three broad phases: early (A.D. 900–1050), high (A.D. 1050–1300), and late (A.D. 1300–1500). Although these divisions are indicative of changes in society, all three phases shared a relatively stable set of beliefs and values that permit them to be grouped together and labeled *medieval*. During the first two phases, drama was performed primarily within churches or monasteries; it is usually called *liturgical drama*. During the third, it flourished in elaborate outdoor productions, some of which continued even after 1500 (when the Middle Ages are usually said to have ended). This type is usually referred to as vernacular religious drama. Most of the plays and productions discussed here are from the late Middle Ages. But before we turn to them, we need briefly to consider drama in the church.

The earliest known example of a liturgical play (one incorporated into the church service or liturgy) dates from about A.D. 970. It dramatized the arrival of three women at the tomb of Christ, the announcement by an angel that Christ has risen, and the subsequent rejoicing.

From *Romanesque Art in Italy*, 1913

The interior of a church like those in which plays were performed during the Middle Ages. Notice the absence of fixed seating, which left space for scenic units, performers, and spectators. In the background is the raised apse that might be used for scenes in heaven or high places, and beneath it is the crypt that might be used to represent the descent into the grave or Hell.

This short play (only four lines of sung dialogue) was performed as part of Easter services. Subsequently, many other biblical episodes were dramatized, but all remained short so as not to interfere with the regular services. These short plays were written in Latin (the language of the church throughout western Europe), were chanted or sung, and were performed by choirboys or members of the clergy.

Around A.D. 1200, some religious plays began to be performed outside the church, and by around 1375 a religious drama had developed independent of the liturgy. Plays of this new type were performed throughout most of western Europe until the sixteenth century, when controversy over religious beliefs and practices (exemplified in the Protestant secessions from the Roman Catholic Church) led to the suppression of these plays almost everywhere. But by that time these religious plays had for almost two hundred years been the major theatrical expression of western Europe. They differed from liturgical drama in being written in the vernacular language of a region rather than in Latin, in being spoken rather than chanted or sung, and in being acted primarily by laymen rather than clergy. They were financed by the community rather than by the church.

This medieval religious theatre in some ways resembled that of Greece and Rome. Like those earlier theatres, it was part of religious festivals in which the entire community was invited to participate. But, though similar in purpose, medieval festivals differed from those of Greece and Rome in how they were organized, financed, and presented.

■ Trade Guilds and the Corpus Christi Festival

THE PRODUCTION of the outdoor religious dramas in England is usually associated with trade guilds that flourished beginning in the thirteenth century. The return of relative stability after centuries of warfare and general uncertainty had by around 1200 encouraged

SOCIETY, ART, AND CULTURE

The First Female Dramatist

The first female dramatist of whom we have any record wrote her plays at about the same time liturgical plays began to be performed. Hrosvitha (c. A.D. 935–c. 975), canoness of a nunnery at Gandersheim (Germany), was, according to her own account, drawn to the comedies of the Roman playwright Terence but, fearing their adverse influence, decided to write others that would show Christian virgins and martyrs triumphing over earthly temptations. It is unclear whether her six plays, *Pafnutius, Dulcitius, Gallicanus, Abraham, Callimachus,* and *Sapientia,* all written in rhymed Latin, were performed during her lifetime. Most of these plays deal with characters martyred for their Christian faith or with young women who overcome the temptations of the flesh. After they were published in 1501, they exerted considerable influence on the didactic drama written during the sixteenth century for performance in schools. Hrosvitha, the first dramatist of the postclassical period whose name we know, is a figure of special interest to those seeking to recover the history of women in theatre.

Hrosvitha's uniqueness also reminds us that the theatre prior to the Renaissance was essentially a male preserve. The plays, even those that focus on female characters, were not only written by men but also acted by them. In general, the attitude seems to have been that only a man truly understands what a woman is or should be. In the Christian era, women were usually viewed as daughters of Eve—weak, easily tempted, and themselves temptresses—requiring guidance and discipline from a father or husband. The Virgin Mary was, of course, always treated as an exception.

increased trade among various parts of Europe, which in turn encouraged an increase in manufactured goods to satisfy the growing demand. Eventually, the need to regulate working conditions, wages, the quality of products, and other matters led craftsmen in various trades—bakers, brewers, goldsmiths, tailors, and so on—to establish guilds to promote the common good of those in each trade. Guilds were organized hierarchically: Each was governed by a council of masters (those who owned their shops and supervised the work of others); under each master were a number of journeymen (those skilled in the trade but who worked for wages) and apprentices (boys or young men who received room and board while learning a trade, usually over a period of seven years). The forces that gave rise to the guilds also encouraged the growth of towns. As the towns and guilds grew, power within each town came to rest primarily with the guilds, because they usually elected the mayor and the council from among their members.

The increased prominence of secular groups seems also to have been at least partially responsible for the church's desire to incorporate ordinary people more fully into its activities. One result was the creation of a new feast day, Corpus Christi. This festival, officially approved in 1311 and observed throughout Europe by about 1350, celebrates the redemptive power of the sacraments of bread and wine (the body and blood of Christ), the mystery that, to the medieval mind, gave meaning to existence: the union of the human and divine in the person of Christ and the promise of redemption through his sacrifice. All biblical events could be related to this festival, and eventually Corpus Christi became the occasion for dramas encompassing everything from the Creation to the Last Judgment. (Previously, plays about the birth of Christ had been done at Christmas, about His resurrection at Easter, and so on according to the church calendar.) Corpus Christi, observed sixty days after Easter, fell variously from May 21 to June 24. Coming during warm weather and

when the days were near their longest, it was favorable to outdoor performance.

The central feature of the Corpus Christi festival was a procession through the town with the consecrated bread and wine. The church sought to involve everyone in the festival by including in the procession representatives from every rank and profession (churchmen, nobles, merchants, craftsmen). This cooperative venture marked the beginning of an association that would eventually lead to the guilds' assumption of a dominant role in the staging of outdoor religious plays. The procession may also be the forerunner of the type of staging eventually adopted in some English towns: mounting plays on wagons and

A double page from the manuscript of the medieval outdoor drama staged at Valenciennes (France) in 1547. At bottom, the text of the play; above, simultaneous drawings of several scenes. At left, Christ is being nailed to the cross; center, the crucifixion; right, the entombment.

performing them at various stops—a combination of procession and performance.

In the British Isles, about 125 different towns produced plays at some time during the Middle Ages. Nevertheless, only a few plays have survived. Most of these are parts of *cycles* (a number of short plays that, taken together, dramatize the Bible from Creation to Doomsday). The surviving cycles come from four towns: York (whose cycle includes forty-eight plays), Chester (twenty-four plays), Wakefield (thirty-two plays), and an unidentifiable town (forty-two plays). All of these date originally from about 1375 and were performed at intervals (that is, regularly but not every year) over the next two centuries. During that time, the cycles underwent many changes as individual plays were rewritten, new ones added, others dropped. The surviving texts show the cycles as they existed near the end of their active production life. All of the plays dealt with the same basic subject: Christian views of God's ordering of existence as revealed in the Bible and in other church writings. Regardless of where they were written, they had many common characteristics and shared conventions.

Conventions of Medieval Theatre

A MAJOR CONVENTION of medieval drama involves the way time is handled. Throughout the Middle Ages, humanity was thought to participate in two kinds of time: eternal and earthly. God, Satan, and human souls exist in eternity—which, unlike physical being, has neither beginning nor end. Thus earthly existence is a short interlude during which human beings must make choices that will determine how they will spend eternity—in Heaven or Hell. Medieval staging often made the human dilemma visible by using a stage that depicted Heaven at one end of a long platform and Hell at the other end. The plays illustrated this situation, especially in the Doomsday (or Last Judgment) play. Because earthly time and place were relatively unimportant, the historical period or geographical location of an event was insignificant. There was little sense of historicity in the plays: Ancient Israelites were dressed in medieval garments, and Old Testament characters referred to Christian saints.

Nederlands Theatre Institute

Pieter Balten's painting *Peasant Fair* (detail) shows a temporary theatre (circa 1540) during the performance of a farce. Notice the raised platform stage (atop barrels) and the hanging curtain that helps to create a backstage area. A prompter stands behind the curtain, while another backstage helper hands a stool to an audience member.

The fluidity of time is also reflected in the structure of the cycles. Rather than treating one of many myths or a restricted story (as the Greeks and Romans did), the medieval cycles encompass the biblical story of humanity from Creation to Doomsday. Seldom was any causal relationship established among the various plays of a cycle or even among the incidents of a single play. Events were thought to happen simply because God willed them. Both time and place were telescoped or expanded as needed.

Staging also involved a number of conventions. There were no permanent theatres, so theatrical spaces were improvised. The principal requirement was an open space sufficient to accommodate a large audience. The stages might be either fixed or movable. Fixed stages were most typically set against buildings on one side of a town square or large courtyard, but they sometimes extended down the middle of a square (and were viewed from two or three sides) or were set up in the ruins of a Roman amphitheatre or other circular space (and were viewed in the round). Movable stages were wagons that could be moved from one location to another.

Regardless of the type of stage or location, the staging conventions were the same everywhere. There were two parts to the stage space: mansions and platea. *Mansions,* used to represent locales, were scenic structures, sufficient to indi-

PRACTICES AND STYLES

Special Effects in Religious Plays

F ar greater marvels could be shown on fixed stages than on pageant wagons. Miraculous events proliferated because they reinforced belief in biblical accounts of the life of Christ. One of the most elaborate of these fixed-stage productions was mounted at Valenciennes, France, in 1547. An account (by H. d'Outreman) published almost one hundred years later gives many details, of which the following are only a few:

> The production lasted 25 days, and on each we saw strange and Wonderful things. . . . [W]e saw Truth, angels, and others descend from very high up, sometimes by visible and sometimes by invisible means. Lucifer flew out of Hell on a dragon without anyone being able to tell how. . . . Jesus was carried to the top of a wall forty feet high by the Devil. . . . The fig tree, when cursed by Our Lord, dried up and its leaves withered in a minute. Other marvels shown at the death of Our Lord included the eclipse, the earthquake, and the splitting of rocks.

> Another account of a play staged at Mons in 1501 tells how water was stored in wine barrels on the roofs of buildings so that during a Noah play the flood could be represented by channeling water through perforated pipes (mounted above the playing area) to create five minutes of continuous rain.

The *Passion Play* as produced by the Arena Stage Theatre (Washington, D.C.).

cate place but not meant to do so fully. A single play might require more than one mansion, and an entire cycle might require as many as seventy. The *platea* was undifferentiated stage space. Once the location of the action was established by relating it to a mansion, the actors could move out and appropriate as much of the adjacent stage space as the action required; this appropriated space then was considered to be part of the place represented by the mansion. Thus the same space might change its identity merely by being associated with a different mansion. Place, then, was almost as fluid as time. There was no proscenium arch or other framing device. The overall setting ultimately symbolized (as the total cycle indicates) the entire universe—human and earthly existence framed by Heaven and Hell.

Costumes were used to distinguish among the inhabitants of Earth, Heaven, and Hell. Secular, earthly characters (no matter the period or place of the action) wore contemporary medieval garments appropriate to their rank, profession, or gender, because no attempt was made to achieve historical accuracy. God, the angels, the saints, and certain biblical characters wore church garments, usually differentiated by adding accessories: Angels wore church robes with wings attached, whereas God was dressed as a high church dignitary and often had his face gilded. Many saints and biblical personages were associated with specific symbols. For example, St. Peter carried the "keys to the Kingdom of Heaven," and the Archangel Michael wielded a flaming sword. Because such visual symbolism was common and well understood in the Middle Ages, it quickly identified characters for the audience. The greatest design imagination went into the costumes of devils, who were fancifully conceived with wings, claws, beaks, horns, or tails. The devils also often wore masks to emphasize their deformities.

There were frequently a number of spectacular special effects. Hell with its horrors was depicted with great care to make it as gruesome as possible. The entrance to Hell was often represented as the mouth of a fire-breathing monster (the "Hell mouth"). Many miracles described in the Bible were staged as convincingly as possible to reinforce faith. Nevertheless, the illusion of actuality was not always a goal, because several widely separated places were usually juxtaposed within a limited stage space and represented by fragmentary scenery. Thus medieval staging ranged between illusionistic and symbolic devices. Overall, conventions permitted rapid switches from broad outline to specific detail, asking the audience to use its eyes in a way analogous to present-day cinematography—focusing in, pulling back, and cutting from one locale to another. Much in medieval staging may now seem naive, but in its time it made efficient use of conventions that evoked the human condition as the medieval mind understood it.

◼ THE WAKEFIELD CYCLE

LET US LOOK at the English cycle staged at Wakefield, a town in central England. The surviving manuscript of this cycle contains thirty-two plays, beginning with the Creation and extending through the Last Judgment. As with all of the cycles, the authors (there appear to have been several) are anonymous. Most medieval artists did not strive for individual glory and recognition, but rather contented themselves with serving God, the church, and the community. Some of the Wakefield plays are borrowed from other cycles, whereas others have qualities suggesting varied origins. Five of the plays are by the same unknown author, usually referred to as "the Wakefield Master." His plays are noted for their details of everyday life and their comic scenes. One of these, *Noah and His Sons,* will be examined more fully later.

The production of the Wakefield cycle was a community effort involving the town council, the church, and the guilds. The council decided the plays were to be given in a particular year, but the church had to agree to this decision because the plays were part of a church festival. The church also had to approve the play texts to ensure that they did not distort church doctrine. There was an official copy of the cycle, which had to be adhered to in performance. The usual rationale for presenting the plays was "to honor God, to edify man, and to glorify the city." Most of the actual work of production was undertaken by the guilds.

The decision to perform the plays apparently was made several months prior to Corpus Christi. One official document is dated September 29, thus permitting nine months of preparation, although it is not certain how much of this time was devoted to preparation. Individual plays apparently were assigned according to a perceived relationship between the guild's specialty and the events of a play. The assignments at Wakefield have not survived, but we know that at other places the Shipwrights, Fishers, or Mariners were assigned plays dealing with Noah (the ark and the Flood), whereas the Goldsmiths were usually given the play in which the Three Kings bring gifts to the Christ child. Sometimes the connections are not immediately apparent. At Chester, the Shepherds' play was assigned to the Painters, whereas at York it was assigned to the Candlemakers (perhaps because they used tallow from sheep in making candles). Each guild was expected to assume the costs of producing its play, and the city council levied fines against those who failed to fulfill their obligations adequately.

At Wakefield, processional staging appears to have been used. Each play was mounted on a pageant wagon (similar to a modern float in a Rose Bowl parade) and drawn through the streets from one playing place to another in the order indicated in the script. No reliable description of a pageant wagon has survived. The wagons were probably as large as the narrow streets would accommodate and were probably designed to meet the requirements of specific plays. Because the same guild always produced the same play, its pageant wagon and scenery could be designed and built to meet the specific requirements of its play. The wagons could be stored and refurbished as needed for subsequent festivals. Each wagon usually had to carry one or more mansions and might require some machinery for special effects. It seems probable that at each playing place the wagon was drawn up alongside a stationary platform that served as the *platea.* The actors sometimes performed scenes in the street. (See the illustration on page 87 for conjectures about how the performance space was arranged.)

At left, a pageant wagon alongside a wheeled platform stage; above, a floor plan of this arrangement; below right, plan of a booth stage, used to show its similarity to the pageant wagon arrangement of the other two drawings. Reconstructions by Glynne Wickham.

In addition to providing the pageant wagon and its equipment, each guild had to supply performers and someone to oversee the production. All of the personnel involved in production were amateurs, but as time went by some became quite skilled and seem to have approached the status of professionals. Surviving records sometimes show that one actor was paid much more than the others; thus it seems likely that he was in charge of the total production (that is, served as director). Some guilds put the same person under contract for several years to stage their part of the cycle. Actors were recruited from the local populace and were not restricted to members of the guild producing that play. We do not know how many rehearsals were held, but the plays were relatively short, and often the same actor played the same role at many different festivals. All of the actors were male, female roles being played by boys or young men.

Costumes, for the most part, consisted of clothing in common use in medieval England and were usually supplied by the actors or borrowed. Church robes, the starting point for ecclesiastical and angelic costumes, could be borrowed or rented from the church, but the costumes of devils had to be made.

Each guild rehearsed and prepared its play separately from the others. No dress rehearsal of the entire cycle was needed, because coordinating the individual plays merely required that the pageant wagons be lined up in the correct order.

The council specified the places at which the plays would be performed; at Wakefield there probably were two or three. Actors were required to be in their pageant wagons by 5 A.M., presumably the starting time. When all was ready, the first wagon moved to the first performance place, where the actors performed the play, and then moved on to the next. Thus all of the plays were performed in the prescribed order at each of the designated places.

On the day of performances, all normal work was suspended; most of the town's residents must have crowded into the places designated for the performances. Word about the performances was usually sent to neighboring towns, and a large number of spectators probably came from outside Wakefield. Provisions for the audience were not extensive, other than choosing sites that permitted a crowd to assemble. The majority of spectators stood, although some seating may have been erected. The windows and roofs of houses overlooking the performance place were in great demand and probably were rented. The council's proclamation provided that sizable fines were to be levied against anyone who disturbed the plays or hindered their procession; carrying weapons was forbidden. Even if the performances began at 5 A.M., they probably required all of the daylight hours (at that time of the year in central England until around 10 P.M.) to complete the full cycle at each of the prescribed stops. That would have made for a very long day, but spectators were as mobile as the wagons and could move from one viewing place to another, watch only some of the plays, move forward or back along the route, and choose how long they wanted to stay. The atmosphere must have been as festive as it was reverential. It was both a holiday and a holy day.

Noah (from *The Mystery Cycle*), adapted by Bernard Sahlins and performed at the Court Theatre (Chicago). The main characters wear slickers as they weather out the flood on the ark.

It is impossible here to examine in detail a performance of the entire Wakefield cycle. Therefore, we will look at one play, considered by many to be one of the best of all of the English cycle plays. It is the cycle's third play, *Noah and His Sons.*

Noah and His Sons

BEFORE THE spectators saw *Noah and His Sons,* they had already viewed two other plays, *The Creation* and *The Killing of Abel. Noah and His Sons,* then, comes very early in the overall cycle of thirty-two plays. This 558-line play is an elaboration of biblical passages from Genesis (chapters 6 through 10).

The play begins with Noah praying to God and comparing God's goodness toward all creatures with the ungrateful responses of those he has created, not only human beings but also Lucifer, whose rebelliousness has caused him to be cast out of Heaven. God, unseen by Noah, continues this lamentation, condemning the wickedness of human beings and promising to destroy them all—except faithful Noah and his family. He then appears to Noah and orders him to build a ship, giving him precise directions about its size and layout. He also orders Noah to take his family and a pair of every known beast into the ship so they may be saved from a flood that will destroy all creatures not on the ship.

The solemn tone of this opening expository scene, which takes up approximately one-third of the play, is abruptly broken when Noah returns home to his wife, who immediately begins to berate him for being an incompetent provider. Their dispute rapidly escalates into an exchange of blows, in which both participate equally. This scene redirects the play's tone toward domestic comedy and relocates the biblical action within the familiar world of the English audience.

Noah then turns to carrying out God's orders and, without any assistance and within a space of twenty-five lines, builds the ship. There follows a lengthy segment during which Noah's three sons and their wives board the ship and seek to persuade Noah's wife to do likewise. Another comic fight occurs between husband and wife, during which they seemingly beat each other thoroughly, before the wife agrees to come aboard (and then only because the water is rising around her). The remainder of the play takes place on the ship, where a year of domestic harmony passes in the midst of anxiety about their plight, as they measure the depth of the water and send out birds in search of signs that land has reappeared. Eventually, the waters recede, and the play ends with prayers that human beings will profit from Noah's example and reconcile themselves to the will of God.

The action of the play is almost equally divided among three parts: One third is devoted to the opening expository scene; one third to the two scenes of bickering between Noah and his wife; and one third to the ship-building and onboard scenes. Time is severely telescoped in the third part. No clues are given as to how much time elapses during the building of the ship, but in the final scene Noah speaks of having endured forty days of rain and of having been on board for three hundred and fifty days.

There are nine roles, of which six are very minor—those of Noah's sons and their wives. They seem to be there only because the biblical source includes them. They have few lines and they do not help build the ship. They figure primarily in the scene in which they assist Noah in coaxing his wife on board. Characterization of the three main roles is simple. God magisterially voices feelings of having been betrayed by his ungrateful creations and announces his decision to destroy them. His benevolence is seen only in his attitude toward Noah and his family. Noah, who claims to be more than six hundred years old, is pious and obedient. His life apparently has been tranquil except where it involves his wife. Despite his wife's claim that Noah is incompetent, he seems unusually efficient in building the ship and carrying out God's instructions. Nevertheless, he would have seemed comi-

cal to medieval audiences because of his inability to control his wife. Noah's wife is clearly very headstrong and independent. She resists being bossed about by anyone and insists on her right to gossip with her friends. She apparently is an industrious housewife, always spinning, and once aboard shares responsibility equally with Noah. All of the roles would have been played by men; having Noah's wife played by a man probably contributed to making the quarreling and fighting more acceptably comic. The realistic bickering and highly physical fights help to balance the necessarily nonrealistic scenes—building the ship, enduring forty days of rain, and floating for a year on the flood waters.

The play seems to demand stylized speech. It is written in sixty-two nine-line stanzas, each using the same structure. The first four lines use

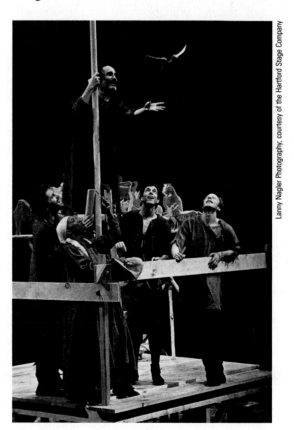

Noah, one part of *The Mystery Plays,* as performed at the Hartford Stage. Adapted by John Russell Brown; directed by Mary B. Robinson.

a double rhyme scheme: The final words of the lines rhyme, as do words halfway through those lines. The fifth and ninth lines are short and rhyme, and lines six through eight, somewhat longer than five and nine, also rhyme. Thus rhythmical speech is a basic structural element.

Only one mansion is required—the ship. It seems likely that a pageant wagon was fitted out to represent a ship and that the ship was initially concealed by a cloth that was gradually removed during the short scene in which Noah supposedly builds it. It also seems likely that the ship was supplied with cut-outs or painted cloths representing animals, because only one line mentions getting "gear, cattle, and company" on board. The initial scene and the scenes with Noah's wife require no mansions. The opening scene probably was played with God standing atop the ship with Noah on the platform adjacent to the pageant wagon. The scenes with the wife also probably were played on the platform. When Noah leaves to build the ship, he declares that he must take his tools along—the only stage property that is mentioned in the play other than the spinning wheel, straps that figure in the beating scenes, and a plumb line that is lowered to measure the depth of the water. The raven and doves sent out to search for signs of life may have been actual birds. The costuming was simple. All of the characters except God would have worn contemporary working-class dress. God would have been costumed in garments associated with the pope or some other high church official.

Because the spectators crowded around the performance space, many spectators saw the actors at close range, and the total configuration of the playing places meant that the performance was viewed from a variety of angles. Thus the spatial relationship between audience and performer and the overall scale differed markedly from those of the Greek and Roman theatres. In addition, the degree of formalization apparently was less than in classical theatres, because most elements of performance in *Noah and His Sons,* though perhaps somewhat exaggerated, were variations on things familiar to the audience.

When the play ended, the wagon moved on to another site and was replaced by the next wagon, bearing a play about Abraham and Isaac. Twenty-nine more short plays would be performed before the day ended.

Other Medieval Theatre and Drama

IN ADDITION to religious plays, several other dramatic types were popular during the Middle Ages, among them moralities, farces, and interludes. *Morality plays* flourished between 1400 and 1550. Unlike the religious plays, which treated biblical or saintly characters, morality plays treated the spiritual trials of ordinary persons. They were allegories about the moral temptations that beset all human beings. The protagonist (often called Everyman or Mankind) was advised and cajoled by personifications of good and evil; most frequently the protagonist succumbed to temptation but was eventually recalled to the path of righteousness by a character called Faith or Mercy or by the grace of God. The most famous morality play is *Everyman,* in which God orders Death to summon the title character (see photo on page 91). Everyman, who has been too busy leading a carefree existence to think about death, now seeks among his companions (Kindred, Knowledge, Five Wits, Beauty, Strength, and so on) for one that will accompany him on his journey, but once they know his destination, they decline his invitation. Ultimately only Good Deeds goes into the grave with him. Through this search, Everyman comes to understand the relationship of his earthly life to salvation.

During the sixteenth century, the morality play was gradually secularized as its original moral concerns were replaced by new ones such as the ideal training of rulers and the content of a proper education. Then, when religious controversies erupted, morality plays were used to attack one's opponents, Protestants or Catholics,

Everyman as produced by the Royal Shakespeare Company. Directed by Kathryn Hunter and Marcello Magni. Sets by Rosa Maggiora; lighting by Chris Davey.

by associating one's own side with good and one's enemies with evil. Such changes moved the morality play increasingly toward a wholly secular drama; thus it served as a transition between the medieval religious drama and the secular drama of Shakespeare's time.

A comic secular drama, *farce,* began to emerge around the thirteenth century, but because the form was not officially encouraged, it remained a minor though highly entertaining type, emphasizing the ridiculous and comically depraved aspects of human behavior. One of the best examples is *Pierre Patelin,* an anonymous French farce of the fifteenth century that dramatizes the story of an impoverished lawyer who buys a piece of cloth from a merchant, whom he invites to dinner to receive his payment. When the merchant arrives, Patelin is in bed, and his wife swears that he has not been out of the house. Patelin pretends madness, beats the merchant, and drives him away without payment for the cloth. This story is loosely joined to a second one in which Patelin agrees to defend a shepherd against a charge of stealing sheep. He counsels the shepherd that during the trial he should answer only "Baa" no matter what anyone says to him. The accuser turns out to be the merchant, who creates total confusion during the proceedings by his alternating charges against

the shepherd and Patelin. In view of this confusion and the shepherd's seeming feeblemindedness, the judge dismisses the case, but when Patelin tries to collect his fee, the shepherd runs away, calling "Baa." Like many farces, *Pierre Patelin* shows clever knaves outwitting each other, but it adds a comic twist by having the seemingly stupid shepherd outwit the experienced lawyer.

The interlude was a nonreligious serious or comic play so called because it was performed between the parts of a celebration (such as the courses of a banquet, usually for some festival or special occasion). It was associated with the rise of professional performers, who developed their art in the specialized entertainments presented in the households of kings and nobles. Eventually these servants were permitted, when not needed at home, to travel about and perform for pay. Thus the interlude is associated with the rise of both the professional actor and the professional theatre.

In addition to those discussed here, many other celebrations utilized theatrical elements, because the Middle Ages was a time when religious and secular ceremony played an important role in people's lives. Amidst the diversity, the religious drama was the most important and characteristic. More than any other type, it appealed to (and actively involved) the largest

An interlude performed during a medieval banquet. In the background St. George is on his horse; he will fight and slay the dragon (center right). The ruler's table is center back. Notice the spectators in the gallery (upper left).

From Pougin, *Dictionnaire...du Théâtre,* 1885

cross section of the populace and most fully embodied those concerns that the age idealized— the biblical vision of human history and destiny.

Comparing Greek, Roman, and Medieval Theatre

THE GREEK, ROMAN, and medieval theatre experiences, then, were alike in some ways and quite unlike in others. For the most part, they were occasional (that is, performances were given on special occasions and not on a continuing, everyday basis, as in modern times), ceremonial (performances were parts of religious festivals and considered offerings to gods), financed by the state, religious or secular organizations, or wealthy citizens, and open to all. They also used many similar conventions: male performers only,

musical accompaniment, large audience spaces, and formalized scenic backgrounds. Greek and Roman theatre used masks for all characters (except in mime); medieval theatre used masks for devils and sometimes for allegorical characters.

There were many differences. In Greek theatre, the chorus played a large role, as did dance. In Roman theatre, the musical element was more equally distributed throughout the play and was associated with the actors more than with the chorus. In medieval theatre, music was plentiful but followed no fixed plan. The theatre structures also differed. But the most important differences were those reflecting basic values. The Greeks seem to have placed great emphasis on moral values and significant issues, whereas the Romans were more concerned with popular entertainment, and medieval theatre was tied to Christian teaching.

Additional Opportunities with InfoTrac College Edition

Can the plays of ancient Greece be relevant today? Many theatre practitioners have found these plays to be appropriate material for addressing contemporary issues. To learn more about how the classics are being performed today, use InfoTrac College Edition to find and read Charles L. Mee's interview with writer and performer Will Power in *American Theatre.*

1. As a class, take up both sides of the argument on "remaking the classics."

2. Will Power describes some of the details of the casting process for his production. In what way did this discussion add to your understanding of this often-difficult process?

Building a Broad Context

■ **First City Dionysia Festival held in Athens (534 B.C.)**

■ Eastern thought and religions develop: Buddhism established by Buddha in India; Confucius develops ethical & social thought in China (both c. 500 B.C.)

■ First five books of the Hebrew Bible (which Jews call the *Torah*) completed (c. 400 B.C.)

■ Alexander the Great (356–323 B.C.) conquers the "known" world. After his death, his generals divide his empire

■ Great Wall of China built (c. 215 B.C.)

■ **Plautus and Terence mark zenith of Roman drama (205–160 B.C.)**

■ Octavian establishes Roman Empire as the Emperor Augustus (30 B.C.)

■ Birth of Jesus Christ (4 B.C.) & crucifixion (c. A.D. 30) *All subsequent dates are A.D.*

■ First Gospels of St. Mark, St. John, St. Matthew (65–85)

■ Rome falls under repeated attacks by Germanic and other tribes (476)

■ Plague spreads through Europe, killing nearly half its population (542–594)

■ Mohammed, founder of Islam, flees from Mecca to Medina (the *Hegira*); first year of Muslim calendar (622); returns to conquer Mecca, which becomes Islam's spiritual center (630)

■ **Possible beginning of liturgical drama (c. 970)**

■ Viking raider Leif Eriksson sails to North America; Pueblo III cliff dwelling cultural period; Chinese perfect their invention of gunpowder (all c. 1000)

■ Pope Urban II calls for a holy war to wrest Jerusalem from the Muslims; at least eight European crusades are launched between 1095 and 1291

■ The Inquisition formed to combat heresy (1231)

■ "Black Death" (bubonic plague) devastates Europe; between 1347 and 1351 almost 75 million die

■ **Festival of Corpus Christi observed throughout Europe (c. 1350)**

■ Florence becomes center of Renaissance arts and Humanist learning under the Medicis (c. 1450)

■ Johann Gutenberg completes first Bible printed with movable type (1462)

■ Columbus becomes first European to encounter Caribbean islands (1493)

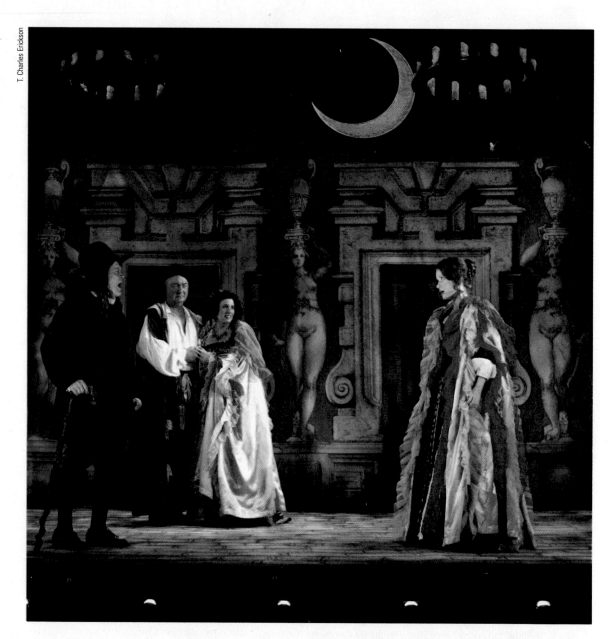

The School for Husbands by Molière, translated by Richard Wilbur; directed by Doug Hughes at the Westport Country Playhouse; scene design by Hugh Landwehr; costume design by Linda Fisher; lighting by Jane Cox; original music by Louis Rosen.

5 :
Creating a Professional Theatre:

ELIZABETHAN ENGLAND, ITALIAN COMMEDIA DELL'ARTE, AND SEVENTEENTH-CENTURY FRANCE

THE THEATRICAL EXPERIENCES we have examined so far were parts of festivals sponsored by governmental or religious authorities, performed on special occasions, and financed by the state or wealthy citizens. Although there were other types of performance, they were considered inferior. Then, during the sixteenth and seventeenth centuries, the role of theatre in European society was redefined.

Creating a Professional Theatre

AMONG THE FORCES that brought about change was a growing secularization of thought as people became more interested in life here and now and less preoccupied with preparing for the life hereafter. As interest in earthly concerns increased, a rebirth of learning occurred in many fields that had long been neglected. This period of rebirth is often referred to as the Renaissance. Scholars, artists, and others turned their attention once more to Greece and Rome, both of which had played a relatively minor role during the Middle Ages, in part because so many classical works had been lost or destroyed while others were ignored because, as pagan creations, they

were considered to be dangerous. Those that had continued to be used were interpreted in ways that obscured their pagan origins. Revived interest in the classical world included Greek and Roman plays and theatrical practices, even though during the Renaissance understanding of the classical theatre was severely limited and often distorted. Nevertheless, educated people began to perceive alternatives to medieval practices, and playwrights began to write plays that imitated or adapted classical subjects and forms or that mingled medieval and classical elements.

The Renaissance spirit of inquiry also extended to religion. During the sixteenth century disputes over church doctrine and practice led to secessions from the Roman Catholic Church and the formation of several Protestant sects. Various factions soon found theatrical performance a good propaganda medium (especially because the majority of the audience could not read), and they exploited it in plays that ridiculed their opponents and upheld their own views. Disputes often erupted into violence, even wars. Rulers were forced to choose sides in religious controversies. In England, the official state religion changed four times during the sixteenth century, and each time many people were executed because of their refusal to accept the changes. These struggles served to shift the center of power to the state and away from the church, which had been the dominant force throughout the Middle Ages.

Under these circumstances, it is not surprising that by 1550 both church and state had begun to look for ways to reduce disturbances. Shortly after Elizabeth I succeeded to the English throne in 1558, she decreed that no plays dealing with religious or political subjects were to be performed. This decree, in effect, was the death knell for the cycle plays. By 1600, they had all but disappeared, not only in England but also throughout Europe, where similar prohibitions existed. A type of theatrical experience—the outdoor religious play—that had enjoyed enormous popularity for more than two hundred years was now forbidden by the same institutions (church and state) that had encouraged and supported it.

Forbidden to perform plays on religious subjects, the theatre became secular and for its subjects it turned to classical literature, historical chronicles, and legends. In part out of necessity, a new kind of drama was born. Perhaps more important, an alternative kind of theatre had to be invented. Because the state, church, and wealthy individuals had withdrawn or curtailed their patronage, other kinds of support had to be found. The theatre was forced to become a commercial enterprise. Rather than remaining occasional (part of a religious festival), officially supported, and free, it became continuous, self-supporting, and sufficiently entertaining to keep a paying public coming back.

Those who had been the most enthusiastic supporters of the religious cycles were the most vehement opponents of a professional theatre. To them, the presentation of plays for the glory of God, the honor of the city, and the edification of citizens seemed worthy goals, but devoting one's life to performing plays for money was considered wasteful and sinful. The guilds that had produced many of the cycle plays in England sought to have the professional theatre banned on the grounds that it took people away from work, encouraged immoral behavior,

spread diseases, and offered cover for seditious activities. Guilds saw the professional theatre in a different light than they had viewed the largely amateur theatre of the Middle Ages.

To survive, professional groups had to be able to play often, had to have a stock of plays sufficiently large and varied to keep the limited available audience coming back, and had to have a performance space large enough to accommodate a sizable number of paying customers and sufficiently enclosed to permit the company to control access and collect entrance fees. They also had to own or control their own costumes, scenery, and other production elements and had to assemble a company of actors and production personnel that could devote full time to theatrical production and performance.

Accomplishing these tasks was difficult because in the sixteenth century acting was not an accepted profession and did not fit into the then-dominant trade-guild scheme under which there was a clear-cut hierarchy of responsibility under which each master was held responsible for the journeymen and apprentices who worked for him. Because actors did not belong to a guild, they were considered "masterless men," meaning that no one was considered to be responsible for them; they fell into the category of vagrants who, because of their threat to the social order, were subject to arrest and punishment. To get around this difficulty, acting companies petitioned noblemen to serve as their patrons; technically, actors became "servants" of these patrons and therefore were no longer masterless. For this reason, during Shakespeare's time the acting companies had such titles as the Lord Admiral's Men, the Lord Chamberlain's Men, and the King's Men as indications of their legal status. Without the patronage of rulers and noblemen, the professional theatre would have had difficulty surviving. Nevertheless, patronage brought little financial support.

If this system protected the companies, it also imposed restrictions, because rulers insisted that every company have a license from the Crown and that every play be approved before

Courtesy of Center Stage/Richard Anderson

In Shakespeare's *King Lear,* Lear loses his position and privilege and is forced to live exposed to the elements in a small hovel. In a recent production of the play by Center Stage (Baltimore), Lear (right) is homeless and uses a discarded cardboard box for shelter.

being performed. Such licensing made it possible for the ruler to ensure that the companies did not perform plays that might stir up political or religious controversy. Despite the legal status that acting companies achieved in England through the patronage of nobles and the licenses issued by the Crown, the London city council (composed of guild members who opposed theatre) sought to forbid performances within the city. Consequently, when permanent theatres were built, they were erected outside the city limits.

Despite these problems, by 1600 English acting companies were creating what many consider the greatest theatrical era the world has known.

■ Shakespeare and the Globe Theatre

THE REPUTATION of the Elizabethan theatre rests above all on the work of William Shakespeare (1564–1616), perhaps the greatest playwright of all time, and the company of which he was a member (the Lord Chamberlain's Men, later the King's Men). Shakespeare was only one of many significant dramatists of his time. Others included Thomas Kyd, Christopher Marlowe, Ben Jonson, John Fletcher, and John Webster, all of whom contributed to making the years between 1585 and 1642 exceptionally fertile.

Theatrical conditions favored the development of playwriting. From the 1580s until 1642, there were always at least two (and sometimes as many as four) companies playing in or around London. Because they performed six times a week (every day except Sunday) in the afternoon (beginning around 2 P.M.) during normal working hours, and because London was still a relatively small city of around two hundred thousand, the companies were in strong competition for audiences. They could not rely on long runs; normally, they changed the bill every day. New plays were performed once and then at intervals from time to time thereafter until they lost their appeal. In the 1590s, a London company produced a new play about every seventeen days. On average a play was performed ten times during one or more seasons before it was dropped from the repertory. New plays were in constant demand, a situation obviously favorable to playwrights, in order to entice the same basic audience group to return again and again to the theatre. Because Shakespeare and his contemporaries did not consider their plays literary works, so much as popular entertainment, they did not initially seek to publish them. Plays began to gain the status of literature in 1616, when Ben Jonson collected and published all his dramas. Shakespeare's plays were not collected and published until several years after his death.

Playwrights had an incentive to be prolific. Once a company had paid the dramatist for a play, it belonged to the company, and the author received no further income from it. A writer who depended entirely on plays for a living had to sell four or five a year. Shakespeare seems to have written about two a year, but he was also

The Swan Theatre, London, 1596. This is the only surviving drawing of an English public theatre made during Shakespeare's lifetime. It shows three levels of seating in galleries, a stage jutting to the middle of an unroofed yard, a roof canopy over part of the stage, and two doors at the rear of the stage (but no "discovery space" between the doors.)

an actor and a major shareholder in his company (that is, he was a part owner of the company's assets and was involved in running the company) and after 1599 was part owner of the Globe Theatre, in which the company performed. Thus he was involved in almost every aspect of the theatre and became wealthier than most of his fellow dramatists.

In addition to a steady supply of new plays, a company needed a performance space. Once the professional theatre began to establish a foothold, buildings intended specifically for theatrical performances began to be erected in Europe for the first time since the fall of Rome. In England, the first was the Red Lion (built in 1567), but the best known of the early playhouses was The Theatre (built in 1576). Others, such as the Swan Theatre, soon followed. Although the English public theatres varied in details, all had similar features that drew on medieval conventions but transformed them.

Let us look at the Globe, the theatre used by Shakespeare's company after 1599 and of which Shakespeare was part owner. Basically round with an exterior diameter of approximately ninety-nine feet, the Globe had three levels of roofed galleries, each about twelve feet six inches deep. These galleries enclosed an unroofed open space (the yard) approximately seventy-four feet in diameter. The stage extended to the middle of the yard. Approximately forty-one feet three inches wide and twenty-four feet nine inches deep and raised five to six feet above the yard, the stage was viewed from three sides by spectators sitting in the galleries or standing in the yard. The stage was sheltered by a roof ("the heavens" or "the shadow") supported by two posts near the front of the stage platform. At the back of the stage platform was a multilevel facade. On the stage level, at least two large doors permitted exits and entrances and served as openings through which stage properties could be moved onto and off of the stage. These doors were the most essential part of the background. Changes of locale were often indicated by the exit of characters through one door, fol-

The New
Globe Theatre

In 1997, a reconstructed Globe Theatre opened in London at a site only two hundred yards from the place where the original structure had stood. The theatre is a twenty-sided polygon, one hundred feet in diameter, with white-washed, half-timber walls and a thatched roof. The stage is raised five feet above ground level; two pillars, painted to look like marble, support the "heavens" decorated with figures of the zodiac. At stage level, the background facade has a large door at either side and a still larger opening at the center. On the second level, there is a large open space that may be used by actors, musicians, or (sometimes) spectators. Plays are staged without scenery, microphones, or spotlights (although floodlights are used to simulate daylight during evening performances). In addition to Shakespeare's plays, others from the same time period are presented. The theatre holds about fifteen hundred people: five hundred standing in the roofless yard and one thousand sitting on benches in the three levels of balconies.

One major surprise for actors performing in the new Globe has been the amount of audience participation. As one actor stated: "I have never performed in any play where the audience became so vocally and physically involved." Another said, "If the audience wasn't saying, 'Oh come on, give her a kiss,' they were booing or hissing at the sexual innuendos." Sir Peter Hall, former director of the Royal Shakespeare Company and the Royal National Theatre, has said about performances at the new Globe: "The essence of Shakespeare's drama is live interaction with a packed audience in a very small space in daylight, challenged to use their imaginations. There's nowhere else in Britain where that's happening."

lowed by the entrance of different characters through another door. Usually, the doors remained unlocalized, but at times they were used to represent houses, city gates, castles, or other places (what they represented, if important, was indicated in the dialogue). There may have been a larger space, called a "discovery space" between the doors that could be used to make "discoveries" (reveal objects or people hidden until the crucial moment); such discoveries were common occurrences in the plays of Shakespeare and other dramatists of the time. Some believe the stage doors were used for this purpose, but others argue that there was something like a small inner stage that could be concealed by a curtain. The second level of the facade included an acting space used to represent balconies (as in *Romeo and Juliet*), windows, battlements, and other high places. There may have been a playing area on the third level as well, but this has not been verified.

Performance of *The Merchant of Venice* at the New Globe Theatre in London. This theatre attempts to duplicate as much as possible both the theatre building/stage and the performance conditions used in Shakespeare's time.

Overall, then, this stage was an adaptation of medieval conventions. The facade served the function of mansions in the medieval stage, while the stage platform served as *platea*. Stage properties, such as tables, thrones, tents, beds, altars, and scaffolds, were sometimes brought onto the stage, usually to meet the demands of the action rather than to localize a scene. This stage also had some things in common with those of Greece and Rome. The background for all scenes was the formalized facade, and the specific location of a scene was established primarily through dialogue. When place was important, the characters named or described it. This conventional way of establishing the setting is sometimes called "spoken decor." This Elizabethan structure and the conventions governing its use greatly facilitated staging because one scene could flow into another without a pause for changing scenery. The playwright had almost unlimited freedom in handling time and place.

The conventions that governed costuming and lighting also resembled those of the medieval theatre. Most characters, regardless of the historical era of the action, were clothed in contemporary Elizabethan garments appropriate to their rank, age, and profession. Other kinds of costumes were used sparingly: Greek and Roman characters were often identified by drapery superimposed on Elizabethan dress; ghosts, witches, fairies, and allegorical figures were dressed in fanciful garments corresponding to accepted ideas of the appearance of such creatures; sometimes racial or national stereotypes (Jews, Moors, Turks) were indicated by dress. Costumes and banners accounted for much of the color and pageantry of Elizabethan theatre, because there were many processions, battles, and celebrations. Maintaining an adequate wardrobe was one of a company's greatest expenses. Lighting was not a major problem, because performances took place in unroofed structures during daylight hours. Darkness was indicated either in dialogue or by torches, lanterns, or candles carried by characters.

Most important was the acting company itself. It was made up of about twenty-five people, of whom about half were shareholders (part owners of the company's assets). The shareholders made all of the important decisions, played most of the major roles, and shared any profit. A number of hired men were paid weekly wages as actors, prompters, musicians, stagehands, or wardrobe-keepers. There were also four to six apprentices, boys who played female roles. All members of the company were male. (There

Sketch (supposedly made in 1595) showing characters from Shakespeare's *Titus Andronicus*. Notice the variety of costumes. The male character standing at center wears drapery suggesting Roman times; the character at extreme right also has some features suggesting the classical era. The others wear Elizabethan costume. Some scholars consider this drawing a forgery.

were no English actresses until 1661.) Because the plays often included a large number of characters, there was much double casting, and because a company usually performed a different play each day, each actor was responsible for a large number of roles. Although the overall performance style was probably not realistic in the modern sense, it was considerably closer to everyday behavior and appearance than that of a Greek performance. Elizabethan actors did not wear masks (except as disguises), all lines were spoken, and behavior was based on that familiar to the audience.

The conventions that most removed the performances from realism were the verse in which much of the dialogue was written, the use of males to play female roles, and the formalized background.

Elizabethan theatre included a considerable musical element. Trumpets sounded flourishes to mark the entrances of kings, to call attention to important announcements, and to serve as signals in the numerous battles. Music accompanied songs and dances in many plays; most performances concluded with a jig (a short, lively music-and-dance piece).

Elizabethan acting companies learned quickly how to make the theatre fully professional and

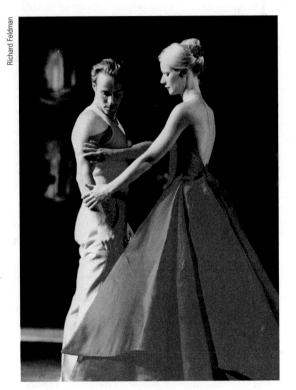

Gwyneth Paltrow as Rosalind in the Williamstown Theatre Festival production of *As You Like It*. A boy apprentice played Rosalind in Shakespeare's day, in part, because acting was thought morally unsuitable for women. Today, moral attitudes have changed so much that we normally assume women will play Shakespeare's female characters.

SOCIETY, ART,
AND CULTURE

On Women Acting

Shakespeare wrote his female roles for boy actors. Although we are inclined to think the playgoer of Shakespeare's day must have regretted not seeing female roles played by actresses, the English not only considered it immoral for women to appear on a public stage, but also apparently believed that boys played female roles more effectively than women could. Thomas Coryat, an Englishman who witnessed some theatrical performances in Venice in 1608, recorded in *Coryat's Crudities* his wonder both at seeing actresses and at their skill: "I saw women act, a thing that I never saw before, . . . and they performed it with as good a grace, action, gesture, and whatsoever convenient for a Player, as ever I saw any masculine Actor."

Women were not allowed to act in public in England, but women of the court sometimes appeared in nonspeaking roles in the lavish Stuart Court masques and even (rarely) performed speaking roles in private plays put on at court. England's Puritans took a dim view of such behavior. In 1633 William Prynne—a Puritan lawyer—sent to press a thousand-page work, *Histriomastix,* in which he basically denounced all actresses as whores. Queen Henrietta Maria, wife of Charles I, who had performed in plays at court, was outraged. Prynne was indicted and convicted of seditious libel, and, after being disbarred from ever practicing law again, was fined £5,000, sentenced to life imprisonment, and had both his ears cut off.

During the English Restoration, women were finally allowed to perform publicly in England. Still, many considered them to be little more than glorified prostitutes. Restoration actresses Moll Davies and Nell Gwynne, each at one time a mistress of King Charles II, did little to dispel this attitude. However, the skill of actresses playing not only female characters but also female characters pretending to be men was apparent. Samuel Pepys' diary records his experience of seeing Nell Gwynne impersonating a man: ". . . then most and best of all when she comes in like a young gallant; and hath the motions and carriage of a spark the most that ever I saw any man have. It makes me, I confess, admire her."

sufficiently attractive and remunerative to support a large number of people. The other important ingredient was the paying audience, among whom backgrounds and tastes varied considerably. The plays usually included something for everyone. Shakespeare's plays have plots as complex as a modern soap opera and often have as much violence as a television police series, but they also use poetic language and other devices that direct attention to the significance of events and provide insights into human behavior so profound that the plays have retained their appeal.

A small general-admission fee permitted one to stand in the yard. Those who wished to sit had to pay a larger fee for admission to the galleries. Entry to the few private boxes in the galleries ("lords' rooms") required a still larger fee. The Globe probably held about three thousand people, although seldom did that many attend. The configuration of the theatre (with the stage jutting to the middle of the yard) meant that no one was very far from the stage. There were no intermissions, and wine, beer, ale, nuts, and playing cards were sold in the theatres by vendors who circulated during performances. The atmosphere must have been somewhat like that of a modern sports event. Keeping the audience quiet and attentive depended on the power of the play and the skill of the performers.

Let us look at *Hamlet,* one of the thirty-eight plays by Shakespeare that have come down to us. It is representative of Elizabethan drama in its story, structure, and conventions, but, one of the world's great tragedies, it is superior to most plays of its time.

Hamlet

LIKE *OEDIPUS REX, Hamlet* concerns a man charged with the duty of punishing the murderer of a king. But Shakespeare uses a broader canvas than Sophocles and includes within his drama more facets of the story, more characters, and a wider sweep of time and place.

Shakespeare organizes his action with great skill. The opening scene, in which the Ghost of Hamlet's father appears at midnight on the castle ramparts, quickly captures attention and establishes a mood of mystery as well as expectation of revelations to come. The remainder of Act I introduces the main characters and establishes the dramatic situation—that Hamlet's father, the former king, has been murdered by his brother Claudius, the present king and new husband to Hamlet's mother, but that no one, other than the Ghost, Claudius, and Hamlet, knows this. The Ghost's revelation of the murder to Hamlet coupled with the Ghost's demand that Hamlet revenge his murder (at the hands of Claudius) is the inciting incident that sets the central action of the play in motion. Hamlet, though he wishes to believe the Ghost's charge, cannot be certain that the Ghost has not been sent by the Devil to tempt him into a deed that will damn his soul. Therefore he seeks confirmation of the Ghost's accusations. He is so torn that in Act II others question whether he has lost his sanity, and he is so disillusioned by his mother's behavior that he rejects Ophelia, the

T. Charles Erickson

Old Hamlet's ghost makes his son take up his sword to avenge his murder in the Long Wharf Theatre (Connecticut) production of *Hamlet.* Directed by Mladen Kiselov; scene design by Douglas Stein; lighting design by Jennifer Tipton; costume design by Paul Tazewell and Michael McAleer; sound and original music by John Gromada.

woman he loves. Hamlet's search for confirmation of the Ghost's charge reaches its climax in Act III, Scene 2, when Claudius' response to a play, whose action parallels the murder of Hamlet's father, establishes his guilt. But this scene also reveals to Claudius that Hamlet is aware of the murder; consequently, Hamlet—who until this point has been the pursuer—now becomes the pursued. The remainder of the play shows Claudius intriguing to have Hamlet killed in ways that will not draw suspicion on himself. Hamlet kills Polonius, thinking it is Claudius eavesdropping on him and his mother; Claudius uses this as an excuse to send Hamlet to England, accompanied by Hamlet's supposed friends Rosencrantz and Guildenstern, with a letter commanding the ruler there to kill Hamlet. But Hamlet escapes and returns to Denmark just in time for Ophelia's funeral.

Shakespeare skillfully interweaves this main plot with the subplot concerning Polonius and his family. The two strands of action are related through Hamlet's love for Polonius' daughter, Ophelia; Polonius' relation to the king as his principal advisor; and Laertes' wish to revenge his father's death after Hamlet kills Polonius and after Ophelia goes mad. The final scene, during which Claudius' plan to have Hamlet killed by Laertes (in a fencing match for which Laertes uses a poisoned foil) ends not only in Hamlet's death but also in that of Gertrude, Laertes, and Claudius, thereby resolving both the main plot and the subplot.

All of the main characters in *Hamlet* are drawn from the nobility or aristocracy. Shakespeare does not tell us the age of his characters or reveal much about their physical appearance. Nevertheless, age and contrast are important. The young and innocent—Hamlet, Ophelia, and Laertes—suffer most.

Many people consider *Hamlet* to be among the most demanding roles ever written for a tragic actor, in part because the actor must project one set of attitudes and responses to the characters and another to the audience. So carefully balanced are the demands that an ongoing controversy has developed over whether Hamlet feigns madness in Acts II and III or whether for a time he actually is mad. Another controversy concerns whether Hamlet procrastinates unduly. Some critics have argued that Hamlet is so sensitive that he cannot at first bring himself to kill Claudius; others argue that it is not Hamlet's sensitivity, but rather his desire to be certain of Claudius' guilt, that causes him to delay and that he acts as quickly as circumstances permit. Hamlet is a sensitive young man who, faced with a series of disillusioning revelations, procrastinates until the final scenes, when—recognizing Claudius' villainy not only against the dead king but also against others—he acts decisively. The actor playing this role is faced with enacting a range of complex emotional responses, delivering ambiguous speeches and actions, and keeping energy under great restraint until the final scenes, when it bursts forth.

Like Hamlet, Ophelia is sensitive. She has little knowledge of the world and is easily led by her father, Polonius. Hamlet's seeming rejection of her and his killing of her father come as such shocks that she becomes truly mad (rather than feigning madness, as Hamlet apparently does). Her brother, Laertes, who is near Hamlet in age, rushes into action instead of hesitating when faced with a situation comparable to that with which Hamlet must deal. Claudius, playing on Laertes' impulsiveness, is able to talk him into a deception (the use of the poisoned foil) contrary to his nature—which he repents, although too late. One may conclude that, whereas Claudius, Gertrude, and Polonius deserve their fates, the young people are victims of their elders' weaknesses.

Claudius is doubtless suave and charming, otherwise it would be difficult to understand how he is able to deceive so many people. He has won the support of the court, he has seduced Gertrude (who apparently is unaware that he has murdered her husband), and he easily takes in Laertes. Not until the final scene do most of the characters perceive Claudius' villainy. Claudius' surface respectability also provides an explanation for Hamlet's hesitation to act hastily or openly, because Hamlet probably would not have been believed had he accused Claudius of murder (his knowledge of the murder depends on a Ghost whose accusations only Hamlet has heard).

Hamlet's mother, Gertrude, is still relatively young (she need be no more than forty); she is a weak and sensuous woman who has been seduced by Claudius and has married him hastily following her husband's death, perhaps to prove to herself that she has sinned out of love. Polonius is a pompous, self-important, verbose politician who gives unsolicited advice and reaches unwarranted conclusions. He is often played as a buffoon, but there is danger in exaggerating his ridiculousness, because this diminishes the obstacles Hamlet must overcome.

Shakespeare's dramatic poetry is generally recognized as the finest in the English language. The usual medium is blank verse, which retains much of the flexibility of ordinary speech while elevating and formalizing it. But many passages are in prose, especially those involving such lower-class characters as the gravediggers and the actors; because these passages often play on words or use slang, the prose is often more difficult to comprehend than the poetry.

Probably the most important element in Shakespeare's dialogue is figurative language. The principal purpose of a figure of speech in dramatic poetry is to set up either direct or indirect comparisons. Shakespeare's superiority over other writers of dramatic poetry lies in his use of comparisons that enlarge the significance without distracting attention from the dramatic situation. His poetic devices partially fulfill the same function as the visual representation of Heaven and Hell on the medieval stage: They relate human actions to the divine and demonic forces of the universe and treat human affairs as significant to all creation.

Shakespeare's language makes special demands on the actor. Figures of speech are likely to seem contrived and bombastic if the actor does not appear to be experiencing feelings strong enough to call forth such language spontaneously. Shakespeare's plays may be damaged in performance if actors do not rise to the emotional demands of the poetry. Therefore, the very richness of expression can be a stumbling block for both performer and reader.

This scene from *Hamlet*, directed by Ingmar Bergman, shows the fencing match between Hamlet and Laertes in Act V. Performed at the Brooklyn Academy of Music.

© Martha Swope

The action of *Hamlet* occurs in many places, but Shakespeare envisioned them all in terms of stage properties, costumes, and the movement of the actors. Scenery was not important, but change of place was. The main stage, discovery space, and upper stage facilitated the flow of one scene into the next. The relatively bare stage was constantly varied by such scenes as the sentry patrols and the appearance of the Ghost in the opening scenes, the elaborate procession and court ceremony in Act I, the play-within-the-play in Act III, the burial of Ophelia and the fight between Hamlet and Laertes in her open grave (a trap-door in the stage floor) in Act V, and the fencing match that leaves the stage littered with corpses at the end of Act V.

Costumes added to the visual effect. Though most of the characters were probably dressed in the garments of Shakespeare's own time, Hamlet was set off from the others by his black mourning clothes amid the bright colors the others wear, the period of mourning for the dead king having been replaced by rejoicing at the marriage of Claudius and Gertrude.

Sounds also added to the overall effect. They include trumpet flourishes, cannons, and, in Act IV, the offstage crowd. But most important was the sound of the actors' voices speaking Shakespeare's poetry.

Hamlet is rich in implications, the most important of which concern the shock of betrayal by those one has most trusted. The betrayals are pervasive—brother of brother, wife of husband, parent of child, friend of friend. After an apparently uneventful youth, Hamlet is suddenly faced with a series of shocking revelations: His father has been murdered by his uncle; his mother has been unfaithful to his father; his mother has accepted his uncle's usurpation of the throne that should have been Hamlet's; and his supposed friends (Rosencrantz and Guildenstern) have become his uncle's spies. It is not surprising that these discoveries make Hamlet suspicious of almost everyone, even of Ophelia, the woman he loves. Considering the nature of the betrayals and the rapidity with which they come, it also is not surprising that both Hamlet and others wonder if he has gone mad. A second theme is the opposing demands made on Hamlet—to avenge his father's death (which seemingly requires him to murder his uncle) and to adhere to Christian teaching (under which the murder of his uncle would be a deadly sin). A third theme concerns the way one crime sets off a chain of evil as the wrongdoer tries to conceal the crime. Everything in *Hamlet* can be traced to Claudius' murder of his brother and the series of deceptions he devises to

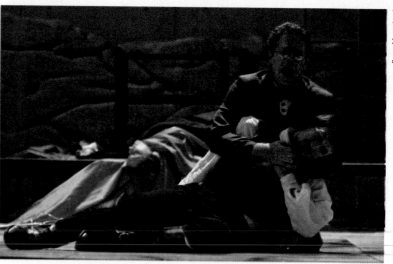

Horatio (Scott Plate) holds the dying Hamlet (Steve Tague) in the Great Lakes Theater Festival's production of Shakespeare's *Hamlet* at the Ohio Theatre, Playhouse Square Center in Cleveland, Ohio.

Roger Mastroianni

hide it. It is this deed that leads to the total destruction of two families.

Another set of implications concerns the nature of kingship and the need to rule oneself before attempting to rule others. This motif is seen especially in the conduct of Claudius and is suggested through the contrasts drawn between Claudius and his dead brother and between Hamlet and Fortinbras (the forceful, uncomplicated prince who is left to return order to the state). These are some implications of the dramatic action, but many others could be suggested, because a play as rich as *Hamlet* cannot be wholly exhausted. Perhaps for that reason, *Hamlet* has transcended its time and place and has appealed to all succeeding generations. It is one of the few plays that has never been out of the active performance repertory.

The English public theatre continued most of the practices of Shakespeare's day until 1642, when civil war brought the forced closure of all theatres until 1660. When performances resumed, practices drastically different from those of Shakespeare's time were adopted. Thereafter, English theatre more nearly reflected practices developed in France during the seventeenth century than it did those of Elizabethan England.

The Theatre Experience in Renaissance Italy

ANOTHER OF THE THEATRE'S great eras occurred in Italy during the Renaissance. It represents a different kind of experience using conventions that would eventually displace those of Shakespeare's theatre and dominate Western theatrical practices until the nineteenth century. The reawakened interest in Greek and Roman thought, literature, and art, which began in the fourteenth century, had by the late fifteenth century led to occasional performances of Roman comedies at the courts of the many small states into which Italy was then divided. In the early sixteenth century, plays imitating classical forms began to be written in Italian. To present such

plays was considered a mark of a ruler's cultural enlightenment, and theatrical entertainments soon became standard features of court festivals given to celebrate betrothals, weddings, births of royal children, visits of emissaries from other states, and similar events. Thus theatre played a role somewhat like that in Greece, Rome, and the Middle Ages, although the occasions were secular and were intended to reflect glory on the ruler. The subject matter of plays and the themes developed in the many events of a festival were usually drawn from classical mythology.

In mounting these festivals, the Italians drew on classical sources, especially *De Architectura* by Vitruvius (a Roman architect of the first century B.C.), who described how a theatre is laid out, as well as the settings appropriate to three kinds of plays: tragedy, comedy, and pastoral. Italian artists sought to re-create what they found in Vitruvius' treatise, but in doing so they transformed it radically, thereby creating the theatre structure and scenic practices that would dominate the European theatre into the twentieth century.

Because they had no permanent theatres, the Italians at first set up temporary performance spaces, usually in large halls of state (comparable in size and shape to the ballrooms of modern hotels). In 1545, Sebastiano Serlio published *Architettura,* in which he showed how to create a performance space within an existing room. He included drawings showing his version of Vitruvius' tragic, comic, and pastoral settings (see illustrations). These drawings fuse classical theatre architecture with Renaissance perspective painting.

The principles of perspective drawing had been developed during the fifteenth century. It is difficult today to appreciate the Renaissance excitement over perspective, which was sometimes viewed almost as a form of magic, because with it the artist seemed to create space and distance on a two-dimensional surface. Given this enthusiasm, it is not surprising that by the sixteenth century perspective had been adapted to stage use.

The acceptance of perspective scenery is of profound importance, because it signaled a movement away from the formal and architectural stage to the representational and pictorial stage. The Greek, Roman, and Elizabethan stages all used a formalized architectural facade as the basic background for all plays; in these theatres, the facade could be modified by the addition of small elements, but no stage property or pictorial element could ever disguise the fixed facade. Any added elements merely suggested (rather than represented realistically) a scene's locale. The mansions of the medieval theatre lay somewhere between the formal and pictorial traditions, because semirepresentational structures were often used to represent two or more places simultaneously. Still, no place was represented in its entirety, and the gaps between places were telescoped. With the coming of perspective, each place was represented in its entirety as seen from a fixed viewpoint. If more than one place was involved, they were shown sequentially, not simultaneously. During the seventeenth century, pictorial representation of place would become the standard for stage scenery throughout Europe, remaining so into the twentieth century.

How to transform a two-dimensional drawing into a stage setting that occupies three-dimensional space was a problem that Renaissance artists had to solve. The solution eventually accepted everywhere was to break up the picture and paint the parts on one of three scenic elements: side wings, backdrops, and overhead borders. Everything painted on the wings, drops, and borders was drawn as seen from a fixed viewpoint located somewhere in the auditorium (originally the seat of the ruler). The floor of the stage raked upward toward the back, giving us our terms *upstage* and *downstage,* and the height

Serlio's floor plan for a theatre set up within an existing hall. The stage is shown at top, the seating arrangement at bottom.

In Serlio's design for the comic scene, the squares on the raked stage diminish in size from front to back, helping create the appearance of depth.

In Serlio's design for the tragic scene, note that the buildings represent those associated with the ruling classes. This is unlike the comic scene where the buildings are shops and dwellings of the middle class.

Serlio, *Architettura,* 1545

Courtesy of the French Cultural Services

Setting by Giacomo Torelli for *Bellerophon*, produced at an opera house in Venice in 1642.

of the side wings diminished as they receded from the audience; both of these features helped perspective achieve apparent depth within a restricted space. The goal was to create a complete and convincing picture.

A pictorialized setting demanded a frame, because otherwise spectators would see around or over the setting, and the apparent scale would be negated. From this need came the *proscenium arch,* used to frame the stage opening (the "picture-frame stage"). Originally, the frame was a temporary structure like the scenery itself, but eventually the advantage of a permanent architectural frame was recognized. The oldest surviving theatre with a permanent proscenium arch is the Teatro Farnese, built in 1618 in Parma, Italy. The proscenium arch soon became a standard feature of theatres and remained so until recently; even today, the picture-frame stage is the most common type.

A setting that depicted a single place in its entirety created another problem: how to move from one locale to another. The solution eventually arrived at used two-dimensional *wings* set up parallel to the front of the stage and in a series from front to back. At each wing position, as many different flats were used (one immediately in back of another) as there were scenes to be depicted during the performance. To change from one set to the next, the visible wings were pulled offstage, revealing others that represented the next scene. The set was enclosed at the back by painted flats, which met at the center of the stage. Several back-scenes (or shutters) could be set up and shifted in the same way as the side wings. (Eventually, *drops* that could be lowered and raised replaced the back-scenes.) *Borders* (two-dimensional cloths, most often representing clouds or the sky) hung above each set of wings and enclosed the scene overhead. Until the nineteenth century, scene changes were usually made in full view of the audience. The front curtain was raised at the beginning of a performance and not lowered until the end. Thus scene shifts were part of the overall visual experience.

The desire to shift scenery was inspired by the love of spectacle and special effects, which the Italians exploited primarily in *intermezzi* (interludes) between the acts of regular plays (which usually did not require any changes of place or special effects). Intermezzi were elaborate complements that suggested parallels between some

Italian Intermezzi
and English Masques

The English developed their own variation on the Italian intermezzi, "masques," which were first performed at the court of Henry VIII. They were most fully developed under the Stuart rulers James I and Charles I between 1605 and 1640. Masques, performed solely for court audiences, were similar in all important respects to Italian intermezzi, except that masques were independent productions, not being inserted between the acts of plays. Like the Italian intermezzi, Stuart masques took their subjects primarily from classical mythology and historical legend; the subjects were developed to draw parallels between some mythical or legendary character and the person who was being honored by the performance. Masques developed an idealized vision of monarchy and nobility, because within the masques the action moved from disorder to order, usually with the ruler or a noble as the transforming agent. Thus masques served not only as an entertainment but also as a justification of the political system.

These spectacular pieces, requiring enormous sums to mount, emphasized music, dance, costumes, scenery, and elaborate special effects. The principal performers were courtiers. Ben Jonson, a major playwright of the day, wrote the majority of the short English texts for the masques, which served primarily to establish a mythical framework. But the principal appeal of the pieces lay in the spectacle created by Inigo Jones, the court architect, who had studied in Italy, where he observed the staging of intermezzi. It is primarily through Jones' work that Italian scenic practices were brought to England, although they were confined to court productions until after 1660.

mythological figure and the person in whose honor the festival was being given; usually the mythic protagonist routed the forces of chaos through magical feats involving elaborate special effects. Music and dance were major features. More effort usually went into the staging of intermezzi than the plays they accompanied.

The appeals of intermezzi were eventually absorbed into opera, a new form that originated in the 1590s out of attempts to re-create the relationship between music and speech found in Greek tragedy. Opera soon became a popular form, combining drama, music, dance, spectacle, and special effects. Opera became the primary medium for popularizing perspective scenery and the picture-frame stage, both of which had developed in the rarefied atmosphere of the Italian courts, where performances were not open to the general public. In 1637, a public opera house in Venice made the pleasures of the court theatres available to the general Italian public. It was so successful that soon there were four public opera houses in Venice.

The Venetian opera houses were in many ways the prototypes of subsequent theatres, not only for opera but also for drama, because they not only incorporated the proscenium arch and perspective scenery but also divided and arranged auditoriums in the way that would remain typical until the late nineteenth century. The division of the auditorium into *box, pit,* and *gallery* reflected the class structure of Europe; it permitted each class to attend the theatre without having to mingle with another class. The auditorium was surrounded by two or more levels of boxes (which permitted well-to-do or snobbish spectators to be more or less private while in a crowded place); on the ground floor was the pit (today's orchestra), less expensive than the boxes and favored by those unconcerned about reputation; above the boxes was the gallery, the least desirable and cheapest seats, usually inhabited by working-class patrons. The popularity of opera, which burgeoned during the seventeenth century, spread throughout Europe, bringing with it the staging practices of Italy.

Commedia dell'Arte

ALTHOUGH MUCH of the theatrical activity in Renaissance Italy was neither professional nor open to the public, one form—*commedia dell'arte*—was both. Commedia dell'arte (comedy of professional artists) and *commedia all'improvviso* (improvised comedy) are terms used to distinguish the plays performed by certain professional troupes from those performed by amateur actors at court (*commedia erudite* or learned

Painting by Pietro Domenico; courtesy of the Civic Museum, Turin

Interior of the Theatre Royal, Turin (Italy) in the 1740s. Notice that the proscenium arch is so thick that it is able to contain a box for spectators on each of three levels. The male actors at left and center are wearing the *habit à la romaine,* an adaptation of classical Roman garb; the actress between them is dressed in the fashion of the eighteenth century. In the auditorium a vendor is selling fruit and drink, and a soldier is posted to keep order. The setting is by Giuseppe Bibiena, noted for monumental painted scenery. Despite the setting's apparent realism, all the details are painted on wings, drops, and borders.

drama). No one knows precisely how or when commedia dell'arte came into being. Some trace it to the mimes and other entertainers of Roman times, whose traditions were supposedly continued thereafter by small wandering troupes. Others see the form as evolving out of improvisations based on the Roman comedies of Plautus and Terence. There are still other theories. Whatever its origin, commedia dell'arte is first mentioned in historical records in the 1560s. By 1600 companies were playing not only throughout Italy but also in France, Spain, and other European countries. Wherever they went, they easily found audiences among both the common people and the ruling classes.

The actor was the heart of commedia dell'arte and almost the only essential element. The commedia companies could play almost anywhere: in town squares or at court; indoors or out; on improvised stages or in permanent the-

atres. If elaborate scenery was available, they used it, but they could function as well against the background of a simple curtain (with slits for entrances and exits). Adaptability was one of their major assets.

The script was a *scenario* merely summarizing the situations, complications, and outcome. The actors improvised the dialogue and fleshed out the action. Although the broad outlines of a script remained the same, the details differed at each performance, depending on the inspiration of the moment and the response of the audience. Many scenarios have survived. A few are tragic, melodramatic, or musical, but the greatest number are comic, revolving around love affairs, intrigues, disguises, and cross purposes.

Improvisation, a distinguishing feature of commedia, was facilitated by the use of the same characters in all the plays performed by the same troupe and by the same actor always playing the

Maurice Sand, *Masques et Bouffons,* 1859

Pantalone and Capitano, two of the "master" characters of the commedia dell'arte.

Preparing a Commedia Performance

When we read about commedia dell'arte, we can easily get the impression that the performers made everything up as they went along. Much of what they did was improvised, but improvisation occurred within a rehearsed framework. For the improvisation to be effective, the performers had always to keep in mind where each scene was headed and what had to be done to make the plot as a whole work. They had to know the outline of the action and, when they inserted *lazzi*, they had to make sure they didn't let the pieces of business get so out of hand as to obscure the plot line.

In 1699, Andrea Perrucci wrote a description of how commedia dell'arte companies operated. A first-hand account, it is one of our most reliable sources of information. Here are some of Perrucci's comments on rehearsal practices:

> The scenario is merely the outline of scenes . . . which are to be acted extemporaneously. . . . The manager or most experienced actor rehearses the scenario . . . until the actors are familiar with the content . . . so they can discover . . . where new *lazzi* can be introduced. . . . [The actors must note] the things that will be needed in the performance, such as letters, purses, daggers, and other properties. . . . After the actors are familiar with what they must do . . . they will be able to run through the scenes and . . . rehearse new material of their own invention. It is wise, however, [when improvising] not to deviate from the plot to such an extent that . . . the audience . . . loses the thread of the plot.

—*Dell'arte rappresentativa, premeditata ad all'improvviso* (1699)

same role with its fixed attributes and costume. Over the years, the actors must have developed sure-fire dialogue and stage business that they could call on as needed. Some pieces of comic business (*lazzi*) became sufficiently standardized to be indicated in the plot outlines. In addition, actors who played the fashionable young men and women were encouraged to keep notebooks in which to record appropriate sentiments from poetry and popular literature, and many lines and actions were probably repeated in various plays. Nevertheless, performances created the impression of spontaneity because no actor could be certain what the others would say or do, and each had to concentrate moment by moment on the unfolding action and respond appropriately.

The *stock characters,* commedia's best-known feature, can be divided into three categories: lovers, masters, and servants. The lovers' roles were the most realistic. Young and handsome, they did not wear masks and were usually dressed in the latest fashions. Each company had at least one pair of lovers, and most had two.

The lovers were often the children of those characters who fell into the category of masters, and their love affairs were typically opposed by their fathers and aided by their servants.

Three masters recurred most often: Pantalone, Dottore, and Capitano. Pantalone was an elderly Venetian merchant, often the father of one or more of the young lovers or a would-be lover himself. His costume consisted of a tight-fitting red vest, red breeches and stockings, soft slippers, a black ankle-length coat, a soft, brimless cap, a brown mask with a large hooked nose, and scraggly gray beard. Dottore, usually Pantalone's friend or rival, was a lawyer or doctor who loved to show off his spurious learning in speeches filled with Latin (often ludicrously incorrect). Despite his supposed wisdom, he was credulous and easily tricked. His dress was the academic cap and gown of the time. Originally the Capitano was one of the lovers, but eventually he was transformed into a braggart and coward who boasted of his prowess in love and war, only to be discredited in both. He usually wore a cape, sword, and feathered headdress, often greatly exaggerated to indicate his braggadocio. He typically was an unwelcome suitor to one of the young women.

The most varied of the commedia types were the servants (the *zanni*—the origin of the English word *zany*). Most companies included at least two, one clever and one stupid, but there might be as many as four. They figured prominently in the action; their machinations kept the plots moving as they sought to help or thwart their masters. Most of the servants were male, but there might be one or more maids (*fantesca*) who served the young women. Typically young, coarsely witty, and ready for intrigue, the female servants carried on their own love affairs with the male servants while helping their mistresses. Occasionally, one was older and served as hostess of an inn or as the object of the older men's affections.

Of the *zanni*, Arlecchino (Harlequin) eventually became the most popular, although originally he was of minor importance. A mixture of cunning and stupidity and an accomplished acrobat and dancer, he was usually at the center of any intrigue. His costume, which began as a suit with irregularly placed multicolored patches, evolved into one with a diamond-shaped red, green, and blue pattern. He wore a rakish hat above a black mask and carried a wooden sword or slapstick (so called because it was slit down the middle so it would make a sharp sound when struck against someone; it is the source of our term *slapstick comedy*). The slapstick figured prominently in the many fights and beatings.

Maurice Sand, *Masques et Bouffons*, 1859

Arlecchino (Harlequin), one of commedia dell'arte's *zanni* characters. Note the slapstick he carries to create the sound effects of comic stage violence.

PRACTICES
AND STYLES

Lazzi

The actors inserted diverse bits of improvised comic stage business (*lazzi*) into commedia dell'arte performances. Most were usable in a variety of plays and could be curtailed or extended as the particular dramatic situation allowed or as the audience's response seemed to justify. A *lazzo* was often used to enliven a performance when audience interest lagged, to create a change of pace, to embroider on a situation, or to fill a gap in the action. Performers often worked out their own variations on established, surefire *lazzi*. Here are two examples involving comic violence, each of which might be elaborated in various ways:

- Two servants loudly threaten each other but are visibly relieved to be held back by others. A Capitano enters and officiously orders them to stop the quarrel. The servants are released and, under the pretense of striking at each other, give the Capitano a beating.

- A servant character (sometimes Arlecchino) persuades a master character (sometimes Pantalone) to hide in a sack that the servant will carry to safety so that his master can avoid a bully that has been pursuing him; the servant then assumes the voice of the bully, then frightens, and eventually beats the sack's occupant.

There are many variations on the sack *lazzo*, but the person in the sack always got punished, usually without discovering who did it. (This *lazzo* was often used in plays showing servants getting even with masters who had unjustly punished them.)

Although each company had a Harlequin-like character, not every company used that name for the character. Name variations include Truffaldino and Trivellino.

Harlequin's most frequent companion was a cynically witty, libidinous, and sometimes cruel servant. His mask had a hooked nose and moustache, and his jacket and trousers were ornamented with green braid. He was variously called Brighella, Scapino, Mezzetino, and Flautino. Another character, Pulcinello, was always a Neopolitan, but his function in the scripts varied. Sometimes he was a servant, but he also might be the host of an inn or a merchant. He had an enormous hooked nose and a humped back and wore a pointed cap. He was the ancestor of the English puppet character Punch. There were many variations, in both name and attributes, on these *zanni*, because each company developed its own version of these types.

A commedia troupe averaged ten to twelve members (seven or eight men and three or four women). Most companies were organized on the sharing plan, although some of the younger actors and assistants may have been salaried. Most troupes traveled frequently, but some were able to settle in one place for considerable periods of time. For example, Molière shared his theatre in Paris with a commedia troupe and

A *lazzo*-like routine from the Dell'Arte Players' contemporary production, *Slapstick.*

Wyn Tucker, courtesy Dell'Arte Players

alternated days of performance with it. (Molière—like many other dramatists of his day—learned much of his comic technique from commedia, and a number of his plays incorporate commedia characters and situations.)

Commedia was most vigorous and popular in the years between 1575 and 1650, but it continued into the last half of the eighteenth century. Its last stronghold was Venice, where two playwrights, seeking to reform and preserve it, contributed to its destruction. Carlo Goldoni (1707–1793), Italy's most famous comic dramatist, began writing scenarios for commedia companies in Venice around 1734. Because he believed the situations in commedia had become hackneyed and vulgar, he refined and sentimentalized the characters and situations. He also believed the usual level of improvisation was inadequate, and he was able to persuade companies to accept scripts with most of the dialogue written out. In addition, he campaigned for the abandonment of masks because he felt they handicapped the actors by hiding facial expressions. Goldoni wrote a number of plays (many

of them still performed) using commedia characters. Had all of the changes he championed been implemented, they would have done away with most of the basic conventions of commedia. He was bitterly opposed by another dramatist, Carlo Gozzi (1720–1806), who emphasized fairy-tale stories and improvisation in his scripts. For a time their battle aroused new interest in commedia, but by about 1775, this theatrical mode largely ceased to be a living form, perhaps because of over-familiarity after two hundred years or because its rather broad, often coarse, farcical humor had lost its appeal in the more refined atmosphere of the eighteenth century.

Although numerous scenarios have survived from the period when commedia was at its peak, they are too bare in outline to convey the flavor of a commedia performance. Goldoni's *The Servant of Two Masters,* though it comes from the last days of commedia and lacks most of the improvisational element, probably brings us as near to the commedia experience as we can come today. Therefore, let us look more closely at this play.

Carlo Gozzi's *The Serpent Woman*, an eighteenth-century commedia dell'arte script, as performed at the American Repertory Theatre. Directed by Andrei Serban; costumes, masks, and puppets by Setsu Asakura; lighting by Victor En Yu Tan.

The Servant of Two Masters

GOLDONI WROTE *The Servant of Two Masters* in 1745 for a Venetian commedia dell'arte troupe that permitted him to write out all of the dialogue. Although this written text eliminated much of the improvisational element, it did not do away with it altogether, because the actors were allowed to improvise much comic business. The script incorporates other of Goldoni's reforms, including taking away the more exaggerated qualities of certain characters. For example, Goldoni's Pantalone has none of the miserly traits typical of the character in earlier scenarios, and Brighella has been deprived of his libidinous and cruel traits. In fact, both have become solid citizens with virtually no ridiculous aspects. As in Goldoni's non-commedia scripts, in *The Servant of Two Masters* middle-class characters are treated with respect, and the women are far more sensible than the men. (Smeraldina's comments on society's double standard for men and women reflect similar ideas found in other plays by Goldoni.) Goldoni has also avoided the coarse, often smutty humor and sexual innuendo of earlier commedia.

Nevertheless, the cast of characters (and the basic traits of each) clearly belongs to commedia.

There are two pairs of lovers (Clarice and Silvio, Beatrice and Florindo), two masters (Pantalone and Dottore), and three servant types (Truffaldino, Brighella, and Smeraldina), although Brighella has been elevated to innkeeper. Silvio has also been given some traits (his exaggerated threats and his easy defeat in the fight with Beatrice) that relate him to the Capitano of other scripts. There are four minor roles (two porters and two waiters), but two actors could easily play the four roles. Thus the company size is probably eleven or twelve—typical for a commedia troupe.

The plot of *The Servant of Two Masters* relies on disguise, coincidence, misunderstanding, and withheld information. When the play opens, Pantalone, believing that his daughter Clarice's fiancé, Federigo Rasponi, is dead, agrees to marry her to Silvio, son of Dottore. Just as this agreement is concluded, Federigo arrives. (This is actually Federigo's sister Beatrice, who has taken on his identity so that she may follow her fiancé, Florindo, who supposedly has killed Federigo in a duel and has fled to Venice from Turin.) Both Silvio and Federigo/Beatrice state their intention to hold Pantalone to his agreement.

Beatrice and Truffaldino, the servant she has hired along the way, take up residence in the inn

Goldoni's *The Servant of Two Masters* as presented at the Piccolo Teatro, Milan, Italy. Theatricality and playfulness are captured in Ezio Frigerio's scene design, which simulates a makeshift stage erected within the ruins of a building. Directed by Giorgio Strehler.

Luigi Ciminaghi: courtesy of the Piccolo Teatro

run by Brighella. Florindo is also staying there and, needing a servant, he, too, hires Truffaldino, who thinks it will be a great challenge to serve two masters without either knowing about the other. The remainder of the play is taken up with Truffaldino's attempts not to be found out. Eventually the truth is revealed and Beatrice and Florindo are reunited, as are Silvio and Clarice, and Truffaldino and Smeraldina (Clarice's maid-servant).

Goldoni is a master of plot development. Everything is neatly set up in the opening scene, and each complication is carefully prepared for and clarified for the audience, even as the play's characters become more confused. Goldoni further demonstrates his skill by making many complications grow out of the characters: Pantalone's haste in arranging another marriage for Clarice is the source of one chain of complications; another grows out of Beatrice's decision to adopt a disguise that serves only to delay her search for Florindo; still another comes from Truffaldino's invention of the imaginary Pasquale (as the friend who serves whichever master he is not at that moment dealing with); and others

come from Silvio's and Dottore's habit of leaping to conclusions. Coincidence is an equally important ingredient: Beatrice arrives at Pantalone's just as the betrothal is concluded; Beatrice and Florindo take up residence at the same inn and employ the same servant; Truffaldino, while unpacking and repacking his masters' trunks, switches items that lead them to discover each other.

The most important character is Truffaldino, who has all of the characteristics of Arlecchino—being both clever and stupid, wearing a black mask and parti-colored costume, and carrying a slapstick. Though the storyline concerns the lovers, it is Truffaldino's stupidity that creates many of the difficulties, just as it is his cleverness that often resolves them. He is the principal source of humor and is onstage more than any other character. He also has the greatest number of opportunities to improvise *lazzi:* dealing with the porters who carry the trunks; trying to reseal letters with chewed bread but always swallowing it because he is so hungry; tearing up an order for a large sum of money and using the pieces to illustrate how to arrange a table; unpacking and

mixing up the contents of his two masters' trunks; and, above all, simultaneously serving dinner to two masters (who are in two separate rooms and unaware of each other's presence). Opportunities to improvise comic business are also provided to other characters, including an argument between Pantalone and Dottore (a traditional feature of commedia); a sword fight between Beatrice and the disappointed lover, Silvio (in which Beatrice wins); the suicide attempts of Beatrice and Florindo (when each thinks the other is dead); the reconciliation of Silvio and Clarice; and the beating of Truffaldino by both Beatrice and Florindo over his mix-ups.

Goldoni wrote for a company that performed in a public theatre of the kind then typical: box, pit, and gallery arrangement of the auditorium, and picture-frame stage with wing-and-drop, perspective scenery. *The Servant of Two Masters* is divided into three acts with a total of ten scenes, although it requires only five settings: a room in Pantalone's house; the courtyard of Pantalone's house; the street in front of Brighella's inn; a room in Brighella's inn; and a street. None of these has great specificity. No furniture is mentioned for Pantalone's house (and probably none was present); a sign identifying it and an entrance to Brighella's inn are the only requirements of that set; four doors are the only practical features of the room in the inn; and no details are noted for either the courtyard or the street. Except for the inn's sign, all of the scenic requirements could have been met from the stock scenery of any theatre of the period. Lighting would have depended on candles or oil lamps.

The Servant of Two Masters does not achieve a high level of characterization or social commentary, but Goldoni was not seeking profundity. He was concerned with providing entertainment for a popular audience by reworking the conventions of a long-familiar form. That he achieved his goal is indicated by the popularity of his play, which has continued to the present day.

Richard Feldman

Truffaldino hangs from a yardarm bundled with ropes to look like a giant fork wrapped in spaghetti in the American Repertory Theatre's production of *The Servant of Two Masters*. Directed by Andrei Belgrader; scene design by Anita Stewart; costume design by Catherine Zuber; lighting by Natasha Katz.

The French Background

THE DEVELOPMENT of the French theatre had been interrupted by the civil wars that grew out of religious controversy in the sixteenth century and recurred in the seventeenth. Stability did not return until around 1625, by which time Cardinal Richelieu, Louis XIII's prime minister, having secured absolute power for the king, set out to make France the cultural center of Europe.

Up to that time, France's theatre had remained under medieval influence. Although religious plays were outlawed in Paris in 1548, the theatre had continued to use simultaneous settings for its plays, most of which required numerous locales. (See the illustration below for a typical stage setting around 1635.) Richelieu believed that the French stage needed drastic reform and looked to Italy for guidance. He advocated adoption of the proscenium stage and perspective scenery and a drama that would adhere to theoretical principles articulated in Italy during the sixteenth century. These principles make up what came to be called the *neoclassical ideal:*

- Firm genre restrictions (tragedy and comedy—which should not be mixed).
- Tragedy should treat royalty and nobles; Comedy should treat middle and lower classes.
- Characters should behave in a manner appropriate to their social status, gender, and ethnicity (*Decorum*).
- All plays should be written in five acts.
- All plays should observe the unities of time (take place within twenty-four hours), place (one location), and action (there should be only one plot).
- All plays should uphold "poetic justice" (punish the wicked and reward the good).

There were other demands, but these were the most important. Neoclassicists believed that the purpose of all drama is to teach and to please.

Although Richelieu and others favored them, these rules were not widely known or accepted in France until 1636, when *The Cid* by Pierre Corneille (1606–1684) became the most popular play yet written in France. Despite its popularity, the play was viciously attacked because it failed to adhere to some of the neoclassical rules. To settle this controversy, Richelieu asked the recently formed French Academy (whose membership was restricted to the forty most eminent literary figures of the day) to deliver a verdict on the play. The Academy praised the play for many of its qualities but faulted it where it deviated from neoclassical rules. For example, although the play observed the unity of time, too many events (including an entire war), had occurred within a twenty-four-hour period. The play failed to observe decorum because the aristocratic heroine agreed to marry the man who had killed her father a few hours earlier. The French Academy's ruling on *Le Cid* is a watershed event in French theatre, because it effectively legitimized the neoclassical view. After 1640, Corneille adopted the new mode, which was later perfected by Jean Racine (1639–1699), especially in his *Phaedra*. The tragedies of

Design by Laurent Mahelot for *La Prise de Marsilly*. Notice that several locales are represented simultaneously.

Courtesy of Bibliothèque Nationale, Paris

The first proscenium-arch theatre in France, built by Cardinal Richelieu in his palace in 1641. Seated in the foreground (from right to left) are Cardinal Richelieu, Louis XIII, and the queen. After Richelieu's death, this theatre was called the Palais Royal. It was used by Molière's company from 1660 until his death in 1673.

Corneille and Racine were to set the standard for serious playwriting throughout Europe until the nineteenth century. On the European continent, these French tragedies were, until around 1800, thought superior to those of Shakespeare.

The transition to the new ideal also required that the theatre structure be altered. To set an example, Richelieu in 1641 had the first theatre in France with a proscenium arch erected in his own palace. By 1650, all of the Parisian public and court theatres had been transformed into picture-frame stages of the Italian type. Thus by the mid-seventeenth century, the Italian order had replaced the medieval heritage.

◼ Molière and Seventeenth-Century French Theatre Practice

J UST AS CORNEILLE and Racine set the standard for tragedy, Molière (1622–1673) set the standard for comedy. Molière began his career as an actor in 1643. Meeting little success in Paris, his company toured the provinces for many years, often competing with commedia companies, from which he learned much about playwriting and how to please an audience. Upon returning to Paris, his company performed in the theatre that Richelieu had built and that had become the property of the Crown upon the cardinal's death. Usually referred to as the Palais Royal, this theatre had a picture-frame stage and a box, pit, and gallery auditorium. Thus Molière performed in a theatre owned by the king but open to the general public. He also shared this theatre (alternating playing days) with a commedia company.

Like Shakespeare, Molière was involved in every aspect of the theatre. He was head of his own company, its principal actor, and its principal playwright. He was not part owner of a theatre building, however.

Despite the differences between the Elizabethan and French stages, their acting companies had many features in common. French companies, like the English, were organized on the sharing plan. They usually included ten to fifteen sharing members, but others were hired as actors, musicians, stage assistants, and so on. A major difference was that French companies

SOCIETY, ART, AND CULTURE

Onstage Audiences

From the 1630s until around 1760, some members of Parisian audiences were seated on stage during performances. This practice apparently originated during the controversy over Corneille's *The Cid,* when the demand to see that play was so great that spectators were allowed to sit or stand in the wings. Sitting on stage soon became fashionable for those who came to the theatre to be seen, and the actors permitted it because they could charge more for onstage seats than for seats in the boxes. That some onstage spectators were determined to give their own performances is indicated in this speech from Molière's *The Bores:*

I was seated on the stage waiting to hear the play, which I had heard praised by several persons. The actors began and everybody was silent when, with a blustering air . . . in rushes a man . . . crying out for a chair, surprising the audience with his great noise which interrupted one of the most beautiful passages in the play. . . . The actors were willing to go on with their parts, but the fellow in seating himself made a new disturbance, and crossing the stage . . . he planted his chair in the middle of the front . . . hiding the actors from three fourths of the house. The yells this aroused would have shamed another man, but he, steady and firm, did not mind at all. [The speech goes on to say that the man moved only so he could talk to another onstage spectator, to whom he insisted on explaining in a loud voice what was coming next.] He got up a good while before the play ended, for these fine fellows, to prove their gentility, are careful above all not to hear the conclusion.

Eventually five rows of benches were permanently installed on either side of the Comédie Francaise's stage and were not removed until 1759, when the premiere of a tragedy by Voltaire was ruined when a ghost could not make its entrance because the stage was so crowded with spectators. When someone among the spectators shouted, "Make way for the ghost," the audience began laughing and never recovered, thus turning a tragedy into an unexpected comedy. This fiasco supposedly motivated the permanent removal of spectators from the stage, allowing it thereafter to be devoted entirely to the dramatic action for the first time since 1636.

included women, who had equal rights with the men and received comparable pay. At the end of each performance, the costs of production were deducted from the receipts, and the remainder was divided among the shareholders. All of the leading companies in Paris (usually two or three) received a subsidy from the Crown, but the sum was not sufficient to guarantee them against loss.

Plays were selected by a vote of the shareholders after hearing a reading of the play. A play might be bought outright, but the more usual method of payment was to give the author a percentage of the receipts for a limited number of performances, after which the play belonged to the company. An acting company usually had in its active repertory fifty or more plays, which were alternated in order to keep the audience coming back.

Casting was simplified because each actor played a limited range of roles. By the eighteenth century, actors were being hired according to "lines of business" (according to the type of characters they played) and remained in those lines throughout their careers. A new actor in the company usually learned roles from the person he or she was understudying or replacing, and therefore many roles came to be played in a traditional manner handed down from one generation to the next. Such practices continued well into the nineteenth century, not just in France but also throughout Europe.

In France, actors were expected to furnish their own costumes, a major expense for the actors. As on the Elizabethan stage, most costumes were contemporary garments, although there were exceptions, especially for Near Eastern, Moorish, and classical characters. Because so many French plays were based on classical myth or history, the costumes for classical characters were of special concern. The typical dress for classical heroes was the *habit à la romaine* (Roman costume), an adaptation of Roman armor, tunic, and boots, which by the late seventeenth century had become highly stylized. Classical female characters, however, wore the fashionable dress of France but with such added exotic touches as ostrich-feather headdresses.

The scenic demands of regular comedy and tragedy were simple. Ordinarily, in compliance with the neoclassical rules, the plays were set in one place and required no scene changes. (Opera and other "irregular" forms were permitted many scene changes and elaborate effects.) Most settings were so generalized in their features (appropriate to a particular kind of play but without individualizing details) that the same set could be used for several different plays. The setting was removed from specificity by using only those stage properties (chairs, tables, beds, and the like) absolutely demanded by the action; thus the stage was largely bare. This emphasis on generalized place served as well to keep down the costs of both scenery and costumes.

Because the theatre performances now took place indoors, lighting was a concern. The available illuminants were candles and oil lamps. The auditorium was usually lighted by chandeliers, and those which hung just forward of the stage, along with a row of footlights at the forward edge of the stage, were the primary lighting sources for the actors, who usually played near the front of the stage. Audiences as well as actors were lighted throughout performances, promoting considerable interaction between auditorium and stage. Sometimes chandeliers were also hung above the stage, but more often overhead or side masking concealed the onstage lighting sources. Along the sides, behind the proscenium arch and each wing position, were vertical poles on which oil lamps were mounted, one lamp above the other. Lamps could also be mounted on horizontal pipes above the proscenium and behind the overhead borders. Reflectors were sometimes

Courtesy of Margaret Mitchell

This drawing conveys the *habit à la romaine* costuming convention that the French used for classical characters.

used to increase the amount of light that reached the stage. At least three methods were used to darken the stage: Lights could be extinguished (although this was awkward if they had to brighten again); open cylinders could be suspended above the lamps and lowered over them to darken the stage, then raised to brighten it; or lamps on rotating poles could be turned toward or away from the visible portions of the stage. Because the intensity of lamps and candles was so low, providing an adequate level of illumination took precedence over all other functions of stage lighting. By modern standards, the level of illumination was very low.

These were the prevailing practices during the years 1658–1673, when Molière performed in Paris. Molière wrote several kinds of plays, many of them resembling commedia and using commedia characters. But his best-known works are comedies of character, among which the most popular is *Tartuffe*.

■ *Tartuffe*

TARTUFFE IS A PLAY about religious hypocrisy. The title character denounces others for their pursuit of worldly pleasures while privately seeking those pleasures for himself. The most likely target of Molière's satire was the Company of the Holy Sacrament, a secret society of the time, whose purpose was to improve morals by being "spiritual police" who spied on the private lives of others. Molière read *Tartuffe* to several people before it was produced in 1664, and the Company immediately organized an attack upon it. The controversy became so heated that Louis XIV forbade further performances. Molière revised the play in 1667, only to have it withdrawn again. But by 1669, the opposition was largely gone, and the play was performed frequently thereafter.

Whether or not Molière had the Company in mind, he was clearly thinking of groups like the Company, who feel that they alone can discern true piety from false, creating conditions under which hypocrites flourish. As in all of Molière's works, in *Tartuffe* the balanced view of life is upheld. To Molière, true piety demands not the abandonment of pleasure but rather the right use of it. The truly devout try to reform the world by actions that set a good example, rather than by pious speeches.

The conflict in *Tartuffe* is established quickly in the opening scene, as Madame Pernelle, Orgon's mother, storms out of the house while denouncing the entire household for failing to appreciate Tartuffe's piety. The conflict is further

Tartuffe as performed at the McCarter Theatre Center (Princeton, N.J.). Here, Orgon (Jim Baker, kneeling) comforts Tartuffe (Richard Risso). Directed by Nagle Jackson.

clarified when Orgon, the head of the household, returning home after an absence, demonstrates more concern for the welfare of Tartuffe than for his own wife. When Orgon's brother-in-law, Cleante, tries to reason with him, Orgon asserts his power by announcing his intention of marrying his daughter, Mariane, to Tartuffe, even though he has promised her to Valère. The news of this proposed marriage leads Valère to start a quarrel with Mariane because he assumes that Mariane has not opposed the plan. But the rift is finally healed through the intervention of Dorine, the outspoken maid. Orgon's son, Damis, also tries to bring his father to his senses by reporting that he has witnessed Tartuffe trying to seduce Orgon's wife, Elmire. When Tartuffe, with an air of injured humility, refuses to defend himself, Orgon denounces Damis and, to protect Tartuffe from such attacks in the future, signs over all of his property to Tartuffe.

Elmire, at last recognizing how deceived Orgon is, seeks to show him his mistake by hiding him under a table to witness Tartuffe's assault on her virtue. Finally convinced, Orgon orders Tartuffe from the house, but Tartuffe, now the owner of the property, declares that rather than moving out, he will have the family evicted. Just as Tartuffe seems triumphant, officers arrest him as a notorious deceiver on whom the king has been keeping watch and return the property to Orgon.

The plot of *Tartuffe* can be divided into five stages: the demonstration of Tartuffe's complete hold over Orgon; the unmasking of Tartuffe; Tartuffe's attempted revenge; the foiling of Tartuffe's plan; and the happy resolution. There are three important reversals. The first (the unmasking of Tartuffe) brings all of the characters to an awareness of the true situation. The resulting happiness is quickly dispelled, however, when Orgon is shown to be at the mercy of Tartuffe. The first two reversals (Orgon turning the tables on Tartuffe; Tartuffe turning the tables on Orgon) have been carefully foreshadowed, but the final one and the play's resolution have not. The contrived (*deus ex machina*) ending (in

which Tartuffe is discovered to be a notorious criminal) is emotionally satisfying in the sense that justice triumphs, but the contrivance is totally unprepared for in the preceding dramatic action.

To prevent any confusion about Tartuffe's nature, Molière uses two acts to prepare for his entrance. The first act includes a lengthy argument by Cleante, the character who apparently represents Molière's point of view, in which true piety is distinguished from false. The structure of *Tartuffe* may be clarified by examining the use of various characters. Cleante appears in Act I, where he performs his principal function: to present the common sense point of view. He does not appear again until Act IV, in which, as well as in Act V, he merely reinforces the ideas he set forth in Act I. Cleante does not influence the action, rather he clarifies the theme.

Although Dorine, the maid, appears in each act, her role is virtually completed after the beginning of Act III, though she has been a major character up to that point. Her frankness and outspokenness serve to show up Orgon's credulity, the lovers' petulance, and Tartuffe's false piety. Her wit and common sense put the exaggerated behavior of others in proper perspective.

Even Tartuffe is given strange treatment when he finally makes his appearance after two acts of preparation. Most of his time onstage is given over to his two "love scenes" with Elmire. Molière seems to take it for granted that the audience will accept the picture of Tartuffe painted by the other characters and that the play need only emphasize one aspect of his hypocrisy. Tartuffe displays his wiles most fully when he is denounced by Damis. Rather than defend himself, he endures the accusations with apparent humility. This scene, more than any other, shows how Orgon has been taken in by Tartuffe.

The lovers, Valère and Mariane, first appear in Act II and are unimportant thereafter. They serve to show the depth of Orgon's credulity and the consequences of it to others, because he plans to marry his daughter to Tartuffe. Their

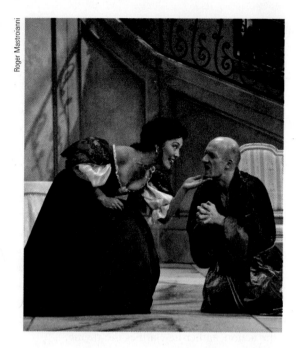

Roger Mastroianni

Elmire (Carie Yonekawa) attempts to let Tartuffe (Steve Tague) know that she hasn't fallen for his pretense of piety in the Great Lakes Theater Festival's production of *Tartuffe* at the Ohio Theatre, Playhouse Square Center in Cleveland, Ohio.

piety, so, too, he emphasizes Orgon's impulsiveness and stubbornness. Orgon errs largely because he acts without considering sufficient aspects of a question. When Tartuffe is finally unmasked, Orgon's character remains consistent; failing to see the difference between hypocrisy and piety, he says: "I'm through with pious men: Henceforth I'll hate the whole false brotherhood." Instead of returning to middle ground, he assumes an equally exaggerated (though opposite) position.

Little indication is given of the age or physical appearance of the characters. Because Molière wrote with his own company in mind and directed them, he did not need to specify every detail in his play. The role of Tartuffe was written for DuCroisy, a large man with a ruddy complexion. No doubt this was one of the sources of humor. All of Tartuffe's talk about scourges and fasting was contradicted by his obvious plumpness and lecherousness. Molière, noted for his expressive face and body, played Orgon; Molière's wife, who was twenty-seven years old in 1669, played Elmire. As was often the case with comic old women, a man played Mme. Pernelle; thus the character was no doubt intended to be seen as ridiculous in her denunciation of pleasure. All of the characters are drawn from the middle or lower classes (in accordance with neoclassical theories of comedy).

In *Tartuffe*, Molière uses the verse form that by that time had become standard in French drama, the *alexandrine* (twelve-syllable lines, with each pair of adjacent lines rhyming). The nearest equivalent in English is the rhymed couplet, although this form seems far less natural than the French alexandrine because English verse, unlike French, uses repeated heavy-stress patterns within lines, and these, in combination with rhymed line endings, encourage a singsong quality. In French verse, in which these internal stress patterns are absent, rhymed endings are far less intrusive. Molière, like most French dramatists until modern times, started a new scene each time a character entered or exited in order to indicate an alteration in motivations or focus

lovers' quarrel that ensues is a source of amusement largely unrelated to the rest of the play.

Although Elmire appears in earlier scenes, most of her lines come in Act IV, where she serves as the instrument for unmasking Tartuffe. This uneven distribution of the role has led some critics to argue that Elmire's moral character is questionable, because she originally seems undisturbed by Tartuffe's advances. Molière probably meant to show Elmire as a reasonably worldly but upright woman who is capable of defending herself without making a fuss about it.

Orgon's role is the one most evenly distributed throughout the play. Although the Tartuffes of the world are dangerous, they can exist only because of the Orgons, because the success of the wicked depends on the gullibility of the foolish. Just as Molière emphasizes Tartuffe's calculated

Molière

olière, born Jean-Baptiste Poquelin (1622–1673), was the son of a prosperous upholsterer and furniture maker. After receiving an excellent education, he abandoned a promising future with his father at the age of twenty-one to join nine other young people in founding the Théâtre Illustre. At this time he took the stage name Molière. He and the other founding members of the Théâtre Illustre then borrowed money and pawned their personal possessions to rent a small theatre in Paris. However, their enterprise failed for a number of reasons: They lacked a repertory of plays that matched their talents; although they were talented, most of them lacked actual stage experience; and they were gullible and overly idealistic regarding the business of theatre.

After the company failed in Paris, it toured the provinces for many years. Molière and his troupe polished their skills and gained experience competing for an audience. Molière began to write plays that used the talents of the company to its best effect. The troupe also became much more knowledgeable about the business of the theatre. In 1658, the company was invited to play for the king, who was sufficiently pleased to let it use a court theatre (the Palais Royal) for public performances. Molière's troupe shared this theatre with a commedia dell'arte company for a time; this contact with the professional comic improvisers from Italy may have influenced his playwriting.

Molière remained in Paris thereafter, often stirring up controversy with plays that satirized obsessive behavior and repressive customs, but enjoying the favor of the king, for whose festivals he wrote entertainments and from whom the company received an annual subsidy. Molière's enemies were often vicious, even spreading the rumor that his wife, some twenty years younger than he, was actually his illegitimate daughter. Molière virtually died on stage, having taken ill while performing the title role in his play *The Imaginary Invalid* and surviving only a few hours. Initially denied a Christian burial because he was an actor, only after the king intervened was he permitted minimal ceremony and burial in consecrated ground.

created by the change of characters on stage. Thus although the action may be continuous, the printed text is divided into numerous scenes. (Such divisions are usually referred to as *French scenes*.)

The unities of time and place are strictly observed in *Tartuffe*. Only a single room is used, and even that requires only a table, under which Orgon can be concealed, and a closet, in which Damis can hide, both used to witness Tartuffe trying to seduce Elmire. No specific use is made of the setting except in these two instances. The action is continuous, or nearly so, and occurs in a single day. All of the episodes, with the possible exception of the lovers' quarrel, are directly related to the main theme of the play. *Tartuffe* is clearly within the neoclassical tradition. It has remained in the repertory almost continuously and has been performed more often than any other play by Molière.

Romanian director Lucian Pintilie directed this radical reinterpretation of *Tartuffe* at the Guthrie Theatre, Minneapolis. In this production the action progresses through various historical periods. In the final act, the rescuers arrive in an automobile. Set by Radu Boruzescu; costumes by Marina Boruzescu; lighting by Beverly Emmons.

Joe Giannetti; courtesy of the Guthrie Theatre

The Elizabethan, Italian, and French Traditions

Although Shakespeare and Molière are among the world's great dramatists and were separated in time by only a few years, they worked within different theatrical traditions. Shakespeare's offered greater flexibility, but before the end of the seventeenth century, it had been replaced by Molière's, probably because the tide of taste was moving steadily toward a preference for representationalism. When the English theatres reopened in 1660, after having been closed for eighteen years, they accepted actresses for the first time in England and adopted the picture-frame stage, perspective scenery, and the neoclassical vision (although never so completely as elsewhere in Europe). During the Restoration, several of Shakespeare's plays were adapted to make them conform more nearly to the neoclassical ideal. For example, at the end of Nahum Tate's adaptation of *King Lear* (1681) only the wicked people died; Lear, Gloucester, and Kent retired to the country, and Cordelia and Edgar married and became the rulers of England. This is the version of *King Lear* that was performed in English theatres until the 1840s.

English theatre between 1660 and 1700, a period usually referred to as the Restoration, was noted principally for its comedy of manners, which focused on the amoral behavior and witty verbal exchanges of the rich and idle upper class. Restoration comedy was concerned above all with sexual conquests, advantageous marriages (in which love played little part), the latest fashions, and a seeming determination to be shocked at nothing. The butts of ridicule included the fop, the old man who marries a young wife, the old woman who tries to appear young, the pretender at wit and sophistication, and the self-deceived. The amoral tone of these plays has made them controversial ever since they were written. Restoration comedy originated with such works as Sir George Etherege's *She Would if She Could* (1668) and *The Man of Mode* (1676) and reached its peak in the plays of William Congreve, especially *Love for Love* (1695) and *The Way of the World* (1700).

Commedia dell'arte influenced many European playwrights. The degree of its influence on English writers of Shakespeare's day is still debated, but it was clearly evident in eighteenth-century English theatre, especially in pantomimes. Commedia's influence on Molière and other French playwrights is undeniable, and this influence continued throughout the eighteenth

Building a Broad Context

- German priest Martin Luther posts his 95 theses denouncing church abuses on church door in Wittenberg (1517), sparking the Reformation movement across Europe

- The Spanish and Portuguese explore the New World; Cortés conquers Mexico (1519)

- Henry VIII divorces first wife, makes himself head of the English church (1535)

- Polish scholar Copernicus claims that the earth revolves around the sun (1543)

- Queen Elizabeth I ascends the throne in England; outlaws the performance of religious and political subjects (1558)

- Japan permits visits of foreign ships (1570)

- Montaigne's *Essays* published (1580)

- Defeat of the Spanish Armada by English (1588)

- Edict of Nantes (1598) gives Protestant Huguenots religious freedom (until Louis XIV revokes it in 1685)

- Dutch bring first African slaves to British North America (1619); Pilgrims on *Mayflower* land at Plymouth Rock (1620)

- French Academy ruling on *Le Cid* controversy establishes neoclassicism as the dominant mode in French drama (1636)

- English Civil War; English theatres closed (1642); Royalists defeated by Puritans (1646); Charles I beheaded (1649); English Parliament calls for restoration of the monarchy and invites Charles II to return from France (1660)

- Taj Mahal completed (1643)

- Descartes writes *Principles of Philosophy* (1644)

- Isaac Newton's experiments with gravity (1664)

- Carlo Goldoni's *The Servant of Two Masters,* incorporates his main reforms of traditional commedia dell'arte (1745)

- Beginning of British Empire in India (1757)

- Jean Jacques Rousseau's *Social Contract;* Mozart tours Europe as six-year-old prodigy (both in 1762)

and into the nineteenth century, even after commedia had ceased to be a separate form.

By the eighteenth century, although there were still obvious differnces among the theatres of various European countries, they shared the same basic conventions. The theatre had made the transition from festival offerings to professional, secular entertainment.

Additional Opportunities with InfoTrac College Edition

There is a long-standing (and apparently irresolvable) debate about the authorship of Shakespeare's plays. Using InfoTrac College Edition, find and read the article "The Business of Bill: Who was Shakespeare?" by William Leahy in the *New Statesman.*

1. Take the author's suggestion to do an Internet search on the "who was Shakespeare" question. Who is most often cited as the person believed to be the true author of the plays?

2. Leahy questions the usefulness of this debate. In your research on the topic, do the "Shakespeare deniers" compel your interest? Do they convince you of the validity of the question?

Interior of the Drury Lane Theatre (London) in 1841. On stage is the wrestling scene from Shakespeare's *As You Like It*. Notice the box, pit, and gallery arrangement of the auditorium, the stage boxes, and the deep apron forward of the stage curtain.

> We should not be surprised if, in the course of the journey, at some point we cannot today ascertain, the road should suddenly turn and astonishing new vistas in art and life should emerge. For human culture is bound by no formula, not even the most recent.
>
> —Otto Brahm, *Freie Buehne für Modernes*

From Romanticism to Realism

THE LATE EIGHTEENTH and early nineteenth centuries brought a reaction against the neoclassical rules that had dominated dramatic writing since the mid-seventeenth century. These rules, although not always followed, had attempted to restrict the action of each drama to a span of twenty-four hours, to one place (additional places were permitted as long as they could be reached without stretching the twenty-four-hour limit), and to one plot (subplots were tolerated only if they were clearly offshoots of the main plot). Neoclassicism also sought to rule out fantasy and supernatural elements. And, because it was grounded in the belief that human nature is the same in all times and all places, it sought to depict universal (rather than historically accurate or individualized) traits, behavior, and visual elements. Settings were so generalized that they could be used in many different productions. For example, if the place of action was a prison, the goal was to depict the essence of a prison rather than any particular prison; therefore, the same set could be used for any prison scene. Similarly, characters were usually dressed in clothing of the period of the performance, no matter what the historical period of the action, because to place characters in a specific historical milieu might suggest that the play's depiction of human behavior was true only for that earlier time and place. Therefore, in the eighteenth century Hamlet wore fashionable eighteenth-century dress, and Macbeth was dressed in the uniform of a British general.

Most of the strictures of neoclassicism were applied only to "regular" drama (that is, comedy and tragedy written in five acts). Perhaps for this reason a number of "irregular" forms gained popularity during the eighteenth century. Many were probably influenced by opera, which had never been subjected to the rules and included numerous special effects, changes of scene, music, dance, and other appeals that were kept to a minimum in regular drama. But by the eighteenth century opera had become an elitist entertainment in most of Europe because of high ticket prices. Consequently, many of its features, in modified form, were brought into the popular theatre through new types of musical drama. England developed the *ballad opera,* which incorporated in an otherwise spoken drama numerous lyrics set to the tunes of well-known popular songs or ballads. The most famous example is John Gay's *The Beggar's Opera* (1728). In France, comparable pieces were called *opéra comique* and in Germany and Austria

Macbeth as costumed about 1775. Macbeth (played by David Garrick, one of England's greatest actors) is dressed as an eighteenth-century British general, and Lady Macbeth (played by Mrs. Pritchard) wears the fashionable dress of that time. In this scene, Lady Macbeth holds the daggers with which she urges Macbeth to kill King Duncan.

English Illustrated Magazine, 1776

Singspiele (of which Mozart's *The Magic Flute* is the best-known example, though it is now performed as an opera). Another popular form was pantomime, in which Harlequin was usually the main character. Harlequin's slapstick became a magic wand, permitting spectacular transformations of people and places; the action was accompanied throughout by music, and there were usually several dances. Thus "irregular" pieces overcame the restrictions imposed by the neoclassical rules, although they were considered inferior to the "regular" dramas.

The Emergence of Romanticism

Toward the end of the eighteenth century, the attitudes that had supported neoclassicism began to change, and several playwrights in Germany, especially members of the *Sturm und Drang* (Storm and Stress) school, began to write serious plays that experimented with both bold subjects and dramatic form. By the early nineteenth century, ideas about appropriateness in dramatic writing had undergone an almost complete reversal, ultimately coalescing to create *Romanticism.* The earlier belief that truth is to be found in "norms" gave way to the conviction that truth is to be found in the infinite variety of creation. According to the romantics, God created the universe out of himself so that he may contemplate himself. Therefore, everything has a common origin and is part of a greater whole. Thus, rather than eliminate details to arrive at norms, one should welcome them in all of their variety. Romantics also believed that the more unspoiled a thing is—the less it deviates from its natural state—the more truthful it is; writers showed a marked preference for poetry about nature and drama about unspoiled human beings living in primitive times or in rebellion against restraints imposed by society. Romantics glorified the writer-genius, who, grasping intuitively the complexity of the universe, rejected the strictures imposed by neoclassicism.

Perhaps the changes in critical attitudes are best summed up in relation to Shakespeare. Although Shakespeare had always been popular in England, where many of his plays held a firm place in the repertory, they were not performed in any other European country until the late eighteenth century. Except in England, Shakespeare was considered barbarous, because his plays were at odds with the neoclassical rules. Even in England, many of the plays were subjected to rewriting intended to bring them more nearly into accord with neoclassical demands. English critics tried to explain Shakespeare's appeal by labeling him a natural genius who,

This painting depicts the riotous confrontation over Victor Hugo's *Hernani* at the Comédie Française in 1830. Hugo's tragedy broke the neoclassic rules governing language as well as the unities of time and place. This enraged supporters of traditional drama but delighted those who supported Romanticism's call for a lifting of restrictions and rules.

despite his ignorance of the rules, had managed to write effective, though flawed, dramas. Nevertheless, they implied, he would have been even better had he known and followed the rules.

During the last quarter of the eighteenth century, Shakespeare's plays began to be translated into other European languages and staged, although at first only in heavily adapted versions. As Shakespeare's reputation grew, the plays were altered less and less, and by the early nineteenth century his works were becoming the standard against which plays were judged throughout Europe. During the nineteenth century, Shakespeare achieved the reputation he has been accorded ever since as the greatest dramatist of all time. Because he had written without regard for the neoclassical rules, he became an argument for ignoring them, and the unities of time, place, and action gave way to stories occurring over many years, in numerous places, and through a tangle of plots. Variety often took precedence over unity. The mysterious and supernatural, which had been deplored by the neoclassicists, became common occurrences in the new drama, as did concern for the characteristic features of specific times and places. Historical accuracy in settings and costumes began to

be favored, although it was not consistently realized until around 1850. In sum, the theatre underwent major alterations during the early nineteenth century. In this new climate, melodrama flourished, becoming to the general public what Shakespeare was to elitist audiences (although Shakespeare was not without appeal to the masses). Romanticism was to be the dominant artistic movement during the first half of the nineteenth century.

Melodrama was the popular-culture manifestation of Romanticism and as such was the most popular dramatic form of the nineteenth century. Melodrama emphasized clear and suspenseful plots in which a virtuous protagonist was hounded by a villain and rescued from seemingly insurmountable difficulties after undergoing a series of threats to life, reputation, or happiness. All important events occurred on stage; typically, there was at least one elaborate spectacular happening (earthquake, burning building, explosion, or the like) and/or scene of local color (festivals or dances using the picturesque customs or conditions of a specific country or city). Typical plot devices included concealed or mistaken identity, abductions, strange coincidences, and hidden documents. Comic relief was often provided by a servant, ally, or companion of one of the principal characters. Perhaps most important, strict poetic justice was meted out: The evil people were punished, and the good were rewarded. The villain might seem triumphant until the final scene, but ultimately he was unmasked and defeated.

Melodrama had a large musical element, as suggested by its name, which literally means "music drama." Originally, there were a number of songs in each play, but, more important, the action was accompanied by a musical score (every theatre in the nineteenth century employed a pit orchestra) that enhanced the action and the emotional tone of scenes. With its simple, powerful stories, unequivocal moral tone, spectacle, and music, melodrama offered compelling and popular entertainment to the mass audiences of the nineteenth century. Many of melodrama's features have been taken over by film. (Recent examples include *Indiana Jones and the Raiders of the Lost Ark* and *Tomb Raider: Cradle of Life*.)

The popularity of melodrama in the nineteenth century is explained in part by fundamental changes in social and economic conditions stemming from the industrial revolution.

As inventions such as the steam engine, power loom, steamship, and locomotive were exploited, the factory system of mass production gradually replaced individual craftsmen, who had been the major producers of goods since medieval times. Because workers had to live near the factories, urbanization accelerated rapidly and created large potential audiences for theatrical entertainment. The largest city in Europe, London, had supported only two or three theatres during the eighteenth century, but between 1800 and 1850, its population doubled and the number of its theatres grew to more than twenty. Its population and number of theatres continued to grow through the remainder of the century. As in television programming today, theatres sought to attract the largest possible audiences. Melodrama and variety entertainment proved to be the answer. Many critics argue that catering to mass taste led to a decline in the quality of theatrical offerings. But eventually theatre managers discovered that they did not have to appeal to everyone, and, during the last half of the nineteenth century, each theatre began to aim its programming at a specific segment of the population or a particular taste.

Because the pattern of melodrama is always the same (good threatened by evil, with the eventual triumph of good), variety was gained through such novelties as exotic locales, ever-more-spectacular effects, increased realism, incorporation into the action of the latest inventions, and dramatizations of popular novels or notorious crimes. A few melodrama theatres included facilities for horseback riding and featured plays with spectacular feats of horsemanship and last-minute rescues by mounted riders. Others installed water tanks to accommodate "aquatic" melodramas. The first important writer of melodramas, the Frenchman Guilbert de Pixérécourt, resolved one of his plays by having the villain destroyed as lava from a volcanic eruption inundated the stage. Dion Boucicault, one of the most popular playwrights of the English-speaking stage between 1840 and 1890, in 1859 used the newly invented camera to reveal the identity of a murderer in *The Octoroon;* and Augustin Daly, an

Frank Leslie's Illustrated Newspaper, 1877

A frontier theatre in Cheyenne, Wyoming. During the nineteenth century, the number of theatres mushroomed as population steadily increased and created a demand for entertainment everywhere. When people moved westward in the United States, the theatre followed.

SOCIETY, ART,
AND CULTURE

Audience Behavior

I t has often been said that the influx of working-class spectators into the nine-teenth-century theatre, and their behavior once there, drove away the more refined segment of the audience. This conclusion is supported by a German visitor's account of his experience in London's theatres:

The most striking thing to a foreigner in English theatres is the unheard-of coarseness and brutality of the audiences. The consequence of this is that the higher and more civilized classes go only to the Italian Opera, and very rarely visit their national theatre. . . . English freedom here degenerates into the rudest license, and it is not uncommon in the midst of the most affecting part of a tragedy . . . to hear some coarse expression shouted from the galleries in a stentorian voice. This is followed, according to the taste of the bystanders, either by loud laughter and approbation, or by the castigation and expulsion of the offender. Whichever turn the thing takes, you can hear nothing of what is passing on the stage. . . . And such things happen not once, but sometimes twenty times, in the course of a performance, and amuse many in the audience.

—Hermann Pücker-Muskau, *Tour in England,*
Ireland, and France, in the Years 1826, 1827,
1828, and 1829

American playwright, in *Under the Gaslight* (1867) was the first to tie a character to a railroad track in the path of an oncoming locomotive and to rescue the character at the last moment.

After electricity became common in the 1880s, electric motors were coupled with treadmills to stage horse or chariot races. To make the race realistic, moving panoramas (long cloths on which a continuous scene was painted) were suspended at the rear of the stage in overhead tracks and pulled between upright spools on either side of the stage. The movement of these panoramas was synchronized with that of the treadmills so that the horses were kept onstage by the treadmills while the scene painted on the panorama rushed by behind them, creating the effect that the horses were racing around a track

A contemporary engraving

The Octoroon, a melodrama by Dion Boucicault, first performed in 1859. Here a man is seeking to prevent the mixed-blood woman he loves from being sold to the highest bidder at a slave auction.

A contemporary engraving

A publicity poster for Augustin Daly's *Under the Gaslight,* the first of many plays to place a character in imminent danger of destruction by an oncoming locomotive.

Scientific American, 1889

A drawing showing an onstage horse race in *The County Fair,* staged at the Union Square Theatre, New York, 1889, using a moving panorama and treadmills connected to electric motors, the speed of which was controlled by the man at upper right.

(see illustration above). The trend was toward ever-more-realistic effects. In the early twentieth century, film inherited this tradition and continued to exploit it. Once the potential of film was established, the theatre largely abandoned such productions.

In melodrama, realistic spectacle, thrilling effects, novelty, suspense, and the vindication of virtue were the major appeals. Melodrama encouraged the development of realism in the visual aspects of theatre while clinging to recognizable and comforting stereotypes in characterization and morality. Let us look more closely at an example of nineteenth-century melodrama.

■ *Monte Cristo*

MONTE CRISTO is a dramatization of Alexandre Dumas père's *The Count of Monte Cristo* (1845), one of the world's most popular novels. Dumas himself dramatized the work in 1848, but it was in twenty acts and required two evenings to perform. Several other dramatizations were made, but the one that eventually held the stage was by Charles Fechter, a French actor who had a long and distinguished career on the stages of France, England, and America. In 1885, James O'Neill (1847–1920) purchased the rights to this version and subsequently made numerous revisions. The text as it now stands is the work of at least several people. O'Neill became so identified with the role of Edmund Dantès that the public would go to see him in no other play; he toured the United States for thirty years in the production. His plight was like that of many actors of recent times who have become so identified with their roles in television series that they have no subsequent careers or are always cast in the same type of role. O'Neill's sense of being trapped by the role is forcefully stated in *Long Day's Journey into Night* (written by his son, Eugene O'Neill, often considered the greatest dramatist America has produced).

Reducing a novel of several hundred pages into a play that could be performed in two or three hours was a formidable task, but not unusual in the nineteenth century, because popular novels were typically dramatized quickly following their publication. Almost all of Charles Dickens' novels were adapted for the stage, and *Uncle Tom's Cabin,* adapted from Harriet Beecher Stowe's novel, became the most popular play of the nineteenth century. Film and television have continued this practice.

Courtesy of the Harvard Theatre Collection

Uncle Tom's Cabin as produced by William Brady in 1901. Eliza (right rear) is about to cross the Ohio River on a piece of ice. The use of dogs and horses by Eliza's pursuers had become common by this time. Note the use of painted two-dimensional scenery (the trees) and the shadows it casts on the rear wall.

The sweep of *Monte Cristo* is nearer to that of Shakespeare's plays than to that of plays by Sophocles or Molière. There are many incidents, though the basic pattern is relatively simple. The hero, a ship's officer named Edmund Dantès, returns from a voyage prepared to marry his fiancée, Mercedes. He runs afoul of three villains: Danglars (the ship's cargo officer), Fernand (who loves Mercedes), and Villefort (a government prosecutor who fears that his brother, Noirtier, will ruin his career if he obtains a letter Edmund is bringing from the deposed emperor Napoleon). These three arrange for Edmund's arrest as a traitor, and he is imprisoned on the notorious penal island, the Chateau d'If. Edmund remains in prison for eighteen years, but during that time an elderly prisoner, Faria, befriends him and reveals the location of his family's vast fortune—the island of Monte Cristo. When Faria dies, Edmund takes the corpse's place in the sack, which—in the prison's burial practice—will be thrown into the sea. Through this ruse, Edmund escapes, recovers the

Faria fortune, and sets out to punish those who have wronged him. While Edmund has been in prison, his betrayers have prospered: Villefort has become minister of justice; Danglars a major financier; and Fernand a general, a peer of France, and Mercedes's husband (after she has been persuaded that Edmund is dead). As the Count of Monte Cristo, Edmund relentlessly tracks down his persecutors and punishes each in turn. By the story's end, all of the villains have been publicly disgraced and are dead.

Like other melodramas, *Monte Cristo* shows goodness victimized and evil triumphant for a time, but ultimately evil is exposed and punished and goodness is vindicated. It differs from most melodramas in rescuing the hero early from danger (at the end of Act II) and in the great amount of time devoted to punishing the villains. By actual time, of course, the hero languishes in prison for eighteen years, but in the play, those years are passed over in the interval between Acts I and II. Edmund is actually seen in prison in only one scene (whereas the novel

Scenes of Suspense and Spectacle in Melodrama

Much of the appeal of melodrama during the nineteenth century lay in the suspense created by placing sympathetic characters in great physical danger and by their last-minute rescue. These scenes were made even more attractive by spectacular scenic contrivances that made the danger seem real and present. One of these occurs in *Uncle Tom's Cabin,* the most popular melodrama of the nineteenth century. The enslaved Eliza, learning that her child, Harry, is to be taken from her and sold, runs away with him. She finds someone who will help her, but she must first get out of Kentucky (where slavery is legal) across the Ohio River (to territory free from slavery). While Eliza waits at an inn for the ferry that will take her across the river, villainous bounty hunters arrive, unaware of her presence. Overhearing their plan to capture her, she slips out through a window, but they see her and give chase. (In some productions, Eliza's pursuers used bloodhounds to track her.) The Ohio River has been frozen over, but the ice has broken into pieces. In desperation, Eliza, clutching Harry, leaps onto a large piece of ice and, as her pursuers look on helplessly, floats across the river where the man who will rescue her is seen waiting. This scene was so popular and well known that it became legendary. Even in the twentieth century, it was not uncommon for people, when circumstances seemed to be closing in on them, to say they felt like Eliza fleeing the bloodhounds.

devotes many chapters to his sufferings). The play omits showing Edmund's recovery of Faria's treasure and his intricate preparations for revenge. Many of the events (especially the way in which Villefort is punished) and character relationships (most importantly in making Albert the son of Edmund and Mercedes rather than of Fernand and Mercedes) differ from those in the novel.

The turning point, Edmund's escape, has a miraculous quality both in the event itself and in Faria's legacy of enormous wealth, which makes Edmund's revenge possible. In this scene, Edmund proclaims himself an instrument of revenge.

Reading the script fails to convey the effect created in performance by Edmund rising from the sea, climbing onto a rock, and proclaiming, "The world is mine." This scene became one of the best-loved moments of nineteenth-century theatre. Following this powerful scene, the villains are punished in the reverse order of their betrayals (Villefort first, then Fernand, and finally Danglars). As each is punished, Edmund announces the score—"One," "Two," "Three"— an accounting so satisfying to O'Neill's audiences that they often counted aloud with him. At the end, the play achieves additional symme-

The Count of Monte Cristo, based on James O'Neill's *Monte Cristo,* at the Kennedy Center, Washington, D.C. The performers are (from left) Anne Beresford Clarke, Patti LuPone, Joaquim de Almeida, Roscoe Lee Browne, Brian McCue, and Tony Azito. Directed by Peter Sellars.

try by implying the possibility of achieving the happiness promised in the opening scene. Though the plot is intricate, the underlying pattern is simple—and deeply reassuring in its inexorable meting out of just rewards and punishments.

Characterization is far simpler than plot in *Monte Cristo.* The main characters are types with few individualizing traits. For example, Edmund seems almost entirely good. When he discovers that Albert, with whom he has arranged a duel, is his son and not Fernand's as he had thought, he abandons his murderous plan and resigns himself to let Albert kill him. Most of the characters are at some point torn briefly between acting honorably and acting out of self-interest; the bad always choose self-interest, and the good choose to act honorably. Melodrama seldom suggests that moral choices are determined by environmental forces; rather, awareness of good and evil is innate, and each character is free to choose right or wrong. Values are viewed as absolute rather than relative (as they are in most current drama).

The characters are always wholly conscious of their motives and feelings and state them to the audience. To prevent any misperception, they use asides to inform the audience (or another character) of reactions they do not wish to share with all those onstage. (The aside, a convention almost as old as drama itself, came under attack in the late nineteenth century as being unrealistic and was eventually abandoned except in self-consciously nonrealistic plays.)

Next to suspenseful and morally satisfying plots, melodrama owed its appeal most to spectacle. By the late 1800s, producers were priding themselves on the realism and authenticity of their costumes and settings. The first act of *Monte Cristo* takes place in 1815 (when Napoleon was in exile on Elba), whereas the other acts occur in the 1830s. Costumes played a major role in marking both passage of time and alteration in the economic and social status of the characters. Much of the "local color" of time and place was created through the dress of sailors, policemen, tavern patrons, and partygoers.

Monte Cristo requires eight sets, two of which were probably simple and very shallow, permitting more complex sets to be erected behind them while a scene was in progress. For example, the Act II scene in Fernand's house involves only a few characters and no unusual physical action. It was probably set up in front of the Chateau d'If setting, the most elaborate of the play, which comes right after it. The Chateau d'If prison setting requires two levels, one of which sinks, concealing the prisoners' cells and revealing the water into which Edmund's body is thrown and the rock onto which he climbs triumphantly.

The demands of the Chateau d'If scene illustrate the changes that had occurred in scenic practices by the late nineteenth century. O'Neill first played his version of *Monte Cristo* at Booth's Theatre in New York. This theatre, opened in 1869, had been built by one of America's greatest actors, Edwin Booth, and probably was the first stage in modern times to have a flat floor and to eliminate the traditional arrangement of wings. Its stage embodied a recognition that the growing emphasis on three-dimensional practicable scenery, furniture, and other details found in real-life places required new ways of handling scenery. Wings had become increasingly unsatisfactory because they were two dimensional, parallel to the front of the stage, and arranged in pairs from front to back. In combination with

From *The Magazine of Art*, 1889

A late-nineteenth-century stage. Notice how the stage floor is divided; notice also the sinking trap, the strong beam of light (either a limelight or carbon arc), and the footlights (lower right corner).

the raked stage floor, wings made it difficult to move large three-dimensional pieces on and off the stage. The flat floor and the absence of wing positions in Booth's theatre permitted scenery to be erected wherever desired and to be moved on and off without hindrance. This theatre also had a number of elevator traps that raised and lowered heavy set pieces hydraulically.

By the late nineteenth century, the stage floor in most theatres was divided into sections a few feet wide, any of which could be removed to create an opening ("bridge") extending completely across the stage. In the second act of *Monte Cristo* the sinking of one part of the setting probably utilized one or more bridges. Upstage was the sea and the rock, both of which became visible as the cells sank. The sea was represented by a painted cloth moved up and down rhythmically by ropes attached to the underside. The sack (containing a dummy) was thrown into the water (no doubt with accompanying splash), and then, after a time, a soaked Edmund rose, probably through a trapdoor, climbed onto the rock, and uttered his triumphant "The world is mine." Such complex spectacle was typical of melodrama. The sets for the final three acts (an inn, ballroom, and forest), though elaborate, could be changed during the intervals between acts. The settings, which provided great variety, had to be designed and constructed with care, because O'Neill toured this production throughout the country beginning in the 1880s and for the next thirty years.

Touring such complex productions was made possible by the development of dependable transportation, which became a reality with the spread of railroads. The first transcontinental line in the United States was completed in the 1860s; by the late 1870s, it was possible to reach almost any area of the country by rail, and numerous theatrical productions were touring with sets, costumes, properties, and actors. Such companies soon became the major purveyors of theatrical entertainment in most of America and remained so until displaced by sound motion pictures in the 1930s.

Pictured here is the final scene from *Monte Cristo*. The acting area is very shallow, but the set is made to seem deep by the use of cut drops—that is, by cutting away portions of each drop so another can be seen through the openings.

Melodrama's visual appeal was further enhanced by lighting, the potential of which had increased greatly after gas replaced candles and oil during the first half of the nineteenth century. For the first time, the stage could be lighted as brightly as desired. Equally important, control over intensity became possible through a gas table, a central location from which all the gas lines ran and from which the supply of gas to any part of the theatre could be controlled. Lights could be dimmed or brightened as desired by one person operating the gas table. It was now possible to darken the auditorium and brighten it again when needed. These improvements encouraged increased concern for atmosphere and mood in stage lighting. Gas also made possible the development and exploitation of the *limelight*, a type of spotlight (from which we get our expression "being in the limelight"). The limelight was made by placing a column of calcium (lime) inside a hood equipped with reflector and lens; onto the lime were directed compressed hydrogen and oxygen along with a gas flame; the lime was heated to incandescence until it gave off an extremely bright light used to create such atmospheric effects as rays of moonlight or sunlight or to focus attention on a character or object. At the end of Act II in *Monte Cristo,* the stage direction reads: "The moon breaks out, lighting up a projecting rock. Edmund rises from the sea, he is dripping, a knife in his hand, some shreds of sack adhering to it." The effectiveness of this scene was greatly enhanced by the limelight.

O'Neill's production of *Monte Cristo* calls attention to another change then underway: Long runs of single plays performed by actors hired for that production only were replacing a repertory of plays performed in rotation by a permanent company (the system that had prevailed since Shakespeare's day). The theatre had begun to adopt those practices that have been typical since the late nineteenth century.

With melodrama, the theatre in the nineteenth and early twentieth centuries achieved its greatest mass appeal. It developed the audience and many of the conventions taken over by film, which displaced it as the prime medium of popular entertainment, especially after sound was added around 1930. And through film this legacy was subsequently passed on to television. Film forced theatre to reassess what it could do most effectively; as a result, theatre largely abandoned attempts to create the kind of realistic spectacle seen in *Monte Cristo,* which can be achieved much more convincingly by film. With their capacity to replicate their products endlessly, film and television were analogous in their effects on theatre to the influence of factories on individual craftsmen in the nineteenth century, making theatre the equivalent of a handcrafted product, one that has difficulty competing in a world attuned to mass production. Theatre had tried to meet the nineteenth-century demand for mass production by mounting elaborate productions and sending them throughout the country by the most efficient means of transportation then available. But theatre ultimately is not a medium adaptable to mass production. Film is. The popular entertainment of the late nineteenth and early twentieth centuries, especially melodrama, was the meeting ground for theatre and film and was crucial in the subsequent history of both.

The Advent of Realism

EVEN AS *MONTE CRISTO* was achieving great popular success, new theories and ideas were undermining the absolutist moral values on which melodrama had depended. Although unanimity of belief was never an actuality, Western civilization throughout the Christian era had looked to the Bible as the ultimate authority on values and moral principles. The biblical version of Creation and subsequent events was often accepted literally. Until the late nineteenth century, the earth was thought to be about six thousand years old, the date of the Creation having been calculated by counting back through the generations that, according to the Bible, had preceded the birth of Christ.

In the late nineteenth century, a number of intellectual and scientific developments (especially in the fields of geology and anthropology) called many biblical passages into question. When geologists began to suggest that the earth is millions (or even billions) of years old, and when anthropologists began to discover animal and human remains thousands of years older than the supposed date of the world's creation, heated controversies resulted. The greatest controversy was provoked by Charles Darwin's *The Origin of Species* (1859), in which he argued (1) that all forms of life have developed gradually from a common ancestry and (2) that this evolution of species involves the natural selection of those best adapted to specific environmental conditions. This theory was, and remains, anathema to those who interpret literally the biblical account of Creation.

Darwin's theories have many implications. First, they suggest that heredity and environment are the primary causes of everything human beings are or do. Second, they suggest that, because human beings have no control over their individual heredity (it is fixed at birth) and little control over their environment (especially during the early years, when an individual's personality and values are being formed), people cannot be held fully responsible for what they do; if blame is to be assigned, it must be shared by the society that has countenanced undesirable hereditary and environmental forces. (Indecisiveness over how responsibility is to be apportioned is the primary cause of contemporary arguments over such issues as the leniency or harshness of court decisions.) Third, Darwin's theories strengthened the idea of progress, because if humanity evolved from simpler forms to its present complexity, improvement must be inevitable. (Many of Darwin's contemporaries believed that progress, even though inevitable, could be hastened with the help of science and technology.) Darwin's theories also contradicted the biblical account of the deliberate, instantaneous creation of humanity with its implication that human beings have been the same (at least biologically) since the time of Adam and Eve. Fourth, Darwin's theories absorbed humanity into nature. Prior to Darwin, human beings, because of their awareness of right and wrong, had always been set apart from and considered superior to the rest of nature. With Darwin, human beings, like other animals, became merely a species to be studied scientifically.

These implications were crucial in the development of the modern temperament, because they suggested that change (rather than fixity) is the norm. Late-nineteenth-century thought began increasingly to support the belief that moral standards are relative to each culture and that concepts of right and wrong may vary widely from one society to another.

The new ideas about human conscience were stated most fully in the writings of Sigmund Freud (1856–1939), the most influential psychologist of the twentieth century. Freud argued that the basic human instincts are aggression and sexuality—self-preservation and procreation. Left alone, human beings would seek to satisfy their instincts without regard for others; therefore, if they are to be integrated into a community, they must undergo socialization. Through rewards and punishments, they learn early what is acceptable and what is unacceptable, and in this process they develop a superego (an interior, subconscious censor or judge), what had previously been called a conscience. Throughout the Christian era, most people had believed that conscience is innate—that human beings have an instinctive grasp of the difference between right and wrong. (Melodrama was built on this premise.) With Freud, a sense of right and wrong is not absolute and does not come from God; it is relative to the individual, family, and societal environment that have produced it. Freud further argued that the process of socialization causes us to suppress many desires and urges (bury them in the unconscious mind) and

to find socially acceptable substitutes that the conscious mind can openly acknowledge. Freud's view of human psychology implies not only that we can never fully understand others but also that we can never be certain of our own motives. To assess people and situations, in addition to noting what is consciously said and done, we must also be aware of the subtext—what is not openly said and done. According to this view, then, not only are moral values relative, but also language and behavior are only partially reliable indicators of a person's state of mind and motives.

Relativity eventually affected every area of thought and action. It initially entered the theatre through realism and naturalism, even though these movements were seeking objective, scientific explanations of human behavior.

Realism and Naturalism

*R*EALISM WAS FIRST recognized during the 1850s, *naturalism* (a more extreme version of realism) during the 1870s. In the theatre, these movements seemed in some ways exten-

A contemporary engraving

An early example of realistic drama, Alexandre Dumas fils' *The Demi-Monde* as staged at the Théâtre du Gymnase in Paris in 1855.

sions of already common practices, especially in the area of spectacle. Since around 1800, emphasis on visual accuracy in scenery and costumes had steadily increased, and one type of realism had already been achieved. Nevertheless, this realism, as is demonstrated by *Monte Cristo,* was exploited primarily as spectacular or picturesque background. In contrast to all preceding movements, realism and naturalism believed that character is determined in large part by environment, and they demanded that settings play an enlarged role—as representations of the environmental forces that have shaped the characters and (consequently) the dramatic action. In other words, setting was conceived as environment and not merely as appropriate or impressive background. One consequence was the belief that each play's scenic needs are unique, because each play's environment is unlike that of any other. Perhaps more important, this approach to setting implies that what a character is and does is relative to specific environmental forces.

The views of realists and naturalists were grounded in the scientific outlook: the need to understand human behavior in terms of natural cause and effect. They restricted their pursuit of truth to knowledge that can be verified through the five senses. They argued that because we can know the real world only through direct observation, playwrights should write about the society around them and should do so as objectively as possible. Given these premises, it was logical that realists and naturalists would write primarily about contemporary subjects (unlike earlier serious dramatists who usually chose historical or mythical subjects) and introduce behavior not previously seen on the stage. Because many of the plays dealt with unsavory social conditions such as poverty, disease, prostitution, and the plight of illegitimate children, conservative critics charged that the theatre had become little better than a sewer, but realists replied that because they were depicting conditions truthfully, they were acting morally, truth being the highest form of morality. Furthermore, the realists argued, what their critics were demanding

was an idealized, nonexistent vision of truth; instead, they declared, if audiences did not like the life portrayed on stage, they should change the society that furnished the models rather than denounce the playwrights who had the courage to portray life truthfully. The real issue was the role of art in society: Should art, as in melodrama, always show good triumphant? If art shows deviations from accepted morality and behavior, should it reaffirm traditional values even though they have not triumphed in this instance? Or should art, as the realists and naturalists argued, follow truth wherever it leads without concern for conformity to social codes and moral values? Ultimately, it was a controversy over absolute versus relative values.

These issues were brought into focus by Henrik Ibsen (1828–1906), a Norwegian playwright often called the founder of modern drama. Ibsen had begun his playwriting career around 1850 with verse dramas about Scandinavian legends, but in the 1870s he abandoned verse and turned exclusively to contemporary subjects. His plays stirred worldwide controversy because the endings of his plays did not reaffirm accepted values. These plays were denied production in many places because they were thought to be immoral and corrupting.

Nevertheless, these plays were widely read and discussed, especially because they were thought to challenge moral values and social norms long considered absolute. Let us look more closely at one of Ibsen's plays, *A Doll's House.*

A Doll's House

IN *A DOLL'S HOUSE* (1879), Nora Helmer is faced with the consequences of having (several years earlier) forged her father's name to borrow the money needed to restore her husband's health (although by law she could not borrow money without her husband's consent). Now, just as happiness seems assured (her husband Torvald is fully recovered and has just been appointed director of a bank), the man from whom Nora

SOCIETY, ART,
AND CULTURE

Critical Reaction
to Ibsen

I t is difficult for us to understand how violent a response Henrik Ibsen's plays evoked when they first appeared. The reaction to *Ghosts* was extreme because, although the disease is never named in the play, both the husband and son of the principal character, Mrs. Alving, are victims of syphilis, a subject considered not only wholly inappropriate in the theatre but also unmentionable in polite society. In addition, the play suggests that her son might have escaped this curse had Mrs. Alving been permitted to leave her husband, as she wished. To many, Ibsen, in introducing into his play both syphilis and divorce, seemed to be attacking the family as an institution and to be violating all standards of decency. The response of some critics and censors was comparable to what might be expected today if one were to propose showing an X-rated movie to children.

When London's Independent Theatre produced *Ghosts*, though only for members of the organization, many critics wrote scathing reviews. George Bernard Shaw, a strong supporter of Ibsen, quotes excerpts from many of these responses in his *The Quintessence of Ibsenism* (1891):

"An open drain; a loathsome sore unbandaged; a dirty act done publicly."
"Garbage and offal." "A piece to bring the stage into disrepute and dishonour with every right-thinking man and woman."

Ibsen's perception of women's role in society was also out of step with the time, when women were wholly subservient to fathers or husbands. In his notes on *A Doll's House*, Ibsen wrote:

A woman cannot be herself in the society of the present day, which is an exclusively masculine society, with laws framed by men and with a judicial system that judges feminine conduct from a masculine point of view.

borrowed the money (Krogstad) threatens to expose her as a criminal if she does not help him keep the job he is about to lose at Torvald's bank. Much of the remainder of the play is taken up with Nora's attempt to conceal the truth from her husband because she is convinced that, because of his deep love for her, he will assume responsibility for the crime and thus be ruined. When exposure comes, he reacts quite differently than she had expected, being concerned only for his own reputation; he declares her so morally corrupt that she will no longer be allowed to raise their three children. When Krogstad unexpectedly withdraws the threat of public scandal, Torvald is jubilant about his escape from ruin and, once certain of his safety, seeks to restore his previous relationship with Nora. She, however, now feels alienated not only from her husband but also her society. She chooses to leave her husband and children because, finding herself in disagreement with both law and public opinion and not yet certain of her own convictions, she does not believe herself capable of meeting her responsibilities as wife and mother. She wishes to consider, freed from the emotional blackmail of home and children, what it means to be a woman in a society that deprives her of all rights. It is this ending that caused outrage and controversy because to many it seemed an attack on the family itself, the very basis of society. The outrage also stemmed from Ibsen's refusal to allow the audience the escape that Torvald had sought—the pretense, following a moment's anxiety, that the old social order was secure. The ending forced consideration of the status of women who, by law, were defined as inferior because a wife was required to have her husband's consent in all matters,

Minnie Maddern Fiske as Nora in a production of *A Doll's House* staged in New York in 1894.

whereas he could act wholly independently, even dispose of property that originally belonged to her, without her consent or knowledge.

Mrs. Linde and Krogstad serve as contrasts to Nora and Torvald. Mrs. Linde has considerable experience, having had to work for a living, though always in positions subordinate to men. She accepts her lot, but what she craves most is someone to look after. Nora, as she herself eventually realizes, has spent her life being treated like a doll, protected from harsh realities but having learned to manipulate men by feeding their fantasies about female helplessness. The mistake for which Krogstad has paid so dearly (forging a signature) is the same one made by Nora, but because women are to be governed by men, her mistake, if revealed, will be laid to the husband's failure to control his wife. Krogstad is shunned by society as morally corrupt, in contrast with Torvald, who is considered a pillar of the community. Despite (or perhaps because of) their experiences, Mrs. Linde and Krogstad (who when young were in love but were separated by circumstances) appear at the play's end much more likely than Nora and Torvald to achieve a satisfying relationship. It is Mrs. Linde who insists that Krogstad not retrieve his letter (revealing to Torvald what Nora has done), because she believes it essential that Nora and Torvald cease their childish games so they can build a mature relationship based on truth and trust. Torvald embodies the attitudes and standards of his society. His condescension toward women, his smug conviction of his own moral superiority, his concern for public opinion and appearances, and his fear of scandal are the qualities against which Nora's situation is measured.

The fifth major character, Dr. Rank, also serves as a contrast to Torvald. Nora can talk freely and share confidences with Rank about things that Torvald would find shocking. Rank probably would have made an excellent husband for Nora (a role he obviously covets) were it not for the congenital disease (probably syphilis) he has inherited from his father. He ultimately faces his unavoidable death with dignity.

Undergirding the characters and action of the play is a basic assumption that character and action are determined by hereditary and environmental forces. What each character is and does is explained by information about background, upbringing, and experience. All of the characters are victims of their environment, although Mrs. Linde and Krogstad, having achieved understanding of their circumstances, ultimately seem capable of rising above them. Ibsen could have made his play melodramatic by depicting Krogstad as villain and Nora as heroine. Instead, all of the characters strive for what they consider to be right; the complications arise from their differing conceptions of proper goals and means for attaining them. Thus they appear to be complex, fallible human beings.

A Doll's House could serve as a model of cause-to-effect dramatic construction. Like most of Ibsen's plays, this one uses a late point of attack. Mrs. Linde, because of her long absence, can believably inquire about the past and thereby motivate revelation of the complex circumstances that have preceded the play's beginning. The first act, then, sets up with seeming naturalness all of the conditions out of which the subsequent action develops logically, though not necessarily predictably.

A Doll's House uses a single setting throughout. It is a *box set* (that is, one that fully encloses the acting space on three sides like the walls of a room, with one side removed). Box sets permitted far more realistic representations of indoor spaces than could be achieved with wings, drops, and borders. The realistic effect was further enhanced by the addition of those furnishings, pictures, drapes, rugs, and bric-a-brac typically found in a real room of the period. Furthermore, instead of standing throughout on a stage largely devoid of furnishings, as had been typical prior to the late nineteenth century, actors now sought to behave as they would in real rooms, rather than letting the sets serve merely as visual backgrounds. In *A Doll's House* the characters seem to live in the setting. Action, character, and environment are intertwined.

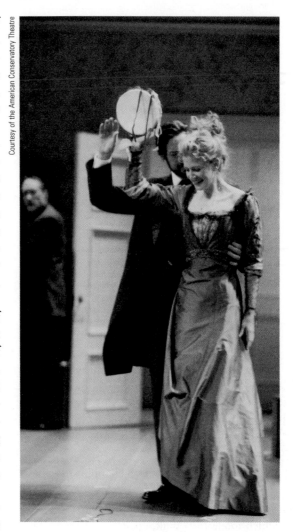

Courtesy of the American Conservatory Theatre

Nora (René Augesen) and her husband, Torvald (Stephen Caffrey), in *A Doll's House* at the American Conservatory Theatre (San Francisco), as directed by Carey Perloff.

Zola and Naturalism

Naturalism, unlike realism, had little success in the theatre, probably because it was too extreme in its demands. Its chief advocate, Emile Zola (1840–1902), thought many realists were more concerned with theatrical effectiveness (building complications, crises, and resolutions) than with truth to life. One of Zola's followers suggested that these temptations could be overcome by thinking of a play merely as a slice of life (*tranche de vie*)—a segment of reality transferred to the stage. The naturalists were far more rigorous than realists in their demands for "truth in art" and for a drama that demonstrated the inevitable laws of heredity and environment. In practice, naturalism emphasized the influence of poverty and other deprivations on the lives of the lower classes, a subject little treated in earlier drama. (Although melodrama often treated lower-class characters, it largely discounted any connection between environment and character. Often the most morally exemplary characters were among the poorest.) Zola, who often compared naturalistic art with medicine, believed that, just as the medical pathologist seeks to discover the cause of a disease so it can be treated, the dramatist should expose social ills so their causes can be corrected. With such rigorous (and often unattainable) goals, it is not surprising that naturalism had a short life and was soon absorbed into realism. The movement produced few plays of importance. Perhaps the best known is Zola's *Thérèse Raquin,* an adaptation of his novel about a woman who, with her lover, kills her husband and then suffers with her lover through many years of regret.

Together, realism and naturalism struck major blows against rigid social codes and absolute values. They laid the foundations on which modernists built.

The Emergence of the Director

THROUGHOUT HISTORY, someone has assumed responsibility for staging plays. In the Greek theatre, the playwright usually staged his own works, and in later times, the heads of companies (or someone appointed by them) had that responsibility. The present-day director, who assumes responsibility for interpreting the script and for approving and coordinating all of the elements that make up a production, is primarily a product of the late nineteenth century.

A convergence of several complex developments led to the emergence of the modern director. One of these developments involved the growing need for someone to coordinate and unify all the elements of a production. From the Renaissance to the nineteenth century, the elements of production, though representational, had been so generalized as to require little attention. Each theatre had a stock of sets (prison, palace, street, country landscape, and so on) that was reused often. To achieve variety, prosperous theatres acquired two or more sets for each general type of scene. Costumes were typically clothing worn in contemporary life, usually chosen or supplied by the actors; some categories of characters (such as classical or Near Eastern) appeared in non-

The Earth, a play adapted from Emile Zola's novel of the same name. Directed by André Antoine at the Théâtre Antoine, Paris, 1902. Notice the many naturalistic details, including the hayloft in the background and the chickens in the foreground.

Le Théâtre, 1902

contemporary dress, but these costumes were so formalized that the same ones could be used for all characters in the same category.

Acting was also conventionalized during the period prior to the nineteenth century, in that actors were hired according to lines of business and always played the same limited range of roles. The actors usually stood near the front of the stage (in part so they would be more visible in the low-intensity lighting of the pre-gas era) and directed their lines as much to the audience as to the other characters. (The auditorium, like the stage, was lighted.) Because there was seldom any furniture on stage, the actors used a pattern of movement that gave the downstage-center position to whichever character had an important speech at that point; when the speech was over, the actor moved away from center stage so the next actor could have that position. Thus there were frequent changes of place determined by a pattern so well understood that the actors did not need to be told when and where to move. Consequently, rehearsals were restricted largely to establishing where entrances and exits were to be made and to such complex action as duels. The person in charge of staging had little to do other than to make sure that all of the elements were assembled and to settle any disputes that arose. There were usually no more than seven to ten rehearsals.

As the nineteenth century progressed and the theatre became more complex, the number and specificity of sets and costumes increased, especially as elaborate spectacle and special effects multiplied. Much of the effect of melodrama depended on split-second timing and precise stage business. The introduction of box sets with furniture also served to alter the movement patterns typical of earlier times. These changes required increased supervision, coordination, and rehearsal. Nevertheless, each area of theatrical production continued for a time to work in relative isolation—scene painters did the sets, seamstresses and tailors the costumes, and so on—with little consultation. Even within an area, the work was often parceled out to several people (for example, each set for a five-set production might be done by a different scene painter). As each element of production became more specific and complex, the need for greater unity and more control became increasingly evident in the late nineteenth century.

The acceptance of the modern director owes most to two influences: the theory of Wagner and the practice of the Duke of Saxe-Meiningen. Richard Wagner (1813–1883), a German now known primarily as a composer of operas, sought to create a "master artwork" (*Gesamtkunstwerk*) through a fusion of all the arts. Opposed to realism, he chose most of his stories from German myth and set his dramas to music, not only to avoid the realistic mode but also to control the way the text was performed. He argued that spoken drama is at the mercy of actors, who are free to speak the lines however they choose, whereas singers are forced to follow the tempo, pitch, and duration dictated by the musical score. He also wished through his music-dramas to create a theatrical experience so overpoweringly empathetic that the audience would be drawn out of its everyday, mundane existence into an idealized, communal, near-religious experience.

To realize his goal, Wagner erected a new kind of theatre building, opened at Bayreuth in 1876. This theatre was the first in the West to do away with the box, pit, and gallery arrangement in favor of a "democratic" configuration, with seating laid out in a fan-shaped pattern that supposedly created equally good seeing and hearing conditions for all. This new auditorium design set the pattern for most twentieth-century theatres. It was also one of the first in which the auditorium was always darkened during performances. Wagner adopted this convention to distinguish between the everyday world (the auditorium) and the ideal realm (the stage), into which the performance sought to pull the audience. Wagner's contribution to the development of the director came from his strong demand for "unity of production"—that is, for productions in which everything has been filtered through a

Sara Krulwich/The *New York Times*

Wagner envisioned a theatre in which the seamless unity of production would create a believable (although not realistic) world that the audience, moved by his mythic tales and powerful music, could easily accept and imaginatively enter. Pictured is Wagner's *Die Walküre* as performed at New York's Metropolitan Opera.

single consciousness to achieve a unified artistic effect. This theoretical position has undergirded most twentieth-century ideas of staging.

Georg II, Duke of Saxe-Meiningen (1826–1914), is now usually considered the first director in the modern sense. Ruler of a small German state, Saxe-Meiningen gained international renown between 1874 and 1890 with his company's tours throughout Europe. The fame of the company did not stem from a new repertory, innovative design, or outstanding acting, but rather from its directorial practices. Saxe-Meiningen exerted complete control over every aspect of production. He designed the scenery, costumes, and properties himself and insisted that they be constructed to his precise specifications in both materials and appearance. Unable to afford well-known actors, he depended on long rehearsal periods (sometimes extending over several months) to achieve the effects he sought. His company was known especially for its crowd scenes, which (unlike those in other companies) were staged with great precision, variety, and emotional power. In Saxe-Meiningen's productions, the total stage picture was worked out carefully moment by moment, and the superior results were seen as convincing arguments for a strong director who can impose his authority and implement his vision. The Meiningen company validated many of Wagner's views, and the need for unified production (to be achieved primarily through the authority of the director) soon became a fundamental tenet of theatrical production.

Die Gartenlaube, 1879

Shakespeare's *Julius Caesar* as produced by Saxe-Meiningen. Shown here is Antony's oration over Caesar's corpse.

The Independent Theatre Movement

B Y THE 1880s, innovative plays by realists and naturalists had appeared, but censorship had kept most of them from production. Similarly, Wagner and Saxe-Meiningen had established the importance of the director, but Wagner had devoted his attention to opera, and Saxe-Meiningen's company was staging mostly poetic drama (by Shakespeare or nineteenth-century playwrights). The new drama and the new staging had remained isolated from each other. They were finally to meet in "independent" theatres.

Throughout most of Europe, plays could not be performed for public audiences until they had been approved by a censor. Some of Ibsen's prose plays were not performed in the 1880s because censors would not license them. On the other hand, "private" performances (those done by a group for its members only) were not subject to censorship. Beginning in the late 1880s, this loophole was exploited by a number of small, "independent" theatres, which were open only to subscribing members and therefore were not subject to censorship. These theatres were able to

accomplish what more established theatres had not: the uniting of the new drama with the new staging techniques.

The first independent theatre was the Théâtre Libre, founded in Paris in 1887 by André Antoine. An enthusiastic follower of Zola and Ibsen, Antoine produced their plays and those of similar writers in settings that reproduced every detail of an environment (in one instance, he hung carcasses of real beef in a butcher-shop set). Like Saxe-Meiningen, he exerted control over every element of production.

Antoine's was only the first of numerous independent theatres. In 1889, the Freie Bühne was founded in Berlin. It was less interested in staging than in providing a hearing for new playwrights. It is credited with launching the careers of playwrights (especially Hermann Sudermann and Gerhardt Hauptmann) associated with the inauguration of modern drama in Germany. In 1891, the Independent Theatre was established in London. Its inaugural production, of Ibsen's *Ghosts,* created an enormous scandal that did much to call public attention to a new type of drama. The Independent Theatre made its greatest contribution by inducing George Bernard Shaw (1856–1950) to begin writing plays. Unlike

Censoring Shaw

Out of the eight thousand plays submitted to the British censor between 1895 and 1909, only thirty were banned from public performance, and three of those were by George Bernard Shaw. One of those plays was *Mrs. Warren's Profession,* which, like most of Shaw's early plays, had its first performance in a private, independent theatre. The play was banned in England because the profession of its title character is prostitution. Although other plays had treated "fallen women," those women either repented their sordid past or were punished. Shaw's prostitute not only refuses to apologize for her past, but she has a clergyman as one of her former clients and (perhaps most shocking) has prospered from it. Shaw states his purpose in his preface to the play:

> "*Mrs. Warren's Profession* was written to draw attention to the truth that prostitution is caused, not by female depravity . . . but simply by underpaying, undervaluing, and overworking women so shamefully that the poorest of them are forced to resort to prostitution."

When Arnold Daly announced plans to produce the play in New York, Anthony Comstock, secretary and special agent of The Society for the Suppression of Vice, warned him not to produce "Bernard Shaw's filthy product." Daly responded by inviting Comstock to read the play or attend a rehearsal, but Comstock refused. Their correspondence was leaked to the newspapers and the production's opening night (1905) was jammed with spectators. Police were called for crowd control. Between two and three thousand people wanting to buy tickets were turned away at the door, and tickets were scalped for the then almost unheard-of price of $40 each. Following the performance, warrants were issued charging the entire cast and crew with "offending public decency."

Reviews in leading newspapers damned the play: the *New York Times* deemed it "unfit"; the *New York Herald* called it "morally rotten"; and *The American* labeled it "illuminated gangrene." (Shaw later pointed out that one of the newspapers most righteous in its condemnation of the play derived considerable revenue by publishing advertising for houses of prostitution.)

Eight months later, those involved with the New York production of *Mrs. Warren's Profession* were cleared of all charges. However, the production was effectively killed after its single Manhattan performance. Shaw later remarked, "To prohibit the play is to protect the evil which the play exposes."

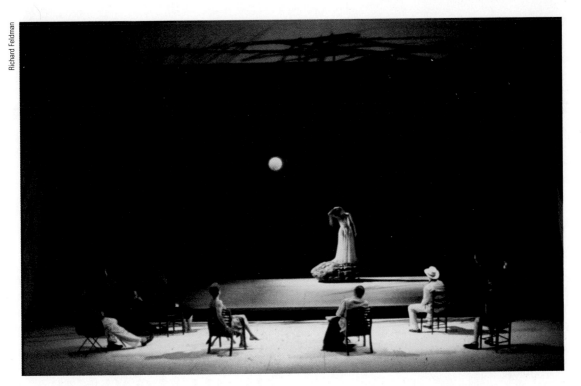

Richard Feldman

Nina performs Treplev's modern play against the background of the lake and the moon in Chekhov's *The Sea Gull,* as produced by the American Repertory Theatre. Directed by Ron Daniels; scene design by Anthony MacDonald; lighting by James Ingalls.

most dramatists of the new school, Shaw chose to write comedies through which he sought to puncture popular prejudices and provoke audiences into reassessing their values. In *Arms and the Man,* he ridiculed romantic notions about love and war; in *Major Barbara* he suggested that a munitions manufacturer is a greater benefactor than the Salvation Army because the manufacturer provides his employees the financial means for bettering their lives, whereas the Salvation Army provides only momentary relief; in *Pygmalion* (later adapted into the musical *My Fair Lady*) he shows how the English class system is related to speech. His other plays include *Man and Superman, Heartbreak House,* and *Saint Joan.* Shaw is considered one of the major playwrights of the twentieth century.

Not only did these independent theatres meet an important need, but also they established a significant precedent, because since that time, whenever established theatres have become insufficiently responsive to innovation, small companies (variously called "art" theatres, "little" theatres, Off-Broadway, or "alternative" theatres) have been formed to meet the need.

Another organization that emerged from the independent theatre movement—the Moscow Art Theatre—was to be of special importance. Founded in 1898 by Konstantin Stanislavsky (1863–1938) and Vladimir Nemerovich-Danchenko (1859–1943), it achieved its first major success with the plays of Anton Chekhov (1860–1904), known primarily for *The Sea Gull, Uncle Vanya, The Three Sisters,* and *The Cherry Orchard,* all of which are set in rural Russia and depict the monotony and frustrations of provincial life. All the characters in these plays aspire to a better life but do not know how (or do not have the initiative) to achieve their goals. They often do not understand their own feelings, and they seek to conceal as much as to reveal their responses. In these plays, subtext is often as important as text. Chekhov does not pass judgment on his characters; rather, he treats all with tolerance and compassion. The plays mix the comic, serious, pathetic, and ironic so thoroughly that they do not fit comfortably into any dramatic type (tragedy, comedy, tragicomedy). Chekhov's plays continue to hold a firm place in the repertory, not only in Russia but also throughout the world.

The Moscow Art Theatre eventually made its greatest impact through Stanislavsky's system of acting, which, described in his books (*My Life in Art, An Actor Prepares, Building a Character,* and *Creating a Role*), became the most pervasive influence on acting during the twentieth century. Stanislavsky's basic premises are these:

1. The actor's body and voice must be trained and flexible so they can respond to all demands.
2. To act truthfully, the actor must be a skilled observer of human behavior.
3. If actors are not merely to play themselves, they must understand a character's motivations and goals in each scene and in the play as a whole, as well as each character's relationship to all the other roles and the dramatic action.

PRACTITIONERS AND THEORISTS

Stanislavsky

Stanislavsky, the Russian creator of the most influential acting system of the twentieth century, was born Konstantin Sergeevich Alekseev, son of a wealthy industrialist. In 1885, he adopted the stage name Stanislavsky; after extensive experience as an actor; he came to recognize that many of his shortcomings as a performer were owing to lack of a systematic approach. In 1898, with Vladimir Nemerovich-Danchenko, he founded the Moscow Art Theatre, which sought to achieve the highest level of ensemble playing in productions that would make the dramatic action clear through simple natural acting emphasizing inner truth rather than external effect. Although the company was successful in achieving most of its goals, Stanislavsky continued his search for a systematic approach to acting. He recorded the first outlines of his system in 1909, and in 1912 he established the Moscow Art Theatre's First Studio to explore the system through training and performances by young actors. Following the Russian Revolution in 1917, the Moscow Art Theatre faltered, but by the 1930s, it was considered by Soviet authorities the model that other companies should emulate. It retained this status into the 1980s.

Stanislavsky was most comfortable with realistic acting but recognized the need to master other styles. He created several studios to explore alternative approaches, but he was never fully satisfied with the results and never felt that his system was complete. He continued to work on it until his death in 1938, publishing several books describing aspects of it.

The final act of Chekhov's *The Three Sisters* as performed at the Moscow Art Theatre.

4. Actors must project themselves into the world of the play and may learn to do so through the *magic if* (that is, through imagining how one would feel or act if one were this specific character in this specific situation).

5. Onstage, the actor should concentrate moment by moment, as if the events were happening spontaneously and for the first time.

Stanislavsky sought in his system to deal with all aspects of acting. What he wrote has been interpreted variously, but it continues to be the best-known attempt to describe what is involved in effective acting.

By the late nineteenth century, realism in the theatre was well established. In some respects, it was the logical culmination of developments that began in the Renaissance, when the picture-frame stage and perspective scenery were introduced. At that time, the stage became essentially representational, and subsequent trends were toward ever-more-convincing pictures. As the nineteenth century progressed, the demand for realistic detail reached a peak. It can be seen in melodrama first and then in realism/naturalism. Melodrama and realism differed, not so much over realistic staging, but over their views of truth and values. Melodrama was grounded in the assumption that human beings innately know the difference between right and wrong, that moral behavior has little to do with environment, class, or wealth. It taught that if one remains faithful to moral principles, everything will eventually work out satisfactorily—that good will win and evil lose. Proponents of realism and naturalism, on the other hand, tended to view the world scientifically rather than morally and to believe that the forces of heredity and environment are the determinants of human behavior. They did not believe that providence intervenes on the part of moral goodness, but rather that it is up to human beings to analyze and discover the causes of undesirable behavior and to alter those causes to achieve the desired results. By challenging melodrama's metaphysical foundations, realism and naturalism undermined the absolutist values that had dominated art since the Middle Ages. A pathway was thereby opened for those ideas and practices that have come to be labeled "modernist."

Additional Opportunities with InfoTrac College Edition

Stanislavsky's influence can be seen in the fact that many current acting teachers trace their training-lineage back to him to affirm their status in the field. Use InfoTrac College Edition to find and read an article about acting coaches: "Almost Famous: What Do the Third-Generation, Post-Stanislavsky Teachers Offer?" by Jean Schiffman in *Back Stage West*.

1. According to the article, how is the current generation of teachers different from the one that came before it?

2. Choose one of the profiles in the article and identify some things you find to be similar to Stanislavsky's teachings and some things you find to be different.

Building a Broad Context

- American Revolution (1775–1783); French Revolution (1789–1799)

- U.S. makes Louisiana Purchase from France for $15 million, effectively doubling U.S. territory (1803)

- Napoleon, Emperor of France, is defeated by allied European forces and exiled to Elba (1814); Napoleon returns and is defeated again at the battle of Waterloo (1815)

- Spain loses its colonies of Colombia, Venezuela, Ecuador, Guatemala, Panama, Santo Domingo, and Mexico as they proclaim independence (all between 1819 and 1824)

- **Victor Hugo's Romantic play *Hernani* causes riots in the theatre due to its defiance of neoclassical rules (1830)**

- Short-lived revolts sweep Europe, sparked by dissatisfaction with monarchies, nationalist urges, and people's desire to have a more active voice in their governments (1848)

- **The melodramatic play adaptation of Harriet Beecher Stowe's novel *Uncle Tom's Cabin* (1852)** becomes one of the most popular melodramas of all time

- Charles Darwin's *Origin of Species* (1859)

- U.S. Civil War (1861–1865); Lincoln assassinated at Ford's Theatre (1865)

- U.S. buys Alaska from Russia for $7,200,000 (1867)

- U.S. ratifies Fourteenth Amendment granting civil rights to blacks (1868)

- First U.S. transcontinental rail route completed; Suez Canal opens (both in 1869)

- Alexander Graham Bell patents the telephone (1876)

- **Ibsen writes *A Doll's House* (1879)**

- "Jack the Ripper" commits brutal mutilation-murders of London prostitutes (1888)

- New Zealand becomes first country in the world to grant women the vote (1893)

Pictured here is Thornton Wilder's *Our Town* as produced by the Acting Company. Directed by Claudia Zelevansky; scene design by Erik Flatmo; costume design by Melissa McVay; lighting by Scott Bolman; sound design by Fitz Patton. When first produced in 1938, *Our Town* seemed much more radical than it does today. The play's nonrealistic staging conventions and nonlinear treatment of time were assimilated into mainstream theatre, like many conventions and practices of the modernist period, so that today they seem commonplace.

In the years following . . . 1885, all the arts changed direction as if they had been awaiting
a signal. . . . In all the arts, 1885 is the point from which we must reckon the meaning
of the word "modern."
—Roger Shattuck, *The Banquet Years*

7: The Modernist Temperament: 1885–1940

B Y THE TIME the independent theatre movement got underway in the late 1880s, another strand of performance—in rebellion against realism—was emerging. This new strand can be viewed as an alternative reaction to many of the same impulses that had led to realism and naturalism. The belief that art should seek to represent human behavior and the physical world (as normatively perceived) had dominated theory and practice since the Renaissance. It was a fundamental premise of realism and naturalism. Beginning in the 1880s, however, one group of artists increasingly rejected this premise and substituted its own subjective visions (usually involving some degree of abstraction and distortion) for the traditional approach that had allowed the audience to compare a subject with its artistic rendering. This rejection of the long-standing relationship between perception and representation is often considered the true beginning of the modernist temperament. No longer shackled to the natural world, artists could now be valued for imaginative perception and formal innovation rather than accurate renditions of recognizable subjects.

Symbolism

T HE FIRST ARTISTIC MOVEMENT to reject representationalism was *symbolism*, launched in 1885. It denied the claims made by realists that ultimate truth is to be discovered through the five senses, arguing instead that truth is beyond objective examination. Because it can be only intuited, it cannot be expressed directly or through wholly rational means; truth can be only hinted at through a network of symbols that evokes feelings and states of mind corresponding imprecisely to our intuitions. Maurice Maeterlinck, author of *Pelléas and Mélisande*, the best known of all the symbolist plays, wrote that the most important element of great drama is the "idea which the poet forms of the unknown in which float about the beings and things which he evokes, the mystery which dominates them."

Unlike the realists, the symbolists chose their subjects from the past, the realm of fancy, or the mysterious present and avoided any attempt to deal with social problems or environmental forces. They aimed to suggest a universal truth independent of time and place that cannot be logically defined or rationally expressed. Thus their drama tended to be vague and mysterious.

Established theatres, finding symbolist drama incomprehensible, were even less inclined to produce it than the works of Ibsen and Zola. Consequently, the symbolists, like the realists and naturalists, established independent theatres in which to perform their plays. The most influential was the Théâtre de l'Oeuvre, founded in Paris in 1893 by Aurélien-Marie Lugné-Poë. The symbolists believed that the most important aspect of a production is mood or atmosphere. They used little scenery, and even that was vague in form and almost devoid of detail. They often placed a gauze curtain (*scrim*) just back of the proscenium so the action would appear to be taking place in a mist or timeless void. Color was chosen for its mood value rather than for representational accuracy. The actors often chanted their lines and used unnatural gestures. The goal was to remove the action from the immediate, everyday world. One can scarcely conceive of productions more unlike those of the realists and naturalists. They so differed from what audiences had become accustomed to that many spectators were baffled. As a movement in the theatre, symbolism soon lost its appeal, and by 1900 had largely ceased. Nevertheless, symbolism is important as the first of the nonrealistic movements that would proliferate in the twentieth century.

PRACTICES AND STYLES

Symbolist Production

The symbolist theatres rejected realism altogether. The motto of the Théâtre d'Art was "the word creates the decor." As one critic put it: "The decor ought to be a pure ornamental fiction which completes the illusion by color and line analogous to the drama. Most often some mobile draperies will suffice to give the impression of the infinite multiplicity of time and place. . . . [T]he theatre . . . ought to be: a pretext for dream." This approach to scenery is exemplified by a setting (for a play about a Christian martyr in Rome) composed of a single gold backdrop on which were glued dozens of red cut-out lions.

About the acting in symbolist theatres, another critic wrote that the actors "have a continual ecstatic air of perpetually being visionaries. As if hallucinatory, they stare before them far, very far, vaguely, very vaguely. Their voices are cavernous, their diction choppy." Audiences were divided between amused or outraged deriders and ardent supporters. About the latter, one critic wrote: "A scattered insanity floats in the air. . . . The very young heads of schoolboys, ecstatic and illuminated, listen to the words of Maeterlinck. . . . [There is] an undercurrent of perversion and craziness."

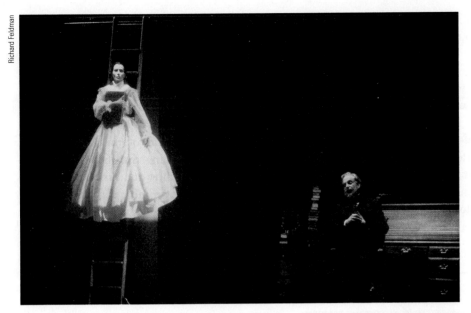

Susan Sontag's play *Alice in Bed* as produced by the American Repertory Theatre evoked the theatrical style of symbolism with its use of scrims and haze to separate the onstage world as a mythic realm quite apart from our physical reality. Directed by Bob McGrath; scene design by Laurie Olinder and Fred Tietz; costume design by Susan Anderson; lighting by John Ambrosone; with interactive films by Bill Morrison.

"Art for Art's Sake"

SYMBOLISM WAS not alone in challenging realism and naturalism during the late nineteenth century. In England, Walter Pater set forth the basic ideas of English Aestheticism, which advocated that the only functions of art were to intensify experience and to provide sensuous pleasure. The movement came to be called "art for art's sake," and Oscar Wilde became its best known playwright and its most eloquent spokesman. In his 1889 essay, "The Decay of Lying," Wilde expresses the basic principles of the movement. Rather than focusing on contemporary subjects and problems, as the realists and naturalists advocated, Wilde claimed that art has an independent life, and that its imaginative power must remain free from the concerns of its time. Instead of art imitating life, he proposed that life imitates art. Wilde argued that nature is not a model to be replicated but raw material to be fashioned and improved upon by fancy. Whereas realism and naturalism strove to use art to expose "the truth," Wilde claimed that "[l]ying, the telling of beautiful untrue things is the proper aim of art." Wilde was not advocating dishonesty; he was freeing art from a responsibility to express anything but itself. This stance has important implications in respect to the mushrooming of artistic styles within the twentieth century. It implies that art should be judged on the creativity of artists to express new vistas rather than to replicate old ones. As such, the stance breaks from adherence to conventional standards regarding both subject and method. We may gain a fuller understanding of Wilde's ideas by looking at the play generally considered his comic masterpiece, *The Importance of Being Earnest.*

The Importance of Being Earnest

WRITTEN IN 1895, the play makes use of the standard devices of the three-act "well-made play": carefully constructed exposition, cause-to-effect arrangement of events, skillful manipulation of withheld information, and startling reversals accomplished by last-minute revelations. Wilde lifts these devices to ridiculous levels, making the inherent artifice of the formulaic pattern laughably evident. He uses stock characters to embody the action: two fashionable bachelors matched with two proper young ladies (one from the city and one from the country), a stern English matron, a governess, an erudite churchman, and appropriately dry servants. The artificiality of the play's language and the self-conscious style called for on the part of its performers resembles Restoration comedy more than realism.

The play begins in the London flat of the fashionable bachelor, Algernon Moncrieff. During a conversation between Algernon and his

T. Charles Erickson

Edward Hibbert plays the strong-minded British matriarch Lady Bracknell in a recent production of Wilde's *The Importance of Being Earnest* at the Long Wharf Theatre (Connecticut). Directed by Doug Hughes; scene design by Hugh Landwehr; costume design by Paul Tazwell; lighting by Donald Holder.

friend Mr. Worthing, we learn that Worthing wishes to marry Algernon's cousin Gwendolen. But before Algernon will give his consent, he wants to know why his friend has a cigarette case engraved "From little Cecily, with her fondest love to her dear Uncle Jack." After all, Algernon knows Worthing's name to be Ernest, not Jack, and he has never heard of this Cecily before now. Worthing explains that he goes by the name Jack in the country and Ernest in town. In the country, he feels he must play the role of a high-minded moral guardian. He therefore invented a wicked younger brother named Ernest, who lives in London, so that he might have a ready excuse to visit London in order to rescue Ernest from the dreadful scrapes he gets into. Algernon understands all too well. He has invented an imaginary friend, an invalid named Bunbury, whom he uses as an excuse to avoid his social obligations in town. Both men have invented personas which free them from social responsibilities and expectations. Lady Bracknell, Algernon's aunt, and her daughter Gwendolen arrive. Worthing proposes to Gwendolen and she accepts, but specifies she could only love and marry him because his name is Ernest; the name of the man she believes she was destined to marry. However, Lady Bracknell reminds Gwendolen that she and her father will decide whom Gwendolen should marry. Lady Bracknell interviews Worthing and, discovering that he is a foundling, refuses her consent.

This synopsis of the events in Act I recounts Wilde's story, but misses the essence of his style. Wilde's use of language (puns, epigrams, hyperbole, and so on) comically reveals the hypocritical attitudes, capricious behavior, and twisted logic of his characters who consistently value artifice over reality and appearances over substance. For example, after Gwendolen agrees to marry Worthing, she remarks, "I hope you will always look at me just like that, especially when there are other people present." Lady Bracknell is pleased to discover that Worthing knows "nothing" because she does "not approve of anything that tampers with natural ignorance," and she purports that the "whole theory of modern education is radically unsound. Fortunately in England, at any rate, education produces no effect whatsoever." Lady Bracknell is also almost wholly devoid of sentimentality and flippantly characterizes Worthing's having lost his parents as "careless" and advises him to "acquire some relations as soon as possible."

Wilde loads the second act with complications and discoveries that sustain the comedic action. In order to get to know "little Cecily," Algernon arrives at Mr. Worthing's country home pretending to be his brother Ernest, and Worthing arrives dressed in mourning declaring that his brother Ernest has died. Cecily brings the two men together and attempts to reconcile their differences, but the fiction of their being at odds has now become true. Worthing orders Algernon/Ernest to leave and storms off. Algernon proclaims his love for Cecily, which she takes as a matter of fact because she has already created a love affair between them months ago in her diary. Far from being a factual record of daily events, her diary is a work of imaginative fiction. She recounts from her diary their engagement, breakup, and reconciliation. She produces letters from him, and when he exclaims that he never wrote her any letters, she retorts, "You need hardly to remind me of that. I remember only too well that I was forced to write your letters for you. . . . [T]he three you wrote me after I had broken off the engagement are so beautiful, and so badly spelled, that even now I can hardly read them without crying a little." Algernon discovers that she, too, finds Ernest the only acceptable name for a prospective husband. Wilde further complicates matters by having Gwendolen arrive, expecting to see her fiancé Ernest. Gwendolen meets Cecily, and the two women learn that each is engaged to "Ernest Worthing." They have tea, but the etiquette of this social ritual barely masks their antipathy. When Worthing and Algernon reappear and clarify who is engaged to whom, the ladies discover that neither man is truly Ernest. The women close ranks and firmly assert that they

are not engaged to anyone if they are not engaged to Ernest. The men console themselves by eating muffins and reaffirming their intentions to be rechristened as Ernest.

In Act III, the conflict reaches its crisis. Lady Bracknell arrives and recognizes Cecily's governess, Miss Prism, as the nanny who many years ago lost a baby in her charge. Miss Prism had mistakenly deposited a novel she had written in the baby carriage and the baby in her handbag, and then inadvertently left the bag at Victoria Station. Worthing produces the handbag which Prism identifies, implicating him as the long-lost baby. Lady Bracknell then reveals that Worthing is her sister's child, General Moncrieff's son, and Algernon's older brother. Furthermore, it happens that Worthing was actually christened "Ernest." Wilde has brought us full circle; the characters' lies have become truths.

The Importance of Being Earnest has been viewed by some as a farcical excuse for clever dialogue and by others as an insightful comic critique on Victorian society. Both views have some validity. Wilde subtitled *The Importance of Being Earnest* "a trivial play for serious people," and it is a rollicking verbal comedy enlisting contrived complications, discoveries, and startling last-minute revelations. Conversely, if one views the play as a critique of Victorian hypocrisy and shallowness, it may appear that Wilde directly treats the concerns of his time despite his "art for art's sake" stance. However, inasmuch as the characters create fictions (lies) which become true as life imitates art, the play supports his critical stance.

The Modernist Influence on Theatrical Visionaries

MODERNISM INFLUENCED all of the arts. From the Renaissance to the twentieth century, the visual arts (including theatrical scenery) had depicted everything in relation to a fixed eyepoint. In the early twentieth century, however, the visual arts no longer always depicted all details of the same picture as seen from one eye-point. The best-known examples are certain of Picasso's paintings, in which various parts of the same subject are painted as though seen from different eye-points. In painting, recognizable subjects were sometimes abandoned altogether, resulting in wholly abstract works. Such painting had to be judged by formal criteria (effectiveness in manipulating line, color, and composition) rather than by the accuracy with which it represented its subject. Similar developments in music displaced melody, so that a composition could be valued not for its melodic and harmonic patterns but rather for its handling of time and atonal relationships. The theatre also participated in these modernist trends. During the early twentieth century, two theorists—Appia and Craig—were especially successful in reshaping ideas about the "art of the theatre."

Born in Switzerland, Adolphe Appia (1862–1928) began with the idea that artistic unity in theatre is fundamental but difficult to achieve because of conflicting elements: the moving actor, the horizontal floor, and the vertical scenery. He sought to replace flat, painted scenery (as well as all decorative detail) with three-dimensional structures as the only proper environment for three-dimensional actors. To overcome the limitations of the flat stage floor, he advocated the use of steps, platforms, and ramps to create transitions from horizontal to vertical planes, thereby making possible greater compositional variety in the total stage picture and the movement of actors.

Appia was also a major theoretician of stage lighting. To reveal the shape and dimensionality of the setting and actor, Appia advocated the use of light from various directions and angles. He considered light the most flexible of all theatrical elements because, like music, it can change moment by moment to reflect shifts in mood and emotion and because it unifies all other elements through its intensity, color, direction, and movement. Appia's views on lighting came at a crucial time—just as the technology needed to implement his theories was becoming available. The incandescent electric lamp was invented in 1879, and as the first medium that did not use an open flame, it gained acceptance rapidly because of its safety. Initially, the wattage of electric lamps was very small, and not until 1911 were lamps available with a concentrated filament of sufficiently high wattage to permit the development of spotlights. By around 1915, most of the technol-

Adolphe Appia's design for the entrance to the underground in Gluck's opera *Orpheus and Eurydice.*

ogy (electric lamps, spotlights, color filters, and dimmers) needed to implement Appia's theories was available and in use.

Edward Gordon Craig (1872–1966) began his career as an actor in the English theatre. Much more militant than Appia, he was always in the public eye because of his controversial views. Craig denied that the theatre is a fusion of other arts; he saw it as a wholly autonomous art whose basic elements—action, language, line, color, and rhythm—are fused by a master artist. He once suggested that actors should be replaced by large puppets (*übermarionetten*), because they, unlike actors, could not impose their own personalities on a production and undermine the master artist's intentions. Like Appia, Craig advocated simplicity in scenery, costumes, and lighting. Both sought to replace the representational approach to visual elements with one concerned with abstract structures that embodied the line, mass, color, texture, and mood appropriate to the dramatic action. Appia and Craig also promoted the concept of the director as the supreme, unifying theatre artist.

The influence of Appia and Craig was reinforced by the German director Max Reinhardt (1872–1943), who was then amending earlier conceptions of the director. During the late nineteenth century, Wagner, Saxe-Meiningen, Antoine, Lugné-Poë, and others had won acceptance for the director, but each of these men, though they differed from each other in his approach to staging, used basically the same mode for every production he staged. As new artistic movements appeared, each movement was faced with the need to establish a theatre specializing in its distinctive style, because each existing theatre was devoted to a single approach in theatrical production. A breakthrough was achieved around 1900, when Reinhardt began to treat each production as a new challenge demanding its own unique stylistic solution. Using this approach, the plays of all movements and periods could be accommodated in the same theatre. For the first time, theatre history became important to directing, because Reinhardt frequently built productions around elements significant to the theatrical context in which a play had originally appeared. Often he tried to re-create the audience-performer spatial relationship. (As examples, he remodeled a circus building to accommodate Greek plays; for a medieval play he transformed a theatre into a cathedral; and he presented many eighteenth-century plays in a

Edward Gordon Craig's design (watercolor and pastel on paper) for *Hamlet* (1926), showing the scene in Act III when Hamlet meets the acting troupe that has arrived at Elsinore.

Reinhardt's production of *Oedipus the King* in the Circus Schumann, Berlin, 1910.

Le Théâtre, 1911

hall of state in an eighteenth-century palace.) He unified some productions around dominant visual motifs and others around theatrical conventions typical of the period when the play was written. Thus knowledge of the theatre's past was crucial in many of his productions.

Reinhardt's method further enhanced the role of the director. Because the stylistic approach to be used in any production was optional, the choice was the director's to make; as the one who chose the vision that would undergird the production, the director was also the arbiter of all choices made by those who worked to implement his vision. Although Reinhardt considered the director's the primary artistic consciousness, he did not, as many of his successors were to do, alter the time or place of a play's action. He believed that the production should serve the script (rather than the script the production, as has become common in more recent times). His productions, viewed from today's perspective, do not seem stylistically as varied as they did to his contemporaries, because most of his productions were still largely representational. Nevertheless, Reinhardt established eclecticism as the dominant directorial approach. Once accepted, eclecticism was (and continues to be) elaborated and extended by others, frequently in ways never envisioned by Reinhardt. With Reinhardt, relativism triumphed in directing (as it already had in many other areas); instead of applying the same approach to all plays (the absolutist's way),

the approach was altered to suit each play (the relativist's way).

New Artistic Movements

THE DECADE between 1910 and 1920 was one of unrest and upheaval, epitomized by World War I. Not surprisingly, this decade saw the emergence of numerous artistic movements, each championing a new perspective on human experience and new ways of expressing this perspective. Three of the most important of these movements were futurism, dada, and expressionism.

Futurism was launched in 1909 by Filippo Tommaso Marinetti (1876–1944), an Italian who glorified the speed and energy of the machine age, which he saw as the key to an enlightened future. Because he thought veneration of the past stood in the way of progress, he declared that all libraries and art museums should be destroyed. The futurists sought to replace old art forms with a number of new ones, among them collage, kinetic sculpture, and *bruitisme* ("noise music" based on the sounds of everyday life). Especially contemptuous of drama that developed leisurely and required no active involvement from its audience, the futurists issued a number of manifestos demanding change. In one of these manifestos, "The Variety Theatre," Marinetti argued that the theatre of his day was devoted almost entirely to historical

PRACTICES
AND STYLES

Futurist Synthetic Plays

The futurists' desire to compress dramatic action into a brief moment is illustrated in the following *sintesi*, reprinted in its entirety.

Synthesis of Syntheses
by Gugielmo Jannelli and Luciano Nicastro

Empty stage: a long dark corridor at the end of which a small red lamp flashes off and on, a long way off. Then, a streak of white light appears like a carpet along the corridor.

Five seconds.

A revolver shot. Scream. Noises. Confused cries.

Pause.

The fresh burst of a woman's laughter.

Simultaneously a door at the back is thrown open by a blow, blinding the audience with a huge, powerful light.

The curtain detaches, and falls. *End of play*

—*Translated by and reprinted with the permission of Victoria Nes Kirby*

drama or photographic reproductions of daily life. He considered such drama to be remnants from "the age of the oil lamp." To reform this theatre, he proposed as a model the variety theatre with its vaudeville acts, jugglers, dancers, gymnasts, and the like because of its dynamic energy and audience involvement. "The Variety Theatre is alone in seeking the audience's collaboration. It doesn't remain static like a stupid voyeur, but joins noisily in the action." Marinetti went on to suggest ways of disrupting the refined and detached behavior of theatre audiences: "Spread a powerful glue on some of the seats. . . . Sell the same seat to ten persons. . . . Sprinkle the seats with dust to make people itch and sneeze."

The futurists proposed to replace existing drama with a "synthetic" drama that would compress into a moment or two the essence of a full-length play. Their desire to speed up life also led them to champion simultaneity and multiple focus. In their performances, several scenes or different kinds of events (musical, pictorial, dramatic) proceeded simultaneously in different parts of the performance-audience space. The futurists sought confrontations with audiences, whose prejudices about what art is or can be they challenged so strongly that their performances often provoked near-riots. Futurism lost much of its appeal during World War I because it praised war as the supreme expression of the aggressive life it championed.

Dada was grounded in rejection of the values that had provoked World War I. When that war broke out, many artists sought refuge in neutral Switzerland, where in 1916 dada was born. Its principal spokesman was Tristan Tzara (1896–1963). Because insanity seemed the world's state, the dadaists sought in their art to replace logic, reason, and unity with chance and illogic. They

A futurist production at the Théâtre de la Pantomime Futuriste, Paris, 1927. Notice the mingling of live performers with nonhuman puppet figures.

Le Théâtre, 1927

presented a number of programs in which, like the futurists, they used simultaneity and multiple focus. Among their favorite forms were "chance poems" (created by placing words in a hat, drawing them out at random, and reciting them) and "sound poems" (composed of nonverbal sounds). They also performed short plays, dances, and music. They recognized no barriers between art forms. Dada was essentially anarchistic, thumbing its nose at a hypocritical, discredited society and the art forms it venerated.

Dada lost much of its energy when the war ended, but some of the most interesting examples occurred after the war. For example, in Cologne, Germany, in 1920 Max Ernst, Hans Arp, and Theodor Baargeld staged a dada event in a glassed-in courtyard entered through a men's toilet. The event included several unrelated features, among them a young woman, dressed as if for her first communion, reciting obscene poems, a pool of blood-red liquid from which a skull and a hand projected, a wooden sculpture to which a hatchet was attached for the convenience of anyone wishing to attack it.

Much of what the futurists and dadaists did seems prankish, intended deliberately to provoke. It is difficult to assess their influence, but the challenges they posed aroused strong emotion and heated debate about such topics as how to define a work of art, the role of audience response, art as an instrument of change, the need for innovation in art, and the relationship of art to its culture. Their influence would resurface strongly after 1960.

Expressionism emerged around 1910 in Germany. It sought to counter materialism and industrialism, which it saw as the principal perverters of the human spirit. Unlike futurism, which glorified the machine age, expressionism charged that the industrial age had turned human beings into machines with conditioned responses and souls shriveled by materialistic values. Its proponents wished to reshape the world to make it conform to what is best in the human spirit and thereby to achieve "the regeneration of man." Unlike futurism and dada, whose theatrical programs were forerunners of today's performance art, expressionism, with its emphasis on text, was more easily assimilated and had a greater immediate impact on theatre than did futurism or dada.

Most expressionist drama focuses on how the human spirit has been distorted by false values. It usually shows the protagonist searching for identity, fulfillment, or a means to change the

Richard Feldman

The Cabinet of Dr. Caligari, a music theatre performance piece by composer/author John Moran, inspired by the 1919 German expressionist silent film of the same name. Note the sharp contrasts and nightmarish reality conveyed through the combination of live action with stylized costumes, slides, film, and a computer-generated landscape. Directed by Bob McGrath; costumes by Catherine Zuber.

world. Because these protagonists have usually been warped by materialism and industrialism, the external world that they see (and that we see through their eyes) is also distorted. The walls of buildings or rooms may lean in threateningly, color may reflect emotion (for example, the protagonist's jealousy may make the sky green rather than blue), movement and speech may be robot-like, or several persons or objects may be identical in appearance (as if machine made). Expressionism typically presents a nightmarish vision of the human situation.

Some of August Strindberg's (1849–1912) plays are often seen as forerunners of expressionism. Perhaps the most important of these is *A Dream Play* (1902), in whose preface Strindberg wrote:

> The writer has tried to imitate the disconnected but seemingly logical form of the dream. Anything may happen; everything is possible and probable. Time and space do not exist. On an insignificant background of reality, imagination designs and embroiders novel patterns: a medley of memories, experiences, free fancies, absurdities, and improvisations.

Strindberg overcame the limitations of time, space, logical sequence, and appearance by adopting the viewpoint of the dreamer. In *A Dream Play,* one event flows into another without logical transition, characters are transformed into others, and widely separated places and times are telescoped in a story about tortured and alienated human beings. From Strindberg the expressionists borrowed many of their techniques.

Expressionism flourished in Germany, especially immediately after World War I, when

Courtesy of National Theatre of Norway

August Strindberg's *A Dream Play* as produced at the National Theatre of Norway.

O'Neill's *"The Hairy Ape"* (Scene 1), in its first production, 1922, at the Provincetown Playhouse. Directed by James Light; designed by Robert Edmond Jones and Cleon Throckmorton.

optimism over the establishment of Germany's first democratic government made the realization of expressionist goals seem possible. The most important German expressionist playwrights were Georg Kaiser (1878–1945) and Ernst Toller (1893–1939). By the mid-1920s disillusionment had replaced optimism, and the popularity of expressionism faded rapidly. Nevertheless, expressionism had attracted a number of writers in various countries. In the United States, several noteworthy expressionist plays were written, the best known of which are *The Adding Machine* (whose accountant-protagonist is little more than an adding machine himself) by Elmer Rice (1892–1967) and *"The Hairy Ape"* by Eugene O'Neill.

Eugene O'Neill (1888–1953), son of James O'Neill and the first American dramatist to win wide and lasting international recognition, is often considered the greatest playwright America has produced. Like many American playwrights of his day, O'Neill was aided in his early career by groups modeled after Europe's independent theatres. In the United States these companies, which began to appear around 1912, were usually called "little" or "art" theatres. O'Neill was discovered by the Provincetown Players, a group that between 1915 and 1929 was concerned with promoting American playwriting. O'Neill's plays, ranging through practically every style, include

The Emperor Jones, Desire Under the Elms, Strange Interlude, Mourning Becomes Electra, The Iceman Cometh, Long Day's Journey into Night, and many more. Let us examine *"The Hairy Ape"* and O'Neill's use of expressionism in that play.

"The Hairy Ape"

"THE HAIRY APE" derives its unity from its central theme: humanity's frustrated search for identity in a hostile environment. When the play begins, the protagonist, Yank, is confident that he and his fellow stokers on an ocean liner are the only ones who "belong" because they make the ship go (and, by extension, the factories and machines of the modern, industrialized society). Yank represents for his fellow workers "a self-expression . . . their most highly developed individual." They do not recognize that their quarters resemble "the steel framework of a cage" or that they themselves resemble Neanderthal men.

The second scene introduces Mildred Douglas, the spoiled daughter of a wealthy steel and shipping magnate. Seen against the natural beauty of the sea, she appears "inert and disharmonious," completely lacking in purpose. In Scene 3, she insists on visiting the stokehole to watch the men shovel the coal that makes the

Mark Portland. Courtesy of the Pittsburgh Public Theatre

O'Neill's "The Hairy Ape" at the Pittsburgh Public Theatre.

ship's engines run. When she sees Yank, she is so horrified that she faints and must be carried away. This is the catalytic moment for Yank, because Mildred's revulsion makes him begin to question all of his beliefs. According to O'Neill, from Scene 4 onward, Yank "enters into a masked world; even the familiar faces of his mates in the forecastle have become strange and alien."

In Scene 5, seeking to reestablish his sense of worth, Yank goes to New York's Fifth Avenue, where the shops catering to the rich and powerful display "magnificence cheapened and made grotesque by commercialism." The people, dressed identically, look like "gaudy marionettes." When Yank tries to get their attention, they ignore him; resorting to force, he strikes at the men, but they remain oblivious to his existence and give their full attention to a monkey-fur coat in the shop window.

In Scene 6, Yank is in jail (called "the zoo"), where the cages run on, "numberless, into infinity." He decides that he will get his revenge by destroying the steel and machinery over which he originally thought he had power. Learning that the IWW (International Workers of the World) opposes the owners of factories and ships, Yank, upon being released from jail, goes to an IWW office (described as "cheap, banal and commonplace") and offers to blow up the IWW's enemies. His offer is greeted with contempt, and he is thrown into the street. In the final scene, Yank arrives at the zoo, where he finds a gorilla that seems to understand him, but when he frees the gorilla it crushes him and throws him into its cage. Yank dies without achieving the sense of belonging that he has so desperately sought.

Yank is symbolic of modern humanity in an industrialized society—cut off from a past when human beings were an integral part of the natural environment and trapped in an existence where they are little better than cogs in the industrial machine. In a speech to the gorilla, Yank sums up his feelings of alienation: "I ain't got no past to tink in, nor nothin' dat's comin', on'y what's now—and dat don't belong."

Only a few of the characters in "The Hairy Ape" have names. Most are representative types or members of groups. In the stage directions, O'Neill writes that, except for slight differentiations in size and coloration, the stokers are all alike. Overall, O'Neill seems to suggest that all human beings in the modern, industrialized world have been distorted—the workers having been reduced to the level of animals, the rich having become useless puppets. These conceptions are embodied in speech and appearance. In Scene 4, almost all of the speeches are described as having a "brazen metallic quality as if [the characters'] throats were phonograph horns," and much of what Yank and others say in this scene is greeted with "a chorus of hard, barking laughter." In the scene set on Fifth Avenue, the rich characters speak in "toneless, simpering voices," and they are masked and dressed to make them look like puppets. In comments on the appropriate performance style for the play, O'Neill suggests that, beginning with Scene 4, everyone whom Yank encounters, "including the symbolic gorilla," should wear a mask. Yank is set off from the other characters because he is the only one who recognizes the need to seek a coherent relationship between himself and his environment. In his search, he meets no one who understands his need, but O'Neill seems to have hoped that Yank's plight would illuminate for the audience an aspect of modern existence.

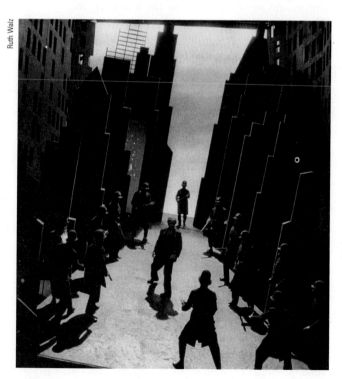

Eugene O'Neill's *"The Hairy Ape"* as produced at the Schaubühne am Halleschen Ufer in Berlin. Directed by Peter Stein.

"The Hairy Ape" is representative of both the outlook and the techniques of expressionism. The episodic structure and distorted visual elements are typical, as is Yank's longing for fulfillment, with its suggestion that society be changed so the individual can achieve a sense of belonging.

By the time O'Neill wrote *"The Hairy Ape,"* the modernist temperament was prominent in all the arts. Yet, many persons still believed in absolute values and considered much of twentieth-century thought and art misguided or dangerous. The modernist and more traditionalist points of view coexisted; perhaps a sign that the fragmentation of standards and values (in both life and art) had become the norm rather than the exception. In this atmosphere of competing values and viewpoints, the varieties of theatrical experience multiplied, and several different styles existed simultaneously.

■ The Postwar Era

BY THE 1920s, modernism dominated "high" art in both Europe and America. The mass audience, nevertheless, still preferred the types of entertainment that had been popular before modernism appeared; as film increasingly met its needs, this audience drifted away from the theatre. The shift was accelerated especially by the almost simultaneous advent around 1929 of sound films and a major economic depression, because not only was film's entertainment potential greatly increased by sound but also its ticket prices were a fraction of those for live theatre. Between 1929 and 1939 approximately two-thirds of all live-entertainment theatres in the United States closed.

In the United States, the majority of those who continued to attend live theatre still preferred some version of realism. New theatrical movements were welcomed first (and often only) by "art" or "little" theatres (the counterparts of European independent theatres). Broadway audiences were not very tolerant of innovation. The peak of post–World War I experimentation on Broadway

The New Stagecraft

The forces that created modernism in Europe had little impact on theatre in America until around World War I in part because before the end of the nineteenth century the professional theatre in the United States had come to be centered in New York, from which companies were sent on tour throughout the country. Around 1896, a group of businessmen was able to gain a near monopoly on touring. Known as the Syndicate, this organization would send out only those productions it thought capable of attracting a mass audience. It opposed the kind of innovations that had triumphed in Europe, and it effectively kept the American theatre in the premodern mode. The power of the Syndicate was challenged and broken in the years between 1910 and 1915 by the Shubert Brothers, but the Shuberts' goals differed little from those of the Syndicate.

Significant change began around 1912 when Americans who had studied and traveled abroad began to adopt the tactics of European independent theatres. Important "little theatres," as they were called in the United States, included the Toy Theatre (founded 1912) in Boston; the Chicago Little Theatre (1912); and the Neighborhood Playhouse (1915), the Washington Square Players (1915), and the Provincetown Players (1915), all in New York. In the beginning, these were amateur groups, although some later became professional.

The first important professional work by an American in the European mode came in 1915 with the production of Anatole France's *The Man Who Married a Dumb Wife*. Designed by Robert Edmond Jones (1887–1954), who had traveled through Europe and spent a year at Reinhardt's theatre in Berlin, this set is usually called the first American expression of the "new stagecraft" (the term used in the United States for the European innovations). Jones, along with Lee Simonson (1888–1967) and Norman Bel Geddes (1893–1958), was to be the major popularizer of the new mode in America. He designed sets for many of Eugene O'Neill's plays, both on Broadway and at the Provincetown Playhouse, and he was the principal designer of Arthur Hopkins' Broadway productions.

Simplification and suggestion (rather than detailed reproduction of the real world) were the hallmarks of new stagecraft design. Jones wrote, "Stage designing should be addressed to the eye of the mind," stimulating the imagination to perceive the underlying feeling of a play rather than stifling the imagination by providing too much. Perhaps more than any other designer, Jones established the style that dominated the American theatre between the two world wars. His influence is still felt through his book, *The Dramatic Imagination* (1941).

came in the early 1920s with Arthur Hopkins' production of an "expressionistic" Macbeth, Robert Edmond Jones' set for which was an arrangement of Gothic arches that leaned ever more precariously as the action proceeded. Three large masks, symbols of the Witches or Fate, hung above the stage throughout (see illustration below). The failure of this production is sometimes said to have made Broadway producers avoid stylistic extremes thereafter and adhere closely to a modified (or simplified) realism, much less detailed than nineteenth-century realism but still basically representational. This type of simplified realism dominated the Broadway theatre from the early 1920s to the 1960s.

In addition to O'Neill, a number of other American playwrights—among them Maxwell Anderson, Elmer Rice, Paul Green, Robert Sherwood, and Lillian Hellman—gained international recognition in the years following World War I. Perhaps the best known is Thornton Wilder (1897–1975), especially for *Our Town* (1938), with its distillation of everyday human experience in small-town America; *The Skin of Our Teeth* (1943), which treats the ability of human beings to survive even the most extreme circumstances; and *The Matchmaker* (1954), which was later transformed into the musical *Hello, Dolly* (1963).

The Federal Theatre and the Group Theatre

THE ECONOMIC DEPRESSION of the 1930s brought a unique development in American theatre, the Federal Theatre Project, the government's first financial support of theatre in the United States. As the depression deepened and unemployment grew, Congress created the Works Progress Administration to provide jobs in many fields, including theatre. The Federal Theatre Project, which existed from 1935 to 1939, was most active in New York, although it had units in forty states. Its primary task was to provide "free, adult, uncensored theatre." It is best remembered for the *Living Newspaper,* a form that aimed at achieving in the theatre something comparable to the printed newspaper. In actuality, it more nearly resembled the documentary film. The most famous living newspapers are *One Third of a Nation* (on slum housing), *Triple-A Plowed Under* (on the government's farm-subsidy program), and *Power* (on rural electrification and flood control). Each of these plays explored a specific problem, along with its causes and proposed solutions. They alternated dramatic scenes (illustrating the effect of existing

Norman Bel Geddes' design for *The Miracle* emphasizes mood over realistic detail, stimulating the audience's imagination to perceive the underlying feeling of the play.

Courtesy of Norman Bel Geddes

Power, a "living newspaper" presented by the Federal Theatre Project. The scene shows an argument before the Supreme Court over the constitutionality of the Tennessee Valley Authority.

social conditions on human lives) with narrative sequences (providing factual information through statistical tables, still photographs, and motion pictures, all projected onto screens). Collaborative creations of many authors, the plays advocated social reform and corrective legislation. This aggressive advocacy eventually contributed to the discontinuance of the Federal Theatre, when in 1939 Congress refused to appropriate funds to continue it.

During the years between the two world wars, Konstantin Stanislavsky became a major influence on American acting after the Moscow Art Theatre toured the United States in the early 1920s. Following that visit, two of Stanislavsky's former students, Richard Boleslavsky and Maria Ouspenskaya, founded the American Laboratory Theatre in New York, where from 1923 to 1930 they taught his approach to acting. But the upsurge in Stanislavsky's influence owed most to the Group Theatre, founded in 1931 by former students of the American Laboratory Theatre and modeled on the Moscow Art Theatre. For the next ten years, it was the most respected theatre in the United States. Among its members were Lee Strasberg, Harold Clurman, Stella

Adler, Elia Kazan, Cheryl Crawford, Robert Lewis, Lee J. Cobb, and Morris Carnovsky—the directors, actors, teachers, and producers who most actively promoted Stanislavsky's system in the United States. During the depression years, the Group Theatre presented many of the best productions on Broadway, most dealing with the pressing economic and social issues of that time. Largely because of internal dissension in the company, the Group Theatre was disbanded in 1941.

Epic Theatre

WHILE SIMPLIFIED REALISM and musicals dominated the theatre in the United States, innovations were common in Europe after World War I. Many made little impact, but a few eventually exerted significant influence. One of the most important was *epic theatre.*

Epic theatre developed in Germany during the 1920s in the wake of expressionism. It is associated above all with Bertolt Brecht (1898–1956), who shared the expressionists' desire to transform society but thought their methods vague and impractical. Brecht's ideas lacked focus at first, but around 1926 he embraced Marxism and its belief that values are determined by the prevailing economic mode of production. Brecht came to view many of the world's problems as the result of capitalism and to believe that they could be solved by the adoption of socialism or communism. Thereafter, he sought to make audiences evaluate the socioeconomic implications of what they saw in the theatre; he was convinced that, if this was done effectively, audiences would perceive the need to alter the economic system and would work to bring about appropriate changes. He was also convinced that his goals could not be attained in the kind of theatre then dominant—one that sought to evoke an empathetic response so overwhelming that the spectators suspended their critical judgment, letting themselves be carried along passively by the performance. In such a theatre, according to Brecht, all the problems raised are solved at the end of the play, and there is no demand that the audience relate what it has seen to the real world. Brecht wished to alter the audience's relationship to the production by encouraging spectators to watch actively and critically.

As a means to his goal, Brecht arrived at the concept of "alienation" (*verfremdung*)—distancing the audience from the stage events so it can view them critically. To achieve alienation, Brecht adopted many conventions not previously used but, through Brecht's influence, have since become common. First, he reminded the audience that it was in a theatre by calling attention to the theatre's means (which formerly had been concealed in the belief that to allow the audience to see them would destroy theatrical illusion). He insisted that lighting instruments be left unmasked; that scenery be fragmentary (merely sufficient to indicate place); that musicians be visible (sometimes on stage); that captions, maps, or other images be projected onto screens; and that when objects were suspended, the ropes supporting them be clearly visible. Actors often sang directly to the audience or commented on the action. Brecht sometimes advised his actors to present their characters rather

than become the characters (as Stanislavsky wished). To help actors achieve distance from their roles, Brecht advised them in rehearsal to speak of their characters in the third person. For example, an actor might verbalize a character's action in "He crosses the stage and says . . ." Such conventions marked a conscious break with practices that had long dominated the stage, the goal having been to make the audience suspend its consciousness of watching a theatrical performance. Brecht did not see the theatre as a place to escape one's problems but rather as a place to recognize problems that are then to be solved outside the theatre.

Brecht sought to achieve alienation by distancing the story through either time or place. According to Brecht, most historical drama treats its subjects from a present-day point of view, thereby creating the impression that conditions, having always been the same, are unchangeable. Brecht, contrarily, sought to make the differences between past and present readily apparent so the audience would recognize that, because the world has changed, it can still be changed if we do not like conditions as they now exist.

Brecht further sought alienation through his handling of the various theatrical elements. He opposed the notion (championed by Wagner and embraced by most of Brecht's contemporaries) that the most effective theatrical production is a synthesis of all the arts, each element reinforcing the others in a fully unified work. Brecht called this practice redundant and wasteful, because each element is seeking to duplicate in its own way what is being done by all of the others. He advocated instead that each element make its own comment. The disparity among elements would then arouse alienation by making the audience assess the varying comments. For example, Brecht's songs often set ironic or disillusioned lyrics to lighthearted tunes; the disparity between melody and words was intended to make the listener more critically aware of the song's implications.

Brecht adopted a number of structural devices to create alienation. Rather than have one scene flow smoothly into another, he wished, as he put it, to call attention to the knots tying the

Bertolt Brecht's *Mother Courage* as produced by the American Repertory Theatre. Directed by János Szász; scene design by Csaba Antal; costume design by Edit Szücs; light design by John Ambrosone.

scenes together. Therefore, he used captions (projected on screens), songs, or other devices to emphasize breaks in the action. Captions also were used at the beginning of scenes to summarize the content of the scene to follow in order to divert attention from story or suspense and direct it to the social implications of the events.

These conventions may suggest that Brecht was heavy-handedly didactic, but he was also intent on entertaining. His stories have many complications and reversals and are leavened with songs and other devices intended to capture and hold attention. In fact, Brecht the storyteller so often subverts Brecht the ideologue that many theatregoers remain oblivious of his desire to provoke social change. Brecht's concept of alienation is often misinterpreted as a demand that spectators be continuously distanced from the events. In actuality, Brecht engages the audience empathetically and then, through some device (such as a song), creates the distance needed to

evaluate what has been experienced during the empathetic moments. Thus there is a continuing alternation of empathy and distance (much like that created through the alternation of episodes and choral odes in Greek drama). One might also get the impression from reading Brecht that settings and costumes played little role in his productions. But, though scenery was restricted in quantity, in Brecht's theatre it was always designed and executed with great care; each piece was meticulously crafted and sometimes intricately detailed. The costumes often looked used and worn, in accordance with the character and situation, but many were elegant. The overall effect was one of considerable richness.

Brecht called his theatre epic because he thought it had more in common with epic poetry (in which dialogue and narration alternate and in which time and place are quickly transformed) than with the dramatic traditions that had dominated the theatre since the

Renaissance. Of Brecht's many plays, perhaps the best known are *The Threepenny Opera, Mother Courage and Her Children, The Caucasian Chalk Circle,* and *The Good Person of Setzuan.* Let us look at the last of these as an example of Brecht's epic drama.

The Good Person of Setzuan

BRECHT WROTE *The Good Person of Setzuan* between 1938 and 1940, and it was first performed in 1943. The play is a parable which

Bertolt Brecht's *The Good Person of Setzuan* as produced at the American Repertory Theatre. The costumes in the background reflect the influence of Beijing Opera, China's major theatrical form. Directed by Andrei Serban; costumes by Catherine Zuber.

Brecht distances from his audience by setting it in China. Brecht's prologue establishes the epic nature of the play. In it narration and dialogue are mingled and time and place are telescoped. The prologue demonstrates the irony that permeates the piece: the waterseller, Wong, having assured the Three Gods, who have come to earth looking for a good person, that everyone is waiting to receive them, can find no one who will give them lodging except the prostitute, Shen Te. In addition, the prologue establishes the situation: The gods find the good person for whom they have been searching—Shen Te—and enjoin her to remain good. When she objects that she cannot be good unless she has the financial security that will permit her to refuse evil, the gods are unmoved, declaring that they "can't meddle in questions of economics." Herein Brecht suggests that not only is economic need the root of evil (because it forces people to do things that are wrong merely to survive) but also that the solution to human problems is not to be found in divine injunctions.

The scenes following the prologue show Shen Te buying a small shop to support herself, only to have greedy relatives and hangers-on descend on her and take advantage of her goodness. When she falls in love with the penniless Yang Sun, who wishes to become a pilot, Shen Te gives him money she needs to pay her bills. On the verge of ruin, she disguises herself as a male cousin, Shui Ta, who suppresses humanitarian feelings and demands that those who want assistance must work—on his capitalistic terms. Thereafter the action is devoted to the conflict between good and evil as seen in the protagonist's two personae. Shui Ta appears for short intervals at first, but eventually takes over, becoming a capitalist boss who exploits workers and does whatever is needed to survive. The other characters suspect that Shui Ta has killed Shen Te. When the gods return disguised as judges before whom Shui Ta is brought, he reveals to them privately not only that he is Shen Te but also that she is pregnant and must provide for her child. But the gods can only admonish Shen Te to be good and to disguise herself less often as Shui Ta. The play ends with Shen Te's dilemma unresolved. An epilogue suggests that it is up to the audience to find a way out, presumably by changing the economic system.

The Good Person of Setzuan alternates short and long scenes. The short scenes serve two purposes: to break up the action and to comment on the long scenes used to develop the action. Brecht makes no attempt to create the illusion of everyday reality. For example, when Wong says he will find a place for the gods to spend the night, he suggests the attempt by circling the stage and pantomiming knocking on imaginary doors that are slammed in his face. This approach allows Brecht to telescope events and to eliminate transitions. Brecht's structural techniques are explained in part by his belief that scenes should be clearly separated as one means of creating alienation. He also insisted that it should be possible to express the social content of each scene in one sentence (a *gestus*) and that all parts of the scene should be clearly related to this statement, which in performance may be projected onto a screen prior to the beginning of the scene.

Brecht oversimplifies characters, because he is principally concerned with social relationships. He is not interested in total personalities or the inner lives of his characters. Instead of names, some characters in *The Good Person of Setzuan* are designated by their social functions, such as Wife, Carpenter, or Policeman. Brecht did not intend to portray well-rounded individuals but rather to interpret social forces. Therefore the action does not exist to display character; rather, character demonstrates social attitude. The only character who seems concerned about morality is Shen Te; the plot progresses in large part through the series of choices she makes about dilemmas created by economic conditions. The other characters are primarily concerned with attaining selfish goals or (in the case of the gods) sustaining a dogmatic view.

Today, many of our most familiar theatrical conventions (no front curtain to hide the stage, the use of fragmentary scenery and visible light-ing instruments, and other practices that call attention to the theatrical medium) derive in large part from Brecht, although Brecht's intention of provoking social change is often ignored.

Artaud and the Theatre of Cruelty

ANOTHER STRAIN of theatre in the 1920s and 1930s focused on forces quite different from those Brecht emphasized; it was concerned with those impulses buried within the unconscious mind. The most influential representative of this strain was Antonin Artaud (1896–1948), whose views, like those of Brecht, were not immediately accepted but, like Brecht's, became influential after his death. Whereas Brecht thought the key to improving the human lot lies in transforming external circumstances, Artaud thought the key lies in confronting internal divisions.

Artaud for a time was a member of the surrealist movement, which flourished during the 1920s. *Surrealism* emphasized one aspect of Freud's teachings: the importance of the unconscious. According to the surrealists, significant truths are those deeply buried in the psyche, suppressed by the conscious mind. In order to expose these "truths," the conscious mind must be subverted. The surrealists promoted dreams, automatic writing, and stream of consciousness as paths through which images, ideas, and experiences buried in the subconscious could escape the conscious mind's control and rise to the surface, where the insights they offered could be utilized. Surrealism made its greatest impact in painting, best known through the work of Salvador Dali, in which familiar objects are used in unfamiliar ways, juxtaposed with unrelated objects, or placed in "dream landscapes" creating visual metaphors that stimulate the imagination and lead to new perceptions. Artaud eventually broke with the surrealists, but his experience with them was crucial to his work both in theatre and in film.

PRACTITIONERS
AND THEORISTS

Peter Brook

and the Theatre of Cruelty

Although Artaud's theories had already influenced some directors and critics, they did not attract wide attention in England and America until Peter Brook began to experiment with them in the early 1960s.

In 1963, Brook, assisted by Charles Marowitz and with support from the Royal Shakespeare Company, selected a group of twelve actors to work with throughout the 1963–64 theatre season. Through exercises they experimented with sound (made with their voices, on their bodies, and with objects), movement, rhythm, and pantomime; they sought to replace clichéd solutions with innovative, nonrealistic means of expression. They also sought to replace the typical pattern of beginning-middle-end development with discontinuous or simultaneous scenes. They performed a "Collage Hamlet" with sequences from Shakespeare's text rearranged, lines from different scenes juxtaposed, characters dropped or blended, and discontinuous fragments inserted. A five-week public showing of the group's work was presented under the title "Theatre of Cruelty." Though what the group did deviated in many ways from Artaud's ideas, critics began to equate Artaud with Brook's experiments, especially following his production of *Marat/Sade* by Peter Weiss (which offered almost endless opportunities for actors—playing inmates of an insane asylum—to make use of Artaudian techniques), one of the most successful and influential productions of the 1960s. In both England and America (where it achieved both long runs and high critical praise), this production was hailed as a practical application of Artaud's theories. With the success of this production, Artaud became widely known for the first time.

Artaud expressed his major ideas about theatre in a series of essays collected in *The Theatre and Its Double* (1938). According to Artaud, the theatre in the Western world has been restricted to a narrow range of human experience, primarily the psychological problems of individuals or the social problems of groups. Artaud considered such theatre insignificant because it failed to touch the most important influences on human behavior, those buried in the unconscious. But if these influences remain buried and unconfronted, they lead to divisions within the person (and between people) and ultimately to hatred, violence, and disaster. Artaud believed that if theatre were used properly, it would free people from destructive impulses. As he put it, "The theatre has been created to drain abscesses collectively."

Artaud was certain that his goals could not be reached through appeals to the rational mind (Brecht's approach), because the conscious mind has been conditioned to sublimate and ignore the very things that need to be examined. Thus, he argued,

Marat/Sade as produced by American Repertory Theatre under the direction of János Szász. Scene design by Riccardo Hernandez; costume design by Edit Szücs; lighting by John Ambrosone.

it is necessary to subvert the audience's defenses. Artaud sometimes referred to this as a "theatre of cruelty," not because it was physically cruel but because it forced the audience, against its wishes, to confront itself. Because he considered the conventions of the established theatre to be directed to the conscious mind, he proposed to replace them with a "new language of the theatre." Believing that the proscenium-arch theatre creates a barrier between performers and spectators, he proposed replacing it with large, undivided spaces such as barns, factories, airplane hangars, and warehouses. Within these spaces he wanted to locate acting areas in corners, overhead on catwalks, and around the walls so as to place the audience in the midst of the action.

Artaud wanted to do away with scenery altogether and replace it with symbolic costumes and properties. In discussing lighting, he wrote of a "vibrating, shredded" effect with pulsating changes (comparable to strobe lighting). He favored great variety in sound, ranging in volume from a whisper to a factory at peak production; he advocated using the human voice not primarily for speech but for yelps, cries, and varied emotional and atmospheric effects. He considered these innovative means capable of bypassing the conscious mind. As he put it,

"Whereas most people remain impervious to a subtle discourse, . . . they cannot resist effects of physical surprise, the dynamism of cries and violent movements, visual explosions, the aggregate of tetanizing effects called up on cue and used to act in a direct manner on the physical sensitivity of the spectators." These conventions were to be coupled with stories of mythical proportions and implications. The ultimate purpose was to break down the audience's defenses, drag suppressed impulses to the surface, and force the audience to face and deal with those things that, if unacknowledged, create hatred and violence.

As this broad survey of theatrical developments suggests, during the years between 1885 and 1940 the modernist temperament achieved dominance. For the first time in history, multiple artistic movements existed simultaneously and challenged each other for supremacy. Some of these movements flourished for a time and then faded, but all left residues that were assimilated into the theatre's mainstream. The diversity of these theatrical forms raised awareness that no single correct approach to theatrical production exists and that each artist is free to offer his or her own vision of truth and human experience no matter how eccentric. Absolutist notions were largely denied, but not wholly abandoned. Similarly, though elitist critics favored the avant-garde, the most popular mode in mainstream theatre remained a modified realism.

Additional Opportunities with InfoTrac College Edition

Many of the movements discussed in this chapter have found new expressions today. Using InfoTrac College Edition, look up the article *Dada Is Back* by Renske Heddema in *Swiss News* to read about the reopened Cabaret Voltaire.

1. Does this cabaret sound as if it has stayed true to the original spirit of dada? Provide evidence to support your conclusion.

2. Of the many movements introduced in this chapter, which style would you most like to see in performance?

Building a Broad Context

■ World's first skyscraper built in Chicago (1885)

■ Sioux chief Sitting Bull arrested and killed by police on Pine Ridge reservation; two weeks later, U.S. troops kill over 200 Sioux at the Battle of Wounded Knee (1890)

■ Oscar Wilde's *The Importance of Being Earnest* is a hit in London (1895)

■ U.S. Supreme Court upholds *Plessy* v. *Ferguson* decision—"separate but equal" doctrine (1896)

■ The British win Boer War (South Africa) fought against the descendants of Dutch settlers (1899–1902)

■ Wright brothers fly motorized plane (1903)

■ Einstein formulates Special Theory of Relativity: $e = mc^2$ (1905)

■ Italian futurism launched (1909)

■ SS *Titanic* sinks on maiden voyage after colliding with an iceberg; 1,513 drown (1912)

■ Assassination of Austrian Archduke Ferdinand in Sarajevo begins WWI (1914); war ends (1919)

■ Dada movement flourishes in Zurich, Switzerland (1916)

■ Tsar Nicholas II abdicates; Lenin leads the Bolsheviks' "October Revolution" (1917); and after years of civil war, fourteen Soviet states form communist U.S.S.R.(1922)

■ German expressionism flourishes (1918–1924)

■ U.S. passes 19th Amendment, granting women the right to vote (1920)

■ Eugene O'Neill's *"The Hairy Ape"* (1922)

■ Mussolini and the fascists gain power in Italy (1922)

■ U.S. stock market crashes on "Black Friday" (1929)

■ Franklin D. Roosevelt elected U.S. president (1932), champions "New Deal" initiatives including the creation of Social Security

■ Hitler is made German chancellor and gains dictatorial powers (1933)

■ Kristallnacht (Night of Broken Glass): All over Germany the windows of Jewish businesses and homes are smashed, synagogues burned down, and Jewish cemeteries vandalized (1938)

■ Conventional start of WWII (1940); U.S. enters WWII after Japanese attack on Pearl Harbor (1941)

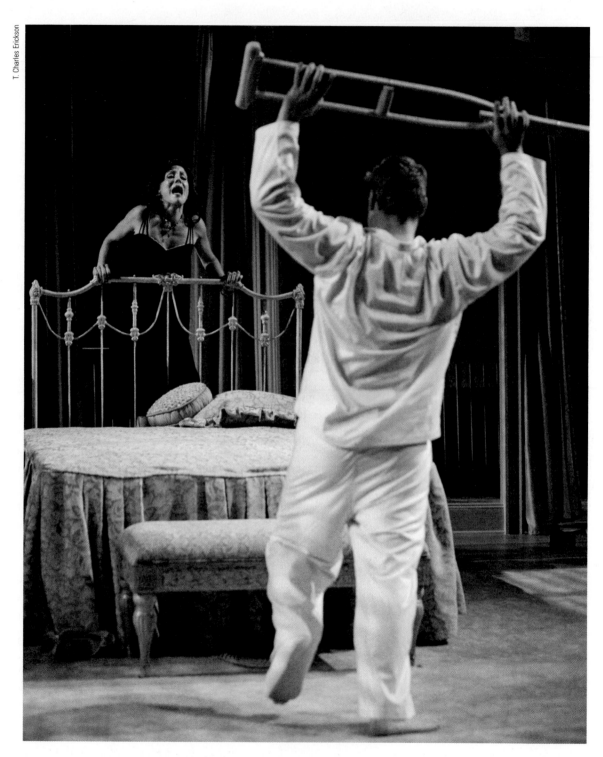

Maggie and Brick square off in the Hartford Stage production of *Cat on a Hot Tin Roof* by Tennessee Williams. Directed by Michael Wilson; scene design by Geoff Cowie; costume design by David C. Woolard; lighting design by Rui Rita.

Reevaluation, Decentralization, and Subsidization

8:

WORLD WAR II disrupted theatrical activity in many countries around the world, and almost everywhere it motivated reassessment of values and theatrical practices. In many countries reassessment led to decentralization of the theatre, which often was accomplished only through financial assistance in the form of subsidization.

Postwar American Theatre

THE UNITED STATES (perhaps because it was geographically removed from the fighting and gained, rather than lost, in optimism) saw little change in its theatre during and immediately following the war years. Modified realism continued to be the major approach in theatrical production, and psychological realism, derived from Stanislavsky, its dominant acting style. In 1947, Robert Lewis, Elia Kazan, and Cheryl Crawford, all former members of the Group Theatre, founded the Actors Studio in New York to provide its members an ongoing opportunity to develop their craft. The Actors Studio was not a school, and there were no fees. The premise was that the actor's training never ends and that experienced performers need a place where they can continue to develop their skills within a group of nurturing peers; once accepted into the Actors Studio (after rigorous auditions), one remained a member for life. Lee Strasberg soon became the studio's director and major teacher and continued as such until his death in 1982. Awareness of the studio's work grew quickly after Marlon Brando, an actor who was briefly associated with the studio, captured the public's imagination with his portrayal of the inarticulate, uneducated, and assertive Stanley Kowalski in Tennessee Williams' *A Streetcar Named Desire* (1947), directed by Kazan. Brando's impact was enormous, not only affecting acting style but also contributing greatly to the influence of the Actors Studio and its version of the Stanislavsky system, usually referred to as "the method." This approach, which concentrated on the actor's belief in the truth of the dramatic moment, could give scenes considerable psychological intensity. A frequent criticism of the method, however, was that actors using it often seemed so self-absorbed that they neglected the technical skills needed to externalize internal feelings and that they mumbled rather than speaking audibly and intelligibly. Members of the Actors Studio included James Dean, Paul Newman, Al Pacino, Robert de Niro, Dustin Hoffman, Shelley Winters, Geraldine Page, and many others who became widely known, especially through their film roles.

Arthur Miller's *Death of a Salesman*, 1949. Lower level, Lee J. Cobb as Willy and Mildred Dunnock as Linda; upper level, Arthur Kennedy as Biff and Cameron Mitchell as Happy. Directed by Elia Kazan; designed by Jo Mielziner.

Eileen Darby

Psychological realism dominated the plays of the postwar period. The two major dramatists were Arthur Miller (1916–2005) with *All My Sons, Death of a Salesman,* and *The Crucible,* and Tennessee Williams (1911–1983) with *The Glass Menagerie, A Streetcar Named Desire,* and *Cat on a Hot Tin Roof.* The Actors Studio's reputation was enhanced by Kazan's direction of several of these plays, on which he collaborated with designer Jo Mielziner. Kazan and Mielziner established the production style that dominated the American theatre from the late 1940s until the 1960s. This style combined psychological realism in acting and directing with simplified, skeletal settings that permitted fluid shifts in time and place. Let us look more closely at a play that is representative of both the period and of the Kazan-Mielziner approach to staging.

Cat on a Hot Tin Roof

Tennessee Williams' *Cat on a Hot Tin Roof* (1955) is a play about mendacity—deception and lying, to both oneself and others. Although divided into three acts, the action is continuous; each act takes up precisely where the preceding one left off; no more time elapses in the play than it takes to perform it. The play, then, has a late point of attack, and the amount of exposition about past events is considerable, although skillfully worked into the action.

The occasion that ostensibly has brought all of the characters together is Big Daddy's sixty-fifth birthday, which coincides with receipt of results of Big Daddy's clinical tests for cancer. Big Daddy and Big Mama are told that he merely has a spastic colon, news that puts them in a highly celebratory mood though based on a lie. The others know that Big Daddy is dying, and because he is extremely wealthy—he owns twenty-eight thousand acres of the "richest land this side of the Valley Nile" and at least ten million dollars in cash—and because he has not made a will, they are concerned with who will inherit his wealth. The obvious candidates are Big Daddy's two sons. The elder, Gooper, a corporation lawyer, is married to Mae and has five children. They covet Big Daddy's wealth and spend most of their time in transparent attempts to ingratiate themselves or to discredit Gooper's younger brother, Brick. A former football star and sports announcer, Brick now concentrates on alcohol. He and his wife Maggie have no children; he is as indifferent to his father's wealth (and everything else) as Gooper is fixated on it. Throughout the play Brick walks with the aid of a crutch, having broken his ankle the night before while attempting to jump hurdles. Both the crutch and the constant resort to alcohol are symbolic of what Williams calls Brick's "spiritual disrepair," born out of his disgust with mendacity.

But if Brick has no interest in Big Daddy's wealth, his wife does. Having escaped a background of genteel poverty, Maggie is determined not to return to it; she sees having a child by Brick as her only hope of avoiding that fate. Unfortunately for her, Brick refuses to touch her, believing that she is to blame for the death of his best friend Skipper, who destroyed himself after Maggie accused him of being in love with Brick. According to Brick, Maggie turned the purest thing in his life into something ugly. His drinking and disgust with the world apparently are related to Skipper's death.

The play concentrates primarily on three characters: Maggie, Brick, and Big Daddy. Big Daddy's situation is the primary motivator of the action, and it is he who forces Brick to acknowledge his own responsibility in Skipper's death. Brick's withdrawal and inaction are a primary spur for others who throughout the play seek to provoke him into action. Maggie, the title character, wants to act but is thwarted by Brick until the final scene.

The first act is devoted almost entirely to Maggie and Brick as she tries to make him understand their precarious position in relation to Big Daddy's wealth. Because Brick has abdicated any concern for life and because they have no children, they are in danger of being disinherited altogether or having to accept whatever Gooper may choose to dole out to them. It is during this scene that Maggie likens herself to a cat trying to hold on to a hot tin roof. Brick refuses to cooperate in her desire to be pregnant. The only time he shows anything more than indifference comes when she (or Big Daddy) insists that they talk about Skipper.

The second act is devoted primarily to Brick and Big Daddy. Much of this act is taken up with Big Daddy trying to work up to a serious talk with Brick. During these preliminaries we find out much about Big Daddy who, beginning in poverty, has made himself rich through his own efforts. He makes it clear that he dislikes Gooper but that he does not want what he has accumulated to be wasted. He sets out, therefore, to find out why Brick drinks, and he ultimately forces Brick to acknowledge that when, in a phone conversation, Skipper admitted his love, Brick had hung up on him. Big Daddy says that it was Brick's unwillingness to face this situation with his friend, rather than Maggie's accusations, that caused Skipper's death. Hurt, Brick in retaliation reveals the truth about the cancer tests. The act ends with both men denouncing liars.

The final act is taken up with a gathering of all the characters except Big Daddy, during which they reveal the truth to Big Mama. Gooper and Mae try to coax Big Mama into approving papers Gooper has had drawn up about authority over the property. She refuses, and Maggie takes control by announcing that she is pregnant. Gooper and Mae accuse her of lying, but later Maggie attempts to make it true by depriving Brick of access to alcohol until he makes love to her. Although what he will do is unclear, he seems to acquiesce.

There is an alternative third act to *Cat on a Hot Tin Roof*, written at the insistence of Elia Kazan, the original director of the play on Broadway. Kazan thought that Big Daddy was too powerful a character not to reappear in the third act (in Williams' original script Big Daddy appears only in the second act) and that Brick should undergo significant change as a result of his confrontation with Big Daddy in the second act. In the Broadway version, Big Daddy does appear in the third act, although primarily to show that he favors Brick and to ask that a lawyer be sent for so he can make a will. In both versions, Big Daddy is later heard offstage howling in pain as the cancer ravages him.

The Hartford Stage production of *Cat on a Hot Tin Roof* by Tennessee Williams. Directed by Michael Wilson; scene design by Geoff Cowie; costume design by David C. Woolard; lighting design by Rui Rita.

In the alternative version, Brick does show change. Early in the act he suggests that Maggie arrange for him to go to a treatment clinic, and later, when Gooper and Mae accuse Maggie of lying about being pregnant, he defends her and subsequently appears to acquiesce to her demands. The overall effect of the Broadway version is to make the play far more positive than Williams wished. He stated that no conversation, "however revelatory, ever effects so immediate a change in the heart or even the conduct of a person in Brick's state of spiritual disrepair." The disagreement between Williams and Kazan illustrates the power that directors may have over a script and how they can persuade playwrights to make changes, even ones they do not approve of.

Despite its great power, *Cat on a Hot Tin Roof* can, from today's perspective, be faulted on two scores—gender and race—though both were treated in ways typical of their time: The play seems almost misogynistic in its representation of women. Both Big Daddy and Brick treat their wives with near contempt, and Mae is shown to be avaricious and calculating. Williams has expressed his admiration and affection for Maggie, but she, as well as the other female characters, apparently believes she has no identity except through her husband. And though Williams himself was homosexual, he treats the very notion of homosexuality as so unacceptable to Brick as to paralyze him psychologically. The play also includes several African American characters. Although how they are treated was not unusual in plays of the time, in *Cat on a Hot Tin Roof* the white characters are by today's standards unthinking or callous in their dealings with the black characters and in their references to blacks in general. Williams seemingly adopts unquestioningly the stereotype (often used for enslaved people in the nineteenth century) that servants are happy to be used and patronized by their "masters."

■ The Musical in Postwar America

ALTHOUGH THE MODIFIED realism of postwar American spoken drama has received more serious study, the musical was the most popular theatrical form in the United States during the twentieth century. Musical drama is not of recent origin. The choral passages of Greek drama were sung and danced; the majority of the lines in Roman comedy were accompanied by music; the Italians developed wholly sung opera; and Shakespeare introduced many songs into his plays. The eighteenth century intro-

**PRACTICES
AND STYLES**

Kazan, Mielziner, and Postwar Production Style

E ric Bentley, in his review of the original production of Tennessee Williams' *Cat on a Hot Tin Roof*, saw the production as exemplary of the production style—developed by Elia Kazan (as director) and Jo Mielziner (as designer)—that dominated post–World War II American theatre. Bentley suggests that this style achieved a kind of grandeur "from the interaction between formality in the setting, lighting, and grouping and an opposite quality . . . in the individual perform-ances. . . . [T]he actors live their roles with that vigilant, concentrated, uninterrupted nervous intensity which Mr. Kazan always manages to give."

Bentley goes on to say: "Jo Mielziner's setting for *Cat on a Hot Tin Roof* consists of a square and sloping platform with one of its corners, not one of its sides, jutting out toward the audience. . . . Around the room steps and space suggest the out-of-doors. The whole stage is swathed in ever-changing light and shade." The most important features of the set were a bed and a combined radio-TV console and liquor cabinet. Bentley concludes: "Such is the world of Elia Kazan, . . . an exterior that is also an interior—but more important, a view of *man's* exterior that is also a view of his interior."

This style, a form of modified realism, dominated the American theatre for much of the latter half of the twentieth century.

duced a number of popular musical forms, including ballad opera and comic opera, and the nineteenth century used music to underscore melodrama's action. When the plays did not require music, some type of music was usually included as an additional entertainment.

Even so, musical comedy did not begin to emerge as a distinct type until the late nine-teenth century. Early examples of musical com-edy usually emphasized the romantic appeal of faraway places or exotic situations; the stories were primarily excuses for songs and ensemble choral numbers, often sung and danced by beau-tiful young women. Around World War I, a change occurred when ballroom dancing and ragtime music, both then in vogue, were intro-duced into musicals; with them came more familiar characters and surroundings. Neverthe-less, storyline remained relatively unimportant, and the emphasis continued to be on spectacular settings, songs, dances, and chorus girls (a pat-tern which continues in many Las Vegas musical entertainments to the present day).

The relationship between music and story as well as the use of songs to convey and develop psychological motivation did not begin to be truly significant until the late 1920s—most notably in *Show Boat* by Jerome Kern and Oscar

The "rumble" scene between the rival gangs, the Jets and the Sharks, in *West Side Story;* composed by Leonard Bernstein; book by Arthur Laurents; lyrics by Arthur Laurents and Stephen Sondheim. Note the chain-link fence and the painted background, which visually modifies the realism of the scene to create a mood and a sense of monumentality to the events. Directed and choreographed by Jerome Robbins; scene design by Oliver Smith; lighting by Jean Rosenthal.

Hammerstein II. The new status of the form was recognized in 1931, when for the first time a musical (*Of Thee I Sing* with text by George S. Kaufman and Morrie Ryskind and music by George Gershwin) won the Pulitzer Prize for the best drama of the year. By 1940, the musical, according to many critics, had become distinctively American and America's most significant contribution to world theatre. It was then on the threshold of perhaps its greatest period. *Oklahoma!* (1943), by Richard Rodgers and Oscar Hammerstein II, is often cited as the first work in which music, story, dance (choreographed by Agnes DeMille), and visual elements were fully integrated so that all contributed significantly to the dramatic action. Rodgers and Hammerstein solidified this approach in such pieces as *Carousel* (1945), *South Pacific* (1949), and *The King and I* (1951). Several other composers and authors in the post–World War II period followed the lead of Rodgers and Hammerstein, among them Alan Jay Lerner and Frederick

Oklahoma! is often credited as one of the first musicals to fully integrate story in a meaningful way with all its visual, aural, and kinetic aspects. Pictured here is its Broadway revival. Directed by Trevor Nunn; choreographed by Susan Stroman; scene and costume designs by Anthony Ward; lighting by David Hersey.

Loewe with *Brigadoon* (1947) and *My Fair Lady* (1956); Frank Loesser with *Guys and Dolls* (1950); and Leonard Bernstein and Arthur Laurents with *West Side Story* (1957).

The popularity of the musical is probably attributable to its multiple appeals. The musical and choreographic elements, sources of pleasure in their own right, can also facilitate storytelling. For example, the lyrics of songs contribute to clarity by expressing emotional response and intention directly, much as soliloquies and asides did in earlier drama. Music, through such conventions as the reprise (the repetition of musical phrases or fragments of lyrics), can connect or recall moments separated in time. Furthermore, music assists in condensing time, as when a song or musical passage is used to show quickly a progression of events that in actuality occurs over a long period. For example, in *My Fair Lady*, the speech lessons that alter the flower seller Eliza's accent so she can pass as a duchess are condensed primarily into one song, "The Rain in Spain." In addition, music establishes mood and builds expectation. Even before the action begins, an overture establishes the general mood of the work to follow, and thereafter music helps to establish the appropriate emotional tone and, through modulations in tempo, key, and volume, to build individual scenes and the work as a whole.

A musical usually provides considerable visual stimulation. Scenic, costume, and lighting designers typically are offered wide scope for their talents in musical productions. There are usually several changes in time and place and a large cast (often with much doubling), which require multiple sets and costumes. Dance usually plays a large role, commenting on the action and forwarding the story much as the songs do. Considering all of these appeals, it is not surprising that the musical has long been among the most popular of theatrical experiences. It is also not surprising that audiences have found in the musical an antidote to the dark vision of humanity offered by much twentieth-century drama.

Courtesy of the Theatre and Music Collection, Museum of the City of New York

Rex Harrison and Julie Andrews in the opening scene of the original production of *My Fair Lady* by Alan Jay Lerner and Frederick Loewe.

Postwar Europe

THESE AMERICAN MUSICALS and plays were quite unlike the theatrical fare typical of postwar Europe. Perhaps because Europe had suffered so much devastation and been subjected to so many atrocities, its postwar mood was much more serious than that of America. In Germany Brecht continued to write plays which tackled social problems. Max Frisch (1911–1991) and Friedrich Duerrenmatt (1921–1990) wrote plays dealing with the corruption and moral responsibility of the individual. In the 1960s, many of the most notable German dramas were based on actual events (a form which came to be called "docudrama"). In 1965 Peter Weiss (1916–1982) extended this form into full-fledged documentary drama with his play *The Investigation*, which took its dialogue directly from the official hearings regarding the exterminations at the Nazi concentration camp in Auschwitz. Although German drama differed from its French counterpart in tone, the drama of both nations drew upon a similar set of questions regarding the very foundations of truth and values.

In France, a group of philosophers known as the existentialists pursued questions regarding truth, values, and moral responsibility in a different way. Jean-Paul Sartre (1905–1980), the best-known existentialist, denied the existence of God, the validity of fixed standards of conduct, and the possibility of verifiable moral codes. He concluded that because none of the institutions (church, state, society) from which we have taken our standards can prove the correctness or necessity of those standards, human beings are "condemned to be free" (that is, people deprived of absolute standards are condemned to choose individually the values by which they will live). He insisted that unquestioning conformity to values established by others is immoral, whereas choosing (and living by) one's own values is to define oneself as a moral being. Sartre's views were persuasive because they came at a time when many Nazis were seeking to escape punishment for war crimes by arguing that they had merely obeyed German laws or carried out their government's policies. The crucial question was, which takes precedence: law and policy (no matter how perverted) or individual moral values? Many Nazis were convicted on the premise that the individual should refuse to obey unjust or inhuman demands, even legal ones. This conclusion, which reflects Sartre's, has been used since then to justify protests of all kinds (nonviolent and violent) against governmental policies as well as local authorities and various institutions.

Albert Camus (1913–1960), another existentialist philosopher and writer, concluded that our situation is absurd because the human longing for clarity and certainty is met with, and forever thwarted by, the irrationality of the universe into which we have been thrown; it is absurd also because we can neither rid ourselves of the desire for order nor overcome the irrationality that stands in the way of order. Camus reasoned that the only recourse is to choose one's own standards and live by them. Both Sartre and Camus were convinced that we can examine our situation and make decisions that permit us to act meaningfully in accordance with those decisions. Both also wrote plays that set their ideas into dramatic action. Among Sartre's plays, the best known are *The Flies* and *No Exit;* among Camus' plays, the best known are *Caligula* and *The Just Assassins.* Although their ideas broke from tradition, their plays expressed them using traditional dramatic structure: showing a protagonist facing a problem, pursuing it through a set of complications to a point of crisis, and making choices that permit a clear resolution.

Eugene Ionesco's *The Chairs* with Richard Briers and Geraldine McEwan. Translated and adapted by Martin Crimp. Directed and choreographed by Simon McBurney; setting by the Quay Brothers; lighting by Paul Anderson; sound by Paul Arditti.

Joan Marcus

Gerry Goodstein

Samuel Beckett's *Waiting for Godot* as produced at the Long Wharf Theatre, New Haven, with the South African actors John Kani and Winston Ntshona.

Absurdist Drama

A GROUP OF PLAYWRIGHTS emerged in France around 1950 who accepted the views of Sartre and Camus about the human condition, but unlike those two writers, the playwrights believed that making rational and meaningful choices was impossible in an irrational universe. For them, truth consisted of chaos and lack of order, logic, or certainty, and their plays embodied this vision in a structure that abandoned cause-and-effect relationships for associational patterns reflecting illogic and chance. Critics came to label drama containing this set of characteristics and viewpoint *absurdist* (derived from Camus' description of the human condition as "absurd"), although the individual playwrights were not consciously working together toward a goal.

Among the absurdist playwrights, who included Eugene Ionesco (1909–1994) and Jean Genet (1920–1986), the most influential was Samuel Beckett (1906–1989). Beckett's play *Waiting for Godot* (1952) brought him and absurdist drama international recognition (see photo on this page). In the play, two tramps improvise diversions while they wait for Godot (who never arrives). As a group, Beckett's plays suggest the impossibility of certainty about anything but the need to accept and endure. Let us examine another of his plays, *Happy Days,* as representative both of his work and of absurdist drama.

Happy Days

THE STORYLINE of *Happy Days* (1961) is very simple. In the first act, Winnie, a middle-aged woman embedded up to her waist in a mound of earth, passes time by following a daily routine, recalling the past, and attempting to communicate occasionally with her husband, Willie, who for the most part remains silent and unseen, hidden behind the mound. The second act follows the same pattern. But now Winnie is embedded up to her neck, unable to turn her head; she is uncertain whether Willie is still alive. She has been forced to adapt herself to an altered routine, but she remains cheerful and brave. At the end of the play, Willie crawls up the mound to Winnie, and in joy she sings a song from *The Merry Widow.* There are no complications, crises, or resolutions in the traditional sense. Rather, themes are introduced and developed.

One major theme is the isolation and loneliness of human beings. It is embodied visually in the setting: a mound of earth beyond which one sees an "unbroken plain and sky receding to meet in far distance." It is even more fully embodied in Winnie's entrapment, which throws her back on her own resources, because she can never be certain whether she is communicating with the only other human being within earshot. The setting and Winnie's entrapment create a metaphor of the human predicament. As in other of his plays, in *Happy Days* Beckett shows human beings isolated in a symbolic wasteland, cut off from all but the most minimal human contact, passing the time as best they can while waiting doggedly or hoping desperately for something that will give meaning to the moment or to life itself.

The play suggests that human beings organize their days around routines to convince themselves that they are in control of their lives.

© George E. Joseph

Irene Worth as Winnie in Beckett's *Happy Days* at the New York Shakespeare Festival's Public Theatre. Directed by Andrei Serban.

That human beings are conditioned to live by routine is reinforced by the bell that awakens Winnie to start her day or whenever she dozes off. Winnie never questions why she is buried in the mound, nor does she wonder at her isolation. She apparently accepts her lot as something to be challenged no more than existence itself. Throughout the play, she remains determinedly cheerful, finding something to wonder at in the smallest occurrence and speaking often of her blessings and of the things that will make this another "happy day." Only occasionally does she show a momentary flash of sadness.

In his plays, Beckett increasingly reduced the scope of action and means to those absolutely essential for projecting his vision. This limited scope of action intensifies the importance of the gestures, stage business, pauses, and language he has scripted in his plays. Their form, structure, and mood cannot be separated from their meaning. They explore a state of being rather than develop an action. Perhaps more than those of any other dramatist, Beckett's plays embody the absurdist vision and methods.

In many ways, absurdism extended the relativist view as far as it could go; it implied that we have no way of proving or disproving the validity of any position. Whereas Brecht suggested that, by examining and weighing arguments, we can arrive at rational conclusions about the changes needed to make the world more just, Beckett suggested that the very notion of rational choice is a delusion. That works embodying such polar visions were often presented in the same theatre for the same audience indicates how varied theatrical experiences had become in the postwar era. Although it did not die out, after the 1960s the appeal of absurdism declined.

■ Decentralization and Subsidization

Tʜᴇ ᴘᴏsᴛᴡᴀʀ ᴘᴇʀɪᴏᴅ also brought interest in making the theatre more readily available beyond established theatre centers. By the end of World War II, professional live theatre in the

United States was confined primarily to New York or to touring productions that originated there. Similarly, in England, the theatre was largely restricted to London, and in France, to Paris. Each of these countries wished to decentralize its theatre by having companies scattered geographically rather than concentrated in one large city. Implementing this goal required money, much of which came from subsidies.

Subsidization is as old as the theatre. It began with the Greeks and remained the primary means of supporting performances until the Renaissance, when the theatre became a commercial venture. Even thereafter, many rulers subsidized the theatre. For example, the king of France provided at least some financial support to all of the companies in Paris during the seventeenth century; and it was by his decree that the Comédie Française was created in 1680. The world's first national theatre, the Comédie Française has continued to the present day and has received governmental subsidies throughout its three-hundred-year history. Seeking to emulate France, the Scandinavian countries, Russia, and most of the small German states (Germany was not united until 1870) founded state-subsidized theatres in the eighteenth century. Most of those theatres still survive and are so geographically dispersed throughout northern and eastern Europe that the countries in those areas were not faced, as were France, England, and America were following World War II, with the need to decentralize their theatres.

The Germanic and Scandinavian countries consider state or municipal funding for the arts a cultural responsibility like that for education. Although these governments do not underwrite all of a theatre's expenses, they own the theatre buildings and subsidize as much as eighty percent of the theatre's operating expenses, making it possible to keep ticket prices relatively low. The companies usually offer seasons of representative plays from the past in combination with new or recent plays. The theatre staffs (including directors, designers, and actors) are employed on renewable contracts, complete with pension plans and other benefits comparable to those for

Courtesy of the Gorki Theater

Chekhov's *The Three Sisters* as produced by the Gorki Theater, Berlin.

workers in industry and government. (Each of these countries also has privately owned and operated theatres run much like Broadway theatres are in America.) These are the companies and practices that theatre workers in England and America looked to as models.

At the end of World War II, France had four state theatres like those in Germany, but all were located in Paris. In 1947, in an effort to decentralize French theatre, the government began to establish dramatic centers in cities throughout France. It later financed several "cultural centers" devoted to various arts activities.

The Postwar British Theatre

ENGLAND, UNLIKE CONTINENTAL European countries, had never awarded government subsidies on the premise that theatre is a business that must be self-supporting. But during World War II, the government began to allocate funds to underwrite performances intended to build the morale of military troops and factory workers. When the war ended, financial support for the arts was continued through an Arts

Council created to decide which organizations should receive funds. Government funding increased after 1948, when Parliament authorized local authorities to devote a percentage of their revenues to the arts. More than fifty cities and towns in Great Britain came to subsidize theatres. Among these provincial theatres and theatre festivals, none grew more rapidly and became more influential than the Stratford Festival in Stratford-upon-Avon.

Although the origins of the Stratford Festival can be traced to 1879, when it became the home of an annual summer festival of Shakespeare's plays, it gained tremendous prestige and popularity in the years following World War II. By 1961 it had been given a new name and charter as the Royal Shakespeare Company (RSC) and, under the direction of Peter Hall, it grew from national to international prominence. Hall leased the Aldwych Theatre in London as a second base so that the company could perform year-round. Between 1964 and 1975, when the RSC was performing in Stratford, the Aldwych hosted the World Theatre Season; major theatre companies from around the world performed there in limited engagements, providing a cross-fertilization of drama and theatre practices that greatly diversified and enriched British theatre and drama. Meanwhile, the RSC was now performing a diversified repertory that featured both Shakespeare and some of the most innovative non-Shakespearean productions of the time. Peter Brook, one of the world's finest directors, was associated with the RSC during the 1960s and staged some of its most influential productions, among them *Marat/Sade* (which critics labeled an example of Artaud's Theatre of Cruelty and which drew wide attention to Artaud's ideas for the first time in England and America) and *A Midsummer Night's Dream* (which utilized circus and acrobatic techniques). The RSC eventually dropped its practice of maintaining a permanent theatre in both London and Stratford, although it still takes some of its productions to London and throughout England on tour. Thanks in large part to government subsidy and support, the RSC ranks among the world's best companies and is recognized as a leader in Shakespearean performance.

The move to decentralize British theatre was to some extent balanced by Parliament's decision to subsidize the formation of a National Theatre in 1949. Numerous challenges delayed its opening for many years. The National Theatre was inaugurated in 1963 as a company led by Laurence Olivier (then perhaps England's foremost actor), but it did not move into its permanent home on the south bank of the Thames until

Courtesy of Robert Ball

The RSC theatre complex in Stratford-upon-Avon contains a large traditional proscenium-arch theatre and a more intimate thrust performance space (one entrance to which is pictured here) as well as a small adjacent performance space. Recently £100 million was granted to renovate this complex and transform the proscenium performance space into a thrust theatre and enhance auxiliary spaces.

1976. The National Theatre has the most elaborate performance facilities in England, with three performance spaces (a thrust-stage theatre, a proscenium-arch theatre, and a flexible theatre). Its repertory of world drama and its overall excellence have made it a major force in world theatre.

A third English group, the English Stage Company (ESC), founded in 1956, made its mark by assisting new playwrights. Its work motivated a reevaluation of the British theatre following its production of John Osborne's *Look Back in Anger* (1956). Prior to this production, the postwar English theatre had been devoted primarily to revivals or innocuous, "proper" dramas. Osborne's play—an attack on the English class system and traditional values—was a slap in the face of "respectability." It brought a new audience into the theatre and inaugurated a new school of writers (the "angry young men"). Within a brief time, the tone of English theatre shifted as the speech and attitudes of disaffected groups brought new vigor to the stage. The ESC, with its willingness to give unknown dramatists a hearing, must be given much of the credit for creating conditions that have continued to encourage an unusual number of outstanding English playwrights since the 1950s.

Among the playwrights who reshaped the English theatre, some of the most important are Edward Bond, Harold Pinter, and Tom Stoppard. Edward Bond has long been one of England's most controversial playwrights. England's Lord Chamberlain refused to license Bond's play *Saved* (1965) as fit for professional public performance, in part because of a scene in which a baby is stoned to death in its carriage. The Royal Court Theatre produced Bond's play despite this by temporarily transforming itself into a private, members-only club. The Lord Chamberlain prosecuted, but the Royal Court Theatre and Bond refused to relent. Bond's next "unapproved" play, *Early Morning*, which portrays Queen Victoria as having a lesbian affair with Florence Nightingale, forced Parliamentary hearings. The result was that the Licensing Act, which had allowed the censoring of plays since 1737, was abolished. All of Bond's plays, which include *Lear, Bingo,* and *War Plays,* depict a world in which the absence of love and compassion has bred callousness so complete that violence is considered normal.

Harold Pinter, often considered England's greatest living dramatist, opened up still another path. His plays, which include *The Birthday Party, The Homecoming, Old Times,* and *Moonlight,* share common characteristics: The action usually involves a small group of people and takes place in a single room; all of the events could occur in real life (sometimes the situations and dialogue suggest naturalism); nevertheless, they create a sense of ambiguity and menace, primarily because the motivations of the characters are never clarified. Because Pinter believes that people use speech to conceal more than to reveal their attitudes and feelings, we often have to guess why they act as they do. It is during the pauses and silences that we often glimpse the unspoken subtext. Among his many honors, Pinter was awarded the Nobel Prize for Literature in 2005.

Tom Stoppard won recognition first with *Rosencrantz and Guildenstern Are Dead* (1967), a play reminiscent of Beckett's, which focuses on two minor characters from *Hamlet* who sense that important events are going on around them but who die without ever understanding the action of which they have been an insignificant part. In his subsequent plays, among them *Jumpers, Travesties, The Real Thing, Arcadia, The Coast of Utopia,* and *Rock 'n' Roll,* he continues to combine verbal wit and highly imaginative action with complex ideas about contemporary perceptions of reality. Stoppard is also an accomplished screenwriter whose 1998 film *Shakespeare in Love* won an Academy Award for best screenplay.

Among Britain's more recent dramatists, several began their careers either in the provincial theatre or in the fringe theatres (comparable to Off-Broadway and Off-Off-Broadway) that mushroomed in number once censorship was

In Tom Stoppard's *Travesties* the main character's memory constructs multiple versions of past events. Among these is a production of Oscar Wilde's *The Importance of Being Earnest.* In this production of *Travesties* by the Long Wharf Theatre, the polite hostility of Gwendolen and Cicely becomes an all-out cat fight. Directed by Gregory Boyd; scene design by Neil Patel; costumes by Judith Dolan; lighting by Rui Rita; sound by John Gromada.

T. Charles Erickson

removed. The plays and experimentation there did much to diversify Britain's theatre. Among the best known of these playwrights are David Hare, Alan Ayckbourn, and Caryl Churchill.

David Hare began his career in fringe theatres with such plays as *Slag,* which focuses on the deprivations and emptiness of working-class life. In his later plays, among them *Plenty* and *A Map of the World,* he extends his concern to include ineffectual intellectuals or bureaucrats on whom he blames the malaise of English society. His later plays have critiqued the church (*Racing Demon*), the judiciary and legal system (*Murmuring Judges*), the British government (*The Absence of War*), and the U.S. post-invasion plans for peace in Iraq (*Stuff Happens*). Hare's literate, often witty plays (also including *Skylight, Amy's View,* and *Breath of Life*) depict a severely flawed world seemingly beyond repair in which situations are rarely as simplistic as we might like to believe. Hare has often directed his own plays, many of them at the National Theatre.

Alan Ayckbourn, England's most popular playwright today, tests plays in his theatre in Scarborough (Yorkshire) before they are brought to London or sent on tour. They deal with con-

temporary middle-class manners and morals seen from a satirical, jaundiced point of view. He is especially admired for his sharp dialogue, intricate situations, and telling observations of human behavior. As time has gone by, his plays have become increasingly less benign. Among his best-known plays are *How the Other Half Loves, The Norman Conquests,* and *A Small Family Business.* His recent plays include *House* and *Garden* (written to be staged on two adjacent stages simultaneously, using the same cast), *Private Fears in Public Places,* and *Improbable Fiction.*

Most of Caryl Churchill's plays have originated in fringe theatres. Many of her plays explore the effect of socioeconomic forces on human relationships, especially those of women. For example, *Top Girls* contrasts famous women of the past (who recall the price they paid for asserting themselves in a male-dominated world) with a group of present-day women (still trapped in a male world that devalues the work of women). Her most popular play has been *Cloud 9,* which explores how social forces determine the stereotyped sexual roles people adopt. This play attracted special attention because, to make her point, Churchill used cross-gender

Caryl Churchill

aryl Churchill is among the most successful of today's British playwrights. Born in England, she grew up in Montreal but returned to England to attend Oxford University. After graduation, she married a lawyer and became the mother of three sons. Because the restrictions of home life left her little time to write or to attend rehearsals, she began her professional career by writing short radio plays. In the late 1960s, Churchill and her husband reoriented their lives: He joined a legal aid center, and she turned to writing plays with feminist and socialist themes. Her first play to be performed in London, *Owners* (1972), concerned housing conditions.

She then began to create plays in collaboration with small ensemble groups—mainly the Joint Stock Company and Monstrous Regiment (a feminist theatre). A subject would be chosen, everyone would become involved in doing research and improvising scenes, and the playwright would bring it all together in a script. The first of these plays, *Light Shining in Buckinghamshire* (1976), concerned the disintegration of an attempt to reform society in the seventeenth century. Churchill's most successful collaboration (as well as her greatest commercial success) came with *Cloud 9* (1979), which grew from a group discussion of Kate Millet's book *Sexual Politics*. The play draws parallels between British imperialism and sexual stereotyping (a relationship underlined by cross-gender and cross-racial casting). Other collaborative projects included *Vinegar Tom* (1976), which argues that preoccupation with witchcraft in the seventeenth century was grounded in the fear of women who did not conform to social norms; *Serious Money* (1987), about the greed that dominates the lives of a group of stockbrokers; and *Mad Forest* (1990), about the lives of Romanians before and after the fall of Ceaucescu.

Churchill's plays, which also include *Top Girls* (1982), *Skriker* (1994), *Blue Heart* (1997), *Far Away* (2000), *A Number* (2002), and a new adaptation of Strindberg's *A Dream Play* (2006), are all as creative in form as they are varied in content. She has used interjected songs and overlapping dialogue, wielded post-structuralist wordplay as well as sparse realistic dialogue and long surrealistic monologues, treated time as fluid or twisted rather than linear, and called for different actors to play the same character in separate scenes. Although Churchill has a strong social conscience, she is not a propagandist. She has stated that her primary concerns are issues of "power, powerlessness and exploitation." By exploring these issues, her plays have encouraged audiences to confront what she considers the corruptive forces of a materialistic society.

Caryl Churchill's *Mad Forest* as produced by the Berkeley Repertory Theatre. Directed by Mark Wing-Davy; scenery and costumes by Marina Draghici; lighting by Peter Maradudin.

Ken Friedman; courtesy of the Berkeley Repertory Theatre

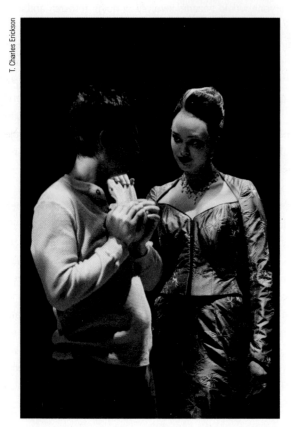

T. Charles Erickson

Martin McDonagh's *The Pillowman*, as produced at the Alley Theatre under the direction of Gregory Boyd. Scene and lighting design by Kevin Rigdon; costume design by Linda Ross.

casting for several of the roles. Recent works include *A Number* (about the ethics of human cloning and the origin of personality) and a new adaptation of August Strindberg's *A Dream Play.*

Other contemporary British playwrights include Patrick Marber with *Closer,* Joe Penhall with *Blue/Orange,* Sarah Kane (1971–1999) with *Blasted* and *4:48 Psychosis,* and Michael Frayn, whose works include the award-winning *Copenhagen* and *Democracy.* Aside from Frayn the most prolific British playwright has been Martin McDonagh, who, over the past ten years, has written a flurry of plays which mix humor with brutal dramatic action. They include *The Beauty Queen of Leenane, The Cripple of Inishmaan, The Lieutenant of Inishmore,* and, most recently, *The Pillowman,* in which a writer of horror stories is interrogated after several local children have been murdered.

Off-Broadway and Off-Off-Broadway

THE CONVICTION THAT THEATRE must be entirely self-supporting persisted longer in the United States than anywhere else. The government had financed the Federal Theatre dur-

Tom O'Horgan's staging of Julian Barry's *Lenny,* based on the life of the comedian Lenny Bruce. The fifteen-foot puppets represent such popular-culture figures as Little Orphan Annie, Boris Karloff, and the Lone Ranger. The musicians are dressed as bandaged accident victims. Scene design by Robin Wagner; costume design by Randy Barcello.

ing the 1930s, not because it valued theatre but because it wanted to reduce unemployment. After the Federal Theatre came to an end in 1939, no further government assistance was given until the mid-1960s. Following World War II, however, a number of nongovernmental groups sought means to decentralize the theatre.

The first important development began in New York City around 1950. Believing that financial conditions forced Broadway producers to cater almost exclusively to mass audiences, theatrical groups found out-of-the-way buildings where low production costs permitted them to offer short runs of plays not likely to appeal to Broadway audiences. These ventures marked the beginning of Off-Broadway. Most groups, working in buildings never intended for theatrical purposes, were forced to experiment with spatial arrangements unlike those in Broadway's proscenium houses. Thus they contributed to the retreat from the picture-frame stage. Many Off-Broadway companies played to small audiences,

because theatres seating more than two hundred people had to adhere to fire and safety provisions more stringent than the companies would have been able to meet. Off-Broadway thus also contributed to the preference for intimate theatres, which steadily increased after World War II (partly because of television, a medium that became available nationwide around 1950).

Off-Broadway proved so attractive that about fifty groups performed there during the 1950s. Of these, the most important was the Circle in the Square, which won critical acceptance both for itself and for Off-Broadway when in 1952 it achieved resounding success with Tennessee Williams' *Summer and Smoke,* a failure on Broadway.

By the 1960s, Off-Broadway had become so successful that theatrical unions insisted on stricter working conditions and higher wages. As a result, production costs rose until the advantages originally offered by Off-Broadway largely disappeared. This prompted the development of

Off-Off-Broadway—in still more out-of-the-way spaces where unions were largely ignored (though most unions eventually approved a special Off-Off-Broadway contract with conditions less restrictive than those in Off-Broadway contracts). Off-Off-Broadway has continued to be the most flexible and diverse venue for productions in New York. Today, as many as 200 groups often are active at the same time.

Of the early Off-Off-Broadway groups, the most important was the La MaMa organization, founded in 1961 by Ellen Stewart. La MaMa provided a place free from restrictions (except those imposed by limited funds) where dramatists could see their plays performed. By 1970, La MaMa was presenting more plays each season than all of the Broadway theatres combined. Although these plays varied enormously, many were determinedly innovative, defying and altering accepted notions of dramatic effectiveness. This free-ranging experimentation in playwriting also extended to directorial techniques. Tom O'Horgan was the most successful of La MaMa's directors. He subsequently directed *Hair, Lenny,* and *Jesus Christ, Superstar* on Broadway, using the approach he had perfected at La MaMa,

which seemingly owed much to Artaud: extensive use of nonverbal vocal sound, over-amplification of sound, highly varied lighting (including strobe), oversized effigies or symbolic stage properties, and the "physicalization" of almost every moment. His productions were colorful and uninhibited. When La MaMa toured abroad, it seemed so innovative that it was asked to establish branches in various countries. Its influence was not merely American but also international. Today, Ellen Stewart continues to lead La MaMa. Recently the city of New York, which had owned the main building La MaMa used, sold La MaMa the building for $1 to ensure the ability of the organization to continue nurturing and encouraging new works for the Off-Off Broadway theatre.

By 1970, the distinctions between Off-Broadway and Off-Off-Broadway were so eroded that they were often indistinguishable. (The type of union contracts under which they operate is their primary differentiation.) A few of these organizations have been especially important. The Circle Repertory Company (1969–1997) produced most of Lanford Wilson's plays as well as new works by many other playwrights. The

The New York Shakespeare Festival's production of Shakespeare's *Measure for Measure.* Directed by Mary Zimmerman; scene design by Dan Ostling.

Manhattan Theatre Club and Playwrights Horizons have also been especially helpful to playwrights. But the most influential of these organizations is the New York Shakespeare Festival Theatre, headed by Joseph Papp until his death in 1991. After a modest beginning in the 1950s, Papp persuaded municipal authorities to let him stage plays free of charge in Central Park. This program became so popular that in 1962 the city built the Delacorte Theatre there. In 1967, Papp acquired the former Astor Library on the edge of Greenwich Village and transformed it into the Public Theatre with five performance spaces. Not only does this organization maintain a heavy production schedule, composed of Shakespeare's plays, revivals, and new plays, but also it provides performance space for many other companies. Several of its productions, most notably *A Chorus Line,* moved to Broadway and garnered Tony Awards. Now headed by Artistic Director Oskar Eustis, the New York Shakespeare Festival/Public Theatre remains an influential force in New York theatre.

Regional Theatres

WHILE OFF-BROADWAY and Off-Off-Broadway were diversifying New York's theatre, decentralization was underway elsewhere. During the 1950s, a few companies—in Washington, Houston, San Francisco, and elsewhere—struggled to survive and ultimately received a major boost from the Ford Foundation, which in 1959 made large grants to several companies that had succeeded in winning local support. Thus the major impetus for decentralization in America came from private rather than governmental subsidy. Decentralization received another boost in 1963 with the opening of the Guthrie Theatre in Minneapolis. Tyrone Guthrie, then one of the world's foremost directors, selected Minneapolis over established theatre centers as the site for his company, and funds were raised locally to construct a new building for it. The

publicity surrounding this theatre aroused considerable interest (or envy) in other cities. Something approaching a boom in the construction of new arts centers followed. Today, almost every major city in the United States has such a complex.

Courtesy of the Paper Mill Playhouse

Michael Healy's *Drawer Boy* demonstrates the increased decentralization of the American theatre. According to *American Theatre* magazine, although it was America's most frequently produced play in 2003–2004 with more than twenty productions across America, it never played on Broadway or even in New York. Pictured here is John Mahoney in the Paper Mill Playhouse's (Millburn, N.J.) 2005 production of the play, reprising his performance from an earlier production at Chicago's Steppenwolf Theatre Company.

SOCIETY, ART,
AND CULTURE

Theatre
across America

New York attracts the greatest attention as a theatrical center, but many other cities also have thriving theatre communities. Seattle has twelve theatres where actors work under Actors Equity (the union for actors) contracts, among them the Seattle Repertory Theatre, A Contemporary Theatre, Intiman Theatre, and the Seattle Children's Theatre. In addition to the Equity companies, there are numerous others covering a wide range of interests and appeal to audiences.

Los Angeles claims to have more than two hundred fifty theatre companies, presenting more than one thousand shows per year. These include a few major theatres, such as the Mark Taper Forum and South Coast Repertory Theatre, but most are small ninety-nine-seat houses, a size that permits them to operate under Equity waiver contracts that offer little pay.

Chicago is estimated to have as many as two hundred theatre companies at any one time. These companies have a strong pool of actors available, from the more than fourteen hundred members of Actors Equity who live in Chicago. The city government recognizes the value of theatre and has helped to finance the upgrading of several theatres, including $18.8 million for the new home of the Goodman Theatre (founded in 1925), noted for giving many now-famous theatre artists their start (among them David Mamet). The Steppenwolf Theatre Company has launched the career of many notable actors (including Gary Sinise, John Malkovich, and Laurie Metcalf). Other notable Chicago theatres include the Court Theatre, Victory Gardens, and Second City (a comedy revue theatre that helped to develop the talents of John Belushi, Dan Aykroyd, Bill Murray, Alan Arkin, Barbara Harris, Mike Nichols, Elaine May, and countless others), as well as several theatres that give voice to the concerns of various audience constituencies: Congo Square Theatre (African American), Teatro Vista (Latino), Rasaka (Asian), Babes with Blades (feminist), and About Face (gay and lesbian).

Other major cities that support a lively theatre scene include Minneapolis, San Francisco, Boston, Denver, Philadelphia, Atlanta, Washington, Houston, and still others too numerous to discuss.

Many smaller cities have long-standing theatre companies of excellent quality with unique missions to serve their audiences. For example, the Perseverance Theatre in Juneau, Alaska (a community of 30,000 accessible only by plane or boat), hosts Alaskan Native performance festivals, educational outreach programs, and special projects with Alaskan artists, and performs new and classical plays both in Juneau and throughout the state on tour.

The *Andromache* segment of *The Greeks,* adapted by John Barton and Kenneth Cavander from works by Aeschylus, Euripides, Sophocles, and Homer, as produced by the Alley Theatre (Houston). Directed by Gregory Boyd; scene and lighting design by Kevin Rigdon; costume design by Susan Tsu.

Subsidization of the Arts in the United States

SUCH CHANGED TREATMENT of the arts, however, probably owes most to the legislation that in 1965 established the National Endowment for the Arts (NEA). Like Britain's Arts Council, the NEA dispenses federally appropriated funds to arts groups throughout the United States. The federal government encouraged states to establish arts councils, and in turn the states encouraged cities and communities to form their own councils. Today, federal, state, and local governments appropriate funds to subsidize the arts. The sums are not large, but that they exist at all marks a major change in American attitudes toward the arts, one that has not gone unchallenged by those who believe that the government should have no role in the arts.

Tax laws also encouraged corporations and foundations to make grants to arts organizations by making all or part of the grants tax deductible. Such grants and subsidies made it feasible for resident theatres to be established throughout the country. These companies are linked through the Theatre Communications Group (TCG), which was created in 1961 with funds supplied by the Ford Foundation. TCG serves as a centralized source of information for more than four hundred not-for-profit professional theatres and provides a forum where common problems can be discussed and solutions sought.

The existence of so many theatres may make theatrical conditions appear more stable than they are. Few of these theatres could exist without financial support from governments, corporations, foundations, or private donors in addition to the revenue they generate through ticket sales. Although the amount of government funding awarded through grants may be small, it is nonetheless very important; studies indicate that each federal grant dollar attracts more than six dollars from private and corporate donations. Unlike many European theatres, for which ongoing governmental support is assured, American theatres receive grants for periods ranging from one to five years and they have no assurance that their grants will be renewed. Consequently, most not-for-profit theatres in the United States devote much of their time to developing grant proposals and soliciting support. Unable to make firm, long-range plans, they must be prepared to alter their programs if

SOCIETY, ART,
AND CULTURE

Subsidization and the NEA

When the National Endowment for the Arts (NEA) was established in 1965, the United States joined the majority of other countries who had long believed that an enlightened government should provide financial support for the arts. In its first year of operation, the NEA had only $2.5 million (slightly more than one cent for each person living in the United States) to distribute among all the arts. At its peak in 1993–94, the NEA's budget was $170.2 million (about sixty-eight cents per capita). But by 1998, its appropriation had shrunk to $98 million. (Meanwhile, the French government devoted approximately $2.3 billion annually to subsidize the arts.)

Although it had faced opposition from time to time, the NEA seemed secure until 1989, when some members of Congress introduced legislation to place strictures on the type of art that could be subsidized; others campaigned to abolish the NEA altogether. Defenders of the NEA argued that the new proposals would impose censorship on the arts, endanger the freedom of expression guaranteed by the Constitution's First Amendment, discourage innovative and challenging art, and advocate officially approved standards for art not unlike those of communist Eastern Europe, which were then being denounced. Supporters of the proposed strictures responded that "this is not a question of censorship. This is a question of whether the American people should continue to subsidize this art with their hard-earned money."

The issues involved in this controversy have not been resolved. On one side, many oppose all subsidies for the arts, believing that art is a commodity that must compete in a free market and that if it deserves support it will find it. On the other side, many argue that market forces are historically short-sighted (most art now considered "great" was unpopular at the time of its creation), and that they would reduce artistic innovation and unfairly favor the economically privileged (those who could afford to experience and participate in arts that others could not). For many, the underlying conflict seemed to be a question of majority values versus the equal opportunity for freedom of expression.

In 1998, the Supreme Court upheld a 1990 law specifying that in making awards the NEA should take into account "general standards of decency and respect for the diverse beliefs and values of the American public." For many, this seemed a defeat for freedom of expression; others hailed it as a victory for majority values. The ruling settled little, especially because the justices who supported it indicated that the ruling was advisory rather than compulsory and neither defined "general standards of decency" nor indicated who should make such decisions. Funding for the NEA has gradually increased over the past several years, though it is still more than $30 million short of its 1993–94 level.

support is not forthcoming. Nevertheless, it is subsidization that has made possible the decentralization of the American theatre.

Most regional theatres offer a season of plays that intermingles revivals of classics with new or recent works. They do not seek long runs and can afford to take greater chances than Broadway does. They have become attractive to playwrights who wish to avoid reshaping their plays to fit the demands of Broadway producers. Several (among them the Actors Theatre of Louisville) now offer festivals of new plays each year.

Broadway and Musicals after Subsidization

DECENTRALIZATION AND SUBSIDIZATION altered the character of Broadway. Formerly the primary producer of new plays in America, Broadway after the establishment of the NEA and regional theatres came to present new works less and less frequently, choosing instead to present plays that had been successful in regional, Off-Broadway, Off-Off-Broadway, or British theatres and that were thought to have the potential for drawing large audiences over an extended period of time. This lessened somewhat the uncertainty of success but did not eliminate it, in part because audiences were not always eager to attend productions of plays with ticket prices ranging from $50 to over $100.

The situation was somewhat different for musicals, which remained Broadway's favorite fare; most of the productions that originated on Broadway were musicals, but many musicals also were tried out first elsewhere. Until around 1968, the type of musical that achieved dominance during and following World War II continued. Some of the best were *Funny Girl* (1964) by Jule Styne, *Hello, Dolly* (1964) and *Mame* (1966) by Jerry Herman, *Cabaret* (1966) by John Kander, and *Sweet Charity* (1966) by Sy Coleman. But beginning in 1968, the musical underwent significant change. The crucial production was *Hair* (1968) with its rock music, barely discernible story, sin-

gle setting, "hippie" dress, strobe lighting, highly amplified sound, and non-confrontational promotion of alternative lifestyles. *Hair* was also the first Broadway production to include nudity and obscene language. It broadened what might be used as subject matter for a musical and explored different ways dance and music might be used to convey thought and dramatic action. Several musicals using the rock idiom followed; perhaps the most successful was *Godspell* (1974) by Stephen Schwartz. Meanwhile, the older type of musical continued sporadically in such works as *Annie* (1977) by Charles Strouse, *La Cage aux Folles* (1983) by Jerry Herman, *Kiss of the Spider Woman* (1993) by John Kander, and *Titanic* (1997) by Maury Yeston, alongside innovative explorations. For example, Michael Bennett's *A Chorus Line* (1975) was innovative in its use of a chorus as the principal character and in its presentational style in which dancers auditioning for a chorus job tell their personal stories. It became one of the longest-running shows in Broadway's history, continuing until 1990.

The most successful innovator of the American musical for the past thirty-some years has been writer/composer Stephen Sondheim, who experimented with various approaches: *Company* (1970) had no chorus and used the principal performers in the song and dance sequences; *Pacific Overtures* (1976) borrowed conventions from Japanese theatre; *Sweeney Todd* (1979), based on a nineteenth-century melodrama, was operatic in its use of music throughout; *Sunday in the Park with George* (1983) took its inspiration from a painting by Georges Seurat and used counterpoint to great effect; *Into the Woods* (1987) deconstructed familiar fairy tales; *Assassins* (1991) interwove vignettes about people who have sought to assassinate presidents of the United States; and *Passion* (1994) focused on compulsive love. Almost all of these depart from the upbeat optimism of previous American musicals; they offer ironic and melancholy views of human behavior and social values and avoid happy endings. Sondheim changed musicals in part by making the songs and music much more

Joan Marcus

Stephen Sondheim's *Sunday in the Park with George* as produced by the Kennedy Center (Washington, D.C.) in a celebration that mounted six Sondheim musicals to honor him as one of the best composers of the American musical theatre. Although the musical was originally produced and directed on Broadway by Harold Prince, Kennedy Center Artistic Director Eric Schaffer directed this production; scene design by Derek McLane.

complex. Rather than writing songs that express an unambiguous emotion or point of view, as was typical in earlier musicals, Sondheim writes lyrics and music that are filled with inner tensions that suggest unacknowledged conflicts or hidden desires and reveal multiple possibilities of meaning. Subtext is a significant element in his lyrics and music, contributing to the sense of ironic acceptance characteristic of much of Sondheim's work. Although Sondheim is much admired, he is also frequently accused of setting the musical on a path that audiences find less satisfying than that of the postwar years.

Despite several successful productions, its critics have often said that after 1970 the American musical lost its vitality. The most popular musicals on the Broadway stage were those imported from England. Andrew Lloyd Webber, with *Jesus Christ Superstar* (1971), *Evita* (1976), *Cats* (1981), *Phantom of the Opera* (1986—which recently overtook *Cats* as the longest running Broadway musical), and *Sunset Boulevard* (1993), became the most successful composer of musicals. His work was joined by other imports from the London stage, among them *Les Misérables* (1985) and *Miss Saigon* (1989) by the Frenchmen Alain Boublil and Claude-Michel Schönberg. Meanwhile the strength of the American musical was reasserted, in part through revivals—among them *Gypsy, Guys and Dolls, Damn Yankees, Carousel, Chicago, Cabaret, The Pajama Game,* and *Sweeney Todd.*

Joan Marcus

The much-praised Broadway revival of *Cabaret*, which featured Alan Cumming as the provocative Emcee. Directed by Sam Mendes; costumes by William Ivey Long; sets by Robert Brill; lighting by Peggy Eisenhauer and Mike Baldassari.

Other factors helped to revitalize the musical and Broadway:

- Dynamic new musicals attracting new audiences
- Renovation of the 42nd Street area and Disney's entrance as a producer of Broadway musicals
- Musicals based on films and pop music

The appearance of dynamic new musicals helped to revitalize the form and attract new audiences to Broadway. *Rent* (1996), by Jonathan Larson, used different forms of contemporary music in adapting Puccini's *La Bohème* to a story about life among the young on New York's Lower East Side—the homeless, people with AIDS, transvestites, and aspiring artists—as they cope with disappointments and revel in their capacity for love. It achieved great popularity (fanned by the death of the author on the eve of the musical's premiere) and won a number of prestigious

awards. *Bring in 'Da Noise, Bring in 'Da Funk* (1996)—conceived and directed by George C. Wolfe with several collaborators—sought through tap dancing in six individualized scenes to evoke the history of African Americans.

Another important factor in the revival of the musical (and Broadway theatre) was the 42nd Street Development Project, which transformed an area of urban blight into something resembling the showplace of Broadway that it had been in the early twentieth century. At great expense, the Disney Corporation refurbished the New Amsterdam Theatre; the Livent corporation remodeled and linked two theatres to create the Ford Center; and the New Victory theatre was revived as a theatre for young audiences. With newly refurbished buildings to support theatrical activity and the removal of striptease clubs, the 42nd Street area became more "family friendly." The Disney Corporation enhanced this image by producing stage versions of its animated films *Beauty and the Beast* and *The Lion King*, which

The musical *Wicked* is based on Gregory Maguire's novel *Wicked: The Life and Times of the Wicked Witch of the West,* which offers a very different look at the land of Oz and the characters made popular in the film *The Wizard of Oz.* Pictured here are Idina Menzel as Elphaba and Kristin Chenoweth as Glinda. Music and lyrics by Stephen Schwartz; book by Winnie Holzman; directed by Joe Mantello; choreography by Wayne Cilento; scene design by Eugene Lee; costume design by Susan Hilferty; lighting by Kenneth Posner; sound by Tony Meloa.

attracted large audiences, including families who did not ordinarily attend Broadway. *The Lion King* also won high critical praise and numerous awards.

Broadway producers have long sought musicals based on material familiar to the general public. A number of musicals derived from films and pop music familiar to the baby-boom generation appeared. Among them: *The Full Monty, Hairspray, Mamma Mia!* (based on the music of the pop group ABBA), *Movin' Out* (based on the music of Billy Joel), and *Lennon* (based on the music and life of former Beatle John Lennon). Despite critics constantly predicting the impending demise of the American

musical, numerous new musicals are touted each season as being under development for Broadway production.

■ American Playwrights after 1960

ALTHOUGH AFTER 1960 Miller and Williams continued to write, they were overshadowed by a new generation of playwrights, among them Edward Albee, Lanford Wilson, David Rabe, David Mamet, and Sam Shepard. During the 1960s, Edward Albee was the most honored American playwright, especially after

Sam Shepard's *The Late Henry Moss* in its world premiere at San Francisco's Magic Theatre, featuring actors Sean Penn (left) and Nick Nolte (right).

the production of *Who's Afraid of Virginia Woolf?* in 1962. He followed that success with *Tiny Alice, A Delicate Balance, Seascape,* and others, but, like Williams and Miller, his reputation gradually faded. Then in 1994 his receipt of the Pulitzer Prize for *Three Tall Women* brought a reappraisal of his work. Since that time he has been prolific and has been especially admired for *The Goat.*

Lanford Wilson began his career in the Off-Off-Broadway theatre. He has written a large number of plays, among them *Balm in Gilead, Hot L Baltimore, Talley's Folly* (Pulitzer Prize, 1980), *The Fifth of July, Burn This, Redwood Curtain,* and *Sympathetic Magic.* The story line in these plays is minimal; the focus is on character relationships and the eventual revelation of hidden feelings, disappointments, and hopes. Wilson's compassionate treatment of the misfits and rejects of society marks him as one of the most humane of contemporary playwrights.

David Rabe wrote most of his early plays in response to the Vietnam War. *The Basic Training of Pavlo Hummel, Sticks and Bones,* and *Streamers* all show the price exacted by violence and war, which leads to the rejection of other more humanizing impulses. His subsequent play, *Hurlyburly,* set in Hollywood, treats characters who apparently are indifferent to the casual cru-

elties they inflict on each other. *Those the River Keeps* develops one of the characters from *Hurlyburly,* whereas *A Question of Magic* concerns difficult decisions about an AIDS patient and assisted suicide. The moral void suggested by several of his plays reflects Rabe's perception of contemporary American society.

David Mamet, who began his career in Chicago, has written many plays, among them *American Buffalo, Glengarry Glen Ross* (Pulitzer Prize, 1984), and *Speed-the-Plow,* about the debasement and distortion of human beings by the materialistic goals of American society as epitomized in its business dealings. Other plays, among them *Sexual Perversity in Chicago,* explore the inability to make personal commitments and establish satisfying relationships. *Oleanna* treats contemporary issues of "political correctness"; *The Cryptogram* traces the disintegration of trust within a family; and *The Old Neighborhood* is a somewhat disguised look at his own family past. In recent years, Mamet has done a great deal of writing for film and television.

Sam Shepard has been among the most prolific and provocative of contemporary American playwrights. He began his writing career in 1964 in the Off-Off-Broadway theatre and for many years thereafter turned out a large number of plays, among them *Chicago, Mad Dog Blues,* and

The Tooth of Crime, without revising the scripts because he considered it dishonest to change what he had originally written. In the mid-1970s, he altered this view and wrote his most successful plays, including *Curse of the Starving Class, Buried Child* (Pulitzer Prize, 1979), *True West,* and *A Lie of the Mind.* Recent, somewhat less successful plays include *Simpatico, Eyes for Consuela, The Late Henry Moss,* and *The God of Hell.* Although there is much variety in Shepard's work, a number of motifs recur: attempts to escape or deny the past, the cowboy and the West as basic American myths, the family as a battleground, and characters caught between empty dreams and an insubstantial reality. Let us look more closely at one of Shepard's finest plays, *Buried Child.*

Buried Child

THE OVERALL DRAMATIC POWER of Shepard's play derives more from its pattern of images and symbols than from its dialogue or story. For example, in Act I a character brings on stage armfuls of corn from a field that the other characters claim has been barren for years. In Act II, he brings in carrots. In the play's last act, he carries the unearthed buried child up a long flight of stairs—with no apparent landing—as we hear the voice of the child's mother relating her surprise at how fertile the field has suddenly become. These images evoke a sense of mystery that pervades the play and open the significance of the action to multiple interpretations.

The play begins by introducing Dodge and his wife, Halie, who are alienated from each other and comically trying to converse while on different floors of the house. We learn that Halie and Dodge have had three sons. Tilden, the oldest, once a star athlete, is living with them again; after having some "trouble," he is now not capable of taking care of himself. Bradley, who cut off his leg in a chainsaw accident, lives nearby and is expected to stop by later in the day. Halie's favorite child, Ansel, died long ago on his hon-

eymoon. The play never makes entirely clear what happened to Tilden or the circumstances of Ansel's death. Instead, Shepard compounds one unexplained event upon another. Tilden enters with his arms full of corn, which he claims is growing on land Dodge and Halie insist is barren. Dodge makes the first reference to the buried child shortly thereafter, but the characters refuse to address it. Thus a few major dramatic questions are established: What happened to this family? Is a child truly buried out back, and, if so, whose child is it? Halie leaves and Act I ends in a series of strange—but symbolically rich—physical actions with little or no dialogue to explain them.

Act II contributes new complications to the action as it introduces two new characters, Vince and Shelly. Vince has told Shelly that this is his family home, but he experiences an identity crisis when first Dodge, whom Vince claims is his grandfather, and later Tilden, whom Vince claims is his father, deny even knowing him. Vince abandons Shelly, ostensibly to get Dodge a bottle of liquor, leaving her with these men who, as far as we know, may or may not be his family. Shelly befriends Tilden while cutting carrots he has brought in from the allegedly barren land. A major discovery occurs for us when Tilden reveals the family's secret. He tells Shelly that there was a baby that Dodge drowned and buried somewhere out back. After this terrifying revelation, Bradley enters. Bradley scares off Tilden and intimidates Shelly into allowing him to place his fingers in her mouth. Act II ends in an air of suspense, as Bradley is gloating over Shelly, Shelly is seemingly in peril, and Vince is nowhere in sight.

Act III begins the following morning. Shelly is no longer frightened and has even begun to think of the house as her home. Halie returns accompanied by Father Dewis (the man she left to have lunch with the day before), having apparently spent the night elsewhere and wearing a different dress. She demands answers from Shelly, but Shelly demands answers to her own questions. This prompts Dodge to finally tell his story of what happened to their family. According to Dodge, everything was splendid until Halie had a baby that could not have been his. Dodge callously admits to drowning this baby. The remaining complications that can be resolved are resolved rather quickly. Vince comes crashing in and Halie recognizes him. For the first time, we (and Shelly) are certain that this truly is Vince's family. Halie retreats upstairs with Father Dewis. Dodge, having finally brought out into the open what he had denied and repressed for so long, proclaims his last will and never speaks again. Vince forces out Bradley and Father Dewis, lets Shelly go, and accepts from Dodge the ownership of the family farm. Meanwhile, Dodge has died unnoticed. The end of the play resembles its beginning: Vince assumes Dodge's opening position on the sofa, and we again hear Halie's voice from upstairs. As she speaks, Tilden enters from out back. This time Tilden carries in his arms the corpse of the baby, wrapped in dirty fabric, up the long flight of stairs to Halie as the lights fade out.

The central theme of *Buried Child* involves evasion and denial of the past. None of the family, except Vince, wants to remember its past. In the end they are unable to escape it, and the action is resolved when the past is acknowledged and the buried child is exhumed. One may view the acknowledgement and acceptance of the past at the end of the play as responsible for the rejuvenation of the land. The play may also be seen as an almost mythic parable about the American dream, represented by the idyllic farm and lives of the characters before their fall from grace. This might explain why Tilden, with his reversion to a childlike state, is the only character who can harvest the abundance that others cynically deny. Ultimately, Shepard's play raises more questions than it answers. For example, we cannot say with absolute certainty who is the father of the buried child. Although a single answer to all the questions raised by *Buried Child* may prove elusive, its dramatic intensity is darkly compelling, and the play continues to be produced frequently on stages throughout America.

During the years between the end of World War II and 1980, the theatre underwent many

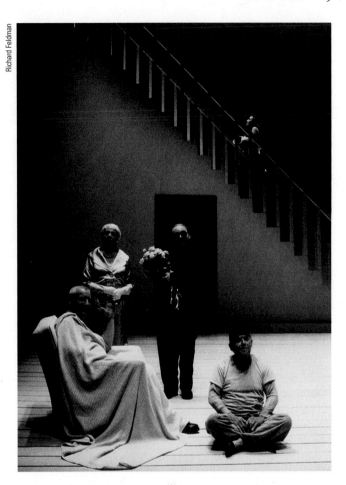

Richard Feldman

Buried Child as produced by the American Repertory Theatre. Directed by Marcus Stern; scene design by Allison Koturbash; costume design by Catherine Zuber; lighting by John Ambrosone.

changes. Perhaps the most significant change was the decentralization of theatre (which saw the establishment of permanent companies where previously there were none) and the increase in subsidization (by both public and private sources). But this period also saw increased questioning of individual values and social conventions. The absurdists extended the challenge to truth and certainty about as far as it could go, but ultimately more far-reaching was the challenge to legal and governmental sanctions of inequities in society. These challenges came to affect almost every aspect of theatre beginning in the 1960s and accelerating thereafter.

Additional Opportunities with InfoTrac College Edition

Theatre—and art in general—provides a unique way of knowing the world. As such it may help to develop perspectives and personal qualities desirable in our society. Using InfoTrac College Edition, find and read Simi Horwitz's "Measuring the Muse" from *Back Stage*. This article covers a conference on research, funding, and advocacy. Participants in the conference argue that art makes "better people." Write a 100- to 200-word position essay agreeing or disagreeing with that premise.

Building a Broad Context

- U.S. drops atomic bombs on Hiroshima (Aug. 6, 1945) and Nagasaki (Aug. 9, 1945); Japan surrenders, ending WWII (Aug. 14, 1945); WWII casualties estimated at thirty-five million killed in warfare and more than eight million in Nazi concentration camps

- U.S. Senator Joe McCarthy's "witch hunt" for American communists and communist sympathizers (1950–1954) ends with the Senate censuring McCarthy for his tactics

- Color TV introduced (1951)

- **Tennessee Williams'** *Cat on a Hot Tin Roof* **(1954)**

- Racial segregation declared unconstitutional (1954); use of non-violent civil disobedience (Rosa Parks and others) to secure civil rights for black Americans (1955)

- United States and Soviet Union develop ICBMs (1956)

- Castro seizes power in Cuba (1959)

- Bay of Pigs invasion of Cuba fails; Berlin Wall constructed, dividing Germany (both in 1961)

- Cuban Missile Crisis (1962)

- President John F. Kennedy assassinated (1963)

- U.S. Surgeon General reports smoking as unsafe; U.S. sends troops to Vietnam (both in 1964)

- **Broadway production of** *Hair* **(1968)**

- Student riots in Paris; Soviet crackdown on Czechoslovakia—"Prague Spring"; civil rights leader Martin Luther King assassinated (all in 1968)

- U.S. lands man on the moon (1969)

- President Richard Nixon visits China; Arab terrorists murder eleven athletes at the Munich Olympic Games (both in 1972)

- U.S. withdraws completely from Vietnam (1973)

- President Richard M. Nixon resigns as a result of Watergate scandal (1974)

- **Sam Shepard's** *Buried Child* **wins Pulitzer Prize for Drama (1979)**

- U.S. and China establish full diplomatic relations; Iranian students seize U.S. embassy in Tehran and hold fifty-two Americans hostage for more than 400 days (both in 1979)

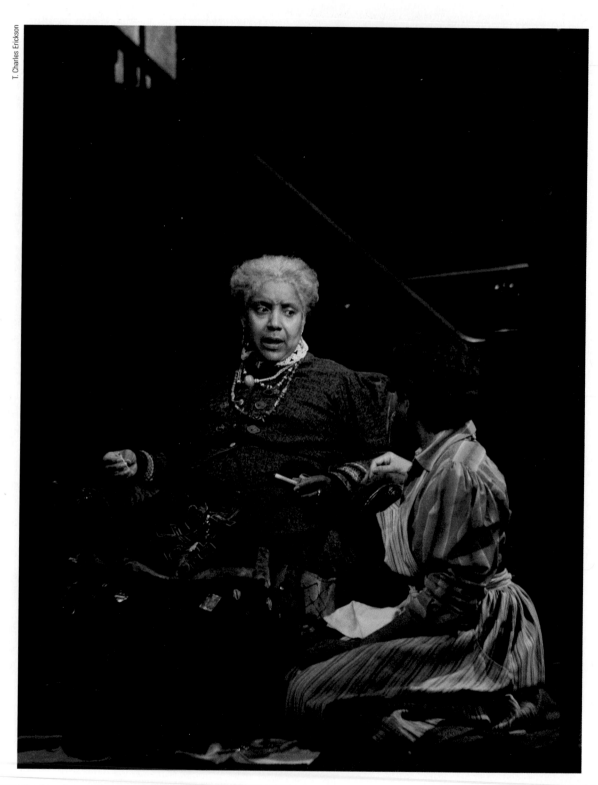

Gem of the Ocean by August Wilson, as performed at Huntington Theatre featuring Phylicia Rashad (left). Directed by Kenny Leon; scene design by David Gallo; costumes by Costanza Romero; lighting by Donald Holder.

Contemporary Theatre and Its Diversity

THE YEARS since the late 1960s have been noteworthy for challenging dominant (primarily white, middle-class) cultural standards and demanding that the diversity of American society not only be acknowledged, but also accepted and celebrated. Efforts have been made to open mainstream theatres to plays about groups previously marginalized or ignored (African American, Asian American, Latino or Hispanic American, Native American, women, gays and lesbians, and others) and also to establish theatres to give these groups their own voice. Still other companies and directors have championed radical change both in theatrical conventions and in ideas about the nature and purpose of theatre. All of these efforts have done much to alter attitudes and practices. Their collective influence has created significant diversity.

Alternative Theatre Groups

IN THE 1960s, the Living Theatre, more than any other organization, epitomized rebellion against established authority in all of its aspects: values, behavior, language, dress, theatrical conventions. When Judith Malina and Julian Beck founded the Living Theatre (1946) in New York, it was devoted to poetic drama. However, during the 1950s Malina and Beck became influenced increasingly by Brecht, Artaud, and anarchist theory. In 1964, its theatre having been closed for failure to pay taxes, it left the United States and until 1968 toured Europe, where it gained a large and enthusiastic following, especially among disaffected young people. In 1968, the Living Theatre returned to the United States with the repertory it had created during its exile. The most extreme of the Living Theatre's pieces was *Paradise Now*. It began with actors circulating among the spectators denouncing strictures on freedom (to smoke marijuana, travel without a passport, go nude in public, and the like). Thereafter during the performance, both spectators and actors roamed the auditorium and stage indiscriminately; many removed their clothing and some smoked marijuana—in other words, many of the strictures they denounced were defied. The performance continued for four or five hours with several scenes proceeding simultaneously throughout the theatre. Actors provoked some spectators into voicing opposition and then overrode them, often by shouting obscenities or even spitting on

them; at the end, the company sought to move the audience into the streets to continue the revolution begun in the theatre. Its aggressive behavior, combined with its anarchistic politics, won the Living Theatre enormous notoriety and called attention to several challenges to long-accepted theatrical conventions, especially those that distinguished the fictional from the real: They treated space and time as real; actors played themselves rather than characters; actors wore their own clothing instead of costumes; the subject matter, political and social issues of the day, was pursued through improvised confrontations rather than through predetermined text.

The Living Theatre also participated in two important changes made by theatre groups during the late 1960s: the introduction of obscene language and nudity. Although obscene language and simulated nudity were common features of early Greek comedy and late Roman mimes, neither had been considered acceptable in legitimate theatrical performances since the fall of Rome. But during the 1960s, the rebellion against accepted attitudes and assumptions that had begun with the civil rights movement gradually passed over into other areas, until almost every standard was challenged. Demonstrations, then common, usually involved the deliberate public violation of some convention or law considered unwarranted or unjust. Continued assaults on the conventions of polite behavior, and the inability of authorities to prevent violations, gained tolerance of behavior previously considered unacceptable.

Nudity and obscenity first came to Broadway in 1968 in the musical *Hair,* a good-natured plea for tolerance of alternative lifestyles. In contrast, the Living Theatre abused spectators who had paid to see its performances but did not agree with their opinions. Rather than being entertained, these spectators were subjected to physical and political intimidation. Why, then, did audiences attend? Novelty and notoriety probably attracted many, whereas others probably came out of sympathy for the group's political goals and defiance of authority; still others probably applauded the group's use of the theatre for purposes other than diversionary entertainment and for insisting on the responsibility of theatre to play an active role in social change. By the early 1970s, however, the group, probably because of its excesses, had lost most of its following.

The Living Theatre's production of *Paradise Now* during which actors mingled with the audience, urged them to remove their clothes (which many did), attacked (even spat on) those who seemed to oppose them, and in general urged the need for revolutionary change.

Ken McLaren; courtesy of the World of Culture, Ltd.

The Bread and Puppet Theatre's *Domestic Resurrection Circus.* The puppets of many sizes are made of "found" materials. The audience usually follows the puppet figures from one place to another.

Still, its influence continued. By the 1970s, though the limits of permissibility were vague, almost any subject, behavior, or manner of speaking was potentially acceptable in the theatre.

Although the most radical, the Living Theatre was not the only group seeking to change society through theatre. Among these, two of the most effective were the Bread and Puppet Theatre (founded in 1961), which used both actors and giant puppets to enact parables (often based on the Bible) that denounced war and the futility of materialism, and the San Francisco Mime Theatre (founded in 1966), which performed satirical pieces promoting civil rights, equality for women, and various other causes. The Bread and Puppet Theatre and the San Francisco Mime Theatre were also two among many theatres that sought to attract audiences by using easily accessible and entertaining forms of theatre to break down the distinctions between high art and popular culture. They borrowed freely from commedia dell'arte, festivals, parades, circuses, and variety theatre in their efforts to form a less materialistic and more accepting society.

Poor and Environmental Theatres

ALL OF THESE GROUPS had limited resources. Most never controlled a theatre and had to perform wherever they could. They were what Jerzy Grotowski, director of the Polish Laboratory Theatre in Wroclaw, Poland, called "poor" theatres. Grotowski also made his own a poor theatre, not out of necessity but out of conviction. He believed that most contemporary theatres had gone astray by depending on the technological devices of other media, especially movies and television. Rather than a technologically rich theatre, then, he sought to create one in which everything not absolutely necessary would be eliminated. He hoped in this way to rediscover the essence of theatre. Eventually, he concluded that only two elements are essential: the actor and the audience.

Because of the actor's central role in performance, Grotowski devoted much of his attention to actor training. He coupled intensive physical exercises with training designed to

Arrangement of the performance space for Grotowski's
The Constant Prince.

remove the performer's psychological inhibitions; he also sought to develop the actor's voice as an instrument capable of exceeding all normal demands. Ultimately, he wished actors to surpass so completely the spectators' own capabilities as to arouse a sense of magic. In performance, actors were permitted to use only those costumes and makeup essential to the action; they were not allowed to change costumes merely to indicate a change in role or psychological condition; properties were minimal; there was no scenery in the usual sense; any music had to be produced by the actors themselves. The performers, deprived of all nonessential and technological aids, had to depend entirely on their own resources.

Grotowski worked in a space that was reconfigured for each production. At first he tried to involve the audience directly in the action, but he concluded that this attempt only made spectators self-conscious. He then concentrated on creating spatial relationships among spectators and actors that would permit the audience to interact unself-consciously. For example, *Kordian,* which takes place in an insane asylum, was staged in a large room throughout which double-decker beds were spaced irregularly; audience members sat on some of the beds, whereas others were used by actor-patients, and the action, which

took place in and around the beds, placed the spectators in its midst, allowing them to function as passive inmates or observers. For *The Constant Prince,* in which the title character patiently accepts mistreatment and suffering, the theatre was arranged so that all of the spectators looked down into a space that resembled a hospital teaching theatre where, as Grotowski put it, psychic surgery takes place (see illustration).

Grotowski viewed the theatre as the modern equivalent of a tribal ceremony. He searched scripts for archetypal patterns of human behavior independent of time and place and developed them (often severely changing the original script) to make both actors and audience confront themselves spiritually. His goals resembled Artaud's, though his means differed markedly. During the late 1960s, Grotowski became a major influence on theatre in Europe and America. His company performed widely, and he conducted workshops for various other theatres and for some of the world's best directors. His influence was further disseminated through his book *Towards a Poor Theatre* (1968). Although few others attempted to restrict resources as severely as he did, many groups adapted his approach to staging and actor training. In the 1970s, Grotowski moved away from theatre into other explorations only partially related to theatre.

The Open Theatre (1963–1974), based in New York and headed by Joseph Chaikin (previously a member of the Living Theatre), was also a "poor" theatre. Like Grotowski, Chaikin concentrated on what he considered essential to theatre. But his work was grounded in contemporary theories of role-playing and theatre games. Above all, he was concerned with "transformation"—a constantly shifting reality in which the same performer assumes and discards roles or identities as the context changes. Reality was treated not as fixed but as ever-changing, implying that, because reality is not fixed, we can reshape ourselves and our society into what we would like them to be. The Open Theatre's scripts, which sought to reveal fundamental moral and social patterns buried beneath trou-

bling contemporary events or preoccupations, usually evolved in its workshops in close collaboration with its playwrights. After selecting a topic of interest, the actors, through improvisations, explored the potentials of situations and characters; the playwright then chose and shaped the discoveries that seemed most effective into a written script. One of the Open Theatre's most successful collaborations was with Jean-Claude van Itallie on *The Serpent*, in which the assassinations of Martin Luther King, Jr. and John F. Kennedy are interwoven with the story of Adam and Eve and other biblical events to suggest that God is a force that sets limits on our behavior and that the Serpent is a force that tempts us to breach those limits. Another successful collaboration resulted in Megan Terry's *Viet Rock*, which (with scenes that moved quickly between battlefields, congressional hearings, and family life) ridiculed bureaucratic justifications of the war in Vietnam and praised the simple pleasures of life that war disrupts and destroys. Such collective creation, explored by several theatres in the 1960s and 1970s, continues to be practiced by some groups.

In 1968, Richard Schechner, having examined various contemporary practices, including those of the "poor" theatres, sought to describe the conventions of an approach to performance that he labeled "environmental theatre." Some of these conventions concern the performance space. "The event can take place either in a totally transformed space or in a 'found' space," Schechner wrote. In other words, space may be adapted to make it appropriate to the action, or a suitable space not requiring alteration may be found (for example, a production depicting war as a game might be performed on a playground). "All the space is used for performance; all the space is used for the audience." That is, the way in which the total space can be used is entirely flexible; any part of the space may be used by performers or spectators, or performers and spectators may be intermingled.

Other conventions relate to what is performed: "A text need be neither the starting point nor the goal of a production. There may be no text at all." Unlike traditional performances (which seek to embody an existing dramatic text), in environmental theatre, performance takes

Courtesy of Richard Schechner

The Performance Group's production of Brecht's *Mother Courage.* Notice the actor-audience relationship in the flexible theatre space.

precedence over text and may be entirely improvisational, leaving no text behind once the performance ends. During a performance, "focus is flexible and variable"—that is, a production need not be shaped by the assumption (typical of traditional theatre) that all spectators must be able to see the same thing at the same time. Instead, several scenes may be going on simultaneously in various parts of the space; spectators are free to choose which they will watch.

Environmental theatre blends categories long treated as distinct during performance:

- Acting space and non-acting space (stage and auditorium)
- Performer and spectator
- Text and performance
- Sequential focus and action and simultaneous focus and action

By doing so, environmental theatre challenges conventions previously considered necessary for effective theatrical production and enjoyable audience experience, suggesting how easy it is to confuse the theatre's essence with its prevailing conventions.

Multimedia, Happenings, and Performance Art

EVEN AS THE "POOR" theatres were restricting their means, other theatres were emphasizing the very elements (electronic and spectacular) that the poor theatres were seeking to eliminate. Living as we do in the "electronic age," it seems inevitable that the theatre would exploit electronic devices. Marshall McLuhan, mass-communication critic, argues that, as electronic media have replaced the printed page as our primary mode of communication, we have become increasingly adept at processing multiple and concurrent stimuli (we watch on television events going on halfway around the world as we simultaneously carry on conversations in our living rooms). McLuhan concludes that we no longer require messages to be received in orderly sequence or one at a time.

Electronic media affected the theatre by creating the desire to make the representation of place in the theatre as transformable as it is in film and television. One result was to reduce the amount and specificity of built scenic elements (because of the time required to shift full-stage sets). Another was to encourage experimentation with "multimedia"—combinations of elements from several media. The best-known multimedia experimentation was done by the Czech designer Josef Svoboda. Around 1958, Svoboda began work on two projects—Polyekran (multiple screen) and Laterna Magika. Polyekran used filmed images entirely but sought to overcome the "visual paralysis" of a single screen by hanging screens of differing sizes at various distances from the audience, projecting different images on each, and changing the images at varying time intervals—thus creating a dynamic visual field and giving the audience a choice of images to watch. Laterna Magika used motion pictures in combination with live actors. Often the performers in the film and on the stage were the same, and at times a live performer seemed to emerge from the screen.

In 1959, Svoboda began to incorporate elements from these experiments into the staging of drama. He also experimented with devices for moving scenic units and platforms in ways intended to make the stage instantly transformable in both configuration and visual appearance. Some of his productions used closed-circuit television, with some scenes performed in a studio miles from the theatre and projected onto screens hung above a stage on which other live scenes were being acted. Closed-circuit television was also used to project close-up images of the actors' faces on screens during moments of crisis. Such experiments by Svoboda and others popularized several practices: using projected still pictures on multiple screens as a scenic background; interjecting filmed sequences into the dramatic action; manipulating the volume, direction, or quality of stereophonic

Josef Svoboda's multimedia design for an adaptation of Maxim Gorki's *The Last Ones* at the National Theatre, Prague. The various fragmentary set pieces at stage level permit multiple scenes to be played simultaneously or in sequence against projected scenes at the rear of the stage. The multiple images create a production of great complexity.

sound; and using closed-circuit television in multiple ways.

These developments are related to others then occurring in the visual arts. Stimulated by dissatisfaction with restrictions imposed by the media in which they worked (for example, two-dimensionality), painters sought to overcome the restrictions by such devices as gluing three-dimensional objects onto paintings. Sculptors, to overcome the static nature of their medium, attached motors to sculptures to make them move or used light to vary the appearance. Out of such experiments eventually came *happenings,* pioneered by the painter Allan Kaprow, who argued that not only the art objects on display but also the space and all of those who attend must be considered essential parts of the total artistic experience. For his first happening in 1959, Kaprow divided a gallery into three compartments, in each of which were several types of visual art and a number of individuals who repetitively performed assigned tasks, while images were projected onto various surfaces, including human beings, and while taped music and sound effects were played. All of those who attended were expected to carry out instructions handed them as they entered. Subsequent happenings varied, but most were multimedia events that shared basic characteristics and, taken as a whole, had implications for theatrical performance:

- They broke down barriers between the arts and mingled their elements.
- They shifted emphasis away from creating a product to participating in a process.
- They sought to provide an experience rather than present a message or single meaning.
- They shifted emphasis from the artist's intention to the participants' awareness.
- They often made each participant a partial creator of the event.

Happenings did much to undermine professionalism and disciplined technique because anyone could participate, and there was no right or wrong way of doing anything. Many aspects of happenings and environmental theatre recall those earlier expressed in dada and futurism.

Perhaps because they were anarchistic, happenings soon passed out of vogue. But the artistic impulse that had prompted them remained and resurfaced in the 1970s as *performance art.* Performance art may intermingle borrowings from (any or all of) visual arts, dance, music, video, and theatre. It may be scripted or improvised. It may or may not make use of props and costumes. Often a solo performance, it may also use multiple performers. It may be highly personal or confrontational, and it often explores issues of sexuality, violence, and power in ways that challenge marketplace values, governmental authority, and the way the media manipulate perceptions (especially of the body as object and commodity). Perhaps the essence of performance art is that there are no rules about what is allowed. Because some performance artists have used nudity, obscenity, unfamiliar conventions, and attacks on authority, it has been at the center of several attempts in recent years to censor art or to curb (or end altogether) government support of the arts.

In 1990, the grants that four performance artists had received from the National Endowment for the Arts were rescinded because portions of their work were considered offensive because of sexuality, nontraditional views of religion, obscene language, or attacks on political and religious opponents. Although the four grants that were rescinded amounted to only a minuscule fraction of what the NEA spent on theatre (let alone on all the arts), the ensuing furor threatened the very existence of the NEA. Not all performance art is transgressive, but much of it calls into question traditional behavior and values or challenges traditional assumptions about art by crossing the boundaries of different art forms to create innovative works.

The major creators of performance art originally came from the visual arts, dance, or music; they were attracted to performance art in part because it disregarded boundaries among the arts, thereby greatly expanding the means of expression. Theatre artists originally found performance art less attractive, perhaps because theatre has always combined elements from various other arts and because performance art tended to deemphasize story/text and to use performers not as actors but as narrators or as objects to be manipulated spatially. For several years now, however, the label "performance art" has been extended by some to include solo theatre pieces by such performers as Eric Bogosian, John Leguizamo, and Spalding Gray (1941–2004). Several artists have also blended theatre, dance, and performance art; among the most notable of them are Laurie Anderson, Pina Bausch, Martha Clarke, Ping Chong, and Meredith Monk.

Aspects of performance art have also been appropriated by music videos and other media adaptations. Because of these alterations and expansions, some critics insist that performance art in the 1990s was swallowed up by theatre and entertainment media on the one hand and the commodity-driven art world on the other.

Richard Foreman frequently writes, directs, and designs the scenery for works that straddle the boundaries some critics have drawn between performance art and theatre. In his play *Benita Canova*, as presented by the Ontological-Hysteric Theatre (New York), one can see his characteristic use of visual line, which, like a diagram of a perspective painting, comments on the director's composition and the audience's expectations of this focus.

T. Charles Erickson

Certainly the performance art of the twenty-first century differs significantly from that of the 1970s, and the term has been applied to so many diverse activities that it has lost specificity. Nevertheless, "performance art" continues to indicate the contemporary tendency to break down barriers between the arts and to help us understand that "performance" can take many forms. Perhaps the most influential force in performance art today is P.S. 122, an organization based in New York.

Postmodernism

THE IDEAS AND PRACTICES of environmental theatre and performance art are related to *postmodernism,* a label that is imprecise but one that suggests major changes in modernism. Most of these changes involve the breakdown of clear-cut categories. With modernism, the crucial battles had involved absolute versus relative standards and values. The triumph of relativism meant that artists did not all have to work in the same style; each could choose the one that seemed most appropriate. In the theatre, directors came to consider each production a prob-lem requiring its own stylistic solution. In addition, many new styles (symbolism, expressionism, surrealism, and the like) enlarged the available choices. Once a stylistic choice was made, however, the director sought to shape every aspect of a production to fit that mode. For modernists, then, though there were many stylistic categories, each was clearly differentiated.

Postmodernism melded categories by ignoring or deliberately violating differentiations and breaching the boundaries between the arts, as in performance art and multimedia; by breaking down the barriers between spectator and performance space, as in environmental theatre; and by removing distinctions between audience and performers, as in happenings. Postmodernists ignored previous distinctions between popular and high culture and often intermingled them, as in the production of *The Comedy of Errors* (at New York's Lincoln Center) in which the Flying Karamazov Brothers (a comic juggling team) not only played key roles but also incorporated juggling and acrobatics into Shakespeare's play.

Another sign of postmodernism is the blurring of distinctions between dramatic forms, as in absurdist and much other contemporary drama.

Peter Brook's production of Jean-Claude Carrière's adaptation of the Sanskrit epic *Mahabharata.* Real fire and water (a small pool and a stream crossing the stage) are permanent parts of the setting. Note the musicians at rear right. Designed by Chloe Oblensky.

Postmodernism also mingles elements from disparate styles, periods, or cultures. Postmodernist architecture is recognizable in large part because of the combination within single buildings of various stylistic motifs and forms from the past. Similarly, directors have utilized conventions borrowed from several cultures. Since the early 1970s, Peter Brook has been exploring the theatrical conventions of various cultures in an attempt to bridge cultural and language barriers. Perhaps the best known of the productions growing out of these explorations is his nine-hour adaptation of the Indian epic, *Mahabharata.* In a somewhat similar vein, the French director Ariane Mnouchkine, working with her company the Théâtre du Soleil, has drawn on Asian performance conventions in productions of several of Shakespeare's plays and in a tetralogy of Greek plays (Euripides' *Iphigenia at Aulis* and Aeschylus' *Agamemnon, The Libation Bearers,* and *The Eumenides*) presented under the title *Les Atrides.* These productions by Brook and Mnouchkine have been performed in major cities throughout Europe and America.

Many aspects of postmodernism came together in the theatre pieces of Robert Wilson, among them *Einstein on the Beach, CIVIL warS, Time Rocker,* and many more. In these pieces, Wilson borrowed from several media, cultures, and historical periods. Although some of Wilson's pieces have included spoken portions, many did not have texts in the traditional sense. They were essentially visual pieces, enhanced by music and sound, in which juxtaposed visual images appeared, disappeared, grew, diminished, and metamorphosed over time. Time was an important element; typically, it was slowed until movement became almost imperceptible, permitting every detail to be experienced; different elements within a scene progressed at different tempos. Because the performance aspects of visual image, time, sound, and movement were equal to if not greater importance than scripted dialogue, it has been difficult for others to restage Wilson's work. Many of his pieces were very long, from four to twelve hours; one lasted seven continuous days and nights. Likewise, the scale of some of his pieces was very large. For example, *CIVIL warS* contained many segments, one each

A segment of Robert Wilson's *CIVIL warS* at the American Repertory Theatre. The tall figure at right is Abraham Lincoln; at left, an owl; at center back, King Lear carrying Cordelia. Design and lighting by Robert Wilson with collaborators Tom Kamm and Jennifer Tipton.

Richard Feldman

staged in West Germany, the Netherlands, Italy, France, Japan, and the United States. It included such disparate historical figures as Abraham Lincoln, Karl Marx, Frederick the Great, Voltaire, and a Hopi Indian tribe, as well as wholly invented present-day and fictional characters. It was intended to reflect all types of conflicts (public and private) that interfere with human relationships. Utilizing twelve languages, it was not meant for an audience from a single culture.

According to Wilson, there is nothing to understand in his pieces, only things to experience, out of which each spectator constructs his or her own associations and meanings. Many spectators have been infuriated or bored by the length and lack of clear-cut intention in Wilson's pieces, but many critics have called him the most innovative and significant force in contemporary theatre. In recent years, Wilson has directed plays and operas, among them Shakespeare's *King Lear,* Euripides' *Alcestis,* Wagner's *Parsifal,* Büchner's *Danton's Death,* and Ibsen's *When We Dead Awaken,* as well as collaborating with others in creating new pieces (among them *The Black Rider,* on which he collaborated with Tom Waits). Even when he has staged classical texts, however, he has avoided using visual elements to merely illustrate what is in the text. Instead, he has sought to suggest other dimensions through imagery not literally (although perhaps thematically) related to the text.

Trends in Directing

POSTMODERNISM HAS INFLUENCED directing in several ways, perhaps most significantly by altering attitudes about the director's relationship to the playwright and the script. Modernists assumed that the director's task is to translate the playwright's script faithfully from page to stage. This assumption incorporated another: that the director can determine a playwright's intentions through a meticulous analysis of the script. Postmodernists, on the other hand, argue that there can be no single "correct" interpretation of a text because words do not convey precisely the same meanings to everyone. Furthermore, once a work is finished, its creator's statements about its meanings have no more authority than anyone else's, because the text and not the author elicits the responses and interpretations. Such arguments free a director to interpret a script as he or she thinks appropriate even if this interpretation is at odds with the playwright's. These views also encourage directors to propose new interpretations of well-known plays. In fact, in recent times, directors have often been judged by the novelty (sometimes more than by the aptness) of their interpretations. Some directors have argued that many classics have come to be so revered that we can see them with a fresh eye only in radical reinterpretations.

Most radical reinterpretations have involved plays by authors long dead. But since the 1980s, some directorial decisions have elicited strong objections from living authors. Samuel Beckett threatened to withdraw his *Endgame* from production at the American Repertory Theatre in Cambridge, Massachusetts, because the director, JoAnne Akalaitis, had relocated the action in a derelict subway station and made one of the leading characters black. In 1994, Beckett's estate forced the closure of an English production of his *Footfalls* because it did not adhere to Beckett's stage directions. In another instance, Arthur Miller threatened to sue the Wooster Group, a New York company directed by Elizabeth LeCompte, to prevent it from using, in a piece called *L.S.D.,* portions of *The Crucible* to illuminate contemporary attitudes about hallucinogenic drugs by juxtaposing them against attitudes about witchcraft in colonial New England as shown in Miller's play. The Wooster Group had previously incorporated portions of Thornton Wilder's *Our Town* into a piece called *Route 1 & 9,* where they were juxtaposed with a black vaudeville routine and a pornographic film. The group's idea was to comment on Wilder's idyllic view of America in which ethnic groups and sex are ignored, as are the industrial wastelands through which run the two highways that give the piece its title.

These productions raise important questions. Can playwrights protect their work from

Beckett's *Endgame* as directed by JoAnne Akalaitis. Beckett felt that Akalaitis changed the essential meaning of his play by setting it in an abandoned subway station, and he threatened to withdraw permission to produce the play. Scene design by Douglas Stein; costume design by Kurt Wilhelm; lighting by Jennifer Tipton.

distortions? Are directors justified in reshaping (even radically altering) a script to suit their own vision even if it distorts the playwright's intentions? What are the implications of demanding that directors adhere to playwrights' notions about how their works should be staged? Should playwrights' preferences be honored even after audience tastes and staging conventions have changed? What is the place of the script in performance? (Does it guide everything else, or is it as malleable as acting, scenery, lighting, and the like?) What is the role of the director (principal creative artist, as in film, or servant of the script)? None of these questions can be answered definitively, but they have created heated debate.

Cultural Diversity

BROADWAY, BECAUSE IT IS a sign of professional acceptance, continues to represent for many people the test for theatre in America. Nevertheless, the number of new productions presented there each season is relatively small, from thirty to forty (as compared to more than two hundred each season in the 1920s). On Broadway, usually no more than twenty-five productions are running at the same time. About thirty-eight theatres are classified as Broadway houses. Their prices range from $35 to $100 for most plays and $50 to $200 for musicals.

During 2005, more than 1,000 not-for-profit theatres scattered throughout the United States presented more than 10,000 different productions in more than 150,000 performances. Although these statistics establish that much more theatrical activity occurs beyond than in New York, they fail to reflect the increase in diversity in American theatres since the 1960s. Today, both Broadway and not-for-profit regional theatres tend to see themselves as serving all segments of society through universal appeals independent of race, class, or gender.

Much of what has happened in theatre since the 1960s calls these assumptions into question. Americans have long accepted the notion that the United States is a "melting pot" without always acknowledging that many groups, because of skin color or ethnicity (African, Asian, Native American, and some Latino/Hispanic), have been denied full absorption into the mainstream where "whiteness" and European cultural values have been accepted as the norm. Still others—women, gays and lesbians, the economically deprived, and the physically disadvantaged—have been denied equity for other reasons. Since the 1960s, most of these groups have rebelled against marginalization and have asserted their determination to have their worth acknowledged and their needs met in the theatre. But some of these groups have come to question the desirability of absorption into the "melting pot" if that means denying or abandoning their own cultures, traditions, and esthetic sensibilities. They have argued that, instead of trying to achieve homogenization, America would be better if it acknowledged, accepted, and valued differences. Efforts to implement these ideas have done much to diversify the American theatre both through plays by and about various groups and through theatres devoted to or sensitive to their needs.

Richard Feldman

The Woman Warrior, adapted by Deborah Rogin from the work of Maxine Hong Kingston. Directed by Sharon Ott; scene design by Ming Cho Lee; costume design by Susan Hilferty; lighting by Peter Maradudin.

African American Theatre

THEATRES AND PLAYS concerned with African Americans have probably made the greatest impact. One of the first African American playwrights to win wide critical acclaim in the postwar period was Lorraine Hansberry (1930–1965) with *A Raisin in the Sun* (1959), a drama about a black family in Chicago. It explored most of the themes that would be significant in subsequent African American drama: integration versus separation of the races; inequities and injustices inflicted on African Americans; aspirations for the good life and the obstacles to achieving one's potential; and maintaining dignity in the face of overwhelming circumstances. *A Raisin in the Sun* was the first play by an African American woman to be presented on Broadway, where it won the New York Drama Critics Circle Award. Although no longer as provocative as it once was, it raises issues about American society that remain to be answered satisfactorily.

African American playwrights and producing organizations have greatly increased since *A Raisin in the Sun* was first produced. Among the early playwrights, one of the most important was Amiri Baraka (LeRoi Jones), who set out to develop a black esthetic. In 1966, he founded Spirit House in Newark, where he promoted a separatist black society and a theatre devoted to the credo "By us, about us, for us." Among his best-known plays are *The Dutchman* and *Slave Ship.* Another important African American theatre was the New Lafayette Theatre, founded in Harlem in 1967, which sought to provide leadership for black theatres in America through an information service and *Black Theatre Magazine.* Unfortunately, because of dissension within the company, it came to an end in 1973.

The most durable of the early companies was the Negro Ensemble Company (NEC), founded in New York in 1968 by Douglas Turner Ward. It produced a wide range of plays meaningful to African Americans but not necessarily written by African Americans. During the 1990s it fell on hard times and eventually gave up presenting

Slave Ship by Amiri Baraka (LeRoi Jones) as produced by the Chelsea Theatre gave the audience a visceral experience of slavery's horrors with its startling use of light and sound in an intimate setting.

Courtesy of Chelsea Theatre

plays. Other African American companies have been established throughout the United States. Among these, some of the best are the Crossroads Theatre Company in New Brunswick, New Jersey; the Lorraine Hansberry in San Francisco; the St. Louis Black Repertory Company; the Penumbra Theatre Company in St. Paul; the New Federal Theatre in New York; Jomandi Productions in Atlanta; and the Providence Black Repertory Company in Rhode Island. There are also a number of black theatre festivals and conferences celebrating African American drama and theatre and discussing common issues.

The upsurge in African American theatrical activity provided a corresponding increase in opportunities for black actors, directors, and playwrights. Lloyd Richards (1919–2006) gained fame in the 1950s with his direction of the original Broadway production of Lorraine Hansberry's *A Raisin in the Sun.* He served as the artistic director of the Yale Repertory Theatre and as dean of the prestigious Yale University School of Drama from 1979 to 1991. Richards was not only a gifted director, but an astute developer of emerging playwrights through his position as artistic director of the National Playwrights Conference at the Eugene O'Neill Theatre Center from 1968 to 1999. Richards is credited with having helped to develop the playwriting talents of Wendy Wasserstein, Christopher Durang, Lee Blessing, David Henry Hwang, and, perhaps most notably, August Wilson. Richards' long-standing collaboration with Wilson began in 1984, when he directed Wilson's *Ma Rainey's Black Bottom.* Richards went on to direct the world premieres of five other August Wilson plays, including *Fences, Joe Turner's Come and Gone, The Piano Lesson, Two Trains Running,* and *Seven Guitars.*

Another successful director, and also a successful playwright, has been George C. Wolfe. Wolfe first gained wide recognition in 1986 as a playwright with his play *The Colored Museum,* a series of eleven exhibits about African American life that combine satire and anger. He next wrote a musical, *Jelly's Last Jam,* which traces the career of Jelly Roll Morton, which had a long run on Broadway. Wolfe also conceived and directed the very popular musical *Bring in 'Da Noise, Bring in 'Da Funk,* for which he earned his first of two Tony Awards for directing. Wolfe won his second Tony Award for his direction of the Broadway production of Tony Kushner's *Angels in America.* Today, Wolfe has begun to direct films (among them HBO's *Lackawanna Blues*) in addition to stage productions. Wolfe also served as the head of the New York Shakespeare Festival Theatre (1993–2005), where he was credited with helping to develop the talents of Pulitzer Prize–winning playwrights Nilo Cruz and Suzan-Lori Parks. Parks is perhaps the most admired of the most recent African American playwrights. Her plays include *The America Play, The Death of the Last Black Man in the Whole Entire World, In the Blood,* and *TopDog/Underdog* (which won the Pulitzer Prize in 2002).

One of the most praised African American playwrights has been August Wilson (1945– 2005). His first success came in 1984 with *Ma Rainey's Black Bottom,* about African American musicians in the 1920s. *Fences,* set in the 1950s, treats a man who might have been a great baseball player had it not been for discrimination in the sport and the effect on him and his family of his sense of waste. It won the Pulitzer Prize in 1985. Others of Wilson's plays include *Joe Turner's Come and Gone, The Piano Lesson* (winner of the Pulitzer Prize in 1990), *Two Trains Running, Seven Guitars, Jitney,* and *Gem of the Ocean.* Wilson's plays, unlike those of several earlier African American dramatists, do not exploit themes of rage about whites so much as concentrate on African American identity and quests for fulfillment and dignity. Wilson felt deeply that African Americans needed separate theatres in which to express their experiences and concerns; his views stimulated much discussion about this issue. Let us look at *Ma Rainey's Black Bottom* as an example of Wilson's work.

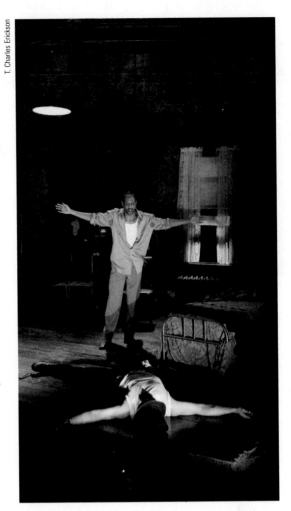

T. Charles Erickson

Topdog/Underdog as produced by the Hartford Stage Company with K. Todd Freeman as Booth (standing) and David Rainey as Lincoln. Directed by Amy Morton; scene design by Loy Arcenas; costume design by Nan Cibula-Jenkins; lighting by Kevin Rigdon.

■ *Ma Rainey's Black Bottom*

THE ENTIRE ACTION of *Ma Rainey's Black Bottom* takes place in a recording studio in Chicago during one day in 1927. When the play opens, two white men—Irvine, Ma Rainey's manager, and Sturdyvant, who is interested only in the money he can make off the musicians—are preparing the studio for the recording they expect to make with Ma Rainey, "mother of the blues," and her band, all of them black. It is clear that the two—especially Sturdyvant—have

no respect for black musicians or their music. The setting is emblematic of the hierarchy they see. It has three parts: the recording booth, raised above and with a view of the recording studio, and, below both, the rehearsal room, where the musicians warm up, exchange good-natured insults, and await their summons to perform.

When the band arrives, without Ma Rainey and her companions, tension begins to rise. It also becomes clear that what the white men

Tina Fabrique as Ma Rainey and Gavin Lawrence as Levee in the Arena Stage production of *Ma Rainey's Black Bottom.* Directed by Tazewell Thompson.

Ma Rainey's choices. He also feels that he has the advantage because Sturdyvant has heard some of his music and has promised to promote it. Levee, somewhat like the white men, feels himself superior to the other members of the band—Cutler, Toledo, and Slow Drag—and believes he and his music will be promoted and that he will get his own band. Much of the early part of the play is spent on Levee's quibbling with the other musicians, who have learned to accept their lot in the white-dominated society and unquestioningly do what they are told. Levee seems to feel that he will be able to move beyond these restrictions. The exchanges between Levee and the other band members define these opposing views and prepare us for troubles yet to come.

When Ma Rainey finally arrives, dressed in furs and other finery, with her nephew, Sylvester, and her girl friend, Dussie Mae, trouble begins. Ma holds one key card—they can't record without her—and her threats to leave eventually get her everything she wants. She recognizes that she may be powerless in the outside world but here she can dominate. Though the white men had decided Levee should play an introduction to Ma Rainey's signature song, she had decided that

expect to record is not what Ma Rainey has told the band they will record, and we see the struggle for power begin to take shape. The band is conditioned to do whatever Ma Rainey says, but a new member of the band, Levee, disagrees with

A scene from August Wilson's *Ma Rainey's Black Bottom* as produced by the Cleveland Play House (with Theresa Merrit in the title role) and directed by Claude E. Purdy.

PRACTITIONERS
AND THEORISTS

August Wilson's
Master Collage

August Wilson wrote a play set in each decade of the twentieth century. Taken as a whole, the individual plays combine to function as a master collage of the African American experience in the twentieth century. Wilson compared his approach to writing individual plays as "working in collages" (wherein one shifts and reorganizes accumulated material until arriving at an overall pleasing composition) and said that he thought of his ten plays as "all one work." Here is a list of Wilson's plays specifying the decade in which they are set and the year they were written:

- *Gem of the Ocean*   set in the 1900s—written in 2003
- *Joe Turner's Come and Gone*   set in the 1910s—written in 1986
- *Ma Rainey's Black Bottom*   set in the 1920s—written in 1984
- *The Piano Lesson*   set in the 1930s—written in 1987
                                       (Pulitzer Prize winner)
- *Seven Guitars*   set in the 1940s—written in 1995
- *Fences*   set in the 1950s—written in 1985
                                       (Pulitzer Prize winner)
- *Two Trains Running*   set in the 1960s—written in 1990
- *Jitney*   set in the 1970s—written in 1982
- *King Hedley II*   set in the 1980s—written in 1999
- *Radio Golf*   set in the 1990s—written in 2005

Sylvester, who has a pronounced stutter, must introduce it with a spoken passage. She demands that they do "takes" until Sylvester gets it right.

After several attempts, he does succeed, but they find that the line to the recording booth was disconnected. Ma Rainey persists in her demand, however, and suggests that she can't go on until someone goes out and buys her a soft drink. During this interruption, Dussie Mae wanders down to the rehearsal room and despite the warning from others about Dussie Mae's relationship with Ma, Levee fondles and kisses her.

Eventually the recording gets completed, after which Sturdyvant informs Levee that he is no longer interested in his music. Levee feels so betrayed and enraged that when Toledo accidentally steps on Levee's shoe, the rage is redirected, and Levee stabs and kills Toledo. Wilson seems to suggest that this violence is an outgrowth of the treatment of blacks that has been discussed and dramatized in the play. *Ma Rainey's Black Bottom* is an exciting play about issues that Wilson would explore many times and in different decades of the twentieth century in subsequent plays.

Latino Theatre

AFTER AFRICAN AMERICAN, Latino (or Hispanic American or Chicano or ?—acceptable terms are a matter of considerable contention) is the most extensively developed alternative theatre in the United States. The first play known to have been staged in what is now the United States was performed by Spanish soldiers near El Paso in 1598. But it was not until the late nineteenth century that Spanish-language theatre became common, first in California, then in Texas, and, by the early twentieth century, in all of the territories bordering Mexico. From 1918 into the 1930s, Los Angeles supported five professional Spanish-language theatres, and professional companies toured widely throughout some parts of the country. During the 1930s, economic depression and the inroads of film ended most of this activity, although amateur theatres continued to fill the need. All of these developments made little impact on the dominant white culture, which remained largely oblivious to them.

Not until the 1960s did Latino theatre begin to make an impression on the wider American consciousness, first through the work of El Teatro Campesino, a bilingual Chicano company founded by Luis Valdez in 1965. Valdez was very successful in calling attention to the plight of migrant workers in California and winning public support for them during a strike by grape pickers. Valdez later turned to writing plays about the heritage and lives of contemporary Mexican Americans. He achieved his greatest popular success with *Zoot Suit* (1976), which mingled traditional Mexican musical forms with Living Newspaper techniques in a play based on an actual case of injustice against a group of young Mexican Americans during World War II. *Zoot Suit,* which enjoyed a long run in the theatre before being made into a film, influenced many other Hispanic American writers to treat similar themes. A prolific playwright, Valdez has written other works that include *Los Vendidos, Corridos, I Don't Have to Show You No Stinking Badges,* and *Bandito.* Valdez is probably best known to the general public for his film work, especially *La Bamba.*

Among the Latino playwrights who have made a significant mark on contemporary American theatre are Maria Irene Fornes, Nilo Cruz, José Rivera, and Milcha Sanchez-Scott. One of the most notable Hispanic American playwrights is Maria Irene Fornes, a Cuban American who began writing plays in 1965. Although she has never achieved wide popular recognition, she has won six awards for Off-Broadway productions. Among her plays are *Fefu and Her Friends,* in which eight women hold a reunion and look back over their lives in a male-dominated world, and *The Conduct of Life,* which draws parallels between political subjugation and the subjugation of women in Latin America. She has also

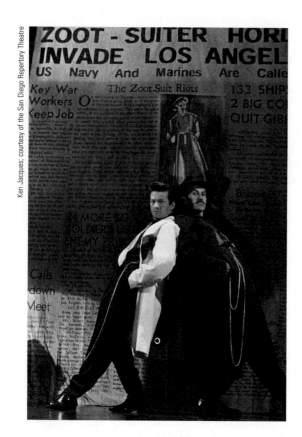

Luiz Valdez's *Zoot Suit* as performed by the San Diego Repertory Theatre, featuring actors David Barrera and Jorge Galvan. Directed by William A. Virchis.

Ken Jacques; courtesy of the San Diego Repertory Theatre

Nilo Cruz's Pulitzer Prize–winning play *Anna in the Tropics* as produced by McCarter Theatre Center (Princeton, N.J.), featuring Jimmy Smits (center, dressed in white). Directed by Emily Mann; scene design by Robert Brill; costume design by Anita Yavich; lighting by Peter Kaczorowski; sound by Dan Moses Schreier.

mentored scores of young Hispanic playwrights, among them Cuban exile Nilo Cruz, who credits Fornes with giving him his start as a playwright. The two met in 1988 in Miami, and Fornes encouraged him to join the now-defunct INTAR Hispanic Playwrights-in-Residence Laboratory in New York. Cruz has said, "I come from the Irene Fornes School, you don't write a play about an idea—you write a play about characters." Cruz is the most recent Latino writer to have gained widespread recognition. When his play *Anna in the Tropics* was awarded the 2003 Pulitzer Prize for drama, it was one of only two plays to have ever been so awarded prior having been staged in New York. Cruz's plays typically focus on characters whose dignity and creative potential are often at odds with the repressive circumstances in which they live. His other plays include *A Park in Our House, Two Sisters and a Piano, Lorca in a Green Dress,* and *Beauty of the Father.* José Rivera has gained considerable attention for his plays *Marisol, Cloud Tectonics, Sueño* (his adaptation of Calderon's Spanish Golden Age drama *Life Is a Dream*), and *References to Salvador Dalí Make Me Hot.* Several critics have noted that Rivera's use of realistic and fantastic

elements coexisting alongside each other reflects the magic realism of Gabriel García Marquez. Recently, Rivera has worked as screenplay writer, and his *Motorcycle Diaries* was nominated for a 2005 Academy Award.

Another notable Latina dramatist is Milcha Sanchez-Scott, daughter of a Colombian father and an Indonesian mother. She was educated partially in England and since the age of fourteen has lived in California. Her first play, *Latina,* concerning women she met while working in an employment agency in Los Angeles, won several awards. Later plays include *Dog Lady, Cuban Swimmer, Evening Star,* and *The Old Matador.* Her best-known work is *Roosters.* Let us examine it as an example of Latina drama.

Roosters

ROOSTERS, WHICH TAKES PLACE in the present-day Southwest, uses cockfighting as its basic metaphor. The father of the family is named Gallo (meaning "rooster," a word also signifying "macho," the male animal focused on his own needs). The primary action of the play

SOCIETY, ART,
AND CULTURE

A National Center
for Latino Performing Arts

Founded by Hugo and Rebecca Read Medrano in 1976, the GALA (Group of Latin American Artists) Hispanic Theatre in Washington, D.C. recently made the transition from a somewhat nomadic theatre to a national center for Latino performing arts. Unlike many Latino theatres in America, GALA's artists and audience are not made up of one particular Hispanic group. The Hispanic community in Washington, D.C. is diverse, and from its beginning GALA's founders saw a need for the different members of that community to join together in a common celebration of Spanish and Latin American drama. As Hugo Medrano has said, "GALA is not Spanish, nor Argentine, nor Puerto Rican. It is Latino in the fullest sense." Consequently, GALA has long presented classical and contemporary plays in Spanish and English that appeal to a broad range of Hispanic backgrounds and interests.

Early on, GALA performed plays in both Spanish and English on alternating days. This created some practical problems. "Many of the actors were bilingual, but it got confusing sometimes about which version we were doing. Occasionally an actor would come out and speak the wrong language [for that performance] or the audience would come to the wrong performance," Rebecca Read Medrano recounts. Hugo Medrano relates that "because some of the actors couldn't speak English, sometimes we would have one actor in the Spanish version and another in the English version." Medrano remembers that for one play, "we even had two directors because one didn't speak English."

In its infancy, GALA operated out of a Washington, D.C. townhouse. The company was surprised when its first production, *La Fiaca* by Argentine Ricardo Talesnik, drew a review and feature article about the group in the next day's *Washington Post* without any of the company having called the press in advance. Despite positive reviews and community support, the theatre spent decades in constant search for a permanent home. It moved from the townhouse location to a church, to an arts center, to the Sacred Heart Catholic School, to the Warehouse Theatre, and finally in 2006 to its new home at the renovated Tivoli Theatre in the Columbia Heights district of inner-city Washington, D.C.

is concerned with the struggle for dominance between the forty-year-old Gallo (who returns home after several years spent in prison for killing a man) and his twenty-year-old son, Hector (who rejects his father's braggadocio in favor of a determinedly unromantic view of himself and his family). Gallo considers it a betrayal that Hector has taken a job working in the fields, because none of the family's male members has ever stooped so low (although such menial work seems the accepted fate of the females who apparently provide financial support while Gallo plays his macho games). Gallo prefers a life focused on cockfighting, winning at which in his eyes justifies any behavior, including cheating, con games, and even murder (it was a fight over a rooster that led to his imprisonment). Hector, on the other hand, dreams of going beyond the mountains (visible in the background) to escape his family and the kind of life Gallo envisions for him.

The struggle between the two men is brought to a head in their attempts to assert ownership of Zapata, a fighting cock that Gallo considers the culmination of his efforts to breed a champion but that has been given to Hector by his grandfather, who died while Gallo was in prison. Hector's determination to take Zapata into the cockfighting ring himself, and to dispose of him after the fight is over, conflicts with Gallo's belief that he is the rightful owner of Zapata and that, as a legendary figure in cockfighting, he should be the one to take Zapata into the ring. The life-and-death nature of their struggle is made clear in a fight between two roosters (represented by actor-dancers), one of whom is viciously killed during a fight for which razors have been attached to the roosters' feet; it is further implied in several references to Zapata as destroying his own offspring. The ultimate parallel between Zapata and Gallo comes when Gallo challenges Hector to a fight with knives, apparently willing to kill his son in order to gain possession of Zapata, a goal that also makes him callously betray his daughter Angela's trust. The struggle is ultimately resolved when Hector overpowers Gallo and reveals that, despite his denunciations of his father, he has been motivated by resentment that his father has ignored his family and failed to offer Hector the love and approval he needed. It is also revealed that Hector has insisted on keeping possession of and disposing of Zapata in order to save his father's life, which is in clear danger from the family whose son Gallo killed and from whose stock Zapata is descended (illegally, through another example of Gallo's chicanery). Once overpowered by Hector, Gallo seems reconciled to his son, finding in him the potential to carry on the macho tradition, although Hector repeats his intention of leaving this kind of life behind.

Set against this struggle between males are the three women of the family: Juana, Gallo's worn-down, thirty-five-year-old wife; Chata, Gallo's fleshy, forty-year-old sister, who "gives new meaning to the word blowsy"; and Angela, Gallo's fifteen-year-old daughter who wears angel wings, plays with dolls dressed as saints, creates a cemetery with headstones bearing the names of those who have offended her, and spends much of her time under the house. Unlike Gallo and Hector, both of whom are described as being

Roosters as produced at the New Mexico Repertory Theatre. As the family gathers around the table, Angela (in the background) makes off with the fighting cock Zapata. Directed by Roxane Rogers; setting by Rosario Provenza; costumes by Tina Cantu Navarro; lighting by Robert Wierzel.

Courtesy of Murrae Haynes, New Mexico Repertory Theatre

unusually handsome, the women are all homely. The men are set off by the women, like colorful roosters surrounded by drab hens, and the women apparently are expected to feel grateful to be associated with these handsome creatures. Juana, who bore her first child at the age of fifteen, has spent her life supporting her family and waiting patiently for the return of Gallo (who apparently in the past has come and gone on whim), adoring him, making possible his macho existence. Chata, who once aspired to home and family but, seduced and betrayed early, has since followed the migrant farm workers, living a life of sexual promiscuity; she is the proverbial "fallen woman with a heart of gold," providing both earthy wisdom, sharp commentary, and momentary comfort. Angela, on the verge of womanhood, clings to childhood and religion as a buffer against hurt. Torn between Gallo and Hector, she on the one hand accepts Hector's view of Gallo as a con man, but on the other hand clearly desires to be loved and accepted by her father. Hers is the most touching betrayal when Gallo, by promising to take her on a trip to the ocean, cajoles her into telling where Zapata is hidden, even though she has given her oath to Hector that she will not do so. Once Gallo has Zapata, he has no more use for Angela. Her disillusionment is intense, and her attempt to retrieve her faith culminates in her levitation, wings spread, a manifestation of the "magic realism" that is characteristic of much Latino literature. The play ends in a suspended moment during which all of the characters seemingly accept themselves and each other.

Roosters is divided into two acts and eight scenes. The elapsed time is unclear but apparently not more than a day or two. The setting is simple: A house, set against a desert landscape with mountains visible in the distance, is raised sufficiently to allow space for Angela to slip under it easily. The porch and yard are the principal playing areas. There is also a chicken-wire enclosure for Zapata and a tree that provides some shade. The atmosphere, shifting easily between realism and fantasy, is characteristic of Latino "magic realism." Overall, *Roosters* is a powerful play that has much to say about machismo, women, love, and psychological need in a male-dominated Latino culture.

There are in the United States more than one hundred Hispanic American theatre groups—Chicano, Puerto Rican, Cuban, and other categories. Some of the best known of these are Repertorio Espanol and the Puerto Rican Traveling Theatre, both in New York; and El Teatro Campesino, El Teatro de la Esperanza, and the Bilingual Foundation of the Arts in California. A large number of cities maintain Hispanic American theatre groups and some cities, including Miami and Chicago, host international festivals of Chicano and Latino theatre.

Asian American Theatre

ASIAN AMERICANS have also made their mark. Asians first came to America in large numbers when Chinese workers were imported in the mid-nineteenth century to help build railroads. Those who remained usually clustered together within cities such as San Francisco, New York, Chicago, Los Angeles, and Seattle. In some of these cities, theatres were established to cater to Asian audiences. San Francisco, for example, maintained a Beijing Opera company until the 1940s. World War II, the Korean War, and the Vietnam War tended to make Americans more aware of Asian cultures and to increase the immigration of Asians to the United States.

When Asian Americans were depicted by white dramatists, they were usually reduced to a few stereotypes: dutiful houseboy, inscrutable detective, wise Confucian patriarch, treacherous dragon lady, or submissive Asian doll-bride. Asian Americans began to rebel against these stereotypes around 1965, writing their own plays and founding their own theatres. Some of the

Should We Write Only about Our Own Culture?

In debates over multiculturalism, an ongoing issue concerns whether playwrights should (or can effectively) write about cultures other than their own. Writers from minority cultures are especially subject to pressure, often being accused of betraying their own heritage when they write critically about it or choose to write about some group other than their own. As Margo Jefferson, an African American critic for the *New York Times*, comments, minority dramatists are often told "that they should not wash dirty linen in public. . . . Put a diverse audience in a theater to see a play set in a particular ethnic, racial or sexual world, and it's clear that the audience members closest to that world feel that outsiders have no right to invade it with their responses."

August Wilson, the African American playwright, felt strongly that he must write about his own culture: "I am more and more concerned with pointing out the differences between blacks and whites as opposed to pointing out similarities. . . . We have different ideas of justice and morality. . . . [B]lacks have been all too willing and anxious to say that we are the same as whites."

On the other hand, Ping Chong, a major Asian American performance/video artist, playwright, and director, argues:

I'm not going to let myself be ghettoized as an Asian-American artist. I'm an American artist . . . we cannot lose sight of the fact that we all live in a society where we have to coexist. It doesn't mean that I have to like your culture. But we have to be sensitive to each other's cultures. I think it extremely naive to think that no one but Asians can write about Asians. It would simply be another point of view. I do make shows about white characters even though I didn't grow up Anglo. Does that mean I shouldn't write about them? . . . I believe it is important to be inclusive; a free society should allow for a multiplicity of views.

Some members of specific cultures believe that their experience is so complex that no outsider can understand or represent it adequately. They may also resent having aspects of their cultural heritage "appropriated" by outsiders who incorporate it into their own works without acknowledging its origins or who distort it through lack of understanding. Daryl Chin, an Asian American critic, writes: "These debates [over multiculturalism] are about feelings of disenfranchisement and exclusion. . . . The reason the debates are so painful is that they strike at the very heart of who people think they are."

Naomi Iizuka's play *36 Views* raises questions concerning the authenticity of cultural artifacts and identities. Pictured is the Huntington Theatre production of the play. Directed by Evan Yionoulis; scene design by Adam Stockhausen; costume design by Teresa Snider-Stein; lighting by Chris Parry; and sound by David Budries.

T. Charles Erickson

most important of the companies were the East-West Players, founded in Los Angeles in 1965 but now centered in New York; the Asian Exclusion Act, founded in Seattle in 1973 and later renamed the Northwest Asian American Theatre; the Asian American Theatre Workshop, founded in San Francisco in 1973; and the Pan Asian Repertory Theatre, founded in New York in 1977. Today, in addition to clusters of Asian American theatres on the East and West Coasts, several midwestern cities maintain Asian American performing arts groups. One of these is Theatre Mu, which blends Asian and Western artistic forms (both ancient and contemporary) to give voice to the experience of the Asian American culture and community.

Several Asian American playwrights have played an important role in the development of Asian American drama and theatre. Frank Chin was the first Asian American playwright to win wide recognition; his *Chickencoop Chinaman* satirized both self-stereotyping and media stereotyping, and his *The Year of the Dragon* was said in 1977 to be the first Asian American play ever produced in New York. Another prominent Asian American dramatist is Philip Kan Gotanda,

whose first play, *The Avocado Kid*, a rock musical, was presented by the East-West Players in 1979. He went on to write *A Song for a Nisei Fisherman, Bullet Headed Birds, The Wash, Day Standing on Its Head, Fish Head Soup, The Ballad of Yachiyo,* and *The Wind Cries Mary.*

The best-known Asian American dramatist is David Henry Hwang, who first came to prominence in 1980 with *F.O.B.* His subsequent plays include *The Dance and the Railroad, Family Devotions, Face Value, Bondage,* and *The Golden Child.* In addition, he has written several works in collaboration with Philip Glass. Still, Hwang's best-known work is *M. Butterfly* (1988), which focuses on race, gender, and politics and suggests that Westerners view "Orientals" (both individuals and nations) as submissively "feminine," willing to be dominated by the aggressive, "masculine" West. Hwang fuses this perception with a real-life story in which a French diplomat carried on a twenty-year relationship with a Beijing Opera performer of female roles (and a spy for the Chinese government) without recognizing that the performer was male.

Other prominent Asian American playwrights include Ping Chong, Elizabeth Wong,

M. *Butterfly* by Henry David Hwang. Directed by John Dexter; scene and costume design by Eiko Ishioka; lighting by Andy Phillips.

Naomi Iizuka, Han Ong, Rick Shiomi, and Rosanna Yamagiwa. Perhaps the most prolific of these in recent years has been Chay Yew. Yew currently serves as both the artistic director of the Asian American Theatre Workshop in Los Angeles and the Northwest Asian American Theatre in Seattle. His plays have been produced throughout America as well as in Malaysia, Singapore, and the United Kingdom. They include *A Winter People* (an adaptation of Chekhov's *The Cherry Orchard* set in 1935 mainland China during the last days of its Nationalist government), *Second Skin, The Long Season* (a musical love story about Filipino immigrants in Alaska, commissioned by the Perseverance Theatre), *Question 27, Question 28* (which treats the experience of Japanese American women detained in American internment camps during World War II), and *A Distant Shore.*

Native American Theatre

THERE HAVE BEEN few Native American theatre groups. The first all-Native American company, the Native American Theatre Ensemble, was founded by Hanay Geiogamah in 1972. With support from the La MaMa company in New York, it presented plays based on myths and contemporary life with the aim of building pride in the Native American heritage. Geiogamah's

plays include *Body Indian* and *49.* In recent years, Geiogamah (now a professor of literature and film and a member of the American Indian

The Denver Center Theatre's production of *Black Elk Speaks,* dramatized by Christopher Sergel based on the book by John G. Neihardt. Directed by Donovan Marley.

SOCIETY, ART,
AND CULTURE

Creating Theatre outside the Box

The theatre of today is more diverse than many people imagine. Individuals who, in another time, might not have been thought of as likely theatre makers are creating theatre that challenges their abilities and the preconceptions others may have about who can do theatre and the purpose of theatre in our society. In short, they are thinking and playing "outside the box."

The United States has dozens of theatre groups and festivals in which senior citizens actively participate. Some of these utilize a "reader's theatre" format, which requires only minimal movement and no memorization. Others perform fully staged musicals. Stagebridge is one of the nation's oldest senior theatres. Located in Oakland, California, it is dedicated to providing opportunities for older adults to use theatre as a way to bridge generations. Since its founding in 1978, Stagebridge has performed for over 250,000 people. Its company, which consists of over one hundred performers and volunteers (whose average age is seventy), performs short plays and workshops at other senior facilities and community centers as well as engages in intergenerational literacy programs with children. In addition to companies like Stagebridge, each year festivals of senior theatre are presented across the nation.

Scores of programs have been developed that provide performance opportunities for children and adults with physical and developmental impairments. For example, the "Dramatically Able" program, operated by the Wild Swan Theatre in Ann Arbor, Michigan, provides teachers with theatre games and performance activities to exercise verbal and nonverbal communication skills, increase awareness of oneself and others, and encourage creativity. The National Theatre Workshop of the Handicapped (NTWH) is a theatre arts training institute for adults with physical disabilities. It offers training in almost all aspects of theatre and brings together disabled and able-bodied actors and playwrights to collaborate on creative performance projects.

The National Theatre of the Deaf (NTD) is one of the oldest and the best known theatre groups involving individuals with a physical impairment. It produces professional-quality theatre that links American Sign Language to the spoken word in a diverse repertory of world drama. Since its inception in 1967, NTD has performed in all fifty states and on all seven continents. It received a Tony Award for theatre excellence in 1977, and in 1986 it was the first American theatre company to perform in the People's Republic of China.

Studies Center at UCLA) has transformed his company into the American Indian Dance Theatre, with nineteen members drawn from a dozen tribes. Among the company's most ambitious works is *Kotuwokan,* a dance-drama about a young Indian's attempt to find his way in the present-day world.

The American Indian Community House in New York has long served as a community center for Native Americans living in New York and has maintained a performing arts program that has sought to revive authentic Native American rituals and performance traditions. Spiderwoman Theatre, founded by three Native American sisters, was the first all-female Native American group in the United States. Another successful Native American company is Naa Kahidi [Clan House] Theater in Alaska, which has performed its adaptations of Tlingit myths at numerous theatre festivals in the United States and Europe. Other Native American performers include Vira and Hortensia Colorado, whose *Walks of Indian Women—Aztlan to Anahuac* traces the history of Native American women since pre-Columbian times. Recently, the plays of Native American playwright William S. Yellow Robe, Jr. have cast a critical eye on the problems facing contemporary Native Americans: the destructiveness of alcohol and chemical addiction, conflicts between traditional Native and popular cultures, problems associated with the rapid rise of casinos on Native American lands, and unemployment. His plays include *Sneaky, Better-n-Indins,* and *Grandfather of the Buffalo Soldiers.*

Theatre by and for Women

WOMEN, REPRESENTING as they do roughly one-half of the world's population, cannot on one level be considered a minority. Nevertheless, throughout the theatre's history they have been relegated to a minor position. Although written about in ancient Greece, for example,

National Theatre of the Deaf production of *Curiouser and Curiouser,* adapted by Larry Arrick from Lewis Carroll's *Through the Looking Glass.*

they did not themselves either write plays or act in them. In England they were not permitted to appear on the stage until 1661, and though prominent as actresses thereafter, seldom did they write plays or attain positions of power in the theatre until recently. In the twentieth century, women began to write plays more frequently, although even those sufficiently successful to have won Pulitzer Prizes (among them Susan Glaspell, Zoe Akins, and Mary Chase) have largely disappeared from memory. Only gradually since World War II have women come to be accepted as directors and heads of theatre companies.

Changes have come about primarily through concern for women's rights, which date back to at least the nineteenth century but were given new energy by the civil rights movement that accelerated in the 1960s. Many women have been concerned primarily with gaining equal rights within the existing system; others have perceived such a clear difference between men (characterized as competitive, aggressive, and violent) and women (seen as cooperative, nurturing, and pacifistic) that they have advocated replacing male with female values. Still others have seen themselves as members of an oppressed group within a white, male, Eurocentric society and have sought alliances with other groups who have been comparably marginalized because of such factors as ethnicity, economic class, or sexual preference. These differences have influenced plays written by women.

Beginning in the 1970s, a number of theatres were formed to present the work of feminist writers. Some of the most important of these have been The Looking Glass Theatre, New Georges, Six Figures Theatre Company, Voice and Vision, Woman Seeking . . . , Spiderwoman Native American Theatre, and the Women's Project and Productions, all in New York; Chrysalis Theatre in Northampton, Massachusetts; Perishable Theatre Women's Playwriting Festival in Providence, Rhode Island; Horizons Theatre in Arlington, Virginia; The Oh Sooo Politically Correct Players and The Theatre Conspiracy in Washington, D.C.; Red Hen Productions in Cleveland, Ohio; Footsteps Theatre Company in Chicago; Root Wym'n Theatre Company in Austin, Texas; Brava! For Women in the Arts and Women's Will in San Francisco; the Latina Theatre Lab in Oakland, California; and the Omaha Magic Theatre. Multiple national festivals of women's theatre have been held in the United States each year. Over the past few decades the number of theatres devoted to addressing the needs and concerns of women and to providing greater opportunities for women in the performing arts has grown considerably.

Many female playwrights have written almost exclusively for feminist theatres and have not sought a broader audience. Others have won recognition in mainstream theatres. Among the best known of the latter group are Marsha Norman, Beth Henley, and Wendy Wasserstein. Norman's first play, *Getting Out,* was voted the best new play by the American Theatre Critics Association in 1977. She is probably best known for *'night, Mother,* winner of the Pulitzer Prize in 1983, in which a woman, having lost all desire to live, matter-of-factly announces to her mother her plan to commit suicide and carries it out. Norman has gone on to write several plays as well as the book and lyrics for the Broadway musicals *The Secret Garden* (for which she won a Tony Award) and *The Red Shoes.* Most recently, she wrote the libretto for the Broadway musical version of *The Color Purple.*

Beth Henley gained early critical acclaim for her play *Crimes of the Heart,* winner of the Pulitzer Prize in 1981. The play, which focuses on the lives of three sisters, begins with the news that the youngest sister has shot her husband because, as she puts it, "I didn't like his looks." Henley later adapted the play into a film that starred Diane Keaton, Jessica Lange, and Sissy Spacek. Henley followed this success with several other plays about colorful characters in small southern towns. Her most recent plays include *Impossible Marriage* and *Family Week.*

Wendy Wasserstein (1950–2006) is best known for *The Heidi Chronicles,* winner of a Tony Award and the 1989 Pulitzer Prize. The action, which begins in the mid-1960s and ends in the late 1980s, traces changes in the political and personal life of the title character as she develops a feminist consciousness and eventually comes to feel that the feminist movement has failed to fulfill its promises. Wasserstein's other plays include *Uncommon Women and Others, The Sisters Rosensweig, An American Daughter, Isn't It Romantic, Old Money,* and *Third.*

Other contemporary female playwrights include Constance Congdon, Tina Howe, Lisa Loomer, Josephina Lopez, Theresa Rebeck, Sarah Ruhl, Naomi Wallace, and many others.

Among the best of contemporary playwrights is Paula Vogel. Her plays include *And Baby*

Makes Seven, The Oldest Profession, The Baltimore Waltz, and *The Mineola Twins.* Let us look at *How I Learned to Drive,* which won the Pulitzer Prize in 1997, as an example of Vogel's work and of a contemporary play by a woman.

How I Learned to Drive

*H*OW I LEARNED TO DRIVE uses learning how to handle an automobile as a metaphor for learning how to navigate one's way through life—from adolescence to maturity. The play's sections are given such headings as "Idling in the Neutral Gear," "You and the Reverse Gear," and "Driving in Today's World." Most of all it is an unusual and sensitive look at a young woman's experience with pedophilia as her Uncle Peck teaches her how to drive even as he is physically obsessed with her. It is difficult to dislike Uncle Peck because he is the only member of Li'l Bit's family who seems genuinely concerned about her happiness and strives to prepare her for the future.

How I Learned to Drive is not organized linearly. Rather it looks at various moments in the protagonist's life, moving easily back and forth from one time period to another as they become relevant to her feelings or anxieties. It ranges from the time when Li'l Bit is eleven until she is approximately 40 years of age. Memory or an association of ideas primarily triggers the shifts in time. Li'l Bit and Uncle Peck are the only complex characters. The others, of which there are many, are played by three actors designated as Male Greek Chorus, Female Greek Chorus, and Teenage Greek Chorus, who fill in wherever needed. The use of a small number of performers playing multiple supporting roles reduces the cast size needed to produce the play, but more importantly they focus our attention on the two main characters, they form the social context for various scenes, and their speeches introduce considerable explanatory and background information. It is through them that we find out much about the family life that surrounds Li'l Bit and Uncle Peck. The family members surrounding Li'l Bit are somewhat insensitive in the way they tease Li'l Bit about her body and in the way they talk to her about sex. The family is also somewhat insensitive in their treatment of Peck. Both more or less isolated within this family, Li'l Bit and Uncle Peck spend considerable time together and the family never seems to suspect that anything unusual is going on between them.

Vogel treats Peck somewhat sympathetically, but she also includes a past for the character that suggests his behavior is part of an ongoing pattern. Although Uncle Peck doesn't want to talk about why he left South Carolina, a scene with his young nephew seems to suggest that it had something to do with an embarrassing situation, perhaps involving pedophilia with a boy because

Courtesy of Actors Theatre of Louisville

How I Learned to Drive as produced by the Actors Theatre of Louisville, featuring Angela Reed as Li'l Bit and John McAdams as Peck. Directed by Leigh Silverman; scene design by Paul Owen; costume design by Lindsay W. Davis; lighting by Tony Penna.

Richard Feldman

How I Learned to Drive as produced by the American Repertory Theatre (Cambridge, Mass.), featuring Debra Winger as Li'l Bit and Arliss Howard as Peck. Directed by David Wheeler; scene design by J. Michael Griggs; costumes by Viola McKenthuen; lighting by John Ambrosone.

Li'l Bit tries to adjust herself to a life in which she cannot find a satisfying unity of body and mind. She and Uncle Peck are bound together forever but in a way that allows no resolution.

How I Learned to Drive requires very little scenery. Two chairs may be used to represent the car, the most important prop, and also to indicate a dining room at home or a restaurant and still other locations. The place of the action is the mind and memory. The play sweeps away most concrete details to focus on the thoughts, desires, and feelings of guilt in its central characters.

How I Learned to Drive is especially unusual in its depiction of a pedophile. It is hard to see Peck in the stereotyped role of a crafty, unloving criminal. Both Li'l Bit and Uncle Peck arouse sympathy. It is Vogel's ability to cut through stereotypes and show us the human side of frailty that marks most of her plays.

Gay and Lesbian Theatre

ALTHOUGH HOMOSEXUALITY has been an occasional topic in drama since the Greeks, it was the primary focus in few plays until recently. Matt Crowley's *The Boys in the Band* (1968), the first play on Broadway specifically about gay men, is often said to have marked a turning point in the acceptability of plays about homosexuality, although all of its characters were still treated as doomed or irrevocably unhappy. Following the Stonewall riots in 1969 (when a group of homosexuals, reacting to years of intimidation in New York, attacked police who were raiding a gay bar), advocates of "gay pride" encouraged greater openness in plays and productions about gay life.

One of the best-known exponents of gay theatre was Charles Ludlam (1943–1987), head of the Ridiculous Theatrical Company from 1967 until his death and author of several plays, among them *Bluebeard, Camille,* and *The Mystery of Irma Vep,* which parodied familiar literary genres and the absurdities of art and life. Ludlam acted in his own plays, often playing several

Uncle Peck invites him to a tree house but makes him swear that he will not tell anyone about it.

Both Li'l Bit and Uncle Peck are damaged people. They want and need love but there are too many warped experiences in their way. Uncle Peck was probably molested as a child and as much as he loves Li'l Bit, he can't let go of his compulsion to seek physical intimacy with her. And Li'l Bit falls into a pattern of behavior after she leaves home that indicates her need for love and sensitivity but that is ultimately self-destructive. It is Li'l Bit who finally finds the strength to separate herself completely from Uncle Peck, with the result that he drinks himself to death while roles, most of them female. Similarly, Harvey Fierstein won mainstream acceptance for his *Torch Song Trilogy* on Broadway in 1981 and for the book of the musical *La Cage aux Folles,* later made into a film.

Beginning in the 1980s, the AIDS crisis generated numerous gay plays, among the first of which were Larry Kramer's *The Normal Heart* and William Hoffman's *As Is,* both in 1985. Later AIDS plays include Cheryl West's *Before It Hits Home,* Terrence McNally's *Lips Together, Teeth Apart,* Paul Rudnick's *Jeffrey,* and Richard Greenberg's *Take Me Out.* Tony Kushner became the most praised American playwright of the 1990s for his *Angels in America: A Gay Fantasia on National Themes,* in two parts: *Millennium Approaches* and *Perestroika.* This epic play, which requires seven hours to perform, treats not only AIDS but also the crisis that faces America as concern for self overwhelms the needs of others, even loved ones. It nevertheless holds out the possibility of change (as suggested in the titles of the two parts). Few lesbian plays have made their way into the mainstream. Jane Chambers' *Last Summer at Bluefish Cove* and Holly Hughes' *The Well of Horniness* are among the best known lesbian plays.

In the 1970s gay theatre companies were formed in major cities throughout the United States. These theatres played an important role in promoting a sense of identity and addressing the concerns and interests of those within the gay, lesbian, and bisexual communities. In 1978, a Gay Theatre Alliance was formed to link gay theatre companies. As is the case with all theatre companies formed during this same time, some of the companies have since closed while others have remained in operation and new companies have formed. For example, New York's TOSOs (The Other Side of Silence), founded by Stonewall riot participant Doric Wilson in 1974, suspended operations after several years and then reopened in 2005 as TOSO II. The WOW (Women One World) Café in New York remains one of the oldest and most prominent theatres devoted to the concerns of women, particularly lesbians. Most

The final scene in Tony Kushner's *Angels in America: Millennium Approaches.* The Angel is played by Ellen McLaughlin; Prior Walter by Stephen Spinella. Directed by George C. Wolfe; scene design by Robin Wagner; costume design by Toni-Leslie James; lighting by Jules Fisher.

major American cities contain such theatres today. For example, the Rhinoceros remains an important producer of gay and lesbian theatre in San Francisco, and Act Out Productions sponsors the Columbus National Gay and Lesbian Theatre Festival in Ohio.

Epilogue

As this chapter indicates, the theatre has become diverse. Although productions seem increasingly unable to achieve universal appeal, each still may capture the attention and fill the needs of a specific group. Broadway's attempt to encompass all tastes often leaves no one satisfied. The strength of the theatre may have come to be its ability to focus and represent the interests of specific communities. Once each community has the opportunity to satisfy its own needs, it may discover the desirability of understanding others and come to recognize that major problems often stem not from the failure to understand one's own culture but rather from the failure to understand other cultures. Ultimately, the need for intercultural communication and understanding may exceed the need for unicultural theatre.

Additional Opportunities with InfoTrac College Edition

Using InfoTrac College Edition, find and read the article "So Many Stories to Tell" from *American Theatre,* which provides transcription from a panel discussion that followed the inaugural Latino Theatre Festival at the Goodman Theatre in Chicago.

1. What are the goals of the Goodman Theatre in offering this festival?

2. How do the panelists respond to the issue of multiple demographics being placed under the umbrella of "Latino"?

Building a Broad Context

First space shuttle flight by the U.S. (1981)

AIDS breaks out (1984); August Wilson writes *Ma Rainey's Black Bottom* (1984)

Milcha Sanchez-Scott writes *Roosters* (1987)

Chinese military cracks down on students and others holding pro-democracy rallies in Tiananmen Square (1989)

Fall of the Berlin Wall and crumbling of the Soviet Union (1990)

U.S. military forces lead multinational "Operation Desert Storm" against Iraq in response to Iraq's invasion of Kuwait (1991)

Bombing of the Federal Building in Oklahoma City kills 160 people in worst-ever act of domestic terrorism (1995)

Paula Vogel writes *How I Learned to Drive* (1997)

September 11 attack on the U.S. in which four domestic planes are hijacked; two are crashed into the World Trade Center in New York; one crashed into the Pentagon; one crashed into a field in Pennsylvania, as 3,025 people are killed (2001)

U.S. military defeats Taliban forces in Afghanistan accused of harboring Al-Qaeda terrorists (2001)

Major cities around the world experience terrorist bombings of transportation systems: Bali (2002), Madrid (2004), London (2005), and Mumbai (Bombay), India (2006)

U.S. leads multinational military force that topples Saddam Hussein's regime in Iraq, although no weapons of mass destruction (the justification for the action) were found (2003)

Tsunami strikes Indonesia (2004)

Hurricane Katrina ravages U.S. Gulf Coast states and inundates New Orleans (2005)

The Dogon, who have lived in the remote Bandiagara escarpment of Mali in West Africa since around A.D. 1400, perform elaborate funeral and fertility rituals wearing a wide variety of masks. Here, the two Dogon performers at left wear rabbit masks related to the mythical antelope Walu, a protector.

10:

Asian and African Theatre

The performance traditions we have examined so far have been confined primarily to European and American theatre. But the theatre varies widely from one culture to another as is readily apparent if we turn our attention to theatre in Asia, Africa, and other regions of the world. In this book it is not possible to look at all the variations. Consequently, we have chosen to consider some aspects of theatre in Asia and Africa. The examples must be limited, because the variations found on those two continents are numerous indeed.

Theatre in Japan

AT ABOUT THE TIME the religious cycles were flourishing in Europe, a very different kind of theatrical experience was being offered halfway round the world in Japan. There Noh theatre was perfected and codified so thoroughly that it is still performed today much as it was five hundred years ago. It came into being in isolation from Western theatre and represents a wholly distinct theatrical tradition.

To understand Noh theatre we need to look at the political and cultural context out of which it developed. During the sixth century A.D. the Buddhist religion arrived in Japan from India and China. With it came a written language and many non-native arts and crafts. In the seventh century an emperor gained power over Japan and took ownership of all land. For some four hundred years Japan flourished under this system, but by the twelfth century the emperor had lost most of his political power. In 1192 he ceded his secular authority to a *shogun* (military dictator), although he retained his status as a near-god in the religious realm. The shogunate became hereditary, although new families won possession of the title from time to time. Japan was ruled in this manner until 1867, when American intervention led to the downfall of the shogunate and the return of power to the emperor.

Under the shogunate, Japan developed a strict social hierarchy. The highest class was the *samurai* (warriors), with the shogun at their head. Below them were three other classes (each with subcategories): merchants; artists and craftsmen; and farmers and peasants. Each rank had a specified code of behavior and mode of dress. Japanese life became highly structured and formalized.

In 1338 the Ashikaga family gained control of the shogunate and retained it for the next two hundred fifty years. One of its goals was to eliminate foreign cultural influences and develop native art forms. Of the native forms, Noh enjoyed special favor.

Noh Theatre

THE MOST SIGNIFICANT developments in Noh theatre began around 1375. At this time, the shogun took the Noh performer and drama-

Courtesy of the National Museum of Tokyo

Noh theatre masks are traditionally made of wood, painted, and handed down for many generations. Whereas there are only five types of masks (aged, male, female, deities, and monsters), there are many variations within these types. Pictured is a mask for the female character in *The Shrine in the Fields*.

tist Kiyotsugu Kan'ami (1333–1384) and his son Zeami Motokiyo (1363–1444) under his patronage and granted them samurai status in his court. Working within this refined atmosphere, these two men gave Noh its characteristic form. Zeami, the greatest of Noh dramatists, wrote more than one hundred of the two hundred fifty plays that make up the active Noh repertory. He also defined Noh's goals and conventions. All the plays in the present Noh repertory were written more than four hundred years ago and are still performed much as they were when written. Noh is thus essentially a product of the fourteenth, fifteenth, and sixteenth centuries.

The major influence on Noh's view of the world was Zen Buddhism, which teaches that ultimate peace comes through union with all being, that individual desire must be overcome, and that nothing in earthly life is permanent. Noh plays typically have as protagonists ghosts, demons, or obsessed human beings whose souls cannot find rest because in life they were devoted to worldly honor, love, or other goals that keep drawing them back to the physical world and its imperfections.

Noh dramas are classified into five types, according to the principal character:

- God plays
- Warrior plays
- Women plays
- Madness plays
- Demon plays

Traditionally, a program is made up of one play from each type, performed in the order given here. These make up a pattern that shows, in the first play, the innocence and peace of the world of the gods; then, in the next three plays, the fall, repentance, and possibility of redemption for human beings; and finally, the glory of defeating the forces that stand in the way of peace and harmony.

Each Noh script is short (often shorter than a Western one-act play) and does not emphasize storytelling. The dialogue serves primarily to outline the circumstances that lead up to, and culminate in, a dance. Above all, Noh is a musical dance-drama that evokes an emotional state and mood. Most of the lines (written partly in verse and partly in prose) are sung or intoned. Even the brief spoken passages are recited in a stylized manner. Ordinary speech is used only when a player comes on stage between the parts of a two-part piece to summarize the first part.

The performers can be divided into three groups: actors, chorus, and musicians. The actors are trained from childhood and expect to devote twenty or more years to perfecting their craft. The five hereditary schools of Noh performance have handed down their traditions and conventions since the fifteenth century. There are two divisions of actors: those who play the secondary character, the *waki,* and the *waki's* followers (whose function is to introduce the drama and lead the main character toward the climactic moment), and those who play the *shite,* the main character, and his or her followers. Two other types of actors also appear in Noh: *kyogen*—actors whose primary skill is in performing the short comic plays that are presented on the same bill with Noh plays but who appear in Noh in the role of commoners, peasants, and narrators—and *kokata,* child actors who, as students, play children or minor roles.

The chorus is composed of from six to ten members (each play specifies the number to be used in that play). They sit at one side of the stage throughout and sing or recite many of the *shite's* lines (especially while the *shite* is dancing) or narrate events. Each play requires two or three drummers and one flute player. No other instruments are ever used. The drummers, in addition to playing their instruments, punctuate the performance with a variety of vocal sounds. There are two stage attendants, whom the audience is supposed to ignore: one to assist the musicians, the other to assist the actors in changing or adjusting costumes or masks and to bring on or remove stage properties as needed. All of the performers and assistants are male.

Courtesy of Kokusai Bunka Shinkokai

Masked performer of the Noh theatre accompanied by musicians.

The *shite* and his companions wear masks of painted wood, many of them passed down for generations. Costumes are rich in color and design, based on the official dress of the fourteenth and fifteenth centuries. Most garments are made of elaborately embroidered silk. Each character has its traditional costume, headdress, hand properties, and positions on stage. The chorus, musicians, and attendants wear stiff shoulder boards and divided skirts, the traditional dress of the samurai.

The Noh stage, standardized for almost four hundred years, is raised about three feet. The two principal areas, the stage proper (*butai*) and bridge (*hashigakari*) are both roofed like the shrines from which they are descended. The roof of the *butai* is supported by four columns, each with its own name and use. By the upstage-right pillar (*shitebashira,* or principal character's pillar), the actor pauses upon entering to tell the character's name and background. While reciting this speech, the actor faces the downstage-right pillar (*metsukabashira,* or gazing pillar). The downstage-left pillar (*wakibashira*) marks the place where the *waki* sits when not directly involved in the action. The upstage-left pillar (*fuebashira,* or flute pillar) marks the flute player's position.

The stage is divided into three areas, although none is separated architecturally except by the pillars (see photo below). The largest area, the main stage, is enclosed by the four pillars and is about eighteen feet square. Back of the upstage pillars is the rear stage (*atoza*), where the musicians and attendants sit. To stage left of the main stage is the *waki-za,* where the chorus kneels on the floor in two rows.

There are two entrances to the stage. The principal one, the bridge, is a railed gangway about six feet wide and forty feet long leading from the mirror room, where the actors prepare for their entrances. In front of the bridge three live pine trees symbolize heaven, earth, and humanity. The bridge is used as an entrance for the musicians and for all important characters. The other entrance, the "slit" or "cut-through" door (only about three feet high and located upstage left), is used by the chorus and the stage assistants. The rear walls of the stage and bridge are made of wood. Painted on the wall behind the orchestra is a pine tree and on the stage-left wall is bamboo, reminders of the natural scenery that formed the background in the earliest years of Noh. There is no other scenery in the Noh theatre. A few stage properties are used, usually miniature skeletal outlines of boats, huts, shrines, and the like, typically made of bamboo. These are set in place and removed as needed by the stage attendant.

The audience views the performance from two sides: in front of the main stage, and facing the stage from alongside the bridge. The theatres used today hold three hundred to five hundred people. Although they are now indoor structures, they retain many outdoor features: the shrinelike roof of the stage is retained in its entirety under the ceiling of the auditorium, and lighting simulates the even distribution of outdoor light.

A Noh stage. At left, the bridge; at center rear, the pine tree painted on the back wall and bamboo on the side wall; at right rear, the *waki-za* (the area used by the chorus). The four upright pillars define the principal acting area. Notice the temple roof above the stage.

Courtesy of Kokusai Bunka Shinkokai

Every element of performance is strictly controlled by conventions that have been established for centuries. Rather than encouraging innovation, Noh seeks to perfect and preserve an art form. Let us look more closely at a Noh play, *The Shrine in the Fields.*

The Shrine in the Fields (Nonomiya)

THE SHRINE IN THE FIELDS (*Nonomiya*) is usually attributed to Zeami. It belongs to the third category (woman play) and is based on episodes from one of the most famous of Japanese novels, *The Tale of Genji*. In the novel, Lord Genji is the lover of Lady Rokujo, but after a time neglects her. During a festival, attendants on Lord Genji's wife publicly humiliate Lady Rokujo when they push her carriage out of the procession and disable it. Humiliated, she decides to leave the capital and go to Nonomiya, where her daughter is being prepared to become the priestess of Ise, the sun goddess. In Nonomiya, Lady Rokujo is called Miyasudokoro. While at Nonomiya, Lady Rokujo is visited by Lord Genji, who brings her a branch of *sakaki* (a sacred evergreen tree) as a sign of his trustworthiness, and begs her to return with him. Although she does not, she is forever after tormented by her humiliation and sense of loss. Lord Genji's visit and Lady Rokujo's response to it are the emotional focus of *The Shrine in the Fields.*

Each Noh play is set in a specific season of the year, named early in the drama, and the mood and imagery of the entire play must be in keeping with that season. In *The Shrine in the Fields* the time is late autumn, the seventh day of the ninth month, the day on which Lord Genji visited Lady Rokujo at Nonomiya. The mood throughout is one of melancholy and bittersweet longing.

As is typical in Noh drama, the introductory scene compresses time and place: an itinerant priest (the *waki* or secondary character) travels—almost instantaneously—from the capital to Nonomiya, where his curiosity is aroused by the seemingly perfect preservation of the shrine although it has long been abandoned. When the ghost of Miyasudokoro (the *shite*) appears in the guise of a village girl, he questions her about the shrine and herself, and gradually it becomes apparent that there is something mysterious about both her and the place. The first portion of the play occurs at dusk, and when the moon (a symbol of Buddha) appears, she vanishes and then returns dressed as the Miyasudokoro of long ago, having changed both mask and costume. As she recalls the festival at which she was publicly disgraced, her emotion builds, and she prays that the attachments that forever draw her back to this place will leave her.

As in all Noh plays, the climactic moment is expressed in dance. The script does little to indicate the length of the dance, which continues in performance for twenty or more minutes. In this final portion of the play, the conflicting attractions of this world and the next are symbolized by

Courtesy of Weatherhill Inc., Tokyo

shrine gate

straw hut   retreat   grave mound   large board hut

well curb with *susuki*   plum tree stand   carriage

From Kunio Komparu, *The Noh Theatre: Principles and Perspectives.*

passing back and forth through the gate of the shrine. At the end, the freeing of her soul is indicated by her departure from the "burning house," a metaphor for the world. In Buddhist teaching, enlightened people are counseled to leave the world as willingly as they would flee a burning building.

In Noh, a number of devices distance the spectator. The language is stylized throughout; most of the passages are intoned or sung; the lines of dialogue are divided in ways that differ markedly from the practices typical of Western drama, so that a single thought may be divided between the *shite* and *waki* or between a character and the chorus; the *shite* sometimes speaks of himself or herself in the third person; and the chorus frequently speaks the lines of both the *waki* and the *shite*. In addition, numerous quotations from or allusions to earlier literary works are embedded in the text.

For *The Shrine in the Fields* the basic appearance of the stage is altered only by the addition of a stylized gate and brushwood fence, and the only property of any significance is the sprig of *sakaki* that Miyasudokoro places at the shrine gate (as Lord Genji had done long ago). During the performance the chorus (seated at stage left) and the musicians and stage attendants (seated at the rear) are visible throughout, becoming part of the visual picture.

The Shrine in the Fields does not seek to tell a story or to develop character so much as to capture a mood, to distill a powerful emotion and to express an attitude about the physical world and human existence.

▋ Other Japanese Theatre Forms

JAPAN DEVELOPED TWO other traditional theatre forms: doll theatre (now usually called *Bunraku*) and Kabuki. The doll theatre, in which the characters are represented by large puppets, came to prominence in the seventeenth century. The puppets went through many changes. Originally,

they were only heads with drapery representing the body: later, hands and feet, and then movable eyes, movable eyebrows, and jointed and movable fingers, were added. Eventually the puppets were doubled in size to their present height of three or four feet and elaborately costumed.

Each puppet is operated by three handlers, all visible to the audience. One handler manipulates the head and right arm, a second the left arm, and the third the feet. A narrator, seated stage left on a platform with the musicians, tells the story, speaks the dialogue, and expresses the feelings of each puppet. He is accompanied by a *samisen* (a three-stringed instrument with a skin-covered base that can be both struck and plucked) and other instruments of lesser importance. The stage itself is long and narrow. Unlike Noh, Bunraku represents all locales scenically, and the scenery is changed as the action requires. Bunraku is probably the most complex puppet performance in the world.

The major writer of plays for doll theatre was Chikamatsu Monzaemon (1653–1724), Japan's greatest playwright. He wrote many kinds of plays but is best known for his five-act history plays and his three-act plays on contemporary life. He was admired above all for his plays about the double suicides of lovers, his sensitive characterizations, and beautiful language.

Kabuki, long the most popular of the traditional forms, also first appeared in the seventeenth century. More open to change than the other forms, it has borrowed many of its plays and conventions from Noh and Bunraku but has adapted them to its own needs. Originally, Kabuki was performed on a stage resembling that used for Noh. But as time passed, it underwent many changes and today bears little resemblance to the Noh stage. The Kabuki stage (especially at the National Theatre in Tokyo) is now framed by a proscenium opening about ninety feet wide but only about twenty feet high. The auditorium is correspondingly wide and shallow, with all seats facing the stage. A raised gangway (the *hanamichi)* connects the stage to the back of the auditorium. Most important entrances and exits are made

Courtesy of Kokusai Bunka Shinkokai

A doll (puppet) theatre performance. Puppets and their handlers are in the foreground. In the background are the musicians and narrators. Notice the painted scenery at left and overhead.

along this gangway, and some major scenes are played there. Thus much of the action occurs in the auditorium in the midst of the audience.

Unlike Noh, Kabuki uses a great deal of scenery, although the settings are not meant to be fully illusionistic. White floor mats are used to represent snow, blue mats to indicate water, and gray mats, the ground. Relatively realistic buildings are depicted frequently, but the entry gates to houses are often removed by stage assistants when no longer needed. These and other conventions constantly call attention to the fictional nature of the performance. Alterations to sets, changes of props, and adjustments to costumes are made in full view of the audience by stage attendants (Japanese stage conventions treat these stage attendants as invisible).

Most Kabuki plays are divided into several acts made up of loosely connected episodes that emphasize highly emotional incidents. The climactic moment in many scenes is reached in a highly stylized pose struck and held (the *mie*) by the principal character. Actors in heroic or villainous roles are offered numerous opportunities to demonstrate their skill through these *mies,* which are greatly admired by Japanese audiences. The most popular of all Kabuki plays is Takedo Izumo's *Chushingura* (1748), the eleven acts of which require a full day to perform. A play about honor and revenge, it tells how forty-seven faithful samurai avenge the wrongs done to their master.

Song and narration are important to Kabuki. Those plays adapted from Noh or Bunraku retain many conventions of the original forms. Therefore, in some plays a narrator or chorus performs some passages. Because the Kabuki actor never sings, passages that must be sung require a chorus. Much of Kabuki action is accompanied by an orchestra, the composition of which varies according to the origin of the play. It often includes flutes, drums, bells, gongs, cymbals, and strings, although the most essential instrument is the samisen.

Kabuki acting is a combination of stylized speaking and dancing. Almost all movement

Female Roles
in Kabuki

For more than three hundred fifty years, the female roles in Kabuki have been played by men. Originally (in the years between 1603 and 1629) Kabuki was performed primarily by women. Perhaps because the performances were erotic, they came to be thought of as encouraging prostitution, and the shogun forbade Women's Kabuki. It was replaced in 1629 by Young Men's Kabuki, but the boys apparently were as seductive as the women, and in 1652, they, too, were forbidden to perform. Men's Kabuki, which has continued to the present, was then authorized, but the performers were required to shave the forward part of the head and avoid emphasis on physical charms. Since that time, some performers have specialized in playing female (*onnagata*) roles, and many Japanese commentaries on Kabuki argue that these male performers capture the essence of femininity far more effectively than any woman ever could. (Feminists argue that the *onnagata* is a male fantasy.)

From a book of advice to actors dating from the early eighteenth century, *The Words of Ayame,* comes this passage about the *onnagata:*

> The *onnagata* role has its basis in charm, and even one who has innate beauty if he seeks to make a fine show in a fighting scene, will lose the femininity of his performance. . . . [I]f he does not live his normal life as if he were a woman, it will not be possible for him to be called a skillful *onnagata.*

borders on dance, distilling the essence of emotions and action into stylized postures, gestures, and movements. Similarly, the spoken lines follow conventionalized patterns of intonation. Roles are divided into a small number of types: loyal, good, and courageous mature men; villains; young men; comic roles (including comic villains); children; and women. All types are played by males, and all require many years of training. Most leading actors come from a few families for whom acting is a hereditary profession. Each family has an elaborate system of stage names, some of them so honored that they are awarded (in elaborate public ceremonies) to those considered undisputed masters of their art.

Kabuki actors do not wear masks, but some roles use boldly patterned makeup to exaggerate the musculature of face or body. Each role also has its traditional costumes, some so heavy (up to fifty pounds) that stage attendants must assist the actors in keeping them properly arranged.

Although Kabuki is highly conventionalized, it includes many elements that resemble, though in exaggerated form, Western usages, perhaps most notably in scenery and lighting, melodramatic stories, and emotional acting. Consequently, Kabuki is the Japanese form that appeals most to Westerners, and in recent years many European and American directors have borrowed Kabuki conventions for productions of

Greek and Shakespearean tragedies (perhaps most notably the Théâtre du Soleil in Paris). Westerners usually understand Japanese conventions only in a general way, and much of what they find attractive they have learned from the Kabuki-derived conventions used in Japanese films about samurai, especially those of Akira Kurosawa. Of all the Japanese forms, Noh remains the least understood in the West.

Japanese Interest in Western Drama and Theatre

BY THE LATE nineteenth century, some Japanese scholars, directors, and playwrights became interested in Western drama. It was probably

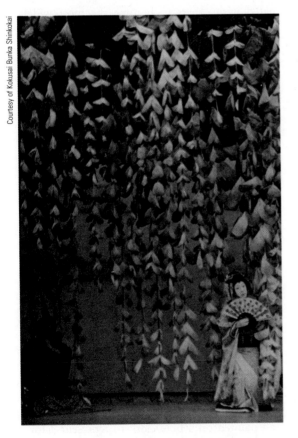

Courtesy of Kokusai Bunka Shinkokai

Unlike Noh, Kabuki uses a great deal of colorful scenery. However, Kabuki scenery decorates the stage rather than conceals it. Here long strings of flower petals are used as a decorative background that suggests the scene's locale.

most admired and studied in Japanese universities, where plays by Shakespeare, Ibsen, Shaw, Chekhov, Strindberg, and others were studied and sometimes performed. Japan's best-known playwrights who were influenced by Western forms include Kobo Abe (1924–1993) and Yukio Mishimi (1925–1970). Writing plays of the Western type has flourished since around 1980, and the Japan Playwrights Association has published several volumes of plays in the Western style in the past ten years. Some contemporary playwrights include Juro Kara, Minoru Betsuyaku, and Masakazu Yamazaki.

Among contemporary Japanese directors, the best known is Tadashi Suzuki, who established his own company, the Suzuki Company of Toga. There he developed a disciplined acting method that synthesized martial arts, Kabuki, and Noh techniques. He staged several productions that were seen in the United States and Europe, some of them adaptations of Greek myths. Many American theatre departments have begun to offer training in the Suzuki method, described in his *The Way of Acting*. In 1993, in collaboration with the American director Anne Bogart, he established the Saratoga (N.Y.) International Theatre Institute (SITI). Yukio Ninagawa, another internationally famous Japanese director, has done many productions of Western and Japanese plays. He has received several international awards in Japan and abroad (including an honorary doctorate from Edinburgh University).

In the past twenty years Japan has built more than two dozen performance halls. Within Japan, contemporary entertainment forms are more popular than the traditional ones, but Japan is determined to support and maintain its dramatic heritage.

Theatre in China

RECORDS OF PERORMANCE in Chinese territories can be traced back to 1767 B.C. After 1000 B.C. there are references to secular entertainments at court, and by 200 B.C. emperors were keeping thousands of entertainers at court who performed what was called the "hundred plays" because of the great diversity of the entertainments. One Chinese emperor established a school to train performers and, according to legend, at one time it included 11,409 students. However, a fully developed drama did not begin to emerge until about A.D. 1000. The first major period of Chinese drama came during the Yuan Dynasty (1279–1368), and about seven hundred titles of Yuan plays have survived. The most complex literary plays were written during the Ming Dynasty (1368–1644). Plays from this period might have as many as fifty or more acts, each with its own title. In the opening act, a secondary character sets forth the author's purpose and explains the story. Succeeding acts introduce many plot strands, all of which are happily resolved in the final scene. Probably the most admired play from the Ming Dynasty is *The Peony Pavilion* (c. 1600), written by Tang Xiansu (1550–1616). In fifty-five acts, it tells a story of a girl who pines her life away for a lover she has seen only in a dream. When he finally appears at her grave, she is resurrected. This play was presented in its entirety (for the first time anywhere) at Lincoln Center in New York in 1999. Although such plays were very popular with readers, they did little to vitalize the theatre. It was not until the nineteenth century that what has come to be called Beijing Opera emerged as a dominant and truly theatrical form. Beijing Opera is a hybrid that evolved from several regional forms brought to Beijing in 1790 to celebrate the emperor's eightieth birthday. Many of the companies remained in Beijing and amalgamated with others to become the most widely known Chinese theatrical form. It is a theatrical rather than a literary form. Instead of a single work, an evening's performance is usually made up of a series of selections from longer works. These are intermingled with acrobatic displays. A text is merely an outline for a performance, and the author is not even listed on the program. All the plays end happily, and each troupe has its own version of the plays they perform.

The traditional Chinese stage was an open platform, usually almost square, covered by a roof supported by lacquered columns. The stage was equipped only with a carpet and two doors in the rear wall (the one on stage right for all entrances and that on stage left for all exits) between which hung a large embroidered curtain. In the beginning, the theatre was based on the layout of teahouses, but in the twentieth century Western-style auditoriums became the standard. The only permanent properties were a wooden table and a few chairs that could be rearranged quickly to indicate a change in place or function. Other conventions include using a wall painted on a blue cloth to represent a fort, city gate, or mountain pass; a whip to indicate that the actor is riding a horse; and many others that are recognized immediately by the audience.

Tan Kian Khoon/Shutterstock, Inc.

Chinese Opera performers wear elaborate costumes and makeup as shown here.

Through such conventions, many places and actions are indicated. Throughout the performance, assistants help the actors with their costumes and rearrange the stage as needed. The audience is expected to ignore these stagehands. The musicians also remain in full view and play a strong role in all performances.

On the relatively bare stage, the actors appear in lavish and colorful costumes and speak, sing, and move according to rigid conventions. In Beijing Opera, the roles are divided into four main types: male, female, painted face, and comic. The male roles (*sheng*) are subdivided into old men (*lao sheng*), young men (*xiao sheng*), and warrior types (*wu sheng*). Actors playing these roles wear simple makeup and (except for young heroes), beards. Female roles (*dan*) are subdivided into quiet and gentle (*qing yi*), vivacious or dissolute (*hua dan*), warrior maidens (*wu dan*), and old women (*lao dan*). The painted face actors (*jing*) have brilliant and elaborate patterns painted on their faces. They include warriors, bandits, courtiers, officials, gods, and other supernatural beings. The comic actors (*chou*) speak an everyday dialect and are free to improvise and tell jokes. They wear white makeup around their eyes and combine the skills of a mime and an acrobat. Except for the clowns, characters render their lines in an extremely stylized manner.

Movement is also highly stylized, and gestures have been fully codified. Methods of walking or running vary with each role. There are about three hundred standard costume items, each intended to describe its wearer's character type, age, and social status through color, design, ornament, and accessories. The complex conventions of Beijing Opera require long and rigorous training that lasts from six to twelve years. Eventually training becomes very specialized as teachers decide which kind of role the student should master.

During the twentieth century, Western drama came to be admired by many in China, but it never became a major force. The most important of the playwrights who were influenced by Western writers was Cao Yu (1910–1996), who wrote about contemporary social problems in *Thunderstorm* (1933) and *The Bridge* (1945).

After the Communists assumed control in China in 1949, Beijing Opera was subjected to reform and many plays were forbidden. Not until the 1980s and the rejection of the "Cultural Revolution" were traditional plays performed once more, but in many instances they were revised to fit the Communist ideal. A number of Chinese playwrights have achieved recognition within China since 1949. Some of the most prominent are Wu Han, Zong Fuxian, Lao

Getty Images

The new Grand Theatre in Shanghai, a $150 million structure of glass and steel, is second only to Beijing's newly built National Theatre complex (a $360 million performance facility).

She, and Sun Huizhu. Two directors have been especially successful in directing spoken drama: Ming Jinghui and Lin Zhaohua.

China has also begun to build major theatrical complexes similar to those in the West. The new Grand Theatre in Shanghai cost about $150 million and includes a main auditorium seating eighteen hundred people and two smaller halls (seating six hundred and two hundred). It is one of Asia's most advanced theatrical structures. In the large auditorium, the main stage, rear stage, and two side stages can be rotated, raised or lowered; its orchestra pit accommodates one hundred twenty instrumentalists. Other Chinese cities, among them Shenzen and Nanking, have built complex opera houses. The new National Theatre Complex in Beijing cost about $360 million. The egg-shaped building, which is 430 feet long and 135 feet high, includes an opera house, a concert hall, and two theatres. It will be interesting to see how these new buildings will affect theatrical production in China.

■ Other Asian Countries

THERE ARE MANY other countries in Asia, each with its own performance traditions, but Japan and China are the best known for their theatrical forms. In India a wide variety of entertainments can be traced back at least two thousand years, and between the first and ninth centuries A.D. drama written in Sanskrit reached an advanced stage before it declined. A number of plays have survived from that period and are available for study. Under British rule from the eighteenth to the twentieth century, India produced diverse types of plays too numerous to trace in detail. The number of languages that are still common in India makes for varied dramatic forms, each of which tends to be popular in specific parts of India.

Other parts of Southeast Asia are noted especially for their work with puppets. For several centuries much of Southeast Asia has been dominated by Muslim standards, which discourages drama being performed by human actors. But where live human performance has been frowned on, performance using puppets has been more easily accepted. Puppetry has flourished in many parts of Southeast Asia, and shadow puppetry has been particularly popular in Indonesia.

■ *Wayang Kulit*

INDONESIAN SHADOW PUPPETRY uses flat puppets, ranging from six inches to three feet in size, made of leather (traditionally from the hide of water buffalo). The puppets are cut and perforated to create intricate patterns of light and shadow when their images are cast onto the screen. *Wayang Kulit* (leather puppets) enacts dramas based on particular sections of the great Hindu epics the *Mahabharata* and the *Ramayana*. In most places this form of theatre maintains a spiritual aspect, and the puppeteer, called a *dalang*, is not only a performance artist but also a spiritual figure. The *dalang* sits between a light source (traditionally a torch or hanging oil lamp) and the screen. The closer the *dalang* moves the puppet toward the screen, the more clearly the shadow of its outline appears. The entire performance is accompanied by a *gamelan*, a gong-chime musical ensemble composed of different types of xylophones, percussion and stringed instruments, flute, and singers.

All the puppets used during a single performance (usually no more than fifty) are manipulated by a single *dalang* who delivers the dialogue (much of it improvised) and narrative passages, sings songs, and inflectionally cues the musicians. It requires great vocal flexibility to suggest so many different characters in a single performance and a strong command of the story and all its characters. In some traditional performances, the *dalang* holds a small wooden striker between his toes and calls forth the character's spirit into the puppet by knocking on the box or stand holding the puppets. This procedure is sometimes referred to as "waking" the

Courtesy of George Burnette

Pictured are two puppets used in *Wayang Kulit* performances. The more intricately perforated puppet is the god Vishnu. Note the differences between this puppet and the other, which represents an earthy comic figure.

puppets and it may last several seconds or several minutes. Characters are differentiated by the size, shape, costume, and color of the puppets as well as by the quantity and arrangement of their perforations. In performance, the puppets seem to flicker into corporeal existence as the *dalang* brings them into the action.

Traditional *Wayang Kulit* performances last from around 8:30 P.M. until sunrise. The different parts of the action relate to the passing hours. First, a problem or situation is established followed by an intrigue, usually in the stronghold of the hero's enemies. Then, the hero appears, accompanied by clownish servants (this phase of the action usually takes place around midnight). The action reaches its crisis in a battle fought by the hero against powerful enemies. Finally, the conflict is resolved and ends in the triumph of the hero over the forces of evil (as the dawn overcomes the night).

Because Asia's cultural sensibility honors tradition, Asian theatre forms have proven less susceptible to change over time than those in America and Europe. However, there remains considerable diversity in Asian theatrical forms.

■ Theatre in Africa

ANOTHER REGION WHERE THEATRE has received too little attention is Africa. Europeans and Americans remained largely ignorant of African performance traditions until the twentieth century. Nevertheless, African performance activities had through the centuries been numerous—religious rituals, festivals, ceremonies, storytelling, and various kinds of celebrations—and had been woven into daily life. These varied widely from one part of Africa to another. When Europeans took control of most of the continent, they brought their own ideas about theatre and tried to establish them there. The presence of the colonialist heritage and indigenous forms created a wide spectrum of performance in Africa. Nevertheless, it is difficult to generalize about theatre in Africa in part because there are more than eight hundred local languages in use, and many local traditions do not always travel well from one part of Africa to another.

During the late nineteenth century, European countries, acting on agreements reached in international conferences, divided up most of

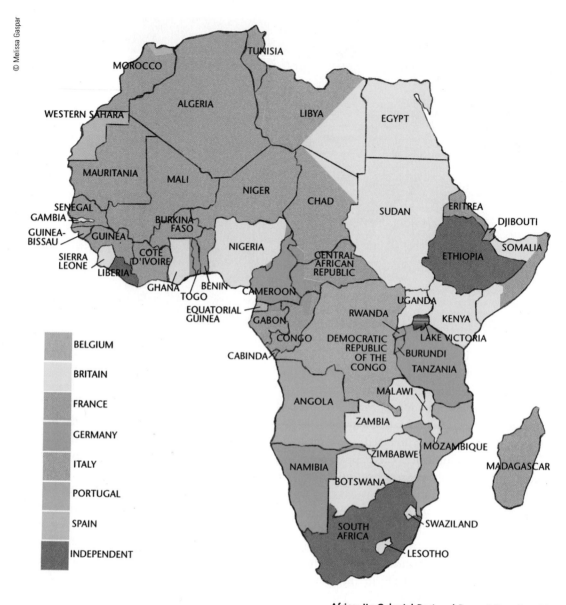

© Melissa Gaspar

Africa: Its Colonial Past and Present-Day Countries
Color areas illustrate European colonization and control of Africa up to 1914 (see color key provided). Names of current African nations and their borders are designated in black. Most African countries did not gain independence until the 1960s, and the lingering effects of European colonization continue to affect Africa to the present day.

Africa among themselves and thereafter sought to impose their languages, governmental forms, and ideas about effective theatre practices on the territories they controlled. Nevertheless, indigenous forms and performance conditions persisted alongside the many European forms that were imported. Because little was recorded about the native traditions prior to the twentieth century, Westerners' knowledge of African theatre has remained limited.

European observers tended to emphasize the linguistic elements of indigenous performances, even though those aspects were often the least important. "Languages" other than words, espe-

SOCIETY, ART,
AND CULTURE

Africa in Four Questions

Test your knowledge of Africa in four quick questions—the answers are included below.

1. How big is Africa?
2. How many people live in Africa?
3. What percentage of Africa's population are dependent on agriculture for their living?
4. What is the most common cause of death in Africa today?

1. Africa contains over 20 percent of the world's land mass: 11,700,000 square miles (roughly three times the size of the United States).
2. More than 900 million people live on the African continent, or about 14 percent of the world's population. More than 70 percent of Africa's population is under the age of twenty-five.
3. Approximately 65 percent of Africa's population makes their living from agriculture; 50 percent of all Africans live on less than $1 a day.
4. AIDS; AIDS has hit hardest in sub-Saharan Africa, where the average life expectancy is 46, compared to 67 in North Africa.

cially drumming and dance, often communicated more to African audiences than words did. To these languages can be added visual imagery, symbolism, gesture, mask, and costume. African performances had traditionally occurred in spatial arrangements quite different from those of European theatres, but the Europeans usually sought to impose the proscenium-arch stage on African performances. In traditional African performances, direct audience participation was usually expected. It was accepted that the dancing, music, and song would induce such communal responses as clapping in rhythm, singing refrains, repeating phrases, or making comments. Dancing and music were important elements in most indigenous performances.

It would be impossible to treat theatrical performance in every country on the African continent, because there are close to fifty separate states. Those in North Africa are dominated by Arab languages and customs; those south of the Sahara are highly diverse. In addition to indigenous languages, much of today's theatre in Africa uses English, French, or Portuguese, depending upon which European country occupied and imposed its demands on the native populations. Most countries still have been unable to rid themselves of their colonial past, though many attempt to do so.

■ Performance in Nigeria

IN LOOKING AT CONTEMPORARY conditions, we have chosen to begin with Nigeria, the most populous African country, as well as one diverse in language groups and performance conditions. It includes more than two hundred fifty different ethnic groups, of which the most important are the Hausa, Yoruba, Ibo, and Fulani. Because public performance was important as a medium of expression and communication, some kind of

Aspects of the colonial past sometimes appear in contemporary African drama and theatre. Here, in *Guest of Honor,* the associations between the past and present form a political statement as the Head Waiter (Alex Muluku) welcomes the audience to his Africa.

"Woyigira" Mujama (the "Dirty Man" Reformed) as performed by Uganda's Katanga Theatre Group, Kampala, Uganda.

performance has gone on throughout the country and throughout the year. One of the major Yoruba festivals was the *egungen,* in which sacrifices were offered and petitions for blessing and prosperity were addressed to the dead. A "carrier" was selected to gather up the accumulated evil of the community and carry it away in a canoe. Some aspects of this ceremony are still common in Nigeria.

The most popular contemporary theatrical form in Nigeria is Yoruba opera (now usually called Yoruba Traveling Theatre). It was developed primarily by Hubert Ogunde, who in 1946 established a professional company (the first in modern Nigeria) with which he toured thereafter. The form consisted of an opening *glee* (or rousing musical number), followed by a topical and satirical story with dialogue, songs, and dances, ending with another *glee.* The emphasis was on entertainment, but there was always a clear moral message. Ogunde created some thirty-eight different operas. His company was tremendously popular and imitated. By 1981 there were some one hundred twenty Yoruba companies. Since then, they have increasingly turned to television, films, and videos, so much so that live performances have greatly declined. (The Yoruba Traveling Theatre is very similar to the Concert Parties in its neighboring country, Ghana.)

English-language plays also became common from around 1900, and drama was introduced into the schools founded by the English colonial

In What Language Should We Write?

O ne of the most controversial questions in Africa today concerns the language in which plays should be written or performed. Because so many tribal languages are spoken by the various groups within each country, the language of the former colonial power (most commonly English or French) is the only one shared (though not always fully understood) by all the groups. Consequently, much of the drama is written in European rather than African languages. One powerful movement insists that native languages should always be used if Africa is ever to escape its colonial past.

The moment you write in English you assume a readership who can speak and read English, and in this case it can only mean the educated African elite or the foreigners who speak the language. This means that you are precluding in terms of class the peasantry, or the workers in Africa who do not read or understand these foreign languages.

—*Ngugi wa Thiong'o, Interview in "Mother, Sing for Me," by Ingrid Bjorkman*
(London, 1989), 3.

government or by religious organizations that were seeking to convert Nigerians to Christianity. English-language theatre flourished, especially after 1960, when Nigeria was granted independence. Some of the country's major playwrights include John Pepper Clark, Ola Rotimi (1938–2000), and Femi Osofisan. But the dominant playwright has been Wole Soyinka, especially since 1986 when he became the first African to be awarded the Nobel Prize for Literature. This has not kept him from being punished by a government that has imprisoned him and threatened him with death for his opposition to certain government policies. He largely gave up writing plays after 1994 to devote his time to human rights activities. Among his plays are *A Dance of the Forests, The Lion and the Jewel,*

Death and the King's Horseman, and *Madmen and Specialists.* Let us look at one of his plays, *The Strong Breed.*

The Strong Breed

T HE STAGING CONVENTIONS used in *The Strong Breed* are much the same as those found in European and American theatres. Consequently, there are few uses that seem strange to an American reader. The difference from European and American drama lies primarily in the subject matter and its treatment, which strongly reflects the *egungen* traditions, but placed in a modern context. The dramatic conventions of the play are largely those found in European and American drama. In *The Strong Breed*, the dramatic action focuses on a ritual that can be traced all the way back to the Greeks—the selection and expulsion of a scapegoat who will take all the problems of the village on himself and carry them away. Eman, a new resident of the village, makes the mistake of thinking that the ritual is observed here as it was in his own community, where a carrier willingly allows the troubles and cares of the village to be loaded onto a symbolic vessel and placed on his head so he can carry it down the river and thereby cleanse the community, making way for happiness and prosperity in the new year. This ritual is of primary importance to the residents of this village, and most of the play is devoted to making certain that a carrier can be found to take the village's troubles before a new year begins. In the village Eman has left, the carrier was honored for his strength, courage, and wisdom, but in the village to which Eman has recently come, the carrier himself becomes the object of loathing and is driven from the village permanently. Consequently, only outsiders are chosen as carriers; they are drugged and hypnotized so they appear happy to receive the beatings, curses, and other forms of abuse heaped upon them.

It is never made clear why Sunma, who seems to be in love with Eman, does not tell him

of the difference in customs here, not even when a girl dragging an effigy appears and lures him into the bush where he can be captured and prepared for the ritual. Eman is so unsuspecting that he even gives the girl one of his garments to put on her effigy. In the action that follows, through a series of flashbacks, we learn that Eman is a descendant of a long line of carriers (the strong breed) and that he has left his own village because he has been devastated when his wife died in childbirth. As in Greek tragedy, Eman finds that he cannot escape his destiny—to be a carrier. Beginning to understand the situation in which he has placed himself, he tries to escape from the villagers, but they become increasingly desperate as midnight approaches and they have no one to carry away the year's burdens. In their panic, the villagers kill Eman, but when they realize what they have done, most are filled with shame. They begin to doubt the traditions they have been taught and turn away from their leaders. Change seems to lie ahead, though it comes too late for Eman.

The Strong Breed develops a number of themes common in Soyinka's plays: the habit of following custom and mistaken beliefs unquestioningly, and the special individual who through dedication and vision awakens the people and leads

Wole Soyinka has written more than a dozen plays that continue to be performed around the world. One common theme in many of his plays is that of ritual. In *Death and the King's Horseman*, pictured here in a performance by the Syracuse Stage (N.Y.), the Elesin (chief minister to the dead king) fails to perform his expected act of ritual suicide, thus jeopardizing the delicate and mysterious balance between the dead, the living, and the unborn.

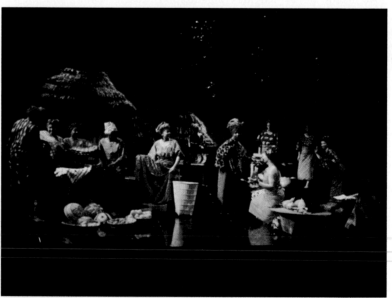

Douglas Wonders

them toward better ways, even though he may become a victim of the society he seeks to benefit. Soyinka may also be suggesting that one cannot escape tradition and therefore must come to grips with it. Soyinka's plays form a bridge between traditional and contemporary performance.

South Africa

THE AFRICAN COUNTRY with which Americans are most familiar is South Africa. The indigenous peoples there are Khoisans, Zulus, Basutos, Xhosas, Swazi Ndebeles, Pondos, and other smaller groups (several of which are often grouped together as Bantus). Europeans began to covet South Africa during the seventeenth century. Around 1650 the Netherlands began to encourage Dutch immigrants to settle there. By 1815 the English also began to gain control over much of the territory, and thereafter there was a struggle between the Dutch, the English, and native groups. The discovery of diamonds in 1867 and gold in 1886 led to the Boer Wars, which by 1902 the English had decisively won. By the 1880s, most of the native peoples were confined to territories not unlike the reservations the U. S. government set aside for Native Americans. The English and Afrikaaners (mostly descendants of northwestern Europeans) eventually joined in 1910 to form the Union of South Africa. The government drew increasing international criticism after 1950, when it established the doctrine of apartheid (the Afrikaans word for "apartness"), a law requiring separate white and nonwhite residential areas. As a result, South Africa essentially became a police state for blacks, wherein much of the black population was moved into townships, best described as shantytowns. They could work in cities but could not live there. Not until 1990 did the government agree to start dismantling apartheid, and in 1994, the country's first democratic elections led to Nelson Mandela, a black lawyer, becoming president. The process of democratizing South Africa still continues.

During apartheid, several groups in South Africa wrote and produced plays that attacked the injustices of apartheid laws and the ways in which various groups were unjustly treated. Perhaps the most influential playwright and performer to come out of Afrikaans theatre is Pieter-Dirk Uys. In addition to his plays, he also performed as a satirical drag character, Evita Bezuidenhout, who highlighted the ridiculousness of apartheid. Other Afrikaaner playwrights included Bartho Smit (1924–1986) and Adam Small. Several black African writers and performers attained popularity during apartheid: Gibson Kente (1932–2004), Mbogeni Ngema, Maishe Maponya, and Matsemala Manaka, all of whom have become very popular in South Africa and in several other countries. The most famous South African dramatist is Athol Fugard. Fugard has been writing about South African issues since 1959. His play *Master Harold and the Boys*

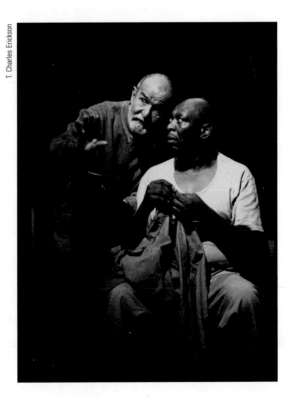

T. Charles Erickson

Athol Fugard in his play *The Captain's Tiger,* which he also directed.

SOCIETY, ART,
AND CULTURE

Theatre of the Struggle

In 1976 the Market Theatre began performing plays in what had formerly been Johannesburg's Indian fruit market. Today they are known throughout the world as South Africa's "Theatre of the Struggle." The struggle was against South Africa's apartheid government and its racist policies. But the Market Theatre has also been criticized at home as well as being celebrated abroad.

Although there were other theatres using their stages to produce anti-apartheid plays, the Market Theatre was one of the first to circumvent a 1965 law that forbade racially mixed casts and audiences. When the Market Theatre drew the attention of South Africa's security police, its producers reminded police of an obscure law: Buildings open to all races prior to segregation were allowed to remain so as long as their exterior had not been altered. Because the fruit market had been open to all and the exterior of its 1912 building had never been altered, it was allowed to remain desegregated. At a time when South African blacks and whites could not live on the same street and socialization with one another was frowned on, the Market Theatre staged Shakespeare's *Othello* with an interracial cast. Still, black artists risked arrest whenever they broke governmentally mandated curfews (for blacks) to attend rehearsals or performances. Among the plays premiered at the Market Theatre was *Bopha* (the Zulu word for "arrest"), in which a black policeman charged with upholding the apartheid laws must deal with his activist son, and *Woza Albert,* which dramatizes how Jesus might respond if he returned to apartheid South Africa and how the government might respond to him.

Since the end of apartheid, the Market Theatre has become a sprawling center for the arts. This has revived old criticisms leveled at the theatre by some South Africans. The Market Theatre's location in the center of urban Johannesburg separated it from the townships, and its close relationship to the Johannesburg City Council seemed to some as if the theatre was collaborating with the very forces those on its stages were decrying. The Market Theatre has been awarded considerable financial assistance to develop its facilities, while all-black theatres with fewer resources have had to fend for themselves. However, few deny that the theatre played an important role in the struggle against apartheid. In 2006 the Market Theatre celebrated its thirty-year anniversary by remounting its 1984 production of Barnie Simon's *Black Dog,* a gripping and controversial anti-apartheid play.

dramatizes how the once-close relationship between Harold, the son of a tearoom's owner, and the establishment's black head waiter is destroyed by the racial arrogance and privilege taught to Harold. Some of Fugard's other plays include *Boesman and Lena; My Children, My*

Africa; Road to Mecca; and *Sorrows and Rejoicings* (which evaluates post-apartheid South Africa). The film version of Fugard's novel *Tsoti,* which treats the relationship between poverty and gang activity in the former townships, recently won the Academy Award for best foreign film.

The abolishment of apartheid left South Africa with many challenges, among them the role of the arts in a culture that had long been split along racial lines. Apartheid had established a duality of culture; European theatrical traditions mainly practiced in state-supported institutions within white urban areas, and indigenous and highly political theatre practiced in rural areas and the townships. Although the post-apartheid government developed policies to transform its former cultural institutions on a national level, many claim that the agencies responsible for implementing these policies lack sufficient funding, experience, and political will to do so. Matters came to a head when, in 2004, the Minister of Arts and Culture dissolved the board of the National Arts Council (NAC)—the head agency overseeing the transformation process. For its part, the NAC has claimed that some of the nine regional provinces have failed to establish funding mechanisms envisioned in the national arts policy. Critic Robert Greig recently summed up the problem: "Is the National Arts Council propping up provinces that can't get their act together and fund artists who live there? Or, by contrast, is it funding rich, urbanized provinces to the detriment of artists everywhere?" Although the South African government has built centers for the arts in cities such as Johannesburg, some claim that these state-funded theatres support a conservative approach to the arts, offer only token support for indigenous performance, and fail to support innovative works that grapple with the economic, social, and political challenges most South Africans face.

Still, the role of theatre as a powerful force to unite the divisions in South Africa's culture seems undeniable. This potential is evinced in the Grahamstown Festival, an annual showcase of the best theatre productions from all over the country, where approximately five hundred theatre events are seen annually.

North Africa

As we have seen, ancient Egyptian rituals were among the earliest performance modes that we know about. Subsequently the areas across North Africa bordering onto the Mediterranean became well known for theatrical entertainments in the Hellenistic and Roman eras. Then in the seventh and eighth centuries all of North Africa was overrun by Muslims; gradually Arabic became the accepted language and Islam the official religion. Because these cultures disliked theatrical performance, it is of little importance here. Not until the nineteenth century (when Egypt was under English domination) did theatrical companies begin to appear, and after 1870 European-style productions began to be available. Singing and dancing were the most important elements, and all roles were played by men.

Tawfig al-Hakim (1898–1931), who wrote some eighty plays, was among the most important Egyptian dramatists of the early twentieth century. His *Sleepers in the Cave* was the opening production of the Egyptian National Theatre in 1935. In the late 1960s, the popularity of theatre gradually was replaced by film and television, of which Egypt is the primary supplier to the Arabic world. Since 1990, Egypt has promoted the annual Cairo International Festival of Experimental Theatre.

Other North African countries (among them Morocco, Algeria, and Tunisia) came under the domination of France and French theatre, especially in the 1960s. Morocco and Tunisia regained independence in 1956; both have since founded national theatres, and their playwrights have for the most part tried to create an Arab form of drama. None of these North African theatres has gained a strong reputation.

A good deal of indigenous African dance-theatre has close ties to the performance of rituals. These Dogon stilt dancers, resting before they execute their intricate dance high atop stilts, are wearing masks and dress in imitation of the long-legged tinetange bird. Their dance is part of their Dama ceremony, which is held to accompany the dead into the ancestral realm and restore order to the universe.

Courtesy of Getty Images

Other African Countries

OTHER AFRICAN COUNTRIES with extensively developed performance traditions include Ghana, Tanzania, Uganda, Kenya, Togo, Sudan, Ethiopia, Sierra Leone, Senegal, Mali, and the Ivory Coast. Unfortunately we can not discuss each of these in depth. African theatre is still handicapped by its colonialist heritage. Rather than judging it by European and American practices, it would probably be best to admire its broad range of theatrical activities, most of which, considering the enormous number of ethnic and linguistic divisions within Africa, understandably appeal to limited and local but often enthusiastic audiences.

Epilogue

IN PART TWO, we have looked at several varieties of theatrical experience. Although those we have examined are important, they do not exhaust the possibilities. Several others from the theatre's long past might justifiably have been selected for study. The theatre is always in flux. It seems likely that the versions with which we are now familiar will change as conditions alter. We can only speculate about what these alterations will be, although we can be sure they will come. Changes are not always welcome, but they are necessary, because theatre can remain vital only by reflecting the dynamics of the culture within which it exists.

Additional Opportunities with InfoTrac College Edition

Using InfoTrac College Edition, find and read Anita Ratnam's "India's Special K" in *American Theatre*, which discusses two forms of Indian theatre from the state of Kerala—*kathakali* and *kutiyattam*.

1. Why isn't *kutiyattam* as well known as *kathakali* outside India?

2. In what ways are *kutiyattam* and *kathakali* different? In what ways are they similar?

3. How have globalization and other economic developments affected India's traditional forms of dance-drama?

PART 3

Theatrical Production

I N PARTS ONE AND TWO, we discussed how theatrical conventions and practices vary widely from one period to another and from one culture to another. So far, we have looked at the theatre from theoretical and historical points of view in an attempt to understand the nature of theatre and varieties of theatrical experience. We will now examine how the theatre functions today.

What follows is an overview of the purposes, principles, materials, and working methods of each of the theatre arts—the varied processes involved in the creation of a production. The primary focus is on typical procedures, although important variations are noted. Topics explored include types of theatrical spaces and how they influence production, collaborative production design, and the work of playwrights, dramaturgs, producers, directors, actors, and designers (scenery, costume, lighting, and sound). Taken together, these topics provide an overview of theatrical production today.

The arrangement of the actor audience relationship influences how the audience perceives the action. Pictured here is a variation of a thrust stage arrangement with the audience on two opposing sides for a production of Shakespeare's *Romeo and Juliet* at the American Repertory Theatre. The illustration on page 288 shows how this stage configuration is used as a part of the overall production design. Directed by Gadi Roll; scene design by Riccardo Hernandez; costume design by Kasia Maimone; lighting by D.M. Wood.

Theatrical Space and Production Design

11

Because the essence of theatre lies in the interaction of performers and audience assembled in the same place at the same time, the physical space in which a performance occurs is a crucial element in the theatrical experience. Like other elements, the theatrical space can be organized in several ways, each with its own potential and limitations.

The Influence of Theatrical Space

THREE BASIC CHARACTERISTICS of any theatrical space influence both audience response and the way in which production elements are used:

- Its degree of formality
- Its size
- Its configuration or arrangement of the actor–audience relationship

The degree of formality that a theatrical space possesses influences audience expectations and their responses. An elaborate theatre building with carpeted lobbies and auditorium, fixed comfortable seating, and complex equipment creates a different set of expectations than does a theatrical space improvised in a warehouse, where the audience sits on the floor, wooden platforms, or folding chairs, and in which the equipment is minimal. The former suggests refinement, permanence (including continuity with the past), and extensive resources; it may arouse expectations of elaborate design, skilled acting, and polished productions. The latter suggests roughness, temporariness (perhaps a deliberate break with tradition), and limited resources; it may arouse expectations of experimentation and the need for imagination to supply what can only be suggested. The audience may also assume that the degree of formality suggests that certain types of responses are more appropriate than others and thereby affects the way in which they respond to staged events. Adult audiences may be less likely to scream and shout in an ornate and elaborately decorated theatre than in a warehouse theatre or an outdoor theatre with informal seating arrangements.

The size of the theatrical space exerts an influence. Very large spaces make it difficult for all members of the audience to see and hear all that the performers are doing or saying. Therefore small details are likely to go unnoticed, and stage business may need to be simplified or enlarged for the audience to see it. Very large performance spaces often seem to encourage increased emphasis on spectacle, and sound may require amplification. More intimate spaces permit greater subtlety in the use of voice, gesture, and facial expression, as well as the effective use of greater detail in costumes and properties. Intimate spaces generally are now preferred over large ones, in part because the close-ups and sound tracks used in television and film have conditioned audiences to expect to see and hear everything clearly. The influence of size (overall scale) on the total theatrical experience accounts for many of the differences among theatres of the past and present. A Greek theatre holding fifteen thousand people demanded performance conventions quite different from those used in today's theatres intended for a few hundred.

Finally, the arrangement or configuration of theatrical space is an important influence. Not only does it define the physical relationship of the performer to the audience, but also it determines how production elements can be used.

There are four common physical arrangements of the actor-audience relationship:

■ **Proscenium-Arch Stage**
The acting area is placed at one end of the space with all of the spectators facing it.
■ **Thrust Stage**
The acting area is surrounded on two or three sides by the audience.
■ **Arena Stage**
The acting area is completely surrounded by the audience on all sides.
■ **Flexible Space**
The relationship of acting and audience areas is variable and flexible.

Overall, then, theatrical space creates an environment that influences the theatrical experience. Let us look more closely at the four basic configurations or arrangements of the actor-audience relationship and their influences.

Four arrangements of theatrical space: proscenium, thrust, arena, and flexible. Flexible space, as the name implies, can take many forms: the audience and performers can remain separated or be intermingled; the configuration can also change during the course of a performance.

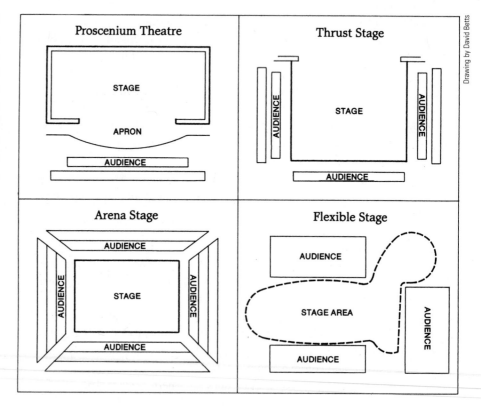

Drawing by David Betts

The Proscenium-Arch Stage

PROBABLY THE MOST familiar type of theatre is still that with a raised stage framed by a proscenium arch, although other types have become increasingly common. The proscenium arch clearly marks the division between stage and auditorium, although some part of the acting platform may extend forward of the proscenium (this extension is called the *apron* or *forestage*). In the auditorium, all of the seats may be on the same level (though usually with the floor raked upward toward the rear to improve the view of the stage), or there may be one or more balconies. In the proscenium theatre, the stage is designed to be seen from the front only. This affects the director's grouping of actors to create stage images and the means used to achieve emphasis and subordination. It also affects the actors' bodily positions, movement, gestures, and use of voice and speech. Because the stage action is oriented in one direction, the designer frequently uses the back and sides of the stage for the scenery, entrances, and exits. The scenery may be as tall as the designer wishes and the space allows, and it may consist of few or many units. The only fundamental restriction is that the audience's view not be obstructed. The lighting designer needs to be concerned with giving three-dimensionality to actors and objects as perceived from the auditorium.

The proscenium stage is usually equipped with a curtain that may be used to conceal or reveal the playing space (although today this curtain is infrequently used). The stage ordinarily has an overhead system of ropes, pulleys, and battens that permit drapes or scenic pieces to be hoisted into the space above the stage or lowered to stage level (typically called a *fly system* because offstage operators "fly" drapes or scenery in or out of the audience's view as framed by the proscenium-arch opening). Usually there is offstage space on either side (called *wings*) to permit the shifting and storing of scenery. There

also may be other specialized machinery for shifting scenery:

- Hydraulic or pneumatic lifts
- Elevators (allowing portions of the stage and its scenery to be lowered or raised)
- Turntables or revolves (allowing portions of the stage to be revolved)

However, such complex machinery is not commonplace because of its cost.

In the proscenium theatre, the action and scenery are usually farther from the audience than in other types of theatres. There may be an orchestra pit or forestage between the first row of seats and the acting area. Because scenery and costumes typically are not viewed at close range, they may be less precisely detailed than in other types of theatres. Likewise, because it is typically seen from only one side, scenery used within the proscenium-arch stage may require only its front side to be completed.

The Thrust Stage

IN A THEATRE with a thrust stage, the seats are usually arranged around three (or occasionally two) sides of a raised platform. The thrust stage brings the audience and performers into a more intimate performer-audience relationship than does the proscenium theatre, because more of the audience is closer to the action than is possible in a proscenium theatre of the same size. The thrust stage also normally lends a more three-dimensional quality to the acting area than does the proscenium stage. However, because the action is viewed from three sides, the director, actors, and designers need to consider how the action will be perceived from three directions simultaneously rather than, as in the proscenium theatre, only one.

The thrust stage discourages realistic spectacle of the type made possible by the picture-frame stage. Tall scenery must be kept to the rear of the platform so as not to interfere with sightlines.

The thrust stage of the Guthrie Theatre (designed by director Tyrone Guthrie, designer Tanya Moiseiwitch, and architect Ralph Rapson) has long been considered one of the finest in the country. Although it could accommodate as many as 1,441, no spectator was more than fifty-two feet from the center of the stage. In 2006 the Guthrie moved to a new home in Minneapolis containing an adapted version of this stage as well as a seven-hundred-seat proscenium theatre and a two-hundred-seat flexible-seating "black box" theatre.

Robert Ashley Wilson; courtesy of the Guthrie Theatre

Although some thrust stages are backed by an area equipped with flying facilities like those of a proscenium stage, extensive use of scenic effects there divides audience attention between the action on the main stage and scenic or lighting effects on a rear stage. Most thrust theatres make no provision for flying scenery, drops, or curtains above the main platform, although lighting instruments are usually mounted in recesses in the ceiling or on a grid above the stage. Generally, furniture, properties, and scenery are shifted by hand on a thrust stage. Some furniture or properties may be mounted on wheeled platforms and moved on and off the stage from the rear of the platform. A few thrust stages have some portions mounted on hydraulic lifts, and there may be several traps in the stage floor.

The Arena Stage

Instead of a raised platform stage, the typical arena theatre has simply an open space left at floor level in the middle of the auditorium. In some arena theatres, the floor of the performance area can be raised or lowered in segments to provide variety in levels or to differentiate locales. The seating is usually a stepped arrangement on four sides of the acting area. In some theatres of this type, the seats are not permanently installed, and the arrangement may be varied at will, but in others comfortable armchair seating of the kind typical of proscenium theatres is used.

Because the arena stage provides a three-dimensional playing area, the director, actors, and designers must be concerned with expressiveness from every angle. In an arena stage, the costumed actors, lighting, furniture, and properties usually play a more significant role in characterizing mood, time, and place than does the scenery because these aspects do not obscure the audience's view. The scene designer may use a few open structures, such as trellises and pavilions through which the audience can see, but ordinarily the scene designer depends more on furniture, properties, and treatment of the stage floor. Provision is seldom made for flying scenery, although a few architectural fragments may be suspended overhead. Occasionally, multileveled settings are used, but they must be constructed so that the audience can clearly see the

An arena stage provides considerable intimacy, as shown here in a production of Shakespeare's *The Taming of the Shrew* at the Arena Stage, Washington, D.C.

George de Vincent, courtesy of the Arena Stage

action on all levels. Screens for projections are sometimes hung at various spots over the acting area, over the audience, or around the walls (the same image may be projected on different screens simultaneously so that all members of the audience can see it), but usually the scene designer must suggest locale, period, mood, and style with a few touches.

Because there is no curtain, all changes are made either in full view of the audience or in semidarkness. Shifting is usually done by hand. Many arena theatres have passageways (vomitoria) running under the seating and opening onto the acting area. These serve as exits and entrances for actors and as means of getting scenic units or properties on and off the stage. Most arena stages are relatively small and intimate. However, because spectators view the production elements from multiple angles, this stage configuration makes special demands on the director's staging and on the production's design to visually communicate from every angle.

Flexible Space

IN A FLEXIBLE STAGE space the relationship of performer to audience is flexible and variable—an arrangement that may change from one production to another or even during the

same performance; in such an arrangement, spectators and actors may be intermingled in multiple playing and seating areas, or the place of performance may shift, as when scenes are played at various sites along a procession route (as in medieval theatre or in some contemporary street theatre), or there may even be a different audience for each scene or at each site, although the configuration of the theatrical space may not have changed.

The intermingling of performers and audiences has occurred primarily since the 1960s. This arrangement usually requires an open space without fixed seating or stage. Many regional and university theatres have such a space, usually in addition to a proscenium or thrust stage. Often referred to as a "black box" (because it is basically a bare room with black walls), it is most frequently used for productions with limited or special appeal—nontraditional works or performance modes, new or untested plays, and low-budget or student productions.

A flexible space may be indoor or outdoor, small or large. The areas used by the performers or by the audience may be varied from one production to the next or even during the course of a single performance. In this type of arrangement, different scenes are sometimes performed at various places within the space simultaneously. Although most theatrical performances seek to have all members of the audience see and

Theatre Architecture

I n *The Shapes of Our Theatres,* Jo Mielziner writes: "All theatre interiors consist of two essential areas: one is 'the auditorium,' which is designed specifically for the audience; the other, designed for the production, we know as 'the stage.'. . . Independently they have no life; together they produce a living theatre. It is therefore the sensitive interrelationship of the two that makes a theatre design either a success or a failure."

In the twentieth century, however, many people have objected to the dichotomy between auditorium and stage and have sought means to bridge them. Laszlo Moholy-Nagy writes: "Stage and spectator are too much separated, too obviously divided into active and passive, to be able to produce creative relationships and reciprocal tensions. It is time to produce a kind of stage activity that will no longer permit the audience to be silent spectators." He suggested building auditoriums with "suspended bridges and drawbridges running horizontally, diagonally, and vertically"; segments of the stage capable of moving toward the spectators to create effects similar to those of close-ups in film; runways that extend completely around the seating area; and other devices that place the spectator in a dynamic relationship with the action.

Marvin Carlson concludes in his *Places of Performance* that, as a result of twentieth-century experiments with theatrical space, "Never before in history has a public had available for its consideration" so many diverse "physical spaces in which theatre today may be presented. . . . In addition to this huge selection of historical spaces, the twentieth century has produced experimental directors who have explored the possibilities of an almost infinite variety of nontraditional spaces:" streets, parks, woodlands, factories, warehouses, and "all manner of public and private buildings."

hear the same things at the same time, those performances using the intermingled arrangement often enlist multiple focus. Some spectators may be watching one scene while others are watching another, or spectators may be able to choose which scenes they will watch, moving about in the space in order to see the scene that has attracted their attention. Sometimes spectators participate in the action and performers may ask them to move or to assist with some task. In other instances, the distinctions between performers and spectators remain clear, and the space each group occupies remains distinct; in still others, performers and spectators share a single, common space. The key is flexibility in the use of all theatrical elements.

Beginning in the 1960s, there was a movement to reject theatre buildings altogether. Some argued that, like museums and concert halls, theatres discourage all except a cultural elite. These innovators sought instead to take performances into parks, streets, and other places where theatrically unsophisticated spectators might discover the theatre. Instead of a building, they advocated the use of "found" space, either adapting a production to fit existing areas or altering existing areas to fit the needs of the production. The variety of audience-performer configurations was great, but all could be reduced to one or some combination of the four basic types of theatrical space. Experimentation with performance spaces reminds us that theatre does not require a permanent structure built especially for it and that all spatial arrangements are merely ways of facilitating the interaction of performers and audiences.

Auxiliary Spaces

IN ADDITION TO THE PERFORMANCE space, theatre buildings usually have a number of auxiliary spaces. Several of these are intended to serve the audience—lobby, restrooms, corridors, exits, and refreshment stands. Others are spaces for theatrical personnel, such as box office and other work space. The amount and type of work space provided in theatres varies widely.

Many theatres, especially those on Broadway, as well as many of those used by low-budget companies, do not include a full range of facilities for the construction of scenery and costumes, nor do they contain storage for equipment or properties not currently in use. Broadway productions are rehearsed elsewhere, costumes and scenery are built in studios far removed from the theatre, and backstage space is often minimally equipped. Broadway theatres host productions rather than serve as the permanent home of a company. Many small companies, such as Off-Off-Broadway groups, even if they are permanent, often function in very limited facilities. Regional and university theatres usually have more extensive facilities.

Courtesy of Jan Mabry, Cornerstone Theatre

Flexible space used in the staging of *Everyman at the Mall*, an adaptation by Shishiri Kurup and Bill Rauch of the medieval play *Everyman*. Here, Kindred and Cousin converse with Everyman while traveling down an up escalator at an actual shopping mall where the play was performed.

Using the Theatrical Space

NORMALLY, IN PLANNING a production little is done to shape the audience and its space. Most directors assume that the audience space of the theatre in which they will be working is fixed—as is the case in the majority of theatres. Although directors must take into account the auditorium's size, shape, sightlines, and

PRACTICES
AND STYLES

Theatre Facilities and Auxiliary Spaces

A well-designed, self-contained theatre (one with facilities for preparing productions as well as performing them) will include all or most of the following:

■ **Scene shop:** A space for the construction, assembly, and painting of scenery as well as storage for equipment, materials, and finished scenery when not in current use.

■ **Property room or shop:** A space for the storage of furniture and bulky props. Large theatres may also have a specialized space for the construction, modification, or repair of stage properties.

■ **Costume shop:** A space for the construction and alteration of costumes as well as facilities for their laundry, dyeing, cleaning, and pressing.

■ **Costume storage:** A space to store costumes or costume pieces so that they may be altered or modified for future use.

■ **Light shop:** A work space for lighting personnel.

■ **Lighting storage:** A storage space for lighting accessories, spare parts, equipment, and instruments.

■ **Control booth(s):** A space for lighting and sound control-board operators during the performances. Ideally, control booths have a full view of the stage and a monitor system so that booth personnel may see and hear the performance as well as communicate with offstage personnel.

■ **Rehearsal room(s):** A room or rooms with space approximating that of each stage space the theatre operates.

■ **Dressing rooms:** Rooms with appropriately lighted mirrors for the application of makeup, restrooms, and showers for the performers and crew.

■ **Greenroom:** A space for the performers to relax before or between scenes and for performers and crew members to assemble to receive instructions or notes.

■ **Business offices:** A box office for taking ticket requests, dispensing tickets, and securing funds; and additional office space for personnel such as dramaturgs, business managers, and artistic directors.

acoustical properties, and the physical relationship it creates between audience and performers, most tend to view these factors as given and unchangeable circumstances. However, some theatrical spaces are designed so that their overall arrangement and audience-actor relationship can be easily altered. In these instances, directors may shape the audience space to suit their production.

Jerzy Grotowski, director of the Polish Laboratory Theatre, made audiences an integral part of his production design. For each production, he had a specific number of spectators in mind (never more than one hundred), and he would permit no more than that number to attend. He also sought to induce the audience to participate in the action unselfconsciously. In his production of *Doctor Faustus,* Grotowski organized the space like a banqueting hall. The audience, treated as friends invited to share Faustus's last meal before the Devil claims his soul (to whom he has sold it many years earlier), sat at the tables, while the action took place on, under, and around the tables. The German director Peter Stein staged several productions in film studios or gutted and rearranged theatre spaces. In his production of *As You Like It,* the court scenes took place in one studio. However, for the Forest of Arden scenes, the audience had to pass through a tunnel to reach another studio in which bleacher-style seating had been erected along the sides. Scenic units, among them a large, live beech tree, a small field of wheat, and a pond filled with water, provided various locations for the action. The Living Theatre often encouraged the audience and actors to use the same space indiscriminately, thereby forcing some spectators to become unwilling participants in the action.

But these are atypical approaches. Directors may try to predict what the makeup of the audience will be and how it is likely to respond, but for the most part they conceive of the audience members as reactors who come to see a production created for them. Normally, the director lets others (through publicity, news releases, and

Grotowski's arrangement of the space for *Doctor Faustus.* The dark figures represent performers, the lighter figures spectators. Faustus is seated at the smaller table at top.

other means) attract as large an audience as possible to the space being used for the production.

Collaborative Production Design

ALTHOUGH THE THEATRICAL space greatly influences the performance and the audience's response to it, the director, actors, and designers select and shape aural and visual signs (within the performance space) to arouse a set of desired audience responses. But the possibilities—in terms of the way one shapes these signs, how skillfully one coordinates them, and how spectators respond to this shaping—are so numerous that the results can seldom be fully controlled. Nevertheless, each production has an overall design—a collaborative assemblage of its many parts.

The audience typically perceives a production's overall design through only two of their senses: hearing and seeing. Sound designers use sound effects and music to convey mood, enhance dramatic tension, and suggest various associations to the audience. Scene, costume,

Fabric runners and chandeliers were added to the basic stage space for the American Repertory Theatre production of *Romeo and Juliet* to designate lanes of performance space and characterize the play's party scene where Romeo meets Juliet. Directed by Gadi Roll; scene design by Riccardo Hernandez; costume design by Kasia Maimone; lighting by D.M. Wood.

T. Charles Erickson

and lighting designers address their work to the audience's sense of seeing. However, it is important to remember that directors and actors also make use of visual and aural aspects. The performers' vocal delivery of the dialogue (inflectional patterns, volume, rhythm and rate) shapes information about character relationships, motivations, emotions, and overall meaning. Likewise, the director's composition of the actors on stage (how much space they use and how they relate to each other as well as to the stage settings, costumes, and properties) may communicate messages quite apart from or in conjunction with the spoken dialogue.

The elements and principles of design form the primary means that the various theatre artists use to create meanings they hope the audience will perceive. The visual design elements—line, shape, space, color, texture, and ornamentation—serve as basic building blocks from which scene, costume, and lighting designers construct various images or patterns. Designers may use these basic elements in very different ways

depending on the meaning they wish to communicate and the response they wish to elicit. The basic principles of design—harmony, balance, variety, proportion, rhythm, and emphasis—help designers use the visual elements effectively. Theoretically, how audiences respond depends on how these aspects of design have been shaped. Study and practice is needed to wield these elements and principles in creative and meaningful ways. Although in such a general discussion they may seem abstract, they are manifested concretely during every moment of a performance.

One of the major challenges of production design arises from the need to coordinate individually conceived parts (in acting, directing, scenery, costumes, lighting, and sound) to create a whole capable of eliciting desired responses and interpretations. Preparing a theatrical production involves the combined efforts of many artists. A common interpretation or goal is usually required for individual artists to coordinate their efforts on various aspects of the production into a cohesive experience for the audience. This process

Julie Taymor
and Coordinated Production Design

Julie Taymor has achieved an enviable reputation for her coordinated production designs. The *New York Times* critic Mel Gussow writes of her production of *Juan Darién*, "The play draws its power from the symbiosis of design, movement and music, melding diverse performance art forms and transforming the stage into a living theatrical organism."

Taymor's ability to coordinate successfully the various aspects of production design may be credited to a number of factors. She has training in movement, highly developed skills in the visual arts, and considerable experience in conceiving and developing new theatre pieces. Taymor began her formal training in 1969 at L'École de Mime Jacques LeCoq in Paris, which emphasizes the physicalization of character and emotion. With LeCoq she also began work with masks, a convention that she has used often in her work as a director and designer. In 1971, Taymor apprenticed with Joseph Chaikin's Open Theatre and Peter Schumann's Bread and Puppet Theatre (both companies were developing new theatre pieces through group discussion and improvisation). The Open Theatre emphasized the actor's movement, whereas the Bread and Puppet Theatre emphasized puppets as "moving sculptures" made from found materials. In 1974, she traveled to Eastern Europe, Japan, and Indonesia to study puppetry, dance, and the visual arts. She remained in Indonesia until 1978, perfecting her use of puppetry, dance, and masks.

When she returned to the United States, Taymor quickly established a reputation as an outstandingly creative visual artist. She designed sets and/or costumes for productions at Baltimore's Center Stage, La MaMa, the New York Shakespeare Festival, and other Broadway, Off-Broadway, and regional theatres. Her sets, costumes, masks, and puppets for the American Repertory Theatre's *King Stag* garnered special praise.

Taymor has won numerous awards for her designs and directing. She is the recipient of a Guggenheim Fellowship and a "genius" grant by the MacArthur Foundation. Her costume design and direction for the Broadway musical *The Lion King* (1998) won her lavish praise and two Tony Awards. Taymor has also expanded into directing films, including a film version of her stage production of *Titus Andronicus*, *Frida*, and the 2006 film *Across the Universe*. Taymor has continued to develop and direct new works for the stage as well, among them the play *Juan Darién* and the opera *Grendel*.

Richard Feldman

The American Repertory Theatre production of Carlo Gozzi's *King Stag* was fancifully stylized through its use of costumes, masks, and puppetry designed by Julie Taymor. Directed by Andrei Serban; scene design by Michael Yeargan; lighting by Jennifer Tipton.

13 includes a treatment of the director's preparations and early process. Here we will concern ourselves with the preparations and early processes of the designers.)

Most designers begin their preparations by familiarizing themselves with the play. Initially, they may read through the play to gain an intuitive feel for it; taking note of their emotional reactions and perhaps specific images that the play evokes. In subsequent readings, the designers try to understand the play as a total structure—its action, characters, themes, language, meaning—because the production design needs to reflect or enhance all of these elements. As designers continue to study the play, they focus increasingly on clues about specific requirements of the play and its overall style. During this process, they accumulate information of various sorts from the play.

Although the play is the primary source of information, designers may also utilize information from other sources. Scene designers may wish to know about decorative motifs, architectural styles, furnishings, and favorite color schemes in use during the period of the play's action. Costume designers may need to determine what clothing was in use at the time of the play's action (characteristic silhouettes, typical textures and materials, dominant colors, ornamental motifs, usual accessories). The designers may also need to be familiar with the manners and customs of the time in order to understand why, when, and how garments or furniture were worn or used. They may wish to explore the stage setting and costuming conventions for which the play was originally written or that were in use when the play takes place. Lighting designers may wish to research the quality of light found in the various locations indicated in the play just as sound designers may wish to explore the soundscapes of these locations. All of the designers may wish to understand the political and social contexts out of which the play came, or they might undertake a variety of other

generally requires much communication and collaboration, but the manner or style in which this takes place varies depending on the individual artists within the production team, the available time, and other constraints that may affect their efforts. The common basis of their collaboration is the play itself and the interpretative focus that will guide the creative choices artists make for a particular production of it. (Chapter

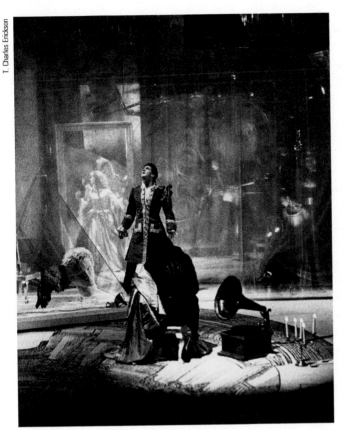

T. Charles Erickson

In *The Illusion,* Tony Kushner's adaptation of Pierre Corneille's seventeenth-century play about love, loss, and redemption, the action not only moves fluidly over time and space but also through different layers of reality. This poses special challenges for its production team. Pictured here is the Hartford Stage Company production directed by Mark Lamos; scene design by John Conklin; costumes by Martin Pakledinaz; lighting by Pat Collins.

explorations, depending upon the production concept. Although the designers may not incorporate all they learn into their designs, the fuller understanding they have gained of the play and its context may stimulate their imaginations.

Before they make sketches, plans and plots (perhaps before they have even begun to study the play and its context in detail), the designers meet with the director and each other to discuss the play and its interpretational focus. The director may use an initial meeting to elicit ideas from the designers and to ask them to participate in formulating this focus. Many directors explain a production concept they have already formulated to the designers at an initial meeting, but remain open to suggestions or to making alterations in the concept. The process of collab-

oration is unique to each group and situation, but communication, respect, and a certain degree of trust are always vital components of any effective collaborative process. A clear production concept or interpretational focus provides a common goal and a framework for the intended meaning or type of experience they wish the audience to have. However it evolves, an interpretational focus must be decided on before the designers can work together effectively and avoid working at cross purposes. Because the work of each designer impinges on that of the others, each designer must be sensitive to the ideas and needs of the others.

The designers may require other information before they begin work. Because each type of stage yields different challenges and

Appia on Hierarchy
in Production Design

Many people have commented on the relative importance of the elements that make up a production. Adolphe Appia, one of the twentieth century's major theoreticians of the theatre, had strong convictions about hierarchy in production design:

The first factor in staging is the interpreter, the actor. The actor carries the action. Without him there is no action, hence no drama. Everything must be subordinated . . . to this element—which takes first rank hierarchically . . . the body is alive, moving and plastic; it has three dimensions. Space . . . must conform to his plastic form, his three dimensions. What else is there: Light! . . . Like the actor, light must become active; . . . it must be put to the service of . . . the actor's dramatic and plastic expression. . . . Here is our normally established hierarchy: the actor presenting the drama, three-dimensional space at the service of the actor's plastic form, light, giving life to both.

—*Adolphe Appia, "Actor, Space, Light, Painting"*

opportunities for the designers, the type of stage (proscenium, thrust, arena, etc.) on which the play will be performed is a primary concern for the designers. Although the theatre's architecture usually predefines the type of stage, some theatres are designed with the capacity to alter the arrangement of the playing space and the resulting performer-audience relationship. Designers also need to know if the director has any special demands (specific floor plan needs such as space for dances or fight scenes, particular costume pieces, or any special lighting or sound effects the director will require, etc.). Moreover, the designers need to know what budget and time constraints apply and what equipment and personnel are available. After they understand the constraints within which they must work—the script, the production concept, the performance

space, the budget, and the personnel—the designers are ready to proceed.

Although each visual and aural element, considered in isolation, is capable of projecting a message and evoking a response, in actuality these elements are seldom wholly separated from each other. In theatrical production, most are present simultaneously, and their relationships change continually as the action develops. Over time each individually created sign or message is modified by others that combine to form the total effect. A theatrical production is therefore a group creation, and the collaboration of the various artists who create it is vital to its effectiveness. The ways in which theatre artists in each area of theatrical production contribute to the overall impact of a theatre performance are explored in the chapters that follow.

Michal Daniel; courtesy of the Guthrie Theatre

Jean Genet's *The Screens* as performed at the Guthrie Theatre. Costumes and scenery for the production combine to suggest a nonrealistic world perhaps set somewhere in the Middle East. Directed by JoAnne Akalaitis; scene design and properties by George Tsypin; costumes by Eiko Ishioka; lighting by Jennifer Tipton.

Additional Opportunities with InfoTrac College Edition

Using InfoTrac College Edition, read about the recently constructed Guthrie Theater Complex in "Minneapolis's New Guthrie Theatre Draws on French Design" by Larry Millett of the *St. Paul Pioneer Press.*

1. What types of actor-audience arrangements are possible at the new Guthrie?

2. What kinds of auxiliary spaces does the new theatre complex provide? How and why might these affect audience experience at the Guthrie?

Nilo Cruz's Pulitzer Prize–winning play, *Anna in the Tropics,* as produced by the McCarter Theatre (Princeton, N.J.). Directed by Emily Mann; scene design by Robert Brill; lighting design by Peter Kaczorowski; costumes by Anita Yavich; sound by Dan Moses.

[A] play in a book is only the shadow of a play and not even a clear shadow of it. . . .
The printed script of a play is hardly more than an architect's blueprint of a house not
built or built and destroyed.
—Tennessee Williams, Afterword, *Camino Real*

12: Playwriting and Dramaturgy

IN THE CONTEMPORARY THEATRE, although a play is typically the beginning point of a production, its creator, the playwright, is usually the theatre artist most removed from the process of play production. It has not always been so. Greek playwrights usually staged their own works. Shakespeare and Molière both wrote plays for the companies in which they acted, apparently knew in advance who would play each role, and were undoubtedly involved in staging their plays. But since the nineteenth century, playwrights have usually worked in isolation—not knowing, while writing, who would act in their plays or if they would be able to find someone willing to produce their scripts. Only a few playwrights today have close ties to theatre organizations. Even those writers fortunate enough to have directors or theatres to collaborate with them on developing scripts usually work alone until the script has reached a point where input from others can be helpful. Thus the initial stage of writing is typically a personal and isolated process.

The Playwright

THE SOURCE OF INSPIRATION for a play cannot be foreseen. It may be a newspaper article, a personal experience, a criminal act for which the motives are unclear, or almost any other source, because the possibilities of drama are ever-present and because almost anything has the potential to stimulate a dramatist's imagination. Each writer has a view of the world or a range of interests that make some subjects more attractive than others. Samuel Beckett was preoccupied with the human predicament in an unknowable universe, whereas Henrik Ibsen was concerned with personal and social morality in an explainable universe. Although both sought to write truthfully, their interests drew them to widely differing subjects, just as their perceptions about human beings and the human condition caused them to treat their subjects distinctively.

The working methods of playwrights also vary widely. Bertolt Brecht began with an outline and then elaborated on it. Victorien Sardou (the most successful French dramatist of the nineteenth century) wrote the climactic scene first and then worked backward from it. Henrik Ibsen made numerous notes about situations and characters, often over a period of years, before actually beginning a play. Paula Vogel, before forming a general plot outline, plays music that she associates with some aspect of the play over and over as she begins the writing process. Sam Shepard has said that he begins with a visual image and starts writing without knowing where it will lead. In some instances plays have been written with the aid of group improvisations. The playwright may present an outline, situation, or idea to a group of performers who then improvise on this material; as story, movement, and dialogue develop, the dramatist selects and shapes what seems most effective until a finished work has emerged. As these variations suggest, there are many different working methods, and writers discover and follow those procedures that work best for themselves.

The mechanics of playwriting also vary widely from one writer to another. (Basic structural patterns, form, and style are discussed in Chapter 3, to which the reader is referred for those aspects of playwriting.) Beckett did most of his writing by hand in bound notebooks. Some writers compose at a typewriter or word processor; others talk into tape recorders. However they proceed, writers seldom arrive at the final version of a script in the first draft. It is sometimes said that plays are not written but rewritten. Some writers spend years refining a script. For example, August Wilson's first draft of *Ma Rainey's Black Bottom* didn't include Levee and the other band members, although in his final version of the play these characters are essential to its conflict. On the other hand, Sam Shepard long refused to revise at all on the grounds that to do so would be like lying because it would deny what he had originally set down.

Because plays are intended for the stage, most writers need to see their work performed before they can be sure they have accomplished what they intended. Lines that look effective on paper may sound contrived when spoken. A playwright needs to be certain that the dialogue places the emphasis of a speech at just the right

The Laramie Project, a collaboratively written play by Moisés Kaufman and members of the Tectonic Theatre Project, as produced by the Philadelphia Theatre Company. The play treats the death of Matthew Shepard, a gay college student who was brutally beaten, tied to a fence, and left to die. Tectonic company members developed the play from hundreds of hours of taped interviews with Laramie residents; they were given additional support by the Denver Center Theatre the New York Theatre Workshop, and the Sundance Theatre Lab.

Courtesy of the Philadelphia Theatre Company

point, that the rhythms are effective when spoken aloud, that speeches make their intended points, that the vocal patterns are appropriate to each character, and that the interaction among characters seems believable. A playwright usually also seeks to make sure that the dramatic action is clear, that revelations create the intended effect, that tension mounts, relaxes, and builds to a climax. In summary, the dramatist must create a play that is effective in performance and not merely on the page.

The types of assistance the playwright needs and can get in developing a script vary widely. An initial step may involve a reading of the play aloud by one or more people (preferably a different person for each character). This not only allows the playwright to hear his or her work, but because others who are present may voice their reactions, it also helps the playwright to get some sense of how an audience responds to the script. Whereas this type of reading usually provides the playwright a basis for revisions, it also creates a problem that every playwright must ultimately deal with: assessing the validity of others' responses. Many listeners may volunteer advice, but advice from one source often contradicts advice from another. In the end, the playwright must decide which responses are valid or helpful. After revisions have been made, the next step may be a staged reading, in which performers, usually with scripts in hand and after some rehearsal, speak the dialogue and walk through the stage action. After assessing the play as presented and the audience's responses, the playwright usually makes further revisions.

Some playwrights are fortunate enough to be members of a playwrights' workshop where scripts can be worked on over a period of time in a process that includes multiple opportunities for rehearsed readings or performances. The Eugene O'Neill Theatre Center in Waterford, Connecticut, is one organization providing this kind of help. Each summer it selects from hundreds of applicants a few playwrights to be in residence for its National Playwrights Conference in which their new works are developed with the help of

Richard Feldman

Several of Sam Shepard's plays grapple not only with the immediate situation of the characters, but also with various aspects of the American mythos. Pictured here is Shepard's *True West* as performed at the American Repertory Theatre.

directors, performers, select critics, and audiences. In the past, all the plays were given a very quick and simple production using modular, gray scenic units and assorted properties. However, under the leadership of the conference's new artistic director, Wendy Goldberg, the individual needs of each play will be assessed on a case-by-case basis. The conference, which has always maintained a balance of very experienced playwrights and less experienced ones, has also initiated a theatre-for-youth pilot program, an international playwright residency in collaboration with Ireland's Abbey Theatre, and guaranteed inclusion of at least one graduate student playwright.

Ultimately, full production is the playwright's goal. In New York, several organizations,

PRACTITIONERS
AND THEORISTS

Playwrights
on Playwriting

Many playwrights do not find it easy to talk about how they work. They may do so in a general way but are usually aware that approaches to writing are enormously variable. Here are what some playwrights have said.

Marsha Norman: "I'm a purist about structure. . . . In plays you have eight minutes at the beginning in which to let the audience know what's at stake, who this is about and when they can go home. I think audiences get real nervous if you don't do that."

David Henry Hwang: "[I]n some ways rehearsal is the worst time to rewrite because you're under a lot of time pressure. If you've spent a year with a play, there's something absurd about rewriting the whole thing in four weeks."

George Bernard Shaw: "Only geniuses can tell you exactly what is wrong with a scene, though plenty of people can tell you something is wrong with it. So make a note of their dissatisfaction; but be very careful how you adopt their cure if they prescribe one."

August Wilson: [On writing *The Piano Lesson*] "I just started writing a line of dialogue and had no idea who was talking. . . . Someone says something to someone else, and they talk, and at some point I say, 'Well, who is this?' and I give him a name. But I have no idea what the story line of the play is. It's a process of discovery."

Wendy Wasserstein: "I rewrite endlessly. . . . [I]f you write comedy, sometimes you can be forcing the comedy by overwriting it. You're trying to make it funny, as opposed to letting the characters speak for themselves."

Arthur Miller: "The very impulse to write, I think, springs from an inner chaos crying for order, for meaning, and that meaning must be discovered in the process of writing or the work lies dead as it is finished."

including the La MaMa Experimental Theatre Club and the Manhattan Theatre Club, assist dramatists to develop their plays through fully mounted productions. In recent years, a few playwrights have had plays given fully mounted productions at multiple regional professional theatres, the intervals between the productions usually being used to revise the play. Among the plays that have gone through this process are Wendy Wasserstein's *The Heidi Chronicles,* August

A readthrough of a new play at the National Playwrights Conference in the Barn Theatre at the Eugene O'Neill Theatre Center, Waterford, Connecticut.

Wilson's *The Piano Lesson,* Tony Kushner's *Angels in America,* and Paula Vogel's *How I Learned to Drive,* all of which won Pulitzer Prizes. Most of the plays now seen on Broadway have profited from some comparable developmental process before being presented there.

Unfortunately, the number of writers who obtain assistance in developing their plays is relatively small. Many playwrights complete their plays without the benefit of staged readings or workshop performances. However it comes into being, the written work will probably seem only partially complete to its author unless it is fully realized through a stage performance; this requires

finding a producer. Playwrights frequently send copies of their plays to various resident theatres, but because these theatres often receive several hundred unsolicited plays each year, they may not read all of them. Some theatre organizations request that playwrights send only a one-page summary and a small excerpt of the unsolicited play; other theatres refuse to read any unsolicited plays. Thus despite playwrights' efforts, some plays are never produced. In fact, relatively few new plays receive fully staged productions in professional theatres.

The difficulties of finding a producer and making contractual arrangements are so complex that most writers prefer to work through an agent. Securing an agent is not easy because agents make their living from a percentage (usually ten percent) of each client's earnings and therefore choose to represent only those they consider potentially successful. Agents can be of great help nevertheless, because they understand the legal and financial aspects of producing and can help to place plays and negotiate contracts.

A producer who is interested in a play may purchase an option on it, which gives the producer the exclusive right to the play for a specified period of time. If the producer decides to stage the play, a contract is drawn up. The Dramatists Guild, an organization to which most playwrights belong and that seeks to protect the rights of playwrights by establishing professional and contractual standards for its members, sets forth the typical provisions of such contracts. The writer seldom relinquishes television, film, amateur, or foreign rights to the producer, because these may eventually be far more financially rewarding than the initial production. The contract usually specifies that the writer must be available for consultation and revisions throughout the rehearsal period, conditions that most playwrights are eager to meet.

During rehearsals, many changes to the written text may be made. Some of these may result

Lynda Griguere, courtesy of the Perseverance Theatre

Among the plays developed in workshop productions at regional not-for-profit theatres before being staged in New York is Paula Vogel's *How I Learned to Drive,* seen here in its first production at Alaska's Perseverance Theatre. Directed by Molly Smith with Timothy Crowe as Peck and Anne Scurria as Li'l Bit. The play was subsequently awarded the Pulitzer Prize in 1998.

from work with a new-play dramaturg (a process discussed later in this chapter). The director, as the artist (next to the writer) most fully involved

Most playwrights find workshops and new-play festivals helpful ways to develop their works. *War of the Worlds,* a play about Orson Welles, was produced for the twenty-fourth annual Humana Festival of New American Plays at the Actors Theatre of Louisville. Conceived and directed by Anne Bogart, this work was created by her SITI company (Saratoga International Theatre Institute) and written by Asian American playwright Naomi Iizuka.

Courtesy of Actors Theatre of Louisville

New Play Development

Playwrights may receive assistance in developing their plays in various ways. Perhaps the most typical ways are through new-play festivals and developmental workshops. Most feel the need to see their work performed, to be allowed time to revise it in light of what has been learned, and then to see it performed again.

One group dedicated to working with writers in this fashion is Playwrights Horizons. Founded in 1971 by Robert Moss to "support and develop the work of contemporary American playwrights, composers, and lyricists," it has presented works by over three hundred fifty different playwrights. Its productions have garnered numerous awards, including six Tony Awards and three Pulitzer Prizes, for its playwrights. Plays are revised and rehearsed, given a limited number of performances, reworked (sometimes over several years), and performed again. Each season Playwrights Horizons presents at least four new plays or musicals in its mainstage season and one or two new works in its studio series. (Studio-series productions are presented on a smaller scale than those produced for the mainstage season.) In addition, Playwrights Horizons not only offers twenty to twenty-five readings of new plays each year and awards commissions for the early development of new works, but also operates a film-development program with Steven Spielberg's Amblin Entertainment. Few organizations maintain such an ambitious ongoing development program for new plays.

Each year several festivals presenting new plays take place across the country. One of the most vital of these has been the Humana Festival of New American Plays hosted by the Actors Theatre of Louisville. Founded in 1976 by Jon Jory, former producing director of Actors Theatre, the festival performs fully mounted productions of at least four full-length new plays as well as presenting a series of short plays (from 1979 to 1989 these were winners of a national one-act play contest, and since then the winners of a national ten-minute play contest). Since its inception, more than seventy-five thousand scripts have been submitted and considered for inclusion in the festival. Over its more-than-thirty-year history, the Humana Festival has produced over three hundred plays representing the works of over two hundred writers. Critics and producers from the United States and abroad attend this major showcase of playwriting talent. Many of these plays have gone on to gain national recognition and numerous subsequent performances.

in maximizing the play's theatrical effectiveness, often makes suggestions for revisions. When based on mutual respect, the playwright-director relationship can be very productive. But sometimes directors make demands that writers think unjustified. When Tennessee Williams' play *Cat on a Hot Tin Roof* was first presented on Broadway, its director, Elia Kazan, cajoled Williams

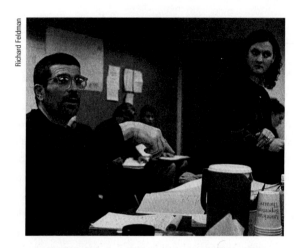

Dramatists and directors often work together closely on new scripts. Seen here is an early rehearsal of the world premiere of David Mamet's *The Old Neighborhood*. At left, Mamet; at right seated atop a table, Scott Zigler, the director.

into rewriting the final act. Williams was so unhappy with the results that when he published the play, he included both his preferred version and the one he had written to please Kazan. Producers may also suggest or demand revisions thought to increase the play's box-office appeal or to keep down costs. Although playwrights' contracts state that they need not make changes they consider undesirable, they often accede to changes rather than risk cancellation of the production or denial of future productions. Many playwrights now prefer to work in regional or Off-Off-Broadway theatres because such organizations are much more sensitive to the writer's wishes than is Broadway, where the sums of money invested make producers less willing to take chances.

Playwrights often revise new plays right up to opening night. Many theatres now have a series of preview performances to which tickets are sold (often at slightly reduced prices) but from which critics are usually excluded. Previews supposedly permit the playwright and the production team to assess audience response for use in fine-tuning the script and production before the official opening takes place and critics write published reviews. Further rewriting may be done following the initial production, but most playwrights feel the

need to put this experience behind them and go on to new projects. Nevertheless, a playwright may continue to rework a script over many years and through several productions. Tennessee Williams, late in his career, wrote new versions of many of his earlier plays.

The Dramaturg

MANY THEATRES now have a dramaturg (sometimes with assistants) on their staff. Although the acceptance of a dramaturg as a valued member of a theatre has grown considerably in recent years, the role of the dramaturg is still not widely understood. This is partly because the duties and working procedures of the dramaturg differ widely from one theatre organization to another.

The dramaturg is not a recent innovation. In Europe the position is usually traced back to Gotthold Ephraim Lessing, an eighteenth-century German playwright and critic. In 1767, upon being asked by the newly created Hamburg National Theater to serve as its resident playwright, Lessing declined but proposed instead that he become its in-house critic, offering advice on the selection of plays, critiquing the company's productions, and publishing a journal through which he might influence public taste by setting forth his theories about the nature and purposes of drama. His offer was accepted and, although the Hamburg National Theater lasted only two years, Lessing's work there established a precedent for later companies. The function he fulfilled later became standard in the many government-owned and subsidized theatres of Germany and elsewhere in Europe. Only gradually did it find favor in English-speaking theatres, in which it has gained ground gradually since the 1960s.

Dramaturgy and Literary Management

IN THE UNITED STATES, the scope of dramaturgy varies widely from one company to another. However, it can be divided roughly into two basic functions: <u>finding, developing, or shaping plays (literary management), and working with directors on specific productions of plays (production dramaturgy)</u>. In some theatres, the role of the dramaturg is confined to the first of these functions, and the person who fulfills this function is often called a literary manager. The literary manager's duties may vary considerably from one company to another, but they almost always include reading new scripts. Almost every not-for-profit professional theatre is inundated annually with new plays that playwrights hope will be produced. Literary managers read, or arrange for others to read, these plays. They choose those few that appear to have sufficient potential to warrant further consideration by the company. Because the volume is usually great, many companies will read only those plays submitted by agents or recommended by people whose judgments they trust.

Literary management may also include new-play development. This involves working with playwrights to help them realize the full potential of their scripts. (This process is sometimes taken over by the director or producer, but, because it is a dramaturgical function, it is discussed here.) New-play development is a delicate process, because it is not so much a matter of advising writers what they should do or demanding that they make certain changes as it is helping them clarify for themselves what they are seeking to do and finding means to do it. Dramaturgs sometimes describe to the writer what they find in the text and ask if that is what was intended. If it is not, then discussions may help the writer clarify what he or she is seeking to do and why it is not coming through. This, or some variation on it, may go on over a long period—before a play has received a reading, following readings of a play before an audience, during and following workshops in which a director and performers work on the play, and during and following partially or fully mounted productions of the play. The goal is to help authors realize as fully as possible the vision they set out to embody.

Although some type of new-play development has probably existed since the beginning of theatre, current practices vary considerably from those typically used earlier in the 20th century, when producers often demanded changes intended primarily to increase the play's box-office appeal, or when directors requested changes based on their ideas about theatrical effectiveness, or when starring performers demanded changes that would enhance their roles or make their roles more

T. Charles Erickson

Playwrights, dramaturgs, and directors often collaborate in the development and production of new plays. *The Learned Ladies of Park Avenue*, David Grimm's freely adapted new translation of Molière's comedy *Les Femmes Savants*, was produced by Hartford Stage for its *Brand:NEW* Festival of New Work. Directed by Michael Wilson; production dramaturgy by Christopher Baker; scene design by Tony Straiges; costumes by Martin Pakledinaz; lighting by Rui Rita; and sound by John Gromada.

IDEAS AND
INFLUENCES

Playwriting
as Collaborative Process

Concern with "new-play dramaturgy" has in recent years served to remind us that the theatre, including playwriting, is a collaborative process, although all of those involved may not be equal partners. In the afterword to the published version of his *Angels in America, Part Two: Perestroika,* Tony Kushner writes:

> The fiction that artistic labor happens in isolation, and that individual talents are the sole provenance of artistic accomplishment, is politically, ideologically charged and, in my case at least, repudiated by the facts. While the primary labor on *Angels* has been mine (defensively, nervously, I hasten to shore up my claim to authorship), over two dozen people have contributed words, ideas, structures to these plays. . . . Had I written these plays without the direct and indirect participation of my collaborators, the results would be entirely different and much the poorer for the deprivation—would, in fact, never have come to be.

Although Kushner graciously acknowledges the contribution of his collaborators, he may "nervously" assert his claim to authorship because of recent disputes between playwrights and dramaturgs over ownership and compensation.

Lynn Thomson, the dramaturg for the late Jonathan Larson's *Rent,* sued the playwright's estate on the grounds that her contributions to the play's development were worth sixteen percent of Larson's royalties. Although Federal Court Judge Lewis Kaplan ruled in favor of Larson's estate, he expressed his belief that Thomson's dramaturgy had played an important role in the "radical transformation of *Rent* from an unproducible work in development into a critically and commercially viable play." However, the judge denied her claim because there had been no contractual arrangement between Larson and Thomson. Legal disputes between dramaturgs and playwrights are rare, but Kaplan's decision does underscore the positive effect of collaboration even as it raises questions about where the credit (and payment) to one person should stop and to another begin.

attractive. Such practices have not disappeared, but it is now more common, especially in not-for-profit theatres, for those working with playwrights to be most concerned with helping the writer achieve the full potential of a script. For this reason, most playwrights prefer to work with one or a series of not-for-profit theatres.

But the old practices have not wholly disappeared, and not all playwrights are enthusiastic about "play development" based on reactions from others. Bruce Miller of Theatre IV in Richmond, Virginia, likens much play development to "a room of strangers who tell the playwright how to rewrite their play." Susan Jonas, dramaturg for

Rent, Jonathan Larson's rock musical adaptation of Puccini's opera *La Bohème*, has been the subject of a lawsuit from the dramaturg, who claimed to have written a sizable portion of it. Directed by Michael Greif; scene design by Paul Clay; costumes by Angela Wendt; lighting by Blake Burba.

the Classic Stage Company in New York, summarizes some of the adverse responses to new-play development: "There is a great deal of criticism directed against the way that new play development is done in this country. Many charge that in the process, dramaturgs and others do a lot of damage trying to normalize the play, using their own preconceived notions of play structure." The playwright's original impulse, which gives a distinctive quality and focus to the play, can become muddied by following the well-meaning advice from others with different perspectives. The playwright must learn which reactions are helpful. A. R. Gurney, one of America's most successful playwrights, has also voiced concern about too many people getting involved in reworking a play: "I think in this country we're committed to developing plays, and many plays I've seen have been rewritten too much. . . . [Y]ou can almost see that too many hands have been on the play. The individual voice is gone."

Literary managers are also usually involved in helping to select a company's season of plays. This usually involves keeping informed about and reading new plays that have been presented elsewhere, especially in the United States and Europe, as well as finding plays from the past that seem particularly relevant to current interests and issues. In considering plays for production,

one of the dramaturg's primary duties is to ask of any play proposed for production this three-part question: Why this play for this audience at this time? Unless compelling answers can be offered, there seems little reason to produce a play.

The literary manager, or the production dramaturg, may also be involved in the selection and preparation of a particular version of a play. If a play was originally written in another language, for example, the challenge of selecting the most effective translation arises. The dramaturg usually examines all of the available translations of foreign language plays and (in consultation with the director) assesses their relative effectiveness. If none is satisfactory, a new translation may be required. If the literary manager is qualified, he or she may make a new translation. More often, the producing theatre commissions someone thought particularly appropriate to make the translation. Plays from the past, even those in English, often pose comparable problems because they may include obsolete phrases, outmoded social customs, or unfamiliar ideas. Sometimes the dramatic or theatrical conventions that shaped a play are barriers to present-day production. The chorus in Greek tragedy almost always creates special challenges for modern productions, as do plays from other cultures.

PRACTITIONERS
AND THEORISTS

Dramaturgs
on Dramaturgy

What is a dramaturg? There is no easy answer because what dramaturgs do varies so widely from one company to another. Here are some attempts to describe dramaturgy and the role of the dramaturg.

Mark Bly (senior dramaturg, Arena Stage, Washington, D.C.): "When pressed for a definition of what it is that I do as a dramaturg, both in a rehearsal hall and in the theater at large, I generally answer, 'I question.' . . . On individual projects, the dramaturg can be that artist who functions in a multifaceted manner helping the director and other artists to develop and shape the sociological, textual, directing, acting, and design values."

Liz Engelman (president of the Literary Managers and Dramaturgs of the Americas) "The joke is the dramaturg doesn't prescribe, but asks questions. So you don't say 'Your play sucks!' You say, 'Why does your play suck?' Then it's up to them to figure out why."

Michael Lupu (senior dramaturg, Guthrie Theatre, Minneapolis): "Simply stated, dramaturgs—that is, individuals holding such a paid or unpaid position in a theatrical institution—are not necessarily indispensable. But dramaturgy—that is, a complex creative, intellectual activity inherent within the universe of drama and theater—is indispensable. There is sufficient proof that bringing a play to life on stage can happen without the involvement of a dramaturg. For practical purposes, though, the production will fail or will not happen at all if dramaturgy is blatantly ignored."

Robert Brustein (former artistic director of the American Repertory Theatre): "The most delicate and difficult function of all remains that of internal critic—finding a way to communicate your views about particular productions, and about the conduct of the theatre, without arousing the defensiveness of the artistic director or hurting the feelings of the company. . . . As the humanist in the woodpile, it is the dramaturg who must act as the conscience of the theatre, reminding it of its original promise, when it threatens to relax into facile, slack, and easy paths."

Decisions must be made about how these challenges may be successfully met in a production intended for the theatre's present-day audience. Sometimes the answer is to adapt the play, a task that may fall to the literary manager or to someone selected by the literary manager and director.

The world premiere of *The Laramie Project* at the Denver Center Theatre. Pictured (left to right) are John McAdams, Barbara Pitts, Greg Pierotti, Amanda Gronich, and Mercedes Herrero.

Production Dramaturgy

PRODUCTION DRAMATURGY is concerned with specific productions. The production dramaturg works most closely with the director but may also work with designers and other members of a production team, as well as with those concerned with publicity, programs, and outreach. The production dramaturg's work used to be (and often still is) considered the responsibility of the director. Some directors refuse to work with dramaturgs, because they prefer to do this work themselves or because they view the dramaturg as usurping one of their functions. The director-dramaturg relationship works best when it is grounded in mutual respect and a desire to explore fully how to make the written text come to life on stage. If disagreements arise, the dramaturg usually retreats to performing only those functions the director specifically requests.

The production dramaturg does not make decisions but helps the director make them by asking questions or supplying information crucial for clarifying the goals of the production and the interpretation of the play. For example, dramaturgs may research the author's life and writings in an effort to understand more fully the concerns that have shaped the play. They may also explore the period or cultural environment in which the play takes place or in which the author lived. They may bring to light what critics have written about the play or what reviewers have said about previous productions. They may examine still other sources to increase the director's understanding of the play and the context out of which it came.

Dramaturgs usually attend rehearsal often. The dramaturg may discuss with the director what he or she was trying to achieve, the disparities between the director's intentions and what the dramaturg saw on the stage, and possible reasons for the differences. These and other types of feedback can assist directors in clarifying and realizing their interpretation of the play.

Dramaturgs often have some responsibility for educating the audience. They may supply information about the play, its past, this production, or other matters that will help those who do publicity to make the play more attractive and accessible to an audience. They may also have some responsibility for the printed program (especially if it includes materials that support and elaborate on the interpretation given the play). If the theatre has an outreach program that takes productions into schools or brings student audiences to the theatre, the dramaturg may have responsibility for assembling auxiliary materials to prepare the audience or make the

Dan McNeil; courtesy of the Denver Center Theatre

experience more meaningful. The dramaturg may also be responsible for "talk back" sessions (discussions between theatre personnel and audiences) following performances.

Overall, then, the dramaturg serves a critical and advisory function, assists in articulating the production team's vision of the production, seeks to help clarify and refine that vision during rehearsals, seeks to prepare audiences for experiencing the production most fully, and helps in evaluating the results after the production ends. Because dramaturgs are involved in the work of every member of the production team, it is often difficult to separate the dramaturgical from other functions, especially those of the director.

Although the playwright and the dramaturg serve different functions in the theatre, their work often converges. The playwright is concerned with creating a play, whereas the dramaturg is concerned with ensuring that the final version of the play realizes the playwright's intentions and that those intentions are embodied on the stage.

The improbable musical with the even more improbable title, *Urinetown,* was a surprise hit in New York. Using InfoTrac College Edition, read more about how this piece was created and became a Broadway phenomenon in "Urinetown Confidential: The Untold Story" by Greg Kotis, the author of the book for the musical.

1. What role did the Fringe Festival play in the success of *Urinetown*?

2. How much time passed between Kotis's original inspiration and the opening on Broadway?

Performers depend on the director to assist them with constructive feedback on their work. Pictured here, Lisa Peterson, the director of Ellen McLaughlin's new version of Sophocles' *Oedipus* at the Guthrie Theatre, gives feedback to members of the production's modern-dress chorus.

Directing is psychology. It's about how to work with other human beings. It's also the art of inducing a psychological effect on a group of people who have come into a theatre to experience that effect. In your mind you're saying to yourself: "What do I want the audience to feel?" From there it's a process of moving toward that feeling with actors, designers, etc., yet allowing yourself to discover the unexpected along the way.
—Mark Lamos in *The Director's Voice*, ed. Arthur Bartow

13: Directing and Producing

ALTHOUGH DIRECTORS have ultimate responsibility for the artistic aspects of productions, they depend on playwrights to provide the plays and producers to secure the necessary resources. The director works with the performers and designers to transform the playwright's work into a particular stage treatment using the resources (money, space, and personnel) the producer makes available. Thus, although the functions of playwright, producer, and director are distinct, they entwine on a practical level. The way they come together varies from one situation to another, but, whatever the starting point, the three functions—writing, producing, directing—ultimately meet in production.

The Producer

PRODUCERS HAVE the financial and managerial tasks of making productions available to the public. Although they may not make artistic decisions directly, they nevertheless influence artistic decisions through their willingness or unwillingness (or ability or inability) to meet the requests of the playwright, director, and other artists. Producers in the Broadway theatre are often accused of placing financial considerations above artistic integrity, but it is their job to stay within a budget and, if possible, to recover the investment made in the production. Someone must carry out the producer's functions, because otherwise productions would never reach the stage.

Although almost all producers have the same basic responsibilities, the specific conditions governing their work vary from one type of organization to another. The producer's responsibilities are most clearly defined in the Broadway theatre. Today, producers of Broadway shows usually are organizations, a group of individuals, or consortia who raise the necessary capital and carry out the other functions of a producer. In return, they receive payment for these services plus a large percentage of any profit. Production costs on Broadway typically run into millions of dollars, and success is unpredictable. Therefore producers usually have to seek financial backing from many people or groups because few individuals are willing to assume all of the financial risk. Producers usually approach prospective investors with a proposed budget that covers

Ayesha Dharker as Rani in the Broadway production of *Bombay Dreams*. The story was simplified and the use of spectacle substantially increased for the New York production in order to broaden the musical's appeal.

and managers, treasurers, ushers and doorkeepers, porters and cleaners, and engineers. Producers also rent space for auditions and rehearsals, lease a theatre for performances, arrange for publicity, and facilitate ticket sales. They are responsible for administering the payroll, keeping financial records, and making reports to investors at specified intervals. Occasionally, productions return very large profits, but a production can run for two or three years and never recover its original investment because the weekly expenses on a large show may consume most of the income from ticket sales, leaving little to repay the money spent before the production opened. The producers are also responsible for closing a show at the end of its run.

The producer's responsibilities are less clearly defined in other situations. Most professional resident companies are ongoing not-for-profit organizations that present a number of plays each year. They often own a theatre or perform in one owned by a municipality or arts organization or in a space leased for an extended period. Although each production has its own budget within the theatre's total budget, such theatre companies are more concerned with financing the ongoing institution than with a single production. Most companies of this type have an artistic director, who is concerned primarily with staging, and a managing director (or producing director), who is concerned with financing and marketing. But both are typically involved in raising money, establishing policy, and choosing the repertory. There is also a board of directors, which must be consulted about many issues that concern the organization's well-being and that may assist in raising funds. Because resident professional companies cannot support their activities entirely from box-office receipts, much time is spent pursuing grants or soliciting contributions. As not-for-profit organizations, they are eligible for grants from foundations, the National Endowment for the Arts, state and local arts councils, corporations, and private donors. Although this form of organization distributes the producer's responsibilities somewhat differ-

expenses up to opening night, weekly operating expenses after the show opens, and a statement about how profits will be divided. Sometimes it takes months, even years, to raise the money needed for a production. Each production is usually capitalized as a corporation or partnership to limit the financial liability of investors.

After producers raise the necessary capital, they negotiate contracts with all of the personnel who will be involved. This process can be difficult, because eleven different unions may be involved—those representing dramatists, directors and choreographers, performers, musicians, stagehands, wardrobe attendants, press agents

SOCIETY, ART,
AND CULTURE

Cross-Cultural
Appeal

ffectively estimating the broad-based appeal of a particular musical is a tricky business, even for veteran producers. This is especially true of musicals that seemingly have an identifiable audience but require cross-cultural appeal to be economically viable.

Andrew Lloyd Webber (*Cats, Les Misérables,* and *The Phantom of the Opera*) has successfully transferred many London musicals to the Broadway stage. Recently, he invested $5 million to produce *Bombay Dreams* (book by Meera Syal and music by A. R. Rahman) in London. *Bombay Dreams* tells the story of a young man—from the lowest level of India's caste system—who rises from the slums to become a film star in "Bollywood" (India's film industry). Along the way, he falls in love with a woman from a higher caste. Despite dismal reviews (*The Times* of London wrote that the "dialogue would test the patience of Mother Teresa"), sufficient numbers of South Asians attended to keep the musical going until it attracted a broader audience and made back its initial investment. Lloyd Webber claimed, "Without the Asian community the London production would have closed in three weeks."

However, London has a historical relationship to India and a much larger South Asian community to draw upon than does New York. The Broadway success of *Bombay Dreams* would depend upon its cross-cultural appeal. Perhaps to fit the tastes of Broadway audiences, Lloyd Webber hired Thomas Meehan (the librettist for the Broadway hits *Hairspray* and *The Producers*) to rework the story. Meehan tightened the story focus onto a few major characters and emphasized its universal theme of lovers divided by rigid class distinctions. Along with changes to the musical's story, its visual aspects and special effects were super-sized for American audiences.

Despite the changes to make the British Bollywood-styled musical more broadly appealing, Broadway critics found it "contrived," and one complained that the musical's Indian components had become "mainly garnish rather than integral elements." Although *Bombay Dreams* had overcome poor reviews in London, its Broadway production closed after having barely recouped for Lloyd Webber and its other producers half of its initial $14 million cost.

ently than is the norm on Broadway, these duties must still be performed, and the managing director or business manager usually assumes a large portion of them.

In community theatre, the organization itself usually serves as the producer, and volunteers carry out many of the duties under the supervision of the organization's officers and board of directors. Some of the duties may be delegated to an individual (president or treasurer) or to a committee. Many community theatres hire only a director and a designer-technician because the purpose of such organizations is to provide an outlet for the talents of people for whom theatre is an avocation.

In educational theatre, the producer's functions may be divided among several people. Usually, the school owns the performance space, and individuals on its payroll in other capacities do most of the supervisory work. The chair of the department or the director of theatre may have responsibilities that combine those of the artistic and managing directors of a resident company. Some theatre programs have a paid business manager who is responsible for keeping accounts, making purchases, running the box office, and handling publicity. In many small schools, the director of each play may have to assume many of the producer's tasks.

Regardless of the type of organization, then, tasks are much the same, though who performs them and the procedures may vary. In all cases, financial support must be provided, contractual arrangements made, space and personnel provided, publicity for productions disseminated, tickets sold, and bills paid. The producer is concerned with the business of show business.

The producer is also often involved in choosing the plays to be produced. On Broadway, it is the producer who selects the play. Often the director and designers are not even contacted until after this basic decision has been made, although increasingly producers bring to Broadway productions that have been successful in regional theatres, Off-Broadway, or abroad (principally London).

Most permanent organizations present a season composed of several plays. In choosing a season of plays, the group may take the following into consideration:

■ The variety of periods and forms being offered
■ The production requirements of each play (including cast size, and scenic, costume, and lighting demands)

■ The total cost in relation to the organization's budget and projected income
■ The tastes of local audiences and probable box-office appeal

During the play-selection process, advice may be sought from a number of sources. (Much of this work may involve a literary manager or dramaturg, as discussed in Chapter 12.)

Professional organizations deal directly with living authors or their agents in negotiating arrangements to produce plays. Amateur production rights are usually handled by play agencies, such as Samuel French or Dramatists Play Service. A play under copyright (which continues for the lifetime of the author plus fifty years) may not be performed without written permission (usually in the form of a contract) from the copyright owners or their authorized agent. Such contracts require that royalties be paid for each performance. Older plays may not require payment if their copyrights have expired, but recent translations or adaptations of older plays may be copyrighted even if the original copyright has expired.

Once the script is selected and production contracts are negotiated, the process of mounting the play begins.

■ The Director

JUST AS THE PRODUCER is concerned with the financial aspects, the director is concerned with the artistic aspects of production. Ordinarily, the director:

■ Decides upon an interpretation of the script and a production concept that will shape its staging
■ Casts and rehearses with the performers
■ Works with the designers
■ Integrates all of the elements into a finished production

In the first of these functions, the director may work closely with a dramaturg, if one is available, or may choose to work alone.

ANALYZING AND STUDYING THE PLAY

REGARDLESS OF WORKING procedures or personnel, the starting point for most productions is a play. Even at this beginning point in the process, many questions face the director: What is the basic story? If the play is a foreign work, what translation is best suited to the production? How might the play's events and their arrangement affect a live audience? Should portions of the script be cut? Should certain scenes be transposed? What is the significance of the play's time and setting? Should these be altered? To answer these questions effectively, the director first needs to understand the play thoroughly on its own terms.

A full understanding of a play usually requires some form of analysis. There is no standard way to analyze a play (one way is described in Chapter 3). Most directors begin by reading the play several times to become familiar with its overall qualities. They may note its structural pattern of preparation, complication, climax, and resolution. Some directors divide a script into short segments (units or beats) defined by the entrance or exit of characters or by major changes in the characters' motivations. They then examine the function of each segment in relation to those that precede and follow it as well as in relation to the play as a whole. Some directors may also note their emotional reactions to certain moments in the play or images that these moments inspire. They may define the "through line" (or "spine") of the action that holds the play together and determines its overall thrust—its themes, point of view, and implications. The director studies all of the characters to understand their individual functions in the play and the challenges and opportunities they pose for the performers who play the roles. The director may note scenic, costume, and lighting requirements in order to work intelligently with the designers. Through such study, the director becomes aware of the opportunities and challenges a play's production poses.

Directors also typically consult other sources so as to understand better the author's point of view and other concerns that may have shaped the play. They may explore the cultural environment depicted in the play and the context from which it emerged. They may also read what critics have written about the play or what reviewers have said about previous productions. They may examine still other sources to increase their understanding of the play. All of this may be

T. Charles Erickson

Director David Warren pointed out the contrast between serious and comedic moments in the Long Wharf Theatre's production of *Twelfth Night*. In this early serious scene Viola finds herself on the coast of a strange country after a storm and shipwreck have separated her from her twin brother, Sebastian. Scene design by James Youmans; costumes by Toni-Leslie James; lighting by Peter Maradudin.

crucial in shaping the director's interpretation of the play and its theatrical production.

If the play is new, the director may work directly with the playwright. This can simplify the director's task, because the playwright can answer many questions the director may have about the play. However, it may also complicate the director's work if what the playwright says he or she intended is not, in the director's opinion, clearly embodied in the play. In the latter case, although the director may suggest revisions, most contracts specify that the playwright cannot be required to alter the play. Still, in an atmosphere of mutual trust and respect, most dramatists welcome insights that the director and the rehearsal process may offer, and they frequently revise a new play right up to opening night (or occasionally throughout the play's preview performances).

After studying the play, the director decides upon an interpretation that accounts for the significance of the play's dramatic action and defines the focus of the production. The director may distill his or her interpretation of the play into a production concept: a short statement that conveys the director's vision for the production. Whether phrased as a metaphor, an action that takes place over the duration of the performance, or as a philosophical statement, a production concept basically defines the focus of the production by articulating what the director will try to realize on stage and communicate to the audience. The concept then becomes an organizational tool for the production team, who will use it as a guide in making the numerous choices about the staging, design, and acting for this particular production of the play.

APPROACHES TO DIRECTING

SEVERAL APPROACHES to directing have become common. One approach stems from the belief that the director serves the playwright by transferring the play as literally as possible from page to stage. Directors who accept this notion of their function usually retain the time and place specified in the text and closely follow (though not necessarily slavishly) the playwright's prescriptions about staging. A second approach stems from a view of directors as translators whose goal is to capture the spirit of the play, although to do this they may depart from

Jean Genet's *The Blacks*, staged in a film studio in Berlin. Directed by one of Germany's most internationally admired directors, Peter Stein.

Ruth Walz; courtesy of the German Information Center

PRACTITIONERS AND THEORISTS

Directors
on Directing

irectors have different notions about their function in respect to how they work with others. Here are the thoughts of several prominent European directors on the director's role in creating theatre.

Adrian Noble *(England):* "I tend to give the actors quite a strong conceptual line on a play because I feel people respond better to a firm framework. . . . I think my job is to work very hard beforehand on the text, and then with the designer, and then with the leading actors, involving them very definitely with the thinking behind the production and the very, very strong idea of it that I have. Once they've grasped the idea they have tremendous freedom within it."

Peter Stein *(Germany):* "The function of the director is not that of the father, but perhaps that of the elder brother. . . . A director's approach should always depend on what is needed for the play. I find that the best stage dynamic comes if I am accepted as a brother who has very good eyes."

Ariane Mnouchkine *(France):* "I'm like a midwife. I help to give birth [to the production]. The midwife doesn't create the woman, and she's not the husband. But still, if she's not there, the baby is in great danger and might not come out. I think a really good director is that. Let's say I am a good director when I don't fail to be that."

Giorgio Strehler *(Italy):* "The undeviating search for the truth of the text, the painstaking search for the dramatic work of art, these are the essential tasks of the director. . . . The problem is the excessive emphasis given to the director's role. . . . Directors have contributed much to the invention of the modern theatre, but they have also often given a skewed image of what 'Theatre' is."

the playwright's specifications. Just as a literal translation of a play from one language to another may distort the spirit of the original, an over-zealously literal production may fail to project a play's essential qualities, especially if the play is from the past or written for another culture with conventions that differ markedly from those familiar to the audience.

This second approach is now the most common, although the way it is applied varies widely from one director to another and even from one production to another. Directors using this approach usually search for a metaphor, dominant theme, or set of conventions that will define the focus—the directorial or production concept—that will shape the production. A Soviet director,

Nikolai Okhlopkov, shaped his production of *Hamlet* around the metaphor of the world as a prison, using a setting composed of cell-like cubicles in which various scenes were played. Perhaps a more common practice is to base a production on an analogy rather than a metaphor, suggesting that the action in a play is analogous to that of another time and place. For example, Orson Welles set *Macbeth* in Haiti, replacing the witches with voodoo priests. Other directors have relocated the action of *Troilus and Cressida* (which is set during the Trojan War) to the American Civil War. Of course, unless carefully formed, the use of a metaphor or analogy can reduce a play's complexities by rigidly limiting its focus.

Peter Brook shaped his widely admired production of *A Midsummer Night's Dream* around a central motif: the potentials and dangers of love. The fantasy scenes in the woods became dreamlike demonstrations to Theseus and Hippolyta, who are about to be married, of the effects of misunderstandings between lovers and about love. To underscore these connections, Brook used the performers cast as Theseus and Hippolyta to also play Oberon and Titania (their parallels in the fantasy world). Most earlier productions of the play had exploited the opportunities for visual spectacle offered by Theseus' court and the enchanted wood. Brook used the same set throughout—a white box (with front

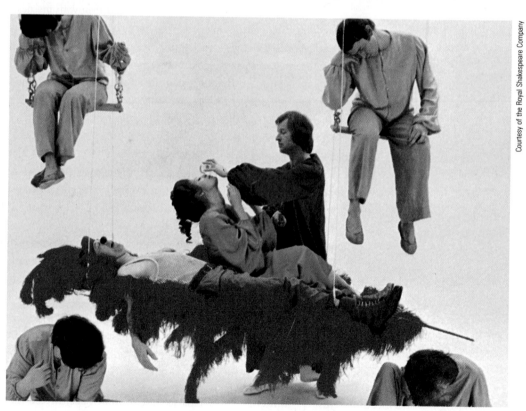

Courtesy of the Royal Shakespeare Company

Shakespeare's *A Midsummer Night's Dream* as performed by the Royal Shakespeare Company under the direction of Peter Brook. At center, Oberon is applying a potion that will release Titania from the spell that has caused her to fall in love with Bottom, seen here atop the bower of red feathers. Instead of being transformed into an ass, as called for in Shakespeare's text, Bottom has been given a clown's nose. Notice the trapeze used for flying in this production, which used many circus conventions, and how the performers stand out against the unadorned white-box setting designed by Sally Jacobs.

and top removed) devoid of decoration. The stage was treated as a space where the fundamental human relationships in Shakespeare's play could be isolated and examined, rather than as a space to illustrate the locales indicated in its story. Most earlier productions had emphasized the magical aspects of the fairy world and had sought to make Puck's flying convincingly real. For the fairy magic, Brook substituted stage and circus magic: Trapezes were used for the flying scenes, and characters on the trapezes performed tricks of stage magic such as keeping plates spinning on sticks. Bottom, rather than being transformed into an ass, became a clown with a red rubber ball for a nose. Thus the magic was translated from fairyland into a context more familiar, though no less magical, to a modern audience. Despite his visual substitutions, Brook altered none of the play's words. His goal was to make audiences consider the implications of certain human relationships rather than concentrate on the spectacle and fantasy.

Ariane Mnouchkine, working with the Théâtre du Soleil in Paris, has used conventions borrowed from Asian (especially Indian and Japanese) theatre in several productions of Shakespeare's history plays and Greek tragedies. She believes that the formalized conventions of Asian theatre can illuminate the repetitive, ritualized power struggles in these plays. Because these conventions are unfamiliar to her Western audience, they draw attention to themselves and encourage the audience to see the more familiar dramatic actions in a fresh light. Mnouchkine's attempt is to "reinvent the rules of the game by which everyday reality is portrayed, revealing it not to be familiar and unchangeable, but astonishing and capable of transformation."

Other variations on this second approach could be cited, but their shared assumption is that fundamental patterns of meaning may be hidden beneath the surface detail of a play. Furthermore, the audience may more fully grasp a play's significance through artistic choices that reveal these deeply embedded patterns. Although

this approach can be effective, if ineptly applied it can distort the play (even without changing a word of its dialogue) by calling attention to bizarre staging rather than illuminating the play's themes and implications through innovative choices.

A third approach to directing places less emphasis on the written play. Using this approach, directors may begin with the play but feel free to reshape it as they see fit. A director who treats the script as raw material to be reshaped for his or her own purposes is sometimes called an *auteur* (French for "author"), because the director is considered the principal creative force. Taken to its most extreme expression, this approach to directing virtually eliminates the playwright (or at least the distinctions between writer and director). Although this is the least common approach, a few directors have achieved startling results using it.

The Polish director Jerzy Grotowski often began with well-known plays, uncovered what he considered to be basic (archetypal) patterns of human behavior in them, and then reshaped the plays (through cutting, rearranging, and relocating scenes for his own purposes), to provoke his audience's self-examination and self-recognition. Perhaps his best-known and most radical reshaping of a play involved Wyspianski's *Akropolis,* one of Poland's most revered classics, set in the royal palace at Cracow on the Feast of the Resurrection. During the action, the walls' tapestries come to life and enact what amounts to a history of Western civilization, at the end of which the resurrected Christ leads all of the figures in a procession to liberate Europe from its past errors. Grotowski saw the play as treating hopes and fantasies that had been destroyed by World War II and the Nazi concentration camps. He reshaped the play so that rather than stressing the possibility of redemption, it depicted "the cemetery of our civilization." The setting became an extermination camp at Auschwitz, and its characters prisoners who, during the course of the play, build cremation ovens and occasionally, in their nightmares, perform scenes based in a distorted way on those in Wyspianski's play. At the end they march into the ovens they have built, following a lifeless figure representing Christ. In such an approach the director's vision overrides the playwright's, and the original script becomes material to be shaped (just as acting, lighting, scenery, and costumes are).

In Robert Wilson's early theatre pieces, the written scripts are inadequate as bases for productions by others. Wilson usually lays out each piece as a storyboard. A master board shows at a glance the development of the entire piece. Wilson elaborates each segment in detailed storyboards before realizing them on stage. (This process can be seen in the illustration below) So tightly entwined is the play with its manner of visual expression that some of Wilson's pieces can properly be said to exist only in their performances. Similarly, performance artists often conceive their pieces as performances rather than as written drama, thereby making it difficult to separate their persona or performance style from the written text; consequently, others may find it quite difficult to stage their works.

Regardless of the approach, directors have to work with others in transforming their vision into

Robert Wilson's storyboard outline of the four acts of his opera *Einstein on the Beach*.

Courtesy of the Byrd Hoffman Foundation

Act 1, Scene 2A, of *Einstein on the Beach* in performance as staged by Robert Wilson. Notice the costume (pants, white shirt, suspenders) worn by most of the characters throughout the opera as one unifying motif.

reality, because at least some production tasks must be delegated to others. The discussion that follows will undoubtedly make directing seem far more rational and precise than it is. Although most directors begin with a reasonably clear idea of what they wish to accomplish, they also make discoveries through their interactions with designers and performers that provide new insights into the play and alter their initial plans. Where directors ultimately arrive may be different from (and more rewarding than) their original destination. But such discoveries are unpredictable, and we must be content with a look at some typical working procedures that directors use.

THE DIRECTOR AND THE DESIGNERS

SOME DIRECTORS (among them Robert Wilson and Julie Taymor) also serve as their own designers, but that is unusual. Because the creation of production designs is a lengthy process, the director meets as early as possible with the designers to discuss the play and the production concept. The director may have already formed his or her vision for the production, or it may evolve out of such discussions. However it is arrived at, if the designers and the director are not to work at cross-purposes with each other,

the production's focus should be clear to everyone involved. Directors should also relate any specific demands they may have, such as the shape of the set, the need for multiple levels, the placement of entrances, specific mood lighting, garments with specific features, and so on.

After the initial meetings, designers must be allowed time to conceive their designs. (Chapters 15–17 provide a fuller discussion of various approaches and procedures used to create production designs.) Then, at subsequent meetings, the designs are considered and a number of questions are usually explored. Do the designs adequately project the production concept? Do they fit the play's action, mood, theme, and style? How do the designs for each aspect (scenery, costumes, lighting, and sound) complement and support each other? Will scenic and costume pieces functionally serve the uses the director has planned for the production's staging? If costume or scenery changes must occur during performance, will the proposed designs permit these changes without undue delays? Can the designs be achieved within the production's budget, personnel, and time constraints? Consideration of such questions during the planning stages can prevent problems and costly last-minute changes. The designs are revised until the director and designers are mutually satisfied.

Nontraditional Casting

Nontraditional casting implies casting performers in roles for which, in the past, they might not have been considered. There are many approaches to this kind of casting. One involves "colorblind" casting—ignoring race or ethnicity and casting solely on the basis of talent and suitability to a role. Although such casting has become relatively common in many professional companies and university theatres, it is still questioned when it leads to mixed-race family groups or when it seems to deny social realities. Commenting on the revival of *Carousel* (with thirteen performers of color in a cast of forty-four), one critic declared it ludicrous that blacks would coexist happily with whites in nineteenth-century coastal Maine and that this was too much to ask audiences to accept. Some observers argue that colorblind casting shifts the question of minority underrepresentation away from the failure of new plays to include minority characters. Others charge that colorblind casting allows cultural differences to be ignored by absorbing representatives of other cultures into the dominant white, Eurocentric culture.

Another approach is "conceptual" casting, which often involves changing the race or ethnicity of some or all characters to bring a new perspective to a play. For the Shakespeare Theatre's 1997 production of *Othello*, director Jude Kelly cast Othello and Bianca with white performers and all of the remaining characters with African American ones. Some critics complained that the casting made the play's lines referring to skin color ridiculous (Desdemona's skin was clearly not "alabaster" nor was Othello's "black"). Others claimed that this controversial "photo negative" casting emphasized the status of Othello and Bianca as "outsiders" to the play's Venetian society and focused attention on the social dynamic of racism that isolates whoever is in the minority. Ironically, the role of Othello has more often than not been cast with a white performer, who affects a black character, in an all-white cast.

Issues related to nontraditional casting are not restricted to race and ethnicity. They also extend to differently abled performers and failures to cast them, even in roles that include characters with those qualities. Because issues related to casting reflect divisions within American society, they are not likely to be resolved until those divisions are healed and greater diversity—and its representation on stage—is embraced.

Richard Feldman

Alice in Bed, written by Susan Sontag and produced under the direction of Bob McGrath at the American Repertory Theatre. The production enlisted the imagery of Lewis Carroll's *Alice in Wonderland* for its carefully coordinated visual elements to create a highly stylized, dream-like world. Scene design by Laurie Olinder and Fred Tietz; costume design by Susan Anderson; lighting by John Ambrosone; films by Bill Morrison.

After the designs are approved, although there may be regular conferences, each artist works more or less independently until the final rehearsals. In the meantime, the director's prime task becomes casting and rehearsing the performers.

■ AUDITIONS AND CASTINGS

AUDITION PROCEDURES and methods vary. One is the "open call," which purportedly allows all of those interested to audition. But even open calls usually restrict access in some way. For example, in professional theatres, Actors Equity may demand that a certain amount of time be devoted to open calls, but these are open only to its members (or to performers who can document their professional eligibility). If there are many applicants, some may be eliminated on the basis of their resumés or preliminary interviews and never actually audition. Even those granted auditions may have only a short time (two minutes is typical) in which to demonstrate their suitability. Under such circumstances, choices may be made on the basis of personal or physical attributes rather than on proven ability.

Many professional producing organizations increasingly depend on casting directors to save them time by creating a small pool of likely candidates. These casting directors sift through resumés, confer with agents, conduct initial auditions, and call on their own memories or videotapes of the performers' previous work. This pool of prescreened candidates is then usually auditioned thoroughly by the director, often in consultation with the casting director, producer, or playwright. The casting process usually progresses from open to closed (or "call-back") auditions. During the latter type, the prospective actors in the narrowed field are generally given more time to demonstrate their suitability for the roles and may be called back several times.

Some directors or producing organizations ask performers to present previously prepared audition material. Frequently actors are asked to perform two short, contrasting monologues unrelated to the play being cast. Sometimes actors are able to study the play being cast and read a passage from it as an audition piece. The director may ask actors to read material they have not previously seen, then give explanations and ask the actors to read the same material again with these instructions in mind. Through this method, called "cold readings," directors try to evaluate the actor's flexibility and quickness in assimilating direction. Some

directors use improvisations or other methods to test the actor's imagination, inventiveness, or physical agility.

Many factors determine final casting. Some roles demand specific physical characteristics (such as being shorter or taller than others) or a particular vocal quality. The director must also consider the emotional range of each role and the actor's potential to achieve this range. Characters often need to be paired or contrasted (in romantic situations, for example), and casting must answer this need. The director must also look at the cast as a whole and assess the way the performers will look and work together. After weighing all of the factors, the director eventually chooses the performers who seem most capable of embodying the qualities he or she is seeking.

■ WORKING WITH THE ACTORS

After casting is completed, the director works to mesh actors with their roles and the dramatic action to bring the script to life on the stage. The director supervises rehearsals, but a director is not a dictator. Actors bring their own insights, many of which may be novel or provocative. Most (though not all) directors are willing to discuss the actors' responses and are sufficiently flexible to adopt those that improve the initial plans. Most directors attempt to create an atmosphere free from unnecessary tensions in which the actors may explore and develop their roles. The director needs to be tactful and understanding, because each actor faces unique challenges and may have favorite working methods. Some actors take criticism gracefully in the presence of others, but others may become argumentative or so embarrassed that they find it difficult to continue.

Throughout the rehearsal process, the director assesses the actors' work and makes suggestions for improvements. Because actors cannot see their work from the audience's point of view, they rely upon the director to do this service for them. Effective directors are usually sensitive listeners and observers, critics, disciplinarians, teachers, and friends. Ultimately, they are the audience's surrogate, because they try to shape the performance in ways that will be most effective for those who will see it.

■ The Director's Means

The director's means include the entire resources of the theatre: the script; the physical and psychological capacities of the actors; the stage space, scenery and properties; costumes and makeup; lighting, and sound. Because each of these elements is discussed elsewhere in this book, the focus here is on the

Nontraditional casting in Shakespeare's *The Taming of the Shrew* as produced by the New York Shakespeare Festival. The place of the action has been moved to the American West in the nineteenth century. Tracey Ullman as Katherine and Morgan Freeman as Petruchio. Directed by A. J. Antoon.

director's work with the actors to shape stage images, movements, gestures, and stage business and to focus voice and speech.

STAGE IMAGES

EACH MOMENT of a performance may be thought of as an image that sends a message to the audience. The director needs to be aware of visual composition not merely to create beautiful stage pictures, but more importantly to form images that convey the situation, emotional content, and character relationships. (In actuality, these images operate in conjunction with the lines and movements of the actors, but left to chance, they can inadvertently contradict the text and lead to audience confusion.) The director uses various devices of visual composition to emphasize what is most important and to subordinate other parts. These devices will be described first as they relate to the proscenium stage and later as they are modified for other types of stage arrangements or configurations.

One of the most important controls over emphasis and subordination is the position of the performers on stage. Certain bodily positions are more emphatic than others. For example, all other factors being equal, the performer most fully facing the audience will be the most emphatic. Similarly, height can be used to achieve emphasis, because, if all other factors are equal, the actor most elevated will be the most emphatic. To vary and control height, the director may have actors stand, sit, kneel, lie down, or mount steps or platforms. The director may also control emphasis by the placement of actors within the stage space or through the creation of spatial relationships. When, for example, a single actor on one side of the stage opposes a large group of actors on the other side, the single actor gains emphasis. Emphasis may also be created through visual focus—as when all of those on the stage look at the same person or object, thereby directing the audience's attention to a specific point. Other ways of gaining emphasis include costume (one example of which would

Director Mary Zimmerman wrote and directed *Metamorphoses*. Pictured here, as produced on Broadway at the Circle in the Square Theatre, the production effectively mixed modern and classical images. Scene design by Dan Ostling; costumes by Mara Blumenfeld; lighting design by T. J. Gerckens.

Courtesy of Dan Ostling

be a brilliantly colored garment amid drab clothing), lighting (using, for example, a spotlighted area while other areas are relatively dark), and scenery (placing an actor in a doorway or against a piece of furniture, for example, to strengthen the visual line). Directors seldom depend on a single source of emphasis; several are often used simultaneously, especially when emphasis needs to be divided among several characters, each requiring differing degrees of emphasis.

When one moves from the proscenium to the thrust stage (which is viewed from three sides) or the arena (which is viewed from four sides), the means to create visual emphasis are more limited. The impact of visual composition lessens when not all of the audience views it

The Game of Love and Chance as produced by the McCarter Theatre under the direction of Stephen Wadsworth, who also provided the English-language translation for this production. In this scene, Wadsworth has created a clear stage image of excited anticipation through his use of stage composition. Note the bodily positions of the performers and how their visual focus and gestures help to direct the audience's focus.

T. Charles Erickson

from the same vantage point. For example, bodily position becomes relatively meaningless, because actors facing one part of the audience may have their backs turned to another. For much the same reason, stage area loses much of its effectiveness, because nearness to one part of the audience may be distance from another part. But most of the other devices apply. Nevertheless, in thrust and arena theatres it is difficult to compose visual images that are expressive from every angle. The director must therefore construct images from a variety of angles throughout the performance so that no one part of the audience is neglected.

The way devices for achieving emphasis are used depends greatly on the stage setting. The placement of doors and furniture encourages some compositional patterns and impedes others. The absence of furniture in settings for many period plays (for example, *Oedipus Rex* and most of the scenes in *Hamlet*) rules out the detailed routine of daily life that is typical in such modern plays as *A Doll's House.* The type of play also affects composition. For example, many of the visual devices appropriate to a farcical commedia dell'arte script such as *The Servant of Two Masters* might be out of keeping with an expressionistic play such as *"The Hairy Ape."*

Some directors consider stage images the legacy of a time when the "picture-frame" stage was the only type in use, and they argue that its conventions have been invalidated by more recent stage forms. Others believe that concern for visual composition leads to a self-conscious or unnatural positioning of performers on stage. They argue that if the performers understand the dramatic situation, they will instinctively group themselves properly. Flexible (or variable) stages pose the greatest problem to the creation of effective stage images, because several scenes may proceed simultaneously in various parts of a space shared by both spectators and performers. This use of theatrical space rejects the traditional view that each moment of a performance should have a major focal point to which every spectator's attention is directed and that should be visible and audible to every member of the audience. However, despite the flexible theatre's use of multiple focal points, each individual scene, even if simultaneously performed with others, creates visual messages, planned or not.

Many objections to the deliberate use of stage images concern the possibility that these compositions will draw attention to themselves and distract attention from the play's action. No doubt poorly conceived or inappropriate compositions may have this effect. But one cannot deny that the stage images that continually form, dissolve, and transform as the audience watches are a major component of any production and that they embody meaning. Therefore, although there may be controversy over the way this element is to be approached, its importance is undeniable.

■ MOVEMENT, GESTURE, AND BUSINESS

ALTHOUGH PARTICULAR images are important, the dominant impression of a performance is one of movement—flow, change, and development. Consequently, movement is among the director's most powerful means of expression. Movement serves many functions.

- It gives emphasis because it catches the eye and directs attention.
- It helps define character and mood.
- It clarifies situation through its tempo and quality.
- It may provide contrast and build scenes to a climax through its type, size, and tempo.

- It provides variety.
- It may indicate dramatic type or style.

Directors work with actors to make sure that their movements focus audience attention on important stage business as well as to assist the performers in making their characterizations distinct. For example, an elderly person normally uses fewer and slower movements than a young person, just as a nervous or angry person moves differently from a casual or relaxed person. Directors may also help performers to shape their movements in order to clarify dramatic situations. Highly emotional scenes normally incite more movement (and more rapid and sharply defined movement) than do quiet moments. Movement may be used to build scenes to a climax, to provide contrast, and to establish tempo. Gradually increasing the amount and size of movement can create a sense of growing confusion, conflict, or development and change. Contrast in movement from one scene to another can point up differences in the play's mood, tempo, and situation, as well as provide variety. Finally, directors may wish to use the performer's movement to reinforce the play's genre or dramatic style. The movement called for by *Oedipus Rex* is typically more stately and formal than that called for by *Cat on a Hot Tin Roof*. For plays that depart from realism, such as *"The Hairy Ape,"* deliberately distorted or stylized movement may be called for.

Movement can be divided into three main types: from place to place, gesture, and business. Each type may be dictated by the script or invented by the director or the performers. Many movements (such as entering, exiting, dancing, or lighting lamps) may be specified in stage directions or dialogue. On the other hand, many older plays include no stage directions, and all movement must be deduced. When devising stage movement most directors take their cues from the script so that the movement not only provides variety, but also embodies the desires and responses of the characters and therefore appears motivated. Character relationships

Anne Bogart

Few contemporary directors are as noted for their work with performers on controversial productions as is Anne Bogart, who helped to popularize an acting technique called *viewpoints.* The technique, which was first articulated by choreographer Mary Overlie, grew out of postmodern dance improvisations and breaks down time and space—the two dominant elements of movement that performers deal with—into different categories. Bogart and others have expanded this technique into a training method that allows performers to generate bold nonrealistic physicalizations while working as an ensemble. Bogart uses viewpoints in her staging to encourage her audience to see familiar plays or subjects in a new light.

Bogart's directing work can be divided into several basic areas. She has created theatrical profiles of significant artists and thinkers. Bogart has provided a provocative combination of Andy Warhol interviews/writings with Dante's *Inferno* in her *Culture of Desire,* playfully reworked Brecht's theories and criticism in *No Plays No Poetry* (for which she won an Obie Award), and explored the creative imagination of Orson Welles' *War of the Worlds.* Bogart has also created new approaches to familiar or classic plays. She set the musical *South Pacific* in a clinic for emotionally disturbed war veterans. Her adaptation of *A Streetcar Named Desire* was set in a German club whose members take turns playing scenes from the play; there were ten Stanleys and twelve Blanches (one of them a man). Third, Bogart has conceived and directed wholly new plays. Her play *Cabin Pressure* examines a theatre audience's experience of suspense and anticipation. Finally, she directs the new plays and operas of others, among them Paula Vogel's *Baltimore Waltz,* for which Bogart was awarded her second Obie.

In 1992, she cofounded with Tadashi Suzuki, the Japanese director and acting theorist, the Saratoga International Theatre Institute (SITI), the goal of which is to "revitalize the theatre from the inside out"; SITI has conducted acting workshops and symposia and has presented plays directed by Bogart and Suzuki. Her work was featured at the Actors Theatre of Louisville's 10th Annual Classics in Context Festival: Modern Masters—Anne Bogart. She has also authored a book on directing and currently serves as the head of the graduate directing program at Columbia University in New York.

Bogart's directing provokes strong, conflicting responses. Because she often adapts or radically stages well-known plays or subjects grounded in our cultural past, her work can seem iconoclastic. As the *New York Times* theatre critic Mel Gussow has pointed out, "Depending on the point of view, [Anne Bogart] is either an innovator or a provocateur assaulting a script."

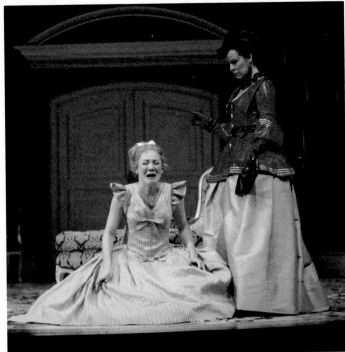

Different types of movement express character emotion and character responses to the emotions of others in *Dangerous Liaisons,* by Christopher Hampton, as produced at the Huntington Theatre (Boston). Directed by Daniel Goldstein; scene design by James Noone; costume design by Erin Chainani; lighting by Mark Stanley.

and emotional connotations are among the most common motivators of movement—feelings of love, anger, and eagerness normally move characters toward each other, whereas disgust, fear, and reluctance separate them. Movement from place to place is the broadest type that directors use in working with the performers.

Gesture, facial expression, and bodily attitude, which together create what is commonly called body language, are of special importance for achieving subtlety and clarity. Gesture normally involves only the hands and arms, but at times the torso, head, feet, or legs may be used gesturally. Gesture can provide a subtle means of gaining emphasis, because a gesture by a performer who is about to speak is usually sufficient to shift attention to that performer at the right moment. Gesture can also convey basic psychological traits: A great many spontaneous gestures may suggest an uninhibited, outgoing personality, whereas few and awkward gestures may suggest the opposite. Bodily attitude—stiffly upright, slumping, relaxed, and so on—is an especially

useful means for conveying emotional attitudes or immediate reactions. So is facial expression, which, though it is not always visible in a large auditorium, is a supplementary aid in conveying a character's response.

Another kind of movement, stage business, involves physical activities such as filling and smoking a pipe, arranging flowers, wrapping packages, eating and drinking, dueling, and so on. Stage business is frequently prescribed by the script, but it may also be invented by the director or performers to clarify action or enrich characterization. Stage business must be carefully timed to make appropriate points and coordinate with dialogue to avoid diverting attention from important lines or action.

In recent years, several nontraditional uses of movement, gesture, and business have become common. Although most stage movement attempts to re-create believable human behavior, some directors may use nonrealistic movement to stylize the production or to physicalize abstract ideas or for still other purposes. Performers may writhe

SITI performers embody esoteric critics in a scene from Anne Bogart's world premiere production of *Cabin Pressure* at the Humana Festival of New American Plays. During the scene the performers pushed this table holding microphones closer and closer to the audience as they spoke, creating a cacophony of voices. Conceived by SITI members and directed by Anne Bogart; settings by Paul Owen; costumes by Walt Spangler; lighting by Mimi Jordan Sherin.

Courtesy of Actors Theatre of Louisville

on the floor in tangled masses, crawl about the set, and perch on various structures. Movement in general has become more uninhibited, and the range of acceptable movement has been considerably extended.

■ VOICE AND SPEECH

T HE DIRECTOR'S MEANS also include the voice and speech of the performers. Just as innovative movement has become important, so, too, has nonverbal vocal sound. In nonrealistic plays, directors may use voice to create dissonance, modulations ranging from the loudest to the softest, cries, yelps, and so on. Nevertheless, the director is still most commonly concerned with voice as a medium for language or song. (Because voice and speech are more fully the performer's concern, they are discussed at greater length in Chapter 14.) The director needs to understand voice and speech thoroughly in order to use them effectively and to coach performers intelligently. In using voice and speech the director has four main concerns:

- The dialogue should be audible and comprehensible to the entire audience.
- The performers' vocal qualities—that which distinguishes any two sounds of like duration, pitch, and volume from each other, such as breathiness or nasality—should be appropriate to their characters.
- The inflectional pattern and volume of the performers should be appropriate not only to their characters but to specific situations and the meaning of their lines.
- The tempo and rhythm of the performers' dialogue should vary appropriately in accordance with the changing dynamics of the action.

The director's means are varied, and, although discussed separately here, they are applied simultaneously in the theatre, first one and then another being given primacy. Through such continuous adjustments, the director seeks to achieve clarity in motivation, action, and meaning, in addition to creating that underlying and indefinable sense of excitement that characterizes theatrical performance at its best.

Rehearsing the Play

REHEARSALS CAN SELDOM be held under conditions approximating those of performance. As a rule, the scenery, costumes, lighting, and properties are not available until the final days, and the rehearsal space is seldom the stage on which the play will be presented. Therefore, the director and performers must rely heavily on imagination during rehearsals.

The typical rehearsal space is a large room (at least as large as the stage) on the floor of which the ground plan of the set is outlined with tape. If there is more than one set, each is indicated with different colored tape. Chairs and tables, as well as improvised doors and levels, help the performers become familiar with the setting. Temporary properties that approximate those to be used in performance are necessary if there is complex stage business, such as serving a meal or fighting a duel. Similarly, rehearsal garments may be needed for plays in which unusual headdresses, hoopskirts, and other unfamiliar features or accessories will appear.

In order to plan rehearsals effectively, the director needs to know how much time will be available. In the nonprofessional theatre, performers are usually available for rehearsal only in the evenings for three or four hours and for a period of four to six weeks. In the professional theatre, a rehearsal period of three to four weeks is typical, with performers available for approximately eight hours each day. A group' that evolves its own scripts may require months to prepare a performance. Whatever the situation, the director ascertains the approximate number of hours available for rehearsals and plans a schedule to utilize the time to maximum advantage. Because all problems cannot be worked on simultaneously, the director divides the schedule into progressive phases.

Any generalized discussion of the rehearsal process makes it seem more standardized than it usually is because rehearsals are shaped to meet the particular demands of each play. However, the typical rehearsal process involves the following phases:

- Read-throughs and "table work"
- Staging or "blocking"
- Working with the performers
- Shaping the performance
- Integrating all the other elements of the production (scenery, costumes, lighting, sound, and so on)

A rehearsal room with the set marked out on the floor with tape.

David Wheeler

The amount of time devoted to reading, discussing, and studying the play varies with the director, with the complexity of the script, and with the experience of the cast. During this period, the director may explain the production concept and clarify the main objectives toward which everyone should be working. Sometimes these early rehearsals are referred to as "table work" because they may involve group reading and study done around a table. However, some directors choose to devote time during the early rehearsals to group activities (such as improvisations and theatre games) intended to familiarize the performers with each other, lessen inhibitions, encourage trust, and otherwise prepare the performers for the work ahead. Whatever method is chosen, early rehearsals usually strive to familiarize the actors with each other, the play they will perform, their roles, and the function of their roles within the play.

Staging or blocking establishes each performer's movements from place to place and each performer's bodily position at each moment. For example, an actor might be asked to enter up center, cross slowly to a sofa down left, and stand facing front. Initially, most directors are concerned only with large patterns of movement; subtleties and refinements come later. When the blocking for one segment is finished, the director moves on to the next, repeating the process until the entire play is blocked. Many directors believe that the initial blocking is merely tentative, and they adjust it as rehearsals proceed. When this is the case, the performers should be made aware that they must be prepared to adjust to changes as they occur. Some directors believe that blocking should evolve out of character relationships and the performers' sense of their roles—a collaborative process among performers and director, which

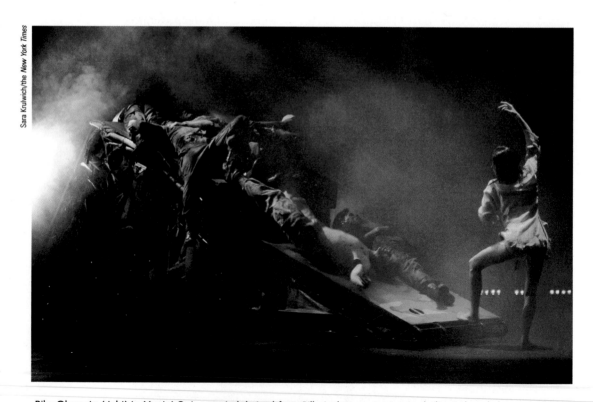

Rika Okamoto (right) in *Movin' Out,* a musical derived from Billy Joel songs as conceived, directed, and choreographed by Twyla Tharp. Scene design by Santo Loquasto; costumes by Suzy Benzinger; lighting design by Donald Holder.

takes longer to develop. Regardless of how the blocking is achieved and when it is set, once it is set the performers should understand where and when they are to move.

After the play is staged, time is typically devoted to deepening the performers' understanding of their lines and blocking. For each act, the director may specify the date by which the performers should have their lines memorized. As with blocking, there is disagreement about the best time for performers to memorize lines (early or after the performers are thoroughly familiar with the roles). However, it is generally acknowledged that it is difficult for performers to achieve subtle characterizations or to build scenes properly if they must continually consult their scripts. During this phase, the director helps the performers to incorporate their lines and movements as clear expressions of the characters' desires, actions, and relationships.

Typically, the director focuses the performers' attention on one segment or scene at a time to clarify the characters' motivations and define their relationships within each segment. A single scene may be repeated many times as these working sessions continue. This allows the performers the repetition needed to memorize their lines and movements as well as a clearer grasp of their specific motivations for what they say and do. If the performers have difficulties, the director may ask them questions or structure improvisations that stimulate responses and attitudes that can then be adapted to the scripted situation. Whatever the process used, it is important that the performers understand who their characters are, what they are doing, why they are doing it, and how they relate to one another.

With musicals, the director's task becomes especially complex during this and later phases of rehearsals. For musicals, a choreographer normally

Richard Feldman

Jonathan Miller (right) directing actors in a production of the eighteenth-century comedy *The School for Scandal* at the American Repertory Theatre.

creates and rehearses the dances separately, just as the musical director rehearses the singers and chorus separately (normally with only piano accompaniment). The director must eventually integrate songs and dances into the whole and devise the transitions that lead smoothly from spoken lines into song and from stage movement into dance.

The next phase of rehearsals usually is dedicated to ensemble playing and shaping the action for an overall effect. At this time, the director fine-tunes transitions between scenes, timing, and the proper emotional dynamics needed to support the progression of scenes. Some directors may go over the same scene repeatedly to achieve the proper timing or intensity, just as they may adjust the pacing of scenes for the sake of variety, but typically the director now works with the performers on progressively larger segments of the action. If the director has not previously allowed the performers an uninterrupted "run-through" of the entire play, almost all directors include at least one at this point in the rehearsal process.

The final phase of rehearsals integrates all of the elements of production. Frequently, this is the first time the performers have rehearsed in the actual performance space with the scenery, lighting, and sound (including, in musicals, the full orchestra) that will be used in performance. Likewise, it is often the performers' first opportunity to rehearse in their costumes and makeup. As might be expected, many adjustments are typically made during these final rehearsals. It is usual to have at least one rehearsal to work out problems with lighting levels and cues, costume and scene changes, sound, music, and properties. This is usually called a "technical rehearsal." Technical rehearsals are then followed by at least two or three dress rehearsals intended to approximate as nearly as possible the conditions of performance. During these rehearsals, difficulties are noted and attempts are made to correct them before the next rehearsal. Some directors invite several people to dress rehearsals to get indications of probable audience response and to prepare the performers for a larger audience. In the professional theatre, preview performances function as a series of additional dress rehearsals, after each of which changes may be made. The changes are then tried out on other audiences until the play opens.

When the play opens, the director's job is considered to be complete, although many directors come back at intervals to revitalize performances. By opening night a production promptbook has been compiled; it records the blocking, stage business, lighting cues, sound cues, and everything that is required to run the show as the director intended.

■ THE DIRECTOR'S ASSISTANTS

THE DIRECTOR USUALLY has several assistants who fulfill a variety of functions. The tasks that these assistants perform can vary widely from theatre to theatre, as can their titles, but their work is of vital importance. At least one assistant takes notes from the director during rehearsals about points to discuss with the performers, designers, or technicians. This individual, sometimes called a rehearsal secretary, may also post notices and keep everyone informed of things they need to know. Another assistant acts almost like a secondary director: attending production conferences, serving as liaison with designers, and coaching or rehearsing scenes with the performers. Typically called the assistant director, this individual performs whatever tasks are assigned by the director. Depending on the size or complexity of the production there may be more than one assistant director. Perhaps the most indispensable of the director's assistants is the stage manager. The stage manager is responsible for running the show at each performance and, during the rehearsal period, for compiling the promptbook, which becomes the blueprint for performances. In the professional theatre, the stage manager may organize and run auditions and, after the show opens, may rehearse the performers if necessary. The stage manager is the director's surrogate during performances, charged with seeing that everything functions as the director intended.

Thinking about the Director's Work

TODAY, NOT ONLY are approaches to directing varied, but so, too, are the plays and the theatrical conventions available. When we attend the theatre, our experiences may also be varied: We may find ourselves confronted with the commonplace and boring, the exotic and puzzling, the novel and exciting, or some combination of these. Such variety often makes it difficult to respond intelligently. Here is a list of questions that may help the theatregoer assess the director's contributions.

1. Was there an identifiable production concept, unifying metaphor, or interpretational approach? If so, what was it, and how was it manifested in the production? To what effect?

2. How closely did the production adhere to the play? Did the production alter time, place, or other aspects of the play? If so, how? To what effect? If not, how did this production make—or fail to make—the play relevant to its audience?

3. How did the director's casting choices influence the production?

4. What effect did the performer-audience arrangement or configuration have on the performance? Did the director's staging take advantage of this relationship? If so, in what ways?

5. Did the director's staging clearly convey the action? How was the staging used to clarify character relationships or emphasize important actions?

6. Did the director's staging create any memorable images or visualizations? If so, which? What overall effect did these have on the production as a whole?

7. Was there appropriate variety in mood and tempo? Did the action, as a whole, build to a climax or have a discernible pattern or shape? What effect did this have on the audience?

8. Did the production make use of any unusual conventions? If so, which? To what effect?

9. Were the production design elements (scenery, costumes, lighting, sound) coordinated to support the action and the production concept? If not, what aspect seemed out of place or inconsistent with the rest? Did the director make any specific use of the design elements? With what effect?

10. Overall, did the production achieve its apparent goals? If not, where did it fall short? With what overall results?

Other questions could be posed, and many of them will arise as other areas of production are examined in the chapters that follow.

Additional Opportunities with InfoTrac College Edition

Broadway producers invest huge sums hoping their show will be a hit. But how do they decide which show will be a hit? Use InfoTrac College Edition to find and read "The Hit Makers: Commercial Producing; How Do Broadway Producers Decide When the Show Should Probably NOT Go On?"

1. Are there any ingredients essential to a hit musical?

2. What steps do producers take to ensure that the musical will have sufficient audience appeal?

3. How do Broadway producers work with regional theatres to develop new musicals?

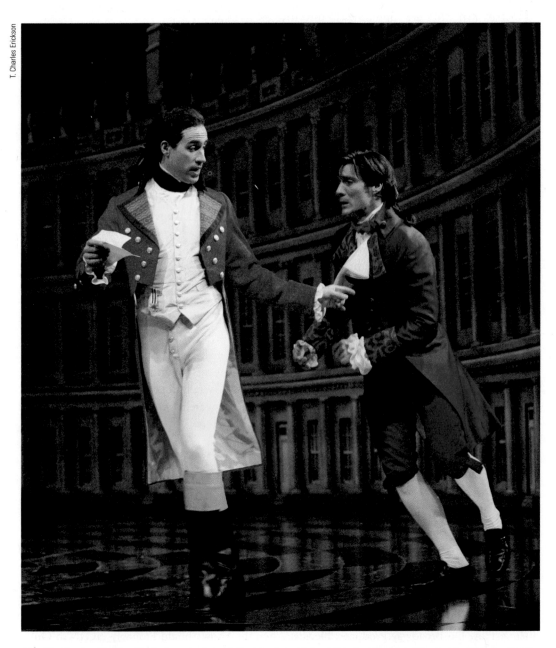

The Huntington Theatre (Boston) production of *The Rivals* by Richard Brinsley Sheridan. Directed by Nicholas Martin; scene design by Alexander Dodge; costume design by Michael Krass; lighting design by Dennis Parichy.

Acting is in many ways unique in its difficulties because the artist has to use the treacherous, changeable and mysterious material of himself as his medium. He is called upon to be completely involved while distanced—detached without detachment. He must be sincere, he must be insincere; he must practice how to be insincere with sincerity and how to lie truthfully.
—Peter Brook, *The Shifting Point*

14: Acting

OF ALL THEATRE PRACTITIONERS, the actor most nearly personifies the stage for the general public, perhaps because the actor is the only theatre artist the audience normally sees. The actor's function is to embody characters that otherwise exist only in the written word and the imagination. What the performers say and do and the way they interact with each other and their surroundings creates a play's action. Though the script may provide the blueprint, the designers the visual context, and the director the overall focus, it is the living presence of the actor that is most essential to the audience's theatrical experience.

Actors are among the few artists (along with dancers and singers) whose basic means of expression cannot be separated from themselves; they must create roles by using their own bodies and voices. The director, designers, and playwright can sit in the auditorium and watch what they have created, but stage performers can never completely separate themselves from what they are creating. Even a filmed stage performance violates the essence of stage acting: the moment-by-moment interaction of the live performer and the live audience. In films, scenes are almost always shot out of sequence and over a span of several months; the actors usually have

only a general notion of how the scenes will fit together; typically film actors do not see the scenes in sequence until the film is ready for release months later. Even then, the performance they (and the public) see has been given much of its shape by the film's editor. Audience response cannot alter or influence what happens during a screening. All of these factors do not make the screen actor's job less difficult than the stage actor's, but they do make it different. Stage actors play scenes in the order specified by the script and complete the entire play at each performance. They must be fully aware of how the action develops, and they must shape their performances to increase and relax tension, vary tempo, create appropriate emphases, and build the action to a climax. They prepare for these tasks through many rehearsals with a director whose critical advice and editing shape the total production, but it is the actors who must re-create the performance each time—and for a new audience, whose immediate feedback continuously influences that performance.

In many ways, acting is an extension of everyday human behavior. Almost everyone speaks, moves, and interacts with others. We also play many "roles," during the course of a day adjusting to changing contexts: home, business, school, recreation, and so on. Perhaps it is not surprising, then, that it is not always easy to distinguish acting talent from certain personality traits or to convince would-be actors that rigorous training is necessary. Nevertheless, acting requires carefully honed skills, because the ability to use behavior expressively in the theatre differs from the ability to function adequately in daily life.

Acting skill is a mixture of three basic ingredients: innate ability (a special talent for acting), training, and practice (or experience). Talent is perhaps most essential, but usually it is not enough in itself; it needs to be nurtured and developed through extensive training and repeated application in performance.

The Actor's Training and Means

I N ACTING TRAINING, though the process of acting as a whole is the ultimate concern, not all of its aspects can be addressed simultaneously. Therefore, different aspects of acting (voice, movement, scene study, and so on) are singled out for specialized attention even as attention is being paid to the interrelationship of the various parts. Ultimately the goal is to integrate all of the parts into a seamless whole.

THE ACTOR'S INSTRUMENT

J UST AS IT TAKES musicians many years of training and practice to master their instrument, actors spend years mastering their instrument. However, unlike musicians, the instrument that actors learn to master is themselves: their body, voice, imagination, concentration, and psychological responsiveness. As the actor's primary means of communicating, the body and voice need to be flexible, disciplined, and expressive. Flexibility is needed so the actor can express physically or vocally a wide range of attitudes, traits, emotions, and responses. But flexibility alone is not sufficient; actors must also be able to control body and voice at will, and such control comes only through understanding, practice, and discipline.

One of the actor's primary challenges is to understand how the body and voice function.

The part of Hamlet requires great imagination and the ability to handle Shakespeare's language as well as stage combat skills. Pictured is Steve Tague in the title role of the Great Lakes Theater Festival's production of *Hamlet* at the Ohio Theatre, Playhouse Square Center in Cleveland, Ohio.

Photo by Roger Mastroianni; courtesy of the Great Lakes Theater Festival

Actors' Thoughts
about Acting

Many well-known actors have been quite articulate about their profession. Here are a few excerpts.

Willem Dafoe *(a member of the Wooster Group and well-known screen actor):* "I think that all the characters I play are basically me. I believe that under the right set of circumstances we're all capable of anything, and that acting allows the deepest part of your nature to surface—and you're protected by the fiction as it happens."

John Barrymore *(one of America's legendary classical actors, known best for his performance as Hamlet):* "Acting is the art of saying a thing on the stage as if you believed every word you utter to be as true as the eternal verities of life; it is the art of doing a thing on the stage as if the logic of the event demanded that precise act and no other; and of doing and saying the thing as spontaneously as if you were confronted with the situation in which you were acting for the first time."

Joseph Chaikin *(leading actor of the Open Theatre):* "Only when [the actor] is awake to the whole event of the piece, rather than just his part, and his interest in what is told in the piece is immediate . . . can his work be organized to each performing situation. What he learns is how to live through the situation each time, instead of just repeating the results. [Otherwise] his performance is without the most essential acting dimension—that of being there and inhabiting the play as it's performed."

Fiona Shaw *(leading contemporary British actress, speaking of her performance as Electra):* "Literature, I think, is humanity's dialogue with itself and an actor is the interpreter of the text of the writer, who is tapping the soul of who we all are. The best one does is to give it expression—the key being one's own grief that reveals a very dark pool of basic grief that everybody has. In the end, I suspect, that dark pool is a very similar pool to everybody else's pool."

Judi Dench *(one of England's major actresses and 1999 Oscar winner for her role in Shakespeare in Love):* "What I like is doing as many different things as possible in the theatre at the same time. I like being in a repertoire of four or five plays. . . . You're kept very much on your toes. . . . It's like a permanent first night and that keeps it very alive; doing a play eight times a week is a killer."

Actors typically begin by learning how the body and voice operate in a general, physiological sense and then proceed to explore how their own body and voice actually are functioning. If one can discover what one's normal body alignment is, how one is breathing, what one's sources of tension are, and so on, one is then in a position to work toward gaining control over one's physical and vocal instrument. The initial goal is to eliminate inhibiting tensions so one can move freely and effortlessly and achieve a resonant, flexible voice; the ultimate goal is control over both body and voice for expressive use in performance.

Because the body and voice are integral parts of a total system that includes psychological forces, it is difficult to achieve physical and vocal freedom and expressiveness without some concern for the psychological processes that may create tension or block creative expression. One popular means of dealing with these has been through improvisational theatre games designed to break down inhibitions, build self-confidence, and foster trust in fellow performers. Other exercises have been borrowed from a variety of sources, both Western and Asian, most of which treat inner impulse, body, and voice as interrelated processes. Therefore, to work on any one of these is to help the others. The goal is to develop a sensitive, skilled, and expressive instrument that the actor can control.

In addition to mastery of body and voice, actors usually seek more specialized training in dancing, fencing, singing, and other skills that increase their ability to play a wide range of roles in a variety of theatrical forms.

■ OBSERVATION AND IMAGINATION

ACTORS REQUIRE highly developed powers of observation and imagination. Because human beings learn about each other in large part through observation, actors need to develop the habit of watching other people (for example, the dominant behavioral patterns of various personality types or age groups). Although observed behavior may not always be directly transferable to the stage, it can be drawn on in creating convincing characterizations.

Willem Dafoe in Eugene O'Neill's *"The Hairy Ape"* as produced by the Wooster Group. Directed by Elizabeth LeCompte; lighting design by Jennifer Tipton.

Mary Gearhart; courtesy of the Wooster Group

Applying Imagination and Observation

All actors use their imaginations and powers of observation to create believable characters with whom they frequently have little in common. However, few actors have the opportunity to test their skills while facing the challenge of playing complex nonhuman characters. Veteran actor André De Shields faced such a challenge in playing a 350-pound gorilla named Graham who is trained to communicate in American Sign Language in Mark Medoff's play *Prymate*.

To prepare for the role, De Shields studied gorillas by reading about them, observing them in zoos and on film, and speaking with a gorilla-behavior specialist. He learned to imitate the dozens of specific sounds that gorillas make, the manner in which they shift their attention every ten to fifteen seconds (because gorillas have a strong sense of peripheral vision, they seldom directly focus on one object for long), and the manner in which they communicate affection or warn others off their territory. He wanted to make certain that his physical actions as Graham were accurate and specific, even though doing so was physically very taxing. Once De Shields had a thorough knowledge of how gorillas communicate and move, he sought to understand why Graham acts as he does and how he might perceive different objects, actions, and events. De Shields then built an imaginative bridge between himself and his 350-pound gorilla character.

De Shields has played a wide variety of roles on Broadway and throughout America's regional theatres including Willy Loman in *Death of a Salesman,* Vladimir in Samuel Beckett's *Waiting for Godot,* and one of the amateur male strippers in *The Full Monty* on Broadway. He originated the role of Graham at Florida State University before playing the part on Broadway.

In addition to the physical rigor and psychological savvy needed to create the character, De Shields also needed great personal courage because he believed that some would find the image of a black man playing a gorilla offensive and potentially racist. But "if you want to explode a stereotype, you don't avoid it," he explained in an interview with the *New York Times.* "You face it down."

Actors must also develop imagination in order to "feel their way" into the lives of others and into fictional situations. The imagination grows when fed by a few particular details or circumstances. For this reason many actors start improvisations or scene work by identifying the *given circumstances* that they are working with: the basic who, what, when, and where that constitute the situation. An actor's imagination also requires specificity to transform the stage world into one that compels belief. To behave believably, the actor handling a plastic pistol imaginatively particularizes it with the properties of a real one (its weight, texture, and deadly potential). Similarly, to embody the character's attitudes convincingly, the actor must imaginatively endow the objects, places, and people with the emotional significance and value they hold for the character. Most imagination techniques are based on behaving as if the fictional world were true. However it may be approached and developed, imagination plays a fundamental role in believable acting.

◼ CONCENTRATION

N O MATTER HOW well actors have mastered the basic skills, they are unlikely to use these skills effectively onstage unless they have also learned to control, shape, and integrate them as demanded by the script and the director. Control is usually achieved only through daily practice and disciplined effort over a long period.

One mark of control and discipline is concentration—the ability to immerse oneself in the situation and to shut out all distractions. Before actors rehearse or perform, they must clear their minds of unrelated personal concerns in order to adopt those of their characters. During rehearsals, actors may need to tune out peripheral noise. They must be able to remain focused on the scene, despite interruptions by the director, and make ongoing adjustments. Well-developed concentration is also required during performance. No matter how often they have performed the roles, actors should make each moment seem as if it were happening for the first time. To create this illusion, actors must concentrate on what is developing around them—not in a general way but on the specific speeches, gestures, and movements of others in the scene—and must respond with the appropriate level of intensity at the appropriate moment.

◼ STAGE VOCABULARY

O VER THE CENTURIES, actors have developed certain ways of doing things onstage because they have proven more effective than others. Many routine tasks have been reduced to a set of conventions that actors are expected to know. Directors take for granted that actors are

André De Shields plays a 350-pound gorilla, and Phyllis Frelich plays the anthropologist who teaches him to use American Sign Language in the Broadway production of Mark Medoff's *Prymate.*

Sara Krulwich/the *New York Times*

familiar with these conventions and give many instructions in a kind of stage shorthand.

Among the basic conventions is the division of the stage into areas, which facilitates giving directions. The term *upstage* indicates the area toward the rear of the stage, and *downstage* refers to the area toward the front of the stage. These terms date from the time when the back of a raked stage actually did slope upward away from the audience and downward toward it. Stage right and stage left refer to the actor's right and left when facing the auditorium. The stage floor may also be spoken of as though it were divided into squares, each with its own designation: *up right, up center, up left, down right, down center, down left.* The actor is also expected to be familiar with body positions. *Full front* means facing the audience; *one-quarter* indicates a quarter-turn away from the audience; *one-half* or *profile* means a 90-degree turn away from the audience; *three-quarter* means a 135-degree turn away from the audience; and *full back* means turned completely away from the audience.

Other terminology may supplement designations of area and bodily position. To *open up* means to turn slightly more toward the audience; *turn in* means to turn toward the center of the stage; *turn out* means to turn toward the side of the stage. Two actors are sometimes told to *share a scene,* meaning that both should play in the one-quarter or profile position so that they are equally visible to the audience. To *give stage* means that one actor gives the dominant stage position to another by facing away from the audience more than the other actor does. In most scenes, emphasis shifts frequently from one character to another, and the actors may constantly be giving and taking the stage according to who needs to be most emphatic at a specific moment. To *focus* means to look at or turn toward a person or object so as to direct attention there. Actors may also be told to *dress the stage* (that is, move to balance the stage picture). Experienced actors make such movements unobtrusively and almost automatically.

Some devices are commonly used to emphasize or subordinate stage business. An object (such as a letter) that is to be important later may need to be planted in an earlier scene. To make sure it is noticed, the actor may hesitate, start to put it one place, then select the final spot. Conversely, some actions need to be masked or cheated, away from the audience. Eating, for example, must be faked to a large degree, because actors can seldom eat the actual food or the amount indicated by the script in the time provided. A convincing illusion of violence on stage (such as a stabbing, shooting, or fistfight) requires careful planning and timing. Sometimes a fight choreographer is employed to make the action both convincing and safe.

In whatever they do, actors normally strive to be graceful, because gracefulness is usually unobtrusive, whereas awkwardness is distracting.

Stage areas.

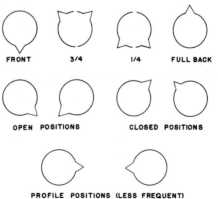

Performer positions.

Movement should be precise and clear, because imprecision suggests vagueness and indefiniteness. (Awkwardness and imprecision can, of course, be used to dramatic effect if they are deliberate.) Actors are better prepared if they are familiar with all aspects of theatrical production, because the more they know about scenery, costumes, and lighting, the better they will be able to utilize these elements in their acting.

■ SCENE STUDY

WHILE ACTORS ARE INVOLVED in gaining control over themselves as instruments, they are simultaneously involved in scene study, based on either scripts as a whole or scenes from scripts. This involves close attention to dramatic action and how it develops. Most actors learn to break scenes into beats or units of action. These are based on alterations in motivation or a change in tactics by a character or some other change such as the entrance or exit of a character. Actors also note changes in tempo and mood and so on. This study is usually preliminary to rehearsing the scenes with other actors. Over time, actors typically study and enact scenes from a wide variety of plays—past and present. This allows them to gain the broadest possible experience in multiple dramatic forms and styles. Scene study and its embodiment in performance (both in the classroom and in fully mounted productions) ultimately bring together all of the elements of actor training.

■ FROM TRAINING TO PERFORMING

PRIOR TO THE TWENTIETH century, would-be actors usually learned on the job. First, they had to be accepted into a company as "utility" actors, roughly equivalent to being apprentices. They then played small roles in a variety of plays and observed the more experienced and established actors closely. Training was essentially a mixture of observation and trial and error. After

a few years, young actors discovered the types of roles to which they seemed best suited and settled into that "line of business," usually for the rest of their careers. But in the late nineteenth century, when resident companies were driven out of existence by touring productions (usually cast in New York with experienced actors), would-be actors were deprived of their traditional training ground. Although some acting schools had existed before this time, the demise of the resident companies was the principal spur to the founding of actor-training programs in the United States. In the twentieth century, actor training gradually gained a foothold in colleges and universities, which have now become the principal trainers of actors, although there are still many actor-training studios, especially in large cities. Today resident theatre companies have become prominent in the United States again, and most of them employ actors who are graduates of universities or other training programs. A few resident companies even have their own schools.

Most training programs stage productions to provide students opportunities to apply what they are being taught. Today's training programs retain some features of the earlier apprentice system, although in today's schools learners often play major roles that in professional companies would be cast with experienced professionals. All training schemes, old or new, attempt (though often in quite different ways) to stimulate and integrate the three foundations of artistic skill: talent, training, and practice.

Although a would-be actor may complete training programs and receive a degree or certificate, there are no exams or boards as there are for lawyers and doctors to certify an actor's readiness to practice the profession. Certification, such as it is, comes from being cast in professional productions. The decision to become a professional actor takes courage, because the number of aspirants greatly exceeds the available jobs. Although there are now more acting jobs in the nation's resident companies than in New York's theatres, many theatre companies still

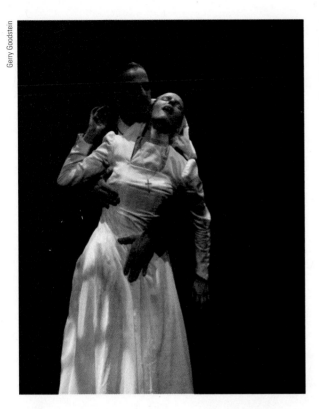

Trained performers conjure intense passion from the given circumstances of the play's action, as Vivienne Benesch (Isabella) and Bruce Turk (Angelo) do here in the New Jersey Shakespeare Festival's production of Shakespeare's *Measure for Measure,* directed by Paul Mullins.

hold auditions and do much of their casting in New York. Though it is possible to be an actor and live in one of the many cities that support professional companies, aspiring stage actors still gravitate to New York, just as aspiring film and television actors gravitate to Los Angeles. Chicago and a few other cities have managed to remain largely independent of both New York and Los Angeles.

Wherever actors live or wish to work, they all face the problem of being cast. To work in the professional theatre, an actor must be a member of Actors Equity Association, the actors' union. But less than one-quarter of Equity's members are ever employed at the same time, and only a small percentage make a living from acting. For most actors, the chances of being cast are improved if they have an agent, whose job it is to help them get employment and whose own income depends on their clients' success, because the agent usually receives at least ten percent of each client's earnings. Despite the odds against success, many people persist, and enough are

sufficiently successful to encourage others to try. Nevertheless, aspiring actors must be prepared to accept rejection as part of their lives. Many, perhaps most, aspiring actors spend more time working as waiters or in temporary office jobs while they make the rounds of auditions than they do performing for pay on the stage. Patience and persistence are necessary attributes of would-be actors.

Most of the procedures involved in casting have already been discussed in Chapter 13. Let us assume that the actor is one of those lucky enough to have been cast and is now ready to create a role.

▌CREATING A ROLE

EACH TIME ACTORS undertake a new role, they are faced with a number of tasks. Perhaps the most basic is to understand the role. (One approach to analyzing script and role is described in Chapter 3.) It is usually helpful to look at the role in relation to four levels of characterization.

1. Biological (What does the script reveal about the character's gender, age, physical appearance, and condition of health?)
2. Sociological (What does the script reveal about the character's profession, social class, economic status, family background, and standing in the community?)
3. Psychological (What does the script reveal about the character's attitudes, likes, dislikes, general emotional makeup, motivations, and goals?)
4. Ethical (What does the script reveal about the character's system of values and choices when faced with crises and conflicts?)

Because a character may have been given many traits, it is also helpful to determine which among these traits are necessary within the dramatic action. Such inquiries form a broad base for further explorations.

The most essential aspects of a role are what the character wants and what the character is willing to do to get it. But though these define the "spine" of a role, the actor needs to examine how they are manifested in each scene, beat by

© Martha Swope

Peter Brook includes actors from many different countries and trained in various traditions in his theatre company so that they may learn techniques from each other that will help them to transcend any one language or style of performance. In this scene from *Mahabharata*, the actors are English, Kenyan, and Polish.

IDEAS AND INFLUENCES

Brecht and Grotowski on Acting

D irectors frequently comment on acting because the actor is the primary material they use to embody their interpretations of scripts. Some directors have envisioned a distinctive purpose for the theatre that places particular demands on the actor. Bertolt Brecht envisioned the "epic theatre," where the actor's job was to observe human relations with a scrutiny that shows them to be changeable rather than naturally fixed. Jerzy Grotowski envisioned the "poor theatre," where the actor's mission was to create a unique encounter with the spectators without relying on other theatrical means. Here are statements about acting by Brecht and Grotowski.

Bertolt Brecht *(one of the twentieth century's major playwrights and directors, explaining the kind of acting he sought for his epic theatre):* "The actor does not let himself be transformed into the man he presents so that nothing of himself is left. He is not Lear, Harpagon, or the good soldier Schweik—he is 'showing' them to an audience. . . . Giving up the idea of complete transformation, the actor brings forward his text, not as an improvisation, but as a quotation. . . . In this sort of acting, where the transformation of the actor is incomplete, three devices can contribute to the alienation of the words and actions of the person presenting them: adoption of the third person, adoption of a past tense, and the speaking of stage directions and comments. . . . Through this threefold process the text is alienated in rehearsal and in general will remain so in performance."

Jerzy Grotowski *(Polish director who exerted great influence on the training of actors beginning in the 1960s):* "One must not think of the spectator while acting. . . . If the actor has the spectator as his point of orientation, he . . . will be offering himself for sale. . . . A sort of prostitution . . . at the same time, he must not neglect the fact of the public . . . he must act vis-à-vis with the spectators . . . he must . . . do an act of extreme yet disciplined sincerity and authenticity. He must give himself and not hold himself back, open up and not close in on himself in a narcissistic way. . . . The most important thing for me . . . is to rediscover the elements of the actor's art."

beat, and how they change and evolve. This investigation helps the actor find the focus of each scene, just as examining individual units in relation to the play as a whole shows how the role builds, grows, or changes.

The actor also needs to examine how the role relates to all of the others in the play. What does the character think of each of the others? How does the character present himself or herself to each of the other characters? What does each of the others think of the character? What is the function of each of these variations within the dramatic action?

The actor needs to understand the script's themes, implied meanings, and overall significance, which demands not only attention to observable relationships among characters and ideas but also sensitivity to subtext—the emotional undercurrents, unexpressed motivations, and attitudes that inform the underlying meaning of their lines. Many plays, notably those by Anton Chekhov and Harold Pinter, depend heavily on subtext because the characters cannot or will not directly address the problems or feelings that lie just beneath the surface. In such scripts, the actor must make the audience sense these unstated elements or else the action will lose much of its power.

The actors also need to examine their roles in relation to the director's interpretation of the script (the production concept). They may wish to talk with the director about their reactions to the interpretation and how it affects their roles; some may even try to persuade the director to alter the production concept. Ultimately, however, the actors must make their roles fit whatever interpretation is being used to shape the production.

■ PSYCHOLOGICAL AND EMOTIONAL PREPARATION

IN ADDITION to understanding the script and the way a role fits into the total concept, the actors must be able to project themselves imaginatively into the world of the play, the specific situations, and their individual characters' feelings and motivations. An actor who has difficulty doing this may need to experiment with ways of inducing empathetic involvement. One method, borrowed from Stanislavsky, is to employ *emotion memory* (searching in one's own past for a parallel situation, recalling the emotion felt at that time, and using that emotion in acting the present scene). Another

Pat Carroll is seen here as the title character in Bertolt Brecht's *Mother Courage and Her Children* as produced by the Shakespeare Theatre in Washington, D.C. under the direction of Michael Kahn.

Joan Marcus

method is to search out people similar to the character and find out more about their situation and feelings. For example, an actor playing a hospital worker may come to understand the character's attitudes and frustrations more fully by spending time in a hospital participating in or observing what goes on there. The most typical method is the use of improvisations and theatre games to explore, in collaboration with other actors, multiple feelings about, and responses to, situations similar to those in the script. Such explorations may be necessary in many different scenes during the preparation or rehearsal process.

◼ MOVEMENT, GESTURE, AND BUSINESS

WHETHER THE DIRECTOR specifies much of the actors' movement or, at least initially, lets the actors position themselves and move about as their responses impel them, actors need to feel comfortable with their blocking and movement. Actors should tell the director if they do not. Most discrepancies can be settled if the actor and director discuss the character's motivations, relationship to other characters in the scene, and the function of the scene. If actors and directors can agree on these points, they can also usually agree on how these points are to be enacted.

Even if the director specifies much of the movement, the actor still must fill in many details—the character's walk, posture, bodily attitudes, and gestures. (For a discussion of movement and its purposes, see Chapter 13.) Actors may find it helpful to approach physical characterization in three steps. First, they need to take into consideration the physical traits required by the action and any changes that occur during the play. Second, they may wish to assess which of a character's physical traits need to be dominant in any given unit or beat. It is sometimes helpful to think of a play as though it had no dialogue; actors would then physically

have to convey their situation, motivations, and emotional responses. This approach, if followed fully, would probably lead to an overabundance of movement (and overacting), but used in the preparatory stages it can stimulate the actors' imagination and provide the actors with a number of choices to explore. It may also require actors to execute each movement precisely, helping them avoid vague, indefinite, and confusing movement. Third, without violating the limits established by the script, role, and production concept, the actors may work for distinctiveness through greater specificity. A physical characterization can be judged by its appropriateness, clarity, expressiveness, and distinctiveness.

◼ VOCAL CHARACTERIZATION

ALTHOUGH ACTORS cannot radically change their dominant vocal traits during a rehearsal period, they may, if they have well-trained voices, modify their vocal patterns considerably for purposes of characterization. The variable factors in voice are pitch, volume, and quality, each of which may be used to achieve many different effects. Typically, the voice is used to speak lines in a manner that evokes or defines emotions, ideas, or situations. The voice is also sometimes used as a type of sound gesture or as a way to create mood through nonverbal dissonances, harmonies, or rhythmical effects.

The variable factors of speech are articulation, duration, inflection, and projection (or audibility). *Articulation* involves the production of sounds, whereas *pronunciation* involves the selection and combination of sounds. A person may articulate sounds clearly but mispronounce words, just as a person may know how to pronounce a word but articulate sounds so imprecisely as to be unintelligible. The well-trained actor should be able to speak clearly or to alter articulation and pronunciation as needed to suit character and situation. One of the most memorable features of Meryl Streep's roles is her vocal characterizations, achieved through control over articulation, pronunciation, and quality.

Duration refers to the length of time assigned to any sound, *inflection* to rising and falling pitch. Both duration and inflection are used to stress some syllables and subordinate others. Without proper stress, words may be unrecognizable. (Try, for example, shifting stress from the first to the second syllable of *probably.*) *Duration* also refers to the number of words spoken per minute. Slowness can create the impression of laziness, old age, or weakness, whereas a rapid rate may suggest tension or vivacity. Inflection (change in pitch) is one of the principal indicators of meaning. Surprise, disgust, indifference, and other reactions may be indicated by tone of voice, and the alteration of inflection can often completely change the meaning of a line or transform a statement of fact into a question. Duration and inflection play key roles in dialects (regional "accents"). Vocal coaches often counsel those working on a southern accent, for example, to end sentences on a rising inflection and to maximize the duration of vowel sounds.

In performance, actors should be both *audible* (which depends on projection or volume) and *intelligible* (which depends primarily on articulation and pronunciation), because the audience needs both to hear and to understand what the characters are saying. Actors must also be concerned with *variety* (which may be achieved through alterations in any of the variable aspects of voice and speech). Nothing is more deadening than hearing all lines delivered at the same pace or intensity. Variety is more easily achieved if the actor clearly understands situation and motivations, because any change in thought or feeling triggers changes in volume, pitch, or quality, as well as in the variable factors of speech.

■ MEMORIZATION AND LINE READINGS

A TASK THAT EVERY actor faces is memorization. It is usually helpful to memorize speeches and movements simultaneously, because they reinforce each other. Furthermore, because blocking is done in relation to specific speeches, this conjunction ultimately becomes fused in the memory.

Memorization is aided by a few simple procedures. Because it is impossible to memorize everything at once, the script may be broken into beats and mastered one at a time. In each, the actors must ultimately not only learn their

Vanessa Redgrave and other actors rehearse for a production of *Antony and Cleopatra* at the Alley Theatre in Houston, Texas.

T. Charles Erickson

own lines but also memorize *cues* (the words or actions of others that immediately precede and trigger their lines) as thoroughly as they memorize their own lines. Before trying to memorize specific lines, it is helpful to study the sequence of ideas or shifts in emotion and tone—the overall development of the beat. Familiarity with sequence and a thorough understanding of the meaning and purpose of each line in a beat are the greatest aids to memorization. (The actual process of memorization requires going over the lines many times, usually while someone else keeps an eye on the script as a check on accuracy as well as to provide the appropriate cues.)

Once the actors have memorized or have become very familiar with their lines, they begin to color their understanding of the lines through the controllable factors of voice and speech to form distinctive line readings. Often these line readings are developed without conscious effort, but the actors must be concerned with timing, pacing, and pauses. They must make sure that speeches, especially long ones, build properly, that their line readings create a sense of spontaneity and conviction, and that their readings are appropriate to character, emotion, and situation.

REFINING THE ROLE

THE FOUNDATION WORK (understanding the role; psychological and emotional preparation; movement, gesture, and business; vocal characterization; memorization) proceeds simultaneously with rehearsals, some of it in isolation, much of it with the director and other actors. In the early phases, different approaches to a scene or aspects of character may be tried and abandoned. Eventually, the major decisions are made, the movement and vocal patterns become clear, and the lines are committed to memory. There follows a period of refining and perfecting the role and integrating it into the whole performance.

This phase is difficult to describe, because it varies with each actor, role, and production. Typically, much of the time is spent on deepen-

ing one's understanding of motivations and relationships. Other concerns during this phase are complex business, precise timing, pacing, and variety. Actors must define each step of their characters' journey throughout the action to ensure that it builds appropriately.

No single role (except in those plays with one character) is complete in itself. It is sometimes said that performing in a play is not acting so much as reacting. The director usually works to achieve the sense of give-and-take, cooperation, and mutual support that characterizes ensemble playing. The goal is a seamless whole rather than a series of separate performances; it can be reached only if all actors are willing to subordinate themselves to the demands of the production. Ensemble playing depends on the actors' awareness of each other's strengths and weaknesses, where they will get support, and where they need to compensate for another's weakness.

DRESS REHEARSALS AND PERFORMANCE

NOT UNTIL DRESS REHEARSALS are actors usually able to work with all properties, settings, costumes, makeup, and stage lighting. Frequently, this is also the first time they have been able to work on the stage that will be used for performances. Thus dress rehearsals may be occasions of considerable stress and exciting discoveries.

Of special importance to actors are their costumes, because they affect not only appearance but also movement and gesture. Actors should find out everything they can about their costumes in advance of dress rehearsals—how a garment may enhance some moments or restrict others, what its possibilities are for use in stage business, and so on. If stage garments will be significantly different from clothing they normally wear, actors are typically provided suitable rehearsal garments early in the rehearsal process. Even if resources or budgets make this impossible, actors should consider from the beginning of rehearsals how they might use their costume and how it might affect their performance. Actors should also give thought to their makeup well before the dress-rehearsal period begins. Although the costume designer may also design the actor's makeup, especially when it is complicated or stylized, the actor should know at least what effects are desired and understand generally how to create them.

Because actors typically rehearse with reasonable facsimiles of the properties they will use in performances, their adjustment to the actual properties is much easier. Still, actors should expect or request extra time to deal with specialty props, such as pyrotechnics (guns that fire blanks, confetti cannons, and so on). Experienced actors

T. Charles Erickson

Mickey Solis as Romeo and Annika Boras as Juliet in the American Repertory Theatre's highly stylized production of *Romeo and Juliet*. Directed by Gadi Roll; scene design by Riccardo Hernandez; costume design by Kasia Maimone; lighting by D. M. Wood.

understand that every aspect of the production—costumes, scenery, properties, lights, and sound—affects their performance and how it will be perceived by the audience. Consequently, they try to gain a working understanding of these aspects and are patient as they are integrated into the production.

Performance is the ultimate goal. The better prepared the actors are, the more confident they will feel on opening night, although it is a rare actor who does not experience some stage fright—which, because it increases alertness, may be turned to advantage. Some actors feel a let-down after opening night and must guard against diminished effectiveness during the following performances. Long runs create special dangers because the actors may begin to perform mechanically because of overfamiliarity with their roles. The best guards against such letdowns are concentration and reminders that each performance is the first for this particular audience. Ultimately, performance offers the actor one of the best opportunities for learning, because the ability to affect or control an audience's responses is a major test of acting skill.

■ Thinking about the Actor's Work

WHEN WE ATTEND the theatre, our attention is focused primarily on the characters, because it is through them that the action develops. But what the actors who play the characters do and say is based on the dramatist's script, just as the interpretation and overall production concept are decided by the director. What actors wear is provided by the costume designer; the stage environment is created by the scenic designer; and much of the mood and emphasis is created by the lighting and sound designers. In such a cooperative venture, it is not easy to isolate the actors' contributions. Perhaps that is as it should be, because usually the director's goal is to create a unified whole rather than a collection of easily distinguishable parts. Nevertheless, even if we cannot determine precisely what is to be attributed to each production element, we often are impelled to make the attempt. Here are some questions that may help us assess the actors' performances and estimate their contributions to the production:

1. Were actors and roles adequately meshed? Were some actors more effective than others? In what ways? How did this affect the action of the play?

2. How did the type of space in which the performance took place affect the actors' tasks? With what results?

3. Were the actors audible? Understandable? Were the vocal characterizations suited to the roles? Were there actors whose voices noticeably enhanced or detracted from their performances? In what ways?

4. Were the physical characterizations suited to the roles? Were there actors whose movement or gestures noticeably enhanced or detracted from their performances? In what ways? How extensively were movement and stage business used? Did they have distinctive qualities? If so, what was the result?

5. Were some actors more effective than others in conveying their characters' psychological attributes and motivations? If so, how and with what effect?

6. Were the relationships among the characters clear? Were some actors more effective than others in creating clear and convincing relationships? If so, how and with what effect?

7. Were any special skills (such as dancing, singing, fencing, dialects, or accents) required of any of the actors? If so, how effectively were the demands met? With what effect on the production?

8. Did the actors make any special use of costume, scenery, properties, or lighting? If so, in what ways and with what effect?

9. Did the actors achieve a sense of "the first time"? Did they work together effectively as an ensemble? If so, with what effect? If not, what interfered? With what result?

10. Overall, were the themes and implications of the play clear? Was the clarity or lack of it attributable to the acting? Script? Directing? Visual design? Total production?

Most of these questions cannot be answered precisely, not only because some of the needed information may not be available but also because, even if the information were available, responses would be at least partially subjective. Answers to each question are likely to vary widely from one audience member to another. Nevertheless, trying to answer these questions as they relate to specific productions or performances will focus attention on the processes and results of acting and will encourage detailed attention to actors' performances.

Additional Opportunities with InfoTrac College Edition

The craft of acting is continuously debated. To see multiple viewpoints on a particular shift in process, use InfoTrac College Edition to find and read "Taking Directions" by Jean Schiffman in *Back Stage West.*

1. Are the respondents in agreement when it comes to the usefulness of stage directions? What about punctuation?

2. Describe one or two of the different approaches to stage directions in detail and then contrast them with the previously dominant approach.

Neil Prince's scene design for *The Umbrellas of Cherbourg* satisfied the musical version's need for multiple locations with a revolving stage framed by (and containing) vertical translucent units. Adapted by Sheldon Harnick and Charles Burr from the film by Jacques Demy; music by Michel Legrand; directed by Jonathan Fox at Two River Theater Company.

Scene Design

THE SCENE DESIGNER is concerned with the organization and appear-ance of the performance space. The designer defines and characterizes the space, arranges it to facilitate the movement of the actors, and uses it to reinforce the produc-tion concept.

The Functions of Scene Design

SCENE DESIGN serves many functions. It defines the performance space by establishing distinctions between onstage and offstage. Through the use of flats, drapes, platforms, floor treatments, or other means, designers delineate the areas that will be used for the dramatic action. Designers may employ a great deal of masking so that people or objects outside a clearly marked area cannot be seen by the audi-ence; or they may use virtually no masking and thereby acknowledge that the place of the action is a stage that continues into the wings as far as the audience can see. In arena and thrust the-atres, the layout of audience seating itself may outline the acting space. In a flexible space, act-ing space and audience space may be intermingled.

Scene design creates a floor plan that shapes movement, composition, character interaction, and stage business. The location of exits and entrances, the placement (or absence) of furni-ture, the presence or absence of steps, levels, and platforms—all the elements of the setting and their arrangement—are among the greatest influences on blocking, visualization, and move-ment. A setting can be organized in many differ-ent ways; arranging it to maximum advantage for a specific production requires careful and cooperative planning by designer and director.

Scene design visually characterizes the acting space. Just how it does so depends on the pro-duction concept. If the concept demands that locales be represented realistically, the designer will probably select architectural details, furni-ture, and decorations that clearly indicate a spe-cific period and locale. For example, the designer might create a setting for *A Doll's House* that suggests a room in a Norwegian house around 1880. Another production concept might demand fragmentary settings with only enough

Kathleen Widomski's evocative scene design for Arthur Miller's *All My Sons* as produced by the Williamstown Theatre Festival.

Richard Feldman

pieces to establish the general character of the locale. Another might rely largely on visual motifs and theatrical conventions from the era when the play was written. A setting for *Tartuffe,* for example, might use decorative motifs and a wing-and-drop setting reflecting the age of Louis XIV. Or the concept may demand that the time and place of the action be altered (such as *Hamlet* being translated to an American Mafia context).

Another way of characterizing the space is to treat it as flexible and nonspecific, a common practice for plays with actions divided into many scenes and set in many places, as is typical in most of Shakespeare's plays. To represent each place realistically would require a large number of sets as well as a great deal of time to change them, thereby interrupting the continuity, rhythm, and flow of the action. On the other hand, to play all of the scenes on the flat floor of an undecorated stage might become monotonous. A common solution is an arrangement of platforms, steps, and ramps that breaks up the stage space, that provides several acting areas that can be used all together or isolated singly through lighting, and that can be localized as

needed through the addition of a few well-chosen properties, pieces of furniture, banners, or images projected on screens, or through other means.

How the scene design characterizes the performance space may make a strong interpretative statement. The setting for Beckett's *Happy Days* visually sums up the human condition as depicted in the play: an individual isolated, trapped, forced to make the best of her lot. For a play about war, the game of chess has been used as a metaphor, with the stage floor laid out in black and white squares and the characters costumed to suggest chess pieces. The settings for *"The Hairy Ape"* incorporate images of human beings caged and dehumanized.

Scene design creates mood and atmosphere. The towering Gothic arches in Norman Bel Geddes' design for the *The Miracle* create a powerful sense of mood atmosphere. (See the illustration on page 176.) On the other hand, Ezio Frigerio's settings for *The Servant of Two Masters* (the illustration on page 118) create a sense of carefree improvisation through details painted on cloths (with slits for entrances) suspended like shower curtains on visible rods.

Michael Yeargan's scene design for the recent Broadway revival of Edward Albee's *Seascape*. Directed by Mark Lamos; costume design by Catherine Zuber; lighting by Peter Karczorowski.

Scene design is only one part of a total design, which includes costumes, lighting, acting, and all the other elements of a production. It should evolve in consultation with those responsible for the other parts of the whole. It is not, as a painting is, complete in itself; it cannot be judged entirely by appearance, because it should not only look appropriate, but also function appropriately.

The Scene Designer's Skills

SCENE DESIGNERS need a variety of skills, many of them pertinent to other arts, especially architecture, painting, interior design, and acting. Like architects, scene designers conceive and build structures for human beings to use.

Although scene designers do not design entire buildings, as architects do, they sculpt space and, like architects, must be concerned with its function, size, organization, construction, and visual appearance. Also like architects, they must be able to communicate their ideas to others through sketches, scale models, and construction drawings that indicate how each element is built and how it will look when completed.

Scene designers, in some aspects of their work, use skills similar to painters, for example, one of the designer's primary ways of communicating with the director and other designers is through sketches and drawings. During preliminary discussions of a production, designers usually make numerous sketches to demonstrate possible solutions to design problems; before these designs are given final approval, they usually are rendered in perspective and in color. For

Courtesy of Richard Isackes

Scene design detail of the act curtain and proscenium for the opera *Falstaff* as designed by Richard Isackes.

final designs, watercolors are the scene designer's most common medium, but pastels and other color media are sometimes used. In addition to making sketches showing entire settings, designers also make painters' elevations—scale drawings of each piece of scenery showing how it is to be painted and the painting techniques to be used. Designers sometimes must paint (or supervise others who paint) the scenery they have designed.

In other aspects of their work, scene designers use the skills of an interior decorator, because many sets are incomplete without furniture, rugs, drapes, pictures, and decorative details. In creating appropriate interiors, designers also need some of the actor's skills because they must understand the characters who inhabit the spaces and whose tastes have dictated the choice of furnishings and decorative features.

Additionally, scene designers need to be grounded in art history (including architecture, crafts, and decorative arts), because in creating settings, designers must be familiar with architectural styles and the history of decorative motifs, furniture, and accessories. In stage settings, such details not only reflect a specific period or place but also indicate the economic status and tastes of the characters. A knowledge of art history also allows designers to draw upon various visual styles. They may wish, for example, to create a setting done in the surrealistic style of Salvador Dali or one that uses a particular artist's color palette. Designers also benefit from a knowledge of stage history so that they may (when appropriate) draw on the theatrical conventions of other times, places, or cultures to connect the play with its original context or to otherwise enhance the production concept.

Scene designers must understand scenic construction techniques (because they must frequently specify how each part of their setting is to be built) and scenic painting (because they must specify the color of each visible surface and the painting techniques to be used). Designers should also be familiar with new materials and technologies and their potential for design purposes. Computer literacy has become increasingly important for scene designers. Most designers now use computer-assisted design or drafting programs to help them in creating or communicating their designs. These programs allow the designer to revise floor plans or construction drawings quickly (with great accuracy). Three-dimensional animation programs can help the designer communicate to others how multiple sets, or parts of them, may move. However, though computer-assisted design and architectural programs are useful tools for designers,

such programs have their limitations and cannot replace the designer's artistic skills and judgment.

Working Plans and Procedures

THERE IS NO STANDARD way of moving through the design process. After having studied the play and discussed the production concept with the director and other designers, most designers make many tentative, preliminary sketches as a means of thinking through possibilities. Much of this preliminary work can be done using computer-assisted design programs. Some designers make a scale model of the empty performance space on which they explore different arrangements of scenic pieces. Some think in terms of design elements—the line, mass, color, or texture needed to capture the

HAMLET

Robert Schmidt's preliminary sketch for a production of Shakespeare's *Hamlet* at the Alabama Shakespeare Festival.

Courtesy of Robert Schmidt

Model of the setting for *Hamlet*.

dominant qualities of the dramatic action or the production concept.

However they work, designers eventually arrive at preliminary designs to present at a conference with the director and the other designers. (Design decisions involve not only how the settings function as acting spaces but also how they relate to costume and lighting designs and the total "look" of the production.) Through a process of reaction and revision, tentative agreement is reached, but before the designs are given final approval, they must usually be rendered as perspective color sketches that indicate how the sets will look on stage when lighted. Scene designers must also supply floor plans (drawn to scale) that show the layout of each set on the stage. Designers may also be asked to construct three-dimensional scale models that show in miniature how each set will look when completed. (It is not unusual for directors to ask for

either a color sketch or a scale model, although in many situations both are expected.)

After the designs have been approved, the next step is to make working drawings. The number and type of drawings needed vary from one type of organization to another. For example, in a permanent company that maintains a stock of scenic units, it may be unnecessary to make working drawings of every flat and platform, because many will be pulled from stock. In the Broadway theatre, every piece is usually built new by union workers who insist on precise drawings for every detail. The designer may have to provide some or all of the following, in addition to perspective sketches, floor plans, and scale models: (1) rear elevations, which indicate the type of construction, materials, and methods to be used in assembling each unit as seen from the rear; (2) front elevations, which show each unit in two dimensions from the front, with

Courtesy of Robert Schmidt

The setting for *Hamlet* in production.

indications of such features as molding, baseboards, and platforms; (3) side elevations, which show units in profile, indicating the thickness and shape of each unit; (4) detailed individual drawings, which show the methods by which such units as platforms, steps, trees, columns, and similar objects are to be built; and (5) painters' elevations, which show the color of the base coat and any overpainting to be used on each unit. With the exception of the perspective sketches, all of the plans are drawn to scale so that the exact size of any object may be determined. In addition to the drawings listed here, designers may need to provide special plans showing how the scenery is to be shifted and how it is to be stored during performance when it is not on stage.

Once the plans are completed, the construction phase can begin. Although designers may not be directly involved in building the scenery, they must approve all work to ensure that it conforms to the original specifications.

Basic Scenic Elements

A COMBINATION OF CHANGING tastes, rising costs, improved materials, and new equipment has steadily diminished the desire for full-stage, realistic settings. Although complete box sets are still seen occasionally, they are far less common than they used to be. The majority of settings today are composed of a few set pieces and stage properties or of steps and levels; they tend to be fragmentary and evocative rather than completely representational, many being wholly abstract. However, traditional stagecraft practices still play a major role in most settings and the

Ming Cho Lee

Ming Cho Lee is often said to be the most influential of contemporary American scene designers. Born in China, he learned landscape watercolor there before coming to the United States in 1949. After studying at Occidental College and UCLA, he went to New York, where he became an assistant to Jo Mielziner, then America's foremost scene designer. Most of Lee's early work was done for groups with limited budgets, among them the New York Shakespeare Festival, for which he was principal designer from 1962 until 1972. During these years, Lee developed the style that was to influence many other designers: abandoning the use of pictorial, painted scenery in favor of defining the space with scaffolding built from metal pipes or wood and combining them with fragments of scenery (usually heavily textured) suggesting collage. Although by 1980 Lee's designs had become more realistic, he is still usually associated with a spare, elegant, minimalist style. He has continued to experiment with innovative materials and multimedia. Though he has seldom worked on Broadway, his influence there is strong because many of its designers are graduates of Yale University's School of Drama, where Lee is head of design training. Each spring for several years, Lee has hosted the Stage Design Portfolio Review, an exhibition of work by student designers from throughout the country at which Lee and a number of other leading designers discuss and offer critiques of the students' designs. This has become a major showcase for young designers seeking to enter the profession.

Lee prefers to work in regional or repertory companies because he feels that is where collaboration is most respected ("the regional theatre atmosphere invites you to behave as part of a family"), whereas on Broadway stars, directors, or producers exert too much control. Lee considers his strengths as a designer to be his sense of proportion and his understanding of the demands and restrictions of various kinds of theatrical space—arena, thrust, or proscenium. Some of his most successful work has been for arena and thrust stages. Lee's recent scene designs include *Stuff Happens* for the Mark Taper Forum (in Los Angeles), and in 2006 he was awarded the Helen Hayes Tribute honoring outstanding lifetime achievement in scene design. (For examples of Lee's work, see pages 231 and 363.)

built pieces (though fewer in number) are usually constructed according to time-tested procedures or variations on them.

Designers use a few basic kinds of scenic units: soft, framed, and three-dimensional. Designers need to understand each kind of scenic unit at their disposal so they can combine them creatively into expressions that are both evocative and practical. Let us look briefly at each type.

Ming Cho Lee's setting for John Osborne's *The Entertainer* at the Guthrie Theatre (Minneapolis). The play draws parallels between the decline in the vitality and fortunes of a family of music-hall entertainers and the British Empire. The play indicates a number of different locations, but Lee's design uses a single setting to suggest all of the locations as well as providing poignant commentary through the figures of the lion (symbol of the empire) and the female figure (a music-hall showgirl dressed in the colors of the British flag, representing Britannia).

◼ SOFT-SCENERY UNITS

SOFT-SCENERY UNITS are typically made of unframed cloth. Usually suspended from overhead, they provide a large area of scenery that can easily be moved, or folded up and stored when not in use. Among the most common soft-scenery units are drops, draperies, scrim, and cycloramas.

Drops are used to enclose settings at the back and to provide surfaces on which scenes can be painted. A drop is made by sewing together enough lengths of canvas or cloth to create an area of the desired size. Typically, the cloth is attached to a wooden or metal batten at the top for support and to another at the bottom to keep it stretched and free from wrinkles. A drop may also have portions cut out so that another drop or object is visible behind it, thereby creating apparent depth and distance. Drops can be raised into, or lowered from, the fly space above the stage; they can be rolled up and stored when not in use.

Draperies may be hung parallel to the proscenium on either side of the stage in a series from front to back in order to mask the sides of the stage in the manner of wings. They may be any color. Black draperies are sometimes used to surround the acting area or to create an enclosing void for a fragmentary setting. Draperies may also be made of canvas or muslin; they may be dyed, or they may have scenes (such as a forest or a distant city) painted on them and be hung in folds to create stylized backgrounds.

Scrim, a specialized curtain made of gauze, appears opaque when lighted only from the front but is transparent when lighted from behind. It can be hung in folds or stretched tightly. It may be used initially as a background for a scene and then become transparent to show another scene behind the first one; it may be used for the appearance and disappearance of ghosts and apparitions; and it can create the effect of seeing a scene through fog, mist, or the haze of memory.

A *cyclorama* is any arrangement of curtains that surrounds the stage area on three sides. It may be composed of draperies, but typically (to avoid the appearance of seams) it is a continuous, tightly stretched curtain suspended on a

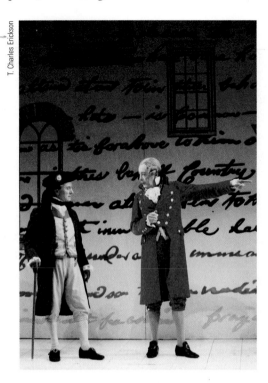

T. Charles Erickson

Michael Yeargan's scene design for *The School for Scandal,* as produced by the McCarter Theatre (Princeton, N.J.), included nonrealistic, moveable framed units. Note the writing and architectural drawings on the units. Directed by Mark Lamos; costume design by Jess Goldstein; lighting design by Stephen Strawbridge.

U-shaped pipe curving around the back and sides of the stage. It is usually neutral or light gray, so that its perceived color may be changed through lighting. It is used to represent the sky, to give the effect of infinite space, and to allow the maximum use of stage space without the need for numerous masking pieces. It is also used as a surface for projections (such as moving storm clouds or abstract, symbolic patterns).

Soft-scenery units are used more extensively on proscenium stages than on thrust or arena stages, where less masking is needed and where scenic units more easily interfere with sightlines.

▌FRAMED UNITS

SOME UNITS ARE framed to make them self-supporting. They are usually relatively small in comparison with soft-scenery units but can be combined to create larger surfaces. The basic framed unit is the *flat.* A flat is a wooden or metal frame covered by a relatively flat surface (either stretched cloth or a thin sheet of wood)

that can be painted or treated texturally. Flats of almost any width or height can be made, but as they become larger, they become less stable, thereby requiring additional support from above or below the stage. Flats may be constructed in a variety of forms, but three basic types are typical: flats without an opening (for walls, etc.); flats with an opening (for doorways, windows, etc.); and flats specifically cut or pieced together to simulate a particular silhouette (such as trees or distant vistas). Most flats have smooth edges so that they can be combined to create larger units, such as the walls of a box set or the exterior of a castle. Occasionally, drops are framed on all four sides.

Screens have become increasingly used as a surface on which to project still or moving pictures. Screens may be used alone or with other screens. They may rest on the floor, or, more commonly, be suspended above the stage. They may be rigged so that they can be raised, lowered, or moved laterally during a performance; they may be of any shape or size and made from almost any material—wide-mesh netting, translucent plastic, textured cloth, and so on. Some of these surfaces blur images, some give texture, and some permit images to bleed through onto other surfaces; on some screens, images can be projected only from the front, and on others, only from the rear. Screens can be used for projected slides or moving images; they may also be used to show offstage or onstage live scenes transmitted to the screens by way of closed-circuit television. There is a wide range of uses for screens, although some options require more advanced technology than is available in many theatres.

THREE-DIMENSIONAL UNITS

SOFT AND FRAMED units are usually two dimensional. Other units, however, especially those that support considerable weight, must be three dimensional. These include (most commonly) steps, ramps, and platforms. Certain other scenic pieces, though they may not always be weight-bearing, are still usually built as three-dimensional forms. These include rocks, tree trunks, and columns. Extensive use of three-dimensional units is most common on proscenium stages or in flexible spaces, but they may also be used sparingly on thrust and arena stages. Three-dimensional objects or fragments of archi-

tecture may be suspended above a thrust or arena stage to suggest what is not shown. How one constructs these various types of scenic units is beyond the scope of this discussion; such processes are described fully in books on scenic practices.

INNOVATIVE MATERIALS AND METHODS

DURING THE PAST two or three decades, there have been many experiments with nontraditional materials. New materials (such as Styrofoam and thermoplastics) and unconventional construction methods (such as molding Plexiglas into weight-bearing forms) have encouraged innovative techniques. The selection of materials and methods depends on the particular circumstances (space, labor, budget, and so on) and on the desired function and effect.

A variety of substitutes for wood may be used. Steel, aluminum, and other metal alloys offer greater strength and support than the same amount of wood, but weigh more and have less flexibility. Steel can be cut and bent to hold different shapes, but this process requires special skills and equipment. Fiberglass (treated with chemicals to make it pliable) may be molded into rocks and other shapes and allowed to

T. Charles Erickson

Dangerous Liaisons by Christopher Hampton at the Huntington Theatre under the direction of Daniel Goldstein. Note how James Noone's scene design uses the large hanging chandeliers and long curved staircase to help suggest period opulence. Costume design by Erin Chainani; lighting design by Mark Stanley.

John Conklin

John Conklin began his career at the Williamstown Theatre Festival in the late 1950s. Today he is known as one of America's most innovative and influential designers. Conklin has designed settings (and often costumes for the same productions) for the Hartford Stage Company, the Goodman Theatre (Chicago), the American Repertory Company, the Chicago Lyric Opera, the Metropolitan Opera, the New York City Opera, the Glimmerglass Opera (where he serves as associate artistic director), and the San Francisco Opera as well as several European opera companies. He has also collaborated with Robert Wilson on designs for many of Wilson's pieces. As a teacher of design at New York University's Tisch School for the Arts, Conklin influences tomorrow's potential scene designers.

Conklin's designs often select images from the different scenes of a play and combine them to create a single setting that remains unchanged throughout except for the rearrangement of a few properties or pieces of furniture. Conklin recalls that for Shakespeare's *Pericles,* "a scattered and fragmented play," he used "a large broken Greek head, a series of yellow rocking chairs and a red curtain—all put together in a collage effect." Such settings have become characteristic of much postmodern theatrical design. But his work is eclectic, some of it very realistic. (For examples of Conklin's work, see pages 9, 53, 291, and 367.)

harden, creating lightweight pieces capable of supporting heavy loads. Styrofoam and urethane may be incised to create the three-dimensional forms of moldings, bricks, and carvings, or sculpted to create figurines and other properties formerly difficult to construct. Such chemically formed or treated materials, however, must be used carefully to avoid toxic poisoning from fumes emitted when subjected to heat or other chemicals. Safety devices, such as respirator masks that filter out harmful fumes or particles, have been developed to protect those who work closely with such materials. Vacuform molds, in which one can duplicate in plastic almost any shape (including armor, swords, or small scenic units), have also become common.

Traditional stagecraft and innovative stagecraft coexist and supplement each other. The basic units discussed here are the building blocks with which designers usually work. Designers must decide which pieces are needed for the settings they have designed, and they must supply the working drawings or indicate which pieces in existing stock are to be used. For pieces using unusual materials or construction methods, designers need to supply detailed drawings and instructions.

■ Assembling and Painting Scenery

Basic scene elements (or units) are constructed, joined together, and painted. The initial stages usually occur in a scene shop.

T. Charles Erickson; courtesy of the Hartford Stage

The Hartford Stage production of Shakespeare's *Pericles,* an episodic play in which characters seek to find lost relatives and to mend relationships in a fragmented, unpredictable world. The setting reflects this fragmentation. The narrator (center left) is dressed in Elizabethan garments, whereas the others are in periodless or modern dress to suggest the tale's timelessness and its relevance to today. Directed by Mark Lamos; designed by John Conklin.

Although in certain instances scenery may be built in the performance space, more often it is built in shops adjoining the stage, or, as is the case for Broadway productions, built in scenic studios far removed from the theatres in which the performances will occur. Regardless of where the construction takes place, after basic units (flats, door frames, doors, steps, platforms, and the like) are constructed (or brought from storage), they are usually combined into larger units (the walls of a room, a door frame and door, platforms and steps, and so on). The way the pieces are assembled depends partially on whether the scenery must be transported from one place to another, whether it must be shifted during the performance, or whether it must be stored during the run of the production. Once erected, scenery for single-set shows may not need to be moved until the production closes. Such sets are typically assembled with permanent joining methods (which provide ample stability), whereas multiple sets may require temporary joining methods so that scenic units may come apart and be moved quickly. Finally, the scenery is painted.

Scene painting makes use of a variety of techniques. Normally, these first require that the scenery be painted with priming and/or base coats to ensure a flat neutral surface upon which other techniques and paint will be applied. Because overpainting adds texture, shading, or details, it requires colors that provide contrast, the degree of which depends on the desired effect. For example, the texture of relatively smooth plaster may be achieved by *spattering* (flicking small drops of paint from a brush onto the base coat) with one color that is slightly lighter and a second that is slightly darker than the base coat, creating the effect of raised and receding surfaces. Rough plaster may be simulated by *rag rolling,* which involves a rolled-up piece of cloth dipped in paint and rolled over the base coat in irregular patterns. Other common painting techniques include *sponging* (dipping a natural sponge in paint and patting it on the surface of the base coat), *scumbling* (simultaneously applying and blending more than one shade of paint on the same surface to give a mottled effect), and *lining* (creating with painted lines the semblance of molding, paneling, door trim, and other details). Most scene designers are accomplished scene painters. They specify the appropriate painting techniques on the painters' elevations and approve the finished painting before it is transported to the stage on which it will be used.

Shifting Scenery Onstage

WHEREAS A SINGLE setting may not require shifting, multiple settings need to be planned so that their individual units can be disassembled quickly and quietly, moved easily, and stored economically. Several different methods are used in shifting scenery: manual, flying, wagons, revolves, and elevators.

The least sophisticated method involves *manual* scene shifting. Using this method, one or more stagehands move each part of a set to some prearranged storage space offstage and bring the elements of a new setting onstage. It requires breaking the setting into small units. Because manual shifting can be used on any stage, however simple or complex, a designer can always rely on it, though a large crew of stagehands may be required to make it efficient.

Another common method of shifting is *flying*—suspending scenic elements above the stage and raising or lowering them as needed. Flying requires a counterweight system composed of battens, lines, and pulleys. Weights sufficient to counterbalance whatever is being flown must be carefully placed into the system. With an adequate counterweight system, a single stagehand can easily raise and lower scenic elements of enormous size and weight. Newer flying systems use electrically controlled winches without counterweights and often provide greater flexibility.

Another common device for shifting scenery is the *wagon* (a platform on casters). The larger the wagon, the more scenery it can accommodate, but many stages do not have sufficient wing space to store or maneuver large wagons. Some stages have permanently installed tracks that guide wagons on and off stage with precision, but such a system has limited flexibility. Wagons can be used singly, in pairs, in groups, or in combination with other shifting devices. The primary advantage of the wagon is that it permits heavy or complex scenic pieces to be shifted more efficiently than by hand.

A revolving stage or turntable is another device for shifting scenery. It may be a permanent

The scene design for this production of *A Midsummer Night's Dream* incorporated an upside-down architectural element, along with the flying of performers in clearly visible harnesses to characterize the action as nonillusionistic and fantastic. Scene design by Michael Yeargan.

T. Charles Erickson

The Odyssey, adapted from Robert Fitzgerald's translation of Homer and directed by Mary Zimmerman, as presented by the Seattle Repertory Theatre. On the isle of the sun, after disobeying the sun god Helios, all but Odysseus are wiped out. Scene designer Dan Ostling enlists only a stylized representation of the sun and the open horizon to characterize the island.

feature cut into the stage floor with a supporting central pivot, or a low circular platform that sits on castors atop the stage floor created for a specific production. A turntable usually bears the weight of two or more settings simultaneously; the individual sets are placed so that each faces the circumference of the circle. Scene changes are made by revolving the stage until the desired setting faces the audience. In the meantime, settings that face the backstage area may be changed for later use. Because of the tremendous weight they normally bear, most turntables are moved by electric motors.

Still another shifting device, the *elevator stage,* raises and lowers segments of the stage. In some theatres, portions of the stage may be lowered to a basement, where scenery is mounted and then raised to stage level. In other theatres, the stage is divided into several sections, each mounted on its own elevator lift that can be raised, lowered, or tilted; these sections can then be used in combinations that create platforms, ramps, or a variety of levels without the need of building and shifting such units in the usual manner. Theatres in which the stage proper is fixed may have a lift that raises and lowers the orchestra pit, so that it can be set below stage level for musicians, raised to the auditorium level and used for audience seating, or raised to stage level for use as a forestage.

Seldom is a single method of shifting exclusively used. Most often, two or more methods are used in conjunction. Designers need to know which methods are available to them and decide which will be used for each unit that must be moved. These decisions are important because audiences may become impatient with delays caused by lengthy scene changes, and such delays can also destroy the rhythm of a production. Today, extremely complicated settings that demand exacting precision in their shifting and coordination with other effects may use computers programmed to orchestrate the total effect. Few theatres now try to hide scene shifts from the audience. Efficiency and speed are the primary concerns.

Set Decoration and Properties

EVEN AFTER the sets are assembled onstage, they are incomplete without set decoration and properties. These elements, though part of the design, are not structural parts of the setting.

Set decoration and properties include such items as banners, coats-of-arms, window draperies, furniture, pictures, and books—anything that completes the setting. Properties may be

IDEAS AND
INFLUENCES

Action and Spectacle

Designers create settings that are appropriate to the play but also provide spectacle through the settings' visual variety and appeal. Can a spectacular design overwhelm a production? What is the proper relation between spectacle and action? Is it different for every play? Here, some of America's most successful scene designers address these questions.

Heidi Landesman (*designer for regional theatres as well as Broadway plays and musicals, among them 'night Mother, Into the Woods, The Secret Garden, and Smokey Joe's Cafe*): "If 'spectacular' means extremely theatrical, then it's all for the good. On the other hand, if it means just a lot of scenery decorated to within an inch of its life, then I don't find 'the spectacle' particularly appealing. But the design for *Les Misérables* . . . it was spectacular in that it created a truly theatrical event, an event that couldn't be reproduced in any other media."

Robin Wagner (*designer for rock concert tours of groups like the Rolling Stones and for such Broadway plays and musicals as* Lenny *[see page 203]*, A Chorus Line, Angels in America *[see page 249], and others*): "How do you draw an event as opposed to the objects that make an event? . . . Theatre design is not about painting or sculpture, it's about life, which is the very essence of theatre. . . . You have to be extremely careful not to snuff out the life of a script visually, because the design is a very powerful instrument. Vision is the strongest sense that a person has and what is there will either support or drown that which has to live in it."

Marjorie Bradley Kellogg (*designer for numerous regional theatre companies, many of which perform in thrust or arena spaces*): "When I was studying Michelangelo, I was taught that one of the great things about his sculptures was that they seemed to be made from the inside out, rather than from the outside in. There is a form there and he was just taking away all the outside junk. That's what positive and negative space is about—the statue is positive and the rest of the marble around it is the negative space. What we tend to think when we look at scenery is that the scenery itself is the positive, whereas what's really positive is the space contained within the scenery. It's positive because that's what the actors are going to be moving through."

T. Charles Erickson

In this production of *Under Milk Wood,* by Dylan Thomas, the textured treatment of the rear wall, the planked flooring, and the careful placement of differing kinds of chairs (some suspended in air) and human bodies create a distinctive setting. Scene design by Michael Yeargan; costumes by Peter J. Hall; lighting by Mark McCullough; directed by Mark Lamos.

subdivided into *set props* and *hand props.* The former is a property either attached to the setting or functioning as a part of the design. The latter is used by the actor in stage business. The designer is always responsible for selecting set props and may also select the hand props. Directors frequently make specific requests regarding hand props because of their intimate connection with the acting. Responsibility for obtaining both types may be assigned to a property master and crew, who may buy, rent, or construct props to the designer's or director's specifications. If the theatre maintains a stock of previously used props, items may be pulled and adapted for reuse. However obtained, set decoration and properties are necessary to complete the design.

Technical Rehearsals, Dress Rehearsals, and Performances

Even after the settings are complete, they must be integrated with the other elements that make up the total production. Typically, this is accomplished during technical and dress rehearsals. A *technical rehearsal* focuses attention on elements other than acting (although typically at least portions of all scenes are performed), so that the various designers and technicians can see if the "technical" elements—in this case, scenery (including scene shifts, prop-

erties, and all stage business involving properties)—are available and are functioning properly both separately and as parts of the whole. Any difficulties revealed by a technical rehearsal are corrected as quickly as possible so that dress rehearsals (in which costumes and makeup are added if they were not included in the technical rehearsals) can proceed as nearly like performances as possible. In complex productions, more than one technical rehearsal may be needed to make certain that all necessary adjustments have been made (including the levels and cues for lighting and sound). Thorough preproduction planning is necessary because it is very difficult to make major changes in scenery at this late point.

Dress rehearsals allow the scene designer to view the settings in use by the actors and stagehands (under conditions that approximate performance). The designer must be available for consultation and changes until the play has opened. On opening night, responsibility for the scenery passes to the stage manager and the stage crews.

The Scene Designer's Assistants and Coworkers

Many people aid the scene designer. In the professional theatre, designers are usually members of the United Scenic Artists Union, and they are usually assisted by members of this

Amphitryon as produced by the Huntington Theatre (Boston). Jupiter (high atop the temple structure, flanked by clouds, with his sidekick Mercury) wants to trade places with Amphitryon (front center) so that he might pitch woo with Amphitryon's beautiful wife, Alcmena. Directed by Darko Tresnjak; scene design by David Gordon; costumes by Linda Cho; lighting design by Frances Aronson.

T. Charles Erickson

or other unions. Established designers often employ one or more assistants who make working drawings, construct models, search for furniture and properties, act as liaison between the designer and the scenic studios—anything the designer may request.

In the nonprofessional theatre, the *technical director* is likely to perform many of these functions. In many theatres, however, the technical director's job is independent of the designer's and of equal status. When a permanent organization produces several shows a year, the designer's job may be divided into its artistic and practical aspects. The designer may then conceive the designs, and the technical director may be responsible for building, assembling, and paint-

ing them. The technical director may also purchase all materials, supervise construction, and be responsible for the crews who run the shows. He or she often serves as a production manager.

In the professional theatre, all people involved in the construction, assemblage, painting, and shifting of scenery are usually members of a union. In other types of organizations, this work is undertaken by assigned or volunteer helpers under the supervision of the designer, the technical director, or a scene shop supervisor. In all types of theatres, during performances the heads of stage crews operate under the supervision of the stage manager. Their duties include the efficient movement and accurate placement of scenery and properties during the performance as well as the maintenance of scenery and properties during the run of the show.

The designer's assistants frequently go unnoticed by the public because little is done to draw attention to them. Often, and especially in the professional theatre, their names do not even appear in the programs. Nevertheless, they are indispensable members of the overall production team; without them the scenery would not be built and painted and could not function efficiently or be shifted during performances.

Thinking about the Scene Designer's Work

THE RANGE OF SCENIC design in today's theatre is great. It may be realistic or abstract. It may incorporate or intermingle elements from almost any period, style, culture, or set of conventions. So much variety can be confusing. The following questions focus attention on crucial aspects of scenic design as an aid to understanding more clearly the designer's contribution to the performance, no matter the situation or mode in which the designer works:

1. How did the type of space in which the production was performed affect the designer's work? How did the designer take advantage of the space's potential and cope with its limitations?

2. Did the scenery define the performance space? If so, in what ways and through what means? If not, with what effect?

3. How did the floor plan affect the action? Were there multiple levels? If so, how did they relate to each other, and how were they used? Were there specific entrances and exits? If so, how did their placement affect the action? Did the arrangement of furniture (or other elements) enhance or inhibit action? How did the overall arrangement affect movement and visual composition?

4. What sorts of scenic units (soft, framed, three-dimensional, or other) were used, and how did these affect the overall setting? Was the setting realistic? Fragmentary? Abstract? What was the overall effect?

5. Were sets (or any parts) changed during the performance? If so, by what means? How long did the changes take? How did the varied settings affect the mood, tension, and tempo?

6. What characteristics did the scenery embody? What did the scenery convey about the characters? Socioeconomic conditions? Period? Locale? How did it affect the play's tone, mood, and atmosphere?

7. Were there any unusual scenic features? Projected images? Highly distinctive effects? If so, how did they affect the performance?

8. How did the scenery relate to the costumes, lighting, and sound? Did they enhance and complement each other? If so, how? If not, in what ways? With what results?

9. Did the setting suggest any specific interpretation of the play? If so, what interpretation? How did the setting convey this interpretation? If it did not, what was the result?

10. How did the scenery contribute to (or detract from) your experience of the production as a whole? What would have been lost if the scenery had been eliminated?

The relevance of each question may vary according to the particular production and setting. There are no absolute answers to many of the questions because responses are inevitably subjective. But so are most responses to art of whatever kind. Nevertheless, formulating answers to these questions forces us to go beyond our usual cursory reaction to scenery and to examine it and its function in production more specifically and critically.

Additional Opportunities with InfoTrac College Edition

Scene Designer George Tsypin's 40,000-pound stage setting for the opera *Grendel* (the mythic monster in the epic Old English poem *Beowulf*) proved something of a monster itself. Use InfoTrac College Edition to find and read "Taymor Meets the Monster" by Eileen Blumenthal and "Irrational Visions: A Maximalist Scenic Designer Describes His Fantastical Architectural Ideas for *Grendel,*" by George Tsypin in the 2006 July–August edition of *American Theatre.*

1. What challenges did Tsypin face in controlling the movements of his trapezoidal twenty-ton set? What challenges did the singers and dancers encounter performing on it?

2. Why did Tsypin create such a behemoth setting? What images does the setting attempt to create? What functions does it need to serve?

Michael Krass' costume design takes center stage in the Huntington Theatre (Boston) production of *The Rivals,* by Richard Brinsley Sheridan. Directed by Nicholas Martin; scene design by Alexander Dodge; lighting design by Dennis Parichy.

The transformation of the human body, its metamorphosis, is made possible by the costume, the disguise. Costume and mask emphasize the body's identity or they change it; they express its nature or they are purposely misleading about it; they stress its conformity to organic or mechanical laws or they invalidate this conformity.

—Oskar Schlemmer, *Man and Art Figure*

16:

Costume Design and Makeup

THE COSTUME DESIGNER is concerned primarily with the visual appearance of characters, but an actor's costume may also affect how the actor moves and feels. Whereas the scene designer helps to define the stage environment within which the action develops, the costume designer helps to define the characters who exist within that environment. Thus the work of the scene designer and costume designer interacts and needs to be coordinated carefully.

The Functions of Costume Design

COSTUME DESIGN serves several functions. Primarily, it helps to define the characters and their relationships. It may establish the characters' social and economic status by distinguishing between lower and upper classes, between rich and poor, or between more and less affluent members of the same group. It may identify occupation (nurse, soldier, policeman) or lifestyle (conservative middle class, fashionable leisure class, disaffected youth). Costumes usually indicate gender and may reflect age (by adhering to stereotypical notions of what is appropriate to each age group). Costumes may also reflect a character's atypicality through dress that departs from the norm. In addition to conveying information about individual characters, costume design can also establish or clarify relationships between characters. For example, in Shakespeare's history plays, in which warring factions are significant, members of the same faction can be related to each other and contrasted with members of rival factions through the line, texture, or color of their costumes. Costume color schemes can also be used to show sympathetic relationships (through compatible colors) or antagonistic relationships (through clashing or contrasting colors) among characters. Changes of costume are often used to indicate changes in a character or an alteration in the relationship among characters.

Costume design may help to establish time and place. If the production concept calls for a realistic approach, the costumes may be based on

Hilary Corbett's costumes for *Gaslight,* at the Walnut Street Theatre (Philadelphia), help to establish the action as taking place in the late Victorian period. Directed by Malcom Black; scene design by Paul Wonsek; lighting by Jerold R. Forsyth.

Jerry Dalia; courtesy of the Walnut Street Theatre, Philadelphia

the clothing worn at the time of the dramatic action (fifth century B.C., Shakespeare's lifetime, present day, and so on); they may indicate a particular country or region (ancient Rome, seventeenth-century France, southwestern United States); a particular kind of place (throne room, battlefield, hospital, farm); or a time of day or occasion (casual morning at home, formal dance).

Costumes (more so than setting and lighting) are likely to retain some realistic qualities because they are worn by actors who must be able to move effectively and appropriately in them and because actors usually draw on real-life behavioral patterns in building their characterizations. Nevertheless, costumes do not always adhere to realistic standards. They may embody a metaphor, symbol, or allegorical concept. For example, in the medieval play *Everyman,* a character called Death summons the title character to his grave; Everyman then tries unsuccessfully to persuade several of his companions (Beauty, Strength, and Goods among them) to accompany him. The costumes need to capture the essence of each character as indicated by its name. On the other hand, a production of *Hamlet* utilizing the metaphor of the world as

prison may embody this perception in more subtle and varied ways.

Costumes may reflect mood and atmosphere. Winnie's neat and refined costume in *Happy Days* (see page 195) contrasts sharply with her entrapped state and reinforces her determined cheerfulness. Costumes may help establish a particular style. In *"The Hairy Ape,"* the fashionable people on Fifth Avenue are dressed like marionettes to reinforce their mechanical behavior. Costumes may reflect formalized conventions or a level of exaggeration, as they do in commedia dell'arte.

Costume can alter an actor's appearance as well as affect an actor's movement. By manipulating line and proportion, the costume designer can make a plump actor appear more slender or a thin actor stouter. Boots may disguise an actor's thin legs; color and ornament can draw attention to an actor's good features and away from weaker ones. Costume also can be used to make a handsome actor plain or misshapen. And, as in many children's plays, actors may be transformed into animals, trees, or fantastic creatures. Light, flexible, and close-fitting garments

PRACTITIONERS AND THEORISTS

Catherine Zuber

atherine Zuber was born in London but makes her home in the United States. She holds a Master of Fine Arts degree from the Yale School of Drama, where she studied scenic design with Ming Cho Lee and costume design with Jane Greenwood. Zuber has designed costumes for many regional theatres, among them Center Stage in Baltimore, where she designed costumes for Ibsen's *Ghosts* (see page 9). In this production, Zuber applied the type of boned ribbing often used for period corsets to the outside of the leading female character's dress in order to convey a sense of the character's confinement. Because the garment and the boning were dark in color, many members of the audience may not have consciously noticed this detail, but Zuber believes it helped the actress to identify and convey this aspect of her character. Zuber has also served as the resident costume designer at the American Repertory Theatre, where she designed costumes for dozens of productions including *The Good Woman of Setzuan* and *The Cabinet of Dr. Caligari*. Catherine Zuber has earned a reputation as a designer who does exhaustive research: "For some projects, you have to be a sociologist. . . . Your task is to examine in close detail what is authentic, always keeping in mind that truth is stranger than fiction. Every shoe, every tie, every shirt collar needs to express the time and place." But Zuber uses her research as a way to support and strengthen her creative choices rather than as a "museum approach" to design. She enjoys that, as an artist, she is sometimes called upon to "invent a world."

Zuber's artistry has earned her wide critical acclaim and several prestigious awards including the 1997 Obie Award for Sustained Excellence in Costume Design, the 2004 and 2005 Lucille Lortel Awards for Outstanding Costume Design, the 2005 Tony Award for Best Costume Design of a Musical (*The Light in the Piazza*), and the 2006 Tony Award for Best Costume Design of a Play (*Awake and Sing*). (See illustrations on pages 9, 119, 171, 180, 215, 357, and 380 for examples of Zuber's work.)

(such as leotards) allow the actor to move and gesture freely, whereas heavy garments (with bustles, trains, and the like) may slow down and restrict movement and gesture. Garments may be designed to help determine the amount, type, and overall pattern of movement and stage business.

Costume may establish the relative importance of characters in the action. Major characters can be made to stand out from minor ones by manipulating any or all of the elements and principles of design. For example, Hamlet is given emphasis in part through his insistence on wearing black (the color of mourning), whereas the others are dressed in colors more appropriate to festivities following the wedding of Gertrude and Claudius.

Costume may underline the development of the dramatic action through costume changes. A

Catherine Zuber's costume design for *Full Circle* by Charles Mee includes an ensemble whose costumes visually link them together through color, texture, and garment choice and whose accessories (note the collection of beer cans worn as necklaces) add ironic commentary on the group.

Richard Feldman

movement from happiness to sorrow or alterations in a character's fortunes, age, or sense of well-being may be underscored by changes in what the character wears. Costume may create both variety and unity, because characters are not only individuals but also parts of a whole. Although each costume may be distinctive in some way, each must fit the total visual style of the production.

Beginning in the 1960s, some groups questioned the need for stage costume at all. Such groups wore the same casual clothing in performance as they did in rehearsal or on the street. Since 1968, nudity has been used in some productions. But both casual clothing and nudity are variations on stage costuming, because both merely extend concepts about what is dramatically appropriate.

■ The Costume Designer's Skills

Costume designers need a variety of skills, many of which are pertinent to other professions (for example: fashion design, visual art, tailoring, sewing, social and cultural history, and acting). Like the fashion designer, the costume designer creates garments for particular types of people to wear for particular occasions or purposes. In creating garments, both types of designers keep in mind gender, social and economic class, activity, climate, and season, as well as stylistic qualities. But unlike fashion designers, costume designers must work within circumstances dictated by the script, director, performance space, and budget. Fashion designers establish fashions; costume designers use fashions. Costume designers must be able to project themselves into any period and create garments not only for present-day fashions but also for those of other eras.

Because they communicate their ideas to others through sketches, costume designers must develop skills like those of the visual artist. They use a multitude of sketches to indicate their preliminary ideas about individual costumes and the overall look of the production. Many designers now use computers to generate sketches. However produced, sketches facilitate discussion of the costumes, their relationship to the other visual elements, and their appropriateness to character, dramatic action, and production concept. Costume designers must also be able to render their final designs in color.

Although costume designers are not always involved in the construction of the garments

Costume designer Junghyun Georgia Lee accentuates the artifice of seventeenth-century high society with exaggerated period wigs and costumes for the Yale School of Drama production of *The Misanthrope* by Molière, translated by Richard Wilbur. Directed by Lisa Channer; scene design by Stuart Polasky; lighting design by Agnieszka Kunska.

they have designed, they often draw upon their knowledge of cutting, draping, patterning, and sewing to achieve the desired effect. Therefore, they need to envision the garments as tailors and seamsters would. Costume sketches should indicate how garments are shaped and the location of seams, darts, and other features that create visible lines and affect cut and fit. Such information is essential for making patterns from which the garments are constructed. Because costume designers also specify the material to be used, they need to be familiar with various fibers (cotton, wool, linen, silk, synthetic fibers) and the characteristics of each. Such information permits designers to choose cloth for appearance, durability, specific use, cost, and other pertinent factors. Designers must also be knowledgeable about weaves, textures, and other qualities, because these are important to the overall appearance of a costume.

Costume designers must be well grounded in social and cultural history (including the visual arts, dance, and theatre) because clothing reflects the mores, standards of beauty, and stylistic preferences of period and place. The more designers know about daily life, occupations, class structure, and favorite pastimes of a society, the better prepared they will be to design garments that reflect the status and function of a character within a specific culture. Because much of our information about clothing of the past comes from painting and other visual arts, a knowledge of art history is helpful. Many productions today draw on theatrical conventions that were in use

Costume sketch by Susan Tsu for Prospero's robe in Shake-speare's *The Tempest* at the Oregon Shakespeare Festival.

when the play was written; consequently, knowledge of theatre history, especially the history of theatrical costuming, may be useful to the designer.

Above all, costumes need to be suited to the characters who wear them. Costume designers must be able to analyze characters in the same way actors do, in terms of each role's significant traits, motivations, feelings, and functions within the dramatic action.

Working Plans and Procedures

THERE ARE NO STANDARD procedures to follow in designing costumes. After the costume designer has studied the play and met with the director and other designers to discuss the production concept, the costume designer begins to create a scheme for the costumes. Because there are usually several characters, and because they appear in many scenes in many different combinations, the designer typically makes numerous tentative sketches and examines them in various combinations to see how they fulfill the needs of individual scenes, whether they sufficiently reflect the progress of the dramatic

action, and how the costumes fit together as a group. There is usually a series of design conferences at which the designers show their sketches and explain their proposals. Through a process of reactions and revisions, tentative agreement is eventually reached. Before final approval is given, however, the designs usually must be rendered in color and in a manner that conveys a clear impression of the final product.

The costumer's working drawing is a color sketch for each costume (although the same basic design may be used for several characters if they are part of a group—soldiers, for example, or members of a mob in which everyone wears variations on the same clothing). This sketch shows the lines and details of the costume as seen from the most distinctive angle. If there are unusual features, the details are shown in special drawings (usually in the margins of the sketch); if the front, back, and sides of a garment all have distinctive features, the costume is usually shown from each of these angles (see illustration above). Samples of the materials to be used in constructing the garment may be attached to each drawing.

Most costume designers use a *costume chart* to communicate their broad organization of the characters' costumes at a single glance (see Table 16.1). It briefly identifies what each character

TABLE 16.1

A Doll's House Costume Chart

Character	Act 1	Act 2	Act 3
Nora	1 Grey wool jacket and skirt + Outerwear (Removes outerwear during act)	2 Outfit 1—grey jacket + maroon and black jacket and blouse	3 Tarantella outfit (After quick-change) 4 Pale blue suit + Outerwear
Delivery Boy	1 Brown and maroon outfit + Outerwear		
Porter	1 Black suit	1	
Helene (The Maid)	1 Black dress with white apron	1	2 Nightgown and shawl
Torvald	1 Black "working" outfit (Later adds outerwear, and then removes it)	2 Trousers, shirt and frock from 1 + maroon tie and gold vest	3 White tie and tails with party mask (Later removed)
Mrs. Linde	1 Distressed burgundy jacket & skirt + Outerwear (Removes outerwear during act)	1	1
Dr. Rank	1 Grey wool 3-piece frock suit (Adds outerwear during act)	2 Outfit 1 + green vest and Green/black tie	3 Black tie and tails
Anne-Marie (Children's Nurse)	1 Navy dress	1	
Ivar (One of Nora's sons)	1 Grey knickerbockers and jacket		
Emmy (Nora's daughter)	1 Gold wool dress with striped pinafore		
Bob (Nora's other son)	1 Blue suit with gold tie		
Krogstad	1 Dark grey suit + Brown outerwear	1	1

A costume chart for a production of Ibsen's *A Doll's House* (Courtesy of Margaret Mitchell)

wears in each of the scenes in which he or she appears. Sometimes color samples of each garment are included so that the range of colors and the overall color scheme can quickly be conveyed. The chart can also be used as the basis for more detailed *dressing lists*. These lists remind the actors (and those who may assist them) which costume pieces they wear in each scene (see Table 16.2 and note how much more detail is provided there as opposed to the broad organization of the costume chart). The costume chart and dressing lists are tools that communicate the designer's intentions and help keep the costumes organized for running the production efficiently.

TABLE 16.2

Dressing List or Card for Nora in *A Doll's House*

Costume #1	Costume #2	Costume #3	Costume #4
Chemise	**Remove:**	**Remove all except:**	**Remove all except:**
Corset w/garters	Grey wool jacket	Corset, chemise	Corset, chemise
Corset cover	**Add:**	**Add:**	and petticoat
Petticoat #1	Black/maroon blouse,	Petticoat #2	**Add:**
Bustle pad	Black/maroon jacket	Fishnet stockings	Brown stockings
Black stockings		Black satin pumps	Brown pumps
Black boots		Red/black skirt	Pale blue skirt
Grey wool jacket		Black embroidered bodice	Pale blue jacket
Grey wool skirt		Jet necklace	Brown coat
Black wool cape		(All rigged for quick change.)	Brown hat
Black hat, maroon flowers		Wig #2	Black gloves
Black gloves		Black shawl	
Gold/onyx earrings			
Wig #1			
Wedding ring			

Courtesy of Margaret Mitchell

◼ Realizing the Designs

Costumes may be borrowed, rented, assembled from an existing wardrobe, or newly made. When costumes must be borrowed, designers look for garments that fit their needs, although they often must accept clothing that is less than ideal. Borrowed clothing can be altered only slightly, because usually it must be returned in the same condition as when it was borrowed. Through the imaginative use of accessories and ornamentation, however, much can be done to alter the appearance of a garment. Borrowing clothing is restricted primarily to nonprofessional theatres and short-run productions.

Costumes from rental houses vary considerably. Some larger agencies buy the costumes from a Broadway or road show when it closes and rent these costumes as a group. Other houses employ staff designers who create costumes for frequently produced plays. In other cases, costume houses assemble a variety of costumes for each period, and from this stock the most appropriate garments are selected for any given show. When costumes are rented, the costume house assumes many of the designer's functions. The director and costumer may give detailed explanations of their interpretation of the play and request specific colors and kinds of garments, but they ultimately may not get precisely what they wanted. Rented costumes normally arrive at the theatre only in time for one or two dress rehearsals, and there is seldom time to obtain replacements or make more than minor changes. Even groups that normally make their own costumes usually rent some articles (such as military uniforms and men's tailored period suits) that are difficult or costly to construct.

Permanent theatre organizations that make their own costumes usually maintain a wardrobe of items from past productions. In this way, a large stock of garments is built up over time. If garments are to be taken from stock, the play is designed with these in mind. The costumer knows what is available and can choose carefully. Existing costumes in the theatre's own wardrobe can be remade or altered to fit new conceptions.

Courtesy of the American Conservatory costumes for Theatre

Costumes create a sense of the period in which the action takes place as well as help to define the characters. Seen here are Elizabeth Raetz as the innocent Cécile and Lise Bruneau as the worldly Merteuil in costumes by Deborah Dryden for Giles Havergal's adaption of *Les Liaisons Dangereuses* at San Francisco's American Conservatory Theatre.

T. Charles Erickson

Edward Hibbert (well known to fans of TV's *Frasier* for his portrayal of Gil Chesterton, the radio station's finicky food critic) in a costume fitting for Oscar Wilde's comic masterpiece *The Importance of Being Earnest* at the Long Wharf Theatre. Fitting Hibbert, who played the strong-minded British matriarch Lady Bracknell, into a period dress offered special challenges.

William Ivey Long

William Ivey Long became involved in theatre, in part, because his parents were involved in doing theatre at The Lost Colony and at the Carolina Playmakers (now the Playmakers Repertory Theatre) in Chapel Hill, North Carolina. Growing up around theatre, Long remembers his childhood home so full of fabric and costumes that they had to clear off the dining room table to eat meals. He had early experiences as a props master and technical director before receiving his undergraduate degree in history at William and Mary. Long then studied art history at the University of North Carolina and eventually studied scene design at the Yale Drama School under Ming Cho Lee. But when Long first moved to New York City after graduating from Yale, he spent his time working with a clothing couturier and making a collection of historical dolls, not designing scenery or costumes. Eventually, his friends convinced him that he should return to theatre and he did. Since then, Long has designed costumes for over fifty Broadway and Off-Broadway plays and musicals, including *Six Degrees of Separation, Miss Saigon, Lend Me a Tenor, The Marriage of Bette and Boo, Contact,* and *The Frogs,* as well as revivals of *Cabaret, Guys and Dolls, Chicago, Private Lives,* and *The Homecoming.* (See an example of his costume designs on page 211.) He has also designed the costumes for opera productions all over the world, for the Rolling Stones' *Steel Wheels* rock concert tour, for a Siegfried and Roy Las Vegas show, and for numerous dance performances. In the process, he has won four Tony Awards for Best Costume Design (*Crazy for You, Nine, Hairspray,* and *The Producers*) and been inducted into the Theatre Hall of Fame.

The procedures and working conditions for creating new costumes vary from one kind of organization to another. In the Broadway theatre, the producer contracts with a costume house to make the costumes. The designer must approve the finished costumes but has little to do with the work beyond supervising fittings. The designer does not need to supply patterns or cutting, stitching, and fitting directions because the costume house provides these services. In resident and nonprofessional theatres, designers may need to supervise construction of their designs. If so, they must be skilled in pattern drafting, draping, and fitting. Again, whether or not they supervise the construction, designers should understand the techniques used to carry out designs so they will know what effects can be accomplished and by what means.

Regardless of who makes the costumes, standard procedures are involved. First, accurate measurements must be made of all the actors. (One of the director's assistants or the stage manager usually makes appointments for actors to have their measurements taken and, later, for fittings.) Second, materials must be bought. Although the designer specifies materials, precisely the right cloth or color may be difficult to find. The designer or another authorized person may need to search for the specified materials or acceptable substitutes. Then, patterns must be drafted as guides for cutting and shaping the materials. At this point, the technical knowledge of the tailor is of great value. Draping may be a more effective method of making some costumes than patterning. For example, Greek garments, which hang from the shoulder in folds and are not fitted to the body, are most easily made by draping the material on a mannequin or a human body. After the patterns are completed, the material is cut and the parts basted together. The first fitting usually takes place before stitching is completed. Actors try on their costumes so the designer can check the fit and appearance because it is far easier to make alterations at this point than later. Finally, the garment is stitched, and ornamentation and accessories are added. A final fitting is arranged to assure that the costume looks and functions as planned.

Many new costumes need to look worn, faded, or tattered. Such garments may need to be *distressed* (that is, treated in ways analogous to overpainting in scenery). They may be washed several times; may be rolled up wrinkled to get a rumpled look; may be sprayed with paint, dye, or bleach to achieve fading or staining; may have the nap worn off the cloth with brushing in strategic places to indicate wear; or may be subjected to a variety of other processes to produce the desired effect.

■ The Costume Designer and the Actor

COSTUME DESIGNERS and actors need to cooperate because each supplements and extends the work of the other. Whenever possible, designers try to consider the strengths and weaknesses of each actor's figure when planning costumes. They must keep in mind the movement demanded of the actor in the production. It is difficult, for example, to climb high steps in a tight skirt, and an actor who must fence may be seriously endangered by billowing shirt sleeves, although these garments may enhance movement in other situations.

For their part, the actors are responsible for exploring the potentials and limitations of the costumes they will wear. Unfamiliar garments may seem awkward initially, but if actors recognize that the clothes in each period emphasize qualities that were admired at that time and allow movements that were then socially useful, beautiful, or desirable, they may use those qualities more effectively. For example, the sleeves of a man's fashionable coat in the eighteenth century would not allow the arms to hang comfortably at the sides (they had to be bent at the elbows and held away from the body), whereas the modern suit coat is cut so the arms are most comfortable when hanging at the sides (outward and upward movements are restricted). Both garments reflect attitudes about appropriate male behavior and consequently encourage some movements and inhibit others. If designers understand the relationship between cut and movement, they can help the actors get the feel of the period by making their garments from authentic period patterns.

The designer can also aid the actors by proper attention to shoes and undergarments. The height of the heel exerts considerable effect on stage movement (high-heel shoes throw the weight forward onto the balls of the feet, whereas flat shoes shift weight toward the heels). Similarly, undergarments affect movement. Hooped crinoline petticoats, for example, will not allow the same freedom of movement as modern underclothing. Corsets can force the body into certain configurations and inhibit action. If costumes encourage appropriate movement, they can be of enormous help to the actor. For optimum effectiveness, however, the actor and director must be willing to explore the possibilities of garments and allow sufficient time for rehearsal in them.

Costume and makeup design by Irene Corey for Prospero in Shakespeare's *The Tempest*, directed by Orlin Corey. The production concept for the play set the action on an island where everything had been affected by underwater forms. Prospero's cloak seems encrusted with coral and his glowing headdress suggests his magic.

Makeup

TRADITIONALLY, MAKEUP has been considered the actor's responsibility. However, in many situations today, the actor's makeup is at least initially the product of design and collaboration. In the professional theatre, the costume designer often conceives of the actor's makeup as a part of the design, especially when a very stylized or complex makeup is required. After the makeup design has been shown to them, professional actors generally apply it themselves. Because actors in the nonprofessional theatre are typically less experienced or adept with makeup than their professional counterparts, the design and application of makeup are sometimes delegated to the costumer, director, or another skilled person. Although the way makeup is handled varies widely, it is treated here in conjunction with costuming because of its intimate connection with the actor's appearance.

Makeup can serve several functions:

- Makeup characterizes (conveying age, state of health, and—within limits—race and basic attitude, such as grumpiness or cheerfulness).
- Makeup aids expressiveness (emphasizing facial features and making them more visible to the audience).
- Makeup restores color and form that are sometimes diminished by stage lighting.

■ Makeup may indicate performance style (as in expressionist plays, where distorted makeup may indicate distorted ideas or behavior, or in Kabuki or Chinese Opera).

When the makeup for a production is designed and supervised by one person, it is usually coordinated through a *makeup plot* (sometimes supplemented by sketches). The plot is a chart recording basic information about the makeup of each character: the base color, liners, eye shadow, and powder; special features, such as a beard or enlarged nose; and any changes to be made during the performance. The plot serves both as a guide for applying makeup and as a check on how the makeup of each actor relates to that of all the others. Sometimes a sketch of each actor's face is made to show how the makeup is to be applied.

■ TYPES OF MAKEUP

Makeup effects may be achieved in two basic ways: through painting and through added plastic, prosthetic, or three-dimensional pieces. Painting involves the application of color, highlights, and shadows to the face or other parts of the body. Plastic makeup includes the addition of such items as false noses, warts, beards, and wigs.

Painted makeup may be divided into four categories:

■ Age groups
■ Straight or character makeup
■ Racial/ethnic groups
■ Special painted effects

Age makeup is of concern only when actors are to play characters whose age differs significantly from their own. Various age groups typically have distinct coloration, highlights, shadows, and lines. These are usually evident on the face as well as on the hands and other visible parts of the body, which must all be made up appropriately or they may destroy the illusion created by facial makeup. A straight makeup utilizes the actor's own basic characteristics without altering them significantly. A character makeup is one that markedly changes the actor's own appearance. The change may involve making the actor seem fatter or coarser, more lean and wizened, or it may emphasize some distinctive facial feature (such as a thin, sharp nose or large, soulful eyes).

Jodi Karjala

Actors applying makeup for a theatrical performance.

Costumes and makeup help lift the Guthrie Theatre's production of *Too Clever by Half* to a farcical level. Note the distortions of the performers' shapes made by the garments and the use of makeup, particularly the prosthetic jutting chin on the figure left of center.

Racial/ethnic makeup emphasizes characteristic skin coloration, eye shapes, and hair color and texture, along with other traits that differentiate Asian, Polynesian, Indian, African, Caucasian, and other subgroups. Special painted effects include clown makeup, distortions for stylistic reasons, and decorative designs painted on the face (such as tattoos and the markings used by some tribal peoples). The materials needed for these and other effects, as well as those required for the most basic stage makeup, are available from manufacturers and makeup supply houses. Almost all makeups begin with a base. However, the base alone is likely to make the actor's face appear flat and uninteresting. Therefore lines, highlights, and shadows are applied over the base. The effects that can be achieved by painting with makeup are almost endless.

Nevertheless, significant transformations in an actor's appearance are most frequently accomplished with three-dimensional elements. For example, a change in the shape of the nose and the addition of a beard and bushy eyebrows can mask an actor's features more completely than painting can. The shape and size of the nose can be changed through prosthetics, usually made from plastics or rubber latex that can be molded into the desired shape. Similar prosthetic pieces can simulate fleshy jowls, a jutting chin, a protuberant forehead, large warts or scars, and other protrusions. They are attached to the face with liquid adhesive and may be removed and reapplied as needed.

The addition of facial hair and wigs, or alterations to performers' existing hair, can also aid in significantly transforming their appearance. Some actors can grow beards and moustaches on demand, but these can also be made or purchased. However, purchased facial hair pieces may not precisely match a particular actor's hair color or fit well. Facial hair pieces may also be made by ventilation. In this process, strands of hair pieces are tied with specialized needles onto a tightly woven net, measured, and precisely cut to fit a specific actor to achieve the desired effect. Ventilated hair pieces have the advantage of precision and durability because the entire piece can be applied with liquid adhesive, taken off, and reapplied many times without damage. The appearance of the actor's hair can be changed significantly through styling and coloring, but wigs may be required for extreme changes or rapid switches. Wigs are now so readily available that they often provide the easiest means of altering hair color and style. Wigs made from materials other than human or plastic hair are seldom satisfactory if a realistic effect is sought. For stylized wigs, various materials may be used: hemp, yarn, confetti, strips of paper, and so on. Baldness can be simulated with a "bald wig." Finally, hair coloration may be altered with dye, although this can be longer lasting than is sometimes desired.

Costume and makeup aid the actor's transformation into the character, although in productions that do not seek realistic effects, makeup may not be used at all; the actor is said to be "presenting" the character rather than attempting to "be" the character, and consequently there is no need to disguise the actor's own appearance. Nevertheless, makeup is still used in the majority of stage productions and completes the visualization of the character that costume design seeks to achieve.

The Costume Parade, Dress Rehearsals, and Performances

WHEN THE COSTUMES are finished, it is usual to have a *dress parade*, during which every costume used for the play is viewed sequentially so that the actors may appear in the correct combinations, in the appropriate costumes, and under lights simulating those to be used in performance. The actors may be asked to perform characteristic actions or special business to make sure the costumes are fully functional. The dress parade allows the designer and director to evaluate the costumes without the distractions of a performance. Problems are noted and corrected before dress rehearsals begin. In the Broadway theatre, the dress parade is held at the costume house; in other organizations, it is usually held onstage. It is normally supervised by the costume designer.

After problems are corrected, the costumes are moved to the dressing rooms in the theatre to be used for the performances. If no dress parade is held, its functions must be accomplished during the technical rehearsals. Dress rehearsals allow the costumes to be seen under conditions as nearly like those of performance as possible. There should be few changes at this time, but any that are necessary need to be made quickly so the actor is not faced with new details on opening night. In most situations, the designer's work is considered complete after opening night.

The Costume Designer's Assistants

THE COSTUME DESIGNER needs several helpers. In the professional theatre, costume designers usually are members of the United Scenic Artists Union, and their helpers may be members of this or other unions. The designer's assistant, usually a younger member of the United Scenic Artists, may make sketches, search for appropriate materials, supervise fittings, act as liaison with the other theatre workers, or undertake any other assigned task.

Pattern drafters, drapers, cutters, tailors, stitchers, and fitters make the costumes. For Broadway productions these workers usually are union members who work at a professional costume house. In regional theatres some of this

The School for Scandal as produced by the McCarter Theatre (Princeton, N.J.). Costume design by Jess Goldstein; directed by Mark Lamos; scene design by Michael Yeargan; lighting design by Stephen Strawbridge.

T. Charles Erickson

work may be done by union members, but much of it is not. In the nonprofessional theatre, almost all of this work is done by volunteer or student labor, although frequently a paid staff person supervises the construction and maintains the theatre's wardrobe.

When the costumes are finished, a wardrobe supervisor takes charge and is responsible for seeing that costumes are ready for each performance. The costumes may need to be mended, laundered, cleaned, or pressed. In long-run productions, garments are replaced when they begin to look shabby. During performances, the wardrobe supervisor is responsible to the stage manager.

Dressers help actors into and out of costumes. The number of dressers depends on the size of the cast and the number and rapidity of costume changes. Sometimes actors need little or no help, but quick changes and complicated garments may require more than one dresser for a single actor. There should be enough dressers to avoid delays, keep performances running smoothly, and ensure that the costumes are in good condition at all times.

Thinking about Costume and Makeup

THE RANGE OF COSTUME and makeup in today's theatre is great. Each may be treated realistically or nonrealistically; each may reflect closely what is indicated by the script or deviate markedly from the script's specifications; or each may be largely ignored (with performers wearing their own clothing and no makeup). Costumes and makeup may make strong stylistic or interpretational statements, or they may be so unobtrusive as to be practically unnoticed. In all cases, the important issues concern why the specific choices were made and how they affect the production. Here are some questions that may contribute to a fuller understanding of choices and their results in the use of costume and makeup:

1. Did the type of space in which the production was staged permit close-range viewing of costumes and makeup? Were details easily visible? What was the overall effect of the space on costumes and makeup?

2. What, if any, specific period, style, or production concept did the costuming convey? If it did so, which? How closely did the approach adhere to the script? If it departed significantly from the script, in what ways did it do so? With what effect?

3. How were the costumes and makeup used to characterize each role? Did they distinguish characters by clarifying specific occupations or professions? Socioeconomic status? Lifestyles? Age of characters? Taste? Psychological traits? If so, through what means? If not, what was the effect of nonspecificity? Were some character traits ignored? If so, which and with what result?

4. Did costumes clarify character relationships? If so, how? With what results? If not, how did they fail to do so? With what results? Did they create appropriate emphasis and subordination? If so, through what means? If not, what prevented them from doing so?

5. Did the costumes enhance or inhibit the performers' movement and business? In what ways? With what results?

6. How were the costumes and makeup used to enhance or alter the actor's appearance? Was this done appropriately in terms of the role? Was the actor's overall physical appearance effective (or ineffective) for the role? In what ways was the effectiveness (or ineffectiveness) attributable to costume and makeup?

7. Were there costume or makeup changes? How did they relate to developments in the dramatic action or alterations in the character's situation or attitudes? Did the changes in costume or makeup clarify the developments? If so, in what ways? If not, why not?

8. Were there any unusual, unexpected, or highly distinctive costumes or makeup? What features or means served to create these effects? Did the distinctiveness enhance or detract from the overall effect?

9. How did costumes and makeup relate to scenery and lighting? Did they enhance and complement each other? If so, how? If not, in what ways? With what results?

10. Overall, how did costume and makeup contribute (or fail to contribute) to the total production?

The relevance of these questions will vary according to the particular production and play. To answer some of the questions about every costume or for the entire cast would be too time consuming; for other questions, adequate answers may require information available only to those actually involved in the creation of the costumes and makeup. Nevertheless, attempts to answer parts or all of these questions will require us to look closely at costumes and makeup and to evaluate their contributions to a theatrical production.

Additional Opportunities with InfoTrac College Edition

How and why did fashion designer Isaac Mizrahi give the characters in the recent Broadway production of *The Threepenny Opera,* the late-1920s musical by Bertolt Brecht (book) and Kurt Weill (music), a startling, punk rock look? Use InfoTrac College Edition to find and read Ruth La Ferla's article "Mack the Debauched Knife, in a Mizrahi and a Mohawk" in the *New York Times.*

1. What does Brecht's hustler Macheath, played by Alan Cumming, wear in the production?

2. In what ways do Mizrahi's costumes for the musical's more conservative characters relate to his costumes for its more licentious ones?

3. How does Mizrahi justify his artistic choices?

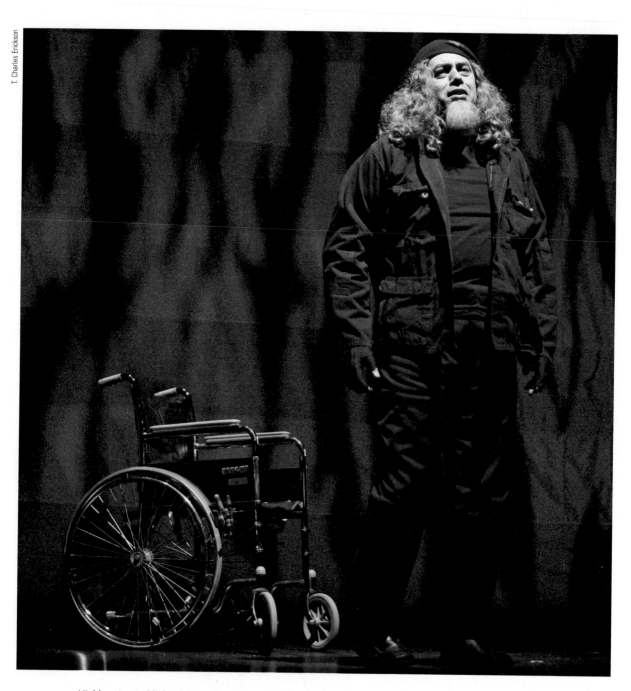

Highly saturated light along with a pattern of light and shadow on the background may create a striking effect, as it does here in *Culture Clash in AmeriCCa*, written, performed, and directed by Culture Clash: Richard Montoya, Ric Salinas, Herbert Siguenza. Presented by the Huntington Theatre.

17:

Lighting and Sound Design

LIGHTING MAKES the other elements of theatrical production visible. But it does much more, because it plays a major role in creating mood and atmosphere, in emphasizing and subordinating visual elements, and in blending the entire stage picture. Stage lighting often escapes conscious notice because it is intangible, takes up no space, and is visible only when it strikes a reflecting surface. Consequently, lighting is often ignored unless it is clearly inadequate or obtrusively obvious. Nevertheless, how light is controlled has a significant, though often subtle, effect on the audience's perception of a performance.

Sound also makes its greatest contribution when it is designed for careful integration with the production as a whole. Because, like lighting, sound depends on electronic means, it is treated here at the end of this chapter's section on lighting design.

The Controllable Qualities of Light

LIGHTING DESIGNERS achieve their goals by manipulating the four controllable qualities of light:

- Intensity (or brightness)
- Distribution
- Color
- Movement

Intensity depends primarily on the number of lamps used and their wattages. It may be increased or decreased in several ways: through the number or types of instruments focused on the same area or object; through the distance of instruments from what is being lighted (brightness diminishes with distance); through the use of dimmers to decrease or increase brightness; and through the presence or absence of color filters. Selective intensity, when used in combination with the other controllable qualities of light, greatly affects the audience's perception of mood and helps to direct their attention.

Distribution refers to both the placement of the light source and the area that it illuminates. Lighting instruments may be mounted almost anywhere in the theatre: in the auditorium, above the stage, on the floor, on vertical or horizontal pipes, or on stands. Lighting effects and the dimensionality of what is being illuminated vary greatly on the direction from which the light comes. A carefully planned distribution of light allows the designer to use frontlighting, backlighting, crosslighting, downlighting, or uplighting, each separately or in various combinations. All light may be directed at one area, or it may be distributed equally or unequally over the entire stage. The lighting designer uses the carefully planned distribution of light to enhance the stage compositions created by the director and the actors, thereby reinforcing the dramatic action.

The visible spectrum of light is divided into colors (red, orange, yellow, green, blue-green, blue, and violet), each of which is distinguishable from the others because it is composed of light waves of a given length. We attribute color to objects because of their capacity to absorb some wavelengths and to reflect others. In stage lighting, filters control the appearance of color through the principle of selective transmission (that is, each color filter permits certain wavelengths of light to pass through and restricts others). A blue filter, for example, screens out or

diminishes other wavelengths. Filtering the light reduces the amount of light that reaches the stage. To avoid unwanted distortions, light from a number of color sources may need to be mixed. For example, a yellow dress illuminated with a highly saturated blue light will appear green on stage, and a red dress illuminated with a highly saturated green light will appear black. Lighting designers therefore may focus multiple instruments on each part of the stage to ensure control over not only intensity but also color using basic principles of *additive color mixing* (mixing different colored light together to produce achromatic white light). Other types of color mixing are also possible and used to produce various tints, shades, hues, saturations, and intensities.

Movement refers to perceptible alterations in any of the controllable qualities. The principal device for creating movement is the control board, which triggers some lamps to be brightened and others dimmed to control intensity, color, or distribution. Lighting instruments may

Multidirectional lighting, torches, and smoke create a strong mood for this scene from Shakespeare's *Cymbeline*. Lighting design by Marcia Madeira; directed by Larry Carpenter; scene design by John Falabella; costumes by David Murin.

Richard Feldman

also be physically manipulated by an operator, as is the case with follow spots, allowing a single instrument to follow an actor's movements. Automated or "intelligent" lighting instruments can be programmed to illuminate different areas of the stage from different angles and to change their filters by remote control. Movement allows light to change moment by moment in accordance with shifting moods and the development of the dramatic action. Its ability to move and change continuously makes lighting the most flexible of the production elements.

■ The Functions of Stage Lighting

Lighting designers selectively shape the controllable qualities of light to fulfill the various functions of light design:

■ Provide appropriate visibility
■ Sculpt dimensionality
■ Reinforce and create stage compositions
■ Enhance mood and atmosphere
■ Support style and production concept
■ Reinforce the action

Apart from artistic considerations, a minimum level of visibility is essential if the performance is to be seen. Having achieved this basic function, lighting affects our perception of dimensionality (mass and form). A three-dimensional structure will appear flat if all of its surfaces are evenly lighted, whereas its shape will be revealed or emphasized by light that varies markedly from one surface to another. Thus the lighting designer can define or alter apparent shape and dimension by manipulating the light's distribution, intensity, and color. This ability to influence perception of mass and form is among the lighting designer's most potent means of creating mood, atmosphere, and stylistic traits. Lighting aids in reinforcing and creating stage compositions. It can selectively reveal or conceal some parts of the stage (or scene). By directing

the eye to the most important elements, it creates emphasis and subordination. On the proscenium stage, the acting (or foreground) areas are usually more brightly lighted than the background, just as the level of intensity at stage level (where the action takes place) is usually greater than on the upper parts of the setting (which are of secondary concern).

Perhaps one of light design's most important functions is to enhance mood and atmosphere. Bright, warm light is associated with gaiety and well-being, cool light with somberness. Glaring white light may create a sense of starkness or clinical probing, whereas low-intensity lighting with many areas of shadow may create an atmosphere of mystery or threat. It is impossible to specify precisely the effect of each use of lighting, because our response is determined by the total context and not merely by the lighting.

Lighting may be used to support the style or the production's concept. If the stylistic goal is realism, the lighting may establish the source of the light (sun, moon, lamps, firelight) and let the source motivate intensity, distribution of light and shadow, color, and movement. Light may reflect the time of day, weather conditions, or season, and it may suggest the play's period through the lighting fixtures used on stage. If the style is not realism, the source of the light and the way it is handled may suggest that as well. Visible light sources may be used to distribute light evenly over the entire stage, establishing the performance space itself (rather than some fictional locale) as the place of the dramatic action. For an expressionistic play, light from very low or sharp angles may be used to distort facial features, or saturated colors may be used to indicate the dominant emotion. The production concept or interpretive focus may be supported by the ways in which light is controlled, the logic this control establishes, and its compositional focus.

Finally, lighting reinforces the action by reflecting the dominant feeling of each scene and the changes in mood, time, and atmosphere from one scene (or location) to the next.

A change in lighting can create a dramatic change in mood even though all the major scenery pieces remain unchanged, as in these two scenes from *Two Sisters and a Piano* by Nilo Cruz. Directed by Brian Kulik; scene design by Mark Wendland; costume design by Anita Yaich; and lighting design by Mimi Jordan Sherin.

Female Pioneers in Stage Lighting

Jean Rosenthal and Tharon Musser have been among the most influential lighting designers in America. Rosenthal (1912–1969) is often said to have created the field of lighting design. When she began working in the theatre (first with Orson Welles and John Houseman in the Federal Theatre Project in 1936), lighting was still the province of the scenic designer or master electrician. From 1938 until her death, Rosenthal was lighting designer (as well as production supervisor) for the Martha Graham Dance Company, and perhaps because light was such an essential element in Graham's pieces, Rosenthal was able to perfect lighting as a distinct artistic statement and creator of a strong sense of mood. Largely because of Rosenthal's pioneering example, lighting design after World War II came to be recognized as a specialized field. Among Rosenthal's numerous designs for the Broadway theatre, the best known are *West Side Story* (see illustration on page 192) and *The Sound of Music*. Rosenthal's book *The Magic of Light* (1972) sums up her views on stage lighting.

Tharon Musser (1925–) is often said to be one of America's most influential lighting designers. A graduate of Berea College and the Yale School of Drama, she did most of her early lighting work for dance companies, especially José Limon's. Her first major Broadway assignment was José Quintero's production of O'Neill's *Long Day's Journey into Night* in 1956. She went on to design for several repertory companies, among them the American Shakespeare Company, for which she lighted twenty-nine productions. Since 1971, she has lighted all of Neil Simon's Broadway productions. She has also designed many musicals, including *Mame* and *A Little Night Music*. Musser has won three Tony Awards and lighted more than one hundred Broadway productions including *A Chorus Line, Dream Girls,* and *The Secret Garden*. She is also credited with several innovations in lighting practice, perhaps most notably computerized lighting, which she introduced to Broadway in *A Chorus Line* (1975). In 2003 Musser was honored with the Ruth Morely Designing Woman Award for her many achievements in stage lighting.

Musser believes that mastery of technical skills alone is insufficient preparation for a young lighting designer. Instead, she strongly advocates a liberal education as the foundation for further training. She has stated that art history courses are more valuable than lighting courses because, though the lighting designer must attain adequate technical training, ultimately that training will be ineffective unless it is combined with a vision that creates paintings with light. She urges young designers to work in regional and summer stock theatres because of the variety of experience those theatres offer and because they permit young designers to try out in a short span of time many ideas that help to develop craft into art.

Changes in lighting may also underscore the rhythmical patterns of scenes and changes in rhythm from one scene to another.

Although it serves many functions, lighting is among the most abstract of theatrical means. It works through suggestion and association rather than through concrete references (as scenery, costumes, and acting usually do). Many lighting designers believe their designs to be most effective when they work in harmony with the other production elements, whether the audience is consciously aware of the light or not.

The Lighting Designer's Skills

LIGHTING DESIGNERS need a variety of skills, many of them pertinent to other professions, such as electrical or optical engineer, computer programmer, display designer, visual artist, electrician, social and cultural historian, and stage director. Like electrical engineers, lighting designers need to understand physics and electronics, because they work with complex instruments and control boards operated primarily by electricity. They need to know how the equipment works as well as the physical principles involved, so that they can make maximum use of the available resources and avoid their inefficient and dangerous misuse. Like optical engineers, lighting designers need to understand the principles of optics and light, because they manipulate the variable properties of light when they use lamps, lenses, reflectors, color filters, and other equipment. The fuller their understanding of the principles and properties of light, the greater their potential for using light effectively for artistic purposes. Although lighting designers work in a more restricted and specialized sphere than electrical and optical engineers, all use the same base of information. Advances in computer technology have created sophisticated, automated lighting instruments, and today's lighting designers typically require computer programming skills in order to use this technology effectively.

In the application of skills, lighting designers have much in common with display designers,

T. J. Gerckens' lighting for *Galileo Galilei*, an opera with music by Philip Glass and libretto by Mary Zimmerman (with assistance by Arnold Weinstein), as presented by the Goodman Theatre (Chicago). Scene design by Dan Ostling and costume design by Mara Blumenfeld.

Courtesy of Dan Ostling

because both use the intensity, distribution, direction, and color of light to focus attention on important elements and to blend the elements into a whole that creates the appropriate mood. The lighting designer's work is usually more complex than the display designer's, however, because in the theatre one is concerned with a space that is used continuously by live, moving actors, whereas in a display the artist usually lights a fixed picture or one in which movement is created by electronically programmed elements.

Like other theatre designers, lighting designers need skills like those of the visual artist, because they usually communicate through visual means. They may demonstrate their preliminary ideas by making many drawings, then render their final designs as sketches that emphasize light and shade—gradations in intensity, dominant direction, distribution—as well as color. Lighting designers must also be able to draft various scale drawings of the stage and auditorium to show the mounting positions of lighting instruments and the areas they are to light. Many designers today use computers to create these drawings.

Although lighting designers may not perform the physical labor required to realize their designs, they must know what has to be done and supply the information needed by those who actually do the tasks. Consequently, like the stage electrician, designers must know what instruments are available; what each can do; what types of lamps, electrical cable, connectors, and the like are needed; where instruments are to be mounted and plugged in; and a host of other details. The designer's practical knowledge must be as extensive as the stage electrician's, although the designer may not be as skilled at installing and operating the equipment.

Lighting designers should be grounded in social and cultural history (including the visual and performing arts), because they often must know what role light played in various periods in the past. They need to be aware of what illuminants (candles, oil, torches, gas, and so on) were available in each period, how each was used, and what qualities of light each generated (so they can re-create or adapt these illuminants for their work as desired). Although today lighting designers normally work entirely with electrical light, they frequently must create the effects of other illuminants. Designers also need to know the conventions that governed stage lighting in each era of theatre history, in case a production requires these.

Lighting designers take an approach more nearly like that of the director than that of any other theatre artist, because they must keep in mind and unify the entire stage picture. Lighting designers must be attuned to the overall needs of each scene as it develops moment by moment, because light is the most flexible of all theatrical means, being instantaneously and continuously variable. Consequently, the lighting designer needs to work closely with the director in realizing the production concept.

■ The Lighting Designer's Working Procedures

THERE IS NO STANDARD approach to the design of lighting. Lighting designers are in a somewhat different position from that of other theatre artists, because lighting is seen only as it is reflected by the actors, costumes, setting, and performance space. Thus what they light is created by others, and frequently lighting designers must adjust their work to enhance that of others rather than proceeding as they would desire. For example, the color of costumes or scenery can be drastically affected by the colors chosen by the lighting designer. They can make general plans, but until the floor plan and setting are agreed upon, lighting designers cannot make firm decisions about the placement and direction of lighting instruments, and until the movement pattern of each actor is established, they cannot know precisely how the light needs to be distributed. Firm color choices must also wait

Jennifer Tipton

Jennifer Tipton is one of today's most admired lighting designers. Her influence is evident not only through her work as a designer, but also through her teaching at the Yale University School of Drama—many of her former students have gone on to distinguished careers in lighting design for Broadway and regional theatres. Tipton has designed for dance, opera, and theatre and has won awards for her excellence in lighting all three. Her lighting designs for dance, among them designs for Paul Taylor, Twyla Tharp, Robert Joffrey, and Mikhail Baryshnikov, have earned her two Bessie Awards in New York and an Olivier Award in London. In theatre, she has designed for Broadway productions, the New York Shakespeare Festival, and many regional companies (including the American Repertory Company, the Goodman Theatre, and the Guthrie Theatre). Her designs have won her numerous awards, including two Tony Awards (the first for Andrei Serban's 1977 production of *The Cherry Orchard* and the second for Jerome Robbins' *Broadway* in 1989), two American Theatre Wing Awards, an Obie Award, three Drama Desk Awards, and a great many other honors. In 2001, Tipton was awarded the Dorothy and Lillian Gish Prize of $250,000 for her work in lighting design. She is also the recipient of the Jerome Robbins Prize and, in 2005, a lifetime achievement award for her outstanding contributions to design.

Tipton is especially known for her work with avant-garde companies and innovative directors such as Robert Wilson, Peter Sellars, and JoAnne Akalaitis. Her design schedule is so busy that she is typically committed to future design projects more than two years in advance. Her recent work includes lighting designs for performance artist Laurie Anderson's *The End of the Moon, O Composite* for the Paris Opera Ballet, and the Wooster Group's *Brace Up!* (Examples of Tipton's lighting designs may be seen on pages 4, 103, 228, 290, 293, 340, and 405.)

until the costume and scene designers have made their decisions. Lighting design therefore seldom becomes as fixed as other design elements do during the planning stages.

Like the other designers, lighting designers should be able to convey their ideas about how the stage should look during performances. The device most frequently used by lighting designers to convey this is value sketches. These sketches emphasize mood and atmosphere or light and shadow. The number and type of sketches depend upon the complexity and variety of the lighting to be used. Instead of sketches (or in addition to them), lighting designers sometimes use a lighting score that breaks the play into scenes or units and indicates in a diagram the time of day, source of light, overall brightness, the desired mood, color, and any other factors

Jennifer Tipton's lighting for Samuel Beckett's *Endgame.* Note how Tipton's use of intensity and distribution helps to suggest that Clov (right) is near the threshold of a confined underground space. Directed by JoAnne Akalaitis.

that will affect lighting design. Some lighting designers have begun using computer simulations to show how the production will look when lighted. Value sketches, lighting scores, and computer simulations all serve as a basis for discussion by the production team of the qualities the lighting should convey.

Lighting designers usually attend several rehearsals to become familiar with the movement patterns and to understand the director's intentions. Increasingly, designers also try out and perfect aspects of their lighting designs (especially color mixing or automated lighting effects) in a laboratory before implementing them. However lighting designers work, they usually do not arrive at fully developed designs until shortly before the instruments are to be hung and focused.

■ Organizing the Distribution of Light

Although value sketches and lighting scores communicate how the lighting should look in terms of mood, atmosphere, and quality, the lighting instruments must still be precisely chosen and placed to achieve these effects. Lighting designers use two primary working plans to organize the distribution of light: *light plots* and *instrument schedules.*

Light plots can be divided into two types: floor plans and vertical sections. The floor-plan plot is drawn to scale and shows, as seen from a top view, the layout of the stage, the setting, and the auditorium. On this plot are indicated the type, size, and position of each instrument and the area it will light. The section plot, also drawn to scale, shows the vertical arrangement (from a side view) of the stage, scenery, and auditorium, and the type, size, and position of each instrument and the area it will light. Together, these plots show the horizontal and vertical distribution of the light sources. Designers often make a separate light plot for each setting and then a composite plot showing all of the settings simultaneously in order to see how

the lighting for each scene relates to that of all of the others. This procedure facilitates the use of the same instruments in multiple scenes. In summary, light plots specify what instruments are to be used and where each is to be mounted. (See illustration below.)

Light plots also take into consideration the three principal types of stage lighting: specific illumination, general illumination, and special

Light plot by David Nancarrow for a production of Shakespeare's *Two Gentlemen of Verona.*

effects. Specific illumination is that which is confined to a limited area. It is used principally for the acting areas, which demand the greatest emphasis and often require variety in intensity, color, and distribution. The principal sources of specific illumination are *spotlights*. Spotlights combine the reflector of the light source with one of several different types of lenses that help concentrate and disperse a beam that can be focused on a specific area. But because a single spotlight can illuminate only a small segment of the stage, lighting designers usually divide the total acting space into several smaller areas. Each area is then lighted separately. At least one spotlight is focused on each area from each side to strike it at an angle of forty-five degrees both horizontally and vertically. More typically, several instruments (mounted at varying levels and angles) are focused on each area. The lighting for each area should overlap into adjacent areas to avoid distracting variations in brightness and darkness as actors move about the stage.

Where instruments are mounted to achieve the desired distribution depends in part on the type of stage. In the proscenium theatre, forward acting areas cannot be lighted effectively from behind the arch, and therefore some instruments are mounted in the auditorium—in ceiling apertures, in vertical apertures at the sides, or on the front of a balcony. Upstage areas are normally lighted by instruments hung back of the proscenium—on the light bridge just behind and above the opening, on vertical pipes at either side of the stage, on pipe battens suspended over the stage at intervals from front to back, on stands, or on the floor. In the arena theatre, all instruments are usually mounted above the acting area and audience or on vertical pipes located where they will not interfere with sightlines. Because performances are viewed from four sides, the acting areas must be lit from all directions. On the thrust stage, most of the instruments are mounted over the platform or in the audience areas, but there may be a space behind the main platform where others are hung. Because the action is normally seen from

two or three sides, lighting on thrust stages is usually a compromise between that used for a proscenium and that used for an arena stage. In flexible or variable performance spaces, lighting may be nothing more than normal auditorium illumination, often no more than is required for visibility. If more selective lighting is used, the instruments may be mounted almost anywhere in the performance space.

General illumination spreads over a much larger area than specific illumination. General illumination is most fully exploited on the proscenium stage, where it serves three functions: to light the background elements (cyclorama, ground rows, drops) not illuminated by spotlights; to blend acting areas and provide a smooth transition from the higher intensity of the acting areas to the lower intensity of the

Courtesy of Dan Ostling

In this scene from *Pacific*, blue downlight spreads evenly over the entire stage creating general illumination, while specific illumination of slightly warmer colored light (at a higher intensity) helps direct our focus on the performer.

IDEAS AND
INFLUENCES

Automated Lighting

Automated lighting, initially developed in the early 1980s to provide a color-changing, programmable moving spotlight for rock concert tours, has proved the most significant development in stage lighting in the past twenty-five years. Early "intelligent" or automated lighting instruments could mechanically pan and tilt on their yoke, thereby allowing a single instrument to light different areas of the stage from different angles on timed cues by remote control. Such instruments reduced the necessary lighting instrument inventory and the number of crew members needed, while they increased the designer's control (particularly over changing color quickly with an internal mechanically rotating wheel of colors). However, at the time, many designers complained that the instruments were torturous to program and were noisy, unreliable, and expensive to buy and maintain.

Since then, numerous improvements have been made to automated lighting instruments. Engineers helped companies to create quieter and lighter motors that could be programmed to internally rotate a reflector and dim, douse, zoom, change gobo patterns (templates that project patterned images), and focus light on cue. Because of their improved ability to focus light with great precision, automated lighting instruments could now project intricately detailed artwork or photographs on high-resolution etched-glass gobos with razor sharpness. Perhaps the most important engineering innovation was the introduction of multiple internal color changers that allowed endless color choices as well as the ability to crossfade or change colors in less than three-tenths of a second or for more than an hour's time.

Automated lighting instruments, although initially more expensive than conventional instruments, are widely used in theatre today. Used properly, automated lighting is so versatile that it may reduce equipment inventory, solve problems of inadequate space in which to hang numerous lighting instruments, and create astonishing effects. But, as with most technology, its effectiveness depends upon its user. Ultimately, as Jennifer Tipton has said, "Technology is always as good as the person using it. Always. And only as good as the person using it."

background; and to enhance or modify the color of settings and costumes. Although general illumination cannot be confined to small areas, its direction can be partially controlled. For example, borderlights may be hung above the acting area and pointed downward or tilted in one direction. Striplights and floodlights may be suspended on battens above the stage, mounted on vertical stands, or placed on the floor. On the arena stage, general illumination plays a minor role, because usually there is no background to light, and the specific illumination covers the entire acting space. On the thrust stage, general illumination may play a larger role, especially if

A scene from the St. Louis Black Repertory's production of Shakespeare's *Macbeth*. Note how the lighting designer has used a lighting instrument within the witches' caldron to uplight Macbeth (center), thereby directing our focus and suggesting mood.

there is a stage house. In flexible or variable spaces, all of the lighting may be general.

Special effects are out-of-the-ordinary demands—among them projections, fires, rainbows, fog, bright rays of light (to simulate sunlight or moonlight), explosions, lightning, strobe lights, and "black" light (ultraviolet light used to pick out specially treated substances on a dark stage).

In making light plots, each type of light (specific, general, and special effects) is considered separately and then as a part of the total unit. The location of all lighting instruments is indicated on the plots.

A wide array of lighting instruments and accessories are available to the lighting designer, who must understand their properties and principles in order to select the appropriate equipment needed to create the desired effects. For example, although both ellipsoidals and fresnels may be considered spotlights because each combines a reflector with a convex lens, fresnels use a thin, specially designed convex lens that reduces heat absorption and diffuses light evenly across its beam. Just as the type of lens may change the properties of light an instrument emits, so too may the type of reflector used. There are also a variety of projectors (capable of projecting still or moving patterns of light, or even whole images) and intelligent lighting instruments that may be programmed to change their focus and their color filters or to create specific patterns of light and shadow on cue from a remote control board. Likewise, there are numerous accessories that can shape the pattern of light and shadow. Among the most common of these are *gobos* (etched glass or metal filters) that selectively block some light from reaching the stage so that patterns of light and shadow are created. Suffice it to say that each instrument and accessory may serve a different purpose depending on its basic properties and how it is used. Therefore lighting designers must understand the basic properties of each type of lighting instrument in order to select the proper instrument to create the effect they wish.

After the light plots are completed, an instrument schedule is made. This is a chart that lists separately each lighting instrument with its specifications (type, wattage, lens, reflector, lamp, and any other pertinent information), mounting position, color filter, area lighted by it, circuit into which it is plugged, and dimmer to which it is connected. The schedule summarizes in tabular form all of the technical information needed for acquiring and setting up lighting instruments. (See the chart on page 410.)

Lighting Instrument Chart

Inst#	Instrument	Position	Focus	Lamp	Circuit	Dimmer	Color	Notes
1	6316 Ellipsoidal	2nd Ante-Pro.	Down-R	1k	202	4	R54	
2	6316 Ellipsoidal	2nd Ante-Pro.	Down-L	1k	203	5	R54	
1	ETC Source 4	1st Ante-Pro.	Center-R	575w	120	1	R60	
2	ETC Source 4	1st Ante-Pro.	Center-C	575w	125	2	R60	
3	ETC Source 4	1st Ante-Pro.	Center-L	575w	123	3	R60	Leaf Gobo
1	VL6	1st Electric	Variable	400w	7	10	Variable	Programmed by Lynn
2	VL6	1st Electric	Variable	400w	14	17	Variable	Programmed by Lynn
3	639 Ellipsoidal	1st Electric	Center-L	1k	1	11	R64	
4	639 Ellipsoidal	1st Electric	Center-L	1k	3	16	R60	
5	639 Ellipsoidal	1st Electric	Center-C	1k	2	14	R60	
6	639 Ellipsoidal	1st Electric	Center-C	1k	4	20	R62	
1	639 Ellipsoidal	2nd Electric	Up-L	1k	27	28	R64	Leaf Gobo
2	639 Ellipsoidal	2nd Electric	Up-L	1k	29	29	R64	Leaf Gobo
3	6" Fresnel	2nd Electric	Up-R	750w	24	22	R62	2" Top Hat
4	6" Fresnel	2nd Electric	Up-R	750w	30	23	R62	2" Top Hat
1	6" Fresnel	3rd Electric	Center-R	750w	44	37	R73	Barndoor
2	6" Fresnel	3rd Electric	Center-R	750w	46	36	R73	Barndoor
1	Par 64	4th Electric	Down-R	1k	54	46	R08	
2	Par 64	4th Electric	Down-R	1k	58	50	R80	
3	Par 64	4th Electric	Down-R	1k	56	48	R08	

A lighting instrument schedule. (Courtesy of Robert Ball)

Setting the Lights, Rehearsals, and Performances

TYPICALLY, THE PERFORMANCE space is not available for work on lights until a few days prior to technical and dress rehearsals. Regardless of how much time is available, the tasks are reasonably standard. Using the light plots and instrument schedule as guides, the master electrician and his assistants mount each instrument and direct it toward the stage area specified in the light plot. The specified light filter is added, the instrument is plugged into the proper circuit, and it is then connected to the designated dimmer. The instruments may be focused tentatively at this time; final focusing may have to wait until the other production elements are added. Among these elements, those most likely to require adjustments in focusing are scenery and the movement or placement of actors.

To expedite these procedures, a number of aids may be used to avoid the need to refer constantly to light plots or instrument schedules. Sometimes at each instrument position the information about the instrument type, color, circuit, and so on is noted on a piece of tape and attached at the spot where the instrument is to be mounted. Sometimes the information about all of the instruments to be hung on a single batten is indicated on a single card. Each designer and/or master electrician usually has his or her own shortcuts for making the complex process of mounting and focusing instruments more efficient. Although most of the work is done by others, the lighting designer is usually present to answer questions or to clarify plans.

Setting and focusing instruments can be time consuming and sometimes disheartening, because it is difficult to confine light precisely. Unwanted lines, shadows, and bright patches may appear; and when the same instruments must be used to light more than one scene or set, an ideal adjustment for one may not be ideal for the others. This process may go on for hours, even days, until the desired results have been achieved.

Cue sheets—indicating the lighting at the beginning of each scene (the dimmers to be used and the intensity setting of each), any changes to be made during the scene, and the cues for the changes—must also be made. Sometimes designers will create a cue synopsis—a listing of each cue, its effect, and how it is created—as a source of communication with the director and others. If there is a memory bank or other preset device, this information is entered into it. The cue sheets become the basis for controlling the lights during performances.

Lighting is usually integrated with the other elements for the first time during technical rehearsals. Alterations may be required at that time, and further adjustments may be made during and after dress rehearsals. This is a crucial time in the lighting designer's work, because many decisions that determine the final design are not definitely made until these rehearsals. At this time, the lighting designer is often called on to compensate for problems in other aspects of production, because it is easier to adjust lights than to make a new costume or to repaint a set at this point in the production process. Some productions, especially those on Broadway, have a number of preview performances, after each of which some adjustments may be required. After a production officially opens, responsibility passes to the light crew.

■ The Lighting Designer's Assistants

IN THE PROFESSIONAL THEATRE, the lighting designer is usually a member of the United Scenic Artists Union, as is the assistant designer (if there is one). The assistant may make sketches and light plots, compile instrument schedules, locate the necessary equipment, and act as liaison between the lighting designer and the rest of the production staff, as well as aid in programming lights, supervising their installation, and compiling the cue sheets.

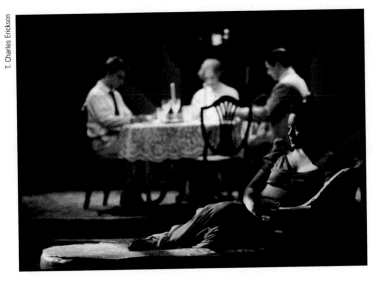

T. Charles Erickson

Robert Perry's lighting for *The Glass Menagerie* by Tennessee Williams. Note how color is used to separate the foreground and background as well as to convey a different mood for both areas. Directed by Joseph Chaikin; scene design by Alexander Dodge; costume design by Sara A. Iams.

The master electrician or lighting crew head works closely with the designer when equipment is being installed and instruments adjusted. After the show opens, the master electrician (or crew head) must see that all materials are properly maintained and check before each performance to see that everything is in working order. These technicians are directly responsible to the stage manager. In the professional theatre, master electricians must be members of the International Alliance of Theatrical Stage Employees union (IATSE).

The lighting crew installs, operates, and maintains all lighting equipment and shifts electrical equipment that must be moved during scene changes. The control-board console operator is of special importance, because this person actually controls the lighting during performances. In the professional theatre, crews usually belong to the union (IATSE). In the nonprofessional theatre, crews are usually students or volunteers.

The Increasing Role of Sound Design

ALTHOUGH SOUND has always played an important role in theatrical production, it has only recently begun to be acknowledged as a separate art of design. Traditionally many have viewed the theatrical use of sound as primarily the craft of recording and playing pre-existing sounds or reinforcing live sound through amplification. However, this view has undergone radical change in recent years. In 1986, the stagehands' union (IATSE) chartered its first sound design chapter, and in 1993 it gained acceptance for a standard labor contract for Broadway and Broadway-tour sound designers. In 1991, John Gromada was awarded an Obie (an award given for excellence in Off-Broadway theatre) for sound design for the New York production of *Machinal.* In the fall of 1993, the Yale School of Drama for the first time admitted sound designers to its design program rather than as previously to its technical crafts division. These developments in effect recognized sound as the fourth

design discipline (along with scenery, lighting, and costume), especially because many theatres now use a complex sound score as well as amplify the performers' voices.

Some maintain that this growing recognition owes to the development of digitized sound that, in conjunction with computers, permits designers to create and manipulate sound waves, not merely record or amplify them. As avant-garde opera and theatre director Peter Sellars has said, "We are beyond the era of sound effects. Sound is no longer an effect, an extra." Sound designer James Lebrecht has been asked to design effects as abstract as "the sound of shimmering light reflecting off a swimming pool at night." Such a request suggests that an effective sound design goes well beyond the basic physics involved and demonstrates the increasing tendency to explore and use sound's esthetic possibilities as an integral aspect of production design.

Sound may be divided into three categories: verbal (the actors' voices), nonverbal (music and abstract sound), and realistic (sound identifiable by recognizable sources). Because the first category has already been discussed in the chapters on directing and acting, little need be said about it here.

The Functions of Sound Design

SOUND MAY fulfill any of four main functions:

- Evoke mood and atmosphere
- Reinforce the action
- Reinforce the performers' voices
- Support the production's style or comments on the action

A mood or atmosphere of gaiety or somberness can be evoked by music, just as mystery or strangeness can be evoked by abstract hollow sounds. Environmental sounds, such as birds singing, may be used to suggest a quiet pastoral scene, or thunder and rain may be used to set the mood for an impending murder.

Sound may reinforce the action by preparing the audience for present or future events or by suggesting offstage events. Gunshots, crashing dishes, doorbells, telephones, and similar sounds may prepare for onstage action or indicate offstage occurrences. Certain identifiable noises may establish the time of day (a rooster crowing is usually associated with daybreak) or season of the year (sleigh bells are usually associated with winter), just as others may place the action outdoors, indoors, in the country or city, or near a specific location such as a railroad or river.

Sound may be live or recorded. But in either case it may be amplified. The actors create live sound, but whether or not it is amplified usually depends on the size of the auditorium, or, in the case of musicals, whether the singing voices need to be amplified to be heard above the musical accompaniment. However, the sound designer may also choose to amplify one or more of the performers' voices for a special effect. Live orchestras are seldom amplified. Most nonmusical dramas do not demand music, but recorded music is often added to underscore an effect, to establish the appropriate mood before the performance begins, or to bridge scenes and cover scene changes.

Sound may comment on the action by giving audiences clues about the response sought by the director. Lugubrious music played during a long pathetic speech can make a comic or satirical comment, or the clashing of cymbals may heighten a pratfall. Thus sound may be used as an additional element that by contrasting or heightening the stage action makes a comment upon it.

■ The Sound Designer's Working Methods and Resources

THE SOUND DESIGNER usually begins by closely examining the play for opportunities to use sound effectively. Some opportunities may be obvious; stage directions may call for the sound of a glass windowpane being smashed, or one character may mention that "the six o'clock train is right on time." However, most opportunities to use sound are less obvious and demand the careful consideration of the designer in consultation with the director. For example, if two characters remain onstage while four or five others exit to play cards in a room offstage, the decision whether or not we hear any of the sounds from this offstage game may add an important nuance or prove distracting.

Most sound designers use their study of the play and their imaginations to develop a *sound score*. The score provides the reason for each intended sound cue (ringing telephone, scene change music, and the like) and approximates its location in the play, its duration, the origin of the sound (what will need to be recorded or used to make the sound, including appropriate information about its style, period, or quality), and the intended treatment of the sound (whether it needs to be distorted, enhanced, and so on). After creating the sound score, the sound designer may present it to the director and other designers for discussion and refinement.

The sound designer then begins to collect sounds to meet the needs of the sound score. The designer may need to research specific effects, music, or environments called for in the play to ensure that the appropriate sounds are selected. Although a wide range of effects is available commercially in sets of recordings labeled as "sound effects libraries," these do not always meet the specific needs of a production. Synthesizers or digital samplers can produce almost any sound, but to achieve the desired quality some sounds may need to be created live or recorded from a live source. Once the intended sounds are found or created, they are recorded on a master tape or entered into a computer and then are edited and enhanced as desired. Computer technology can also be used to alter a recorded sound's duration, pitch, and reverberation, as well as to change its quality by rewriting its digital signature. Sounds can be mixed, fused, and adjusted by a number of other

The effectiveness of the most spectacular moment in the musical *Miss Saigon*, the arrival and departure of a helicopter, depended as much on realistic sound effects as it did on lighting.

techniques to produce almost any desired effect. Likewise, the range of recording equipment has increased so that most organizations now own some type of recording equipment that allows them to create the effects most appropriate to their needs. In the professional theatre, a tape or compact disc approximating the sound that is planned for the production is often used for some rehearsals, allowing sound designers to evaluate the effectiveness of their designs and to make ongoing adjustments. An audio technician or engineer sometimes assists the designer during this process of collecting, recording, and modifying sound.

The designer then creates a *sound plot*, which is similar to the sound score but much more detailed in its organization. It designates a letter or number for each cue, specifying its function, its script page, its duration, its playback system (tape deck, digital player, computer, or whether it will be made live), and its source direction (what speaker or speakers it should be played through and their location). On the basis of these decisions, the designer creates a show tape or disc (as it will be used in the production). Sound must then be integrated into the production with all appropriate information written into the stage manager's promptbook. Cue sheets must be created for the personnel who will oper-

ate the sound during the performances. During technical and dress rehearsals, sound levels and lengths of cues may need to be adjusted and the show tape or disc altered to reflect these changes. Backup tapes or discs are made in case anything should happen to the original. After the production opens, the sound designer's work is considered to be ended, and responsibility passes to the stage manager and sound operator.

Effective execution of a sound design requires a sound system of high quality. Some groups have only the simplest of recorder/playback units, whereas others have very elaborate systems. An effective system allows all of the controllable factors of sound—pitch (or frequency), quality (or timbre), volume (or amplitude), direction, and duration—to be varied in relation to each other and in accordance with the demands of the production. Complete flexibility in direction, for example, requires a series of speakers located at various spots on the stage and in the auditorium so that a sound (such as that of an airplane) can begin on one side, seem to approach, pass overhead, and pass out of hearing on the other side. Effective placement and control are made more complex by the acoustics of the space in which sound may reverberate or be reflected off of various surfaces.

Mixed-Media Productions

MIXED- (OR MULTI-) media productions
may combine elements from several
media, but characteristically they mingle live
action (which may include dance) with projected
still or moving pictures and stereophonic sound
and music.

Several factors may explain the popularity of
multimedia, but perhaps the most important of
these are contemporary changes in artistic taste
and audience perception. Influenced by film, television, and our interaction with computers,
many of us expect time, place, and focus to shift
rapidly, without long delays. This being the case,
many playwrights have begun to write accord-
ingly. In general, the result has been a more fluid
treatment of the stage space instead of cumber-
some full-stage, three-dimensional stage settings.
Significant advances in computer and other electronic technology have been adapted for theatri-

cal use, making it possible to program many
effects and to control them with great precision.
For these reasons, traditional settings have been
largely supplanted by those created with a few
built pieces combined with effects created
through light and sound. The stage has become
technologically more complex, while stage settings have become less illusionistic.

A notable feature of multimedia productions
has been the liberal use of projected images—
often of still pictures, frequently several shown
simultaneously on a number of screens. The
images may be fragments of the same picture, or
each may be unlike the others. All are usually
chosen for their appropriateness to the mood or
theme of the piece; some may suggest comparisons between the dramatic events and those of
other times and places. For example, a production of Shakespeare's *Troilus and Cressida*—
which takes place during the Trojan War—might
project images of wars in various periods and

Jarka Burian

Josef Svoboda's setting for Richard Wagner's *Die Götterdämmerung* at the Royal Opera, Covent Garden, London. Large lenses were used to magnify features as in a film close-up (see figure left). The background is composed of similar lenslike surfaces.

Josef Svoboda and Multimedia

Josef Svoboda (1920–2002) gained international acclaim as a designer, in part because of his extensive use of multimedia. Born in the Czech Republic and trained as an architect, he became chief designer at the National Theatre in Prague in the 1950s. From that time, he experimented continuously with means of applying new technology and materials to scenography. By 1966, his ability to create dynamic stage environments capable of almost continuous alteration led *The Times* of London to hail him in an article as "the world's leading scenic designer." In addition to his work in the Czech Republic, Svoboda designed for leading directors and theatre companies in the United States, England, France, Germany, Belgium, Switzerland, and many other countries.

Several of Svoboda's projects combined filmed or closed-circuit images with live stage action. Among the most complex of these productions was Luigi Nonno's opera *Intoleranza* in Boston. In addition to the live stage action, other scenes were staged simultaneously in a number of studios, some as far as three miles away from the theatre. These studio scenes were projected onto numerous screens located on the stage, thus intermingling several separately staged scenes. As Svoboda described it: "All these studios were joined with each other by audio and visual monitors, so that the actors could see the conductor in relation to themselves, the actors in the studio could see what was being played on the stage, and . . . the actors on the stage see what was played in the studios."

Svoboda was also concerned with the stage's ability to alter scale in ways that create emphasis and subordination comparable to that achieved by close-ups in film. In a production of Wagner's opera *Die Götterdämmerung* in London, he placed on stage large lenses that served as scenic elements but that, when characters moved behind them, magnified those characters, making them much larger than the other live actors onstage. (See illustration on page 415.) The manipulation of light (in color, direction, and intensity) in relation to these lenses also created varied visual effects. Svoboda was a pioneer in exploring the potentials for stage use of emerging technologies.

places, thereby suggesting the similarity of all wars. Filmed sequences may also be used in various ways. Footage of real events may be used to supply a context for a play's action; filmed sequences using the play's actors may be injected into the action to give it greater scope; or filmed sequences and live sequences may be coordinated. Closed-circuit television can be used to project onto large screens close-ups of the actors' faces, portions of the action, or even of the audience. Projections (whatever the type) are often accompanied by stereophonic, directional sound or music. Performance art and the theatrical pieces of such directors as Robert Wilson are examples of multimedia productions in which nonverbal elements take precedence over a written text. (See pages 2, 225, 226, 340, and 415 for examples of multimedia production design.)

In these and other ways, multimedia productions, which depend heavily on the work of the lighting and sound designers, have enlarged the ways in which theatrical means are used and probably will continue to do so as new technology is developed and adapted to stage use.

Thinking about Stage Lighting and Sound

STAGE LIGHTING is among the most difficult production elements to evaluate, because it usually attracts attention not to itself but to the actors, scenery, costumes, or directing. Unless we have difficulty seeing, are distracted by shadows on the actors' faces, are annoyed by glare, or are fascinated by some beautiful or spectacular lighting effect, we may not think about the lighting. Yet light is an essential production element both for the sake of artistry and for the sake of visibility. Sound is perhaps more immediately noticeable, but how and when it is used can have a profound effect on emotional response to a stage moment and our understanding of its significance. Our attention to the lighting and sound choices made by their designers can enhance our understanding of any theatrical production. Here are some questions that may contribute to a fuller understanding of stage lighting and sound:

1. How did the type of theatrical space used for the production (proscenium, arena, thrust, flexible) affect the use of lighting?
2. What overall approach governed the lighting and sound? Did they suggest recognizable sources? Were they used to suggest a specific time of day, period, or place? If so, how? With what effect? Were the lighting and sound dictated by stylistic or interpretational considerations? If so, what were the results?
3. How did lighting and sound affect (or help to create) mood and atmosphere? Did mood and atmosphere change? If so, how? With what results?
4. How effectively did the lighting designer use the controllable qualities of light? How did the light's color and intensity affect your perception of costumes and scenery? How did the distribution of light on stage affect your focus and attention? Did the designer use direction (frontlighting, downlighting, backlighting, crosslighting)

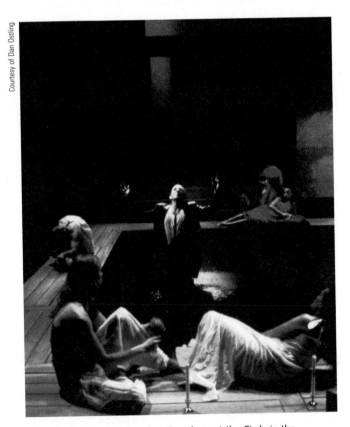

Courtesy of Dan Ostling

Metamorphoses as produced on Broadway at the Circle in the Square Theatre. Directed by Mary Zimmerman; lighting designer T. J. Gerckens; scene designer Dan Ostling; costume designer Mara Blumenfeld.

to emphasize certain areas and features or to deemphasize others? With what effect?

5. Was sound and lighting used to underscore or reinforce the development of the dramatic action or clarify the production concept? If so, how? With what results?

6. Were there any unusual lighting or sound effects? If so, which and with what results? Did these call undue attention to themselves at any point? If so, how?

7. How did the lighting enhance or fail to enhance the acting, scenery, costumes, and makeup? Was it unified with all the other elements?

8. How did the sound enhance or fail to enhance the acting, lighting, and scenery? Was it unified with the other elements? Was sound used to comment upon the action? If so, in what ways? With what results?

9. Overall, how effectively did lighting contribute to the total production?

10. Overall, how effectively did the sound contribute to the total production?

The relevance of each of these questions may vary with the particular production and play. Furthermore, some of these questions may not be answerable because there is not adequate information or because the lighting and sound cannot be isolated from other production elements or the total context. Nevertheless, attempting to answer some or all of these questions can make us examine lighting and sound more closely and lead us to appreciate more fully their contributions to theatrical production.

Afterword

WE HAVE NOW looked at the theatre from several angles: the basic characteristics of theatre as entertainment and as an art form; approaches to evaluating performances; the way plays are written and structured; ways in which the theatrical experience has varied in the past and the way it continues to change in the present; how each of the theatre arts functions today and how all are combined to create the performances we see in the theatre. Taken together, these explorations provide a foundation for a fuller understanding and appreciation of the theatre.

But a foundation is just that—something to build on rather than a finished structure. What one chooses to do with the foundation is as important as the foundation itself. It can be abandoned, or it can be a basis for further growth. Whether your understanding and appreciation of the theatre will continue to develop depends upon whether you attend theatre often and enjoy the experience.

Additional Opportunities with InfoTrac College Edition

Lighting designers Jules Fisher and Peggy Eisenhauer have been working together on theatre and film projects for over twenty years. Use InfoTrac College Edition to read about how Eisenhauer met Fisher and became his assistant in the *American Theatre* case study/interview "Jules Fisher and Peggy Eisenhauer;" search with keywords for projects the two have worked on together.

1. What qualities are essential to such a long-standing working relationship in the theatre?

2. Why did Eisenhauer want to work with Fisher? Why did Fisher decide to take Eisenhauer as his professional partner?

absurdist drama A term used to describe certain plays of the post–World War II period. The writers of these plays believed that the human condition is absurd because the desire for clarity and order is met only by the irrationality of the universe, thus making rational or meaningful choice impossible. Absurdist plays abandoned the logic of cause-to-effect relationships for associational patterns reflecting the illogical nature of the human situation. Two of the most prominent absurdist playwrights were Beckett and Ionesco.

agon In Greek Old Comedy, a debate over the merits of the "happy idea."

antagonist The primary opponent of the leading character in a dramatic action.

arena stage Type of theatre with audience seating on all sides of the performing space; also known as theatre-in-the-round.

art for art's sake A late nineteenth century movement, which asserted that the only functions of art were to intensify experience and to provide sensuous pleasure. In this respect it challenged the scientific outlook of realism and naturalism, their focus on contemporary subjects, and their tacit agenda for social change.

backdrop *See* **drop.**

backstage The areas beyond the visible performance space, especially the workspaces of the backstage personnel, such as stage crews and technicians.

batten A pipe suspended above the stage by lines that permit it to be raised or lowered; scenic pieces or lighting instruments may be hung from it. Wooden battens are attached to the top and bottom of drops to keep the cloth stretched and free of wrinkles.

blocking The placement and movement of the actors on stage moment by moment, usually planned by the director.

border A short curtain or piece of painted canvas hung parallel to the front of the stage and in a series from front-to-back, used to mask the overhead space. Striplights mounted behind the borders are called borderlights.

box set A setting or set that fully encloses the acting space on three sides like the walls of a room, resembling a box with one side removed.

bunraku A Japanese form of doll or puppet theatre.

butai The primary acting area in the Japanese Noh theatre, which includes areas associated with the four pillars (shitebashira, wakibashira, fuebashira, metsukabashira) and specific characters and functions.

character makeup Application of makeup intended to markedly alter one or more of an actor's natural facial features.

characterization That which delineates a person or differentiates that person from others, typically operating on four levels: physical, sociological, psychological, and moral.

choregus A wealthy citizen in ancient Greece who helped finance the training and costuming of the chorus. One choregus was chosen for each competing dramatist.

chorus In Greek drama, a group of actors who spoke, sang, and danced in unison; the choral songs and dances, usually commenting on the action, separated the play into episodes. In Renaissance drama, a single character who commented on the action or served as a narrator.

chou The comic characters in Chinese opera.

city Dionysia The principal Athenian festival (held in honor of the god Dionysus) at which plays were performed.

climactic plot structure An arrangement of a play's events wherein, typically, scenes build sequentially in a cause-to-effect relationship from inciting incident to the climax or resolution.

climax The highest point of interest or suspense, typically the moment that determines the outcome of a play's action.

comedy A form of drama based on some deviation from normality in action, character, or thought treated as to arouse laughter or ridicule and which ends happily.

commedia dell'arte A type of performance that emerged in Italy during the sixteenth century. Starting from a scenario that merely outlined the situation, complications, and outcome, the actors improvised the dialogue and action. Each actor always played the same stock character, who wore his or her distinctive costume and mask. The most popular characters were the **zanni**, or comic servants, whose contrivances served both to create and resolve complications. Commedia companies played through-out Europe and enjoyed great popularity everywhere until the middle of the eighteenth century.

complication Any new element that serves to change the direction of a play's dramatic action.

conventions Theatrical and dramatic practices, devices, and procedures that are mutually understood and accepted by both theatre practitioners and audiences. Things seldom happen in the theatre precisely as they would in life, but audiences easily overlook and accept these deviations if they understand the conventions being used. When initially introduced, a convention may be misunderstood; it gains acceptance through continued usage. Some common conventions are Shakespeare's use of soliloquies, characters breaking into song or dance in the midst of a scene in musicals, and the rapid and visible changes that shift the action from one locale to another in many kinds of plays.

costume chart A broad organizational chart used to indicate what costumes and accessories each actor will wear in each scene. It may also be used by costume crews as a guide for dressing the actors during performances.

crew The backstage personnel who assist in mounting and running a production. There are usually separate crews for scenery, costumes, properties, lighting, and sound.

crisis The final turning point in the action of a play, usually brought about by the revelation of those things that have been partially or entirely unknown by one or more of the principal characters.

cue The words, actions, or other prearranged indications that serve as signals for actors to go on to their next line or action, or for lighting, sound, or other crew members to execute some agreed-upon change.

cue sheet A list of cues that will serve as the basis for making changes in lights, sounds, or other production elements during the course of a performance. Cue sheets also indicate the changes to be made, along with any other information needed to carry out the appropriate action.

cycle plays In the Middle Ages, a series of short plays dramatizing events drawn from the Bible, often extending from the Creation to Doomsday.

cyclorama Any arrangement of cloth or other material (including plaster) that curves around the rear of the stage and partially down the sides. Usually neutral in color, it is often lighted to represent the sky or used as a projection surface.

dada An early twentieth century movement that sought to replace logic, reason, and unity in art with change and illogicality.

dalang The performer who speaks the dialogue and manipulates the shadow puppets used in Wayang Kulit. *See* **Wayang Kulit.**

dan Female roles in Chinese opera; divided into quiet and gentle females (qing yi); vivacious or dissolute females (hua dan); warrior maidens (wu dan); and old females (lao dan).

decorum A principle supporting French Neoclassic drama that suggested characters should behave in a manner appropriate to their social status, gender, and ethnicity.

denouement ("unraveling" or "untying") The final portion of a play, it extends from the crisis to its end. It may resolve the conflict, make sense of the various stands of action, answer the questions raised earlier, or solidify a theme.

deus ex machina A Greek term meaning "the god from the machine," referring to the common practice of flying in a god to resolve a difficult dramatic situation. Later it came to mean the use of any unprepared-for and unexpected means of resolving an action. *See* **machina.**

dimmer A device for altering the flow of electrical current and thereby selectively changes the intensity of particular lighting instruments.

discovery The introduction of information or revelations of sufficient importance raise a complication.

dramatic action Not only what the characters do but also why they do it, in relation to some question, problem, or theme that forms the central focus of the play as a whole.

dress parade A procedure used by the costume designer to make certain that costumes have been completed as designed and function appropriately. For each scene, the actors don their costumes, appear together, and perform characteristic actions under lights simulating those that will be used in performance.

dressers Wardrobe personnel responsible for assisting actors with costume changes during performances.

dressing lists Lists of all the costumes and accessories worn by each performer and used by dressers or the performers to ensure that all the correct items are worn in the appropriate scenes.

drop A hanging unit made of lengths of cloth sewn together and attached at the top to a batten that supports it and to another at the bottom that keeps it stretched and free of wrinkles. Scenes of various sorts may be painted on drops. Drops usually serve as backgrounds (backdrops) for the action.

eccyclema The platform, rolled or pushed out through the central doorway of the ancient Greek skene, used typically to display the corpses of characters slain offstage.

egungen A traditional Nigerian New Year's ceremony which ends with the sins of the community being loaded onto a "carrier" who cleanses the village by taking them away.

elevations Scene designers' two-dimensional scale drawings that communicate detailed information to others regarding the appearance and construction of each scenic unit; these typically include front, rear, and side views as well as the desired paint treatment.

environmental theatre A type of performance, especially during and after the 1960s, in which acting and audience space may be intermingled to achieve interaction between spectators and performers.

epic theatre A theatrical form, usually associated with Bertolt Brecht, that emerged in the 1920s. Brecht sought to distance ("alienate") spectators emotionally in order to help them more objectively watch and judge what it saw. Ultimately Brecht hoped his audiences would relate what they saw in the theatre to conditions in society and then seek to alter the sociopolitical system. Brecht called his theatre "epic" because the alteration of dialogue and narration, with its frequent shifts in time and place, had more in common with epic poetry than with traditional drama.

episodic plot structure An arrangement of a play's events wherein its scenes jump from one to the next, often separated by time or place, without necessarily building a cause-to-effect relationship between them.

existentialism A philosophical position that gained popularity following World War II, especially through the writings of Jean-Paul Sartre, and carried over into playwriting by Sartre and Albert Camus. The argument of the existentialists was that there are no longer any certainties and that human beings are condemned to choose their own values and to live by them, whether or not these values are accepted by others.

exposition The setting forth of information about events, characters, and the present situation that precede the play's point of attack. Typically, exposition is most abundant in the opening scene, where it is used to clarify the situation, establish the identity and relationship of the characters, and set forth the present situation, although it may occur throughout the play.

expressionism An artistic movement that flourished, especially in Germany, from around 1910 to about 1924. Believing that the industrial age had turned human beings into machine-like creatures, expressionism sought to undermine materialist values and create "the new man," who would reshape the world in accordance with the needs of the human spirit. Expressionist drama made extensive use of distortion and grotesque imagery to portray the present human condition. Expressionism found its way into American drama, as in O'Neill's *The Hairy Ape.*

farce A type of comic, secular drama that usually emphasizes situation over character or idea. Coincidence, misunderstanding, ridiculous violence, and rapid pace are its typical ingredients.

flat A basic scenic unit composed of a covered frame existing in various types, the most common being wall, door, or window flats; two or more of which may be joined to create a larger scenic surface.

flying A method of shifting scenery in which scenic elements may be suspended overhead and lowered into or raised out of audience view as needed. *Flying* also refers to the raising and lowering of performers by cables attached to a body harness.

footlights A row of striplights mounted at floor level at the front of the proscenium stage or around the outer edges of a thrust stage.

French scenes The division of a printed play into new scenes with each entrance or exit of a character. French drama long used this organization of dramatic action to indicate an alteration in the motivations or focus created by the change of characters on stage.

front of the house That part of the theatre forward of the stage and the activities and persons associated with it: audience, ushers, box office, and the like. Often used as the opposite of **backstage.**

futurism A movement launched in early twentieth century Italy that glorified the speed and energy of the machine age and sought to replace traditional art forms with new ones. These new forms included "synthetic" drama which compressed into a moment or two the essence of a full-length play, the use of simultaneously staging different scenes or events in different parts of the performance and audience spaces, and various attempts to induce confrontational audience/performer interaction.

gas table The controlboard for a lighting system that uses gas as the illuminant.

general illumination Stage lighting that spreads over a relatively large area, serving one or more of three functions: (1) lighting all background areas not illuminated by spotlights; (2) blending the acting areas together and providing a smooth transition between the high intensity of the acting areas and the lower intensity of the background; (3) enhancing or modifying the color of settings and costumes.

gesamtkunstwerk A German term meaning "master artwork," usually associated with the opera composer Richard Wagner. Wagner believed that a theatre production should create a unified illusion and that all choices should be filtered through a single consciousness to achieve this unified effect.

glee A rousing musical number and the opening number in Yoruba opera.

gobo A thin template made of metal or glass into which a pattern is generally cut that, when inserted directly into the lighting instrument's focal point, projects a pattern of shadows by obstructing some portion(s) of the light.

green room A room in the theatre where all of the actors and crewmembers can assemble to relax or receive instructions.

habit à la romaine The usual costume worn by actors playing Greek or Roman heroes in neoclassical theatre; a stylized adaptation of Roman armor, tunic, and boots.

hanamichi A raised gangway or walkway that connects the front of the stage to the back of the auditorium; important entrances and much of the action take place on this gangway.

hand props *See* **properties.**

happenings Multimedia performance events, pioneered by visual artists in the 1950s and 1960s, that sought to (1) break down the barriers between the arts and between performers and spectators, (2) shift emphasis from creating a product to participating in a process, and (3) shift emphasis from communicating an artist's intention to enhancing the participant's awareness.

hashigakari In the Noh theatre, a long bridge leading from the dressing room to the stage; used as the principal entrance for actors and musicians.

hell mouth In medieval theatre, a specific mansion representing Hell and often portrayed as the mouth of a beast.

inciting incident An occurrence that sets the main action of a play in motion.

independent theatre movement A trend that began in the 1880s and continues to the present, originating because major theatres would not produce certain new plays, either because of indifference or because official censors would not license the plays for production. Independent theatres, which could avoid censorship by performing only for their subscribers, were able to introduce and gain acceptance for many new plays. In the twentieth century, variations on this original plan have been used whenever the theatre has been unresponsive to new forms of writing or production. Twentieth-century independent theatres have been labeled little theatres, art theatres, fringe theatres, alternative theatres, Off-Broadway, Off-Off-Broadway, and so on.

instrument schedule A chart used by lighting designers listing each lighting instrument with its specifications (type, wattage, lens, reflector, lamp, and any other pertinent information), mounting position, color filter, the area it lights, the circuit into which it is plugged, and the dimmer to which it is connected.

intermezzi Interludes between the acts of Italian court drama that acted as elaborate compliments suggesting parallels between some mythological figure and the person in whose honor the festival was being given. Eventually, the spectacular appeals of intermezzi were absorbed into opera.

jing Chinese opera characters represented in part by elaborate patterns painted on the actors' faces.

kabuki The most popular of the traditional Japanese theatrical forms; it uses highly stylized settings, acting, costumes and makeup in its performance of melodramatic stories.

komos An exit to feasting and revelry.

kyogen Japanese short farces performed as interludes between Noh plays.

lazzi Improvised comic stage business or routines based on character type and situation.

light plots These come in two basic types: floor plans and section plots. A floor plan oriented light plot shows, as seen from a top view, the layout of the stage, the setting, and the auditorium. On this plot are indicated the type, size, and position of each lighting instrument and the area it will illuminate. Section plots show the layout of the stage, the setting, the auditorium, and lighting positions from a side view. Taken together, these plots show the horizontal and vertical distribution of the light sources in conjunction with the stage setting and auditorium.

limelight The first effective spotlight, consisting of a hood equipped with a reflector, lens, and a column of calcium (lime) onto which hydrogen and oxygen were directed, along with a gas flame. The flame in combination heated the lime to incandescence, creating an extremely bright light. Its frequent use as a follow spot gave rise to the phrase, "in the limelight."

lines of business The division of acting into a few categories defined by the character types they included. Until the late nineteenth century, an actor was employed in terms of his or her line of business. Actors usually began their careers as utility actors and played supernumerary roles until they discovered the character type for which they were best suited. Most actors then continued in that line of business for the remainder of their careers.

liturgical drama The incorporation of drama into or performed in conjunction with the church service or liturgy.

liturgical play A play incorporated into or performed in conjunction with the church service or liturgy.

living newspaper A form that developed within the Federal Theatre Project, financed by the U.S. government during the 1930s to relieve unemployment. Each Living Newspaper treated a single pressing problem (such as slum housing) and advocated social reform and corrective legislation to solve the problem. The Federal Theatre Project ended in 1939 when Congress, offended by the partisan stance of the Living Newspapers, refused to appropriate funds to continue it.

ludi A Roman term, literally meaning "games," that referred to the religious festivals at which theatrical performances were given.

machina A crane like device used to simulate flying in the Greek theatre. *See* **deus ex machina.**

magic if A key aspect of Stanislavsky's system through which actors project themselves into the world of the play; actors imagine how they might feel or act if they were a particular character in a particular situation.

major dramatic question The most significant question raised by the inciting incident; a question which, typically, will be pursued throughout most of the play.

makeup plot A chart recording basic information about the makeup of each character.

mansion The basic scenic structure in the medieval theatre used to represent locale. As many mansions as were needed to indicate the locales of a play's action were present simultaneously on platforms or wagons. After the place of the action was indicated by associating it with a specific mansion, the performers used as much of the adjoining platform space as was needed for the action. *See* **platea.**

melodrama A form of drama, especially associated with the nineteenth century, based on a clear distinction between good and evil. Typically a virtuous protagonist seeks to overcome seemingly insurmountable threats created by a villain. Suspense is created and increased until the last moment, when the villain is punished and the protagonist rescued and rewarded. Melodrama often incorporates elaborate spectacle and originally used music to create mood and to underscore emotional responses.

messenger scene A standard part of Greek tragedy used to describe violent events that have taken place offstage. Greek sensibilities forbade enacting scenes of violence onstage. *See* **eccyclema.**

mie A highly stylized pose struck and held by a principal character in Japanese Kabuki.

morality plays In the late medieval theatre, plays of an allegorical nature that treated the spiritual trials of ordinary persons.

naturalism A late nineteenth-century form of extreme realism whose chief spokesman was Emile Zola. The naturalists argued that plays should be a slice of life that demonstrates the effects of heredity and environment. Naturalism was the first artistic movement to treat working-class characters with the same seriousness accorded the middle and upper classes by earlier movements. In the twentieth century, naturalism is often used as a label for plays that seek to recreate the details of everyday life, especially its seamy side.

naumachia A staged or mock sea battle; one of the most spectacular of the Romans' theatrical entertainments.

neoclassicism The set of rules, conventions, and beliefs that dominated much drama and theatre from the Renaissance to the end of the eighteenth century. Neoclassicism recognized only two legitimate forms of drama (tragedy and comedy), arguing that the two forms should never be mixed. Tragedy should treat serious stories of kings and nobles, whereas comedy should treat the domestic world of the middle or lower classes. According to the neoclassicists, plays should be written in five acts, observe the unities, and uphold poetic justice in their endings.

neocolonialism The residue of attitudes, practices, and power structures left over from occupation/domination by foreign states/cultures; especially noteworthy in (but not restricted to) Africa and parts of Asia.

new stagecraft A term used in the United States for its early assimilation of European modernist innovations. Simplification and suggestion were the hallmarks of this trend which valued the ability of scene design to evoke mood and stimulate the imagination more than its ability to create a detailed reproduction of the real world.

onnagata Female roles played by male actors in Japanese Kabuki theatre.

orchestra The "dancing place;" in ancient Greek theatre, the space in which the chorus sang and danced.

overpainting Any modification of the base coat; overpainting is used to simulate textures, materials, decorations, or conditions.

pageant wagon In the medieval theatre, a platform on wheels that each play was mounted on and moved from one playing place to another thereby achieving processional staging.

panorama A scenic element in the nineteenth-century theatre; a continuous scene painted on a long expanse of canvas that could remain fixed or be rigged to move, giving the effect that characters, though remaining on stage, were moving from one place to another.

parabasis In Greek Old Comedy, choral passage addressed directly to the audience most frequently filled with advice on civic or other contemporary problems.

parodoi The spaces at either side of the orchestra between the skene and the auditorium in the Greek theatre, used primarily as entrances and exits for the performers, especially the chorus.

parodos The processional entrance of the chorus in the Greek theatre.

performance art A contemporary type of presentation, often by a solo performer, that typically intermingles elements from various arts. Performance art usually encourages spectators to derive from the presentation whatever is meaningful to them.

platea In the medieval theatre, an undifferentiated stage space in front of the mansions.

plot The arrangement of a play's incidents or the overall structure of its action. Thus it differs from story, which may have begun long before the play begins.

point of attack The moment within the overall story wherein the playwright begins his or her treatment of events.

poor theatre A phrase, introduced by Jerzy Grotowski, to identify a type of theatre that discards all technological aids not essential to theatrical performance. Grotowski concluded that there are only two essential theatrical elements: the actor and the audience.

postmodernism A term used to describe certain contemporary artistic tendencies, among them the blurring of distinctions between dramatic forms and the mingling of elements from disparate styles, periods, and cultures.

producer The person responsible for financing a production, making contractual arrangements with those involved, leasing a theatre, publicizing the show, selling tickets, and handling all other aspects relating to the business and managerial side of theatrical production.

production concept Sometimes called the directorial concept; a metaphor, dominant idea, or set of conventions used by a director to shape a production; also referred to as an interpretational focus.

promptbook A copy of the script in which the blocking and stage business of the actors, cues for lighting and sound, and all other information needed by the stage manager have been entered.

properties Onstage objects of two types: (1) set properties, required to complete or decorate the set, and (2) hand properties, used by the actors in their stage business.

proscenium arch An architectural feature that frames a stage opening to keep spectators from seeing around or over the stage setting.

protagonist The principal character in a dramatic action.

realism An attempt in writing and production to represent characters and events as they are observed in real life. Scattered attempts at realism are found throughout theatre history, but, as a movement, realism emerged in the 1850s, grounded in the scientific outlook and the belief that human behavior can best be explained in terms of hereditary and environmental influences. Realists argued that because we can know the real world only through direct observation, playwrights should write only about the society around them as objectively as possible.

regional theatre Term used to designate ongoing not-for-profit theatres throughout the United States. Such theatres are sometimes called resident theatres.

repertory The total group of plays a company chooses for presentation. A repertory company is one that alternates performances of several productions.

restoration The period in English history following the restoration of Charles II to the throne in

1660, extending to about 1700. In theatre, the period is noted for its comedy of manners, which focused on the amoral behavior and witty verbal exchanges of the idle upper class.

revolving stage A circular platform or segment of the stage floor mounted on a central pivot. When it is revolved, one setting comes into view as another moves out of sight.

romanticism A dramatic style that emerged during the early nineteenth century which rejected the strictures imposed by neoclassicism. Romanticism favored infinite variety over standardized norms of neoclassicism and glorified the writer as a genius who operated beyond the limitations of stultifying rules.

samisen A three-stringed musical instrument used as the primary accompaniment in Japanese Bunraku theatre.

satyr play A short comic or satiric play that followed each set of three tragedies at the City Dionysia in Greece. Its chorus was composed of satyrs (half-man, half-goat creatures), and its story usually poked fun at some Greek myth.

scaenae frons The façade enclosing the back and sides of the stage in the ancient Roman theatre. It served as background for all types of plays.

scrim A curtain or drop made of gauzelike fabric. When lighted only from the front, it appears opaque. When lighted from the back, it appears translucent.

sheng Male roles in Chinese opera; divided into young men (xiao sheng); old men (lao sheng); and warriors (wu sheng).

shite The principal character and his followers in Japanese Noh theatre.

sightline The line of vision from any audience seat to any point on stage. Often used to indicate how much of the stage action can be seen from any part of the house.

skene The scene house in the Greek theatre; literally meaning a hut or tent, the word probably derives from the structure used originally as an offstage place where actors could change costumes. It is the source of our word "scene."

soliloquy A speech given by a character who is alone on stage; generally represents a character's inner thoughts through this convention.

sound score The score provides the reason for each intended sound cue and approximates when it should be played, its duration, as well as information about its source, its playback, and any special treatment it may need.

specific illumination Stage light confined to a limited area, usually produced by spotlights.

spoken decor Locale established through character speech rather than representation scenically.

spotlight A lighting instrument composed of a metal housing, a reflector, lamp, and lens designed to illuminate restricted areas with a concentrated beam of light. The major types of spotlights are plano-convex, fresnel, and ellipsoidal.

stage business Detailed action performed by the actor, such as filling and smoking a pipe or setting a table; often prescribed by the script but may be invented by the actors or the director to clarify or enrich action or characterization.

stage house The stage and all of the space above it to the roof.

stage manager The individual responsible for running the show during performances, making sure that everything functions as intended.

stock characters Easily recognizable broad character types.

straight makeup Application of makeup intended to make visible or enhance an actors natural facial features without significantly altering them.

striplight A lighting instrument composed of a series of lamps usually mounted in a rectangular trough and used for general illumination. There are three basic types of striplights: (1) footlights, mounted in the floor at the front of the stage; (2) borderlights, hung from battens above the stage in a series from front to back; and (3) miscellaneous striplights, used to light backings, the cyclorama, or other scenic elements.

sturm und drang A German term meaning "storm and stress" used to identify a group of German playwrights who wrote serious plays that experimented with bold subjects and dramatic form in the late eighteenth century.

subplots Events or actions of secondary interest which often provide contrast to or commentary on the main plot.

subtext Unstated motivations, ideas, or tensions beneath the surface of a play's text. Often the subtext is more important than the text.

summer stock Companies that perform only during the summer, typically in resort areas, and produce a series of plays, often one each week.

supernumerary Extra characters with non-speaking roles in the ancient Greek theatre.

surrealism A movement, especially in the 1920s, emphasizing the importance of the subconscious. Believing that the most significant truths are those buried in the unconscious, surrealists sought to release these suppressed forces by exploring dreams, automatic writing, and stream-of-consciousness.

symbolism A movement that emerged in the late nineteenth century, symbolism was the first of several that sought to counter the influence of realism and naturalism. Rather than seeking truth through direct observation of the world around them, symbolists argued that truth can only be intuited and that these intuitions can be expressed only indirectly through symbols.

technical director A position found primarily in resident and educational theatres, the technical director is usually responsible for implementing the designer's plans: purchasing materials, supervising the building, assembling, and painting of sets, and overseeing the crews that run the shows.

technical rehearsal One of the final rehearsals, usually immediately preceding dress rehearsals, devoted primarily to making sure that all of the technical elements (scenery, costumes, makeup, lighting, sound, and properties) are ready and are functioning as planned.

theatre of cruelty Antonin Artaud's label for the type of performance he advocated to force audiences to confront the violent impulses suppressed within their unconscious minds. Although he acknowledged that such confrontations might be cruel, Artaud thought them necessary to overcome violence and divisiveness if the theatre is to fulfill its goal of "draining abscesses collectively." Little heeded during his lifetime, Artaud later exerted major influence on theatrical practice, especially during the 1960s.

theatre-in-the-round *See* **arena stage.**

theatron The "seeing place;" in ancient Greece, the slope upon which the audience sat to see the plays performed, and the origin for our word "theatre."

thrust stage Type of theatre with audience seating arranged around three, or occasionally two, sides of a raised platform.

tragedy A form of drama that presents a serious action and maintains a serious tone (although there may be moments of comic relief). The protagonist is usually one who arouses our sympathy and admiration but who encounters disaster through the pursuit of some goal, worthy in itself, conflicting with another goal or principle.

trap An opening in the stage floor that allows performers to appear or special effects to materialize from beneath the floor.

unities Neoclassicism demanded that three unities be observed: unity of time (which usually was interpreted to mean that all events should occur within twenty-four hours); unity of place (which typically required that the action occur in the same place); and unity of action (which typically required that there be only one plot). Most other movements have considered unity of action necessary, although interpreting it more liberally than the neoclassicists, but have rejected the unities of time and place.

waki The secondary character and his followers in Japanese Noh theatre.

wayang kulit The performance form and term for leather puppets that a dalang manipulates in a shadow puppet performance.

well-made play Term used to describe logically constructed plays following the pattern of careful exposition and preparation, a series of complications that creates growing suspense and builds to a climactic moment, after which all-important questions are resolved. Although most of these features can be found in plays from the time of the Greeks onward, the term *well-made play* is associated with Eugène Scribe, the popular nineteenth-century French playwright who reduced these traditional playwriting techniques to a formula. Although "well-made play" is now often used condescendingly, Scribe's practice has supplied the pattern for much realistic playwriting since his time.

willing suspension of disbelief Samuel Taylor Coleridge's description of the audience's complicity in accepting stage events; although we know that the events of a play are not real, we agree for the moment not to disbelieve them.

wings From the Renaissance onward, a major scenic element consisting of pairs of flats set up parallel to the front of the stage and arranged in a series from downstage to upstage. They were used in conjunction with two other major scenic elements: drops or shutters (flats that met at center back) used to enclose the rear of the stage, and borders used to complete the scene overhead. Today, the term is most often used for the offstage space on either side of the stage.

yoruba opera (or Yoruba Traveling Theatre) The most popular form of entertainment in Nigeria. It includes an introduction composed of song and dance, followed by a topical play, and concluding with another section of song and dance. It is very similar in form to the Concert Party of neighboring Ghana.

zanni The servants of the commedia dell'arte; origin of the word *zany.*

Bibliography

This bibliography lists some of the many important books on theatre. The divisions correspond to those in the text. All works are in English.

PART ONE

Chapter 1
The Nature of Theatre

Brook, Peter. *The Empty Space.* New York: Avon Books, 1969.

Esslin, Martin. *The Field of Drama: How the Signs of Drama Create Meaning on Stage and Screen.* New York: Methuen, 1987.

Lahr, John, and Jonathan Price. *Life-Show: How to See Theatre in Life and Life in Theatre.* New York: Viking Press, 1973.

Rozik, Eli. *The Roots of Theatre: Rethinking Ritual and Other Theories of Origin.* Iowa City: University of Iowa Press, 2002.

Schechner, Richard. *Performance Theory.* New York: Routledge, 1988.

Styan, J. L. *Drama, Stage and Audience.* New York: Cambridge University Press, 1975.

Turner, Victor. *From Ritual to Theatre: The Human Seriousness of Play.* New York: Performing Arts Journal Publications, 1982.

Wickham, Glynne. *Drama in a World of Science.* Toronto: University of Toronto Press, 1962.

Wilson, Glenn. *The Psychology of the Performing Arts.* London: Croom Helm, 1985.

Chapter 2
Performance, Audience, and Critic

Bennett, Susan. *Theatre Audiences: A Theory of Production and Reception.* New York: Routledge, 1997.

Blau, Herbert. *The Audience.* Baltimore: Johns Hopkins University Press, 1990.

Esslin, Martin. *An Anatomy of Drama.* New York: Hill & Wang, 1976.

Kauffmann, Stanley. *Theatre Criticisms.* New York: Performing Arts Journal Publications, 1984.

Lahr, John, and Jonathan Price. See under Chapter 1.

Sontag, Susan. *Against Interpretation and Other Essays.* New York: Doubleday, 1966.

Styan, J. L. See under Chapter 1.

Vena, Gary. *How to Read and Write about Drama.* New York: Arco, 1988.

Chapter 3
The Play

Barranger, Milly S. *Understanding Plays,* 2d. ed. Boston: Allyn and Bacon, 1994.

Barry, Jackson G. *Dramatic Structure: The Shaping of Experience.* Berkeley, Calif.: University of California Press, 1970.

Beckerman, Bernard. *Dynamics of Drama: Theory and Method of Analysis.* New York: Knopf, 1970.

Esslin, Martin. *The Field of Drama.* New York: Methuen, 1987.

Fergusson, Francis. *The Idea of a Theatre.* Princeton, N.J.: Princeton University Press, 1949.

Grote, David. *Script Analysis.* Belmont, Calif.: Wadsworth, 1985.

Hayman, Ronald. *How to Read a Play.* New York: Grove Press, 1977.

Heffner, Hubert. *The Nature of Drama.* Boston: Houghton Mifflin, 1959.

Heilman, Robert B. *Tragedy and Melodrama: Versions of Experience.* Seattle: University of Washington Press, 1968.

Kerr, Walter. *Tragedy and Comedy.* New York: Simon & Schuster, 1967.

Scanlan, David. *Reading Drama.* Mountain View, Calif.: Mayfield, 1988.

Styan, J. L. *The Elements of Drama.* New York: Cambridge University Press, 1960.

Weales, Gerald. *A Play and Its Parts.* New York: Basic Books, 1964.

PART TWO

Banham, Martin, ed. *Cambridge Guide to Theatre.* Cambridge: Cambridge University Press, 1995.

Brockett, Oscar G., and Franklin J. Hildy. *History of Theatre,* 9th ed. Boston: Allyn and Bacon, 2003.

Carlson, Marvin. *Theories of the Theatre: A Historical and Critical Survey, from the Greeks to the Present,* rev. ed. Ithaca, N.Y.: Cornell University Press, 1994.

Duerr, Edwin. *The Length and Depth of Acting.* New York: Holt, Rinehart and Winston, 1962.

Izenour, George C. *Theatre Design.* New York: McGraw-Hill, 1977.

Laver, James. *Drama: Its Costume and Decor.* London: Studio Publications, 1951.

Leacroft, Richard, and Helen Leacroft. *Theatre and Playhouse: An Illustrated Survey of Theatre Building from Ancient Greece to the Present Day.* London: Methuen, 1984.

Oenslager, Donald. *Stage Design: Four Centuries of Scenic Invention.* New York: Viking Press, 1975.

Oxford Companion to the Theatre, 4th ed. London: Oxford University Press, 1983.

World Encyclopedia of Contemporary Theatre. 6 vols. London: Routledge, 1994–2001.

Chapter 4
Festival Theatre: Greek, Roman, and Medieval Theatre Experiences

Arnott, Peter D. *Greek Scenic Conventions in the Fifth Century B.C.* Oxford: Clarendon Press, 1962.

———. *Public and Performance in Greek Theatre.* London: Routledge, Chapman and Hall, 1989.

Beacham, Richard C. *The Roman Theatre and Its Audience.* Cambridge, Mass.: Harvard University Press, 1992.

Beare, William. *The Roman Stage: A Short History of Latin Drama in the Time of the Republic,* 3d ed. London: Methuen, 1963.

Bevington, David. *From Mankind to Marlowe: Growth in Structure in the Popular Drama of Tudor England.* Cambridge, Mass.: Harvard University Press, 1962.

Bieber, Margarete. *The History of the Greek and Roman Theater,* 2d ed. Princeton, N.J.: Princeton University Press, 1961.

Chambers, E. K. *The Mediaeval Stage.* 2 vols. Oxford: Clarendon Press, 1903.

Collins, Fletcher. *The Production of Medieval Church Music-Drama.* Charlotte: University of Virginia Press, 1971.

Craik, Thomas W. *Revels History of Drama in English.* Vol. 2, *1500–1576.* New York: Barnes & Noble, 1980.

———. *The Tudor Interlude: Stage, Costume, and Acting.* Leicester: University of Leicester Press, 1958.

Deardon, C. W. *The Stage of Aristophanes.* London: Athlone Press, 1976.

Duckworth, George E. *The Nature of Roman Comedy.* Princeton, N.J.: Princeton University Press, 1952.

Hunter, R. L. *The New Comedy of Greece and Rome.* New York: Twayne, 1985.

Kitto, H. D. F. *Greek Tragedy,* 2d ed. London: Methuen, 1950.

Kolve, V. A. *The Play Called Corpus Christi.* Stanford, Calif.: Stanford University Press, 1966.

Nicoll, Allardyce. *Masks, Mimes and Miracles.* New York: Harcourt Brace Jovanovich, 1931.

Ogden, Dunbar. *The Staging of Drama in the Medieval Church.* Newark, Del.: University of Delaware Press, 2002

Pickard-Cambridge, A. W. *The Dramatic Festivals of Athens,* 2d ed. Rev. by John Gould and D. M. Lewis. Oxford: Clarendon Press, 1968.

Potter, Robert. *The English Morality Play: Origins, History and Influence of a Dramatic Tradition.* London: Routledge and Kegan Paul, 1975.

Salter, F. M. *Medieval Drama in Chester.* Toronto: University of Toronto Press, 1955.

Sommerstein, Alan. *Greek Drama and Dramatists.* New York: Routledge, 2002.

Tydeman, William, Michael J. Anderson, and Nick Davis, eds. The *Medieval European Stage 500–1550.* Cambridge: Cambridge University Press, 2001.

Vince, Ronald W. *A Companion to the Medieval Theatre.* New York: Greenwood Press, 1989.

Walton, J. Michael. *Living Greek Theatre: A Handbook of Classical Performance and Modern Production.* Westport, Conn.: Greenwood Press, 1987.

Webster, T. B. L. *Greek Theatre Production,* 2d ed. London: Methuen, 1970.

Wickham, Glynne. *Early English Stages, 1300–1660.* 3 vols. New York: Columbia University Press, 1959–1979.

Wiles, David. *Greek Theatre Performance.* Cambridge: Cambridge University Press, 2000.

Chapter 5
Creating a Professional Theatre: Elizabethan England, Italian Commedia dell'Arte, and Seventeenth-Century France

Andrews, Richard. *Scripts and Scenarios: The Performance of Comedy in Renaissance Italy.* Cambridge: Cambridge University Press, 1993.

Astington, John N. *English Court Theatre, 1558–1642.* Cambridge: Cambridge University Press, 1999.

Barroll, J. L., et al. *Revels History of Drama in English.* Vol. 3, *1576–1613.* New York: Barnes & Noble, 1975.

Beckerman, Bernard. *Shakespeare at the Globe, 1599–1609.* New York: Macmillan, 1962.

Bentley, Gerald E. *The Profession of Dramatist in Shakespeare's Time, 1590–1642.* Princeton, N.J.: Princeton University Press, 1971.

———. *The Profession of Player in Shakespeare's Time, 1590–1642.* Princeton, N.J.: Princeton University Press, 1984.

Bjurstrom, Per. *Giacomo Torelli and Baroque Stage Design.* Stockholm: Almqvist and Wiksell, 1961.

Bradley, David. *From Text to Performance in the Elizabethan Theatre: Preparing the Play for the Stage.* New York: Cambridge University Press, 1992.

Cairns, Christopher, ed. *Scenery, Set, and Staging in the Italian Renaissance.* Lewiston, N.Y.: Edwin Mellen Press, 1996.

Callaghan, Dympna. *Shakespeare Without Women.* New York: Routledge, 2000.

Clubb, Louise G. *Italian Drama in Shakespeare's Time.* New Haven, Conn.: Yale University Press, 1989.

Duchartre, Pierre L. *The Italian Comedy: The Improvisation, Scenarios, Lives, Attributes, Portraits and Masks of the Illustrious Characters of the Commedia dell'Arte.* Trans. by R. T. Weaver. London: Harrap, 1929.

Graves, R. B. *Lighting the Shakespeare Stage, 1567–1642.* Carbondale, Ill.: Southern Illinois University Press, 1999.

Gurr, Andrew. *Playgoing in Shakespeare's London.* Cambridge: Cambridge University Press, 1987.

———. *The Shakespearean Playing Companies.* Oxford: Oxford University Press, 1996.

Hewitt, Barnard, ed. *The Renaissance Stage: Documents of Serlio, Sabbattini, and Furttenbach.* Coral Gables, Fla.: University of Miami Press, 1958.

Howarth, W. D., et al., eds. *French Theatre in the Neo-Classical Era, 1550–1789.* Cambridge: Cambridge University Press, 1997.

Ingram, William. *The Business of Playing: The Beginning of the Adult Professional Theater in Elizabethan London.* Ithaca, N.Y.: Cornell University Press, 1993.

Knutson, Roslyn L. *Playing Companies and Commerce in Shakespeare's Time.* Cambridge: Cambridge University Press, 2001.

Lawrenson, T. E. *The French Stage in the XVIIth Century: A Study in the Advent of the Italian Order,* rev. ed. Manchester: Manchester University Press, 1984.

Lea, Kathleen M. *Italian Popular Comedy: A Study of the Commedia dell'Arte, 1560–1620.* 2 vols. Oxford: Clarendon Press, 1934.

Lough, John. *Paris Theatre Audiences in the Seventeenth and Eighteenth Centuries.* London: Oxford University Press, 1957.

McCarthy, Gerry. *The Theatres of Molière.* London: Routledge, 2002.

Mittman, Barbara G. *Spectators on the Paris Stage in the Seventeenth and Eighteenth Centuries.* Ann Arbor, Mich.: UMI Research Press, 1984.

Mongredien, Georges. *Daily Life in the French Theatre in the Time of Molière.* London: Allen and Unwin, 1969.

Nicoll, Allardyce. See under Chapter 4.

Oreglia, G. *The Commedia dell'Arte.* New York: Hill & Wang, 1968.

Orgel, Stephen, and Roy Strong. *The Theatre of the Stuart Court: Including the Complete Designs . . . Together with Their Texts and Historical Documentation.* 2 vols. Berkeley, Calif.: University of California Press, 1973.

Orrell, John. *The Human Stage: English Theatre Design, 1567–1640.* New York: Cambridge University Press, 1983.

Schwartz, Isidore A. *The Commedia dell'Arte and Its Influence on French Comedy in the Seventeenth Century.* Paris: H. Samuel, 1933.

Scott, Virginia. *Molière : A Theatrical Life.* Cambridge: Cambridge University Press, 2000.

Smith, Winifred. *The Commedia dell'Arte.* New York: Columbia University Press, 1912.

Stern, Tiffany. *Rehearsal from Shakespeare to Sheridan.* New York: Oxford University Press, 2000.

White, John. *The Birth and Rebirth of Pictorial Space,* 2d ed. London: Faber & Faber, 1967.

Wickham, Glynne. See under Chapter 4.

Wickham, Glynne, et al. *English Professional Theatre, 1530–1660.* Cambridge: Cambridge University Press, 2000.

Wiley, W. L. *The Early Public Theatre in France.* Cambridge, Mass.: Harvard University Press, 1960.

Chapter 6
From Romanticism to Realism

Antoine, André. *Memories of the Théâtre Libre.* Trans. by Marvin Carlson. Coral Gables, Fla.: University of Miami Press, 1964.

Bentley, Eric. *The Playwright as Thinker: A Study of Drama in Modern Times.* New York: Reynal, 1946.

Bogard, Travis, et al. *Revels History of Drama in English.* Vol. 8, *American Drama.* New York: Barnes & Noble, 1977.

Booth, Michael R. *English Melodrama.* London: Herbert Jenkins, 1965.

Booth, Michael, et al. *Revels History of Drama in English.* Vol. 6, *1750–1880.* New York: Barnes & Noble, 1975.

Carter, Lawson A. *Zola and the Theatre.* New Haven, Conn.: Yale University Press, 1963.

Davis, Tracy. *Actresses as Working Women: Their Social Identity in Victorian Culture.* New York: Routledge, 1991.

Donohue, Joseph W. *Theatre in the Age of Kean.* Oxford: Blackwell, 1975.

Glasstone, Victor. *Victorian and Edwardian Theatre.* Cambridge, Mass.: Harvard University Press, 1975.

Grimsted, David. *Melodrama Unveiled: American Theatre and Culture, 1800–1850.* Chicago: University of Chicago Press, 1968.

Hunt, Hugh, et al. *The Revels History of Drama in English.* Vol. 7, *1880 to the Present Day.* Barnes & Noble, 1978.

Koller, Ann Marie. *The Theatre Duke: Georg II of Saxe-Meiningen and the German Stage.* Stanford, Calif.: Stanford University Press, 1984.

McConachie, Bruce A. *Melodramatic Formations: American Theatre and Society, 1820–1870.* Iowa City: University of Iowa Press, 1992.

McCormick, John. *Popular Theatres of Nineteenth-Century France.* New York: Routledge, 1993.

Meisel, Martin. *Realizations: Narrative, Pictorial, and Theatrical Arts in Nineteenth-Century England.* Princeton, N.J.: Princeton University Press, 1983.

Moynet, Jean-Pierre. *French Theatrical Production in the Nineteenth Century.* Binghamton, N.Y.: Max Reinhardt Foundation, 1976.

Odell, G. C. D. *Shakespeare from Betterton to Irving.* 2 vols. New York: Scribner's, 1920.

Quinn, Arthur H. *A History of the American Drama from the Beginning to the Civil War,* 2d ed. New York: Appleton-Century-Crofts, 1943.

———. *A History of the American Drama from the Civil War to the Present Day,* 2d ed. New York: Appleton-Century-Crofts, 1949.

Rowell, George. *The Victorian Theatre,* 2d ed. London: Oxford University Press, 1979.

Southern, Richard. *Changeable Scenery: Its Origin and Development in the British Theatre.* London: Faber & Faber, 1952.

Stein, Jack M. *Richard Wagner and the Synthesis of the Arts.* Detroit: Wayne State University Press, 1960.

Stephens, John R. *The Profession of the Playwright: British Theatre, 1800–1900.* London: Cambridge University Press, 1992.

Vardac, A. N. *Stage to Screen: Theatrical Method from Garrick to Griffith.* Cambridge, Mass.: Harvard University Press, 1949.

Waxman, S. M. *Antoine and the Théâtre Libre.* Cambridge, Mass.: Harvard University Press, 1926.

Chapter 7
The Modernist Temperament: 1885–1940

Appia, Adolphe. *The Work of Living Art and Man Is the Measure of All Things.* Coral Gables, Fla.: University of Miami Press, 1960.

Artaud, Antonin. *The Theatre and Its Double.* Trans. by Mary C. Richards. New York: Grove Press, 1958.

Bablet, Denis. *The Revolution of Stage Design in the Twentieth Century.* Paris: Amiel, 1977.

Braun, Edward. *The Director and the Stage: From Naturalism to Grotowski.* New York: Holmes and Meier, 1982.

Brecht, Bertolt. *Brecht on Theatre.* Trans. by John Willett. New York: Hill & Wang, 1965.

Brockett, Oscar G., and Robert R. Findlay. *Century of Innovation: A History of European and American Theatre and Drama since 1870,* 2d ed. Boston: Allyn and Bacon, 1991.

Brustein, Robert. *The Theatre of Revolt: An Approach to Modern Drama.* Boston: Little, Brown, 1964.

Clurman, Harold. *The Fervent Years: The Story of the Group Theatre in the Thirties.* New York: Hill & Wang, 1957.

Craig, Edward Gordon. *On the Art of the Theatre,* 2d ed. Boston: Small, Maynard, 1924.

Davis, Hallie Flanagan. *Arena.* New York: Duell, Sloane and Pearce, 1940.

Deak, Frantisek. *Symbolist Theater: The Formation of the Avant Garde.* Baltimore: Johns Hopkins University Press, 1993.

Gordon, Mel. *Dada Performance.* New York: PAJ Publications, 1987.

Gorelik, Mordecai. *New Theatres for Old.* New York: Samuel French, 1940.

Greene, Naomi. *Antonin Artaud: Poet without Words.* New York: Simon & Schuster, 1970.

Innes, Christopher. *Avant-Garde Theatre 1892–1992.* New York: Routledge, 1993.

Kirby, Michael. *Futurist Performance.* New York: Dutton, 1971.

Larson, Orville K. *Scene Design in the American Theatre, 1915 to 1960.* Fayetteville, Ark.: University of Arkansas Press, 1989.

Melzer, Annabelle. *Latest Rage the Big Drum: Dada and Surrealist Performance.* Ann Arbor, Mich.: UMI Research Press, 1980.

O'Connor, John, and Lorraine Brown, eds. *Free, Adult, Uncensored: The Living History of the Federal Theatre Project.* Washington: New Republic Books, 1978.

Patterson, Michael. *The Revolution in German Theatre, 1900–1933.* London: Routledge and Kegan Paul, 1981.

Roose-Evans, James. *Experimental Theatre: From Stanislavsky to Peter Brook,* new rev. ed. London: Studio Vista, 1984.

Shafer, Yvonne. *American Women Playwrights, 1900-1950.* New York: Peter Lang, 1995.

Styan, J. L. *Max Reinhardt.* Cambridge: Cambridge University Press, 1982.

Volbach, Walther. *Adolphe Appia, Prophet of the Modern Theatre.* Middletown, Conn.: Wesleyan University Press, 1968.

Willett, John. *Expressionism.* New York: McGraw-Hill, 1970.

———. *The Theatre of Bertolt Brecht.* New York: New Directions, 1959.

Chapter 8
Reevaluation, Decentralization, and Subsidization

Beauman, Sally. *The Royal Shakespeare Company.* New York: Oxford University Press, 1982.

Berkowitz, Gerald M. *New Broadways: Theatre across America, 1950–1980.* Totowa, N.J.: Rowman & Littlefield, 1982.

Bigsby, C. W. E. *A Critical Introduction to Twentieth-Century American Drama.* Vol. 2, *Williams/Miller/Albee.* New York: Cambridge University Press, 1984.

Boardman, Gerald. *American Musical Comedy: From Adonis to Dreamgirls.* New York: Oxford University Press, 1982.

Brockett, Oscar G., and Robert R. Findlay. See under Chapter 7.

Brustein, Robert. See under Chapter 7.

Cook, Judith. *The National Theatre.* London: Harrop, 1976.

Esslin, Martin. *The Theatre of the Absurd,* rev. ed. New York: Doubleday, 1969.

Findlater, Richard. *Twenty-Five Years of the English Stage Company.* London: Methuen, 1981.

Gorelik, Mordecai. See under Chapter 7.

Gottfried, Martin. *Broadway Musicals.* New York: Abrams, 1979.

Hirsch, Foster. *A Method to Their Madness: The History of the Actors Studio.* New York: Norton, 1984.

Patterson, Michael. See under Chapter 7.

Roose-Evans, James. See under Chapter 7.

Segel, Harold B. *Twentieth-Century Russian Drama.* Baltimore: Johns Hopkins University Press, 1993.

Styan, J. L. *Modern Drama in Theory and Practice.* 3 vols. New York: Cambridge University Press, 1981.

Chapter 9
Contemporary Theatre and Its Diversity

Abramson, Doris E. *Negro Playwrights in the American Theatre.* New York: Columbia University Press, 1969.

Aronson, Arnold. *American Avant Garde Theatre.* New York: Routledge, 2000.

Betsko, Kathleen, and Rachel Koenig. *Interviews with Contemporary Women Playwrights.* New York: Beech Tree Books, 1987.

Biner, Pierre. *The Living Theatre,* 2d ed. New York: Horizon Press, 1972.

Bradby, David. *Director's Theatre.* New York: St. Martin's, 1988.

Brater, Enoch, ed. *Feminine Focus: The New Women Playwrights.* New York: Oxford University Press, 1989.

Brockett, Oscar G., and Robert R. Findlay. See under Chapter 7.

Brook, Peter. See under Chapter 1.

———. *The Shifting Point: Forty Years of Theatrical Exploration, 1946–1987.* New York: Harper and Row, 1988.

Brustein, Robert. *Revolution as Theatre: Notes on the New Radical Style.* New York: Liveright, 1971.

Burian, Jarka. *The Scenography of Josef Svoboda.* Middletown, Conn.: Wesleyan University Press, 1971.

Byrd Hoffman Foundation. *Robert Wilson: Theatre of Images.* New York: Byrd Hoffman Foundation, 1984.

Case, Sue-Ellen. *Feminism and Theatre.* New York: Routledge, 1988.

Chinoy, Helen K., and Linda Jenkins, eds. *Women in American Theatre,* 2d ed. New York: Theatre Communications Group, 1987.

Clum, John M. *Acting Gay: Male Homosexuality in Modern Drama.* New York: Columbia University Press, 1992.

Croyden, Margaret. *Lunatics, Lovers and Poets: The Contemporary Experimental Theatre.* New York: McGraw-Hill, 1974.

DeJongh, Nicholas. *Not in Front of the Audience: Homosexuality on Stage.* New York: Routledge, 1992.

Eyre, Richard, and Nicholas Wright. *Changing Stages.* New York: Knopf, 2001.

Goldberg, Roselee. *Performance Art: From Futurism to the Present,* rev. ed. New York: Abrams, 1988.

Grotowski, Jerzy. *Towards a Poor Theatre.* New York: Simon & Schuster, 1968.

Hill, Errol, ed. *The Theatre of Black Americans.* 2 vols. Englewood Cliffs, N.J.: Prentice Hall, 1980.

Huerta, Jorge. *Chicano Theatre: Themes and Forms.* Ypsilanti, Mich.: Bilingual Press, 1982.

Itzin, Catherine. *Stages in the Revolution: Political Theatre in Britain since 1968.* New York: Methuen, 1981.

Kanellos, Nicolas. *A History of Hispanic Theatre in the United States: Origins to 1940.* Austin, Tex.: University of Texas Press, 1990.

Kerensky, Oleg. *The New British Drama: Fourteen Playwrights since Osborne and Pinter.* New York: Taplinger, 1979.

Kirby, Michael. *Happenings.* New York: Dutton, 1965.

Kolin, Philip C., ed. *American Playwrights since 1945: A Guide to Scholarship, Criticism, and Performance.* Westport, Conn.: Greenwood Press, 1989.

Kostelanetz, Richard. *The Theatre of Mixed Means.* New York: Dial Press, 1968.

Kumiega, Jennifer. *The Theatre of Grotowski.* London: Methuen, 1985.

Marowitz, Charles. *Prospero's Staff: Acting and Directing in the Contemporary Theatre.* Bloomington, Ind.: Indiana University Press, 1986.

Marranca, Bonnie. *The Theatre of Images* [Robert Wilson, Richard Foreman, Lee Breuer]. New York: Drama Book Specialists, 1977.

Pasolli, Robert. *A Book on the Open Theatre.* Indianapolis: Bobbs-Merrill, 1970.

Pottlitzer, Joanne. *Hispanic Theatre in the United States and Puerto Rico.* New York: Ford Foundation, 1988.

Roose-Evans, James. See under Chapter 7.

Sanders, Leslie C. *The Development of Black Theatre in America: From Shadows to Selves.* Baton Rouge, La.: Louisiana State University Press, 1988.

Seller, Maxine S., ed. *Ethnic Theatre in the United States.* Westport, Conn.: Greenwood Press, 1983.

Shank, Theodore. *American Alternative Theatre.* New York: Grove Press, 1982.

Shyer, Laurence. *Robert Wilson and His Collaborators.* New York: TCG, 1989.

World Encyclopedia of Contemporary Theatre. See under Chapter 3.

Chapter 10
Asian and African Theatre

Banham, Martin., ed. *A History of Theatre in Africa.* Cambridge: Cambridge University Press, 2004.

————. *African Theatre: Playwrights and Politics.* Bloomington, Ind.: Indiana University Press, 2001.

————. *The Cambridge Guide to African and Caribbean Theatre.* Cambridge: Cambridge University Press, 1994.

Barber, Karin, et al. *West African Popular Theatre.*

Bloomington, Ind.: Indiana University Press, 1997.

Bowers, Faubion. *Japanese Theatre.* New York: Hermitage House, 1952.

Brandon, James R. *The Cambridge Guide to Asian Theatre.* Cambridge: Cambridge University Press, 1993.

Breitinger, Eckhard, ed. *Theatre and Performance in Africa.* Bayreuth: Bayreuth University Press, 1997.

Ernst, Earle. *The Kabuki Theatre.* New York: Oxford University Press, 1956.

Etherton, Michael. *The Development of African Drama.* London: Hutchinson, 1982.

Gibbs, James. *African Theatre: Playwrights and Politics.* Bloomington, Ind.: Indiana University Press, 2001.

Gibbs, James. *Wole Soyinka.* London: Macmillan, 1986.

Gray, John. *Black Theatre and Performance: A Pan-African Bibliography.* Westport, Conn.: Greenwood Press, 1990.

Hironaga, Shuzaburo. *Bunraku: A History of Japanese Puppet Theatre.* Osaka: Bunrajyza Theatrem 1959,

Komparu, Kunio. *The Noh Theatre: Principles and Perspective.* New York: Weatherhill, 1983.

Kruger, Loren. *The Drama of South Africa: Plays, Pageants, and Publics since 1910.* New York: Routledge, 1999.

Leiter, Samuel L. *The Art of Kabuki: Plays in Performance.* Berkeley, Calif.: University of California Press, 1979.

————. *New Kabuki Encyclopedia.*, rev. ed. Westport, Conn.: Greenwood Press, 1997.

Mrazek, Jan, ed. *Puppet Theater in Contemporary Indonesia: New Approaches to Performance-Events.* Ann Arbor, Mich.:University of Michigan Press, 2001.

Ngugi Wa Thiong'o. *Decolonizing the Mind: The Politics of Language in African Literature.* Portsmouth, N.H.: Heinemann, 1986.

Obafemi, Olu. *Contemporary Nigerian Theatre.* Bayreuth: Bayreuth University Press, 1997.

Ortolani, Benito. *The Japanese Theatre: From Shamanistic Ritual to Contemporary Pluralism,* rev. ed. Princeton, N.J.: Princeton University Press, 1995.

Powell, Brian. *Japan's Modern Theatre: A Century of Change and Continuity.* Curzon Press, 2002.

Rubin, Don, ed. *The World Encyclopedia of Contemporary Theatre.* Vol. 3, Africa. New York: Routledge, 1997.

Sakanishi, S. *Kyogen.* Boston: Marshall Jones, 1938.

Scott, A. C. *The Kabuki Theatre of Japan.* New York: Collier, 1966.

Suzuki, Tadashi. *The Way of Acting.* New York: Theatre Communications Group, 1986.

World Encyclopedia of Contemporary Theatre. See under Chapter 3.

PART THREE

Chapter 11
Theatrical Space and Production Design

American Theatre Planning Board. *Theatre Check List: A Guide to the Planning and Construction of Proscenium and Open Stage Theatres.* Middletown, Conn.: Wesleyan University Press, 1969.

Burris-Meyer, Harold, and Edward C. Cole. *Theatres and Auditoriums,* 2d ed. with supplement. Huntington, N.Y.: Krieger, 1975.

Cogswell, Margaret, ed. *The Ideal Theater: Eight Concepts.* New York: American Federation of Arts, 1962.

Green, Peter Arthur. *Design Education: Problem Solving and Visual Experience.* London: Batsford, 1974.

Howard, Pamela. *What Is Scenography?* London: Routledge, 2002.

Ingham, Rosemary. *From Page to Stage.* Portsmouth, N.H.: Heinemann, 1998.

Izenour, George C. *Theatre Design.* New York: McGraw-Hill, 1977.

Jones, Robert E. *The Dramatic Imagination.* New York: Meredith, 1941.

Maier, Manfred. *Basic Principles of Design.* New York: Van Nostrand Reinhold, 1977.

Mielziner, Jo. *Shapes of Our Theatres.* New York: Clarkson N. Potter, 1970.

Schubert, Hannelore. *Modern Theatre Buildings: Architecture, Stage Design, Lighting.* New York: Praeger, 1971.

Sommer, Robert. *Design Awareness.* San Francisco: Rinehart Press, 1972.

Chapter 12
Playwriting and Dramaturgy

Cardullo, Bert, ed. *What Is Dramaturgy?* New York: Peter Lang, 1995.

Cohen, Edward M. *Working on a New Play: A Play Development Handbook for Actors, Directors, Designers, and Playwrights,* 2d ed. New York: Limelight Editions, 1997.

Cole, Toby. *Playwrights on Playwriting.* New York: Hill & Wang, 1961.

Dramatists Sourcebook. New York: Theatre Communications Group (frequently updated).

Jonas, Susan, et al., eds. *Dramaturgy in American Theater: A Source Book.* Fort Worth, Tex.: Harcourt Brace, 1997.

Packard, William. *The Art of the Playwright.* New York: Thunder Mouth Press, 1997.

Savran, David. *In Their Own Words: Contemporary American Playwrights.* New York: TCG, 1988.

Smiley, Sam. *Playwriting: The Structure of Action.* Englewood Cliffs, N.J.: Prentice Hall, 1971.

Chapter 13
Directing and Producing

Ball, William. *A Sense of Direction: Some Observations on the Art of Directing.* New York: Drama Book Publishers, 1984.

Bartow, Arthur. *The Director's Voice: 21 Interviews.* New York: TCG, 1988.

Benedetti, Robert. *The Director at Work.* Englewood Cliffs, N.J.: Prentice Hall, 1985.

Bloom, Michael. *Thinking Like a Director.* New York: Faber and Faber, 2001.

Bradby, David. See under Chapter 9.

Braun, Edward. *The Director and the Stage: From Naturalism to Grotowski.* New York: Holmes and Meier, 1982.

Brook, Peter. See under Chapter 9.

Clurman, Harold. *On Directing.* New York: Macmillan, 1972.

Cohen, Robert, and John Harrop. *Creative Play Direction,* 2d ed. Englewood Cliffs, N.J.: Prentice Hall, 1984.

Cole, Toby, and Helen K. Chinoy, eds. *Directors on Directing,* rev. ed. Indianapolis: Bobbs-Merrill, 1963.

Delgado, Maria M., and Paul Heritage, eds. *In Contact with the Gods? Directors Talk Theatre.* Manchester: Manchester University Press, 1996.

Farber, Donald C. *From Option to Opening: A Guide for the Off-Broadway Producer,* rev. 4th ed. Wolfeboro, N.H.: Longwood, 1989.

———. *Producing Theatre: A Comprehensive Legal and Business Guide,* 2d ed. New York: Limelight Editions, 1997.

Hodge, Francis and Michael McLain. *Play Directing: Analysis, Communication, and Style,* 6th ed. Boston: Allyn and Bacon, 2004.

Jones, David R. *Great Directors at Work: Stanislavsky, Brecht, Kazan, Brook.* Berkeley, Calif.: University of California Press, 1986.

Langley, Stephen. *Theatre Management in America, Principles and Practice: Producing for Commercial, Stock, Resident, College and Community Theatre,* rev. 2d ed. New York: Drama Book Publishers, 1990.

Newman, Danny. *Subscribe Now!: Building Arts Audiences through Dynamic Subscription Promoting.* New York: TCG, 1983.

O'Neill, R. H., and N. M. Boretz. *The Director as Artist.* New York: Harcourt Brace, 1987.

Reiss, Alvin. *The Arts Management Reader.* New York: Audience Arts, 1979.

Shagan, Rena. *The Road Show: A Handbook for Successful Booking and Touring in the Performing Arts.* New York: ACA Books, 1984.

Thomas, James. *Script Analysis for Actors, Directors and Designers.* Boston: Focal Press, 1992.

Whitmore, Jon. *Directing Postmodern Theatre: Shaping Signification in Performance.* Ann Arbor, Mich.: University of Michigan Press, 1994.

Wills, J. Robert, ed. *The Director in a Changing Theatre.* Palo Alto, Calif.: Mayfield, 1984.

Chapter 14
Acting

Benedetti, Robert L. *The Actor at Work,* 9th ed. Boston: Allyn and Bacon, 2004.

Berry, Cicely. *Voice and the Actor.* London: Virgin, 1993.

Chaikin, Joseph. *The Presence of the Actor: Notes on the Open Theatre, Disguises, Acting and Repression.* New York: Theatre Communications Group, 1991.

Cohen, Robert. *Acting Professionally: Raw Facts about Careers in Acting,* 6th ed. New York: McGraw-Hill, 2003.

Cole, Toby, and Helen K. Chinoy, eds. *Actors on Acting: The Theories, Techniques, and Practices of the Great Actors of All Time as Told in Their Own Words,* 4th ed. New York: Crown, 1995.

Hagen, Uta. *Respect for Acting.* New York: Macmillan, 1973.

Harrop, John, and Sabin Epstein. *Acting with Style,* 2d ed. Englewood Cliffs, N.J.: Prentice Hall, 1989.

Lessac, Arthur. *The Use and Training of the Human Voice.* New York: Drama Book Publishers, 1987.

Lewis, Robert. *Advice to the Players.* New York: Theatre Communications Group, 1989.

Machlin, Evangeline. *Speech for the Stage.* New York: Routledge, 2003.

McGaw, Charles J., Larry D. Clark and Kenneth L. Stilson. *Acting Is Believing,* 8th ed. New York: Wadsworth, 2003.

Potter, Nicole. ed. *Movement for the Actor.* New York: Allworth Press, 2002.

Spolin, Viola. *Improvisation for the Theatre,* rev. ed. Evanston, Ill.: Northwestern University Press, 1983.

Stanislavsky, Constantin. *An Actor Prepares.* Trans. by Elizabeth Reynolds Hapgood. New York: Theatre Arts Books, 1936.

————. *Building a Character.* Trans. by Elizabeth Reynolds Hapgood. New York: Theatre Arts Books, 1949.

————. *Creating a Role.* Trans. by Elizabeth Reynolds Hapgood. New York: Theatre Arts Books, 1961.

Yakim, Moni, with Muriel Broadman. *Creating a Character: A Physical Approach to Acting.* New York: Applause, 1993.

Chapter 15
Scene Design

Arnold, Richard L. *Scene Technology,* 3d ed. Englewood Cliffs, N.J.: Prentice Hall, 1994.

Aronson, Arnold. *American Set Design.* New York: Theatre Communications Group, 1985.

Bablet, Denis. *Stage Design in the Twentieth Century.* New York: Amiel, 1976.

Bay, Howard. *Stage Design.* New York: Drama Book Publishers, 1974.

Bellman, Willard F. *Scenography and Stage Technology: An Introduction.* New York: Harper and Row, 1977.

Burdick, Elizabeth B., et al., eds. *Contemporary Stage Design.* Middletown, Conn.: Wesleyan University Press, 1975.

Corey, Irene. *The Mask of Reality: An Approach to Design for the Theatre.* Anchorage, Ky.: Anchorage Press, 1968.

Davis, Tony. *Stage Design.* Crans-Pres, Celigny, Switzerland: RotoVision, 2001.

Howard, Pamela. See under Chapter 11.

Jones, Robert Edmond. See under Chapter 11.

Larson, Orville K., ed. *Scene Design for Stage and Screen: Readings on the Aesthetics and Methodology of Scene Design for Drama, Opera, Musical Comedy, Ballet, Motion Pictures, Television and Arena Theatre.* Westport, Conn.: Greenwood Press, 1976.

Mielziner, Jo. *Designing for the Theatre.* New York: Atheneum, 1965.

Oenslager, Donald. *Scenery Then and Now.* New York: Norton, 1936.

Parker, W. Oren. *Sceno-Graphic Techniques.* Carbondale, Ill.: Southern Illinois University Press, 1987.

Payne, Darwin. *The Scenographic Imagination,* 3d ed. Carbondale, Ill.: Southern Illinois University Press, 1993.

Pecktal, Lynn. *Designing and Drawing for the Theatre.* New York: McGraw-Hill, 1995.

Smith, Ronn. *American Set Design 2.* New York: Theatre Communications Group, 1991.

Sporre, Dennis J., and Robert C. Burroughs. *Scene Design in the Theatre.* Englewood Cliffs, N.J.: Prentice Hall, 1990.

Wolf, R. Craig, and Dick Block. *Scene Design and Stage Lighting,* 8th ed. New York: Wadsworth, 2002.

Chapter 16
Costume Design and Makeup

Anderson, Barbara, and Cletus Anderson. *Costume Design.* New York: Holt, Rinehart and Winston, 1984.

Barton, Lucy. *Historic Costume for the Stage.* Boston: Baker's Plays, 1935.

Corey, Irene. *The Face Is a Canvas: The Design and Technique of Theatrical Makeup.* New Orleans: Anchorage Press, 1990.

Corson, Richard, and James Glavan. *Stage Makeup,* 9th ed. Boston: Allyn and Bacon, 2000.

Emery, Joy S. *Stage Costume Techniques,* 2d ed. Englewood Cliffs, N.J.: Prentice Hall, 1992.

Ingham, Rosemary, and Liz Covey. *The Costume Designer's Handbook: A Complete Guide for Amateur and Professional Costume Designers.* Portsmouth, N.H.: Heinemann, 1992.

Motley [design firm]. *Designing and Making Stage Costumes.* London: Herbert Press, 1992.

Payne, Blanche. *History of Costume from the Ancient Egyptians to the Twentieth Century.* New York: Harper and Row, 1965.

Pecktal, Lynn. *Costume Design: Techniques of Modern Masters.* New York: Back Stage Books, 1993.

Russell, Douglas. *Costume History and Style.* Englewood Cliffs, N.J.: Prentice Hall, 1983.

———. *Stage Costume Design: Theory, Technique and Style,* 2d ed. Englewood Cliffs, N.J.: Prentice Hall, 1985.

Smith, C. Ray, ed. *The Theatre Crafts Book of Makeup, Masks, and Wigs.* Emmaus, Penn.: Rodale Press, 1974.

Chapter 17
Lighting and Sound Design

Ballou, Glen, ed. *Handbook for Sound Engineers.* Indianapolis: H. W. Sams, 1987.

Bellman, Willard F. *Lighting the Stage: Art and Practice,* 3d ed. New York: Broadway Press, 2001.

———. *Scenography and Stage Technology.* See under Chapter 14.

Bergman, Gosta M. *Lighting in the Theatre.* Totowa, N.J.: Rowman & Littlefield, 1977.

Burian, Jarka. See under Chapter 10.

Collison, David. *Stage Sound.* New York: Applause Theatre Books, 1990.

Essig, Linda. *Lighting and the Design Idea.* New York: Harcourt Brace, 1997.

Gillette, J. Michael. *Designing with Light,* 3d ed. Mountain View, Calif.: Mayfield, 1993.

Jones, Robert E. See under Chapter 11.

Jones, Tom Douglas. *The Art of Light and Color.* New York: Van Nostrand Reinhold, 1973.

Kaye, Deena, and James LeBrecht. *Sound and Music for the Theatre,* 2d ed. Boston: Focal Press, 2000.

Keller, Max. *Light Fantastic: The Art and Design of Stage Lighting.* Munich: Prestel Verlag, 1999.

Leonard, John A. *Theatre Sound.* New York: Routledge, 2001.

McCandless, Stanley R. *A Method of Lighting the Stage.* New York: Theatre Arts Books, 1984.

Moody, James L. *The Business of Theatrical Design.* New York: Allworth Press, 2002.

Palmer, Richard H. *The Lighting Art: The Aesthetics of Stage Lighting Design,* 2d ed. Englewood Cliffs, N.J.: Prentice Hall, 1994.

Parker, W. Oren, and R. Craig Wolf. See under Chapter 15.

Rosenthal, Jean, and Lael Wertenbaker. *The Magic of Light.* Boston: Little, Brown, 1972.

Warfel, William B. *The New Handbook of Stage Lighting Graphics,* rev. ed. New York: Drama Book Publishers, 1990.

Warfel, William B., and Walter R. Klappert. *Color Science for Lighting the Stage.* New Haven, Conn.: Yale University Press, 1981.

Watson, Lee. *Lighting Design Handbook.* New York: McGraw-Hill, 1990.

Credits

CHAPTER 1

Page 2 Sara Krulwich/the *New York Times;* page 4 T. Charles Erickson; page 7 Joan Marcus; page 8 © George E. Joseph; page 9 Richard Anderson; courtesy of Center Stage; page 12 T. Charles Erickson; page 13 Bob Marshak; page 15 Karl Hugh; © Utah Shakespearean Festival; page 19 Joan Marcus

CHAPTER 2

Page 22 Richard Feldman; page 24 T. Charles Erickson; page 25 Richard Feldman; page 29 T. Charles Erickson; page 30 Bob Marshak; page 33 T. Charles Erickson

CHAPTER 3

Page 36 T. Charles Erickson; page 40 Courtesy of the American Conservatory Theatre; page 42 T. Charles Erickson; page 45 T. Charles Erickson; page 46 Joan Marcus; page 49 Courtesy of the Goodman Theatre; page 53 Courtesy of the Atlanta Shakespeare Company; page 53 T. Charles Erickson; page 53 T. Charles Erickson

CHAPTER 4

Page 54 © Gerry Goodstein; page 56 T. Charles Erickson; page 58 From Baumeister, *Denkmaler des Klassischens Alterums,* 1888; page 60 From Dorpfeld-Reisch, *Das Griechische Theatre,* 1896; page 61 Courtesy of the Embassy of Greece; page 61 From Ernst Fiechter, *Antike Griechische Theaterbauten,* 1936; courtesy of Dr. Charlotte Fiechter; page 63 From *Monumenti Inediti,* 2, 1879; page 65 Courtesy of the Guthrie Theatre; page 66 Donald McKague; courtesy of the Strafford Shakespearean Festival Foundation of Canada; page 68 Courtesy of Guthrie Theatre; page 69 T. Charles Erickson; page 71 From Robert, *Die Masken der Neueren Attischen Komoedie,* 1911; page 72 D'Espouy, *Fragments d'Architecture Antique,* 1, 1901; page 76 Courtesy of the University of Iowa Theatre; page 77 Courtesy of the Museo Nazionale, Naples; page 79 From Laumann, *La Machinerie au Théâtre,* 1897; page 80 From *Romanesque Art in Italy,* 1913; page 82 Courtesy of the Bibliothèque Nationale, Paris; page 83 Nederlands Theatre Institute; page 85 Courtesy of the Arena Stage Theatre; page 87 From Wickham, *Early English Stages,* 1, 1959; Courtesy of Routledge Publishers; page 88 Matthew Gilson; courtesy of the Court Theatre; page 89 Lanny Nagler Photography; courtesy of the Hartford Stage Company; page 91 Sara Krulwich/the *New York Times,* page 92 From Pougin, *Dictionnaire...du Théâtre,* 1885

CHAPTER 5

Page 94 T. Charles Erickson; page 97 Courtesy of Center Stage/Richard Anderson; page 98 Bapst, *Essai sur l'Histoire du Théâtre,* 1893; page 100 John Tramper; courtesy of the International Shakespeare Globe Centre; page 101 Reproduced by permission of the Marquess of Bath, Longleat House, Warminster, Wiltshire, England; page 101 Richard Feldman; page 103 T. Charles Erickson; page 105 © Martha Swope; page 106

Roger Mastroianni; page 108 Serlio, *Architettura,* 1545; page 108 Serlio, *Architettura,* 1545; page 108 Serlio, *Architettura,* 1545; page 109 Courtesy of the French Cultural Services; page 111 Painting by Pietro Domenico; courtesy of the Civic Museum, Turin; page 112 Maurice Sand, *Masques et Bouffons,* 1859; page 114 Maurice Sand, *Masques et Bouffons,* 1859; page 116 Wyn Tucker; courtesy Dell'Arte Players; page 117 Richard Feldman; page 118 Luigi Ciminaghi; courtesy of the Piccolo Teatro; page 119 Richard Feldman; page 120 Courtesy of Bibliothèque Nationale, Paris; page 123 Courtesy of Margaret Mitchell; page 124 Randall Hagadorn; courtesy of the McCarter Theatre Center for the Performing Arts, Princeton, N.J.; page 126 Roger Mastroianni; page 128 Joe Giannetti; courtesy of the Guthrie Theatre

CHAPTER 6

Page 132 From *London Interiors,* 1841; page 134 *English Illustrated Magazine,* 1776; page 135 Courtesy of the Maison de Victor Hugo, Paris; page 136 Frank Leslie's *Illustrated Newspaper,* 1877; page 137 A contemporary engraving; page 138 A contemporary engraving; page 138 *Scientific American,* 1889; page 139 Courtesy of the Harvard Theatre Collection; page 141 Joan Marcus; page 142 From *The Magazine of Art,* 1889; page 143 Albert Davis Collection, Hoblitzelle Theatre Arts Library; Harry Ransom Humanities Research Center, University of Texas at Austin; page 145 A contemporary engraving; page 148 Courtesy of the Harry Ransom Humanities Research Center, University of Texas at Austin; page 149 Courtesy of the American Conservatory Theatre; page 150 *Le Théâtre,* 1902; page 152 Sara Krulwich/the *New York Times;* page 153 *Die Gartenlaube,* 1879; page 155 Richard Feldman; page 157 Fred Fehl; courtesy of the Hoblitzelle Theatre Arts Collection, Harry Ransom Humanities Research Center, University of Texas at Austin

CHAPTER 7

Page 160 T. Charles Erickson; page 163 Richard Feldman; page 164 T. Charles Erickson; page 166 Courtesy of the Adolphe Appia Foundation, Schweizerische Theatresammlung, Geneva; page 167 Courtesy of The Collection of the McNay Art Museum, Gift of Margaret Batts Tobin; page 168 *Le Théâtre,* 1911; page 170 *Le Théâtre,* 1927; page 171 Richard Feldman; page 171 Courtesy of National Theatre of Norway; page 172 Vandamm. The Billy Rose Theatre Collection, the New York Public Library for the Performing Arts, the Astor, Lenox and Tilden Foundations; page 173 Mark Portland. Courtesy of the Pittsburgh Public Theatre; page 174 Ruth Walz; page 176 Reprinted from R. E. Jones, *Drawings for the Theatre,* by permission of the publisher, Routledge, New York; page 177 The Billy Rose Theatre Collection, the New York Public Library for the Performing Arts, the Astor, Lenox and Tilden Foundations; page 179 Richard Feldman; page 180 Richard Feldman; page 183 Richard Feldman

CHAPTER 8

Page 186 T. Charles Erickson; page 188 Eileen Darby; page 190 T. Charles Erickson; page 192 The Billy Rose Theatre Collection, the New York Public Library for the Performing Arts, the Astor, Lenox and Tilden Foundation; page 192 Joan Marcus; page 193 Courtesy of the Theatre and Music Collection, Museum of the City of New York; page 194 Joan Marcus; page 195 Gerry Goodstein; page 196 © George E. Joseph; page 197 Courtesy of the Gorki Theater; page 198 Courtesy of Robert Ball; page 200 T. Charles Erickson; page 202 T. Charles Erickson; page 202 Ken Friedman; courtesy of the Berkeley Repertory Theatre; page 203 © Martha Swope; page 204 Courtesy of Dan Ostling; page 205 Courtesy of the Paper Mill Playhouse; page 207 Courtesy of Susan Tsu; page 210 Joan Marcus; page 211 Joan Marcus; page 212 Joan Marcus; page 213 Courtesy of the Magic Theatre; page 215 Richard Feldman

CHAPTER 9

Page 218 T. Charles Erickson; page 220 Ken McLaren; courtesy of the World of Culture, Ltd.; page 221 Craig Hamilton; page 222 © 1968 Jerzy Grotowski and Odin Teatrets Forlag; courtesy of H. Martin Berg; page 223 Courtesy of Richard Schechner; page 225 Courtesy of Jaromir Svoboda; page 226 T. Charles Erickson; page 227 Martha Swope; page 228 Richard Feldman; page 230 Richard Feldman; page 231 Richard Feldman; page 232 Courtesy of Chelsea Theatre; page 233 T. Charles Erickson; page 234 Courtesy of the Arena Stage; page 234 Richard Termine; courtesy of the Cleveland Play House; page 236 Ken Jacques; courtesy of the San Diego Repertory Theatre; page 237 T. Charles Erickson; page 239 Courtesy of Murrae Haynes, New Mexico Repertory Theatre; page 242 T. Charles Erickson; page 243 Joan Marcus; page 243 Terry Shapiro; courtesy of the Denver Center Theatre; page 245 T. Charles Erickson; page 247 Courtesy of Actors Theatre of Louisville; page 248 Richard Feldman; page 249 Joan Marcus

CHAPTER 10

Page 252 Courtesy of Getty Images; page 254 Courtesy of the National Museum of Tokyo; page 255 Courtesy of Kokusai Bunka Shinkokai; page 256 Courtesy of Kokusai Bunka Shinkokai; page 257 Courtesy of Weatherhill Inc., Tokyo; page 259 Courtesy of Kokusai Bunka Shinkokai; page 261 Courtesy of Kokusai Bunka Shinkokai; page 262 Tan Kian Khoon/Shutterstock, Inc.; page 263 Getty Images; page 265 Courtesy of George Burnette; page 266 © Melissa Gaspar; page 268 Courtesy of Eckhard Breitinger; page 268 Courtesy of Eckhard Breitinger; page 270 Douglas Wonders; page 271 T. Charles Erickson; page 274 Courtesy of Getty Images

CHAPTER 11

Page 276 T. Charles Erickson; page 278 T. Charles Erickson; page 280 Drawing by David Betts; page 282 Robert Ashley Wilson; courtesy of the Guthrie Theatre; page 283 Geeorge de Vincent, courtesy of the Arena Stage; page 285 Courtesy of Jan Mabry, Cornerstone Theatre; page 287 © 1968 Jerzy Grotowski and Odin Teatrets Forlag; courtesy of H. Martin Berg; page 288 T. Charles Erickson; page 290 Richard Feldman; page 291 T. Charles Erickson; page 293 Michal Daniel; courtesy of the Guthrie Theatre

CHAPTER 12

Page 294 T. Charles Erickson; page 296 Courtesy of the Philadelphia Theatre Company; page 297 Richard Feldman; page 299 A. Vincent Scarano; courtesy of the Eugene O'Neill Theatre Center; page 300 Lynda Griguere; courtesy of the Perseverance Theatre; page 300 Courtesy of Actors Theatre of Louisville; page 302 Richard Feldman; page 303 T. Charles Erickson; page 305 Joan Marcus; page 307 Dan McNeil; courtesy of the Denver Center Theatre

CHAPTER 13

Page 310 T. Charles Erickson; page 312 Sara Krulwich/the *New York Times;* page 315 T. Charles Erickson; page 316 Ruth Walz; courtesy of the German Information Center; page 318 Courtesy of the Royal Shakespeare Company; page 320 Courtesy of the Byrd Hoffman Foundation; page 321 Babette Mangolte; courtesy of the Byrd Hoffman Foundation; page 323 Richard Feldman; page 324 © Martha Swope; page 325 Courtesy of Dan Ostling; page 326 T. Charles Erickson; page 329 T. Charles Erickson; page 330 Courtesy of Actors Theatre of Louisville; page 331 David Wheeler; page 332 Sara Krulwich/ the *New York Times;* page 333 Richard Feldman

CHAPTER 14

Page 336 T. Charles Erickson; page 338 Photo by Roger Mastroianni; courtesy of the Great Lakes Theater Festival; page 340 Mary Gearhart; courtesy of the Wooster Group; page 342 Sara Krulwich/the *New York Times;* page 345 Gerry Goodstein; page 346 © Martha Swope; page 348 Joan Marcus; page 350 T. Charles Erickson; page 352 T. Charles Erickson

CHAPTER 15

Page 354 T. Charles Erickson; page 356 Richard Feldman; page 357 Joan Marcus; page 358 Courtesy of Richard Isackes; page 359 Courtesy of Robert Schmidt; page 360 Courtesy of Robert Schmidt; page 361 Courtesy of Robert Schmidt; page 363 Courtesy of the Guthrie Theatre; page 364 T. Charles Erickson; page 365 T. Charles Erickson; page 367 T. Charles Erickson; courtesy of Hartford Stage; page 368 T. Charles Erickson; page 369 Courtesy of Dan Ostling; page 371 T. Charles Erickson

CHAPTER 16

Page 376 T. Charles Erickson; page 378 Jerry Dalia; courtesy of the Walnut Street Theatre, Philadelphia; page 380 Richard Feldman; page 381 T. Charles Erickson; page 382 Courtesy of Susan Tsu; page 383 Courtesy of Margaret Mitchell; page 384 Courtesy of Margaret Mitchell; page 385 T. Charles Erickson; page 385 Courtesy of the American Conservatory costumes for Theatre; page 388 Courtesy of Irene Corey, from her book *The Face Is a Canvas: The Design and Technique of Theatrical Makeup;* page 389 Jodi Karjala; page 390 Courtesy of the Guthrie Theatre; page 392 T. Charles Erickson

CHAPTER 17

Page 396 T. Charles Erickson; page 398 Richard Feldman; page 400 T. Charles Erickson; page 400 T. Charles Erickson; page 402 Courtesy of Dan Ostling; page 405 Richard Feldman; page 406 Courtesy of David Nancarrow; page 407 Courtesy of Dan Ostling; page 409 Stewart Goldstein; courtesy of the St. Louis Black Repertory; page 410 Courtesy of Robert Ball; page 411 T. Charles Erickson; page 414 T. Charles Erickson; page 415 Jarka Burian; page 417 Courtesy of Dan Ostling

Index

A

ABBA, 212
Abbey Theatre, 297
About Face, 206
Abraham, 81
Absence of War, The, 200
Absurdist drama, 195–196, 227
Across the Universe, 289
Act Out Productions, 249
Acting, 337–353
  actor's instrument in, 338, 340
  in *Akropolis,* 320
  business in, 343, 349
  concentration and, 342
  costumes and, 344, 351–352
  creating a role in, 345–348
  critical perspective and, 30
  director and, 151, 316, 337,
    342–343, 347–349, 352
  dress rehearsals for, 351–352
  elements of theatre and, 7
  gesture in, 342, 349
  in Japanese theatre, 259
  lifelikeness in, 16
  lighting design and, 402
  line readings and, 350–351
  memorization and, 350–351
  modernist temperament and, 162
  movement in, 342, 344,
    349, 350
  observation/imagination in, 338,
    340–342
  performance for, 351–352
  production design and, 288
  psychological/emotional prepara-
    tion for, 348–349
  refining the role in, 351
  scene design and, 357
  scene study in, 344
  stage vocabulary and, 342–344
  style and, 52
  theatrical space and, 281
  training/performing and,
    344–345

  from training to performing,
    344–345
  vocal characterization in,
    349–350
Acting company, 100, 121–122, 160
Acting space, 355
Action
  acting and, 337, 348
  in *Cat on a Hot Tin Roof,* 188
  of contemporary theatre, 222
  costume design and, 377, 379
  director and, 315, 327, 330
  in *Doll's House,* 149
  dramatic (*See* Dramatic action)
  falling, 43
  in *Hamlet,* 103, 106
  in *How I Learned to Drive,* 248
  in *Importance of Being Earnest,*
    165
  lighting design and, 399–400,
    407
  in *Ma Rainey's Black Bottom,* 233
  modernist temperament and,
    162, 167, 178, 180, 181, 183
  in *Noah and His Sons,* 89
  in plays, 37, 38
  in postwar America, 193
  production design and, 290
  rehearsals and, 334
  rising, 42, 43
  in *Roosters,* 237–238
  scene design and, 355, 370
  sound design and, 412
  in *Strong Breed,* 270
  Svoboda and, 416
  in *Tartuffe,* 127
  theatrical space and, 281, 284
  unifying, 39, 40
  in *Wayang Kulit,* 265
Actor-audience relationship,
  279, 280
Actors. *See also* Performers
  acting and (*See* Acting)
  assistants to, 392
  auditions/castings and, 323–324

  in China, 263
  commedia dell'arte, 112–113
  of contemporary theatre,
    219–220, 221–222, 223
  costume design and, 377–379,
    383, 386, 387
  costume designers and, 387
  director and, 150, 151, 152,
    323–327
  elements of theatre and, 7
  in England, 101
  festival theatre, 62
  film, 345
  in France, 122, 123
  in *Hamlet,* 104, 105, 106
  in Japanese theatre, 259, 260
  lifelikeness and, 16
  lighting design and, 398, 403,
    407, 410, 416, 417
  makeup and, 388, 389, 390, 391
  modernist temperament and,
    162, 166, 178
  in *Noah and His Sons,* 90
  in Noh theatre, 255, 256
  production design and, 287–288
  professional, 344–345
  professional theatre and, 96
  rehearsal and, 332
  in Rome, 75, 77
  screen, 337
  stage, 337, 345
  television, 345
  theatrical space and, 279, 280,
    281, 282, 283, 287
  Wakefield cycle and, 87
Actors Equity, 206, 323
Actors Equity Association, 345
Actors Studio, 187, 188
Actors Theatre, 209, 300, 301
Actors Theatre of Louisville,
  247, 328
Actresses, 102
Adaptability, 112
Adding Machine, The, 172
Additive color mixing, 398

Adler, Stella, 177
Advocate, The, 35
Aeschylus, 58, 64, 207, 228
Afer, Publius Terentius, 73, 74, 75, 92, 112
Africa, theatre in, 265–267
African American theatre, 231–233
African theatre. *See* Asian/ African theatre
Agamemnon, 64, 228
Age groups, makeup and, 389
Agon, 71
Ajax, 64
Akalaitis, JoAnne, 229, 230, 293, 404, 405
Akropolis, 319
al-Hakim, Tawfig, 273
Alabama Shakespeare Festival, 359
Albee, Edward, 212–213, 357
Alcestis, 64, 229
Aldwych Theatre, 198
Alekseev, Konstantin Sergeevich, 156
Alexander the Great, 39, 71
Alexandrine, 126
Alice in Bed, 163, 323
Alice in Wonderland, 323
Alienation, 178
All My Sons, 188, 356
Allegorical concept, costume design and, 378
Allegory, 45
Alley Theatre, 202, 207, 350
"Almost Famous: What do the Third-Generation, Post-Stanislavsky Teachers Offer?", 158
Amateur production rights, direct-ing/producing and, 314
Amblin Entertainment, 301
Ambrosone, John, 163, 179, 215, 248, 323
America. *See also* American play-wrights; United States
　Grotowski influence on, 222
　postwar, 190–193
　postwar theatre in, 187–188
　theatre across, 206
America Play, The, 233
American, The, 154
American Buffalo, 213
American Conservatory Theatre, 40, 149, 385
American Daughter, An, 246
American Indian Community House, 245

American Indian Dance Theatre, 245
American Laboratory Theatre, 177
American playwrights, 212–214
American Repertory Company, 366, 404
American Repertory Theatre
　Alice in Bed at, 163, 323
　Brustein and, 306
　Buried Child at, 215
　CIVIL warS at, 228
　Endgame at, 229
　How I Learned to Drive at, 248
　King Stag at, 289, 290
　Mother Courage at, 179
　Romeo and Juliet at, 278, 288, 352
　School for Scandal at, 333
　Serpent Woman at, 117
　Servant of Two Masters at, 119
　True West at, 297
　Zuber and, 379
American Shakespeare Company, 401
American Theatre, 92, 205, 250, 275, 374, 418
Amphitheatres, 78
Amphitryon, 372
Amplification, 280, 412
Amy's View, 200
An Actor Prepares, 156
Analogy, director and, 318
And Baby Makes Seven, 246–247
Anderson, Laurie, 226, 404
Anderson, Maxwell, 176
Anderson, Paul, 194
Andrews, Julie, 193
Andria, 73
Andromache, 207
Andronicus, Livius, 72
Angels in America, 232, 249, 299, 304
Anna in the Tropics, 237, 294
Annie, 209
Antigone, 64
Antoine, André, 150, 153, 167
Antony and Cleopatra, 32, 350
Appia, Adolphe, 166–167, 292
Apron, theatrical space and, 281
Arcadia, 199
Arcenas, Loy, 233
Architecture
　postmodernist, 228
　production design and, 292
　scene design and, 357, 358

theatre, 284
Architettura, 107
Arena stage, 280, 282–283, 292, 306, 362, 408
Arena Stage Theatre, 85, 234
Arena theatre, 326, 355, 407
Aristophanes, 71
Aristotle, 38, 39, 41
Arkin, Alan, 206
Arms and the Man, 155
Arp, Hans, 170
Art
　defined, 10, 14
　high, 10, 12
　low, 10, 12
　modernist temperament and, 163
　performance, 224–227
　realism/naturalism and, 146, 161, 163
　theatre as form of, 9–16
　value and, 18–21
"Art for art's sake," 163
Art history
　costume design and, 381
　scene design and, 358
Artaud, Antonin, 181–183, 184, 198, 204, 219
Articulation, acting and, 349, 350
Artistic director, 312
Arts
　decorative, 358
　performing, 403
　visual (*See* Visual arts)
Arts Council, 197–198
As Is, 249
As You Like It, 14, 15, 101, 132, 287
Asakura, Setsu, 117
Asian/African theatre, 253–275
　in Africa, 265–267
　in China, 261–264
　director and, 319
　in Japan, 253–254
　Japanese interest in Western drama/theatre and, 261
　Noh theatre and, 254–257
　in North Africa, 273
　other African countries and, 274
　other Asian countries and, 264
　other Japanese theatre forms in, 258–261
　performance in Nigeria and, 267–269
　Shrine in the Fields (Nonomiya) and, 257–258
　in South Africa, 271–273

Strong Breed and, 269–271
Wayang Kulit and, 264–265
Asian American theatre, 240–243
Asian American Theatre Workshop, 242, 243
Asian Exclusion Act, 242
Asides, 45, 140
Assassins, 209
Assistant director, 334
Assistants
   costume designer's, 391–392
   director's, 334, 386
   lighting design and, 411–412
   in Noh theatre, 255
   scene designer's, 371–372
Astor Library, 205
Atlanta Shakespeare Company, 53
Atmosphere
   costume design and, 378
   director and, 324
   festival theatre and, 66, 88
   lighting design and, 397, 399, 404, 405
   modernist temperament and, 162, 174
   professional theatre and, 103, 110, 116
   scene design and, 356
   sound design and, 412–413
Atoza, in Noh theatre, 256
Attitude
   acting and, 342
   bodily, 329
Audibility, acting and, 349, 350
Audience, 23–35. *See also* Spectators
   acting and, 337, 343, 350, 352
   behavior, 27, 28, 137
   of *Carousel,* 322
   characters and, 44
   of contemporary theatre, 219, 220, 221
   critical perspective and, 29–32
   director and, 317, 319, 324, 325–326, 327, 330
   dramaturgy and, 307–308
   in England, 103
   in France, 121, 122
   Greek, 66
   of *Hamlet,* 104
   history of, 27, 28
   independent theatre and, 153
   interactivity and, 18
   in Italy, 109
   Japanese theatre and, 258, 259

lighting design and, 397, 402, 407
mass, 75, 136, 174, 175, 203
melodrama and, 144
modernist temperament and, 162, 169, 174, 178, 179, 180, 183
of *Monte Cristo,* 140
nature of theatre and, 5, 6, 7–9, 13–14
in Noh theatre, 256
playwriting and, 297
production design and, 287–288, 291
professional theatre and, 96
rehearsal and, 334
in Rome, 75
scene design and, 355
of *Servant of Two Masters,* 119
sound design and, 412
theatrical space and, 279, 281, 282, 283, 285, 287
Wakefield cycle and, 87
who is, 26–29
Audience space, 355
Auditions, directing/producing and, 312, 323–324, 334
Auditorium
   acting and, 337, 343
   in China, 262
   director and, 151, 152
   Drury Lane Theatre, 132
   festival theatre and, 60, 75
   Goldoni and, 119
   lighting design and, 397, 406, 407
   nature of theatre and, 8
   Theatre Royal, 111
   theatrical space and, 281, 282, 284, 285
Augesen, René, 40, 149
Automated lighting, 405, 408
Auxiliary spaces, 285, 286
Avocado Kid, The, 242
Awake and Sing, 379
Ayckbourn, Alan, 200
Aykroyd, Dan, 206
Azito, Tony, 140

B

Baargeld, Theodor, 170
Babes with Blades, 206
Bacchae, The, 64, 65
Back-scenes, 109

Back Stage, 21, 52, 216
Back Stage West, 158, 353
Backlighting, 398
Baker, Christopher, 303
Baker, Jim, 124
Baker, Stephen, 42
Bakker, Sara Kathryn, 15
Balance, production design and, 288
Bald Soprano, The, 38–39
Baldassari, Mike, 211
Ballad of Yachiyo, The, 242
Ballad opera, 133, 191
Balm in Gilead, 213
Balten, Pieter, 83
Baltimore Waltz, The, 247, 328
Bandito, 236
Bankhead, Tallulah, 32
Banquet Years, The, 161
Baraka, Amiri, 231, 232
Barcello, Randy, 203
Barn Theatre, 299
Barrera, David, 236
Barringer, Heather, 45
Barry, Julian, 203
Barrymore, John, 339
Barton, John, 207
Bartow, Arthur, 311
Baryshnikov, Mikhail, 404
Baschky, Richard, 76
Basic Training of Pavlo Hummel, The, 213
Bausch, Pina, 226
Beauty and the Beast, 211
Beauty of the Father, 237
Beauty Queen of Leenane, The, 202
Beck, Julian, 219
Beckett, Samuel
   acting and, 341
   Endgame by, 229, 230, 405
   plays by, 195–196
   playwriting and, 295, 296
   scene design and, 356
   Stoppard and, 199
   Waiting for Godot by, 13
Before It Hits Home, 249
Beggar's Opera, The, 133
Beginning, of play, 41–42
Behavior
   acting and, 337
   audience, 27, 28, 137
   characters and, 44
   dramatic action and, 38
   realism/naturalism and, 145, 161
Beijing Opera, 262, 263
Bel Geddes, Norman, 175, 356

Belgrader, Andrei, 119
Bellerophon, 109
Belushi, John, 206
Benesch, Vivienne, 345
Benita Canova, 226
Bennett, Michael, 209
Bentley, Eric, 6, 191
Benzinger, Suzy, 332
Beowulf, 374
Bergman, Ingmar, 105
Bergson, Henri, 50–51
Berkeley Repertory Theatre, 202
Bernstein, Leonard, 192, 193
Betsuyaku, Minoru, 261
Better-n-Indians, 245
Bibiena, Giuseppe, 111
Bilingual Foundation of the
    Arts, 240
Bingo, 199
Biological characterization, acting
    and, 346
Birthday Party, The, 199
Bjorkman, Ingrid, 269
Björnson, Maria, 13
Black, Aaron, 24
Black, Malcolm, 378
Black Dog, 272
Black Elk Speaks, 243
Black Rider, The, 229
Black Theatre Magazine, 231
Blacks, The, 316
Blank verse, 105
Blasted, 202
Blessing, Lee, 232
Blocking
    acting and, 350
    rehearsal and, 332–333, 334
Blue Heart, 201
Blue/Orange, 202
Bluebeard, 248
Blumenfeld, Mary, 325, 402, 417
Blumenthal, Eileen, 374
Bly, Mark, 306
Board of directors, directing/produc-
    ing and, 312, 313–314
Bodily attitude, director and, 329
Body, acting and, 338, 340
Body Indian, 243
Body language, director and, 329
Boesman and Lena, 272
Bogart, Anne, 261, 300, 328, 330
Bogosian, Eric, 226
Boleslavsky, Richard, 177
Bolman, Scott, 160
Bombay Dreams, 312, 313
Bond, Edward, 199

Bondage, 242
Booth, Edwin, 141
Booth's Theatre, 141
Bopha, 272
Boras, Annika, 352
Borders, 109
Bores, The, 122
Boruzescu, Marina, 128
Boruzescu, Radu, 128
Boublil, Alain, 30, 210
Boucicault, Dion, 136, 137
Box, 111, 119, 132, 151
Box set, 149, 151
Boycott, 11
Boyd, Gregory, 200, 202, 207
Boys, female roles by, 100–101, 102.
    See also Men
Boys from Syracuse, The, 76
Boys in the Band, The, 248
Brace Up!, 404
Bradley, Scott, 42
Brady, William, 139
Braggart Warrior, The, 73
Brahm, Otto, 133
Brand:NEW Festival of New Work,
    303
Brando, Marlon, 187
Brava! For Women in the Arts, 246
Bread and Puppet Theatre, 221, 289
Breath of Life, 200
Brecht, Bertolt
    acting and, 347, 348
    Bogart and, 328
    contemporary theatre and,
        219, 223
    modernist temperament and,
        177–181, 182
    nature of theatre and, 5
    playwriting and, 295–296
    postwar Europe and, 193
    scene design and, 394
Breuer, Lee, 49
Bridge, in Noh theatre, 255
Bridge, Andrew, 13
Bridge, The, 263
Briers, Richard, 194
Brigadoon, 193
Brightman, Sarah, 13
Brill, Robert, 211, 237, 294
*Bring in 'Da Noise, Bring in 'Da
    Funk,* 211, 232
British theatre, 197–202, 209
Broadway
    action/spectacle on, 370
    after subsidization, 209–212
    audience and, 26–27, 29

Bombay Dreams on, 312, 313
of *Cat on a Hot Tin Roof,*
    189, 190
Cat on a Hot Tin Roof on, 301
contemporary theatre and,
    230, 231
criticism and, 31
De Shields on, 341, 342
directing/producing and, 311,
    314, 335
dress parade on, 391
gay/lesbian theatre on, 248, 249
IATSE and, 412
Lake on, 32
Lee and, 362
Long and, 386
Metamorphoses on, 417
modernist temperament and,
    174, 175, 176, 177
Musser and, 401
nature of theatre and, 9, 19
Oklahoma! on, 192
playwriting and, 299, 302
Rosenthal and, 401
scene design and, 360
Seascape on, 357
Taymor and, 289
theatrical space and, 285
Threepenny Opera on, 394
Tipton and, 404
Urinetown on, 309
Wicked on, 46
Broadway, 404
Brook, Peter
    acting and, 337, 346
    Mahabharata and, 227, 228
    Midsummer Night's Dream and,
        318–319
    nature of theatre and, 6, 7, 8
    RSC and, 198
    Theatre of Cruelty and, 182
Brooklyn Academy of Music, 105
Brooks, Avery, 25
Brothers, The, 73
Brown, John Mason, 32
Brown, John Russell, 89
Browne, Roscoe Lee, 140
Bruneau, Lise, 385
Brustein, Robert, 306
Büchner, Georg, 229
Budget
    costume design and, 380
    directing/producing and,
        311–312
Budries, David, 12, 242
Building a Character, 156

Bullet Headed Birds, 242
Bunraku, as Japanese theatre form, 258, 259
Burba, Blake, 305
Buried Child, 45, 214–215, 217
Burn This, 213
Burr, Charles, 24, 354
Business
    acting and, 343, 349
    directors and, 327, 329–330
Business manager, directing/producing and, 313
"Business of Bill: Who was Shakespeare?, The," 130
Business offices, 286
Butai, in Noh theatre, 255
Butler, Sam, Jr., 49

C

Cabaret, 209, 210, 211, 386
Cabaret Voltaire, 184
Cabin Pressure, 328, 330
Cabinet of Dr. Caligari, The, 171, 379
Caffrey, Stephen, 40, 149
Caird, John, 30
Cairo International Festival of Experimental Theatre, 273
Caligula, 194
Callimachus, 81
Cambridge Guide to World Theatre, The, 253
Camille, 248
Camino Real, 37, 295
Campbell, Douglas, 66
Camus, Albert, 194, 195
Capitalism, 178
Captain's Tiger, The, 271
Captions, 179
Captives, The, 73
Carlson, Marvin, 284
Carnovsky, Morris, 177
Carolina Playmakers, 386
Carousel, 192, 210, 322
Carpenter, Larry, 398
Carrière, Jean-Claude, 227
Carroll, Lewis, 245, 323
Carroll, Pat, 348
Carson, Terrence A., 49
Carthaginian, The, 75
Cast, of *Oedipus Rex,* 70
Casting, 123, 322, 323–324, 345
Casting directors, 323
Cat on a Hot Tin Roof, 186, 188–190, 191, 217, 301, 327

Cats, 27, 210, 313
Caucasian Chalk Circle, The, 180
Cause-to-effect arrangement, 39, 40, 163
Cause-to-effect dramatic construction, 149
Cavander, Kenneth, 207
Cenci, The, 55
Censorship, 9, 11, 153
Centeno, Augusto, 17
Center Stage, 9, 97, 289, 379
Chaikin, Joseph, 222, 289, 339, 411
Chainani, Erin, 329, 365
Chairs, The, 194
Chamberlain, Lord, 199
Chambers, Jane, 249
Chance poems, 170
Channer, Lisa, 381
Chaplin, Charlie, 12
Character makeup, 389
Characterization
    acting and, 340, 346, 349–350
    biological, 346
    character and, 44–47
    costume design and, 378
    dramatic action and, 38
    ethical, 346
    of *Monte Cristo,* 141
    of *Oedipus Rex,* 69–70
    of *Servant of Two Masters,* 119
    sociological, 346
    vocal, 349–350
Characters
    acting and, 342, 343, 344, 346–350, 352
    in *Akropolis,* 319–320
    auditions/casting and, 323–324
    in *Cat on a Hot Tin Roof,* 188–189, 190
    in *CIVIL warS,* 229
    commedia dell'arte, 112, 114–115, 116
    of contemporary theatre, 220, 223
    costume design and, 377, 379, 380, 382
    director and, 150–151, 315, 323–324, 324, 325, 327
    in *Doll's House,* 148–149
    of Elizabethan theatre, 100
    in France, 120, 123
    in *Good Person of Setzuan,* 180–181
    in *"Hairy Ape,"* 173–174
    in *Hamlet,* 103, 104–105
    in *Importance of Being Earnest,* 164–165

    individualized, 44
    makeup and, 389, 391
    in medieval theatre, 85
    in *Menaechmi,* 77
    modernist temperament and, 178
    in *Monte Cristo,* 140
    nature of theatre and, 13–14
    neoclassical rules and, 133
    in *Noah and His Sons,* 88, 89, 90
    in Noh theatre, 256
    in *Oedipus Rex,* 69
    in *Othello,* 322
    playwriting and, 297
    plot and, 38, 41, 44–47
    production design and, 290
    realism/naturalism and, 146
    in religious/morality plays, 90
    Roman/Greek, 74, 100
    in *Roosters,* 238–239
    in *Servant of Two Masters,* 117, 118–119
    stock, 113–114, 164
    sympathetic, 44, 45
    in *Tartuffe,* 125–126, 127
    typified, 44
    unsympathetic, 44, 45
    Wayang Kulit and, 265
    women, 81
Charles I (England), 110
Charles II (England), 102
Chase, Mary, 245
Chekhov, Anton, 155, 156, 157, 243, 261, 348
Chelsea Theatre, 232
Chenoweth, Kristin, 212
Cherry Orchard, The, 155, 243, 404
Chicago, 210, 213, 386
Chicago Little Theatre, 175
Chicago Lyric Opera, 366
Chickencoop Chinaman, 242
Children, as audience, 66
Chin, Daryl, 241
Chin, Frank, 242
China, theatre in, 261–264
Chinese Opera, 389
Chiton, 65, 66, 71
Cho, Linda, 372
Chong, Ping, 226, 241, 242
Choregoi, 62
Choregus, 62
Choreographer, 7
Chorus
    defined, 45
    festival theatre and, 60, 62–63, 65, 67, 71

Chorus, continued
  Greek/Roman/Medieval theatre
     and, 92
  in Noh theatre, 255
  in Rome, 74, 75
Chorus Line, A, 205, 209, 401
Chou, in China, 263
Chrysalis Theatre, 246
Church
  drama in, 80, 82, 86
  professional theatre and, 95–96
Churchill, Caryl, 200–202
Chushingura, 259
Cibula-Jenkins, Nan, 233
Cid, The, 120, 122
Cilento, Wayne, 46, 212
Cinematography, 86
Circle in the Square, 203
Circle in the Square Theatre,
     325, 417
Circle Repertory Company, 204
Circus Maximus, 78
Circus Schumann, 168
City Dionysia, 58, 59, 62, 66,
     70, 93
CIVIL warS, 228–229
Clark, John Pepper, 269
Clarke, Anne Beresford, 140
Clarke, Martha, 226
Classic Stage Company, 305
Clay, Paul, 305
Cleveland Play House, 234
Climactic plots, 41
Climax, 43, 103, 297, 315, 327, 337
Closed-circuit television,
     224–225, 416
Closer, 202
Cloud 9, 200, 201
Cloud Tectonics, 237
Clurman, Harold, 177
Coast of Utopia, The, 199
Cobb, Lee J., 177, 188
Coleman, Sy, 209
Coleridge, Samuel Taylor, 15
Collaboration
  playwriting and, 204
  production design and, 287–293
Collaborative production design,
     287–293
"Collage Hamlet," 182
Collins, Pat, 291
Color mixing, 398, 405
Color Purple, The, 246
Colorado, Hortensia, 245
Colorado, Vira, 245

"Colorblind" casting, 322
Colored Museum, The, 232
Colors
  costume design and, 377,
     378, 387
  in England, 100
  lighting design and, 397, 398,
     399, 403–404
  modernist temperament and,
     162, 167
  production design and, 288
  in Rome, 75, 77
  scene design and, 359
Colosseum, 78
Columbus National Gay and Lesbian
     Theatre Festival, 249
Comédie Francaise, 122, 135, 197
Comedy
  in France, 120, 121, 122, 123
  Greek, 66, 70–72, 220
  independent theatre and, 156
  in Italy, 107
  musical, 191
  neoclassical rules and, 133
  plays and, 39, 47, 49, 50–51
  Restoration, 128, 164
  Roman, 72–74, 75, 77, 78,
     79, 190
  Second City and, 206
Comedy of Errors, 76, 227
Comic opera, 191
Commedia all'improvviso, 111
Commedia dell'arte, 111–116,
     117–119, 128, 221, 378
Commedia erudite, 111–112
Commonwealth Shakespeare Com-
     pany, 22
Communication
  lighting design and, 411
  production design and, 290, 291
Communism, 178, 263
Community theatre, 313–314
Company, 209
Company of the Holy
     Sacrament, 124
Complexity of means, 16, 17–18
Complications, 42, 43, 165, 315
Composer, 7
Computer simulations, lighting
     design and, 405
Comstock, Anthony, 154
Concentration, acting and, 338, 342
"Conceptual" casting, 322
Concert Parties, 268
Conduct of Life, The, 236

Conflict, 42, 45, 124–125, 165,
     180, 265
Congdon, Constance, 246
Congo Square Theatre, 206
Congreve, William, 128
Conklin, John, 9, 53, 291,
     366, 367
Constant Prince, The, 32, 222
Contact, 386
Contemporary theatre, 219–250
  African American theatre in,
     231–233
  alternative theatre groups in,
     219–221
  Asian American theatre as,
     240–243
  cultural diversity in, 230–231
  directing and, 229–230
  happenings and, 224–227
  How I Learned to Drive as,
     247–248
  Latino theatre in, 236–237
  Ma Rainey's Black Bottom as,
     233–235
  multimedia and, 224–227
  Native American theatre as,
     243–245
  performance art and, 224–227
  playwriting and, 295
  poor/environmental theatres in,
     221–224
  postmodernism in, 227–229
  Roosters as, 237–240
  women and, 245–247
Contemporary Theatre, A, 206
Contracts, directing/producing
     and, 312
Contrast, director and, 327
Control, acting and, 342
Control booth(s), 286
Coordinated production design, 289
Copenhagen, 202
Copyright, 314
Corbett, Hilary, 378
Corey, Irene, 388
Corey, Orlin, 388
Corneille, Pierre, 120, 121, 122, 291
Corporation, directing/producing
     and, 312
Corpses, 61
Corpus Christi, 11
Corpus Christi Festival, 80–83, 93
Corridos, 236
Coryat's Crudities, 102
Costume chart, 382–383

Costume design, 377–388, 391–392.
    See also Costume designers
costume designer/actor and, 387
costume designer's skills in,
    380–382
functions of, 377–380
realizing designs in, 384–387
working plans/procedures and,
    382–383
Costume designers, 193, 287, 290,
    352. *See also* Costume design
Costume house, 391
Costume parade, 391
Costume requirements, director
    and, 315
Costume shop, 286
Costume storage, 286
Costumes
    acting and, 344, 351–352
    in China, 263
    of contemporary theatre,
        220, 222
    critical perspective and, 30
    design of (*See* Costume design)
    designers of (*See* Costume
        designers)
    director and, 150–151, 152,
        324, 325
    distressed, 387
    Elizabethan theatre and, 100
    festival theatre and, 65
    in France, 123
    in *Hamlet,* 106
    lighting design and, 402, 403,
        404, 408, 417
    live performance and, 25
    Long and, 386
    makeup and, 5, 324, 351, 352,
        388–393
    in medieval theatre, 85
    modernist temperament and,
        167, 179, 183
    of *Monte Cristo,* 140
    nature of theatre and, 5, 7, 16
    neoclassical rules and, 135
    in Noh theatre, 255
    production design and, 288
    professional theatre and, 96
    realism/naturalism and, 140, 146
    rehearsal and, 331
    in Rome, 75, 77
    scene design and, 357
    sound design and, 412
    spectacle and, 47
    style and, 52

Taymor and, 289
theatrical space and, 280, 285
of *Titus Andronicus,* 101
Wakefield cycle and, 87
Count of Monte Cristo, The,
    138–144, 146
County Fair, The, 138
Court Theatre, 88, 206
Covent Garden Theatre, 28
Coworkers, scene designer's,
    371–372
Craig, Edward Gordon, 166, 167
Crawford, Cheryl, 177, 187
Crawford, Michael, 13
Crazy for You, 386
Creating a Role, 156
Creation, The, 88
Crimes of the Heart, 246
Cripple of Irishmaan, The, 202
Crisis, 43, 165
Critic, 23–35
    of contemporary theatre, 226,
        229, 237
    director and, 315
    form in drama and, 49
    of melodrama, 136
    perspective of, 29–32
    playwriting and, 297
    problems with, 32–34
    qualities needed by, 34–35
Critical perspective, 29–32
Criticism, 30, 31, 32–34, 324
Crosslighting, 398
Crossroads Theatre Company, 232
Crowley, Matt, 248
Crucible, The, 188, 229
Cruz, Nilo, 233, 236, 237,
    294, 400
Cryptogram, The, 213
Cuban Swimmer, 237
Cue sheets, 411
Cue synopsis, 411
Cues, 351
Culei, Liviu, 65
Cultural diversity, 230–231
Cultural environment, 315
Culture, 10, 12, 14, 18–19,
    227, 241
Culture Clash, 396
Culture Clash in AmeriCCa, 396
Culture of Desire, 328
Cumming, Alan, 211
Curiouser and Curiouser, 245
Curse of the Starving Class, 214
Cycles, 83, 84, 86–88, 96

Cyclops, 64
Cyclorama, scene design and,
    363–364
Cymbeline, 398

D

Dada, 169–170, 185, 225
Dada Is Back, 184
Dafoe, Willem, 339, 340
Dalang, 264, 265
Dali, Salvador, 181, 358
Daly, Arnold, 154
Daly, Augustin, 136–137, 138
Damn Yankees, 210
Dan, in China, 263
Dance
    contemporary theatre and,
        225, 226
    costume design and, 381
    festival theatre and, 92
    in Japanese theatre, 259–260
    nature of theatre and, 5, 7, 8, 16
    neoclassical rules and, 133
    in Noh theatre, 255
    in postwar America, 192, 193
    in *Shrine in the Fields
        (Nonomiya),* 257
    Taymor and, 289
Dance and the Railroad, The, 242
Dance of the Forests, A, 269
Dangerous Liaisons, 329, 365
Dante, 328
Danton's Death, 229
Darwin, Charles, 144–145, 159
Davies, Moll, 102
Day Standing on Its Head, 242
de Almeida, Joaquim, 140
De Architectura, 107
de Niro, Robert, 187
De Shields, André, 341, 342
Death and the King's Horseman,
    269, 270
Death of a Salesman, 49, 50,
    188, 341
*Death of the Last Black Man in the
    Whole Entire World, The,* 233
"Decay of Lying, The," 163
Decentralization, 196–197, 205, 209
Decorative arts, scene design
    and, 358
Decorum, 120
Degree of formality, in theatrical
    space, 279
Delacorte Theatre, 205

Delicate Balance, A, 213
Dell'Arte Players, 116
DeMille, Agnes, 192
DemiMonde, The, 145
Democracy, 202
Dench, Judi, 339
Denoument, 43
Denver Center Theatre, 243, 296, 307
Design
    collaborative production, 287–293
    costume (*See* Costume design)
    director and, 316, 321, 323
    lighting (*See* Lighting design)
    scene (*See* Scene design)
    sound (*See* Sound design)
Designer-technician, 314
Designers
    acting and, 337, 352
    costume, 193, 287, 290, 352
        (*See also* Costume design)
    directing/producing and, 311, 314
    directors and, 321, 323
    display, 402–403
    dramaturgy and, 307
    lighting, 193, 288, 290, 352
        (*See also* Lighting design)
    nature of theatre and, 7
    production design and, 287–293
    scene/scenic, 193, 287–288, 290, 352, 377, 404 (*See also* Scene design)
    sound, 287, 352 (*See also* Sound design)
    theatrical space and, 281, 282
Desire Under the Elms, 172
Deus ex machina, 61–62, 125
Dialogue, 100, 101, 105, 116, 117, 165, 180
    in *Buried Child,* 214
    director and, 330
    in Noh theatre, 254–255
    playwriting and, 296–297
    in postwar Europe, 193
    production design and, 288
Diction, 45–47
Die Götterdämmerung, 415, 416
Die Walküre, 152
Dimensionality, lighting design and, 399
Directing, 30, 52, 229–230, 311.
    See also Directors
    approaches to, 316–321
    directors on, 317

production design and, 288
    sound design and, 417
Director-dramaturg relationship, 307
Directors, 311, 314–330, 335
    acting and, 151, 316, 337, 342–343, 347–349, 352
    actors and, 150, 151, 152, 323–327
    analyzing/studying play as, 315–316
    approaches to directing by, 316–321
    artistic, 312
    assistants to, 334
    auditions/casting and, 323–324
    board of, 312, 313–314
    casting, 323
    of contemporary theatre, 227, 228
    costume design and, 380, 382, 385, 387
    criticism and, 32–33
    designers and, 321, 323
    dramaturgy and, 303, 306, 307, 308, 314
    emergence of, 150–152
    lighting design and, 398, 403, 411
    managing, 312, 313
    modernist temperament and, 167, 168
    playwriting and, 297, 300–301
    production design and, 287–288, 290, 291, 292
    rehearsal and, 331–334
    scene design and, 359, 360
    sound design and, 413
    stage images and, 325–327
    technical, 372
    theatrical space and, 281, 282, 285, 287
    working with actors as, 324
    writers and, 319
Director's means, 324–330
Director's Voice, The, 311
"Dirty Man" Reformed, 268
Discipline, acting and, 342
Discovery/discoveries, 42–43, 99, 165
Distant Shore, A, 243
Distribution, lighting design and, 397–398, 399, 403, 405–410
Dithyrambs, 66
Diversity
    in Asian theatrical forms, 265
    audience and, 28, 29
    contemporary theatre and (*See* Contemporary theatre)

cultural, 230–231
    modernist temperament and, 183, 184
    in theatre, 3, 6
Doctor Faustus, 287
Docudrama, 193
Dog Lady, 237
Dogon, The, 252
Doll theatre, 258
Doll's House, A
    cause-to-effect arrangement in, 40
    character/characterization in, 44
    costume chart for, 383
    director and, 326
    dramatic action in, 38
    dressing list for, 384
    plot in, 41, 42, 43
    realism/naturalism and, 146–149
    scene design and, 355
    spoken language in, 47
Domestic Resurrection Circus, 221
Don Giovanni, 33
d'Outreman, H., 84
Downlighting, 398
Downstage, 108, 343
Drama
    absurdist, 195–196, 227
    Aristotle and, 39
    contemporary theatre and, 224
    epic, 180
    in France, 120
    Greek, 57, 63
    learned, 111–112
    liturgical, 80, 93
    medieval theatre and, 90–92
    in Middle Ages, 79–80
    modernist temperament and, 168–169, 170–171
    musical, 190
    nature of theatre and, 5
    plays as (*See* Plays)
    in postwar Europe, 193
    religious, 91, 92 (*See also* Religious plays)
    Roman, 78–79, 93
    Sophocles and, 44
    symbolist, 162
Dramatic action, 107, 146, 270, 297
    acting and, 344
    costume design and, 378, 379–380, 382
    director and, 316, 324
    lighting design and, 398, 399
    in plays, 38–41, 45
Dramatic Imagination, The, 175, 355

Dramatic poetry, 105
Dramatists Guild, The, 300
Dramatists Play Service, 314
Dramaturg, 302, 306, 314
Dramaturgy, 302–308
  literary management and,
    302–306
  production, 307–308
Draperies, scene design and, 363
Drawer Boy, 205
Drawing, 108, 361
Dream Girls, 401
Dream Play, A, 171, 201, 202
Dress parade, 391
Dress rehearsals, 334, 351–352, 371,
    391, 410
Dress the stage, acting and, 343
Dressers, 392
Dressing lists, costume design and,
    383, 384
Dressing rooms, 286
Drops, 109
  scene design and, 363
Drury Lane Theatre, 132
Duerrenmatt, Friedrich, 193
Duke of Saxe-Meiningen, 151,
    152–153, 167
Dulcitius, 81
Dumas, Alexandre, 138, 145
Durang, Christopher, 232
Duration, 47, 330, 349, 350,
    413, 414
Dutchman, The, 231

E

Early Morning, 199
Earth, The, 150
East-West Players, 242
Eccyclema, 61
Eclecticism, 168
Edinburgh University, 261
Education theatre, 314
Egungen, in Nigeria, 268, 269
Egypt, theatre in, 59
Egyptian National Theatre, 273
Einstein on the Beach, 228,
    320, 321
Eisenhauer, Peggy, 211, 418
El Teatro Campesino, 236, 240
El Teatro de la Esperanza, 240
Electra, 56, 64
Electronic media, 224
Elements, of theatre, 6–9
Elevator stage, scene design and, 369
Elitist culture, 10, 12, 14

Elizabethan theatre. *See also* England;
    Shakespeare, William
  musical element of, 101
  reputation of, 97
Ellipsoidals, 409
Emotion memory, 348
Emotional preparation, acting and,
    348–349
Emperor Jones, The, 172
Emphasis
  acting and, 337, 343, 352
  director and, 325, 326
  production design and, 288
Empty Space, The, 7
En Yu Tan, Victor, 117
End, of play, 43
End of the Moon, The, 404
Endgame, 229, 230, 405
England. *See also* Elizabethan theatre;
    Shakespeare, William
  France and, 107
  postwar theatre in, 197–202
  religion in, 95
  Shakespeare/Globe Theatre in,
    97–103, 134–135
  theatre in, 5, 27, 28
  tradition in, 128–129
  women acting in, 102
English Aestheticism, 163
English Restoration, 102
English Stage Company (ESC), 199
Entertainment
  nature of theatre and, 6, 12
Environment
  cultural, 315
  of *Doll's House*, 149
  independent theatre and, 153
  realism/naturalism and,
    145, 146
  Zola and, 150
Environmental theatres. *See*
    Poor/enviromental theatres
Ephemerality, 16
Epic drama, 180
Epic theatre, 177–180, 347
Episodic plots, 41
Ernst, Max, 170
ESC. *See* English Stage
    Company (ESC)
Ethical characterization, acting
    and, 346
Ethnicity, nontraditional casting
    and, 322
Eugene O'Neill Theatre Center, 232,
    297, 299
Eumenides, The, 228

Eunuch, 73
Euripides, 41–42, 58, 64, 65, 207,
    228, 229
Europe
  dramaturg in, 302
  Grotowski influence on, 222
  postwar, 193–194
Eustis, Oskar, 205
Evening Star, 237
Everyman, 45, 90, 91, 378
Everyman at the Mall, 285
Evita, 210
Existentialist, 194
Expenses, directing/producing and,
    312
Exposition, 41, 43, 163, 188
Expressionism, 170–172, 174, 177,
    185, 227
Eyes for Consuela, 214

F

Façade
  on Elizabethan stage, 108
  in Globe Theatre, 99–100
  in Roman theatre, 74
Face Value, 242
Facial expression, director and, 329
Falling action, 43
Falstaff, 358
Family Devotions, 242
Family Week, 246
Fantasy, 133
Far Away, 201
Farce, 47, 91
Fashion designer, costume design
    and, 380
Fechter, Charles, 138
Federal Theatre, 176–177, 202–203
Federal Theatre Project, 176,
    177, 401
Feedback, from audience, 8
Fefu and Her Friends, 236
Female roles, in Kabuki, 260
Fences, 232, 233, 235
Fergusson, Francis, 38
Festival theatre, 57–93
  in ancient Egypt, 59
  of ancient Greece, 57–58, 60
  comparing
    Greek/Roman/Medieval the-
    atre, 92
  conventions of medieval theatre,
    83–90
  Corpus Christi Festival and,
    80–83

Festival theatre, continued
  drama and, 79–80, 90–93
  Greek comedy in, 70–72
  history of, 93
  medieval theatre and, 90–92
  Menaechmi and, 76–77
  Middle Ages and, 79–80
  performance of *Oedipus Rex* in, 66–70
  performers and, 62–63, 65–66
  Roman drama/theatre and, 78–79
  Roman theatre experience and, 72–74
  Roman theatrical context and, 74–75
  Theatre of Dionysus, 60–62
  trade guilds and, 80–83
Fierstein, Harvey, 249
Fifth of July, The, 213
Figurative language, 105
Figure of speech, 105
Film
  acting and, 337
  contemporary theatre and, 224
  live performance v., 24, 25
  melodrama and, 144
  nature of theatre and, 16, 18
  postwar American theatre and, 187
  sound design and, 416, 417
Film actors, 345
Financial aspects, producer and, 314
Financing, directing/producing and, 312
Fish Head Soup, 242
Fisher, Jules, 249, 418
Fiske, Minnie Maddern, 148
Flat, scene design and, 364
Flats, 109
Flexibility
  acting and, 338
  sound design and, 414
Flexible space, 280, 283–285, 355, 356
Flexible stage, 25, 327
Flies, The, 194
Floodlights, 408
Flute pillar, in Noh theatre, 256
Fly system, theatrical space and, 281
Flying, scene design and, 368
Flying Karamazov Brothers, 227
F.O.B., 242
Focus, acting and, 343
Footfalls, 229
Footsteps Theatre Company, 246

Ford Foundation, 205, 207
Foreman, Richard, 226
Forestage, theatrical space and, 281
Forms
  of plays, 47, 49–51
  of theatrical experience, 55
Fornes, Maria Irene, 236–237
  49, 243
42nd Street Development Project, 211
4:48 Psychosis, 2, 202
Framed units, 364–365
France
  absurdist drama in, 195
  background in, 119–121
  England and, 107
  existentialists in, 194
  Molière and, 121–124, 127
  seventeenth-century theatre practice in, 121–124
  Tartuffe in, 124–127
  traditions in, 128–129
France, Anatole, 175
Frasier, 385
Frayn, Michael, 202
Frederick the Great, 229
Freie Buehne für Modernes, 133
Freie Bühne, 153
French Academy, 120
French scenes, 127
Fresnels, 409
Freud, Sigmund, 145, 181
Frida, 289
Frigerio, Ezio, 118, 356
Fringe Festival, 309
Frisch, Max, 193
Frogs, The, 386
Front elevations, scene design and, 360–361
Frontlighting, 398
Fuebashira, in Noh theatre, 256
Fugard, Athol, 11, 271–273
Full Circle, 380
Full front, acting and, 343
Full Monty, The, 212, 341
Funny Girl, 209
Furies, The, 64
Futurism, 168–169, 170, 185, 225
Fuxian, Zong, 263

G

GALA. *See* Group of Latin American Artists (GALA)
GALA Hispanic Theatre, 238
Galileo Galilei, 402

Gallery, 111, 119, 132, 151
Gallicanus, 81
Game of Love and Chance, The, 326
Gamelan, 264
Games, theatre and, 12–14
Garden, 200
Gardner, Howard, 20
Garrick, David, 134
Gaslight, 378
Gay, John, 133
Gay Fantasia on National Themes, A, 249
Gay/lesbisn theatre, 248–249
Gay Theatre Alliance, 249
Gazing pillar, in Noh theatre, 256
Geiogamah, Hanay, 243, 245
Gem of the Ocean, 216, 233, 235
General illumination, 406, 407–409
Genet, Jean, 195, 293, 316
Genre, 120
Georg II (Germany), 152. *See also* Duke of Saxe-Meiningen
Gerckens, T. J., 325, 402, 417
Gershwin, George, 192
Gesamtkunstwerk, 151
Gesture
  acting and, 342, 349
  costume design and, 378
  directors and, 327, 329–330
Gestus, 181
Getting Out, 246
Ghosts, 9, 147, 153, 379
Give stage, acting and, 343
Given circumstances, acting and, 340
Glaspell, Susan, 245
Glass, Philip, 242, 402
Glass Menagerie, The, 188, 411
Glee, in Nigeria, 268
Glengarry Glen Ross, 213
Glimmerglass Opera, 366
Globe Theatre, 26, 97–103
Gluck, 166
Goat, The, 213
Gobos, 409
God of Hell, The, 214
Godspell, 209
Golden Child, The, 242
Goldoni, Carlo, 116, 117–119, 129
Good Person of Setzuan, The, 180–181
Good Woman of Setzuan, The, 379
Goodman Theatre, 49, 206, 250, 366, 402, 404
Gordon, David, 372
Gorki, Maxim, 225

Gospel at Colonus, 49
Gotanda, Philip Kan, 242
Government
    Chicago city, 206
    Federal Theatre and, 202–203
    postwar British theatre and,
      197–198
    Roman/Greek, 74
    subsidization and, 196–197, 207
Gozzi, Carlo, 116, 117, 290
Grahamstown Festival, 273
Grand Theatre, 263, 264
Grandfather of the Buffalo Sisters, 245
Gravity, in Roman theatre, 74, 78
Gray, Spalding, 226
Great Lakes Theater Festival, 106,
    126, 338
Greece, 57–72
    comedy in, 70–72
    comparing ancient theatres to, 92
    Globe Theatre and, 100
    Italy and, 107
    Oedipus Rex and, 66–70
    performers in, 62–63, 65–66
    religious theatre and, 80
    theatre in, 5, 6, 18, 57–58, 60
    Theatre of Dionysus in, 60–62
    tragic dramatists in, 64
Greek theatre, 92. *See also* Greece
Greeks, The, 207
Greenberg, Richard, 249
Greenroom, 286
Greenwood, Jane, 379
Greif, Michael, 305
Greig, Robert, 273
Grendel, 289, 374
Griggs, J. Michael, 248
Griguere, Lynda, 300
Grimm, David, 303
Gromada, John, 4, 103, 200, 303, 412
Grotowski, Jerzy, 32, 221, 222, 279,
    287, 319–320, 347
Group of Latin American Artists
    (GALA), 238
Group Theatre, 176, 177, 187
Guest of Honor, 268
Guilds, trade, 80–83, 86, 87, 96
Gurney, A. R., 305
Gussow, Mel, 289, 328
Guthrie, Tyrone, 66, 205, 282
Guthrie Theatre
    Bacchae by, 65
    decentralization and, 205
    Entertainer at, 363
    festival theatre and, 68, 69
    Lupu and, 306

    Night of the Iguana by, 36
    Oedipus at, 45, 310
    Screens at, 293
    Tartuffe at, 128
    thrust stage of, 282
    Tipton and, 404
    Too Clever by Half at, 390
Guys and Dolls, 193, 210, 386
Gwynne, Nell, 102
Gypsy, 210

H

Habit à la romaine, 123
Hair, 204, 209, 217, 220
Hairspray, 212, 313, 386
"Hairy Ape, The," 172–174, 185,
    326, 327, 340, 356, 378
Hall, Peter, 99, 198
Hamburg National Theater, 302
Hamlet
    acting of, 338
    Barrymore as, 339
    costume design and, 378
    director and, 326
    language of, 47
    at Long Wharf Theatre, 4
    modernist temperament and, 167
    Okhlopkov and, 318
    plot of, 43
    production styles of, 53
    on professional theatre, 103–107
    scene design and, 356, 359,
      360, 361
    Stoppard and, 199
    tragedy of, 50
Hammerstein, Oscar II, 191–192
Hampton, Christopher, 329, 365
Han, Wu, 263
Hanamichi, 258
Hand props, 371
Hansberry, Lorraine, 231, 232
Happenings, contemporary theatre
    and, 224–227
Happy Days, 356, 378
Hare, David, 31, 200
Harmony, production design
    and, 288
Harris, Barbara, 206
Harrison, Rex, 193
Hart, Charles, 13
Hartford Stage, 29, 42, 89, 186,
    190, 303, 367
Hartford Stage Company, 233,
    291, 366
Hashigakari, in Noh theatre, 255

Hauptmann, Gerhardt, 153
Haze, 163
Healy, Michael, 205
Heartbreak House, 155
Heidi Chronicles, The, 246, 298
Hellman, Lillian, 176
Hello, Dolly, 176, 209
Henley, Beth, 246
Henry VIII (England), 110
Hepburn, Katharine, 32
Herman, Jerry, 209
Hernandez, Riccardo, 45, 69, 278,
    288, 352
Hernani, 135, 159
Hersey, David, 30, 192
Hierarchy, in production design, 292
High art, 10, 12
Hilferty, Susan, 42, 46, 212, 231
Hippolytus, 64
History
    art (*See* Art history)
    of contemporary theatre, 251
    costume design and, 381
    of Elizabethan/Italian/French
      traditions, 129
    of festival theatre, 93
    lighting design and, 403
    modernist temperament, 185
    reevaluation/decentralization/sub-
      sidization and, 217
    of Romanticism to Realism, 159
    stage, 358
    theatre, 382, 403
Histriomastix, 102
Hoffman, Dustin, 187
Holder, Donald, 19, 164, 216, 332
Homecoming, The, 199, 386
Homer, 207
Hopkins, Arthur, 175, 176
Horizons Theatre, 246
Hot L Baltimore, 213
House, 200
How I Learned to Drive, 40–41, 42,
    247–248, 251, 299, 300
How the Other Half Loves, 200
Hrosvitha, 81
Hua dan, in China, 263
Hughes, Holly, 249
Hugo, Victor, 30, 31, 135, 159
Humana Festival of New American
    Plays, 300, 301, 330
Huntington Theatre, 12, 216, 242,
    329, 336, 365, 372, 376, 396
Hurlyburly, 213
Hwang, David Henry, 232, 242,
    243, 298

I

I Don't Have to Show You No Stinking Badges, 236
IATSE. *See* International Alliance of Theatrical Stage Employees (IATSE)
Ibsen, Henrik
    Doll's House by, 38, 41, 146–149, 159
    Ghosts by, 9, 153
    modernist temperament and, 162
    playwriting and, 295, 296
    When We Dead Awaken by, 229
    Zuber and, 379
Iceman Cometh, The, 172
Iizuka, Naomi, 12, 242, 243
Illumination, 406–409
Illusion, The, 291
Images, 214, 325–327
Imaginary Invalid, The, 127
Imagination, acting and, 338, 340–342
Immediacy, 16, 18
Importance of Being Earnest, The, 163–165, 185, 200, 385
Impossible Marriage, 246
Improbable Fiction, 200
Improvisation, 112–113, 116, 117–119, 223, 356
Improvisation for the Theatre, 23
In the Blood, 233
Inciting incident, 42, 43, 103
Independent Theatre, 147, 153
Independent theatre movement, 153, 155–157, 161
Independent theatres, 162
India, theatre in, 264
Individualized characters, 44
Indonesia, theatre in, 264
Industrial revolution, 136
Industrialism, 170, 171
Inferno, 328
Inflection, acting and, 349, 350
Innate ability, acting and, 338
Innovation
    critic/criticism and, 33, 34
    modernist temperament and, 161, 170, 174, 175, 177
    in Noh theatre, 257
Innovative materials/methods, 365–366
Instrument, actor's, 338, 340
Instrument schedules, 405, 409, 410, 411

INTAR Hispanic Playwrights-in-Residence Laboratory, 237
Intelligence, theatre and, 20
Intelligent lighting instruments, 408, 409
Intensity, lighting design and, 397, 399, 403
Interculturalism and Performance, 219
Interior decorator, scene design and, 357, 358
Interludes, 109
Intermezzi, 109–110
International Alliance of Theatrical Stage Employees (IATSE), 412
Intiman Theatre, 206
Into the Woods, 209, 370
Intoleranza, 416
Investigation, The, 193
Investors, directing/producing and, 311, 312
Ionesco, Eugene, 38–39, 194, 195
Iphigenia at Aulis, 64, 228
Isn't It Romantic, 246
Italy
    commedia dell'arte in, 111–116
    opera in, 190
    Servant of Two Masters in, 117–119
    theatre experience in, 107–111
    traditions in, 128–129

J

Jackson, Nagle, 124
James, Toni-Leslie, 33, 249, 315
James I (England), 110
Japan, theatre in, 253–254, 258–261
Japan Playwrights Association, 261
Jean Cocteau Repertory Theatre, 55
Jefferson, Margo, 241
Jeffrey, 249
Jelly's Last Jam, 232
Jesus Christ, Superstar, 204, 210
Jing, in China, 263
Jinghui, Ming, 263
Jitney, 233, 235
Joe Turner's Come and Gone, 232, 233, 235
Joint Stock Company, 201
Jomandi Productions, 232
Jonas, Susan, 304–305
Jones, Inigo, 110
Jones, LeRoi, 231, 232

Jones, Robert Edmond, 172, 175, 176, 355
Jonson, Ben, 97, 98, 110
Jory, Jon, 301
Juan Darién, 289
Judgment, 29–32, 33–34. *See also* Criticism
Juggling, 6
"Jules Fisher and Peggy Eisenhauer," 418
Julius Caesar, 153
Jumpers, 199
Just Assassins, The, 194

K

Kabuki, 258–261, 389
Kahn, Michael, 348
Kaiser, Georg, 172
Kamm, Tom, 228
Kan'ami, Kiyotsugu, 254
Kander, John, 209
Kane, Sarah, 2, 202
Kani, John, 195
Kaprow, Allan, 225
Katanga Theatre Group, 268
Kaufman, George S., 192
Kaufman, Moisés, 296
Kazan, Elia, 177, 187, 188, 189, 190, 191, 301–302
Kellogg, Marjorie Bradley, 370
Kelly, Jude, 322
Kennedy Center, 140, 210
Kente, Gibson, 271
Kern, Jerome, 191–192
Killing of Abel, The, 88
King, Martin Luther, Jr., 223
King and I, The, 192
King Hedley II, 235
King Lear, 97, 128, 229
King Stag, 289, 290
King's Men, 96, 97
Kingston, Maxine Hong, 231
Kiselov, Mladen, 4, 103
Kiss of the Spider Woman, 209
Kokata, in Noh theatre, 255
Komos, 71
Komparu, Kunio, 257
Kordian, 222
Koturbash, Allison, 215
Kotuwokan, 245
Kramer, Larry, 249
Krutch, Joseph Wood, 50
Kunska, Agnieszka, 381
Kurup, Shishiri, 285

Kushner, Tony, 232, 249, 291, 299, 304
Kyd, Thomas, 97
Kyogen, in Noh theatre, 255

L

La Bamba, 236
La Bohème, 211, 305
La Cage aux Folles, 209, 249
La Ferla, Ruth, 394
La Fiaca, 238
La MaMa, 204, 243, 289
La MaMa Experimental Theatre Club, 298
La Prise de Marsilly, 120
Lackawanna Blues, 232
Lake, The, 32
Lamos, Mark, 291, 311, 357, 364, 367, 371, 392
Landwehr, Hugh, 94, 164
Language. *See also* Diction
  in Africa, 269
  body, 329
  Craig and, 167
  as diction, 46, 47
  dramaturgy and, 305
  in *Importance of Being Earnest*, 164
  in Noh theatre, 258
  obscene, 219, 220
  production design and, 290
Lao dan, in China, 263
Lao sheng, in China, 263
Laramie Project, The, 296, 307
Larson, Jonathan, 211, 304, 305
Last Ones, The, 225
Last Summer at Bluefish Cove, 249
Late Henry Moss, The, 213, 214
Laterna Magika, 224
Latina, 237
Latina Theatre Lab, 246
Latino theatre, 236–237
Latino Theatre Festival, 250
Laurents, Arthur, 192, 193
Lazzi, 113, 115, 118
Lear, 199
Learned drama, 111–112
Learned Ladies of Park Avenue, The, 303
Lebrecht, James, 412
LeCompte, Elizabeth, 229, 340
Lee, Eugene, 46, 212
Lee, Ming Cho, 231, 362, 363, 379, 386

Legrand, Michel, 24, 354
Leguizamo, John, 226
Lenaia, 70
Lend Me a Tenor, 386
Lennon, 212
Lenny, 203, 204, 370
Leon, Kenny, 216
Lerner, Alan Jay, 192, 193
Les Atrides, 228
Les Femmes Savants, 303
Les Liaisons, 385
Les Misérables, 7, 30, 31, 210, 313, 370
Lesbian theatre. *See* Gay/lesbian theatre
Lessing, Gotthold Ephraim, 302
Lewis, Robert, 177, 187
Libation Bearers, The, 64, 228
Licensing, professional theatre and, 96–97
Licensing Act, 199
Lie of the Mind, A, 214
Lieutenant of Inishmore, The, 202
Life Is a Dream, 237
Lifelikeness, 16
Light in the Piazza, The, 379
Light plots, 405–407, 409, 410, 411
Light Shining in Buckinghamshire, 201
Light shop, 286
Lighting
  acting and, 344, 351
  automated, 405, 408
  costume design and, 378
  critical perspective and, 30
  design for (*See* Lighting design)
  designers for, 288, 290, 352
    (*See also* Lighting design)
  director and, 151, 324, 325
  Elizabethan theatre and, 100
  in France, 123–124
  functions of stage, 399–402
  melodrama and, 143
  modernist temperament and, 166–167, 178, 181, 183
  Off-Off-Broadway, 204
  production design and, 288
  scene design and, 356, 357
  sound design and, 412
  spectacle and, 47
  style and, 52
  theatrical space and, 281, 282
Lighting accessories, 409
Lighting crew, 411–412
Lighting cues, rehearsal and, 334

Lighting design, 397–412, 415–418
  controllable qualities of light in, 397–399
  female pioneers in, 401
  lighting designer's assistants in, 411–412
  lighting designer's skills in, 402–403
  lighting designer's working procedures in, 403–405
  organizing distribution of light in, 405–410
  performances and, 410–411
  rehearsals and, 410–411
  setting lights in, 410–411
Lighting designers, 193, 288, 290, 352. *See also* Lighting design
Lighting instruments, 409
Lighting requirements, director and, 315
Lighting scores, 405
Limelight, 143
Lincoln, Abraham, 40, 228, 229
Lincoln Center, 227, 262
Line
  costume design and, 377, 378
  memorization of, 349–350
  modernist temperament and, 167
  playwriting and, 296
  production design and, 288
  scene design and, 359
Line readings, acting and, 350–351
Lining, scene design and, 367–368
Lion and the Jewel, The, 269
Lion King, The, 7, 211–212, 289
Lips Together, Teeth Apart, 249
Literary management, 302–306
Literary Managers and Dramaturgs of the Americas, 306
Little Night Music, A, 401
Liturgical drama, 80, 93
Living Newspaper, 176
Living Theatre, 219, 220, 221, 222, 287
Loesser, Frank, 193
Loewe, Frederick, 192–193
London Times, 31
Long, William Ivey, 211, 386
Long Day's Journey into Night, 138, 172, 401
Long Season, The, 243
Long Wharf Theatre
  Hamlet by, 4, 103
  Importance of Being Earnest by, 164, 385

Long Wharf Theatre, *continued*
    Travesties by, 200, 412
    Twelfth Night by, 33, 315
    Waiting for Godot by, 195
Look Back in Anger, 199
Looking Glass Theatre, The, 246
Loomer, Lisa, 246
Loquasto, Santo, 332
Lorca in a Green Dress, 237
Lord Admiral's Men, 96
Lord Chamberlain's Men, 96, 97
Lorraine Hansberry, 232
Los Vendidos, 236
Lost Colony, The, 386
Louis XIII (France), 119, 121
Louis XIV (France), 124
Love for Love, 128
Low art, 10, 12
L.S.D., 229
Ludi, 72
Ludlam, Charles, 248–249
Lugné-Poë, Aurélien-Marie, 162, 167
LuPone, Patti, 140
Lupu, Michael, 306
Lysistrata, 71

M

M. Butterfly, 242, 243
Ma Rainey's Black Bottom, 232,
    233–235, 296
MacBeth, 134, 318, 409
Machina, 61–62
Machinal, 412
Mad Dog Blues, 213
Mad Forest, 201, 202
Madmen and Specialists, 269
Maeterlinck, Maurice, 161, 162
Magic Book of Light, The, 401
Magic Flute, The, 134
Magic Theatre, 213
Mahabharata, 227, 228, 264, 346
Mahelot, Laurent, 120
Maimone, Kasia, 278, 288, 352
Major Barbara, 155
Major dramatic question, 42
Makeup, 5, 324, 351, 352, 388–393
Makeup plot, 389
Malina, Judith, 219
Malkovich, John, 206
Mame, 209, 401
Mamet, David, 206, 212, 213
Mamma Mia!, 212
Man and Art Figure, 377
Man and Superman, 155

Man of Mode, The, 128
Man Who Married a Dumb Wife,
    The, 175
Managing director, 312, 313
Manhattan Theatre Club, 11,
    205, 298
Mann, Emily, 237, 294
Mansions, 84–85, 86, 90, 100, 108
Mantello, Joe, 46, 212
Manual scene shifting, scene design
    and, 368
Map of the World, A, 200
Maradudin, Peter, 33, 202, 231, 315
Marat/Sade, 182, 183, 198
Marber, Patrick, 202
Marinetti, Filippo Tommaso, 168–169
Marisol, 237
Mark Taper Forum, 206, 362
Market Theatre, 272
Marketing, directing/producing
    and, 312
Marlowe, Christopher, 97
Marowitz, Charles, 182
Marquez, Gabriel Garcia, 237
Marranca, Bonnie, 219
Marriage of Bette and Boo, The, 386
Martha Graham Dance
    Company, 401
Marx, Karl, 229
Marxism, 178
Masks
    festival theatre and, 65, 71, 75,
        77, 79, 92
    nature of theatre and, 5, 13
    Noh theatre, 254, 255
    professional theatre and,
        101, 116
    Taymor and, 289
Masques, 110
Mass, scene design and, 359
Mass audience, 75, 136, 174,
    175, 203
Master Harold and the Boys, 271–272
Matchmaker, The, 176
Materialism, 170, 171
McBurney, Simon, 194
McCarter Theatre, 53, 294, 326,
    364, 392
McCarter Theatre Center, 56,
    124, 237
McDonagh, Martin, 202
McGrath, Bob, 163, 171, 323
McGuinness, Frank, 56
McLaughlin, Ellen, 45, 69, 249, 310
McLuhan, Marshall, 224

McNally, Terrence, 11, 249
Meaning, director and, 330
Measure for Measure, 204, 345
"Measuring the Muse," 216
Medea, 64, 73
Media, 17–18, 224–227
Medieval theatre, 83–92
Medoff, Mark, 341, 342
Medrano, Hugo, 238
Medrano, Rebecca Read, 238
Mee, Charles L., 92, 380
Melodrama, 44, 47, 51, 135–144,
    145, 146, 157, 191
Memorization, acting and,
    350–351
Men. *See also* Boys
    actors of male/female roles, 65,
        87, 100–101, 260, 273
    as dominant audience, 66
    female characters written by, 81
Menaechmi, The, 73, 76–77
Merchant of Venice, The, 100
Merry Widow, The, 195
Metamorphoses, 325, 417
Metaphor
    costume design and, 378
    director and, 316, 317, 318
Metropolitan Opera, 152, 366
Metsukabashira, in Noh theatre, 256
Middle, of play, 42–43
Middle Ages, 79–80, 95–96,
    107, 157
Midsummer Night's Dream, A, 198,
    318, 368
Mielziner, Jo, 188, 191, 284, 362
Mies, 259
Milk Wood, 371
Miller, Arthur, 49, 50, 188, 212,
    213, 229, 298, 356
Miller, Jonathan, 333
Millet, Kate, 201
Mime, 79, 92, 220
Mimicry, 5
Mineola Twins, The, 247
Minority cultures, 241
Minority theatres, 28
Miracle, The, 356
Misanthrope, The, 381
Mishimi, Yukio, 261
Miss Saigon, 210, 386, 414
Mitchell, Cameron, 188
Mixed-media productions,
    415–417
Mizrahi, Isaac, 394
Mnouchkine, Ariane, 228, 317, 319

Modernism, 165, 174, 175, 227
Modernist temperament, 161–184
    Artaud in, 181–183, 184
    epic theatre in, 177–180
    Good Person of Setzuan as,
        180–181
    "Hairy Ape" as, 172–174
    Importance of Being Earnest as,
        163–165
    influence on theatrical visionaries
        in, 165–168
    new artistic movements in,
        168–172
    postwar era in, 174, 176
    symbolism in, 161–163
    Theatre of Cruelty and,
        181–183, 184
Moholy-Nagy, Laszlo, 284
Moiseiwitch, Tanya, 66, 282
Molière, 94, 115–116,
        121–128, 139
    dramaturgy and, 303
    Misanthrope by, 381
    playwriting and, 295
Monstrous Regiment, 201
Monzaemon, Chikamatsu, 258
Mood
    acting and, 344, 352
    costume design and, 378
    in *Cymbeline*, 398
    diction and, 46
    director and, 327
    dramatic action and, 38, 41
    festival theatre and, 63, 65
    lighting design and, 397, 399,
        404, 405
    modernist temperament and,
        162, 166, 167
    music and, 47
    of performance, 24
    in postwar Europe, 193
    scene design and, 356
    in *Shrine in the Fields
        (Nonomiya)*, 257
    sound design and, 412
Moonlight, 199
Moral level, of characters, 44
Morality plays, 90
Morton, Jelly Roll, 232
Moscow Art Theatre, 155, 156,
        157, 177
"Mother, Sing for Me," 269
Mother Courage and Her Children,
        179, 180, 223, 348
Mother-in-Law, 73

Motivation
    director and, 315, 330
    dramatic action and, 38
    plot and, 43
Motokiyo, Zeami, 254
Motorcycle Diaries, 237
Mourning Becomes Electra, 172
"Mousetrap," 4
Movement
    acting and, 342, 344, 349, 350
    Asian/African theatre and, 263
    costume design and, 378, 379,
        380, 387
    director and, 327, 329–330
    lighting design and, 397,
        398–399, 405, 410
    modernist temperament and, 182
    playwright and, 296
    Taymor and, 289
Movin' Out, 212, 332
Mozart, Wolfgang Amadeus, 33
Mrs. Warren's Profession, 154
Multiculturalism, 241
Multimedia
    contemporary theatre and,
        224–227
    sound design and, 415
    Svoboda and, 416
Multimedia productions. *See* Mixed-
        media productions
Multiple Intelligences Theory, 20
Murmuring Judges, 200
Murray, Bill, 206
Music
    of contemporary theatre, 222,
        225, 226
    in Elizabethan theatre, 101
    festival theatre and, 63, 65, 92
    melodrama and, 136
    modernist temperament and, 166
    nature of theatre and, 5, 7, 8, 16
    in play, 45, 46, 47
    in postwar America, 191,
        192, 193
Musical comedy, 191
Musical drama, 190
Musicals
    after subsidization, 209–212
    in postwar America, 190–193
    rehearsal and, 333–334
Musicians, 62, 75, 255, 263
Musser, Tharon, 401
My Africa, 272–273
My Children, 272
My Fair Lady, 155, 193

My Life in Art, 156
Mystery Cycle, The, 88
Mystery of Irma Vep, The, 248
Mystery Plays, The, 89

N

Naa Kahidi, 245
NAC. *See* National Arts Council
        (NAC)
Narration, 180
National Arts Council (NAC), 273
National Endowment for the Arts
        (NEA), 207, 208, 209,
        226, 312
National Playwrights Conference,
        232, 297, 299
National Theatre, 171, 198–199,
        200, 225, 258, 263, 416
National Theatre Complex, 264
National Theatre of the Deaf
        (NTD), 244, 245
National Theatre Workshop of the
        Handicapped (NTWH), 244
Native American theatre, 243–245
Native American Theatre
        Ensemble, 243
Naturalism, 145–146, 149–150,
        157, 161, 163
Naumachia, 78, 79
NEA. *See* National Endowment for
        the Arts (NEA)
NEC. *See* Negro Ensemble Company
        (NEC)
Nederlands Theatre Institute, 83
Negro Ensemble Company
        (NEC), 231
Neighborhood Playhouse, 175
Nemerovich-Danchenko, Vladimir,
        155, 156
Neoclassical ideal, 120, 128
Neoclassical rules, 133, 135
Neoclassical tradition, 127
Neoclassical vision, 128
New American Shakespeare
        Tavern, 53
New Amsterdam Theatre, 211
New Comedy, 71–72
New England, theatre in, 5
New Federal Theatre, 232
New Georges, 246
New Globe Theatre, 99–100
New Jersey Shakespeare Festival, 345
New Lafayette Theatre, 231
New Mexico Repertory Theatre, 239

New-play development, 303, 305
New-play dramaturgy, 304
New Victory theatre, 211
New Voices Project, 26
New York City Opera, 366
New York Shakespeare Festival, 8, 196, 204, 289, 324, 362, 404
New York Shakespeare Festival Theatre, 205, 233
New York Theatre Workshop, 296
Ngema, Mbogeni, 271
Nichols, Mike, 206
Nigeria, Asian/African theatre and, 267–269
'night, Mother, 246, 370
Night of the Iguana, 36
Nightingale, Benedict, 31
Nine, 386
No Exit, 194
No Plays No Poetry, 328
Noah and His Sons, 86, 88–90
Noh theatre, 253, 254–257, 261
Noh Theatre: Principles and Perspectives, The, 257
Nonprofessional theatre
    costume design and, 384
    lighting design and, 412
    makeup and, 388
    rehearsals and, 331
    scene design and, 372
    volunteer/student labor in, 392
Nonrealistic movements, 162
Nonspecific space, 356
Nontraditional casting, 322, 324
Nonverbal sound, 412
Normal Heart, The, 249
Norman, Marsha, 246, 298
Norman Conquests, The, 200
Norms, 134, 145, 146
North Africa, theatre in, 273
Northwest Asian American Theatre, 242, 243
Not-for-profit organizations, 312
Not-for-profit theatres, 28, 230, 303, 304
NTD. See National Theatre of the Deaf (NTD)
Ntshona, Winston, 195
NTWH. See National Theatre Workshop of the Handicapped (NTWH)
Nudity, 219, 220, 380
Number, A, 201, 202
Nunn, Trevor, 30, 192

O

O Composite, 404
Objectivity, 16–17
Observation, acting and, 340–342
Octoroon, The, 136, 137
Odyssey, The, 369
Oedipus, 45, 73, 310
Oedipus at Colonus, 49, 64
Oedipus Rex
    character/characterization of, 44
    director and, 326
    festival theatre and, 60, 62, 72
    Hamlet and, 103
    movement in, 327
    performance of, 66–70
    plot of, 41, 42, 43
    by Sophocles, 60, 64, 67, 69, 73
    tragedy in, 50
Oedipus the King, 42, 66, 168
Of Thee I Sing, 192
Off-Broadway, 202–205, 209, 289, 314, 386, 412
Off-Off-Broadway, 202–205, 209, 213, 285, 302
Offstage, 355
Ogunde, Hubert, 268
Oh Sooo Politically Correct Players, The, 246
Ohio Theatre, Playhouse Square Center, 106, 126, 338
O'Horgan, Tom, 203, 204
Okhlopkov, Nikolai, 318
Oklahoma!, 192
Old Comedy, 71
Old Matador, The, 237
Old Money, 246
Old Neighborhood, The, 213, 302
Old Times, 199
Oldest Profession, The, 247
Oleanna, 213
Olinder, Laurie, 163, 323
Olivier, Laurence, 198–199
Omaha Magic Theatre, 246
One-half, acting and, 343
One-quarter, acting and, 343
One Third of a Nation, 176
O'Neill, Eugene, 138, 172–174, 176, 185, 340, 401
O'Neill, James, 138, 140, 141, 143, 172
Ong, Han, 243
Onnagata, in Japanese theatre, 260
Onstage, 355, 391

Ontological-Hysteric Theatre, 226
Open call, 323
Open Theatre, 222–223, 289, 339
Opera, 110–111, 123, 133–134, 190, 191
    ballad, 133, 191
    Chinese, 262
    Falstaff, 358
    Yoruba, 268
Opéra comique, 133
Orchestra, 60, 67, 74
Oregon Shakespeare Festival, 382
Oresteia, 64
Origin of Species, The, 144, 159
Ornamentation, production design and, 288
Orpheus and Eurydice, 166
Osborne, John, 199, 363
Ostling, Dan, 204, 325, 369, 402, 407, 417
Othello, 272, 322
Other Side of Silence, The (TOSO), 249
Our Town, 17, 160, 176, 229
Ouspenskaya, Maria, 177
Overacting, 349
Overlie, Mary, 328
Owners, 201

P

Pacific, 407
Pacific Overtures, 209
Pafnutius, 81
Pageant wagon, 86, 87, 90
Painted effects, makeup and, 389, 390
Painters, scene design and, 357–358
Painters' elevations, scene design and, 361
Pajama Game, The, 210
Pakledinaz, Martin, 19, 291, 303
Palais Royal, 121, 127
Pan Asian Repertory Theatre, 242
Pantomime, 134, 182
Paper Mill Playhouse, 205
Papp, Joseph, 205
Parabasis, 71
Paradise Now, 219, 220
Parados, 71
Parichy, Dennis, 336, 376
Paris Opera Ballet, 404
Park in Our House, A, 237
Parker, Dorothy, 32

Parks, Suzan-Lori, 29, 233
Parodoi, 60, 66, 67
Parodos, 66, 67, 71
Parsifal, 229
Partnership, directing/producing
    and, 312
Passion, dramatic action and, 38
Passion, 209
Passion Play, 85
Pastoral, 107
Pater, Walter, 163
Patronage, 96
Payroll, directing/producing
    and, 312
Peasant Fair, 83
Pelléas and Mélisande, 161
Penumbra Theatre Company, 232
Peony Pavilion, The, 262
Pepys, Samuel, 102
Perception, dramatic action and, 38
Performance, 23–35.
    See also Production
    acting and, 351–352
    in ancient Egypt, 59
    of contemporary theatre, 222,
        223–224
    costume design and, 391
    director and, 325
    as element of theatre, 6–7, 9
    lighting design and, 410–411
    movement and, 327
    in Noh theatre, 257
    of *Oedipus Rex,* 66–70
    play and, 37
    preparing a commedia, 113
    professional theatre and, 96
    scene design and, 371
    Wakefield cycle and, 86–87, 88
    watching a, 24–25
Performance art, 224–227
Performance Group, 223
Performance space
    audience and, 26
    costume design and, 380
    festival theatre and, 60, 86, 90
    lighting design and, 399,
        403, 410
    nature of theatre and, 5
    postmodernism and, 227
    professional theatre and, 96,
        98, 107
    scene design and, 355
Performer-audience relationship,
    281, 292

Performers. *See also* Actors
    acting and (*See* Acting)
    of contemporary theatre, 222,
        223–224
    directing/producing and, 311
    director and, 315, 323, 325,
        326–327, 327, 329, 330
    festival theatre and, 62–63,
        65–66
    modernist temperament and, 183
    nature of theatre and, 5, 8
    in *Noah and His Sons,* 90
    in Noh theatre, 255
    play and, 37
    playwriting and, 296, 297
    production design and, 288
    rehearsal and, 331–334
    in Rome, 75
    spectators and, 18
    theatrical space and, 283,
        284, 287
Performing, acting and, 344–345
Performing arts, 403
Pericles, 366, 367
Perishable Theatre Women's Play-
    writing Festival, 246
Perseverance Theatre, 206, 243, 300
Persians, The, 64
Perspective, 107–109
Perspective drawing, 107
Perspective scenery, 108, 120,
    128, 157
Phaedra, 73, 120–121
Phantom of the Opera, The, 7, 13,
    27, 210, 313
Philadelphia Theatre Company, 296
Philoctetes, 64
Phormio, 73
Physical level, of characters, 44
Piano Lesson, The, 232, 233, 235,
    298, 299
Picasso, 166
Piccolo Teatro, 118
Picture-frame stage, 128, 157, 326
Pierre Patelin, 91
Pillowman, 202
Pinter, Harold, 199, 348
Pit, 111, 119, 132, 151
Pitch, 47, 330, 349, 350, 413, 414
Pittsburgh Public Theatre, 173
Pixérécourt, Guilbert de, 136
Places of Performance, 284
Platea, 84–85, 86, 100
Plato, 39

Plautus, Titus Maccius, 73, 74, 75,
    76, 93, 112
Playmakers Repertory Theatre, 386
Plays, 37–54. *See also* Production
    absurdist drama and, 195–196
    analyzing/studying, 40, 48,
        315–316
    in Asian/African theatre (*See*
        Asian/African theatre)
    character/characterization of,
        44–47
    critical perspective and, 30
    criticism of, 32–33
    directing (*See* Directing)
    dramatic action of, 38–41, 45
    dramaturgy and (*See* Dramaturgy)
    festival theatre and, 58
    form in drama, 47, 49–51
    independent theatre and, 153,
        155–157
    medieval theatre, 83–90, 90–93
    in Middle Ages, 79–80
    during Naturalism
        (*See* Naturalism)
    nature of theatre and, 5, 6, 7,
        9, 14
    in Noh theatre, 254
    playwright/playwriting of (*See*
        Playwright/playwriting)
    plot of (*See* Plot)
    in postwar America, 187–193
    in postwar Europe, 193–194
    producing, 311–314
    production design and, 290
    reading, 37–38
    during Realism (*See* Realism)
    religious, 80, 84, 90
    during Romanticism
        (*See* Romanticism)
    in Rome (*See* Rome)
    satyr, 58, 64, 70
    style in drama, 51–52
    varieties of theatrical experiences
        through, 55
    watching, 24–25
Plays for the Theatre, 40
Playwright-director relationship, 301
Playwright/Playwriting, 295–302
    acting and, 337
    American, 212–214
    audience and, 23
    criticism of, 32, 33
    directing/producing and, 311
    director and, 316–317, 323

Playwright/Playwriting,, continued
   modernist temperament and,
     163, 172, 176
   nature of theatre and, 7, 8, 9
   sound design and, 415
Playwrights Horizons, 205, 301
Plenty, 200
Plot, 41–43. *See also* Storyline
   of *Buried Child,* 214–215
   of *Cat on a Hot Tin Roof,*
     188–189
   of *Doll's House,* 146–148
   episodic, 41
   in France, 120
   of *Good Person of Setzuan,*
     180–181
   of *"Hairy Ape,"* 172–173
   of *Hamlet,* 103–104
   of *Importance of Being*
     Earnest, 164
   of *Ma Rainey's Black Bottom,*
     233–235
   of *Menaechmi,* 76–77
   of *Monte Cristo,* 139–140
   neoclassical rules and, 133, 135
   of *Noah and His Sons,* 88–89
   of *Oedipus Rex,* 67–68
   of *Pierre Patelin,* 91
   in Roman comedy, 75
   of *Servant of Two Masters,*
     117–118
   of *Shrine in the Fields*
     (Nonomiya), 257
   of *Tartuffe,* 125
Poetic justice, 120, 136
Poetics, 38, 39
Point of attack, 41, 43
Point of view, director and, 315
Polish Laboratory Theatre, 221, 287
Polyekran, 224
Poor/environmental theatres,
   221–224, 225, 227, 347
Popular culture, 10, 12
Poquelin, Jean-Baptiste, 127. *See also*
   Molière
Postmodernism, 227–229
Postwar America, 190–193
Postwar American theatre, 187–188
Postwar British theatre, 197–202
Postwar era, 174–176
Postwar Europe, 193–194
Postwar production style, 191
Pot of Gold, 73
Power, 176, 177
Preparation, director and, 315

Previews, playwriting and, 302
Prince, Harold, 13, 210
Principal character's pillar, in Noh
   theatre, 255
Prior censorship, 11
Private Fears in Public Places, 200
Private Lives, 386
Producer
   directing/producing and,
     311–314
   director and, 323
   dramaturgy and, 303
   playwriting and, 299–300
Producers, The, 313, 386
Producing, 311–314.
     See also Producer
Producing director, 312
Production. *See also* Performance;
     Plays
   critical perspective and, 30
   criticism of, 32–34
   design, 287–293
   directing (*See* Directing)
   director and, 150, 151, 152
   as element of theatre, 6, 7–9
   independent theatre and, 153
   lighting design and, 399
   mixed-media, 415–417
   modernist temperament, 162,
     167, 168
   play and, 37
   postwar, 191
   producing, 311–314
   professional theatre and, 96
   in Rome, 75
   styles of, 53
   symbolist, 162
Production design, 287–293
Production dramaturgy, 307–308
Professional actors, 344–345
Professional organizations, direct-
   ing/producing and, 314
Professional theatre, 95–130
   acting and, 345
   assistants in, 391
   commedia dell'arte and,
     111–116
   creating a, 95–97
   director and, 323
   in France, 119–121, 121–124
   Globe Theatre and, 97–103
   Hamlet and, 103–107
   Italy and, 107–111
   lighting design and, 411, 412
   makeup and, 388

   modernist temperament and, 175
   Molière and, 121–124
   playwriting and, 299
   rehearsal and, 331
   scene design and, 371–372
   Servant of Two Masters and,
     117–119
   Shakespeare and, 97–103
   sound design and, 414
   Tartuffe and, 124–127
Profits, directing/producing and,
   311–312
Programs, for live performance, 24
Projection, acting and, 349
Prometheus Bound, 64
Pronunciation, 349, 350
Properties
   acting and, 351, 352
   director and, 152, 324
   of play, 46, 47
   production design and, 288
   professional theatre and, 100
   rehearsal and, 331
   scene design and, 369, 371, 372
   theatrical space and, 280, 282,
     283
Property room/shop, 286
Proportion
   costume design and, 378
   production design and, 288
Props, 371
Proscenium arch, professional theatre
   and, 109, 111, 121, 123,
     162, 183
   audience and, 27
   festival theatre and, 66, 85
Proscenium-arch stage, 280, 281
Proscenium curtain, 66
Proscenium stage, 25, 292, 325,
   399, 407
   professional theatre and, 120
Proscenium theatre, 407
Providence Black Repertory Com-
   pany, 232
Provincetown Players, 172, 175
Provincetown Playhouse, 172
Prymate, 342
Prynne, William, 102
P.S. 122, 227
Pseudolus, 73
Psychological characterization, acting
   and, 346
Psychological level, of characters, 44
Psychological preparation, acting
   and, 348–349

Psychological realism, 187, 188
Psychological responsiveness, acting and, 338
Public Theatre, 196, 205
Publicity, 307, 312, 314
Puerto Rican Traveling Theatre, 240
Puppetry, 289
Puppets, 258, 259, 264–265
Purdy, Claude E., 234
Purpose, dramatic action and, 38
Pygmalion, 155

Q

Qing yi, in China, 263
Qualities
    of critic, 34–35
    of dramatic form, 47, 49
    of light, 397–399
    style and, 51–52
    of theatre, 16–18
Quality
    in acting, 349, 350
    in lighting design, 405
    in music, 47
    in sound design, 413
Quay Brothers, 194
Question 27, Question 28, 243
Question of Magic, A, 213
Quintero, José, 401
Quintessence of Ibsenism, The, 147

R

Rabe, David, 212, 213
Race, nontraditional casting and, 322
Racial/ethnic groups, makeup and, 389, 390
Racine, Jean, 120–121
Racing Demon, 200
Radio Golf, 235
Rag rolling, scene design and, 367
Raisin in the Sun, A, 231, 232
Ramayana, 264
Reading, a play, 37–38
Real Thing, The, 199
Realism, 133–134, 138, 140, 144–149, 150, 151, 157
    modernist temperament and, 161, 163, 164, 174
    in postwar America, 192
    postwar American theatre and, 187, 188
    psychological, 187, 188
Realistic sound, 412

Rear elevations, scene design and, 360
Rebeck, Theresa, 246
Red Hen Productions, 246
Red Lion, 98
Red Shoes, The, 246
Redwood Curtain, 213
References to Salvador Dali Make Me Hot, 237
Regional theatres, 205, 209, 391–392
Rehearsals
    acting and, 342, 351
    directing/producing and, 312, 330–334
    dress, 334, 351–352, 371, 391, 410
    lighting design and, 405, 410–411
    technical, 334, 371, 391, 410
Reinhardt, Max, 167–168
Rejection, acting and, 345
Religious drama, 91, 92
Religious plays, 80, 84, 90
Renaissance, 95, 107–111, 157, 161, 165, 180
Rent, 211, 304, 305
Repertorio Espanol, 240
Resolution, 43, 45, 315
Response
    audience, 27, 28
    reviewer, 35 (*See also* Critic)
Restoration, 128
Restoration comedy, 128, 164
Reviews, 30–32
Revolving stage, 368–369
Rhinoceros, 249
Rhyme scheme, 89–90
Rhythm
    director and, 330
    lighting design and, 402
    modernist temperament and, 167, 182
    playwriting and, 297
    production design and, 288
Rice, Elmer, 172, 176
Rice, Tim, 7
Richards, Lloyd, 232
Richelieu, Cardinal, 119–120, 121
Ridiculous Theatrical Company, 248
Rigdon, Kevin, 202, 207, 233
Rising action, 42, 43
Rita, Rui, 186, 190, 200, 303, 412
Rivals, The, 336, 376
Rivera, José, 236, 237

Road to Mecca, 273
Robbins, Jerome, 192, 404
Rock 'n' Roll, 199
Rodgers, Richard, 76, 192
Role
    creating the, 345–348
    refining the, 351
Roll, Gadi, 278, 288, 352
Rolling Stones, 370, 386
Roman theatre, 92. *See also* Rome
Romanticism, 133–144
Rome
    drama in, 78–79
    dramatists in, 73
    Globe Theatre and, 100
    Greece v., 74
    Italy and, 107
    Menaechmi in, 76–77
    nudity/obscene language in, 220
    religious theatre and, 80
    theatre in, 18, 72–75, 78–79, 92
Romeo and Juliet, 99, 278, 288, 352
Roosters, 47, 237–240, 251
Root Wym'n Theatre Company, 246
Rosencrantz and Guildenstern Are Dead, 199
Rosenthal, Jean, 192, 401
Ross, Linda, 202
Rotimi, Ola, 269
Route 1 & 9, 229
Royal Court Theatre, 2, 199
Royal National Theatre, 99
Royal Opera, 415
Royal Shakespeare Company (RSC), 26, 91, 99, 182, 198, 318
RSC. *See* Royal Shakespeare Company
Rudnick, Paul, 249
Ruhl, Sarah, 246
Rylance, Mark, 26

S

Saint Joan, 155
Samisen, 258
San Diego Repertory Theatre, 236
San Fransisco Mime Theatre, 221
San Fransisco Opera, 366
Sanchez-Scott, Milcha, 236, 237, 251
Sapientia, 81
Saratoga International Theatre Institute (SITI), 261, 300, 328, 330
Sardou, Victoria, 296
Sartre, Jean-Paul, 194, 195

Satyr play, 58, 64, 70
Saved, 199
Scaenae frons, 74
Scenario, 6, 112, 116
Scene design, 355–374
    assembling/painting scenery in,
        366–368
    assistants/coworkers for, 371–372
    basic scenic elements in,
        361–366
    functions of, 355–357
    performances and, 371
    rehearsals and, 371
    scene designer's skill in, 357–359
    set decoration/properties and,
        369, 371
    shifting scenery onstage in,
        368–369
    working plans/procedures in,
        359–361
Scene/scenic designers, 193,
        287–288, 290, 352, 377, 404.
        See also Scene design
Scene shop, 286
Scene study, 344
Scenery. *See also* Setting
    acting and, 344, 352
    assembling/painting, 366–368
    in Booth's Theatre, 141
    commedia dell'arte, 112
    of contemporary theatre, 222
    critical perspective and, 30
    director and, 152, 324, 325
    in France, 123
    in *Hamlet,* 106
    in *How I Learned to Drive,* 248
    in Italy, 109, 110, 111
    Kabuki, 261
    lighting design and, 402, 403,
        406, 410, 417
    live performance and, 24, 25
    modernist temperament and,
        162, 166, 167, 178, 181, 183
    nature of theatre and, 7, 13
    in Noh theatre, 256, 261
    perspective, 108, 120, 128, 157
    production design and, 288
    professional theatre and, 96
    realism/naturalism and, 146
    scene design for (*See* Scene
        design)
    of *Servant of Two Masters,* 119
    shifting, 368–369
    sound design and, 412
    style and, 52

theatrical space and, 281,
        282, 285
    Wakefield cycle and, 86
Scenic designers. *See* Scene/scenic
        designers
Scenic elements, 361–366
Scenic requirements, director
        and, 315
Schlemmer, Oskar, 377
Schmidt, Robert, 359, 360
Schönberg, Claude-Michel, 30, 210
School for Husbands, The, 94
School for Scandal, The, 333, 364, 392
Schumann, Peter, 289
Schwartz, Stephen, 46, 209, 212
Screen actor, 337
Screens, scene design and, 364–365
Screens, The, 293
Scrim, 162, 163, 363
Script
    acting and, 337, 342, 345,
        347, 348
    costume design and, 380, 393
    director and, 324
    makeup and, 393
    rehearsal and, 332
Scumbling, scene design and, 367
Sea Gull, The, 155
Seascape, 213, 357
Seattle Children's Theatre, 206
Seattle Repertory Theatre, 205, 369
Second City, 206
Second Skin, 243
Secret Garden, The, 246, 370, 401
Selective intensity, 397
Self-censorship, 11
Self-Tormentor, 73
Sellars, Peter, 33, 140, 404, 412
Seneca, Lucius Annaeus, 73, 74,
        78–79
Serban, Andrei, 117, 196, 290, 404
Serious Money, 201
Serlio, Sebastiano, 107, 108
Serpent, The, 223
Serpent Woman, The, 117
Servant of Two Masters, The, 116,
        117–119, 129, 326, 356
Set decoration, 369, 371
Set properties, 369, 371
Set props, 371
Setting. *See also* Scenery
    acting and, 351
    costume design and, 378
    of *Doll's House,* 149
    in France, 123

in Globe Theatre, 100
    for *Hamlet,* 360, 361
    independent theatre and, 153
    in Italy, 109
    lifelikeness in, 16
    lighting design and, 399,
        403, 408
    of *Ma Rainey's Black Bottom,* 233
    modernist temperament and,
        162, 166, 179
    of *Monte Cristo,* 140, 141
    neoclassical rules and, 133, 135
    of *Pericles,* 367
    postwar American theatre
        and, 188
    realism and, 140
    realism/naturalism and, 146
    Roman/Greek, 74
    scene design and, 355–356, 358,
        361–362, 368
    spectacle and, 47
    in *Tartuffe,* 127
    of Wilson's plays, 235
Seven Against Thebes, 64
Seven Ages of the Theatre, The, 57, 95
Seven Guitars, 232, 233, 235
Sexual Perversity in Chicago, 213
Shakespeare, William
    Asian performance and, 228
    As You Like It by, 132
    Cymbeline by, 398
    Flying Karamazov Brothers
        and, 227
    French tragedies and, 121
    Hamlet by, 47, 50, 359
    history plays of, 377
    Japanese theatre and, 261
    Julius Caesar by, 153
    MacBeth by, 176
    Measure for Measure by, 345
    Midsummer Night's Dream by,
        318, 319
    modernist temperament and, 182
    Monte Cristo and, 139
    nature of theatre and, 4, 12, 13,
        14, 15, 16
    neoclassicism and, 134–135
    Othello by, 272
    Pericles by, 366, 367
    playwriting and, 295
    plot and, 41
    professional theatre and, 96,
        97–103, 128–129
    Roman dramatists and, 73,
        76, 79

Romeo and Juliet by, 278
songs in plays by, 190
Stratford Festival and, 198
style of, 52
Taming of the Shrew by, 283, 324
Tempest by, 25, 382, 388
traditions and, 128
Troilus and Cressida by, 415
Twelfth Night by, 33
Two Gentlemen of Verona by, 406
Wilson and, 229
Shakespeare in Love, 199, 339
Shakespeare Theatre, 322, 348
Shape, production design and, 288
Shapes of Our Theatres, The, 284
Share a scene, acting and, 343
Shareholders, 100, 122
Shattuck, Roger, 161
Shaw, Fiona, 339
Shaw, George Bernard, 147, 153–155, 261, 298
She, Lao, 263–264
She Would if She Could, 128
Sheng, in China, 263
Shepard, Sam, 212, 213–215, 217, 296, 297
Sheridan, Richard Brinsley, 336, 376
Sherwood, Robert, 176
Shifting Point, The, 337
Shite, in Noh theatre, 255, 257, 258
Shitebashira, in Noh theatre, 255
Short Organum for the Theatre, A, 5
Short-run productions, 384
Show Boat, 191–192
Shrine in the Fields (Nonomiya), The, 254, 257–258
Shubert Brothers, 175
Shutters, 109
Side elevations, scene design and, 361
Siegfried and Roy, 386
Siguenza, Herbert, 396
Silverman, Leigh, 247
Simon, Barnie, 272
Simon, John, 32
Simon, Neil, 401
Simonson, Lee, 175
Simpatico, 214
Singing, 13
Singspiele, 134
Sisters Rosensweig, The, 246
SITI. *See* Saratoga International Theatre Institute (SITI)
Six Degrees of Separation, 386

Six Figures Theatre Company, 246
Size, in theatrical space, 279–280
Skene, 60–61
Sketches
    costume design and, 380–381, 382
    lighting design and, 403, 404, 405, 411
    makeup and, 389
Skin of Our Teeth, The, 176
Skriker, 201
Skylight, 31, 200
Slag, 200
Slapstick, 116
Slapstick comedy, 114–115
Slave Ship, 231, 232
Slaves, as audience, 66
Sleepers in the Cave, 273
Slice of life, 149–150
Small, Adam, 271
Small Family Business, A, 200
Smit, Bartho, 271
Smith, Molly, 300
Smith, Oliver, 192
Smits, Jimmy, 237
Smokey Joe's Cafe, 370
Sneaky, 245
Social commentary, 119
Socialism, 178
Societal level, of characters, 44
Society for the Suppression of Vice, The, 154
Sociological characterization, acting and, 346
Soft-scenery units, 363–364
Soliloquies, 45
Sondheim, Stephen, 192, 209–210
Song, 45, 75, 191, 193, 330
Song for a Nisei Fisherman, A, 242
Sontag, Susan, 163, 323
Sophocles
    Andromache and, 207
    character/characterization of, 44
    Electra by, 56
    as Greek tragic dramatist, 64
    Monte Cristo and, 139
    Oedipus by, 45, 49, 310
    Oedipus Rex by, 50, 60, 64, 67, 69, 73
    Oedipus the King by, 66
    plot and, 42
    satyr play and, 58
    Shakespeare and, 103
    style of, 52
Sorrows and Rejoicings, 273

Sound
    acting and, 352
    Artaud and, 183
    Brook and, 182
    defined, 46
    design for (*See* Sound design)
    designers for, 287, 352 (*See also* Sound design)
    director and, 324
    in *Hamlet*, 106
    nonverbal, 412
    production design and, 288
    realistic, 412
    theatrical space and, 204, 280
    verbal, 412
Sound cues, rehearsal and, 334
Sound design, 397, 412–418. *See also* Sound designers
    functions of, 412–413
    mixed-media productions and, 415–417
    role of, 412
    sound designer's working methods/resources in, 413–414
Sound designers, 287, 352. *See also* Sound design
Sound of Music, The, 401
Sound plot, 414
Sound poems, 170
Sound score, 413
South Africa, Asian/African theatre and, 271–273
South Coast Repertory Theatre, 206
South Pacific, 192, 328
Southeast Asia, theatre in, 264
Southern, Richard, 57, 95
Soyinka, Wole, 269–271
Space
    acting, 355
    audience, 355
    auxiliary, 285, 286
    flexible, 280, 283–285, 355, 356
    nonspecific, 356
    performance (*See* Performance space)
    rehearsal, 331
    theatrical (*See* Theatrical space)
Spattering, scene design and, 367
Speaking, 13, 259
Special effects
    director and, 151
    festival theatre and, 85, 86
    lighting design and, 406–407, 409, 412

Special effects, continued
  neoclassism and, 133
  professional theatre and, 109
Specific illumination, 406–407
Spectacle
  diction and, 46
  director and, 151
  dramatic action and, 38
  festival theatre and, 67
  of *Monte Cristo,* 138, 140, 141
  in play, 47
  professional theatre and, 109
  realism/naturalism and, 146
  scene design and, 370
  theatrical space and, 280, 281
  thought and, 45
Spectators. *See also* Audience
  behavior of, 137
  of contemporary theatre, 219,
    220, 222, 223–224
  director and, 327
  in France, 122
  in Italy, 109
  modernist temperament and,
    162, 178, 179, 183
  at *Mrs. Warren's Profession,* 154
  in *Noah and His Sons,* 90
  in Noh theatre, 258
  performance and, 23–25
  performers and, 18
  production design and, 287
  qualities of theatre and, 16
  response to play, 15
  theatrical space and, 283, 284, 285
  Wakefield cycle and, 87, 88
Speech, 16, 89–90, 151, 183, 255,
    297, 330, 342, 349–350
Speed-the-Plow, 213
Spiderwoman Native American
    Theatre, 246
Spiderwoman Theatre, 245
Spielberg, Steven, 301
Spinella, Stephen, 249
Spirit House, 231
Spoken decor, 100
Spolin, Viola, 23
Sponging, scene design and, 367
Sponsors, 11
Spotlight, 143, 407, 409
St. Louis Black Repertory
    Company, 232
St. Paul Pioneer Press, 293
St Louis Black Repertory, 409
Stage
  acting and, 343
  areas of, 343

arena, 280, 282–283, 292, 306,
    362, 408
in China, 262, 263
contemporary theatre and, 224
director and, 151, 324, 325–327
Elizabethan, 108
in England, 121–122, 128
flexible, 327
in France, 121–122, 123
Globe Theatre, 98–100
in Greece, 108
in *Hamlet,* 106
in Italy, 108, 109, 110
Japanese theatre and, 258
lighting design and (*See* Lighting
    design)
in medieval theatre, 84–85
melodrama and, 143
modernist temperament and,
    166, 175, 181
nature of theatre and, 8, 13,
    14–15
in nineteenth century, 141
in Noh theatre, 255–256
Off-Off-Broadway, 204
performer positions on, 343
picture-frame, 128, 157, 326
production design and, 288,
    291–292
proscenium (*See* Proscenium stage)
proscenium-arch, 280, 281
revolving, 368–369
Roman, 74, 75, 77, 108
scene design and (*See* Scene
    design)
in *Shrine in the Fields
    (Nonomiya),* 258
sound design and
    (*See* Sound design)
in *Strong Breed,* 269
Svoboda and, 416
thrust, 280–283, 292, 325, 362,
    407–409
variable, 327
Wakefield cycle and, 87
Stage actor, 337, 345
Stage attendants, 255
Stage business, 329, 334,
    343, 371
Stage compositions, lighting design
    and, 399
Stage Design Portfolio Review, 362
Stage history, scene design and, 358
Stage house, 409
Stage images, 325–327
Stage manager, 334, 386, 392

Stage proper, in Noh theatre, 255
Stage vocabulary, acting and,
    342–344
Stagebridge, 244
Staging
  directing/producing and, 312
  director and, 316
  Kazan-Mielziner approach
    to, 188
  rehearsal and, 332
  Wakefield cycle, 86
Standards, in postwar Europe, 194
Stanislavsky, Konstantin, 155,
    156, 157, 158, 177, 178,
    187, 348
Steel Wheels, 386
Stein, Peter, 174, 287, 316, 317
Steppenwolf Theatre Company,
    205, 206
Sticks and Bones, 213
Stock characters, 113–114, 164
Stoppard, Tom, 199, 200
Story
  in *Buried Child,* 214
  dramatic action and, 38
  playwriting and, 296
  in postwar America, 191, 192
Storyline. *See also* Plot
  of *Happy Days,* 195
Storytelling, 5, 6, 193, 254
Stowe, Harriet Beecher, 138, 159
Straiges, Tony, 303
Straight makeup, 389
Strange Interlude, 172
Strasberg, Lee, 177, 187
Stratford Festival, 198
Stratford Shakespearean Festival, 66
Strawbridge, Stephen, 364, 392
Streamers, 213
Streetcar Named Desire, A, 187,
    188, 328
Strehler, Giorgio, 118, 317
Strindberg, August, 171, 201, 202,
    261
Striplights, 408
Stroman, Susan, 192
Strong Breed, The, 269–271
Strouse, Charles, 209
Stuart Court, 102
Stuff Happens, 200, 362
Sturm und Drang school, 134
Style
  in *Importance of Being Earnest,*
    164–165
  lighting design and, 399
  plays and, 51–52

postwar production, 191
production design and, 290
sound design and, 412
Styne, Jule, 209
Subplots, 43, 133
Subsidization, 196–197, 207–212
Sueño, 237
Summer and Smoke, 203
Sundance Theatre Lab, 296
Sunday in the Park with George,
209, 210
Sunset Boulevard, 210
Supernatural elements, 133
Supernumeraries, 62, 70
Suppliants, The, 64
Surrealism, 181, 227
Suspense, 43, 138, 140
Suzuki, Tadashi, 261, 328
Suzuki Company of Toga, 261
Svoboda, Josef, 224, 225, 415, 416
Swan Theatre, 98
Sweeney Todd, 209, 210
Sweet Charity, 209
Swiss News, 184
Symbol, 45, 214, 378
Symbolism, 161–163, 227
Symbolist drama, 162
Symbolist production, 162
Sympathetic characters, 44, 45
Sympathetic Magic, 213
Syndicate, 175
Synge, John Millington, 6
Syracuse Stage, 270

T

Take Me Out, 249
Tale of Genji, The, 257
Talent, acting and, 338
Talley's Folly, 213
Taming of the Shrew, The, 324, 383
Tartuffe, 124–127, 356
Tate, Nahum, 128
Taylor, Paul, 404
Taymor, Julie, 7, 25, 26, 289,
290, 321
Teatro Farnese, 109
Teatro Vista, 206
Technical director, 372
Technical rehearsals, 334, 371,
391, 410
Technicians, 7
Tectonic Theatre Project, 296
Tempest, The, 25, 26, 382, 388
Tempo, 47, 327, 330, 337, 344
Tension, acting and, 337

Texture
costume design and, 377
production design and, 288
scene design and, 359
Tharp, Twyla, 332, 404
Theatre
African American, 231–233
arena, 326, 355, 407
art/value of, 18–21
Asian/African (See Asian/
African theatre)
Asian American, 240–243
by/for women, 245–247
community, 313–314
contemporary (See Contemporary
theatre)
costume design and, 381
decentralization and, 196–197,
205, 209
defined, 6
education, 314
elements of, 6–9
epic, 177–180, 347
festival (See Festival theatre)
as form of art, 9–16
gay/lesbian, 248–249
history of, 5, 27, 28, 55, 382, 403
Latino, 236–237
medieval, 83–93
minority, 28
Native American, 243–245
nonprofessional (See Nonprofessional theatre)
not-for-profit, 28, 230, 303, 304
Off-Broadway/Off-Off-Broadway,
202–205
poor/environmental, 221–224,
225, 227, 347
professional (See Professional
theatre)
proscenium, 407
qualities of, 16–18
regional, 205, 209, 391–392
subsidization and, 196–197,
207–212
thrust, 326, 355
women and, 247–248
Theatre, The, 98
Theatre and Its Double, The, 182
Théâtre Antoine, 150
Theatre Communications Group
(TCG), 207
Theatre Conspiracy, The, 246
Théâtre d'Art, 162
Théâtre de la Pantomime
Futuriste, 170

Théâtre de l'Oeuvre, 162
Théâtre du Gymnase, 145
Théâtre du Soleil, 228, 261, 319
Theatre for a New Audience, 25, 26
Theatre history, 5, 27, 28, 55,
382, 403
Théâtre Illustre, 127
Theatre IV, 304
Théâtre Libre, 153
Theatre Mu, 242
Theatre of Cruelty, 181–183, 184,
198
Theatre of Dionysus, 60–62
"Theatre of the Struggle," 272
Theatre Royal, 111
Theatrical production, section 3
Theatrical space, 279–287
arena stage in, 282–283
auxiliary spaces in, 285, 286
director and, 327
flexible space in, 283–285
influence on, 279–280
proscenium-arch stage in, 281
thrust stage in, 281–282
using, 285, 287
Theatrical visionaries, 165–168
Theatron, 60
Theme
acting and, 348
in *Buried Child,* 215
director and, 315, 317
in *"Hairy Ape,"* 172
in *Hamlet,* 106–107
in *Happy Days,* 195–196
in plays, 42
production design and, 290
in *Strong Breed,* 270–271
Theory of Wagner, 151
Thérèse Raquin, 150
Thespian, 58
Third, 246
36 Views, 12, 242
Thomas, Dylan, 371
Thoroughly Modern Millie, 19
Those the River Keeps, 213
Three-dimensional units, 365
Three Sisters, The, 155, 157
Three Tall Women, 213
Threepenny Opera, The, 180, 394
Through the Looking Glass, 245
Thrust stage, 280–283, 292, 325,
362, 407–409
Thrust theatre, 326, 355
Thunderstorm, 263
Thymele, 60
Time, lighting design and, 399

Time Rocker, 228
Times, The, 313, 416
Tiny Alice, 213
Tipton, Jennifer, 4, 103, 228, 230, 290, 293, 340
   automated lighting and, 408
   lighting design by, 397, 404, 405
Titanic, 209
Titus Andronicus, 26, 101, 289
Toller, Ernst, 172
Tomb Raider: Cradle of Life, 136
Too Clever by Half, 390
Tooth of Crime, The, 214
Top Girls, 200, 201
Topdog/Underdog, 29, 233
Torch Song Triology, 249
Torelli, Giacomo, 109
TOSO. *See* Other Side of Silence, The (TOSO)
Touring, 141, 175
Towards a Poor Theatre, 222, 279
Town council, 86, 87–88
Trachiniae, 64
Trade guilds, 80–83, 86, 87
Tragedy, 39, 44–45, 47, 49–50
   in France, 120, 121, 122, 123
   Greek, 57, 58, 63, 64, 66, 70
   independent theatre and, 156
   in Italy, 107
   neoclassical rules and, 133
   Roman, 78, 79
Tragicomedy, 47, 156
Training, acting and, 338, 344–345
Tranche de vie, 150
Transportation, touring and, 141
Travesties, 199, 200, 412
Trinity Repertory Theatre Company, 53
Triple-A Plowed Under, 176
Troilus and Cressida, 318, 415
Trojan Women, The, 64
True West, 214, 297
Trust, production design and, 291
Truth
   absurdist drama and, 195
   in plays, 52
   in postwar Europe, 194
   realism/naturalism and, 163
   from Romanticism to realism, 134, 146–150, 156, 157
   symbolism and, 161
   universal, 161–162
Tsoti, 273
Tsu, Susan, 207, 382
Tsypin, George, 293, 374

Tumbling, 6
Turn out, acting and, 343
Turntable, 368–369
Twelfth Night, 22, 33, 315
Two River Theater Company, 24, 354
Two Sisters and a Piano, 237, 400
Two Trains Running, 232, 233, 235
Typified characters, 44

U

Ullman, Tracey, 324
Umbrellas of Cherbourg, The, 24, 354
Uncle Tom's Cabin, 138, 139, 140, 159
Uncle Vanya, 155
Uncommon Women and Others, 246
Under the Gaslight, 137, 138
Unifying action, 39, 40
Union members, 391–392
Union Square Theatre, 138
Unions
   acting and, 345
   directing/producing and, 312
   scene design and, 372
United Scenic Artists Union, 372, 391, 411
United States, subsidization of arts in, 207–209. *See also* America; American playwrights
Unity, 40–41, 52, 135, 166, 172
Universal truth, 161–162
Unsympathetic characters, 44, 45
Uplighting, 398
Urinetown, 309
Utah Shakespearean Festival, 15

V

Valdez, Luis, 236
Value
   art and, 18–21
   history of theatre and, 5
   of theatre, 19
Value sketches, 405
Values
   art and, 12
   festival theatre and, 92
   of melodrama, 144
   modernist temperament and, 170–171, 174
   in *Monte Cristo,* 140
   in postwar British theatre, 199
   in postwar Europe, 194
   realism/naturalism and, 146
   women and, 15

van Itallie, Jean-Claude, 223
Variable stage, 327
Variety
   acting and, 344, 350
   director and, 150, 327
   in dramatic action, 38
   in *Monte Cristo,* 141
   production design and, 288
   Romanticism and, 134, 135, 136
   scene design and, 373
Verbal sound, 412
Victory Gardens, 206
Video, contemporary theatre and, 225, 226
Viet Rock, 223
Viewpoints, 328
Vinegar Tom, 201
Visibility, lighting design and, 399
Visionaries, 165–168
Visual arts, 10, 12, 16, 225, 226, 289, 381, 403
Vitruvius, 107
Vocabulary, acting and, 342–344
Vocal characterization, acting and, 349–350
Vocal qualities, 330
Vogel, Paula, 40, 246–248, 251, 296, 299, 300, 328
Voice
   acting and, 338, 340, 349–350
   directors and, 330
   sound design and, 412
Voltaire, 122, 229
Volume, 47, 330, 349, 350, 414
Vomitoria, theatrical space and, 283

W

wa Thiong'o, Ngugi, 269
Wadsworth, Stephen, 326
Wagner, Richard, 151–152, 153, 167, 178, 229, 415, 416
Wagner, Robin, 203, 249, 370
Wagon, scene design and, 368
Waiting for Godot, 13, 195, 341
Wakefield cycle, 86–88
Waki, in Noh theatre, 255, 256, 257, 258
Waki-za, in Noh theatre, 256
Wakibashira, in Noh theatre, 256
Walks of Indian Women-Aztlan to Anahuac, 245
Wallace, Naomi, 246
Walnut Street Theatre, 378
Wanamaker, Zoë, 56

War of the Worlds, 300, 328
War Plays, 199
Ward, Douglas Turner, 231
Wardrobe supervisor, 392
Warhol, Andy, 328
Warren, David, 33, 315
Wash, The, 242
Washington Square Players, 175
Wasserstein, Wendy, 232, 246, 298
Way of Acting, The, 261
Way of the World, The, 128
Wayang Kulit, 264–265
Webber, Andrew Lloyd, 13, 210, 313
Weill, Kurt, 394
Weiss, Peter, 182, 193
Well of Horniness, The, 249
Welles, Orson, 300, 318, 328, 401
West Side Story, 192, 193, 401
Westport Country Playhouse, 94
When We Dead Awaken, 229
Who's Afraid of Virginia Woolf?, 213
Wicked, 46, 212
Wickham, Glynne, 87
Wilbur, Richard, 94, 381
Wild Swan Theatre, 244
Wilde, Oscar, 163–165, 185,
    200, 385
Wilder, Thornton, 17, 160, 176, 229
Williams, Tennessee, 217
    as American playwright, 212, 213
    Camino Real and, 37
    Cat on a Hot Tin Roof by, 186,
      188–190, 191, 217
    Glass Menagerie by, 411
    Night of the Iguana by, 36
    playwriting and, 295, 301–302
    Summer and Smoke by, 203
Williamstown Theatre Festival, 101,
    356, 366
Wilson, August, 216, 232, 233–235,
    241, 296, 298–299
Wilson, Lanford, 204, 212, 213

Wilson, Michael, 186, 190, 303
Wilson, Robert, 228–229, 320, 321,
    366, 404, 417
Wind Cries Mary, The, 242
Wing-Davy, Mark, 202
Wings, 109, 141, 281, 355
Winter People, A, 243
Wizard of Oz, The, 212
Wolfe, George C., 211,
    232–233, 249
Woman Seeking. . ., 246
Woman Warrior, The, 231
Women
    acting, 102
    as audience, 66
    characters, 81
    in England, 100–101
    festival theatre and, 57, 71
    first dramatist, 81
    in France, 122
    Japanese theatre and, 260
    plays and, 15
    in Rome, 75, 79
    theatre by/for, 245–247
Women One World (WOW), 249
Women's Kabuki, 260
Women's Project and
    Productions, 246
Women's Will, 246
Wong, Elizabeth, 242
Wooster Group, 229, 339, 340, 404
Words of Ayame, The, 260
Works Progress Administration, 176
World Theatre Project, 26
World Theatre Season, 198
Worth, Irene, 196
WOW. *See* Women One World
    (WOW)
Woza Albert, 272
Writers
    director and, 319
    dramaturgy and, 304

playwriting and, 296, 298, 299,
    300, 303
Wu dan, in China, 263
Wu sheng, in China, 263
Wyspianski, Stanislaw, 319–320

X

Xiansu, Tang, 262
Xiao sheng, in China, 263

Y

Yale Repertory Theatre, 232
Yamagiwa, Rosanna, 243
Yamazaki, Masakazu, 261
Year of the Dragon, The, 242
Yeargan, Michael, 290, 357, 364,
    368, 371, 392
Yellow Robe, William S., Jr., 245
Yew, Chay, 243
Yionoulis, Evan, 12, 242
Yonekawa, Carie, 126
Yoruba opera, 268
Yoruba Traveling Theatre, 268
Youmans, James, 33, 36, 315
Young Men's Kabuki, 260
Yu, Cao, 263

Z

Zanni, 114, 115
Zeitgeist, 45
Zhaohua, Lin, 264
Zigler, Scott, 302
Zimmerman, Mary, 204, 325, 369,
    402, 417
Zipprodt, Patricia, 65
Zola, Emile, 149–150, 153, 162
Zoot Suit, 236
Zuber, Catherine, 9, 119, 171, 215,
    357, 379, 380